THE CHANCELLORS

The

CHANCELLORS

ROY JENKINS

MACMILLAN

First published 1998 by Macmillan

an imprint of Macmillan Publishers Ltd
25 Eccleston Place, London SW1W 9NF
and Basingstoke

Associated companies throughout the world

ISBN 0 333 73057 7

Copyright © Roy Jenkins 1998

1 3 5 7 9 8 6 4 2

A CIP catalogue record for this book is available from
the British Library.

Typeset by SetSystems Ltd, Saffron Walden, Essex
Printed and bound in Great Britain by
Mackays of Chatham plc, Chatham, Kent

CONTENTS

INTRODUCTION

THIS BOOK RECORDS THE CAREERS OF the nineteen men who were Chancellor of the Exchequer between Gladstone's last appointment to the office and Attlee's first. It attempts also to describe their personalities, characters and social backgrounds. Partly for this reason, but partly also because the leaves of dead budgets curl quickly, it does not in general confine itself to the Chancellorship of the Chancellors. With four exceptions, for which there are specific reasons (explained below) it tries to look at the evolution of their whole lives.

I started in 1886 because I saw the book as being to some extent a follow-on from my life of Gladstone, because that year is a natural break-point in British politics, and also because it gave me, as it were, a running start with Lord Randolph Churchill and Sir William Harcourt, two of the most colourful, although not, in the case of Churchill at least, most distinguished occupants of the office. (I have placed Churchill rather than Harcourt first, because although the latter had a brief Chancellorship before the former came to the Treasury, the plenitude of Harcourt's career was more in the 1890s whereas Churchill's was effectively finished by the end of the 1880s. And I have made similar alterations of order where a very brief early Chancellorship – Hicks Beach, Neville Chamberlain, Snowden – might have wrenched the subject away from his quintessential period.) And I ended with Hugh Dalton because I do not much like writing about the living or going over ground I have already covered, and the greater number of Dalton's dead successors – Cripps, Gaitskell, Butler, Macleod – had already been subjects of essays by me. Furthermore Dalton was an unusual man of considerable interest, not wholly admirable, but now rated below his deserts. And he neatly rounds off a series starting with Harcourt, as there were many characters in common between the two men, similarities of which Dalton was both aware and proud. What Harcourt would have thought is not known.

The four Chancellors whom I have treated differently were Asquith, Lloyd George, Baldwin and Winston Churchill. They were four out of the six in the series who subsequently became Prime Minister, but this is not in itself the reason why I have applied a different method. (The other two Prime Ministers, Bonar Law and Neville Chamberlain, I have subjected to my regular meander over their whole lives.) Of Asquith and Baldwin I had already published biographies. Therefore, just to maintain the continuity, I confined myself to very short essays dealing exclusively with their brief (very brief in Baldwin's case) periods at the Exchequer. On Churchill I had written nothing, but it seemed to me ludicrous to attempt my overall appraisal of his long, splendiferous and fluctuating career within the confines of a thirty-page essay. I therefore decided to write only about his four and a half 1920s years at the Treasury, now a largely forgotten and, if remembered, ill-esteemed period of his life. These years proved a rewarding segment of his life, in some ways showing his Chancellorship in a more favourable light than is the conventional verdict, and displaying his vast energy, many-faceted occupations and sometimes ill-judged exuberance, which at the age of just over fifty were even more in evidence than sixteen years later when he started his premiership. He therefore provided ample material for a time-concentrated but, in the scale of this book, full-length essay.

Something the same was true of Lloyd George, although leading to a different shape of result. His Chancellorship (and particularly his 1909 'people's budget') had figured prominently in my first and now long-ago foray into early-twentieth-century history, *Mr Balfour's Poodle*. His later career, which took him as far away from the affairs of the Treasury as from the hills of North Wales, was almost as spectacular and swooping as that of Churchill. It has been subject to extensive and sometimes deep biographical excavations, which indeed is still continuing as John Grigg moves to his fourth and maybe his fifth volume. I therefore approached Lloyd George with considerable caution, and eventually decided on a two-barrel approach. The first deals with his Chancellorship, paying more attention to his lesser-known budgets of 1910–15 than I had hitherto done, and the second, which started life as a lecture given at his birthplace as part of the 1995 Criccieth Festival, attempts to set him in the galaxy of the thirty-five Prime Ministers who had come before him and the fifteen who have come afterwards. It is the only part of this book which was not written specially for it.

Even apart from this out-of-category quartet, the essays vary a good deal in length, and not wholly in accordance with the pattern I would have expected. I did not assume there would be great stores of fascinating information to be tapped in the careers of C. T. Ritchie, Sir Robert Horne and Sir Kingsley Wood, and those assumptions proved to be true, although all three provide the interest of explaining how they ever got to the job, and Wood was a better than average Chancellor. It was however easy to deal with them within essays a little longer than those which, for quite different reasons, sufficed for Asquith and Baldwin.

What I would never have guessed in advance was the identity of the two who spontaneously called forth the longest essays: Austen Chamberlain and Philip Snowden. Austen, the least forceful of the three Chamberlains, had a long and variegated ministerial career, starting in 1895 and ending only in 1931, embracing two Chancellorships, one when he was forty and the other when he was fifty-five, as well as becoming the only Conservative leader in this century, so far at least, who was never Prime Minister. This last attribute was, I fear, an epitome of his role as a 'nearly man' of politics, less talented but even more long-suffering than R. A. Butler. But his remarkable interest for a dull man lay not so much in his spanning so many chapters of political history and so many different offices of state as in his ability to survive without fatal psychological damage being moulded, just as though he had been placed in one of those metal presses which were a feature of the Birmingham background from which sprang the remarkable Chamberlain success story, into the same physical shape as his father, although made of very different mental and emotional material.

Philip Snowden was a mule, without pride of ancestry or, childless, of posterity, compared with Austen Chamberlain. But he was a still more rewarding subject, an idealistic mordant cripple from the recesses of the Pennines, who gradually shifted his raking fire from the harshness of capitalism to the sentimentalities of socialist aspiration. Despite the mutual dislike – contempt on Snowden's part – which existed between him and Ramsay MacDonald, he was the inevitable Chancellor of the Exchequer of the first two Labour governments and of the first days of his 'National' coalition. Snowden was neither an easy colleague nor a nice man, but he was a formidable parliamentarian and minister, who deserves far more attention than he currently receives.

The two Chancellor/Prime Ministers, other than the four who I have treated specially, were Bonar Law and Neville Chamberlain. They necessarily require fairly long essays. Both of them were, in differing ways, better Chancellors than they were Prime Ministers. They were both men of somewhat melancholic disposition and narrow competence.

They were both products of provincial business culture, Glasgow in one case, Birmingham in the other, although shot through, more strongly in Chamberlain's than in Law's case, with a social reform conscience. They were also both obvious reactions as party leaders against the more emollient styles of their predecessors, Balfour and Baldwin. In the Balfour/Law case, and to a lesser extent in the Baldwin/Chamberlain one, it was also a shift from a higher to a more workaday style. Both their careers had tragic ends.

The remaining five were all men of considerable contemporary interest and impact but of whom it is difficult to say that they left a deep imprint upon the history of the country. They represented between them a wide range of provenance. Michael Hicks Beach (Lord St Aldwyn) was the English country gentleman as Chancellor. G. J. Goschen was the City financier as Chancellor, with as much of cosmopolitanism as of Britain in his background. Reginald McKenna, with a French mother and an Irish father, was the lad o' parts as Chancellor; he also became a great City figure, but post rather than pre his Treasury experience. John Simon was the epitome of the ambitious advocate as Chancellor. John Anderson (Waverley) equally epitomized the powerfully thrusting civil servant and wholly reliable administrator, whether in India or at home, as Chancellor.

I find it difficult to imagine any of this quintet as Prime Minister, although that is perhaps true of nearly everyone until they actually occupy the top post, and I doubt if any of them ever saw 10 Downing Street as being closely within their grasp, or its occupancy their primary and realistic motivation. This is despite the facts that Queen Victoria's eyes once flickered towards Goschen as a possible but constitutionally improper alternative to Gladstone, and that Winston Churchill wrote a formal early 1945 letter saying that, if he and Eden were both killed on the journey to Yalta, Anderson would be the best successor.

Taken together the post-Gladstonian Chancellors were a disparate lot, with no very obvious sinews of provenance, style or policy connecting them. They all however had at their service (or as some might say were at the service of) the department with the highest authority in Whitehall and partly as a result the opportunity to be one of the foremost members of the governments to which they belonged. But this was essentially an opportunity rather than a guarantee. No one could say that C. T. Ritchie was more dominant than Joseph Chamberlain, or Reginald McKenna (in 1915 and 1916) more so than Lloyd George, although even in these two cases the Chancellors were quite good at standing up to the stars who twinkled over their heads. Equally, Kingsley Wood from 1940 to 1943, competently though he performed, was not remotely the second (or the third or the fourth) man in the Churchill Coalition.

Two of these examples, however, were from wartime, with the unusual structures of government which then evolved; and Ritchie's appointment was a careless mistake by Balfour. For the rest, with the clear exception of Robert Horne (but that again was in the special circumstances of a coalition government) and the more doubtful exceptions of Goschen, Hicks Beach and Austen Chamberlain (in his first phase), all nineteen of my subjects were in the top three of their governments, and mostly carried power and a political weight second only to that of the Prime Minister.

The only office which provided anything like a steadily competing bastion of fame and power was the Foreign Office. But although working backwards, Bevin was ahead of Dalton in 1945–7, Eden ahead of Anderson in 1943–5 and Curzon ahead of Horne in 1921–2, the boot has mostly been on the other foot. Two interesting jousting grounds between the two departments were provided in the second Baldwin and the second MacDonald governments, which between them held office from 1924 to 1931. Under Baldwin, Austen Chamberlain was a very senior Conservative Foreign Secretary who with the Locarno Treaties secured the last achievement of his long ministerial career and was rewarded with both the Nobel Peace Prize and the Garter. But Winston Churchill, a surprise appointment to the Exchequer in view both of his very recent Conservative adherence and of his reputation for erratic judgement, was a more powerful influence on the central policies of the government.

Equally, in the succeeding Labour government, Arthur Henderson was not only the anchor of the party machine but also a Foreign Secretary who won wide international repute (and incidentally another Nobel Prize – which no British Foreign Secretary has since achieved). This did not prevent him being completely routed in his principal clash – at the Hague War Debts Conference of 1929 – by the Yorkshire stubbornness of the half-socialist idealism and half-embittered jingoism of his Chancellor colleague Philip Snowden. 'I might as well go home,' Henderson said after a few days of the conference. 'That's about it, Arthur' was Snowden's unyielding reply. The Exchequer victory was not made less striking by the fact that Snowden was foolishly wrong and Henderson wisely right.

This power, verging upon pre-eminence, the Treasury and successive

Chancellors owed largely to Gladstone, surprisingly aided by Disraeli, for it was exceptional to have them pulling in the same direction on the same rope. Prior to Disraeli's Chancellorship in the 1851 Derby government and Gladstone's in the 1852–5 Aberdeen one, the Exchequer was by no means the most sought-after or the most powerful office. Althorp had been an important figure in the Grey government, but the occupants of the office under Melbourne, Peel and Russell (Francis Baring, Henry Goulburn and George Cornewall Lewis) were far from dominating. The Home and Foreign Secretaries in all these governments were figures of greater fame. And it was not just a question of personality, for up to and over the 1840s Peel government a large part of the fiscal policy was controlled by the Board of Trade, with Gladstone first as Vice-President under the non-active Ripon and then as President himself.

From about the mid-century point onwards all this changed dramatically. Disraeli was the agent of the Chancellor becoming outwardly second, and Gladstone, although never nominally so until after the death of Palmerston in 1865, gave his eleven budgets of the 1850s and 1860s such a sweep and force that their presentation became a fixture of the national life comparable with Derby Day or the State Opening of Parliament. In addition their substance became so central to the then limited machinery of government that he greatly enhanced not only his own influence but the institutional power and prestige of Treasury officials in Whitehall.

Disraeli's contribution was somewhat paradoxical, as befitted his character. By splitting the Tory party in 1846 he so weakened it for a generation both in electability and in personnel that it enjoyed only short snatches at minority office with Derby in the Lords as (three times) the only possible Prime Minister. Disraeli himself was just as inevitably (and triply) the only possible leader of the House of Commons. And as he each time combined this position with being Chancellor so he elevated that office institutionally, complementing the way in which Gladstone was increasing its policy dominance during the same two decades, which incidentally were those of Britain's most unchallenged commercial supremacy.

The 1870s and the 1880s were less vaulting decades for the Chancellor and the Treasury. In his first government (from 1868) Gladstone made Robert Lowe (later Viscount Sherbrooke) Chancellor. Lowe was an awkward, admirable, rather non-administrative man, who was not a great success at the Exchequer. In 1873 he was moved, as a result of a departmental scandal not touching his honour, to the Home Office, and Gladstone, which he was only too inclined to do, resumed personal control of the Treasury for the last unfortunate year of that, on the whole, notable and successful government.

From 1874 to 1880, Disraeli's only period of real power, Stafford Northcote was Chancellor, as he had been during his chief's brief February-to-December 1868 premiership. And after 1876, when Disraeli became Beaconsfield, Northcote was leader of the House of Commons as well. A worthy figure whose career included having been twice Gladstone's private secretary (inhibiting for opposing the Grand Old Man in the House of Commons) and co-author of the Trevelyan–Northcote report on open and competitive recruitment to the civil service, he was a serious but not a flamboyant politician. In the next parliament he was the butt of Randolph Churchill's Fourth Party, and became nicknamed 'the Goat' but not for the same reason that Lloyd George attracted that sobriquet. He did not enhance his office, but nor could he be held to have let it down.

In the 1880s and the second Gladstone government the Prime Minister began by foolishly again doubling up and becoming Chancellor as well as First Lord of the Treasury. It was difficult to see what purpose was served by this exhausting arrangement other than that of achieving the clear all-time record of introducing thirteen budgets. At the end of 1882, however, Gladstone was persuaded to give up the double burden and appointed H. C. E. Childers who, although a serious man with a very serious bearded appearance, was a less than averagely distinguished Chancellor who brought less than average strength to the government. It was perhaps an example of a Prime Minister making a weak appointment to a department in which they themselves have specialized, a Selwyn Lloyd to an Anthony Eden.

After Childers there begins my series of nineteen. Ten of them were Oxbridgians, five from each, an unusual balance between the two universities over that sixty years. (Foreign Secretaries split ten to two in favour of Oxford, Prime Ministers five to three and Viceroys of India six to three). Only three of the Chancellors were Etonians (Randolph Churchill, Hicks Beach and Hugh Dalton (as against six among the Foreign Secretaries) and another five from major boarding schools (three from Rugby and two from Harrow). Only two of the Chancellors had serious landed property (Hicks Beach and Harcourt, but the latter not inheriting until nearly the end of his life). Another six of them were or became commercially rich, and three others earned large fees as leading advocates. Two began their lives in humble circumstances, and another six (including two sons of Nonconformist ministers) at the very modest end of the middle class. None ended in poverty, for that, even before the practice of 'selling their lives dearly' to publishers and the Sunday newspapers became the practice, has rarely been the lot of ex-senior ministers. But at least three were mildly financially embarrassed towards the end of their lives. None of the nineteen was a crook, or even, *pace* Baldwin on Horne (see p. 236), a full cad, but several of them, including the two most famous, would have found embarrassing a modern degree of investigation into their personal finances.

Their policies varied considerably, although probably less than their styles, as did the circumstances of war and peace, secure prosperity or near bankruptcy, trade upswing or downswing, in which they had to operate. But none of them, hardly even Dalton, accepted responsibility for the overall economic, as opposed to the purely fiscal, health of the nation as subsequent Chancellors from Cripps onwards have done. They took the ups and downs of the trade cycle almost as acts of God, and no more tried to claim credit for the good years than to accept blame for the bad ones. Pre-1914 at least this applied just as much to a radical and pro-active Chancellor like Lloyd George as to a money-market-orientated one like Goschen, or a cautious follower of official Treasury advice like Austen Chamberlain in his first (1903–5) spell as Chancellor.

The job of the Chancellor was seen as preserving fiscal balance and maintaining the national credit whatever the state of the seas which had to be navigated. It emphatically did not include trying to determine the state of the economic weather. Fiscal balance involved public expenditure discipline on the one hand (which gave the Treasury much of its authority over other departments) and on the other the careful fostering of taxable resources, almost entirely for their actual and potential revenue yield and hardly at all for wider policy purposes. It was rather like a skilled and dedicated gamekeeper looking to the supply of pheasants or grouse, not only for the forthcoming season but for future years as well. Maintaining national credit depended upon prudent debt management, keeping interest rates sufficiently low not to make servicing the national debt an intolerable burden on the budget, but not so low as to threaten borrowing ability. This balance was struck without much regard to the lateral effects of interest rate policy, to the consequences for industrial investment or to building activity for instance. It so happened that Britain up to 1914, the first twenty-eight years of this book's sixty-year span, was mostly a low-interest country, but that was a desirable consequence of the good standing of the national credit rather than a stimulus sought for its own sake.

Most of these assumptions survived the First World War or at least were revived after it. Philip Snowden's two short Labour Chancellorships were based upon them as strongly as had been the reigns of Goschen and Hicks Beach. Indeed Snowden was more severe on the public expediture side than they had been. Winston Churchill between Snowden's two Chancellorships and Neville Chamberlain after his second were in differing ways less Gladstonian and more interventionist. Churchill with his derating proposals proclaimed the specific intention of giving a stimulus to industry, and Chamberlain, apart from actively encouraging much cartelization of traditional industries in decline, saw the low interest rates which he achieved from 1932 onwards as a fine instrument for recovery through house-building.

In the Second World War the Chancellors fluctuated between Simon's business-as-usual attitude, although with some quite heavy taxation increases, through the much more Keynesian approach of Kingsley Wood, to the 'steady as she goes' caution of John Anderson. Then came Dalton, pushing cheap money harder even than Chamberlain had done and firmly using taxation for the first time, although both Harcourt and Lloyd George had veered in this direction, as a direct route to equality rather than as a means of raising revenue in a way that could be plausibly presented as fair between the classes. But, sharing economic power first with Herbert Morrison as Lord President and then with Stafford Cripps as Minister of Economic Affairs, he did not succeed in bringing together (indeed hardly tried to do so) the overall allocation of resources.

Among the Chancellors, as has been said, were to be found six future Prime Ministers. This left five who, during the period covered, took over 10 Downing Street for the first time without having gone through the Treasury experience. They were Rosebery, Balfour, Campbell-Bannerman, MacDonald and Attlee. None of these claimed to know much about economic or financial affairs, and, with the exception of Attlee, were less successful Prime Ministers than the six who had served at the Exchequer. Baldwin however rather broke the pattern. Although in many ways the most successful politician of the inter-war years, he was very much in the category of a laid-back Prime Minister. His seven months as Chancellor (preceded, however, by fours years as Financial Secretary to the Treasury) seemed to slip over him like water over the back of the cliché'd duck. As a former Chancellor who behaved as though he had not been one, he was balanced, at a slightly later period, by Harold Wilson, who gave the reverse impression.

More fundamentally I believe that the attempt to draw patterns out of these nineteen disparate lives is a tenuous and even sterile exercise. It is like trying to break a cipher from an imperfect text. Perhaps happily, Chancellors do not come as die-stampings. They are almost, but not quite, as variegated as a random selection of any nineteen reasonably successful men. They all had somewhat more than average ability and substantially more than average ambition. The reason for bringing them together is not to prove a point, but the belief that there is some interest in all their lives, and the hope that between them they illustrate some of the currents and some of the quirks of the river of British politics as it flowed from Gladstone to Attlee.

Roy Jenkins
30 August 1997

Lord Randolph Churchill

It is an ironical thought that, a century after his death, Lord Randolph Churchill should be best known as a father. It is ironical because in life an intensely personal fame, sought and achieved, was his forte, just as parenthood or any other form of domestic activity most certainly was not.

Churchill lived less than forty-six years, and for the last two or three of them was in pitiable physical and mental decline. He became a member of Parliament at the age of twenty-five in 1874, but did not make a national mark until after the 1880 election. He then had three years or so as a brilliant parliamentary gadfly, tormenting almost equally Gladstone in his second premiership and Stafford Northcote, Churchill's nominal leader in the Commons. This period was followed by two and a half years – no more – when he was at the centre of Conservative politics, Salisbury's most prominent if not most trusted colleague. He had two six-month experiences of office, first as Secretary of State for India and then as Chancellor of the Exchequer as well as leader of the House of Commons. The one was brought to an end by the defeat of Salisbury's minority government, the other by Churchill's own resignation, which was ill tempered, ill judged and almost certainly not intended to be taken seriously. But Salisbury had by then had enough of Churchill, and was not a man to prevent the suicide of a nuisance. Thereafter Churchill retained his interest (could he mount a come-back?) but not his power until the early 1890s when the shades began to close around him.

Was he ever near to being a serious statesman? Undoubtedly he had some high political talents. He had a gift for mordant, wounding, sometimes very funny phrases. And having thought up the most outrageous attack he had the nerve to deliver it, without fear of offending taste or friends or damaging his own repute. Like Disraeli before him, Joseph Chamberlain among his near contemporaries and F. E. Smith after him, he was strong on insolence. He also had other attributes necessary to make his words resound and his fame increase: a mnemonic name, an idiosyncratic appearance, and a good delivery, whether on the platform or in the House of Commons. In addition he had sporadic charm, although intermingled with offensive and often pointless rudeness.

But did he have supporting qualities underneath his brash and slightly vulgar charisma? That is the basic question with which the rest of this essay will be concerned. It was generally assumed that he was not educated ('Of course he isn't,' Harcourt said, 'if he were he'd be spoiled'), but in fact he had got a perfectly respectable second class in history at Merton College, Oxford, together with the sustenance of one of those tutors who was prepared to say that it might easily have been a first. He was however always slapdash in his facts and unrooted in any coherence of political belief. 'Shuffle up the cards and try again' was his most consistent motto. Yet most of his officials in both the India Office and the Treasury thought that he was a good minister. In the latter department this was the more striking because he was surrounded by 'Gladstonians', in the sense not only that they took the GOM's attitude to candle-ends (which Churchill intermittently shared), but that they had personally served him. And it is difficult to think of any two late-nineteenth-century politicians whose style had less in common than that of Gladstone and Churchill.

Gladstone's respect for dukes, or 'Scotch toadyism to the aristocracy' as Dilke more brutally put it, did not extend to the Marlboroughs. In an 1882 account of Gladstone's conversation he was recorded as saying, 'There never was a Churchill from John of Marlbourgh down who had either morals or principles.' While the style and rhythm of this sentence was not very convincingly Gladstonian, it is nonetheless the case that the sentiment contained an important fragment of the truth. None of the six Dukes of Marlborough who had by that time succeeded the victor of Blenheim had added to the lustre of the family name (nor can anything different be said of the subsequent quartet). The fifth duke, although a talented gardener, had in addition seriously dissipated the family fortune, and had to abandon the fine arboreal estate (now the site of Reading University) where he had exercised his botanical skills. The sixth duke was almost equally extravagant. It later required several grafts of American heiresses to keep in the family Vanbrugh's palace at Woodstock, but that at least has been both retained and maintained.

In this line Randolph Churchill's father, the seventh duke, although not a very exciting figure, was probably the one with the highest sense of public service. He was an MP for a decade or so and Lord-Lieutenant of Ireland for four years. His wife (Randolph's mother) was a Londonderry daughter and something of a battleaxe. She was devoted to her second son, and sought to promote his political interests with more determination than tact. She survived him and at the time of his death wrote a letter of bitter reproach to Salisbury for not having saved her son from destroying his own political career. Her elder son, although in many ways like Lord Randolph, but without his bursts of inspired energy, did not call forth the same degree of maternal feeling. He too predeceased her, and was always known as Blandford, an ill-fated name to which his life and personality were well matched, even during the short nine years during which he held the dukedom. The main imprint that he left on Blenheim was that of selling off the outstanding picture collection, an act of which Lord Randolph deeply disapproved, even though his own pattern of life hardly amounted to careful stewardship.

Lord Randolph Churchill's background, therefore, while nominally that of the high aristocracy, did not have a wholly secure foundation of esteem, public service or affluence. It was subtly different from that of a Cavendish, a Russell, a Cecil or a Stanley. What was remarkable was that as a branch from this doubtful trunk, he should, for two generations in the male line but no more, have started such a combination of his own streak of lightning through the sky and his son's many-splendoured genius.

Randolph Churchill's qualities, although flamboyant and never steady, were well short of genius. But how far were they above the political 'pranks' (Salisbury's word for Churchill's habits of behaviour) of an essentially immature young man without much warmth of heart or depth of brain? Gladstone thought that he had not 'a single grain of conviction in him except in the abstract' (whatever the last phrase meant). Salisbury as early as 1884 saw him as being the antithesis of the Soudanese Mahdi, who then occupied his thoughts about as much as did Randolph, and who 'pretends to be half-mad and is very sane in reality'. Balfour, who had been an early Churchill ally, although also a detached one as was always the way with Balfour, said that he had 'the manners of a pirate and the courage of a governess'.*

---

* Professor Roy Foster, who quotes this in his succinct and penetrating 1981 biography of Churchill, aptly commented that the epigram, if reversed, would have applied very

How did Churchill see himself? Although he was always, even well before his destructive illness, subject to moods of black depression, the conceit of his more sanguine periods was probably best summed up in an April 1882 letter to *The Times*, when he wrote of the need for 'a statesman who fears not to meet and who knows how to sway immense masses of the working classes, and who either by his genius or his eloquence, or by all the varied influences of an ancient name, can move the hearts of households'. A pretence of modesty was maintained by leaving a cloak of ambiguity as to whether this mythical 'clothed in white samite' statesman was supposed to be Salisbury (whose leadership Churchill was temporarily promoting over the despised Stafford Northcote) or himself. But there can be no doubt which he thought had the greater eloquence and command over the masses.

The early months of 1874, when he was just twenty-five years old, contained two of the most important departure points of Churchill's life. In February, after a hard fight in spite of it being the family borough lying respectfully at the park gates, he was elected member of Parliament for Woodstock. And in April he was married in Paris to Jennie Jerome. She was a twenty-year-old American whom he had met at Cowes the previous August and had become engaged to on the third evening of their acquaintanceship. It was unquestioningly a courtship of passion, although the marriage to which it led, except in its early days, was more notable for its first offspring than for its sustaining companionship. Winston Churchill was born at the end of November 1874 and his brother Jack just over five years later. Nevertheless it lasted, in a fluctuating and somewhat rackety way, for the remaining twenty-one years of Randolph Churchill's life. Lady Randolph subsequently made two further marriages before her death in 1921 at the age of sixty-seven. The first was to George Cornwallis-West, a Scots Guards lieutenant two decades her junior, and lasted fourteen years before ending in divorce; West then married Mrs Patrick Campbell. The second in 1918 (when she was sixty-four) was to Montagu Porch, a quiet Somerset gentleman who was a junior Colonial Service official in Nigeria and was even more junior to his wife than Cornwallis-West had been.

In 1874 however Jennie Jerome was a *jeune fille en fleur* apparently suitable to become one of the first and (by virtue of her elder son) the

---

well to Balfour himself. Foster's view was that Churchill always behaved essentially as a character in a political novel with 'all the trappings, opportunism and triviality characteristic of the genre'.

most famous of the American wives and mothers who have been so frequent a feature of British political life for at least a century from the 1870s. That was the decade when their importation started, as was accurately recorded by Trollope, always a sensitive social barometer, who portrayed the growing need and greed of the British aristocracy which made their sustenance so desirable in *The Way We Live Now* (1875), and also described a notable example who carried off a most desirable heir in *The Duke's Children* (1880). Unlike Isabel Boncassen, the heroine (or at least the victor) of the latter work, however, Jennie Jerome was not exactly a girl from the golden west. In the first place she had passed most of her adolescence in Paris and been educated there. And second, while her looks were undoubtedly striking, she quickly assumed an appearance which was hard, imperious and above all self-indulgent. She was the antithesis of a flaxen-haired, *ingénue* singing her way gaily and undemandingly through a musical-comedy cornfield.

Her father, Leonard Jerome, was a New York financier of verve and considerable but fluctuating fortune. When the Duke of Marlborough approached him about a heavy marriage settlement (what else were rich Americans for?) he found him difficult, ostensibly because of his disapproval of women's weak position under English property law, but it may also have been due to his heavy losses in the Stock Exchange fall of 1873. Winston Churchill's statement in his intensely filial 1906 biography that his grandfather 'owned and edited the *New York Times*' seems to have owed everything to pietistic feeling and nothing to truth. What Jerome was strong in was New York race-tracks, having founded both Jerome Park and the Coney Island Jockey Club. Eventually, after some haggling, he settled the equivalent of a modern £2.5 million on the couple. It was far from enough for them to avoid a constant state of indebtedness.

For some time Churchill devoted more attention to his wife than he did to the House of Commons. Indeed his approach to serious politics was by the circuitous route of Dublin. When his father was appointed Irish Viceroy in 1876 he accompanied him there, set up house in one of the Phoenix Park lodges and acted as a sort of supernumerary private secretary. During the Dublin years he believed himself to have acquired a close understanding of and sympathy with the Irish, and he certainly made lasting friendships with an unusual group of indigenous career-makers who clustered around the house at Howth of Gerald Fitzgibbon. Fitzgibbon himself advanced from (Irish) Solicitor-General to Lord Justice of Appeal during Churchill's Dublin sojourn; the others were mostly graduates of Trinity College and Protestant (although they included the fashionable Father James Healy of Bray who, in conjunction with that parish's former vicar of 200 years before, showed that worldliness could be an ecumenical quality in County Wicklow). But they were not of the landed and alien ascendancy. They were more akin to Bloomsbury, or the Brattle Street associates of Emerson, Holmes and Longfellow in Cambridge, Massachusetts, or even to the Raymond Mortimer/Desmond Shaw-Taylor set at Long Crichel, than to an aristocratic clique. They included, apart from Fitzgibbon and Healy, Michael Morris (later as Lord Killanin Lord Chief of Justice of Ireland), David Plunkett and Provost Mahaffy of Trinity. They were Unionists but not uncritically so. Churchill loved their high-talking, hard-drinking and misogynous society. Lady Randolph was never of the party during his many Howth Christmases over the next dozen years. He always liked unorthodox recreations. In the 1880s he had a share of a house in Paris and was more likely, when he needed respite, to slip away there or to Howth than to an English country-house party.

His Irish connections and sympathy led Churchill to deliver at a Woodstock farmers' dinner in the autumn of 1877 what was widely interpreted as a 'Home Rule' speech. In fact his words did not strictly bear such an interpretation, although they amounted to a very sharp criticism of British rule in Ireland, which was quite something from the Lord-Lieutenant's son. His father gave him an ambiguous vote of confidence, saying that on such an occasion he assumed he was drunk. In the House of Commons his problem at this stage was non-attendance rather than indiscretion. At the 1880 election when he attempted to make much of the splendour of the Disraeli government's external record, his Woodstock opponent was able damagingly to point out that Churchill had been present for only three of the Parliament's 217 divisions on foreign affairs.

His speeches were as rare as his votes, but given his age (still under thirty) and his unfamiliarity with the ways and rules of the House they could be remarkably presumptuous. In 1878 he helped to kill a County Government Bill which had been brought forward by the President of the Local Government Board, the curiously named George Sclater-Booth. Churchill, rather presaging some of his later speeches, made the name of its sponsor half the count against the bill. Despite the evolution of his self-proclaimed status as the first of the Tory Democrats and an early prophet of a classless Conservatism, there was a strong strain of anti-middle-class snobbery which ran through several of his speeches.

From the great height of Blenheim there was nothing he liked better than looking down on bourgeois pretension. Mr Sclater-Booth, who was in fact a respectable Balliol Wykehamist and a fellow of the Royal Society, was denigrated for displaying all the pomp of minor ministerial authority and of 'a double-barrelled name, so often associated with mediocrity' as well as presuming to meddle with matters above his concern. A President of the Local Government Board might deal with 'the Poor Law, with sanitary questions, with the salaries of inspectors of muisance', but not with historic forms of government in the counties.

It was all very much of a piece with his bestowal of the department-store name of Marshall and Snelgrove upon the combination of R. A. Cross, the Lancashire banker who became Disraeli's Home Secretary, and W. H. Smith, the stationer–statesman. Even more strongly did it come out when he denounced Smith for seeking to exclude Ireland from the operation of the 1884 Reform Bill on the ground that it would give the franchise to peasants who lived in 'mud-cabins', 'I suppose'. Churchill said,

> in the minds of the lords of suburban villas, of the owners of vineries and pineries, the mud-cabin represents the climax of physical and social degradation. But the franchise in England has never been determined by Parliament with respect to the character of the dwellings. The difference between the cabin of the Irish peasant and the cottage of the English agricultural labourer is not so great as that which exists between the abode of the right honourable member for Westminster [Smith] and the humble roof which shelters from the storm the individual who now has the honour to address the Committee.

When in the same year, switching his aim from members of his own party on to Liberal targets, Churchill had mocked Gladstone for being a self-advertiser comparable with the purveyors of 'Colman's mustard, Holloway's pills and Horniman's pure tea', the GOM sadly remarked that it was 'a curious fact that real vulgar abuse always and only emanated from scions of the highest aristocracy'.

Vulgar or not, Churchill had a brilliant gift for phrase-making accompanied by the brazenness never to suppress his own most outrageous thoughts. He pinned on to Gladstone the unforgettable label of 'an old man in a hurry', and he mocked his favourite tree-cutting recreation with the thought that 'the forest laments so that Mr Gladstone may perspire'. At a more serious level it is impossible to think of a more effective (or more seditious) slogan than 'Ulster will fight and Ulster will be right'. In the 1870s Disraeli had denounced Salisbury as 'a great master of gibes and flouts and jeers'. In the late 1880s, however, there can be no doubt that Randolph Churchill, who after a period of alliance became Salisbury's greatest bugbear, proved himself an even greater master of these weapons than the by then somewhat weary marquess.

Before Churchill could exploit these exceptional if not very profound gifts he had to get himself re-elected for Woodstock in 1880 and establish himself in the new parliament in a way that he had not done in the previous one. The first hurdle he cleared by a margin of only sixty votes – but it was of course on a Conservative ebb-tide. The second he sailed over more triumphantly by the shock tactics of setting up the 'Fourth party', with himself as the self-proclaimed but nonetheless natural leader. Its name came from a typical piece of quick-footed effrontery by Churchill himself. One night in the first year of the new parliament the sonorous cliché that there were 'two great parties of state' rolled out of the mouth of a member. Parnell interrupted with 'three' and Randolph Churchill with 'four'. It was the second interjection which got the laugh and made the impact. Thereby Churchill's little band had made sufficient impact that the claim, while presumptuous, was not ludicrously so, and therefore stuck.

The 'four' had a double meaning, for they were not only the fourth party but also had four members. The others were Arthur Balfour, Sir Henry Drummond Wolff and John Eldon Gorst. Balfour, who eventually came to much more than Churchill, partly because he had eighty-two years (as opposed to Churchill's forty-six) in which to do it, was then a languid young man who, although a few months Churchill's senior, was very much the junior partner. He was also the one who quickly flaked off when he saw a conflict between membership of the group and his family loyalty to his uncle Salisbury. The other two were already middle-aged. Gorst was a lawyer/politician who was reputed to have made a big organizational contribution to the Conservative victory in 1874 but one unrecognized by any preferment in the subsequent Disraeli government. Wolff was a diplomat/politician with a touch of an adventurer about him. He was probably more at home in the Middle East than in London, but he had parliamentary verve and he was the member of the quartet with whom Churchill remained on most consistently good terms.

It was Wolff who seized on the issue which brought the quartet together and into prominence. In the first days of the new parliament he led the attack on Bradlaugh, the atheist member for Northampton, who although elected four times, at the general election and at three subsequent by-elections, was prevented from either swearing or affirming his way into the House for the whole of that five-year parliament. Churchill quickly poured his oratorical resources into the gap which Wolff had opened. Three days later he made a histrionic (some might say hysterical) speech on the issue which culminated in his throwing a pamphlet of Bradlaugh's on the floor of the House of Commons and stamping upon it.

Churchill's motives were about as cynical as they could have been, but his tactics were brilliant. The cynicism was manifold. First his religious conviction, while making him what might be called a staunch political Anglican, could hardly be regarded as a tenth that of Gladstone, who nonetheless took a Voltairean position towards what he regarded as the unattractive aberrations of Bradlaugh. Second, the Bradlaugh pamphlet, which Churchill treated with so much physical contempt, was an attack on the royal family, and Churchill was anxious, following a bitter 1876 quarrel with the Prince of Wales involving a lady (his brother's rather than his own), abusive letters and nearly a duel, to repair relations with that leader of rakish fashionable society which was his own natural habitat; and the stamping incident did indeed make some considerable progress in this direction. Third, Bradlaugh's campaigning activities extended to denouncing archaic state pensions, of which one of the least defensible examples was the £4,000 a year (£200,000 today) which the Dukes of Marlborough continued to receive in recognition of their ancestor's military prowess.

Anti-Bradlaughism, as developed by Churchill, Wolff and the others, was nevertheless an excellent ploy for the objectives which the Fourth party had in its sights. These were to offer a more spirited opposition to the Gladstone government than was forthcoming from the official party leaders, and thereby to undermine Sir Stafford Northcote and his almost equally staid colleagues of the Tory 'old gang'. For what purpose were they to be undermined? Motives are mostly mixed, but the nearest approach to an accurate answer is to say that it was first to provide amusement, almost a form of parliamentary foxhunting, for two potentially bored young men (Churchill and Balfour) supported by two more middle-aged whippers-in (Wolff and Gorst); second to promote the fame and prospects of Lord Randolph Churchill; and third (and later) to advance to somewhat imprecise but not ignoble concept which was given the name of Tory Democracy.

The attempt to combine these three objectives led to considerable paradoxes and strains, not least in relation to who were their heroes and who were their devils. Disraeli was the first hero. He had been an exponent of stylish and adventurous politics (in contrast with North-cote), he liked patting rebels on the head, which he conspicuously did to Lord Randolph and co. until the spring of 1881, and after that he had the even greater advantage of being dead, which meant that there was no danger of his repudiating them. On the other hand and within a few years Churchill was calling for 'a casting off and burning of those old, worn-out aristocratic and class governments from which the Derby–Dizzy lot, with their following of county families, could never, or never cared to, extricate themselves'. The problem was that if Churchill proclaimed himself the harbinger of a new Toryism he could hardly convincingly align himself with the head of the last Conservative government.

He had something of the same trouble with Salisbury. In the early days of the Fourth party it had half been a lobbying organization to get Salisbury, the leader in the Lords, elevated above Northcote and proclaimed the overall chief and therefore the obvious next Prime Minister. This might have the beneficial side-effect of humiliating Northcote to an extent which made him throw up even the downgraded Commons leadership and thus create a possible vacancy for Churchill. 'Young man in a hurry' although he undoubtedly was (still only thirty-three in 1882), even he may not have seen himself as being able to leap quite so soon to the centre of the citadel. But the promotion of Salisbury was key to his early strategy. In 1883 he pursued it on the issue of who should unveil Disraeli's statue in Parliament Square and wrote two letters to *The Times* of such unrestrained offensiveness to Northcote that, for the first time (but by no means the last), hardly any Conservative MP would speak to him.

By the following year, however, his next effort at self-promotion brought him into direct conflict with Salisbury. He switched his attention from Parliament to the country, and in particular to the 'great industrial boroughs', to use the almost romantic phraseology which he began to develop about them, and sought to capture the National Union of Conservative Associations, to give it a cutting edge comparable with Joseph Chamberlain's National Liberal Federation, and to use it as a weapon to cleave his way to the forefront of the party. Salisbury, as the effective founder of 'villa Conservatism', the elevator of the proprietors of 'vineries and pineries' whom Churchill so despised, was not at all keen on the latter's attempt to mobilize the mob for the Tory party. But at this stage Salisbury out-manoeuvred rather than took him head-on. Churchill, thinking that in rugby terms he had gained a realistic amount of ground, suddenly kicked for touch.

This may have been sensible – and indeed led to his entering a Cabinet within a year and becoming Salisbury's principal lieutenant within two – but it left several of his allies, most notably Gorst, running in the wrong direction and began a pattern of leaving his friends out on a limb which became one of his least attractive attributes. He successively let down – not perhaps with vicious intent but with devastating consequences for his reputation: Gorst; his other allies on the National Union Council; many leaders of provincial Conservatism; Joseph Chamberlain, with whom he tried to form some sort of Radical/ Unionist partnership after the Home Rule split (and who does not perhaps deserve too much sympathy because in general he was so much a man who got his retaliation in first); the Conservative Committee in the Central division of Birmingham; Sir Michael Hicks Beach, who after Churchill's resignation remained his best friend on the Conservative front bench; and, worst of all, Louis Jennings, MP for Stockport, who, after Churchill's fall, devoted his political life to an almost servile relationship with him until in March 1890 he was so affronted and disillusioned with Churchill's behaviour that he never again communicated.

This destroyed Jennings's political purpose and he died prematurely in 1893. Churchill was lucky that his widow was not provoked into recriminating against him in the way that Lady Randolph, and even more so the Dowager Duchess of Marlborough, did to Lord Salisbury at the time of Churchill's own death three years later. Mrs Jennings confined herself to a dignified request to Winston Churchill, when seven or eight years later he was preparing his life of his father, that a memorandum giving Jennings's own account of the split should be included in an appendix. It was, and honour was mutually satisfied. Nonetheless it is impossible not to be struck by the unspoken assumption of all concerned that Lord Randolph was entitled to be judged by different standards than other people. To damage him was 'to break a butterfly upon a wheel'. For him to break someone else was unfortunate, but great campaigns under great generals necessarily involve casualties.

The policy platforms upon which Churchill mounted his guns were as inconsistent as his personal affiliations. It was difficult to tell whether his fire would come from the left or the right. He was the arch exponent of the view that the business of opposition is to oppose, and he moved in whatever direction gave him most opportunity to make mischief, like wind blowing into an area of low pressure. On the first issue for the new parliament (of 1880) he mounted the high horse of religious intolerance, made piquant rather than portentous only by the wit and impudence with which he pretended that Gladstone's espousal of Bradlaugh's cause meant that the Grand Old High Churchman has suddenly been converted to atheism, republicanism and contraception.

Two or three years later he attacked the Gladstone government's Egyptian invasion with all the anti-imperialist fervour (if not quite the moral authority) which Gladstone himself had deployed against Disraeli's jingoism in the Midlothian campaign. But when the prospect of the third Reform Bill came into the centre of British politics in 1884 Churchill's stance was at first highly conservative. In a speech in Edinburgh at the end of 1883 he advanced a whole series of arguments, some of principle some of circumstance, against any early extension of the franchise. He was so negative that both Arthur Balfour and Lord Elcho (a nice combination) who were sharing the platform with him thought it necessary to repudiate what he had said. This chilling reception, and his decision to contest Birmingham at the next election (Woodstock faced extinction as a separate borough), concentrated his mind most wonderfully. Within a few months he denounced the mediocrity of 'an unchanging mind' and swung into a vigorous advocacy of the assimilation of the county to the borough franchise.

This was as nothing compared with his switch of position on Ireland. Winston Churchill, in his truly brilliant young man's biography of his father (he wrote it between the ages of twenty-seven and thirty), strenuously endeavoured to maintain that Lord Randolph was always consistent in his opposition to Home Rule. Such a defence is the more striking because Winston Churchill, in spite of his romantic pietism towards the father whom he hardly knew, is in general willing to evacuate, although often under a smokescreen of inaccurate and highly selective quotation, untenable pieces of ground. This is one reason, combined with its intense readability in spite of its two-volume tombstone shape, why the biography is brilliant. But on Lord Randolph's opposition to Home Rule he sticks: 'to the repeal of the Parliamentary Union he [Randolph Churchill] was always unalterably opposed'. 'No Unionist politician has a clearer record.' Against the charge of opportunism and inconsistency he has 'an unassailable defence'.

It is curious that Winston Churchill, already by the time of publication of his book a Liberal junior minister and soon to be both a leading member of a Home Rule Cabinet and a truculent opponent of Ulster at the time of the Curragh 'mutiny' in 1914, should have chosen such unpromising terrain on which to dig in, in defence of his father's consistency. Randolph Churchill had been a principal agent of the alliance with Parnell over the summer and autumn of 1885, which had brought down the second Gladstone government and had then garnered the Irish vote to the Conservatives in the towns. In pursuit of this objective he had sought to undermine Spencer's 'law and order' decisions, and by so doing had done much to swing both that ex-Viceroy and Harcourt to Home Rule. In and out of government he had opposed Coercion Acts, despite the fact that by 1885 at latest the only realistic alternatives for Ireland were Home Rule or a harsh period of 'resolute government'. He had often been tolerant of Irish obstructionism in the House of Commons; he liked parliamentary mischief. He had been party to several murky negotiations with Parnell. And he had expressed contempt for obscurantist Ulster politicians.

When therefore he went to Belfast in February 1886, whipped up religious as well as political intolerance and coined his immortal Ulster slogan there was a widespread feeling that he was motivated more by opportunism than by principle. And the jaunty and cynical tone in which he wrote to his friend Fitzgibbon within a few days of this speech would have done little, had it been known, to dispel suspicion: 'I decided some time ago that, if the GOM went for Home Rule, the Orange card would be the one to play. Please God it may turn out to be the ace of trumps and not the two . . .'

In a sense all of Randolph Churchill's political initiatives were the equivalent of choosing a card from his hand, sometimes almost at random, and banging it down on the table. Sometimes his ploys were wildly contradictory, as when, having been violently against imperialist expansion from Alexandria to Suakin (in the Red Sea), he gloried in the main event of his brief Indian Secretaryship being the annexation of Burma. Sometimes the initiatives were foolhardily courageous, as in 1889, when, while attempting in a series of speeches to rehabilitate himself with the Tory party, he launched his campaign at Walsall with a great attack on the evils of the drink trade and of the brewers, a group of gentlemen whose public spirit caused them to provide much of the foundation and finance of West Midlands Conservatism.

Insofar as there was a streak of consistency behind his juvenile lurchings it lay in his own unique capacity to communicate with working-class audiences in big industrial cities and in his desire to

prevent the Tory party being staid, bourgeois and dull. This was marred
by what a *Spectator* obituary described as 'his instinctive rowdyism'. He
liked an occasional provincial riot and a disorderly House of Commons.
He was good, until his powers began to fail, at riding them both. He
was an effective and offensive popular orator. Yet he did not rant, but
nor did he much elevate his audiences. Personal mockery was his most
frequent weapon. It was often funny mockery, but it was not particularly
good-naturedly so. He rarely tempered his raillery with caution about
his victim's reaction, and as a result he gave deep offence several times
to those with whom he was either attempting, or was soon to attempt,
to work closely. This was notably true of Hartington at the end of 1885
and of Chamberlain in early 1887. Hartington he compared in a
somewhat convoluted metaphor to a boa-constrictor, endlessly and
visibly digesting large lumps of the radical programme. But it was
probably the serious conclusion of the passage rather than the joke
which left lasting resentment:

> There is nothing democratic about the Whig. He is essentially a cold
> and selfish aristocrat who believes that the British Empire was erected
> by Providence and exists for no other purpose than to keep in power a
> few Whig families, and who thinks that our toiling and struggling
> millions of labourers and artisans are struggling and toiling for no
> other purpose than to maintain in splendour, opulence and power the
> Cavendishes and the Russells.

His speeches mostly give the impression of being prepared rather
than spontaneous (unlike Gladstone's), but quickly prepared with an
easy flow. In general he had a dangerous gift of fluency, which made his
political letters much too long. Lord Salisbury, during their few years of
political intimacy, must have groaned as yet another swollen and
unsolicited missive arrived from his bumptious lieutenant.* But he also
had a great gift, not for profound political thought, but for inventing
the wounding phrase and the amusing analogy. These qualities (and
indeed the whole flavour of his oratory) are epitomized in a passage of a
January 1884 speech at Blackpool in which he set his sights on the

---

* Salisbury may indeed have been tempted to anticipate Lord Elgin's laconic treatment
of Lord Randolph's son. Winston Churchill as a young Under-Secretary for the
Colonies addressed a vast memorandum to Elgin (who was his Secretary of State) which
ended, a little portentously, with 'These are my views, W. S. C.' 'But not mine, E.' was
the only addition which the Colonial Secretary made to the document.

highest peak in the mountain range and sought to describe Gladstone's method of receiving a deputation at Hawarden Castle:

It has always appeared to me somewhat incongruous that the great chief of the Radical party should reside in a castle. But to proceed, one would have thought that the deputation would have been received in the house, in the study, in the drawing room or even in the dining room. Not at all. Another scene had been arranged. The working-men were guided through the ornamental grounds, into the wide-spreading park, strewn with the wreckage and ruin of the Prime Minister's sport. All around them, we may suppose, lay the rotting trunks of once umbrageous trees: all around them, tossed by the winds, were boughs and bark and withered shoots. They came suddenly on the Prime Minister and Master Herbert [the fourth son and MP for Leeds], in scanty attire and profuse perspiration, engaged in the destruction of a gigantic oak, just giving its last dying groan. They are permitted to gaze and to worship and adore and, having conducted themselves with exemplary propriety, are each of them presented with a few chips as a memorial of that memorable scene.

Is not this, I thought to myself as I read the narrative, a perfect type and emblem of Mr Gladstone's government of the Empire? The working classes of this country in 1880 sought Mr Gladstone. He told them he would give them and all other subjects of the Queen much legislation, great prosperity, and universal peace; and he has given them nothing but chips. Chips to the faithful allies in Afghanistan, chips to the trusting native race of South Africa, chips to the Egyptian fellah, chips to the British farmer, chips to the manufacturer and the artisan, chips to the agricultural labourer, chips to the House of Commons itself. To all who leaned upon Mr Gladstone, who trusted in him, and who hoped for something from him – chips, nothing but chips – hard, dry, unnourishing, indigestible chips . . .

These gifts of mockery, impudence and popular oratory, harnessed to his tactics of self-promotion, virulence against the government and browbeating of his own leaders, were substantially successful. When, in the early summer of 1885, Salisbury had his chance to put together his first government, which had to survive without a parliamentary majority at least until November (because the slow passage of the Redistribution of Seats Bill made an earlier election impossible), Churchill's presence in the Cabinet was regarded as essential. Indeed his position looked so strong that he tried to make his own terms for entry, and to some extent succeeded, although typically overplaying his hand. Salisbury offered him the India Office, which Professor Foster, on the ground that it had been occupied by Salisbury himself and by Hartington, regarded as a traditional crown prince's pillow. Even discounting that, it was in itself acceptable to Churchill. It appealed to his imagination, and as he had just spent four months in the sub-continent, looked appropriate to the informed public.

His overplaying lay in trying to stipulate the shape of the rest of the government. Primarily he demanded that his long-standing butt, Stafford Northcote, who was also long-suffering, should be banished from the leadership of the House of Commons and elevated to misty eminence in the Lords. In this he eventually succeeded in forcing Salisbury's hand, partly because the latter half wanted it forced. Northcote was given the rare dignity for a non-Prime Minister of a political earldom from scratch, and the even rarer honour of being allowed to call himself First Lord of the Treasury. Salisbury, uniquely, was always happy to detach this title from the premiership, thus enabling him to concentrate his attention and his physical presence on the Foreign Office. When he gave the title to W. H. Smith in 1887 and to Balfour in 1891 and again in 1895 it meant something, for they were leaders of the House of Commons. But in the case of the Earl of Iddesleigh it was all honour and no power, for he had practically nothing to do.

With his other conditions Churchill was less successful. He secured minor appointments for Gorst and Wolff (Balfour of course could and did look after himself), but he failed in his other objectives of excluding from the Cabinet R. A. Cross, the Marshall or maybe the Snelgrove of his earlier joke, together with such other members of the Conservative 'old gang' as Richmond, Manners and Carnarvon. He thus began the government in a somewhat confrontational mood both with his Prime Minister and with nearly half the Cabinet who were there in spite of him. To balance this there was the good impression which, according to all his biographers, he made as a department chief. He impressed by his hard work, his quickness of comprehension and his surprising modesty and courtesy with officials. There was also the natural enjoyment which the more buoyant ones always derive from serving a 'star'. They like the enhancement of the prestige of the department which flows from such a ministerial chief, and find that anecdotes about his idiosyncrasies embellish their social lives.

The chorus of praise was not universal (when is it?). An important official (Bertram Currie) after several favourable phrases wrote: 'I never heard him express any large or statesmanlike views, and in my secret heart I thought him rather deficient in quality.' Perhaps more significant, the Viceroy (Dufferin) in a letter to the Queen's private secretary referred to 'my little master at the India Office', not the most obvious expression of affection or respect.

Dufferin, who following Ripon's liberal five years was almost as hard-line a Viceroy as Ripon's immediate predecessor Lytton, was not a steadying partner for Churchill. He led him into the war for the annexation of Burma, which while it added the name of the ancient kingdom of Ava to his own marquisal title did little but confuse Churchill's record. He played an ambiguous role in relation to Churchill's resistance to the appointment of the Queen's son (the Duke of Connaught) as Commander-in-chief of the Bombay Presidency, an issue on which Churchill presaged his December 1886 flounce by threatening resignation within five weeks of taking up office. And, much the most serious, Dufferin encouraged Churchill to disappoint all the hopes which he had aroused among Indian educated opinion during his four-month visit. The culmination of this sad process was his Birmingham denunciation, during the November election campaign, of a delegation from this group as 'three Bengalese baboos', who had disgracefully been allowed to appear in the Town Hall of that city alongside John Bright.

As the last example shows, Churchill's fault as a minister, and one for which Dufferin cannot be blamed, was his constant addiction to partisan demagogy. It came out strongly when he used his presentation of the Indian budget to the House of Commons for an astonishing personal attack on Ripon, whom he had extravagantly praised ('nothing but the change from Lytton to Ripon saved us from a second Mutiny') a few months before. In one of his most vicious dismissive passages he described the high-minded former Viceroy as having been 'dulled and made sullen by the narcotic effects of Indian life'. It might have just been acceptable at a provincial mass meeting (although hardly an aid to the good opinion of a much respected statesman of Empire), but in the presentation of a departmental budget it was about as appropriate as a comic hat on a bishop, and caused a mixture of amazement and offence. He was sufficiently aware of this that he wrote a letter of semi-excuse to Dufferin, saying that 'the first law of nature and governments' was self-preservation and that he had to mount a pre-emptive strike against the possibility of 'a second Midlothian campaign', with Gladstone denouncing Tory extravagance in India. Whether or not this was persuasive with the Viceroy, who was at least nominally a Liberal, it did not deflect

Dufferin from expressing pleasure and relief when, six months later, Kimberley returned to the India Office. There is no reason to dissent from Professor Foster's view that during his brief reign 'Churchill ruthlessly subordinated important issues of Indian development to British electoral considerations . . .'

Such subordination did not avail and the result of the November election was indisputably a Conservative defeat (only 249 seats), although it was less clearly a Gladstone victory, both because of the overhanging presence of eighty-three Parnellite MPs and because there was practically no issue, and least of all the dominating one of the government of Ireland, on which there was a prospect of getting the 333 Liberals into the same lobby. After a swashbuckling campaign Churchill lost to Bright in the Central division of Birmingham by 4,216 votes to 4,989. As he had also been nominated for and was safely returned by South Paddington, this involved no exclusion from Parliament. It was merely the prestige, as he regarded it, of representing a great popular constituency which eluded him. This was a constant desire. As late as 1893, when he was already far gone in physical decline, he was still playing with the idea of contesting the hazardous Central Bradford in place of the secure South Paddington. And his 1885 Birmingham failure cannot have been made any more palatable to him by the quiet success of Arthur Balfour, who was soon to displace him as the Conservative crown prince, in a similar Manchester constituency.

None of this prevented the six-month interval between the first and the second Salisbury governments being the high plateau of Randolph Churchill's career. He was essentially an opposition politician (who behaved as such even when he was in government) and this was the last occasion when he was able to play this role aided by the qualification, paradoxical but necessary for arousing full interest, that it looked as though he might soon be in office. But the plateau, although high, was also extremely uneven. Almost everything he said contradicted some recent or future statement. The one consistency lay in his ability to arouse interest. Alone with Gladstone, Salisbury and Joseph Chamberlain, he was graded 'Class 1' by the Central News Agency, which meant that his speeches got almost verbatim reporting, as opposed to the one column which was the ration of Dilke, Granville, Hartington and Spencer, or the half-column which was the allocation of Hicks Beach, Harcourt and several others.

Particularly on Ireland Churchill was like a door banging in the wind. He was against the Coercion Bill which sealed the fate of the

Salisbury government, but he was in favour, for a time at least, of the more drastic measure of prosecuting the National League and arresting the Nationalist MPs. This was to be balanced by a major measure of Irish land reform. During the period of the run-up to the first Home Rule Bill and its defeat after the long-drawn-out second reading debate he was working more closely with Chamberlain, a reluctant member of the Gladstone government until his March resignation and always an implacable opponent of the bill, than with any leading Conservative. His own special contribution was to discover and exploit the Ulster issue, which could be made into the biggest boulder in Gladstone's path, and one to which the GOM was peculiarly blind. Yet here too Churchill boxed the compass. A short time before he had been talking about 'foul Ulster Tories', and the Reverend Richard Kane, a fine forerunner of the Reverend Ian Paisley, who was a principal organizer of his seditious Ulster Hall meeting, had only a few weeks before been threatening that if Churchill set foot in the province 'things would be made very unpleasant for him'.

It was the lack of inhibition in their expression which gave to his often foolish and nearly always ill-considered ideas a spontaneous vividness. Thus, when he made an 1886 lurch towards Protectionism (a few months at the Treasury subsequently put him back on a firm Free Trade line) he denounced Gladstone for the sin of trying to force 'filthy foreign wines', instead of honest beer, down the throats of good xenophobic Englishmen.

In appraising his tergiversations during 1885 and 1886, years of turbulent and febrile politics, it should be taken into account that his own life had come fully to match the turbulence and the febrility of the political scene. His health was already poor. At the age of thirty-seven he looked old and ill. Wilfrid Scawen Blunt thought that he must have had a stroke. And his doctor, the fashionable but indiscreet Robson Roose, fuelled rumours of his precarious health and maybe of the cause, the syphilis which Roose had diagnosed in 1883. At the best Churchill was living on the edge of his nerves, effectively separated from his wife (who was much engaged with Count Kinsky, an Austrian diplomat in London), drinking and smoking heavily, and rushing wildly from the Carlton Club, where he made his London headquarters, to provincial meetings, to Paris, to Howth, to Labouchère's house on the Thames and to other occasional centres of non-restful recreation. It was widely expected that he might succumb at any moment to a nervous breakdown.

Why, in these circumstances, did the eminently sane Salisbury appoint him to the key position in his second government? The administration was formed at the end of July (1886) after an election result which left the Gladstonians with under 200 seats, but with the Conservatives nonetheless dependent on the Liberal Unionists (sixty Whigs and a dozen Chamberlainite Radicals) to defeat an alliance of Liberal Home Rulers and the usual eighty or sixty Parnellites. Salisbury may have felt that he had no one else. Balfour, not even in a Cabinet until later that year and with his sobriquet still to be changed from 'Pretty Fanny' to 'Bloody Balfour' by his performance as Irish Chief Secretary in 1887–8, was not ready for it. Hicks Beach, who soon had temporarily to retire because of bad eyesight, had not proved a success as Commons leader either in office or in opposition, and was willing to defer to Churchill. W. H. Smith, who in fact led the Commons with a dour dependability after Churchill had flounced, was regarded as too dull and perhaps too bourgeois to be a first choice.

Salisbury had probably half fixed his mind on Hartington for the second place. Although these two unglossy hereditary grandees did not particularly get on with each other (Salisbury was too intellectual for Hartington, and Hartington too lazy for Salisbury) the Tory leader saw a coalition with the Whigs as probably desirable and recognized that this meant Hartington as at least leader of the House of Commons. But when Hartington would not enter without Chamberlain (an amazing reversal of their enmity of less than two years before) Salisbury decided that was too much, went ahead with a purely Conservative government and found himself with an empty space near the top.

There was a more positive reason as well. Salisbury saw his particular role as teaching the Tories to be a governing party despite the franchise extensions of 1867 and 1885. He concentrated on 'villa Conservatism' at the more respectable end of this task, while Randolph Churchill, better with the city-centre roughs, offered a good balancing of the ticket. Churchill also looked the key to the avoidance of trouble with the party machine, a consideration which has rarely been far from the minds of Conservative leaders, which is perhaps a reason why they have so often led their party into government. In addition, as a reserve side-thought, there may have been a feeling that, if Churchill were to prove an impossible colleague, and there were already enough indications that this could not be ruled out, it was best that he should have enough rope for his public hanging of himself to be a spectacular and salutary event.

This is precisely what happened. Churchill began unsteadily well. His House of Commons performance aroused great interest, rather in the way that an inebriate trying to wheel a barrow across a tightrope would have done. Churchill was nervous, but he got to the other end of the wire, in the sense of disposing of the debate on the address and of some necessary financial business before sending the House away until January, in reasonably good order. Curiously he aroused comment by excessive diligence, no doubt a result of his nervousness. He dined in the House night after night, equally probably a result of the abeyance of his marriage, and was a fixture on the front bench until late-night adjournments.

Then, after an 'incognito' October visit to Berlin, Vienna and Paris, where he enjoyed both poking his finger into foreign policy (the despised Iddesleigh was Foreign Secretary) and finding that his incognito advanced rather than discouraged press interest, he devoted his autumn to quarrelling with his colleagues. Altercations with Iddesleigh went without saying. Next were his relatively rational disputes with the two service ministers, W. H. Smith the Secretary for War even more than with Lord George Hamilton the First Lord of the Admiralty. But he also managed to find time for minor skirmishes with Ritchie, Cranbrook, Manners, Chaplin and Stanley. And, quite early in the life of the government, he indulged in a celebrated abuse of Hicks Beach, fluctuatingly his best ally, in front of Lord George Hamilton, the memory of which never faded from the minds of either Beach or Hamilton. Only Chamberlain, supporting the government on Ireland but still regarded with apprehension and even repugnance by most Tories, commanded his starry-eyed admiration.

Salisbury observed all this with a mixture of detachment and disapproval. He probably began to think that Churchill was not long for his government when he received from him an early November letter containing the following piece of petulance:

> I am afraid it is an idle schoolboy's dream to suppose that the Tories can legislate – as I did, stupidly. They can govern and make war and increase taxation and expenditure *à merveille*, but legislation is not their province in a democratic constitution . . . [Chaplin] is the natural leader of the Tories in the House of Commons, suited to their intellects and their class prejudices. I certainly have not the courage and energy to go on struggling against cliques, as poor Dizzy did all his life.

Churchill interspersed his quarrels with vastly publicized speeches in the country, the first at Dartford in suburban Kent at the beginning of October and then at the end of the month two in Bradford at the annual meeting of what he regarded as his private army, the National Union of Conservative Associations. These speeches, without in themselves risking a break, were designed to drive his colleagues further than they wanted to go in the direction of social reform and collaboration with the Liberal Unionists of the Chamberlain tendency. The tone of the speeches was also very much that of a head of government rather than of a loyal lieutenant.

What was still more remarkable, particularly as it suggested a high degree of self-discipline, was his other main activity of the autumn. Churchill was the only Chancellor,* apart from Iain Macleod (cut off by death after only five weeks in office), who never presented a budget. But this did not mean that it is unknown what he would have done. On the contrary he set himself in November (five months early) to work out with his officials, whose warm co-operation he had secured by a mixture of surprising them with his politeness and reassuring them by retreating from his Protectionism as rapidly (and frivolously) as he had advanced toward it, the full details of a 'big' budget. It was 'big' in the sense that it pulled up almost every plant in the garden, looked at its roots and replanted it in a somewhat different place. But it did not seek to alter the shape of the garden. It used conventional taxation methods, but used them in a restless way.

He proposed to provide nearly £5 million of new money to lubricate the local government reform for which he was urgently pressing, and about the same amount to reduce income tax from eightpence to fivepence in the pound and (a nice anti-regressive touch) to abolish the tea duty. Those generosities were to be paid for partly by a major reduction in the sinking fund, and partly by a series of indirect taxation increases, mostly non-regressive, on horses, wine (very unGladstonian that) and cartridges. The complex of death duties was to be simplified, the total yield somewhat increased, but coming from a shift to a graduated inheritance tax. This could be regarded as a younger son's charter, although Lord Randolph was past the hope of much direct personal advantage.

This draft budget achieved half of its room for manoeuvre through improvidence. It could be argued, quite plausibly, that the sinking fund at £28 million, nearly a third of the total budget, was too stringent, too much of a charge upon the present for the sake of the future. It was also liable, two rather contradictory effects, both to exterminate the national

* But see footnote on p. 94.

debt by approximately 1930 (assuming there was no 1914) and on the way to drive up the price of scarce Consols etc., to a height which made their redemption excessively expensive to the Exchequer. There was therefore quite a strong case for moderating the rate of debt retirement, although it might have been better to gear the reduction to some need more national than Lord Randolph Churchill's desire to make a splash. But it was not obviously sound finance. In consequence it doubled Churchill's wish to show himself an 'economist' on military expenditure, and as there were upward pressures from the War Office even more than the Admiralty this led him into a direct and unwinnable clash with the decent stolidity of the face which had launched a thousand news-stands. In Salisbury's quest for suburban Conservative support, as opposed to Churchill's more romantic but less reliable hopes of prole-tarian Tories, W. H. Smith was a more reliable ally and therefore a difficult man to beat.

When he had completed his draft budget in early December Churchill told officials that he did not wish to trouble his mind with it again until the time came for its presentation in the spring. This sounded impressively orderly, and was buttressed by the argument that in the New Year he would need to have his mind free for the new session and his duties as leader of the House rather than as Chancellor of the Exchequer. It was also a striking illustration of how, in the years of splendid isolation and of budgets without macro-economic responsibility, a Chancellor could operate free of day-to-day or even month-to-month restraints. No modern Chancellor would dream of sealing up an April budget in early December. And even in 1886–7 Churchill showed a curiously mechanistic insensibility for such an 'instinctual politican', as he was often described, by believing that he could do so. In the first place his budget was very doubtfully received when he presented it to the Cabinet (much too far in advance) in December. Salisbury complained to him about its effect on Hertfordshire country gentlemen – which was a very bad sign, for Salisbury, if he had been well disposed on general political grounds, would have cared little about his worthy but unexciting neighbours. And Churchill in his locked-up budget had also set himself on a public expenditure collision course which made it unlikely that he would survive to present it.

Only a couple of days after he had encountered the Cabinet's chilly reception of his proposals he plunged into his resignation course. The surrounding circumstances were oddly chosen. On the evening after the Cabinet meeting he dined with Chamberlain and told him that a crisis was imminent. In return he appears to have got the false information that Liberal reunion, with Gladstone retreating from Home Rule, was approaching. This was surprising misinformation, for neither Gladstone nor Chamberlain had any real desire to work with each other again, but it had the effect of increasing Churchill's restless sense that time was short. Chamberlain was not in fact eager to provoke him into resignation, for he subsequently opined that Churchill had resigned at the wrong time on the wrong issue (who does not?). What is probably the case is that they were both so addicted to playing the 'big game' in politics that they talked each other up, like two gamblers, into ever more attention-stealing gestures.

On the next day, a Saturday, Churchill stayed in London and gave a grand dinner for, *inter alia*, Salisbury, the Prince of Wales and Goschen, who at least was not forgotten from Lord Randolph's social list. On the Monday afternoon he went to Windsor to 'dine and sleep', travelling each way with Lord George Hamilton, who as First Lord of the Admiralty was one of his principal Cabinet adversaries. After dinner with the Queen he retired to his suite and wrote, on Windsor writing paper, a substantial letter of resignation, which however concentrated on the narrow issue of army and navy estimates. On the Tuesday morning he took the letter back to London and despatched it to Salisbury. Given his tendency to 'impulsiveness, variability and bullying' (in Salisbury's phrase about him) this letter required treatment as little more than a bargaining ploy. Churchill added strength to this interpretation by twice seeing W. H. Smith, his principal departmental adversary, in the next two days. But Salisbury saw it as too good an opportunity to miss. He had had more than enough of Churchill and he seized this as a very good chance to dispose of him without too much repercussion. He took his stand on Smith's side because 'the outlook on the continent is very black'. It was his primary duty as Prime Minister to look to national security, and therefore coolly accepted the resignation. Although the Christmas holiday was then a much less extended affair than it is today, it was nonetheless difficult to think of a worse choice of date from Churchill's point of view, or a better one from Salisbury's, than the evening of 22 December, which was when the latter's letter arrived. The old marquess was a more skilled if quieter tactician than the young populist.

On receipt of Salisbury's reply Churchill retired to the Carlton Club and wrote his second letter from there. In this he endeavoured to widen the issue and to give himself some sort of manifesto of departure. He then went to the theatre and after that to the offices of *The Times*, where he proffered his Carlton Club letter to give the editor (Buckle) a scoop for the next morning. Both the Queen and Lady Randolph received their first news of the sensation from the columns of Mr Buckle. Neither was pleased at the method of communication. Nor was Salisbury, even though he had received his copy at a ball in the middle of the night. And Buckle did not even repay Churchill with editorial support.

The most vivid indication of how badly Churchill had miscalculated is supplied by an account of his next two days. He clung on to his room in Treasury Chambers and spent Boxing Day and one or two subsequent ones forlornly sitting there and writing letters of explanation and false optimism to his mother and potential political allies. By the New Year Salisbury had got Goschen, nominally a Liberal Unionist and a man who gave far more financial confidence than did Churchill, to accept the Exchequer. (Churchill was held to have 'forgotten Goschen' in over-estimating his own indispensability, but as his action was essentially irrational any reason given was *ex post* rather than causative.) W. H. Smith filled the other half of Churchill's vacated responsibilities.

Churchill spent January thrashing around for some political alliance or strategy which would give him a future, and failed to find one. Parliament did not resume until 27 January, so that he could not make his 'resignation' speech until five weeks after the event, another indication of how ill had been his sense of timing. Then he made another speech on 31 January. They were neither of them *sur place* disasters, but neither were they oratorical triumphs, and they were certainly not feats of alliance-building. The more strongly he justified his position the more he widened the gap between himself and Salisbury, or at least gave Salisbury the excuse to say that he did, for, however softly he had cooed, the chances of Salisbury having him back into the government were neglible. Nor did the Liberals want him, although Harcourt purported to admire these speeches and Gladstone, surprisingly and a little later found him one of the most 'courtly' men that he had ever known. (This is an indication of how ineffective Churchill had then become; it was the equivalent of the sort of Tory tribute which now might be paid to Mr Tony Benn.) Hartington, with whom a possible combination had been mooted, appeared to discard this possibility in a speech at Newcastle following Churchill's two House of Commons efforts. And even Chamberlain, touchily offended, as many brutal men often are, by a passage in Churchill's 31 January speech, wrote unfriendily.

Discouraged by all this, Churchill in early February fled to North

Africa and then to Italy, and remained away until late March. Passing through Paris in both directions, his principal contact very typically had become General Boulanger, the 'man on a white horse' and meretricious Minister of War who made the grand old Duke of York, with his movement up and down the hill, seem a master of decisive action. Churchill's seven weeks abroad were said to have improved his health. They certainly did not improve his political prospects, which were bad when he left and worse when he came back. The fact was that he was finished, hard if fitfully though he tried for the subsequent four years or so, and pitifully though he went on, even when in the early 1890s his diction became slurred, his mind confused and his speeches an agony of embarrassment for his listeners, particularly if they were his friends. He died in January 1895, aged forty-five. Except for Pitt there had been no other British politician of the parliamentary period who had attained the front rank of fame and died so young. But the contrast with Pitt could nonetheless hardly have been greater. Pitt was Prime Minister for nineteen of his forty-six years. Churchill had eleven months in office and was without rival in attracting so much attention and achieving so little.

SIR WILLIAM HARCOURT

WILLIAM GEORGE GRANVILLE VENABLES VERNON HARCOURT, a boisterous politician, sometimes known as 'the Great Gladiator' and an amalgam of attributes subsequently possessed by Hugh Dalton, Willie Whitelaw, Richard Crossman and Roy Hattersley, is one of the most neglected areas in the somewhat over-ploughed terrain of modern political biography. He was briefly Solicitor-General, then Home Secretary for five years and twice Chancellor of the Exchequer, and led his party in the House of Commons from 1894 to 1898. He was also a richly anecdotal figure. Yet, as far as I am aware, nothing has been published about him since A. G. Gardiner, a leading Liberal journalist (editor of the *Daily News*), buried him in 1923 – which was late, for Harcourt died in 1904 – under a handsome, wise and readable, but over-generously proportioned, two-volume tombstone life.

As his multiplicity of christian names implies, Harcourt came of high patrician stock, which was mingled with a strong episcopal strain. His paternal grandfather was a notable Archbishop of York, who carried the traditions of the eighteenth century deep into the nineteenth. Edward Ebor, as he signed himself for much of his life, became a bishop (of Carlisle) in 1791 at the age of thirty-three, appointed by Pitt, was translated to York seventeen years later by the Duke of Portland, and remained primate of the Northern Province until 1847, when at the age of ninety a small footbridge in the archiepiscopal park at Bishopsthorpe collapsed under his weight and he succumbed to a chill consequent upon his immersion. He had sixteen children by his Leveson Gower wife (sister of the first Duke of Sutherland); of these William Harcourt's clergyman father was the fourth son. This William Harcourt (*père*) did not however match his own father's ecclesiastical preferment, not rising above a country rectory and a canonry of York. He was however a considerable amateur scientist and the effective founder of the British Association.

He also became the Archbishop's eventual heir and the patrimony to which he succeeded, even when stripped of the *ex officio* splendour of York, was a massive one. In 1830 the Archbishop inherited huge south Oxfordshire estates, which had been accumulated at various times over the previous seven centuries, from his second cousin, Field Marshal the third and last Earl of Harcourt. These included Nuneham Courtenay, five miles downstream from Oxford, and Stanton Harcourt, which although only ten miles away by crow's flight was a good twenty-five miles upstream by the meandering course of the Thames. It was a condition of this inheritance that the Archbishop, who as a younger son of Lord Vernon had been known by that surname, should change his name to Harcourt. He thought the reward well worth the switch, and henceforward was not only known as Archbishop Harcourt, but spent as much time (or more if his period in his London house for attendance at the House of Lords be included) on the banks of the Thames as on those of the Ouse. Indeed, he preached his farewell sermon in York Minster nine years before he vacated the archbishopric.

The subject of this essay was three years old when he ceased to be William Vernon and became William (Vernon) Harcourt, often referred to as W. V. H. When he was twenty his uncle, George Granville Harcourt with his more famous wife Frances Lady Waldegrave, who changed husbands three times without bothering to change her name, became master and mistress of Nuneham and Stanton. In 1861 he was succeeded by W. V. H.'s father and ten years later by W. V. H.'s elder brother Edward. Edward Harcourt, much more than his father, was a self-conscious Oxfordshire magnate. He was also a firm Tory, who wished to (and became) MP in that interest for the county. Even before he succeeded he found the prospect of his brother becoming Liberal MP for Oxford City distinctly distasteful, and did not hesitate to remonstrate direct. Such family apostasy quite spoilt his view of the dreaming spires, which was one of the amenities of Nuneham. On another occasion he protested that William had 'no landed ideas', and provoked the splendid and typical riposte: 'You have the land, and may leave the ideas to me.' There is also a story (maybe apocryphal) that, during a Carlton Club encounter, Sir Thomas Gladstone, the elder and equally Tory brother of the Grand Old Man, complained to Edward Harcourt: 'Mr Harcourt, you and I have two very tiresome brothers.'

Later, however, personal although not political relations between the Harcourt brothers were completely restored, aided by W. V. H.'s ejection from Oxford City in 1880. Edward Harcourt died in 1891 and was succeeded by a son who never married (although he had tried; his bride-to-be, a daughter of Dean Liddell of Christ Church and therefore a sister of Alice [in Wonderland], died suddenly only a few hours short of the altar) and he himself died (young) at Monte Carlo in March 1904. Then, by an irony which aroused much comment, Sir William Harcourt, most famous for his 'death duties' budget of 1894, at the age of seventy-six and in the last six months of his life, succeeded his nephew in the ownership of one of the grandest landed estates of the Thames Valley. And, by a double irony, he discovered that it was nearly bankrupt, with the quick double succession duties, when he himself died six months later, almost completing the process.

On his mother's side W. V. H.'s provenance was relatively uncomplicated. Matilda Harcourt was the daughter of Colonel Gooch, and the granddaughter of Bishop Gooch, an unusually mobile prelate who moved without ascending from the see of Bristol to that of Norwich to that of Ely. The double (or by some reckoning quintuple episcopal strain in W. V. H.'s ancestry may have contributed to making him one of the most Erastian of all politicians who were firmly but not piously Anglican. This erected a sharp divide between him and Gladstone, who was his effective chief for twenty-six of his thirty-six years in the House of Commons. Gladstone regarded the Church as a divine mystery. Harcourt regarded it almost as a department of state, 'the parliamentary church', as he sometimes referred to it.

His paternal lineage, natural ebullience, liking for more or less good-humoured controversy, physical size, intellectual equipment of a first-class advocate although not perhaps of a greater profoundity, combined to give him a personality of swashbuckling self-confidence. He was (mostly) an unsentimental radical with a grand manner. It was succinctly expressed by Charles Dilke, who wrote in the late 1870s of a meeting which had been 'sufficiently interesting to keep Harcourt and a Duke standing for three hours – putting Harcourt first because he was the more august'.

This may be an appropriate moment to pursue the reasons which provoked me to compare Harcourt with four politicians of the past fifty years. He was like Dalton in that he was very partisan from an essentially moderate position. Neither was remotely extremist, but they both liked denouncing their opponents and did so in clanging language which often caused resentment. They were both large booming men with a tendency to bluster, who saw themselves as cheerleaders, instilling social and intellectual confidence into their less favoured supporters. They were both cynical and addicted to political gossip. Their intellectual equipment was about equal: high facility of comprehension and expression, without much subtlety or originality. This reflected itself in their oratory, which was effectively declamatory but struck few emotional chords. Harcourt, however, had an unusual gift of elaborate but genuinely funny mockery. He also had an edge over Dalton in that his social self-confidence was more deep-seated and his family life, while interspersed with some tragedies (but that was habitual in Victorian life) was less bleak. Dalton, in spite of his Etonian noise, was socially insecure, and his emotional life was a hollow shell.

With Willie Whitelaw the likeness was less. Apart from anything else, Harcourt was unusually articulate. But they both had a capacity to act as invaluable seconds-in-command to leaders with whom they had little affinity, Harcourt to Gladstone, Whitelaw to Mrs Thatcher. In addition, they also both built up stores of affection by being the butts of many anecdotes in which they appeared as caricatures of themselves. Harcourt however aroused more hostility than Whitelaw, with whom the proportion of affection to mockery has always been high.

In the case of Hattersley the comparison is provoked by his pulsating partisan loyalty (as with Dalton) and his ability to make a story against himself funnier by virtue of his inherently comic character (as with Whitelaw). But Hattersley is a better writer, with a wider range of literary interest, than any of these. Harcourt's range exceeded his only in Greek and Latin authors, where he had the thorough grounding of a clever member of the Victorian upper class.

The joker in the pack of four is Richard Crossman. At first sight he is remarkably unlike Harcourt. His sense of party loyalty, or, some would say, any other sort of loyalty, was minimal. He made a speciality of scoring own goals, and enjoyed shocking the susceptibilities of his own side more than overwhelming the enemy. Yet reading some of Harcourt's argumentative writings, of which, particularly in his early middle age, there was a vast outpouring, mainly on international questions and written from a quasi-juridical point of view, I was constantly reminded of the habits of mind of someone with whom I had had close dealings, and eventually tracked the likeness down to Crossman. There was the same touch of intellectual brutality, the same desire to instruct by shocking, the same willingness to change opinions with bewildering rapidity, the same ability to grip an audience by, as it were, riding a bicycle of argument straight at a cliff edge and holding the listeners spellbound by waiting to see whether he would go over it or by what feat of dialectical gymnastics he would at the last moment jerk himself away to safety.

All these comparisons of varying validity lead to the view that Harcourt, despite his view of himself as an essentially eighteenth-century figure, Whig in lifestyle if sometimes Radical in opinions, dealing a little impatiently with the rather bourgeois politics of the end of the nineteenth century, had in many ways a twentieth-century *mentalité*. In this he contrasted violently with Gladstone, for although Gladstone's life was a magnificent vehicle for interpreting the nineteenth to the twentieth century he was nonetheless a figure almost impossible to imagine in the worlds of Dalton, Whitelaw, Hattersley or Crossman.

Harcourt was born in York in 1827. Neither that year nor its neighbours were vintage years for politicans. It was not until 1830 that a clear alpha in the shape of the third Marquess of Salisbury emerged. It was a decade or two later that the champions with whom Harcourt fought most of his main jousts were born. Hartington, Spencer, Joseph Chamberlain, Morley, Dilke, Parnell, Rosebery, Balfour, Randolph Churchill were in varying degrees just as much his juniors as Disraeli, Gladstone, John Bright and Granville were his seniors.

Harcourt therefore had a lot of generational elbowroom, but he threw part of it away by entering the House of Commons unusually late for such an assured member of the governing class. He was forty-one when he was first elected for Oxford City in 1868. Only John Morley among senior ministers of the period was later, and Morley was a journalist not a patrician. Even Joseph Chamberlain, who also had to make his own way and complained that he had almost left it too late, was an MP by thirty-nine.

It was indeed the case that there were several unorthodox features in the early career of William Harcourt. The first was that he attended no traditional school. For a few years from the age of eight he was at a small preparatory establishment at Southwell, the seat of the Nottinghamshire bishopric, but his father did not approve of public schools, and when the time for one of them came he was sent instead to reside with about five other boys in a tutorial group run by a Canon Parr near Salisbury. When the Canon was 'preferred' to be Vicar of Preston (Lancashire), which may be thought an odd preferment, Harcourt (and his brother) went with him and stayed there for six or seven years. The company was restricted, but the regime was intellectually both demanding and successful. It was nearly all work and no play, but at the end of it Harcourt was an accomplished classicist with enough knowledge of history, both ancient and modern, for his speech and his writing in later life to be almost over-adorned with mostly mocking historical parallels. He had become a considerable mathematician, so much so that, almost at the last moment, he was switched from following his brother to Christ Church and went to Trinity College, Cambridge.

At that remarkable institution, still more the 'middle kingdom' of the fenland University than Christ Church then was of Oxford, he arrived as a 'gentlemen commoner' in the autumn of 1846. Despite his unorthodox earlier education and consequent lack of ready-made friends, Harcourt appears to have patronized Trinity and Cambridge, rather than vice versa. His early letters have a strong affinity to Keynes's first-term comment on King's just over half a century later: 'I have had a good look round the place and come to the conclusion that it's pretty inefficient.' Harcourt quickly became a member of the Apostles, or the Society (of twelve) which from F. D. Maurice and Tennyson through Henry Sidgwick, Leslie Stephen, G. E. Moore, Lytton Strachey, Maynard Keynes and Bertrand Russell to Anthony Blunt, has represented the radical chic of the University. He became a dominant Union figure, speaking mainly in the Peelite interest, and he secured high but not pre-eminent honours in both the mathematical and the classical triposes. His easy superiority owed something to his height (which at six feet three and a half inches was more unusual 150 years ago than it is today) and youthful good looks, which later turned to an embonpoint which would have subjected the bridge at Bishopsthorpe to as much strain as it received from his grandfather. His lack of a school background seemed to give him a greater sophistication than his contemporaries. He was very much a Cambridge 'blood', although not one who looked towards Newmarket. Nor was he an aesthete. He had a muscular intellect firmly turned in a public service direction: law and history were his natural interests.

Although his tripos performances made such a prospect perfectly possible he did not at this stage seek a Trinity fellowship, and abandoned Cambridge for London in 1851. Eighteen years later, however, he was elected to the newly founded Whewell Professorship in International Law, which carried with it a fellowship as well as a fine set of rooms in Trinity, and continued to occupy that chair until 1887, which span covered his five years as Home Secretary as well as his first short spell as Chancellor of the Exchequer. Although full-term residence was not required he regularly spent solid autumn weeks in Cambridge, delivering serious courses of lectures.

In the London of the 1850s he lived a life typical of a well-connected young man of talent without significant money of his own. Before and for a time after his call to the bar in 1854 he supported himself by journalism, first for the *Morning Chronicle*, which was a Peelite journal (although Peel himself was of course dead), and then for the *Saturday Review*, founded in 1855, which shot its darts in all directions. He lived comfortably, first in St James's Place and then in a suite of rooms at the top of Paper Buildings in the Temple with a fine view across the Thames. He enjoyed a varied and fashionable social life ranging from the Cosmopolitan Club (which had Bohemian tinges) through exchanging mementoes with Rachel the great French actress (and courtesan), weekends at Nuneham, Saturdays (later) at Lady Waldegrave's Strawberry Hill, men's dinners such as one where he sat between the Dukes of Bedford and Newcastle whom he noted as being more shy of one another than he was of either.

By the late 1850s his legal practice was becoming busy and in the 1860s very prosperous. Although his intellectual interests were in public international law, he did a lot of work at the parliamentary bar and enjoyed rich pickings from the spate of private railway legislation. He never aspired to live as a full-scale magnate but rather in 'orchids and cigars' style in a mock-Tudor mansion of the sort favoured by Joseph Chamberlain. He seemed to have no financial worries until he inherited the Nuneham estate in the last year of his life.

In 1859, the birth year of the Liberal party, to which he was to devote his last four decades, he broke two pieces of new ground. In the spring he fought his first election, and in the autumn he got married. His attitude to both categories of enterprise had hitherto been ambiguous. Immediately after Cambridge he had repulsed overtures from the Duke of Bedford to promote him for a safe Whig seat. This was partly because he did not then see himelf as an orthodox party politician and partly on the ground that he wished to make his own reputation and secure his financial independence before entering Parliament.

His 1859 electoral excursion did not contradict this for it was more a tilt at a windmill than an approach to a political career. He went to Kirkcaldy, which was a long way and where he had practically nil previous connection, and mounted an independent challenge to the sitting Whig member, a bucolic local squire and coalowner. The venture came within eighteen votes (in a poll of 600) of succeeding, but it did not advance his political prospects, for he was widely accused of being a Carlton Club 'plant' (which he was not) and in his letters he treated his campaign more as a prank than as a serious foray. However, he aroused sufficient local affection that when, six months later, he went back with his new bride for a farewell visit he received presents worth, in modern terms, approximately £6,500. Few MPs after half a lifetime of elected service, let alone a maverick one-time candidate, could achieve that today.

His marriage (at the age of thirty-two) was short-lived and tragic, through no fault of either husband or wife, but taken together with his second one, which occurred seventeen years later, and some other circumstances, it prompts reflection on his attitude to women. He was rarely without female friends. He had been something of a stage-door johnnie as the time of his Rachel encounter; in the middle 1850s he had nearly married (why not is unclear) a Miss Bulteel, a Devon MP's daughter, who subsequently married General 'Fritz' Ponsonby, Queen Victoria's long-serving and liberal-minded private secretary, and with Mary Bulteel he remained on close letter-writing terms for the rest of his life; for his enjoyment of the Kirkcaldy campaign the main sources are his letters to Lady Melgund, soon to be Minto and mother of a Viceroy; and a decade or so later Lady Ripon, wife of another future Viceroy, was an important confidante.

His first wife, whom he married after a brief acquaintanceship, was Thérèse Lister, whom he described as 'a Radnorshire woman'. In spite of the geographical label, her dead father had been a Staffordshire gentleman. Her mother, who was the queen of the family chessboard, was Lady Maria Theresa Lewis, a sister of the Earl of Clarendon who was intermittently Foreign Secretary between 1853 and his death in 1870, and currently the wife of Sir George Cornewall Lewis, who in a somewhat shadowy way was both a Home Secretary and a Chancellor of the Exchequer. Miss Lister was therefore well connected politically. Harcourt was not indifferent to this, and he particularly valued the link with Lewis. But he also embraced his bride and her family with the affection which was natural to his warm nature. There was no reason to doubt his connubial bliss, even if his letters leave an impression that it was the novelty of the married state rather than an individual passion for Miss Lister which seized his imagination.

His enthusiasm for this may have been assisted by the remarkable ease with which a modest but fashionable domestic establishment could be set up in 1859: 'I have already secured a small house in Pont Street which leads out of Chesham Place . . .', he wrote to his sister. 'It has three rooms on the ground floor, two nice drawing-rooms, then two bedrooms, and on the third floor three very good rooms besides servants' wings. The offices are particularly good and the rent is only £120 [£6,000 today] which is very cheap.'

In these circumstances he had two years of much proclaimed but probably genuine felicity. After eleven months a son was born and christened Julian after his great Cambridge friend Julian Fane. The boy died suddenly at the age of sixteen months. A year later Thérèse Harcourt produced a replacement son, who survived for sixty years, but herself died on the day of the birth. Then George Cornewall Lewis died (aged sixty) two months later, and Harcourt who had originally had the child christened Reginald, after his almost equally great Cambridge friend Reginald Cholmondeley, had him rechristened Lewis at Nuneham, with Clarendon as godfather. It had been a terrible year for Harcourt, and it left him as a peculiarly devoted father, which devotion was fortunately reciprocated by the boy. As a child, as an adolescent, as a young and then an early-middle-aged man (he was forty-one when William Harcourt died) Lewis or 'Loulou' Harcourt was always an inseparable companion and latterly a dedicated private secretary to his father.

This aspect of domesticity apart, however, William Harcourt for at least the next thirteen years, and maybe beyond, lived an essentially bachelor life. When in 1874 Charles Dilke lost his wife in circumstances very similar to those in which his own had gone, Harcourt successfully pressed him to come and share his house for a few months, saying 'We will live together as if in college rooms.'

A year or so after that, Harcourt, aged almost fifty, married his second wife. She was called Elizabeth Cabot Ives, and as her name implies was of impeccable American East Coast stock. It was interesting as well as impeccable, for her father was J. L. Motley, who had not only been American minister in London (the heads of mission of the future superpower were only allowed the rank of ambassador from the 1890s) but was also the author of the *Rise of the Dutch Republic*, a work perhaps even more famous than read. She was described as 'an extraordinarily pretty young widow'. Despite these attributes there is the strong impression that, apart from producing a son in 1878, who lived until 1962 and was a Liberal MP and minor playwright, she was an almost totally lay figure in the subsequent life of Harcourt. There is no reason to think they were unhappy. They were often apart, but such was the

English upper-class habit of the time (cf. the Gladstones), and when they were he wrote frequently if impersonally. But there is equally little reason to think that they had any great impact on each other's lives.

Harcourt was a man of very warm affections (and very hot disaffections), but he also liked a masculine-orientated life and society. He was not, I think, remotely homosexual. He was a macho figure (not that the two categories are mutually exclusive) who in both his correspondence and his conversation liked a Victorian version of men's locker-room chaff with an addition of classical tags and historical allusions. Throughout his political life he was a famous giver of luncheon and dinner parties, first at his house in Grafton Street and then, when the lease of that expired, a little higher up Mayfair in Brook Street. He was also an enthusiastic partaker of the copious food and drink which he provided. He was hospitable and gregarious, and specialized in cross-party dinners, even at times when tension and bitterness made them rare events. To be warmly entertained at his table was however no guarantee against being virulently denounced by him in the House of Commons within a few days. With Joseph Chamberlain after the Home Rule split he had a particularly strong private friendship/public enmity relationship, although after a few years even that sedulously preserved friendship faded under the strain.*

These political entertainments were as often as not purely masculine. And this was to some extent true of his country entertaining. Until 1883 he had no non-London house of his own, although he frequently took autumn tenancies of fishing or shooting lodges in the Western Highlands. Then, in his mid-fifties, he suddenly acquired a long lease from the Crown that he described as 'twenty-two acres of the choicest spot in the New Forest'. It was alleged to be the site on which William Rufus had spent his last night before meeting his fatal arrow. Harcourt did not help the unspoilt amenity of the Forest. He covered one of the acres with a gabled, many-bedroomed and several-balconied three-storey villa in what he described as 'Queen Anne cottagey' style, as well as a good

---

* Harcourt and Chamberlain had a good deal in common: the loss of wives in childbirth followed by American replacements, a liking for self-indulgence in large over-heated modern houses, a self-conscious manliness with a theoretical belief that the roughest of blows could be exchanged between well-matched opponents without the impairment of respect or friendship, perhaps a shared streak of vulgarity. But they were divided by one great difference. Harcourt was notorious for the hottest temper in politics. But he was generous, warm-hearted and quick to forgive and even apologize. Chamberlain, *per contra*, had a brooding implacability. Harcourt in other words was much the nicer man.

part of the other twenty-one with elaborately laid-out gardens. But he gave himself enormous and continuing pleasure.

Surprisingly in view of his broad-acred background he regarded Malwood, as he called it, as the finest spot in England, and therefore in the world. He retreated there whenever he could and was always trying hard to get his friends to visit him. He could hardly write a political letter without including a pressing invitation. Sometimes the recipients proved elusive – John Morley particularly so – but he got the Gladstones for a two-day stay in 1889 and the GOM wrote in his diary – where he did not have to be polite – that the house and garden were 'a marvellous creation'.

It was however almost always his male political colleagues rather than couples or general house parties whom or which Harcourt wanted for Malwood. I do not think that he disliked women, provided that they knew their place. He was, for instance, much more successful than Gladstone in handling the Queen. He could be mildly susceptible to pretty wives; and such female visitors as there were to Malwood were almost all wives. Both his sons married late, and Malwood was never a house for girls.

On women's rights Harcourt was the ultimate male chauvinist. In his opposition to female suffrage he was of course far from being alone among leading Liberal politicians. Gladstone was at best equivocal, and Asquith, a quarter of a century younger than Harcourt and a statesman who could never be accused of misogyny, was until 1918 equally hostile to votes (or seats in Parliament) for women. But Harcourt struck a note which was more offensive. 'I am coming up to London on Tuesday only to vote against the women,' he wrote in April 1892. And at about the same time, having admittedly been much provoked by the machinations in the Women's Liberation Federation of the formidable (and intolerable) 'Countess Rosalinda', as he engagingly referred to Lady Carlisle, he complained of 'suffering under deluges of female correspondence which satisfy me more than ever of the total incapacity of the sex for public affairs'.

After Kirkcaldy Harcourt stood aside from electoral politics for another eight and a half years. He sought no candidature in the election of 1865, Palmerston's last. This was despite his reputation as a leading commentator and controversialist on the hinge between law and international politics having been greatly enhanced in the preceding four years by the American Civil War. On the basic merits of that struggle he was a firm partisan of the North, much more so for instance than were Palmerston or Gladstone. But he was more interested in being a pundit than a partisan, and pronounced with authoritative impartiality sometimes against the legal claims of the North, sometimes against those of the South. The vehicle for his pronouncements was a series of letter/articles in *The Times* written under the pseudonym of 'Historicus', at once a little pretentious and pointless, for his identity was never intended to be concealed. He was successfully seeking a reputation, and a secret reputation is not much use. His words resounded not only around Westminster, Whitehall and the Temple, but in Washington and Richmond, Virginia too.

These letters constituted the platform of repute from which Harcourt was a few years later offered his Cambridge chair. They also made him, while still a junior barrister aged only thirty-seven, better known than most MPs. And they were not without some remunerative spin-off. As unsolicited contributions, often at variance with editorial policy, they were not paid for by *The Times*. But when in 1865 Russell as Foreign Secretary asked Harcourt to give his opinion on some related points he suggested a fee of up to £500 (£25,000 today). Harcourt's reply was a very good example of getting the best of both worlds with grandeur: 'As to what you say anent "payment", International Law is my passion rather than my profession. What I have done was solely with a view of being of use to you and the country . . . But if the F. O. choose to send an *honorarium quelconque* to my clerk I shall not be too proud to accept it . . .'

With the approach of the 1868 election, which turned out to be the watershed between the confusion of mid-century politics and the clear-cut two-party partisanship of the next fifty years, Harcourt came under increasing demand both as a speaker and as a possible candidate. In spite of his family affiliations he regarded himself as firmly on the Liberal side of the divide, even though of the two champions he probably had more temperamental affinity with Disraeli than with Gladstone. Disraeli in 1866 was said to have offered him 'a safe Welsh [Tory] seat' (where in Wales were such seats?). He visited Disraeli a few times at Hughenden and sent Lady Beaconsfield on her deathbed what sounds the singularly inappropriate present of a consignment of full-strength Trinity Audit Ale. But these were only superficial ripples, illustrative more of Harcourt's taste for the company of the famous than of any political fluctuation. Indeed his first real barnstorming speech in the country was a 'breakfast' in the Philharmonic Hall, Liverpool where he brought the audience to their feet with a violent denunciation of Disraeli for seeking to drag the Queen into politics with 'the most wicked, the most dangerous and the most unconstitutional course which was ever pursued by a great party or by a public minister in this century'. It was always a characteristic of Harcourt, as his official biographer pointed out, that 'he could not be content with beating a man but wanted to roll him in the dust as well'.

However his shafts excited the faithful, and his Philharmonic Hall speech led on to a strong demand that he should stand for Liverpool. In the event, in spite of (or perhaps because of) the dismay of his brother, he preferred an alternative Oxford invitation, and turned out to be wise. On the Thames he was comfortably elected. On the Mersey he would almost certainly have gone down to defeat. Most of Lancashire was disappointing for the Liberals. Harcourt's comment on this pattern of results was interesting both for illustrating his taste for cynical clanging phrases (which again sets ringing in my mind the echoing bell of Dalton's private conversation) and for giving a foretaste of the paradox of his support for Gladstone on Home Rule. He stuck to the GOM in 1886 because he disliked almost equally the Tories and the Irish. In 1868 he wrote: 'It is provoking that the Lancashire places should have gone so wrong. I take it to mean nothing else but hatred of the Irish, who like the niggers are most hated where they are best known.'

Harcourt's legal and political reputation was such that many thought he would go straight into the government, probably as Solicitor-General. But Gladstone had two more parliamentary senior law offices available, and instead offered him the politically semi-detached post of Judge Advocate-General. Harcourt, who would probably have accepted the Solicitorship, declined, saying that he preferred to cut his teeth in an independent role. This he proceeded to do for nearly five years, exercising his independence very firmly, and clashing directly with Gladstone on at least two issues: the Education Bill of 1870, where Harcourt's devotion to a wholly secular system ran hard up against Gladstone's sacerdotalism; and the abolition by Royal Warrant of the sale of army commissions. On the first issue he conducted a correspondence with his already venerable Prime Minister which, while courteous in form, had an underlay of splendid insolence for a first-term back bencher, particularly one who undoubtedly saw his future in a ministerial direction.

On the second issue he approved of the objective but not of Gladstone's imperious method of proceeding by prerogative: 'Strafford died on the block and Clarendon [not his dead wife's uncle but a greater predecessor] was disgraced for pretending ... that the Crown was the supreme governor and regulator of the Army'. There could be little doubt either about Harcourt's fearlessness or about his ability to provide ringing, wounding and more or less accurate historical support for his arguments.

As something of an anti-climax after all this (and as a sign too of generosity on Gladstone's part) Harcourt did eventually become Solicitor-General. In the autumn of 1873 when the five-year-old government was on its last legs, two of the most distinguished lawyers ever in combination to be law officers, Coleridge and Jessel, became respectively Chief Justice and Master of the Rolls. Henry James (not the novelist but the future Lord James of Hereford) and Harcourt replaced them, but only for a few months until the government resigned after heavy electoral defeat in February 1874. It was not a glorious initial period of office for Harcourt. He and his senior colleague jointly gave unwelcome and probably wrong legal advice to Gladstone that he had vacated his Greenwich seat by becoming Chancellor of the Exchequer (as well as Prime Minister) in the summer, and by so doing helped to precipitate the disastrous election, although the result was unlikely to have been much better at any other time.

The main footprint in the sand which was left by Harcourt's brief tenure of the Solicitor-Generalship was that he became known to history as Sir William Harcourt. He strenuously resisted the knighthood which was habitually bestowed on the law officers – almost entirely on snobbish grounds. He regarded it as an honour for lesser men than himself. Gladstone told him that it was necessary that the rank should be attached to certain distinguished offices and that he should accept it in order to keep up the prestige of knighthoods. He, unfailing in impudence, told Gladstone that an even better way of doing this would be for Gladstone to accept one himself. However, he succumbed, and it was not until a hundred years and a few months later (in 1974) that law officers escaped from what was to some the indignity. In the interim such a disparate group as Sir John Simon, Sir Stafford Cripps, Sir Hartley Shawcross and Sir Geoffrey Howe were labelled as though they were members of an Arthurian round table.

Although Harcourt in 1852 had told his mother that 'I have made friends with Gladstone, who is the man of all those going I have most respect for', their relationship in the period of that statesman's first government, which was in many ways his most successful, was not such as to create any particular bond of loyalty. The Gladstone/Harcourt nexus was not improved by a violent clash in the summer of 1874 over the Public Worship Bill, an anti-ritualist measure, which Gladstone in a small minority vehemently opposed, and which Harcourt in a large majority aggressively supported. Liturgically they were each in their logical positions, but it was nonetheless somehow the wrong way round. The impudent David with the sling had the big battalions on his side and Goliath in the shape of the former Prime Minister was left to expostulate from the fringe. The clash created lasting resentment. Harcourt therefore shed no tears over Gladstone's withdrawal from the leadership, and give his strong support to Hartington, the new Liberal leader in the Commons.

Gladstone was never for Harcourt the king over the water. On the substance of Gladstone's great onslaught on Disraeli's foreign policy, which began with his 1876 pamphlet on the Bulgarian atrocities and ended with his Midlothian campaigns of 1879–80, Harcourt, always resolutely anti-jingo, broadly agreed with him. He nevertheless thought Gladstone's methods showed a lack of consideration for Hartington. But he assured Dilke that there was no fear of a return from Elba: 'He [Gladstone] is *played out*. His recent conduct has made all sober people distrust him.'

Nor did Harcourt much like Gladstone's oratorical style. It was too earnest and uplifting for his taste. His own was based much more on ridicule and humour. And as Harcourt was advancing at this stage to becoming the second most accomplished Liberal speaker – Bright was fading and Rosebery had not then developed the special brand of florid but glamorous eloquence which became his hallmark in the late 1880s and 1890s – there may have also been some element of jealousy. Harcourt however conspicuously lacked Gladstone's ability to hold an audience spellbound with words which appeared to owe everything to his feeling of the moment and not to midnight oil. Harcourt, by contrast, was a contrived speaker. He could sometimes begin a debating speech in the House of Commons with boisterous unprepared humour of the moment. But he then quickly reached for his written text which, while often full of well-turned epigrams and elaborate mocking comparisons, gave the impression that he was heavy on his feet and too much of a professional advocate, lacking in spontaneous sincerity. Dilke made an odd comment in 1885 to Loulou Harcourt, who was ever at his father's side: 'Your father always makes his speeches three times,' he was recorded as saying. 'The first time they are sublime, the second they are very good, and the third time they are only fairly good. He makes the first in conversation to one of his intimate friends or colleagues, the second in talk at the dinner table, and the third in public.'

Even after the Midlothian campaign and the result of the 1880 general election it was Harcourt's wish, as it was even more strongly the desire of the Queen that Hartington, the titular Liberal leader, should be Prime Minister. But this was swept aside by the force of Gladstone's personality and following. The outcome did not prevent Harcourt being offered a senior post in the new administration, to which his standing in Parliament and the country by this time, fully entitled him. He was indeed elevated above his own expectations and even desires at the time. He had hoped to be Attorney-General with a view to succeeding to the Lord Chancellorship. This was a curiously legal concentration of hopes and direction for such a self-confident and ambitious politician aged only fifty-two. Instead he became Home Secretary, the senior secretary-ship of state, although the holder is often exceeded in Cabinet weight by the Foreign Secretary. This Cabinet appointment necessitated his re-election for Oxford, and he failed at the fence. His victory at the general election had been by no more than 112 votes and this turned itself at the by-election to defeat by fifty-eight. Samuel Plimsoll, the seaman's friend, immediately offered to resign his Derby seat in Harcourt's favour, who was there elected unopposed.*

Oxford, however, repercussed behind him. It had been building up a reputation as a peculiarly corrupt constituency and on this occasion his Conservative opponent had overdone it to such an extent (he appeared to have spent £7,500, the equivalent of a modern £375,000) that a commission of two judges not only annulled the election but recommended that the seat be left unfilled, as a sort of collective punishment, for the duration of the parliament. Harcourt presided over the Home Office with a truculent confidence, marred by occasional deficiences of proportion, for the next five years. During this period he considerably improved his relations with Gladstone, and perhaps for the first time, while remaining miles short of sycophancy, came to under-stand the latter's unique force.

On criminal justice matters Harcourt was on the whole liberal, and

---

* He remained member for that Midland railway town over four parliaments until 1895, when he was again defeated and retreated, which was beginning to become a Liberal habit, to the Celtic fringe, a loyal MP once again retiring in his favour. Within a few weeks he was to be returned for West Monmouthshire and sat as the forerunner of Aneurin Bevan as the representative of the miners and steelworkers of Ebbw Vale and Tredegar for the last nine years of his life.

provoked remonstrances from the Queen for what she regarded as his softness in submitting remissions for her to sign. Like many subsequent Home Secretaries he was horrified by the incidence of false conviction, and partly for this reason had pronounced himself against the death penalty in 1878. But the time being far from ripe for implementing such a reform he took his decisions under the existing law without agonizing. He reprieved rather against his will the 'Babbacombe murderer', whom the hangman had three times failed to execute, and he was persuaded by other capital cases to change his attitude to the alcoholic licensing laws.

Previously he had been an extreme licensing libertarian. But he decided that in 80 per cent of the cases where he had sent men to the gallows drink had been a strong contributory factor to the crime – as with many other lesser ones. This pushed him towards temperance reform and he became a strong advocate of local option on closing hours and reduction in the number of licensed houses. This was indeed a big factor in the loss of his Derby seat, the beer barons of nearby Burton-on-Trent mounting a lavish campaign against him. The temperance cause was fortunately more popular, at any rate with the Nonconformist leaders of opinion, in the Welsh valleys.*

In his broader Cabinet capacity Harcourt was a resolute ally of Gladstone – almost his only reliable one after John Bright's 1882 departure from the government – in resisting imperialist adventures. He could not exactly be described as a 'peace-at-any-price' man; his temperament was too bellicose for that. But one of his most consistent attachments was to a raft of ideas which embraced the conviction that Britain had more colonies than were good for it, that alliances were dangerous and that increased expenditure on armaments provided more provocation than safety. He was suspicious of all 'forward' imperial policies and gave currency to a good phrase about the menace of 'prancing pro-consuls'.

However, he balanced his distrust of the military by an overreaction to Fenian terrorist threats in London, and to some extent Liverpool and Manchester too, and by an immature enthusiasm for turning himself into a police generalissimo. His instinctive dislike of the Irish and his

---

* I do not think that he allowed his 'conversion' to affect his personal habits, perhaps setting the pattern for a near analogy with his demi-namesake, a rich Liberal MP of two generations later. After Harcourt Johnstone had delivered to his Middlesbrough constituents a great denunciation of the social evils of gambling it was unkindly pointed out that he was himself frequently to be seen at both Newmarket and Monte Carlo. 'Oh, but I can afford it' was his bland reply.

unrestrained boisterousness came together in an immoderate combination. He may have been against 'prancing pro-consuls' on the frontiers
of empire but he was susceptible to the idea of prancing police chiefs in
the heart of the metropolis. He even instructed the Commissioner of
Police to ride alongside the Queen's carriage whenever she was in
London, a form of protection more ostentatious than efficient.

More seriously he set up the Special Branch (of the Metropolitan
Police) for surveillance of Irish terrorist activity, and as a by-product
was fully informed about Parnell's relations with Mrs O'Shea six or
seven years before the scandal broke. He pronounced himself unable to
spare the time for much non-police business at the Home Office, and
encouraged the transfer of some of the Home Secretary's habitual
business to Dilke at the Local Government Board. In April 1883 he
introduced an emergency Explosives Bill which he got through all its
Commons stages in an afternoon, with the Lords being equally expedi-
tious in the early evening. Then, having alerted the Queen to give Royal
Assent that same night, the arrangements for getting the bill to Windsor
by special train broke down. This was the sort of semi-farcical contretemps in which Harcourt enterprises sometimes ended. He was always
on the edge of being a figure of fun, always liable metaphorically to lose
his trousers at the end of Act II, and to do so to widespread laughter and
enjoyment.* I cannot however cite the Explosives Bill as an example of
Harcourt's over-excited approach to police powers and Irish threats
without remembering that, ninety-one years later, another Home Secretary introduced at short notice a Prevention of Terrorism (Temporary
Provisions) Bill and carried it through all its parliamentary stages by
breakfast time the next morning.

Nevertheless Dilke's remark that Harcourt fancied himself as a
Fouché (Napoleon's chief of police) had more than an element of truth
in it and led to at least one unfortunate consequence for the second

---

* An extreme example of this was provided in January 1882, when Harcourt addressed
a party rally in Burton-on-Trent (probably before his temperance conversion but
without any suggestion that he had made excessive use of the main local product) and,
talking about a pending by-election in rural Yorkshire, expressed his enthusiasm 'for a
bit of ducking' and thought the local opportunities made this 'very likely'. *The Times*
report, apparently as a result of a deliberate joke by a compositor, substituted an 'f' for
the 'd' in ducking. This caused immense hilarity, and copies of the offending edition
changed hands (Brighton was appropriately where the market reached its peak) for up
to a sovereign (at least £50 today). Victorian prurience was of course at play, but the
joke was made much funnier by the fact that it was Harcourt and not, say, John Morley
who was being reported.

Gladstone government. It meant that its first four years were almost completely barren of any major domestic reform. The third Reform Act (extending household suffrage to the counties) was always intended to come towards the end, for the basis on which a parliament was elected could not easily be changed with destroying the validity of the existing one. The early years were dominated by Ireland. But the middle stretch, and particularly the session of 1883 (when Harcourt's police obsession was at its height), should have seen two major measures of local government reform, a Government of London Bill followed by a general measure for the rest of the country, and they were both announced in the Queen's Speech. For London it was proposed to democratize and extend the City Corporation so that its writ ran over the whole four-million-population inner area of what soon (under the Conservatives) became the London County Council.

There was a snag. The City of London like any provincial borough controlled its own police. The police in the rest of the metropolis was, as today, directly under the control of the Home Secretary. Harcourt absolutely refused to consider giving up this prerogative. Gladstone and the majority of the Cabinet could not agree that a Liberal government should take away (from the City) such a small element of democratic control over the police as there was in the capital. The result was impasse. Harcourt killed the London Bill and the wider measure got blocked behind it. It was a striking example of Harcourt's irascible stubbornness as well as of the unpredictability of some of his attitudes. He was the embodiment of the phrase 'a radical in every department but his own', and he was well on the way by the end of that government in 1885 to having established his reputation as a politician of the front rank but an awkward colleague.

The government resigned on 9 June 1885 as a result of a twelve-vote defeat on a clause of the Finance Bill. It would not have been a resigning issue had the Cabinet not already been in a state of disintegration. Ten out of sixteen ministers had on different issues and from different points of view threatened or submitted resignations. But much the greatest cause of the demoralization was a complete inability to agree on an Irish policy. Ireland also had another influence on the defeat. As the first fruit of a tentative alliance between Parnell and the Conservatives, thirty-nine members of the Irish party voted against the government.

That unholy alliance was never consummated. But the rituals of courtship were carried a considerable distance. Carnarvon, the new Irish

Viceroy, had a long meeting, concealed even from the Cabinet, with Parnell in a dust-sheeted Mayfair house ('negotiating in secret with treason' in the words of Balfour's 1882 attack on Gladstone?). The new government did not proceed with an Irish Coercion Bill and stood back from a Nationalist attack on the law-and-order decisions of Spencer, the previous Viceroy. And in the November election the Irish vote in London and the Lancashire towns was mobilized in favour of the Tories.

Gladstone rather welcomed such developments. Over those months his mind was moving inexorably towards the proclamation of Home Rule as a great act of belated justice towards Ireland, an expiation of England's sins from Cromwell to the Famine, and a crusade to which he was prepared to devote the rest of his life. With a shaft of political shrewdness such as often accompanied his moral purposes, he could see that Home Rule might be best, and certainly most quickly, carried through by the Tories, with their command over the House of Lords. Such an approach was at least worth a try.

Harcourt's attitude could hardly have been more different, even though the result of these developments was to land him (unlike half the members of the previous Cabinet) at Gladstone's side, and indeed as his principal lieutenant, for the remainder of the Grand Old Man's political life. Harcourt never saw Home Rule primarily in terms of justice, still less as an expiation or a crusade. This would have been an improbable stance for the Irish-despising, secret-police-loving and dynamite-chasing Home Secretary of 1883. It was essentially political partisanship which brought him along. First, he was a tremendous believer in 'our side against their side'. Party was mostly more important to him than ideology. Second, he was able to persuade himself that it was the Tory flirtation with Parnell over the second half of 1885, towards which he had none of Gladstone's benevolence, which had undermined the prospect for continuing British authority in Ireland. In particular he resented the Tory failure to defend Spencer's administration.

He was thus able to get somewhat ill-temperedly to a Home Rule destination, but by a very different route and in a very different mood from that which had brought Gladstone there. And he was later able to add the argument of an 'economist' (in the nineteenth-century sense of the word, when it meant someone in favour of low public expenditure). He discovered that the cost of the police was 2s 6d per head in England, 1s 11d in Scotland and 6s 10d in Ireland. 'That is the cost of resolute government' was his dismissive conclusion. It was a far cry from the high sentiments of the 'union of hearts'.

Nevertheless these various considerations were enough to make Harcourt available to be Chancellor of the Exchequer in Gladstone's third (and first Home Rule) government, which was formed in late January 1886. In some ways this was unfortunate, for it kept Chamberlain out of the one job (to which Gladstone would however in any case have been unlikely to appoint him) from which he might have found it difficult to resign, and it also gave Harcourt the opportunity to be awkward about the financial clauses of the Home Rule Bill. To offset this it gave Gladstone an effective deputy who brought genuine parliamentary strength of his own, which John Morley, the third member of the triumvirate which ran the Liberal party for the next eight years, dedicated an adjutant for Irish affairs though he was, did not possess.

In this first brief period at the Treasury (the government lasted only five and a half months) Harcourt proved himself a ferocious economist. He was confronted with a deficit, but one which he could meet by reducing debt repayment. The issue became one of whether some increase in the naval estimates, whch were already in the pipeline and after such a brief interval of Conservative government could be largely attributed to previous Liberal policy commitments, should be allowed to stand and be met by taxation rises. To avoid this he set upon the First Lord of the Admiralty, the Marquess of Ripon, and the War Secretary, Henry Campbell-Bannerman, not exactly a sabre-rattling pair, with unrelenting violence. Within three weeks of the formation of the government he was threatening resignation, and there is a clear impression that he went too far both for his Prime Minister (whose mind was concentrated on other things) and for his Treasury officials, with whom however he became in general very popular, in spite of his often farcical outbreaks of short-term wrath.

In the event he was called off by pressure from both these seconds, rather like a dog being separated from the throat of another (or rather another two), after he had secured a reduction of £2 million. As a result he was able to introduce a standstill budget, with no new taxation. This first tenure of the office was little more than a dummy run for his second and notable Exchequer performance in 1892–5.

Before that, however, Harcourt had first to go through an election campaign which reduced his party to 191 MPs (compared with the 333 which they had achieved in 1885 before the split); and then to sustain six years in opposition, with the leadership duties increasingly devolving upon him, as Gladstone, advancing to the age of eighty-two by the end of the parliament, concentrated upon Ireland and became fitful in his routine attendance. It was during these years that Harcourt built up his reputation as a parliamentary trouper. He had been an international lawyer of distinction in his early middle age. In his fifties he was a strong and interesting, although often tiresome and by no means steadily liberal, Home Secretary. In his sixties he was a notable Chancellor of the Exchequer. But transcending all these compartmentalized achievements there was the steady growth over his thirty-six-year membership of his reputation as a House of Commons man. He was best in opposition, and he had plenty of experience of that, a total of twenty-two years out of thirty-six, although none of them on the back benches. His arrogance and grandeur of manner never led him to the modern habit of expressing his superiority by attending the House of Commons as little as he could decently get away with. This may have been partly due to the much greater and more deserved prestige of the House a century ago. To Harcourt, Liberal partisan and on some issues radical reformer though he was, the British House of Commons was unquestionably the greatest deliberative assembly in the world, and its powers the finest jewel in the crown of the almost impeccable 1689 settlement.

'When I am ill I am in bed, when I am well I am in the House of Commons,' he once said, relishing the aphoristic effect of exaggerating the counterpoise. But there was underlying truth. Four days a week he would sit for nine hours a day in the House, mostly with his feet on the table and his hat tipped over his eyes, but surprisingly alert and ready, not only occasionally to deliver the aria of a prima donna, but also to intervene on little points when he could force the government on to the defensive. He had the essential (but rare) parliamentary trouper's attribute of being willing to make bad speeches as well as good ones rather than see his side's case neglected. He was not a fastidious orator. Nor was he a sensitive one. He was splendidly unresentful of hard blows delivered from the other side, and was devoted to cross-party friendships, trying almost desperately, as we have seen, to preserve one with Chamberlain (and to a lesser but perhaps for that reason more successful extent with Hartington and Henry James) even when excoriation and not merely opposition had become the keynote of their public exchanges. The corollary of this was that he often under-estimated the wounding effect of his own rough denunciations. But on the whole there was a steady advance in the affection, sometimes mocking sometimes admiring, in which he was held across the House of Commons. He was a prize bear in the circus.

His judgement was not always up to his brio. The most crucial issue with which the opposition had to deal during the second Salisbury government was the devastating blow struck to their hopes by the Parnell divorce case. Until it broke, the Liberal party appeared to be riding high for victory at the forthcoming general election, with a big enough majority to intimidate the House of Lords and provide Gladstone with a crowning triumph at the end of his sixty-two years in Parliament.

This fair prospect disappeared in November 1890. The evidence given against Parnell, which made him appear ridiculous as well as deceitful, and his disdainful refusal even to attempt an answer, threatened the always precarious alliance between Irish Catholics and British Nonconformists, the latter providing the bulk of the Liberals' provincial support. The issue confronting the Liberal leadership (which for relevant decision-making was the triumvirate of Gladstone, Harcourt and Morley) was whether Gladstone should proscribe Parnell as an Irish leader with whom he could not work. Harcourt was unhesitating that he must do so. He and Morley represented the GOM at an ill-timed National Liberal Federation conference in Sheffield, from which he wrote as follows: 'I have to report to you that the opinion was *absolutely unanimous and extremely strong* that if Parnell is allowed to remain as the leader of the Irish Party all further co-operation between them and the English Liberals must be at an end.'

Morley concurred, Gladstone was for once uncertain and between them they concocted a letter from Gladstone to Parnell which was at first intended to warn him off from automatically seeking re-election as leader, but which, when it was delivered too late for this purpose but nevertheless published, became an excommunication. The 'union of hearts' then dissolved in the bitterness of the Committee Room fifteen split in the Irish Parliamentary party and in Parnell's rat-in-a-corner denunciation of Gladstone as 'an unrivalled sophist'. And the hopes for a great majority in 1892 shrank into a narrow margin with the Irish holding the balance and a shaky Commons passage for the second Home Rule Bill which emboldened the Lords for their contemptuous rejection.

Of course it could be argued that Parnell dug his own grave and that without the excommunication and the protection 'of the credit of the G.O.M.' (which Harcourt claimed was its necessary purpose) there would not have been a majority at all in 1892. But it could also be argued (as, quietly, did two such differently authoritative figures as Spencer and Asquith) that there would have been far less damaging bitterness had the Irish been left to make their own untrammelled decision. Harcourt was indisputably a powerful influence for precipitate action. And part of his motive was his old anti-Irish genie rising up in the bottle. He smacked his lips too enthusiastically over Parnell's downfall. In contrast with Gladstone's dismay and persistent liking for the fallen 'uncrowned King of Ireland', Harcourt wrote to his wife: 'To me I confess it is a relief to have done with such a rascal. I feel some satisfaction in remembering that I have never shaken hands with him.' In the crusade for Home Rule Harcourt was a heavyweight ally of Gladstone's, but also a bloody-minded one.

It was in this mood that he entered the dispiriting government of 1892. Unlike Rosebery, the epitome of self-regard who reluctantly became Foreign Secretary, he did not play hard to get. He went back to the Treasury with private complaint about the awfulness of the prospect but with no public hesitation. Yet he was truculently unhelpful to Gladstone, who complained that if he had had two Harcourts to deal with he could not have carried on the government. The truth was that Harcourt did not have his heart in the main purpose of the administration and that, at nearly sixty-four, he was tired of having a chief, however illustrious, on top of him. But it was his own goose and not Gladstone's that he cooked with his truculence.

With most of the 'nearly Prime Ministers' there has been some trait of character which expressed itself in crucial circumstances and did much to explain their failure to climb to the topmost branch. But in Harcourt's case it was even more sharply pinpointed than with the others. The crucial moment was at 10 p.m. on the night of 12 February 1893, the eve of Gladstone's marathon speech introducing the second Home Rule Bill. There was some muddle and dispute about the financial clauses of the bill, for which Treasury errors were partly responsible and from which Harcourt tried to disengage. That afternoon he had received a letter on the issue from John Morley, Irish Secretary and his closest political friend for at least the past seven years. This had the effect of sending him, like an intermittent volcano, into eruption. And in his 10 p.m. letter he poured out his lava over the eighty-three-year-old Prime Minister, who read the disagreeable and threatening missive the following morning, as he prepared for his great high jump of the afternoon. This Morley – more than Gladstone – regarded as unforgivable, and Morley at that stage had curiously more importance for Harcourt's future than did the Prime Minister. Morley expressed his disapproval in terms at once lucid and lashing: 'What you do is ostentatiously to hold aloof from the business, and then when others do the best they can, you descend upon them with storm and menace. That you should have on such a morning written as you have done to Mr G. is the kind of thing that Brougham* would have done, and nobody else that I have read of in modern public life.'

As Harcourt had at the time, true to his 1886 habit, been bombarding his other Cabinet colleagues with intemperate attacks upon their estimates, this lost him almost his last and certainly his most crucial Cabinet friend. The public expenditure letters which he wrote were at once wounding and frivolous. They were like speeches which he might have made in the Cambridge Union nearly fifty years earlier. When Spencer, the First Lord of the Admiralty, wrote, 'I cannot banter like you, but I fear I can be angry,' he ought to have become cautious, but he merely raked still more bombinating fire round in the direction of the Education Minister, Arthur Acland.

The result was a terrible weakness of support, far below his deserts in early 1894. And Harcourt's self-awareness grew so that he, who had thought for at least the past year that Gladstone was well past the capacity for the job, was humiliatingly forced to urge him to stay on, not out of respect but out of self-protection. Harcourt had no Cabinet allies. If Morley would not support him, and that was a direct price of 12/13 February 1893, no one else would. And so, when Gladstone eventually went, the first choice not merely of the Queen but of the whole Cabinet was Rosebery rather than Harcourt. Gladstone himself would have preferred Spencer, but he was not asked. Nor were the Liberal MPs, who would almost certainly have come out for Harcourt, as would the Liberal activists in the constituencies. It did not avail, and Rosebery, who was a less good Liberal, an ineffective and a less skilled parliamentarian and, above all, a much less nice man, was chosen. The sting was in the last comparison. Harcourt who was fundamentally warm-hearted and generous was passed over, on grounds of personal unacceptability, in favour of Rosebery, who was selfish, quick to take offence and unforgiving.

Rosebery's government was not a success and left a damaged Liberal party which took nearly ten years to recover. A more open question is how many weeks or months it took several of the marginal but crucial Rosebery supporters to regret their choice. Certainly Harcourt and Morley were back on close terms of alliance well within the sixteen

* Brougham, who became a great friend of Gladstone's in later life, had as a young Lord Chancellor under Grey been a notorious and reprobate figure, who on one occasion took the Great Seal with him to Scotland, under the mistaken impression that this would insulate him against being dismissed while he was on holiday.

months which was the length of the Rosebery premiership. Spencer remained more loyal to Rosebery as Prime Minister so long as he held that office and tried to act as a bridge between the leaders of the two Houses, who were effectively not on speaking terms. But in the post-government disputes, which led up to the flouncing resignations, first of Rosebery in October 1896 and then of Harcourt in December 1898, he was more on Harcourt's side. Kimberley, who succeeded Rosebery both as Foreign Secretary in 1894 and as Liberal leader in the Lords in 1896 and who in the former capacity received heavy lashing from Harcourt's tongue and pen, followed much the same course as Spencer.

Harcourt's own behaviour in response to such a final and crushing defeat of his legitimate ambitions was a mixture of the good and the bad. In mitigation of the latter it must be remembered that the reasons for which he was passed over were of the most insulting. It could not be pretended, as with Curzon in 1923, that it was because he was in the wrong House of Parliament. As with Butler in 1957 (and again in 1963) it was that his character and/or personality were measured by his colleagues and, however mistakenly, found wanting.

Despite this he made no attempt to stand out from serving under Rosebery. Such a refusal would have made it impossible to carry on the government, and this course was strongly urged upon him by his devoted son. Instead he got on with his own departmental business. Within six weeks of his great disappointment he produced one of the four or five most notable budgets of the nineteenth century, and carried it through all its stages with a skill, and even a good-humoured tact, which made the government's majority seem much more secure than it was. It was in a sense a perverse performance. If only he could in the preceding months have lavished on his own colleagues the same tolerant good temper that he displayed to his opponents in the House of Commons he might easily have been Prime Minister instead of Chancellor of the Exchequer. But maybe that 1894 budget left more of an imprint than anything which the head of a dying government could have achieved.

The essence of the budgetary problem with which he was confronted was that he had to meet a deficit of nearly £5 million, large by the standards of those days, but arising almost entirely from increasing defence (mainly naval) expenditure, and therefore non-controversial with the Conservatives. This he dealt with in four ways. First, and not very heroically, he reduced debt repayment. Then he made a small increase in the beer and spirit duty. Next he put up income tax from sevenpence to eightpence, but making a total abatement for those with incomes under £500 (£25,000 today), thus introducing the principle of a graduated direct tax, in which direction he would like to have gone much further, but was persuaded that, in combination with his fourth proposal, it would have been over-egging the custard for a single year. This fourth proposal was much the most bold at the time and much the most pregnant for the future. He ended the gross discrimination in favour of land in assessment of what could roughly be called 'death duties'. Hitherto land and settled personalty had been subject only to a very low rate of probate duty. Only free or unsettled personalty had been liable to estate and succession duty as well. Harcourt, the landed scion without landed ideas, ended the discrimination in favour of land and brought all forms of property left at death into a uniform and somewhat higher rate of tax.

The budget went through with curiously little public protest, although the Chancellor had to engage in long argumentative corre-spondence with the Duke of Devonshire (Hartington) and the Queen. (He claimed however to have received a visit of congratulation from Lord Rothschild.) Twelve days before the budget Rosebery presented him with a memorandum which was in effect an attack upon its whole approach and principle. Loulou Harcourt recorded: 'WVH much amused by the high Tory line taken by R.' WVH however reacted with energy as well as amusement and immediately went home and wrote a 2,000-word reply (he was always very fluent), of which the intransigent (and self-righteous) tone may be gauged from the following passage:

> You are not, as I am, old enough to remember the great battle fought by Mr Gladstone in 1853 on the succession duties. That contest secured for him the lasting hatred of the landed proprietors, and the enthusiastic support of the Liberal Party. The fears which your memorandum express are a faint echo of the panic and terrorism of the time. The Tories openly and the Whig magnates covertly feared and hated his policy. He had however the advantage of the courageous and strenuous support of Aberdeen and Granville. I have no doubt that we shall have a 'formidable enemy' in those who find themselves deprived of monopolies which they ought never to have possessed, and the privileges which enrich them at the expense of their poorer fellows. That this class may be alienated from the Liberal Party I am not disposed to dispute.
>
> If it be so, the Liberal Party will share the fate of another Party which was founded 1,894 years ago, of which it was written that it was

'hard for a rich man to enter into the Kingdom'. I think it is highly probable that there are many young men who will go away sorrowing because they have great possessions.

He invited Rosebery to a Cabinet joust on the basis of the two memoranda, a challenge from which the Prime Minister wisely resiled, making use of a small concession in the scale of duty which Harcourt had offered as an excuse for his lack of valour. The result however was that the budget and the Chancellor's subsequent conduct of the Finance Bill, which was both Harcourt's finest hour and the Rosebery government's sole significant achievement, was carried through in spite of the Prime Minister. Harcourt's success did not therefore put him in a better temper with his Prime Minister. He probably felt that it merely underscored the injustice of his supersession. Spencer wrote at the end of the summer trying to persuade him to take to the platform and rally support for the Liberal cause, a task for which he was normally enthusiastic. But on this occasion he was implacably unforthcoming. 'I don't know why you should suppose that I should depart from my fixed resolution not to make any public speech,' he replied on 2 September. 'Why should I? You and your friends have informed me sufficiently frankly you do not regard me as fit to lead. Why then should I pretend to take the initiative only in order that you may repudiate me? As you know I am not a supporter of the present government.'

This was rough and not very generous stuff from the leader of the government party in the chamber on which its existence depended, and it set the tone for the remaining nine months of that government's unhappy life. As in 1885 so in 1895 a casual defeat in the House of Commons provoked the end of a moribund government. The difference was that in 1885 Gladstone resigned, whereas in 1895 Rosebery dissolved. The election was a Liberal rout. Their number fell to 177. Rosebery, reviving a dying convention that peers did not campaign, hired a yacht and sailed round the north of Scotland, calling at remote fishing ports to receive news of defeat for his colleagues and disaster for his party. He had some moments of satisfaction: Harcourt went down in Derby, as did Morley in Newcastle.

Rosebery took the opportunity of the débâcle to behave even worse than Harcourt had done in the previous September. He announced to his colleagues (through Spencer) that as his connection with Harcourt had been purely official, and as the life of the government was over, he had no intention of renewing any contact with him.

The fundamental truth was that the Liberal Party had little hope of full recovery until both of them were out of the way. For this consummation to be achieved another three and a half years had to pass. In the meantime however some sort of Liberal opposition had to be carried on in the House of Commons. The House of Lords did not matter so much. There were only forty Liberal peers and most of them did not turn up. But in the Commons the conventions of opposition and the role of the 'popular party' (even if it had reduced itself to remarkable unpopularity) had to be maintained. And for this fortitude in adversity Harcourt was once again at his best. He got himself returned for West Monmouthshire before the new parliament met, and he kept the show on the road. He was the old entertainer, but he also achieved sporadic tactical victories over a government with an inflated majority but no great sense of direction.

Even after he had given up the leadership at the end of 1898 he could not keep away from the House of Commons. He was habitually there, still on the front bench, mostly sustaining Campbell-Bannerman, his successor, although probably occasionally oppressing him. At the 'khaki election' of 1900 he stood again and was adequately returned. When King Edward VII at last succeeded to the throne a year later he wrote and offered Harcourt a 'non-Prime Ministerial' peerage, that is one from the sovereign direct and therefore without any political strings. But he did not enhance the offer by specifying that it would be a viscountcy, which was 'rations' for a former Home Secretary or Chancellor, let alone one who had been both, was so nearly Prime Minister and had achieved such a special position in the House of Commons. It ought indeed to have been an earldom, for which there was the recent Tory precedent of Stafford Northcote (a lesser man than Harcourt) transformed into Earl of Iddesleigh in 1885. But I doubt if Harcourt would have accepted in any event. He was not quite a great statesman, but he was a great commoner, and he was right to stay in the Commons until he died, which he did in the autumn of 1904, a few days short of his seventy-seventh birthday, and in a particularly easy way. He was at his newly inherited Nuneham Courtenay property, concerned with lack of liquid resources for death duties and maintenance but otherwise at reasonable ease. He spent a routine evening writing a few letters, went quietly to bed, read an article by Morley in the *Nineteenth Century* and died in his sleep.

George Joachim Goschen

GEORGE JOACHIM GOSCHEN WAS NOT ONLY allegedly forgotten in life by Randolph Churchill. In death he has also been one of the more forgotten of Chancellors, indeed in relation to his abilities the most forgotten of the lot. For his epoch he had a long life, with an early and continuing official success, which was the more remarkable in a second-generation immigrant who bore several traces of his provenance. He was never a magnetic popular figure, but he was regarded as a safe pair of hands for difficult jobs, a man moreover who managed to wrap his firm and sometimes rigid views in a cloak of magisterial impartiality, a sort of nineteenth-century Sir John Anderson (later Viscount Waverley). Honours were showered upon Goschen, including late in life a brief Chancellorship of the University of Oxford and, perhaps as even greater assuagement of old age, his opinion was widely sought and his advice mostly heeded.

Goschen, or Göschen as he was known for at least the first thirty-five years of his life, traced his ancestry back to a Lutheran minister who functioned in Saxony in the early seventeenth century and was chiefly useful to establish the non-Jewish credentials of the Göschens on which the future Chancellor seemed excessively keen. These appear to have been impregnable, despite the Kaiser having muttered to King Edward VII when the youngest Goschen brother was proposed as (British) ambassador to Berlin in 1908 something about 'a whiff of the ghetto'. (It should be added that Wilhelm II later became enthusiastic about the appointment.)

The interesting figure however was G. J. Goschen's grandfather, who bore exactly his own names and, having originated in Bremen, became a Leipzig printer and publisher who not only launched Goethe and Schiller upon the reading public but was their intimate friend. It was almost too good to be true: the place, the trade, the epitome of the liberal German culture of the turn of the eighteenth into the nineteenth century. But the Napoleonic Wars were hard on the prosperity and urbanity of the central German lands, and in 1814 William Henry Göschen, the third son of the publisher, emigrated to England, where he set up with a partner the merchant banking and trading business of Frühling and Göschen, which was as rich in profits as its partners were in umlauts.

This Göschen of the intermediate generation was an impressive but ambiguous figure. He was determined to make his life as well as his fortune in England. He married an English wife (although one with the not excessively English name of Ohman) and between them they brought up ten English children, although two of the five daughters married Germans. He settled first in a small Stoke Newington villa (where G. J. Göschen was born in 1831) and later in a larger but not pretentious or commanding house in what was then the open country between Blackheath and Eltham. It was a typical progression for a rising City man. But he did not shake off his Leipzig inheritance. Mammon meant more to him than to his father, and maybe than to his eldest son too (although G. J. Göschen was always deeply respectful towards money and the rights of property, even if not obsessed by a desire to go on making it) but Göschen *père* was also deeply involved with Central European culture. He sent that son to a German school for three formative years from eleven to fourteen, and in his own later life he reverted to spending long periods of semi-holiday in Germany.

There was also ambiguity in W. H. Göschen's attitude to the direction of his son's success. That the son was capable of achieving it seems to have been unquestioned. When, at the age of thirty-one it was felt he had to choose between pursuing his career as a great merchant and concentrating on public service in what was then the foremost country in the world, his father inclined to the latter course – the honour to the son of an immigrant was greater – although pointing out to him that it meant he would have to make do with such money as he had already accumulated (was it enough to sustain a peerage? he interestingly queried) instead of advancing to the wealth of a Rothschild or a Baring.

G. J. Göschen's relentless success began very soon after his return from his German school. He was sent late to Rugby, which somewhat over-robust school, with Thomas Arnold three years dead and the future Archbishop Tait installed as headmaster, retained a good part of its Tom Brown tradition. Göschen, no doubt with some Germanic pedantry, and maybe a touch of a German accent as well, was an obvious target for a full Rugbeian welcome, and he only just survived the first year. Thereafter, however, having got on to terms (to some extent his own) with the school, he rose inexorably to be head boy and to win the English, history and Latin prizes. He also had a successful career at Oriel College, Oxford, then just past its greatest days as the home of Newman, Keble, Pusey and Samuel Wilberforce, but still one of the more interesting houses. He was President of the Union and was placed in the first class in both Mods and Greats. There was some suggestion that in spite of his intellectual power his 'scholarship' was deficient, but in view of his performance that suggests an Oxford pedantry at least as strong as the German version which had to some extent been knocked off him at Rugby.

Despite these triumphs (for which his father rewarded him with £2,000 – the equivalent of £100,000 today), he was recalled on leaving Oxford in 1854 to the counting house. The Buddenbrooks side of his family life asserted itself. There was no serious question of the bar, or of the pursuit of further academic distinctions, or of an early parliamentary seat. On the contrary, he was plunged into merchant life at the rough end. In a manner reminiscent of Neville Chamberlain's sisal-growing experience in the Bahamas nearly forty years later, he was sent to look after the firm's interests in what is now the South American Republic of Colombia, and kept there for two years. This was partly because he had formed a matrimonial intention which his father regarded as doubtfully desirable and certainly premature. However he persisted, and a year after his return married Lucy Dalley, who appears to have given him unruffled contentment, unmarred by any views or activities of her own until 1898, when she predeceased him by nine years.

After another year, and still aged only twenty-seven, he joined the Court of the Bank of England, which was a remarkably early recognition of his City success and repute. At this stage, he was known in high mercantile circles as 'the fortunate youth', a sobriquet which carries with it a flavour of the debonair somewhat at variance with the impression of portentous early gravitas which provoked the comparison with Anderson, who was chairman of the Board of Inland Revenue at thirty-seven and permanent secretary of the Home Office just before he was forty.

During the late 1850s and early 1860s Göschen both became the leading figure in Frühling and Göschen and gained fame as the author of an 1861 book on *The Theory of Foreign Exchanges*. This was a work on the frontier between an academic treatise and a practical City man's handbook, but with sufficient logic, lucidity and command of detail to achieve respect from both directions. It became a classic guide and went through many editions and translations. In the firm itself, Frühling had died in 1841 and had been succeeded as a partner by Wallroth, who in turn had died in 1857, leaving the equivalent of a modern £8 million, W. H. Göschen was becoming old (he died in 1866) and his four younger sons were too young for much responsibility (although two of them had to take it after the mid-1860s). G. J. Göschen was therefore pivotal. He did not seek a shift to politics, but when an opportunity was thrust upon him in 1863 he did not hesitate to make the decisive bifurcation.

There were then four MPs for the City of London, and the Liberal party of Russell and Palmerston commanded sufficient mercantile and banking support that until 1874 there was not a Tory among them. Indeed Lord John Russell himself had been a member for the City until he opted for an earldom in 1861, as had Lionel de Rothschild, who however was not allowed to sit because of non-recognition of a Jewish oath for eleven years following his first election. In 1863 a death precipitated the second City by-election of that 1859 parliament. Göschen, to his considerable surprise but also gratification, was approached to stand by two of his Bank of England colleagues who were prominent in Liberal affairs. In the nineteenth century constituencies were not all regarded as equal passports to the House of Commons. There was a certain hierarchy, although one varying with subjective judgement. Thus, as we have seen, Lord Randolph Churchill had a recurring urge to sit for a great provincial city instead of for South Paddington, and Gladstone, rather *per contra*, preferred Midlothian to the safer Leeds. The City was unique in that, Russell and half a century later Balfour perhaps being exceptions, its representatives were regarded almost as legates of commerce* in contrast with the young men of wealth and/or family who had made arranged marriages with boroughs by the agency of party whips or local magnates. Göschen rightly regarded it as a considerable honour to be so chosen by the age of thirty-two, and although he sat for the City for only seventeen of his thirty-seven years in the House of Commons always regarded himself as carrying a special responsibility for the interests of men of property. He

---

* In my first years in the House of Commons this was still symbolized by their sitting for budget day on the government front bench in top hats, rather like envoys from the Porte in a Venetian group painting.

was against aristocratic privilege, although it had occasionally to be used as an ally in a defensive battle, but he was much in favour of the protection of wealth, particularly that earned through individual enterprise, which was more a feature of the nineteenth- than of the twentieth-century City.

However in 1863 he stood upon a platform which made him an 'advanced Liberal' by Palmerstonian standards. He was in favour of extending the franchise, of the ballot, of the abolition of Church rates and of the removal of religious disabilities from the universities as from official life. He was as vehemently in favour of local government reform for the whole nation as he was (naturally) against any invasion of the special rights and privileges of the City of London. For a few days after the issue of his election address the whole Göschen family was on tenterhooks. His father in Karlsbad found that the strain of waiting for daily bulletins undid the beneficial effects of his cure. His wife in London wrote that the tension was almost unbearable. As the only point at issue was whether or not he should get an unopposed return it may be thought by those who have endured tight counts that the nervousness was extreme. However all was well, and in the summer of 1863 with Palmerston having another two and a quarter years to live, with Gladstone in full command at the Treasury, with the outcome of the American Civil War still apparently open and Lancashire suffering heavily from its effects, and with the infinitely complicated Schleswig-Holstein question becoming the dominant issue in Europe, Göschen took his seat on the government side of the House of Commons.

From the beginning he was immensely favoured. Within eight months he was approached by Palmerston to second the address at the beginning of 1864 session, and was memorably told by the great man when he asked about domestic reform: 'Oh, there is really nothing to be done. We cannot go on adding to the Statute Book *ad infinitum*.' Lord Richard Grosvenor, who was to become Gladstone's last Whig Chief Whip, was the mover and Göschen was no doubt seen as a commercial, bourgeois and even faintly radical balance to the broad-acred (as well as urbanly rich) landed interest of the Westminsters. Göschen was later to write about his own speech on this occasion: 'I was extremely successful.' Although a high degree of self-satisfaction was undoubtedly one of his enduring characteristics, it appears on this occasion to have been well founded. It was a very hard-line free market speech which foreshadowed many of his later attitudes and showed how much more difficult even than Gladstone he would have found adapting to the 'constructive radicalism' which rapidly gained ground in the Liberal party from 1880. He praised 'the noble bearing of Lancashire operatives during the terrible privations of the cotton famine' but all that he offered in return was that 'the restrictions which now impede the free circulation of labour as well as of land will be temperately reconsidered'. In other words – a perfect statement of his *laissez-faire* position – the working classes should be happy to give up trades union rights in return for the removal of entail, settlements and other (mostly) aristocratic restrictions on the free sale of land. When, many years later, he reflected on this speech and defensively commented, 'as it has been often urged, with reference to my political and social tendencies, that I showed little sympathy with the working classes, and little understanding of the problems of poverty and distress, I may be excused if I recall what I said in this speech . . .', it could be regarded as a classic example of *qui s'excuse s'accuse*. He worshipped the market and believed that those who were its victims should show a patriotic stoicism.

Patriotism, perhaps rather exceeding that of most native-born subjects of Queen Victoria who took their Englishness for granted, was his other leitmotif. He was not an unthinking jingo, and was on the whole critical of the tinsel showiness of Disraeli's foreign policy in the 1870s, and in particular of the *de facto* annexation of Cyprus, which he regarded as a useless acquisition and one which he found gravely compromised Britain's 'clean hands' reputation in the eastern Mediterranean when he became ambassador to the Porte a few years later. But in general he was a great defender of Britain's imperial prerogatives, a firm believer in the 'blue water' school of strategy by which the wide-margined supremacy of the Royal Navy must at all costs be maintained. (Over a long interrupted span of twenty-nine years, exactly the same as that which covered Winston Churchill's two First-Lordships, he was twice the political head of the navy.)

Furthermore his opposition to Home Rule for Ireland was made almost irrational by the virulence of his disapproval of the 'disloyalty' of Irish Nationalists. This disapproval amounted to incomprehension. In spite of his firm conviction that he stood for a 'thoughtful' approach to politics, he never put forward any constructive alternative policy for Ireland. Home Rule was clearly against the interests of business, of the rights of property, of tidy administration, and (superficially at least) of Britain's power, and that was surely enough. He never thought of visiting Ireland, even though he was so eager to use it as a reason to break, and to urge others to break, from the Liberal party. Whether or not because of over-compensation for his German background, he became a classic example of a man *plus royaliste que le roi*, more imperialist (almost) than the Queen–Empress, over what he saw as British interests.

Whatever views he was expressing Göschen never presented them with much oratorical flair. His strongly supportive and almost hagiographic official biographer, Arthur Elliot, a sporadic Liberal Unionist MP, struck on this issue a note of depressing frankness: 'His voice was not good, nor his gestures and bearing graceful.' Yet we are assured that such was the force of his logic and the respect commanded by his somewhat self-righteous disinterestedness that he several times made the most persuasive speech at critical junctures. He also balanced his lack of the physical attributes of a commanding orator with a gift for a good phrase. In 1885, in almost his last Liberal pronouncement, 'he would not give a blank cheque to Lord Salisbury'. A year or so later, with a choice between Home Rule and coercion, he 'would never surrender to crime or time'. In 1903, when he fought against Tariff Reform as his last battle, he 'would be no party to a gamble with the food of the people'. And when Joseph Chamberlain at the peak of his mid-1880s radicalism had mordantly demanded 'what ransom will property pay', the phrase was borrowed from Göschen, who had pejoratively used it to him, in private conversation, a few days before.

What is indisputable is that Göschen acquired a quick and early House of Commons reputation for being a man of substance, somewhat comparable with that which Asquith equally quickly acquired a quarter of a century later, although Asquith had at once more political force and more private humour than Göschen. In both cases it led to early promotion, which with Göschen may have been over-promotion. In the autumn of 1865, Russell, Prime Minister in the wake of Palmerston's death, offered him the Vice-Presidency of the Board of Trade, the office which Gladstone had accepted with some disgruntlement from Peel in 1841. Göschen accepted more enthusiastically than Gladstone, as well he might with only two and a half years of parliamentary experience. But before the new parliament met in January 1866 the Prime Minister had decided to upgrade the offer to the Chancellorship of the Duchy of Lancaster, made vacant by Clarendon becoming Foreign Secretary, and to include with it membership of the Cabinet. At the age of thirty-four, Goschen (as we may henceforth call him, for the umlaut went out as office came in) took his seat on the front bench alongside Gladstone, the new leader of the House, and only three other Commons Cabinet ministers. It was an extraordinary promotion over the heads of such diverse but more resonant figures as John Bright and Hartington. The jealousies aroused were considerable and raised eyebrows were almost universal among Goschen's colleagues. Some even thought that the resentment contributed to the foundering of the Russell government's franchise reform bill that spring, but this seems an exaggerated view. What is certain is that the inability to carry this bill was fatal to Russell and his ministers, that by June of the same year they were all out, with Goschen's first and not very demanding experience of government having lasted only five months.

It had however served the purpose of giving him a position in the Liberal hierarchy, and when the first Gladstone government came in two and a half years later he was an almost automatic choice for the tail-end of a notable Cabinet; he became President of the Poor Law Board. In the meantime he had been returned for the third time for the City, securing there his one marked electoral success, for he was not in general a vote-attracting figure. But in 1868 he came top of the poll, leading the other two Liberals and one Conservative who were also elected. The presence of the single Conservative was however the beginning of the writing on the wall for Liberal hegemony in the City.

The Poor Law Board was the forerunner of the Local Government Board (which then went through various post-1918 metamorphoses to become the Ministry of Health, then the Ministry of Housing and Local Government before, having shed both health and social security on the way, it settled down into the great wen of the Department of the Environment). Goschen's administrative achievement was to work out a scheme for putting together the local government functions of the Poor Law Board and those scattered over the Home Office and the Privy Council and thus making a basis for the Local Government Board. But he was much less successful with his attempt to reform both the structure of local government in the counties and the basis of local taxation. Partly this was because the issues lay on a fault-line in his political outlook. At this stage he believed strongly in a democratic and rational structure for local government. But he also believed, and this became almost an obsession with him twenty years later, that the poor must not have any control over the administration of the Poor Law. If they did they would debauch themselves and the national finances. And as county local government, through the Boards of Guardians, was then primarily concerned with the provision of relief, indoor or outdoor, his two positions were almost impossible to reconcile.

He also showed a considerable tactlessness in dealing with the susceptibilities of country gentlemen, which led to an uncomfortable number of Liberals of this species joining with the Tories to vote against him in the House of Commons. Florence Nightingale, although not a country gentleman of either persuasion, well captured this aspect of Goschen when she wrote: 'I don't think he will ever do much. He is a man of considerable mind, great power of getting up statistical information and Pol. Econ. but with no practical insight. It is an awkward mind – like a pudding in lumps.'

Altogether it was a relief for the government and a lucky promotion for Goschen when, in the spring of 1871, Childers resigned on health grounds and Gladstone moved him up to be First Lord of the Admiralty. There was little obviously nautical about Goschen. He provoked the mocking jingle 'Goschen has no notion of the motion of the ocean,' and was widely thought to have inspired W. S. Gilbert's satirical characterization of the First Lord in *Pinafore*. The counting house rather than the quarter-deck was his natural habitat. But his Admiralty connection was not to be finally terminated until after the turn of the century. By then he had assumed a sea-dog air with a fondness for reefer jackets and yachting caps. Already in the early 1870s he went native on Admiralty matters and tempered his economist's approach to life with the firm conviction that naval expenditure was special. Gladstone came up against one of the awkward lumps in Goschen's pudding in late 1873, when his failure to get the Admiralty estimates down was a powerful factor in provoking him into his ill-fated dissolution of Parliament in early 1874, which led to Disraeli's only period of sustained majority power.

This defeat also led to Gladstone's temporary withdrawal from the Liberal leadership and to the beginning of Goschen's permanent estrangement from the party. There was however no connection between the two developments. In spite of Gladstone including Goschen in 'one of the best instruments of government that ever was constructed', as he described his first administration, there was little affinity between the two. Goschen was lucky to have survived the Conservative semi-landslide of 1874, and, in contrast with his position at the head of the poll in 1868, he scraped home for the City in fourth place as the only Liberal there elected and with his majority over the last Conservative candidate reduced to a handful. Thereafter he decided that discretion was the better part of valour, and for the 1880 election retreated from the City to the hills, or at least to the Yorkshire dales, by becoming member for Ripon.

In the meantime however he had performed the first of his pro-consular roles as well as establishing himself as an independent servant of the state who knew about money. In the last third of the nineteenth century Egyptian bonds were a favourite high-yielding stock of the bourses of Europe. But the debt was always top-heavy in relation to the resources of Egypt, and in the spring of 1876, despite the injection of cash resulting from Disraeli's purchase of the Suez Canal shares in the previous year, the Khedive's government teetered on the brink of default. Goschen was asked by the Council of Foreign Bondholders, an international organization although centred in London and powerful although private, to negotiate on their behalf with the Egyptian govern-ment. Typically in all respects, Goschen successfully carried through this property-sustaining mission, which could be regarded as bleeding the Egyptian fellahin in the interests of London and Paris *rentiers*, while stipulating that he should not himself receive a penny of profit or commission. He secured the promulgation of the Khedival decree of 18 November 1876, which is generally known in Egyptian history as the 'Goschen decree'. He was also responsible in this phase for the first involvement in the affairs of Egypt of that great future pro-consul Evelyn Baring, later first Earl of Cromer.

This Levant exercise did not predispose Goschen in favour of Gladstone's anti-Turkish crusade which was launched in that autumn of 1876. When Goschen dined with the Queen on his return he deprecated Gladstone's 'wild, senseless agitation of the country'. And by six months or so later, when he had uncompromisingly opposed the bill for the extension of the borough franchise to the counties, which was likely to be a central measure of the next Liberal government, he had cast off most of his Liberal or even Whig garments. The habit of being a Tory in Liberal clothing settled easily upon him. In these circumstances it was odd that he made quite an effort to get a new (for him) Liberal constituency for the 1880 election. Ripon adopted him, partly on the recommendation of their local marquess, and that was odd too for Lord Ripon was a 'hot Liberal', in the nice phrase sometimes used in those days of enthusiastic politics, and one who remained not only with Gladstone over Home Rule but with Campbell-Bannerman and Asquith through the social reforms of the 1906 parliament. Already in 1878 the eponymous marquess described himself to Goschen as 'pretty nearly the greatest radical in Ripon.'

There was yet another oddity. When Goschen had been safely elected and Gladstone had been swept back into office it was accepted on both sides that he was not eligible for the Cabinet because of his intransigence on franchise reform. Instead Gladstone offered him the great post of Viceroy of India, and was 'amazed' at his refusal. Goschen's motives were a mixture of reluctance to be away for four or five years from his young family (the youngest of the Goschen's six children had been born only in 1875) and suspicion that, even with Hartington at the India Office, he would find the policy of the second Gladstone government too soft both for the 'big game' with Russia in the mountain fastnesses of Afghanistan and for relations with the native races in the plains of India itself. As a result the offer reverted to Goschen's Yorkshire patron. Lord Ripon both accepted the offer and pursued a notably liberal policy in Calcutta.

Goschen meanwhile was persuaded by Granville, the Foreign Secretary, to accept a special ambassadorship to Constantinople, where the European Powers were endeavouring to persuade and/or force the Sultan to carry out the stipulations of the Congress of Berlin in relation to Greece, Montenegro and Armenia. This role he was prepared to undertake provided it did not involve giving up his seat in Parliament, which consequence was avoided by making it a short-term appointment without a stipend. Goschen stayed in Constantinople for almost a year, achieving considerable success with the Porte, in spite of (or maybe because of) looking at the time uncannily like Mrs Thatcher's minister Patrick Jenkin (now Lord Jenkin of Roding). His wife and some of his family were with him for much of the time, the Bosphorus apparently being judged both healthier and more accessible than the banks of the Hoogly river. He behaved with aplomb and authority, whether dealing with the Sultan, his fellow ambassadors or the home government. In his despatches and letters he treated Granville like a colleague (if anything a rather junior one) rather than an instructing authority.

Back in England in the summer of 1881 Goschen was able to continue to build up his reputation as being more sought after than seeking. He refused the GCB to keep himself free of obligation to the government, which he hardly ever supported in difficult divisions – from the Irish Land Bill to the Transvaal. Nonetheless there would probably have been an eager response (although with Gladstone more reticent than the Whig members) to any suggestion that he might be prepared to join the Cabinet. A year later, however, when there was a reshuffle in the wake of the Phoenix Park murders, Gladstone made him a formal offer to be Secretary of State for War. What he conspicuously did not do was to offer him the Exchequer, which was also available and which might have been more tempting. Gladstone pronounced the interesting and probably sound dictum that 'no man connected with the City can make a good Chancellor'. Childers went to the Treasury and Goschen, refusing the War Office, notched up another *nolo episcopari*.

In 1883 he achieved a still further refusal, but for different reasons and in different circumstances. Speaker Brand retired and Gladstone offered government support for the vacancy to Goschen, as second choice after the future Lord Chancellor Herschell had refused. For once he was disposed to accept, even though it involved going into a political cul-de-sac at the age of fifty-two. At least it involved no commitment to evolving Liberal policies. Then Goschen's oculist was called in and apparently advised that during scenes of Commons excitement he would be able to see little except an inchoate and more or less inseparable mass of members before him. So he again declined, and applied himself for the remaining eighteen months of that parliament to opposing the third Reform Bill and refusing to recognize that there were any problems special to Ireland which firm government would not cure.

It followed that when Gladstone embraced Home Rule in the autumn of 1885 Goschen's reaction was so predictable as hardly to be of interest. Indeed there is an impression that Goschen became rather an insensitive bore to the other leading Liberals who reluctantly but determinedly split from Gladstone. For them the moment of decision was one of sadness. They wished that Gladstone had not forced it on them. For Goschen, by contrast, it was one of exhilaration. For the first time for several years it gave him some political allies. His loyalties were not torn. He had not been a Gladstonian Liberal for nearly ten years and to be able to avail himself of the Liberal Unionist exit was a bonus. At the London Opera House meeting in April 1886, following the introduction of the Home Rule Bill, which, probably prematurely for the interests of Unionism, brought Hartington and Salisbury for the first time to the same platform, Goschen, despite his oratorical limitations, was by common consent thought to have made the best speech. He was the one who had no inhibitions and most had his heart in the new alignment.

Fortunately, however, he retained inhibitions about what was constitutionally proper and what was not. As a result he resolutely refused invitations from the Queen to go to Osborne in the aftermath of the Conservative Commons defeat in January 1886 on the 'three acres and a cow' amendment, and to provide a focus for a moderate coalition which would save her from having to send for Gladstone. With greater propriety, self-restraint and regard for the long-term interests of the monarchy than Disraeli had shown in 1880, Goschen firmly told the Queen that it was her constitutional duty to give Gladstone the opportunity to form his third government. Goschen was delighted to fight his policy, but he had no desire to prevent it being put to the test by encouraging the Queen to behave dangerously and improperly. It was perhaps his finest hour. It also showed that he had a rare capacity to distinguish, even at the height of battle, desirable ends from unacceptable means.

Then, not for the first time, electoral embarrassment struck Goschen. He never seemed to handle his constituencies elegantly. Ripon, in spite of the Marquess's assurance that he was the most radical man there, was already beginning to find Goschen both right-wing and remote by 1883. That however did not greatly signify, for the borough's hold on life was distinctly tenuous. The 1885 Redistribution of Seats Bill terminated its separate constituency existence. Despite his growing estrangement from the party Goschen once more sought a new Liberal seat and secured one – Edinburgh East – which was dangerously close to the beat of Gladstone's eagle wings. For that first election under the new arrangements, when there was no leader's commitment to Home Rule and when a degree of ecumenicism prevailed across the 333 at least nominal Liberals who were elected, that did not matter too much. Goschen fought on a very right-wing platform but his only opponent was a way-out radical whom he comfortably led by 4,337 to 1,929. Eight months later, by the summer election of 1886, with the first Home Rule Bill defeated, the political landscape had been transformed. On the whole it was improved for Liberal Unionists. There had been a swing to Unionism (the unseceding official Liberals declined to only 195 seats), and still more importantly they were given a free constituency run by the Conservatives. As a result they were nearly all comfortably returned.

The major exception was Goschen. He had the excuse that lack of Conservative opposition was not a special 1886 bonus for him. He had already enjoyed it in 1885. Nevertheless the magnitude of his defeat was humiliating. He went down to a local Gladstonian Liberal by 3,694 to 2,253. Worse was to come. He remained out of the House of Commons for six months, but when he became Chancellor of the Exchequer over the turn of the year 1886/7 it was obviously urgently necessary that he be found a seat. There was a vacancy in the Exchange division of Liverpool, which in those days had the advantage, almost tailor-made for Goschen, of a large business vote, and he decided to risk the contest. He lost it, but only by seven votes. It was nonetheless a severe jolt. This vacancy had at least occurred naturally, but the next one had to be contrived. Lord Algernon Percy, the member for the Westminster constitency known as St George's, Hanover Square, resigned with the utmost grace. The trouble was first that it sounded more like the venue of a fashionable wedding than a democratic constituency, and second that it made Goschen completely dependent upon Conservative votes. Had he held Edinburgh or won Liverpool the result would have owed something to his distinctive Liberal Unionist contribution. In St George's he was just a Tory poodle. His retreat there symbolized his Conservative subservience even more than did his joining the Carlton Club, six years later.

The story of Lord Randolph Churchill's flounce from office in December 1886 and the question of whether his impetuousness had really allowed him 'to forget Goschen' belongs to a previous essay. What is certainly the case is that Goschen's acceptance of office, even though it made him the solitary so-called Liberal in an entirely Conservative Cabinet, and even though it caused some fluttering in the dovecots of those who were attempting to put together a Liberal Unionist party organization (particularly in Edinburgh, where a great banquet in his honour had to be put off at less than a week's notice) caused no surprise among the political cognoscenti. Thirteen years out of office had not made him indifferent to its charms. Unlike the majority of his colleagues he would have welcomed a coalition immediately after the 1886 election, and failing a general move would probably have been susceptible to a unilateral invitation, had one been immediately forthcoming, which it was not. On the former occasion, as six months later, he wanted Hartington's seal of approval, which he got without difficulty, and at the end of the year he tried to get two fig-leaves in the form of Lansdowne and Northbrook entering the Cabinet with him, but when that came to nothing he was far from making it a condition.

Salisbury, by offering, and Goschen, by accepting, the Exchequer concluded a mutually advantageous deal. Goschen got the senior office for which he seemed most suited and he got it in a Conservative government, which was the only one in which he could by then feel at home. Salisbury got a confidence-giving figure without real political strength of his own or the desire to cut too high a profile, which was exactly what he wanted as an antidote to Randolph Churchill. Whether Goschen was a good Chancellor is more problematical. His main and real achievement was the conversion in 1888 of the core of the national debt from a 3 per cent to a 2.75 and ultimately 2.5 per cent basis. For the rest he was a stolid and uninnovating Chancellor. His American academic biographer of 1973, Professor Thomas Skinner, captured almost perfectly the feeling that a safe pair of hands had also been a rather dull pair of hands when he wrote: 'Yet there remains a feeling that he failed to accomplish much of what needed to be done.' Perhaps Gladstone had been right in seeing a City connection as a bar to a great Chancellorship. A City Chancellor was liable to be a man of the money markets, capable of a major technical achievement like the conversion of 1888, but not of wider horizons. Maybe Goschen himself half appreciated this, for in 1895 after the interval of the Gladstone/Rosebery governments, he declined to go back to the Treasury. The fact that Salisbury offered him the return showed that his long (five-and-a-half-year) Chancellorship had been far from a disaster. The fact that he preferred to switch back for his final five years in government to his old post at the Admiralty showed that, despite his tendency to self-satisfaction, he had a realistic appreciation of his own talents and limitations.

He introduced six budgets, all of them in the conventional spring season, the contents fairly conventional as well, and the first four of them on a rising tide of prosperity which made their formulation and reception relatively easy. All of his budgets produced surpluses, and surpluses substantially in excess of those which he had estimated. This was not because he was particularly effective in holding down expenditure. At first he inherited the effects of Randolph Churchill's obsessive attempt at stringency. But from 1889 onwards, when he and the Cabinet had accepted Lord George Hamilton's Naval Defence Bill with its plan for laying down seventy new ships over five years, he was on an escalator which led permanently out of the bargain-basement 'small budget' finance of the mid-Victorian period. He was the last Chancellor not to breach the £100 million frontier, but he was also the Chancellor who made it almost inevitable that all his successors of either party would operate beyond it. By 1900, Goschen's last year in office – although no longer at the Exchequer – total expenditure, assisted by the South African War but never again to fall significantly, was above £150 million.

When there is added to Goschen's endorsement of naval demands the provision for free education which he accepted in his 1891 budget and the need for additional local government 'own resources', an old commitment of his dating back to 1870 which assumed new force with the County Councils Act of 1888, the increase in expenditure over which he presided became formidable by the standards of the times.

The only significant offset was the £1.5 million saved by his successful conversion operation of 1888. Public expenditure (including local taxation grants) rose between his first year as Chancellor and his last from £87.5 million to £97.5 million.

It was not therefore a rigid parsimony of expenditure which led to Goschen's persistent unconvenanted surpluses. It was very much more his instinctive caution in estimating revenue. He developed what became almost an obsession with the exhaustion of traditional sources of indirect revenue. Tobacco and alcohol, he sought to demonstrate in his 1887 budget, were tired giants; their buoyancy was gone. This proved to be wholly unfounded, in both the short and the longer term. In the longer term they proceeded triumphantly through the Boer War, the Great War and the Second World War to provide vast revenue. In the short term alcohol bounced up even within Goschen's Chancellorship and benevolently slapped him in the face. Eighteen-eighty-nine was a year of alcoholic surge when 'some men rushed to the beer barrel, some to the spirit bottle and others to the decanter'. Even more however, the British fortified their intake of rum, which went up by 12 per cent in a single year. Why? They could hardly all have been celebrating the centenary of the French Revolution with more enthusiasm than Mrs Thatcher summoned up for the bi-centenary. The result was what Goschen called the 'stupendous, the sensational' figures, which like vintages or weather records recalled the 'great drinking year of 1875–6'. But what indeed had happened in that earlier financial year, apart from Gladstone's first withdrawal from the Liberal leadership and the quietest year of Disraeli's premiership, neither of which were obvious excuses for bacchanalia?

Goschen's basic prognosis of what was happening to taxation yields was therefore false, and it led him into a heresy from the true church of Peel and Gladstone (the latter in his budgetary not his Home Rule phase), who were Goschen's natural economic forebears. Peel and Gladstone believed in simplifying and narrowing the base of indirect taxation. Goschen, coming nervously to assume that existing seams were running out, believed in widening the base: 'It is better service to the State to increase the number of sources of revenue than to attempt to find simplicity . . .', he said in 1889. This led him not merely to throw Peel out with the bath water but also to complicate his budgets with over-ingenious proposals, several of which foundered. The one which became a joke, even though basically sensible, was the van and wheel tax of 1888. It was designed to make vehicles, according to their weight, pay for the upkeep of roads and was supplemented by a horse tax of £1 on every 'pleasure horse', £5 on racehorses and £15 on horse-dealers. It was unpopular for populist reasons, became mockingly known as the 'veal and ham tax', and eventually had to be humiliatingly abandoned. The horse tax went down with the 'veal and ham'.

Goschen's other major failure was with his 1890 proposal for using the proceeds of an increased whisky duty to compensate publicans who suffered under the power given to local authorities to reduce the number of licensed premises. This offended not only the distillers and the publicans but also the temperance lobby, which regarded the payment of such compensation as the 'wages of sin'. This compensation provision also had to be withdrawn, which further retreat pointed to some lack of political adroitness on Goschen's part. Some of the 'whisky money', being allocated to local authorities, then found its way into a very modest beginning of technical education, although the whole saga considerably discredited the principle of hypothecation of a national tax for local authority use.

This restless and sometimes ineffective search for broadening the basis of indirect taxation led him to produce cluttered rather than bold budgets. Combined with another of his nostrums, which was that even the most impoverished should, as a matter of civic cement, make some contribution to national revenue, led him to keep taxes alive as the 'skeletons of our [fiscal] regiments'. He could for instance have abolished the tea duty in his 1890 budget but chose instead to keep it in being at a low level because otherwise there would have been a whole class of teetotal and non-smoking working men who would have paid no taxation of any sort. This was very unGladstonian, and indeed the Grand Old Man, firm inegalitarian though he was, had rebuked Goschen two years before for being 'too much in favour of property and too little in favour of the general consumer'.

Goschen also showed a bias in favour of indirect as opposed to direct taxation. In the course of his five years he succeeded in widening the gap between the two from 54.4 per cent indirect to 45.5 per cent direct to 55.9 per cent indirect to 44 per cent direct. When Harcourt confronted him with these figures he somewhat disingenuously claimed that his two reductions in income tax, which between them brought the rate down from eightpence to sixpence in the pound, should not be allowed into the calculation because income tax, at any rate at eightpence, had been an emergency national defence measure in 1885 and was not to be considered as part of the permanent structure of taxation.

More convincingly however he rested on his record in carrying through his great conversion, in providing an extra £2 million a year for the navy, and about the same amount for local government, in financing the beginnings of free education, and doing it all while paying off £59 million of debt (of a total of approximately £700 million) and relieving income taxpayers of £4 million and some indirect taxpayers of lesser amounts. There is a lot to be said for being at the Exchequer during an economic upswing, even if, in accordance with the conventions of the time, Goschen took no more credit for it than he would have accepted blame for a downswing. Either was more an act of God than a responsibility of the Chancellor. But it nonetheless made life easier to have a buoyant revenue. With it, he was a competent although not a great Chancellor, cautious, convoluted and too interested in the techniques of financial manipulation: a great financier maybe, but not a great minister, rather the equivalent, often said to be a mistake, although there are not many examples to prove or disprove it, of a leading advocate being Foreign Secretary.

Apart from the conversion the other dominant non-budgetary event of Goschen's Chancellorship was the first Baring collapse in the autumn of 1890. That unfortunate firm, whose fluctuations from complacent superiority to disaster have been without parallel had got into a grossly over-exposed position in the Argentine as well as in Russian bonds. Its liabilities were about £20 million, a sum which applying the crude but roughly appropriate factor of fifty, was curiously approximate to the Singapore exposure 105 years later. A sense of unease began to pervade the City in mid-October, but it was the end of the first week in November before discreet panic began to set in. There remains, however, a considerable smokescreen over what happened in 1890 as there does over what happened in 1995. Neither of the two lives of Goschen nor such a distinguished historian as Philip Ziegler in his *The Sixth Great Power: Barings 1762–1929* tells us exactly what degree of government intervention saved Barings in the 1890s. What is clear, however, is that no one, except possibly William Lidderdale, the distinctly non-patrician Governor of the Bank of England (when the trouble was over Goschen recommended him for a GCB on the ground that he was 'not rich enough for a baronetcy'), covered themselves with glory.

Lord Revelstoke, the holder of one of the innumerable Baring peerages who was then the leading member of the firm, certainly did not. He was described by Ziegler as 'not the most likable of men [whose] arrogance and complacency had alienated many who would otherwise have sympathised fully . . .' Nor was he the most competent of men. But he at least paid the price of the selling up of his London house and a severe cut in his standard of living. Lord Rothschild, already the leader of the City and likely to be even more pre-eminently so, even if suffering a bit from nuclear fallout after the collapse of Barings, adopted an air of mournful pessimism. 'I fear they are a'gonna,' was his attitude to Barings. But he managed to arrange a staunching loan of £3 million from the Bank of France to the Bank of England. Other City eminences, according to Goschen, varied between a state of 'blue funk' and being 'quite demoralized'.

Goschen himself was not much better. He contributed one sleepless night and several visits to the City. He was full of criticism of others for flapping round ineffectually. But he was himself obsessed with a conviction that government credit, for which the Governor of the Bank and others were insistently asking, must not be pledged on behalf of a private firm. How could he defend it before the House of Commons? Once again, as with 'veal and ham' and the licensed victuallers, he was weakened by his lack of an easy self-confidence in dealing with the Conservative party, in whose maintenance in power, for Ireland and other reasons, he slavishly believed, but in which party he was not instinctively at home. Balfour or W. H. Smith could and would have perfectly easily defended such an intervention.

On the crucial days, Friday and Saturday, 14 and 15 November, Goschen by good fortune was due to speak in Dundee. It was decided that for him to cancel his engagement would add to the panic. So he departed, and Salisbury and Smith assumed joint ministerial responsibility for dealing with the crisis. It is not exactly clear to what extent they directly reversed Goschen's *non possumus*, but by a flexible sleight of hand they met the Bank and the City halfway, agreed that for a short period the Bank and the government would share any losses, and got round the awkward corner. Goschen, as he sat down to lunch in Dundee on the Saturday, had the pleasure of receiving a telegram informing him that the crisis was over and that all had been resolved. He hoped from the sidelines that it was *more or less* within his policy.

This meant that Goschen, for all his portentous reputation and genuine quality of intellect and character, had shown himself inadept at dealing not only with the House of Commons but also with his heartland of the City. When W. H. Smith died just under a year later these considerations were decisive in keeping Goschen out of the Commons leadership. A year or so before it would have been very difficult for Salisbury to have avoided giving it to him. Now a combination of the rise of Balfour and of Goschen's own limitations meant that it was easy to bypass him. Salisbury tactfully put it all on his not being a nominal Conservative.

Goschen accepted his supersession with good grace. But it decisively marked the beginning of the gradual and honourable descent from his maximum political influence. Rather typically he repaired his nominal deficiency by joining the Carlton Club two years later, almost overdoing his credentials by having himself proposed by Salisbury and seconded by Balfour, and also underlining his abeisance by resigning from Brooks's a year after that, surely a supererogatory gesture, for Fox's old citadel had become at least as full of Liberal Unionists and even Conservatives as of Gladstonian Liberals. But it was too late for Goschen to count as one of W. S. Gilbert's 'little Conservat*ives*' and qualify for the number-two spot to Salisbury.

In any event, by October 1891 he was over sixty, not youthful for his age, and, although he had another nine years of full political life ahead of him, was showing several signs of an increasing rigidity which cut him off from easy relations with his colleagues. In the three opposition years from 1892 to 1895 his sense of unyielding outrage at both Gladstone's second Home Rule Bill and Harcourt's 'death duties budget' (despite the few paving steps which he himself had taken in 1889) made him a vehement rather than persuasive opposition spokesman, even apart from the fact that, as a parliamentary gladiator, he was not in the same class as Harcourt, let alone the GOM. Nor was he in the inner quartet of Salisbury, Balfour, Devonshire and Chamberlain which, particularly when the 1895 government became a full coalition and not merely an alliance of support as in 1886–92, provided the strategic Unionist leadership.

In these circumstances he was perhaps lucky to be offered a second Chancellorship. He hesitated only long enough to make sure that there was no risk of Chamberlain, who became safely settled in the Colonial Office, being appointed to the Treasury in his place, and then said that he would prefer the Admiralty. There the former cautious Chancellor presided for five years over a regime of determined extravagance. Naval estimates, which had been under £10 million when he had been Gladstone's First Lord in 1871, had risen to £29 million by his final year, and over a half of the increase had taken place during his second term. The personnel strength had risen from 61,000 when Goschen had first gone to the Admiralty to 85,000 when he returned in 1895 and to 112,000 when he finally left in 1900. He turned the old adage on its head, and as a gamekeeper turned poacher was very effective. He was a fine servant of conventional naval opinion. Salisbury's 1896 expostulation, after Goschen had sent him an 'admirals' benefit' paper, arouses sympathy: 'There is something, if I may put it so, theological in the absolute confidence of the counsels given by your advisers . . .'

Goschen was also a solid obstructionist in the path of the new co-ordinating Committee of Defence which Salisbury endeavoured to set up under Devonshire after 1895. It was an ineffective forerunner to the Committee of Imperial Defence which Balfour established in 1903. A substantial reason why it was ineffective in the 1890s was that Goschen was determined to make it so. Altogether he was a powerful advocate of a big navy, but otherwise a backward-looking First Lord. His performance was almost perfectly captured by a *Punch* cartoon of the week he laid down office. It showed him leaving the Admiralty, in court dress with a sword, bearing his seals of office, and being saluted by a diminutive Mr Punch in ordinary seaman's uniform, standing on a step and with an expression at once appraising and approving saying: 'Good-bye, Sir; and *Good Luck*! You've done such a lot for the Service, we're all sorry to lose you.'

Goschen naturally and reasonably expected a peerage, but he made rather a fuss about its form. He wrote to Salisbury saying that he could not determine his title until he knew what rank he was to get and that he hoped his enoblement would not be announced as 'one of a batch'. He hinted hard that a viscountcy was merely rations for a retiring Cabinet minister and that his long service might entitle him to something higher. Salisbury's secretary succinctly if brutally wrote on the back of the letter: 'Accepts Viscountcy: would have liked an Earldom.' He became Viscount Goschen of Hawkhurst, Hawkhurst being the small Kent town which rather confusingly adjoined the substantial East Sussex house and estate of Seacox Heath, which had been his country base since 1874. Salisbury from the strength of his own high rank (and refused higher one) no doubt reflected on Goschen's bourgeois pretension.

When Goschen withdrew from office and retreated to the House of Lords he had six and a quarter years to live. They might have been a sad evening. He was naturally uxurious and his wife had died in 1898. And on a variety of grounds he felt his ambitions only about three-quarters fulfilled and the recognition of his services a little less than it ought to have been. Loneliness with a touch of sourness could have been his final lot. But this was not so. He had a wide range of interests and friends – many of them literary. And he found three themes of activity, none wholly foreseeable, which illuminated his old age. First he published a filial but attractive and successful life of his grandfather, the Leipzig publisher. He had been working sporadically at it for a decade or more, but retirement concentrated his mind and it came out, in the two volumes which were biographically *de rigueur* at the time, in early 1903.

Later in the same year he began a brief (three and-a-quarter year) Chancellorship of Oxford. Although he might be accounted lucky to have slipped in between a predecessor as illustrious as Salisbury (who himself had thirty-five years earlier followed Derby, elected in the wake of Wellington) and a successor as unforgettable as Curzon, he was elected unopposed. Rosebery had nibbled at a contest, but always liking the palm without the dust had withdrawn when support seemed weak, and waited to be beaten by Curzon in 1907. Goschen enjoyed Oxford, and took it seriously, as he did everything in his life, although he visited it for little more than the annual Encaenia. He recoiled with dismay at the suggestion that he might pay another adjacent visit and open a college building. Apart from the Encaenia itself the Vice-Chancellor, he insisted, must in that week be given full and unchallenged sway. In his long inaugural list of honorands Goschen included Asquith, Marconi (of wireless telegraph fame), the Speaker (Gully) of the House of Commons and John Singer Sargent. Harcourt, surprisingly, declined.

The third theme was more political and also marked Goschen's first tack to the left (or at least the centre) for thirty or more years past. He remained a firm Free Trader, which conviction indeed fitted in perfectly with all his other attitudes. He had never liked Joseph Chamberlain, thrown together though they had been by the defence of the Union. So when Chamberlain, in that same year of 1903, raised the banner of Protectionism and Imperial Preference, Goschen was moved by brain and emotion alike to oppose him as strongly as he could. He disliked the crudity, the demogogy and the intellectually slipshod nature of the Tariff Reform case. Moreover Chamberlain had impertinently captured the Liberal Unionist machine for his heresy. In association once again with the Duke of Devonshire (and with Hicks Beach, C. T. Ritchie and Lord James of Hereford) Goschen felt the scent of battle in his nostrils and rallied to fight his last campaign, delivering mighty rebukes to what he regarded as Chamberlain's cheap-jackery. A successful defensive battle was fought for Free Trade, but it presented Goschen with something of a dilemma, for this successful campaign was a powerful contributory factor to the Liberal landslide of 1906. Goschen wanted to defeat Chamberlain, but he did not want to elect Campbell-Bannerman as Prime Minister. However, there was something elegiacally satisfactory about his last campaign bringing him back into respectful relations with those such as Asquith, who was the leading hammer of Chamberlain's fallacies, from whom he had been for so long estranged.

Goschen was lucky in the manner of his death, singularly like that of his old *vis-à-vis* William Harcourt. He was active up to his last days and then died suddenly and quietly in his sleep. John Morley, in an odd judgement, although he spoke with expertise on the subject, thought he was one of 'the cleverest men' he had ever known. Goschen thought of himself as essentially a moderate man, although others may think his moderation had a built-in right-hand bias. 'The Duke of Devonshire', he once said, 'is like myself, a moderate man, a *violently* moderate man.' Professor Skinner was probably nearest to the truth in thinking that, while Goschen embodied nearly all nineteenth-century bourgeois virtues, his fatal flaw was a lack of sympathy with those who had failed to climb up the ladder as successfully as he had done himself. He instinctively blamed the casualties of society rather than society itself. As a result he was virtuous but limited, a very able man but an only moderately (and not even a violently moderately) attractive one.

Sir Michael Hicks Beach

AMONG THE CHANCELLORS BETWEEN GLADSTONE AND 1914 there are only two whose names have lost almost all historical resonance. Goschen and Austen Chamberlain may be a little marginal but no one can doubt the place in history of Randolph Churchill, William Harcourt, Asquith or Lloyd George. This is not so with Michael Hicks Beach (1885–6 and 1895–1902) or C. T. Ritchie (1902–3). In the latter case this is not surprising as Ritchie was Chancellor only for fourteen months, introduced only one budget and was of a quiet disposition, a poor speaker and more a technocrat than a politician.

The fading of Hicks Beach is more surprising, for he and Lloyd George have been the only Chancellors since Gladstone (who did eight in a row) to introduce a continuous series of seven annual budgets. (Neville Chamberlain was their nearest rival with six.) Furthermore Beach was a political Chancellor who, although not a great orator, had clear views of his own, and was always a factor in any Conservative leadership discussions. There is only one biography of him, a two-volume work with all the appearance of a faithful family tombstone produced by his youngest and unmarried daughter, Lady Victoria Hicks Beach, sixteen years after his death. In fact however it is highly readable (more readable than read, I suspect), lucid and perceptive, one of the best examples of a family biography. It portrays him as a gruff but handsome figure, dutiful and austere, intimidating to those who did not know him (and occasionally to those who did), with a high sense of public service, perhaps a little self-righteous, but with genuine modesty and kindness. He confused his identity by changing his name for the last ten years of his life, but that, being a frequent habit of British politicians of his period, is hardly a sufficient explanation of his descent into obscurity. In 1906, on his retirement from the House of Commons, he became the Viscount St Aldwyn, and then in 1915, for no very obvious reason, he was elevated to an earldom. It was a surprising 'step' for the

Asquith government to bestow upon a seventy-seven-year-old Conservative who had not held office for thirteen years. It had the effect of
giving him, for the last year of his life, a rank attained by few politicians
who had not been Prime Minister, Lord Chancellor or Viceroy.

Although Hicks Beach started from scratch in the peerage, he was
the ninth holder of the baronetcy which dated from the first years of
James I's creation of such a rank, and was well established in the triangle
of good east Gloucestershire land between Cirencester, Lechlade and
Bibury. His father, who had been briefly member of Parliament for that
part of the county, died young in 1854, and he succeeded at the age of
seventeen to 4,000 acres there, the baronetcy and, after an interval of
ten years, the constituency. He also owned an estate of 8,000 acres in
Wiltshire. Of all the other post-Gladstone Chancellors, the one whose
provenance, both geographically and socially, was most akin to that of
Hicks Beach was Stafford Cripps, the Robespierre of the 1930s but later
the essential saviour of the economic reputation of the Attlee government. They both, Beach and Cripps, came from a secure background
with many connections in the South Cotswold countryside which has
been rich from wool to corn to weekend commuters; they both found
Bristol a convenient city to represent in Parliament; and they both, from
different angles, pursued a politics of intellectual quality and austere
principle.

Beach was never a magnate. He owned no urban land or mineral
rights and enjoyed no ground rents or mining royalties. During the
agricultural depressions of the late 1880s and early 1890s he was
positively embarrassed. He had to let Williamstrip Park, the oddly
named mansion of his Gloucestershire estate, and moved into the much
more modest and inconveniently placed (for a railway) manor house of
the Wiltshire estate at Netheravon and stayed there until 1897, when it
was compulsorily purchased by the War Office as an extension of the
Salisbury Plain training area. Even then he did not return to Williamstrip but moved into the smaller Coln St Aldwyns Manor on the same
estate.

He was always a devoted and careful estate manager, never employ-
ing a full-scale agent, even when he was Chancellor. During his
ministerial years he never had much spare cash and when he returned to
Dublin in 1886 for his second Irish spell (which involved some upkeep
and entertaining expense in Chief Secretary's Lodge) he had to
be helped out by a private subvention, raised primarily by his colleague
W. H. Smith, the rich newsagent. When out of office after 1892 he

Lord Randolph Churchill in his prime
and a fine overcoat.

Lady Randolph, as hard cut as
her jewels.

Three 'swells' on a Rothschild lawn in 1890: W. H. Trafford;
Natty, 1st Lord Rothschild; and R. C.

Harcourt, 'the Great Gladiator', did not allow the force of his partisan radicalism to impair his sartorial turnout.

Malwood, 1890: the luxuriance of the gables dwarfing even Harcourt as he stands on his terrace.

'A Frontbench Fixture', Harcourt by Harry Furniss *c.* 1900. This drawing of his predecessor but fifteen as Chancellor, and the one he most admired, was bequeathed in 1962 by Hugh Dalton to the present author, his ninth successor in that office.

Goschen as British Ambassador to the Porte *c.* 1881.

Although Goschen, as First Lord of the Admiralty, was said to have 'no notion of the motion of the ocean' he makes a reasonably convincing appearance as an old sea dog with two generations of his descendants.

Michael Hicks Beach as a young landowner (*aet* 23) in 1860.

Williamstrip Park, near Cirencester, the core of his land.

At 11 Downing Street (at 65) in his last year of office.

C. T. Ritchie, then President of the Board of Trade, at Westminster, 1897.

drew a ministerial pension which in those days was available on a declaration by the applicant that his private fortune was inadequate to maintain his position in life. In 1905, having drawn the pension again since his retirement in 1902, he voluntarily renounced it.

In the year after his father's death Hicks Beach went from Eton to Christ Church and in 1858 secured a first in the new honours school of jurisprudence and modern history established by the Oxford legislation of 1854. His intellectual equipment was therefore considerable, but he was not of a scholarly or even a literary disposition. He had great powers of concentration but in later life he used them almost exclusively for his parliamentary or estate management work. He did not impatiently seek any seat which could get him into the House of Commons. He waited six years after Oxford until, in the last year of Palmerston's premiership and life, a vacancy came up in his own territory. Nonetheless he was out to be a man of government and not a silently unambitious squire of the shires.

It was not a good period for upwardly clambering Tories, and Disraeli, the epitome of such a category, enjoyed office for only four and a half years between his forty-second and his seventieth birthdays. Hicks Beach, who was a Disraeli fan and protégé, as well as being at the same time utterly unlike him (which combination well illustrated the flair of Disraeli's leadership) was lucky that the long years of Whig hegemony were on the wane by the time he entered the House of Commons and wholly over by his thirty-seventh birthday, at which early age he became Chief Secretary for Ireland, although he was not in the Cabinet until two years later. Already during the Derby/Disraeli government of 1866–8 he had experienced junior office, first at the Poor Law Board and then at the Home Office. Shortly before becoming an MP he had married the eighteen-year-old daughter of a Gloucestershire country neighbour. This first wife, Caroline Elwes, survived only eighteen months before dying in childbirth, as did her child. This tragedy had the effect for nearly a decade of turning Hicks Beach very much in upon himself and gave him a reputation for aloof melancholy. In 1874, he married again, this time a daughter of the Devon-based Earl Fortescue. Lady Lucy Hicks Beach became the mother of his four children and survived him.

While Beach was Chief Secretary the Duke of Marlborough became Lord-Lieutenant, and his younger son, Lord Randolph Churchill, installed himself in Phoenix Park as an unofficial private secretary. Their joint presence in Dublin led to Beach becoming (and to some extent remaining, in spite of being subject to abuse, betrayal and other of Randolph's amiable little habits) his best political ally. They were both relatively liberal on Ireland, although Churchill swivelled more violently.

The open-mindedness of Hicks Beach on Ireland did not however overlap into any reservations about Disraeli's jingoism on the Eastern question and his generally forward imperial policy. Beach did not sympathize with either Derby (the son of Disraeli's old chief) or Carnarvon, both of whom in early 1878 resigned against sabre-rattling. He was therefore offered and accepted promotion to fill Carnarvon's vacant place as Secretary of State for the Colonies. His two years in this senior position were not altogether happy for he was caught in crossfire between the Prime Minister, to whom as a rapidly promoted young minister he was heavily indebted, and Sir Bartle Frere, an obstreperous pro-consul in South Africa, to whom he was more sympathetic than was Disraeli. Frere's obstreperousness led on to the British disaster of Isandlwana at the hands of the Zulus in January 1879, which involved not only the death in action of the Prince Imperial, the only son of the Emperor Napoleon III, but also one of the few British colonial defeats of the nineteenth century.

Beach's first experience of a senior department – from the age of forty-one to forty-three – was therefore by no means an unqualified success. Nonetheless he had acquired a certain position in the Tory hierarchy, which in no way diminished during the next five years in opposition when the weak leadership of Stafford Northcote was constantly assailed by Randolph Churchill's Fourth party. Beach endeavoured to perform a mediatory role, both in the House and in the country, and when a truce (more with Salisbury than with Northcote) was reached in July 1884 he was persuaded to take over the chairmanship of the National Union (of Conservative Associations) as the man most acceptable to both sides.

That year of 1884 was for him one of advance on several fronts. In May he had made what was until then (and maybe ever) his best speech in the House of Commons. It was four months after the despatch of General Gordon to Khartoum and eight months before his death there. Beach attacked the half-heartedness of the Gladstone government's support for the expedition. It was one of those speeches which lead to talk the next day about a future Prime Minister having been revealed. There are, however, many more such speeches than Prime Ministers. Nonetheless in the early autumn of that same year he was nominated by his party to negotiate with Hartington, another unconsummated future

Prime Minister of many years' standing, on the Redistribution of Seats Bill, which was an essential key to the unlocking of the door to the passing of the third Reform Bill. This negotiation achieved little, partly because neither Hartington nor Beach had much grasp of the detail, and partly because it was soon subsumed in a more elevated negotiation between Salisbury and Gladstone. But Beach's initial nomination indicated that in a future Conservative Cabinet he was likely to be in the upper third.

This was reinforced when, in June 1885, he moved the successful amendment to the Finance Bill which brought a happy release to the second Gladstone government. With the electoral mechanism in a state of limbo until the Seats Bill was through, Salisbury then formed his first (and minority) administration before dissolving in the autumn. The first intention was that Beach should go back to the Colonial Office, a very considerable department in those days as was shown by Joseph Chamberlain choosing it above all others ten years later. However, by joining Randolph Churchill in vetoing the unfortunate Stafford Northcote for the Exchequer and the leadership of the House of Commons, Beach inadvertently secured these two positions for himself. He came to the Treasury, in the view of its astringent and Gladstonian diarist, Edward Hamilton, never having 'shown any aptitude for finance'. Hamilton also thought that Lady Lucy Beach showed an excessive eagerness quickly to take over 11 Downing Street. Hamilton always had an engaging initial reluctance to warm to his Chancellors, and then found the best in almost all of them. When Beach finally left the Treasury, nineteen years later, Hamilton was almost ecstatic with praise:

> I am more sorry than I can say to lose him personally. He is certainly one of the very ablest men I have ever served; and he has many excellent qualities besides, notably (1) his thoroughness combined with assiduity ... (2) his faculty of deciding – of making up his mind and making it up the right way; (3) his power of criticising – no slip, omission or mistake ever escaping him, and (4) the goodness of his judgement. I put him very high as Chancellor of the Exchequer. His measures and the way he expounded and conducted them will secure him a place not far off Pitt, Peel and Mr G.

Hamilton's one point of criticism was that Beach 'would have had more influence with his colleagues had he managed them with a little more tact – had there been more of the *suaviter in modo* mingled with the *fortiter in re*'. This chimed in with Beach's forbidding capacity to administer a snub, which led to his being given the sobriquet of 'black Michael', as well as with Goschen's enjoyable remark, 'Beach is the only man I know who habitually thinks angrily.' But all this was far in the future in 1885. He then came to the leadership of the House instinctively believing that Randolph Churchill would have done it better, which showed more modesty than judgement. His first term at the Treasury was one of the only four Chancellorships without a budget* – he merely brought in a bill giving him power to borrow an extra £4 million and thus cover the effect of his own amendment to his predecessor's proposals. In these circumstances he inevitably did not make great impact on fiscal policy.

As leader of the House his most controversial intervention and, because of its varying effect on the positions of others, his most seminal one too, was his refusal, in the Maamtrasna hangings debate of 17 July 1885, to defend the hard-line decisions of Spencer, the previous Liberal Viceroy. This had a considerable influence on driving Spencer towards Home Rule. If the Conservatives would not support difficult 'resolute government' decisions, what was the point of believing there was any alternative to letting the Irish go their own way? And it consolidated the tentative Conservative/Irish Nationalist alliance which persisted over the November general election. Yet Beach's position, unlike that of several of his colleagues, was far from being cynically opportunistic. He was naturally sympathetic to Irish aspirations and instinctively antipathetic to both Ulster sectarian populism and the 'hard rent' Southern landlord approach. Had the cards fallen otherwise he could easily have become a supporter of a Dublin parliament, resolutely but uneasily though this is denied by his daughter and official biographer. Yet, such are the dictates of party politics, he found himself devoting the spring of 1886 to organizing the defeat of Gladstone's first Home Rule Bill. The most devastating blows were struck by Hartington and Chamberlain, but Beach, once Salisbury had recoiled from conciliation at the turn of the year 1885/6, organized the broad Conservative base on to which these former Liberals could put the icing.

The defeat led to the second general election within eight months, and the coming to power, with a large majority when the support of the Liberal Unionists was secure, as it was on anything to do with Ireland,

---

* Two of the others were Lord Randolph Churchill and Iain Macleod, but Beach unlike them had the opportunity to come back to the Treasury and produce a whole litter of budgets. So did Neville Chamberlain, the fourth of the quartet.

of the second Salisbury government. Beach's position in this government was less central than it had been in the first. The Chancellorship and the leadership of the House were again combined, but in the hands of Churchill and not of Beach, who reverted to the post of Chief Secretary for Ireland, which he had first occupied twelve years before. The exact motivation for these arrangements is obscure. Beach recognized that Churchill, to whom he was well disposed at the time, even though he was to be grossly abused by him six weeks later, had a fame and popular support which overwhelmingly entitled him to the second place in the government. But Salisbury in a letter written at the time (not to Beach) indicated that the prior consideration was to use Beach's experience and authority in the Irish Office, which had become the most demanding of Cabinet posts, and that Churchill's ill-fated appointment only followed from this.

In fact the Beach arrangement did not work out much better than did that of Churchill, although it ended less flamboyantly. Beach was too disposed to special Irish ameliorative measures to suit the new hard-line mood of Salisbury and his other principal colleagues. He was soon in dispute with them on railway nationalization and on landlords' rights. Beach felt isolated both ideologically and geographically (having to be in Dublin for at least half the year), and this sense of loneliness, despite their up-and-down relationship, was increased when Randolph Churchill flounced out of the government at Christmas. Then Beach became afflicted with a devastating eye infection, which at times completely incapacitated his sight. He withdrew from the Irish Office in March 1887. Arthur Balfour was appointed in his place and approached the task of imposing 'twenty years of resolute government' on Ireland with a new conviction and enthusiasm. Beach remained in the Cabinet as Minister without Portfolio for a short time, but then withdrew entirely. In February 1888, however, his eyesight having substantially recovered, he came back as President of the Board of Trade, and served out the remaining four and a half years of that long parliament without much trouble or excitement.

This and the three-year Liberal interlude which followed took Beach to his fifty-eighth year, by which time it might have been expected that, with his ocular infirmity and his uncompulsive attitude to politics and promotion, his thoughts would have been turning towards a combination of the House of Lords and spending more time with his broad Wiltshire and Gloucestershire acres. Instead he began the long Chancellorship on which his quiet reputation (and certainly his earldom) essentially depends. Just as in 1886 he had deferred to Randolph Churchill, so in 1895 Goschen deferred to him.

It is remarkable how unmagnetic a pull the Exchequer exercised upon Conservative politicians at this period. Hicks Beach was eager to see the claims of another in 1886, Goschen did not want it in 1895, and Austen Chamberlain, the incumbent in 1903–5 and 1919–21, disliked it almost equally in both periods. Liberals, on the other hand, seemed to enjoy the office. Certainly Gladstone did, and he was joined, to some considerable extent, by Harcourt, Asquith and Lloyd George.

The Hicks Beach Chancellorship was sharply divided into two periods, the easy years of his first four budgets, all of which coincided with a long upward roll of the trade cycle, for which the Unionist government showed almost as little disposition to claim credit as the opposition did to deny its existence. Harcourt indeed got very close to mocking the Chancellor for living in this soft climate and avoiding the testing moral rigour of an economic downswing: to such an extent was the state of trade regarded by both sides as an act of God rather than a triumph or a disastrous consequence of government policy.

These easy years produced a consistent buoyancy of revenue which made Beach a very bad Chancellor if the test be ability accurately to predict the fiscal outcome, and a very good one if it be that of financial ease with more than adequate resources with which to finance commitments and still pay off debt or reduce taxation. Expenditure was also rising fairly rapidly, so that whereas Beach had inherited commitments of £98 million from Harcourt, he allowed them to rise to £118 million in his last peacetime, that is pre-South African War, year. This was led, although by no means exclusively caused, by Goschen's extravagant big-navy policy at the Admiralty. Even with these mounting commitments, however, Beach was able to redeem debt at an average rate of about £7.5 million a year (as against an outstanding total of about £650 million) together with mild taxation reductions. Beach's budgets during the period were cautious and unexciting. They were however simple and clear. Sir Bernard Mallet, the monumental chronicler of *British Budgets* (who in three volumes covered those from 1887 to 1933) wrote that his 1896 speech was 'as on subsequent occasions singularly excellent in form'. Despite the bewildering logic of this phrase Mallet gave his praise substance by citing some of the long-term comparisons with which Beach embellished his 'steady as she goes' budget. In the previous twenty years the population had increased by 19 per cent but expenditure by 68 per cent, mainly on account of the army and the navy. However Beach argued that the direct taxpayer (that is the prosperous group in the community) had met the bulk of the additional burden, for in the half-century and a little more since the beginning of the Peel government direct taxation had risen from 27 per cent to 48 per cent of the total, and (necessarily) indirect taxation had fallen from 73 per cent to 52.

Two years later Beach also produced some interesting but heavily contrived figures designed to show that, although British defence expenditure was crudely higher than that of rival powers, it was not disproportionate in relation to either the population or the acreage of the British Empire (which of course covered about half the globe at the time): 'For every thousand square miles of Empire we spend in defence £5,664, France spends £9,523, Germany £28,654 and Russia £4,454. For every thousand inhabitants of the Empire we spend £174, France £399, Germany £560 and Russia £298.'

There was a certain engaging naivety about these arguments which fitted in with a comment on one of his later budgets that 'it might have been prepared by a schoolboy'. But, it might be added, only by a singularly straightforward and clear-headed one. He was neither an iron nor an imaginative Chancellor, but he steered the national finances round the £100 million expenditure barrier reef and into a smooth expanse of open water beyond with skilful acceptability. This was partly, to quote Mallet again, because of 'his adherence to the conception of his great office which treats finance as finance and not as an instrument of policy'. This was intended as a compliment, although several of the most notable future Chancellors – Lloyd George, Churchill, Neville Chamberlain, Stafford Cripps – would not have regarded it as such.

The pattern of his Chancellorship was perhaps most like that of R. A. Butler, who however certainly did not have the mind of a straightforward schoolboy. They both successfully rode four years of upswing and then came unstuck at the beginning of their fifth year. Butler's trouble was an electioneering budget in 1955. That was not Beach's weakness. The 'khaki election' of late 1900 had hardly begun to loom when he ran into his 1899 budget turbulance, and in any event electioneering was not his style. But in a year of strong economic upswing, and as it turned out on the eve of the South African War, he made the mistake of reducing the sinking fund for the first time since Goschen had done so ten years before. Not only Harcourt, reinvigorated by this monstrosity, but most of the other financial pundits came down on him like a ton of bricks. 'The Chancellor of the Exchequer up to this time has had a pretty easy life,' Harcourt, the great but ageing gladiator, thundered. 'He was the heir of a highly solvent estate. He has reduced it to a declaration of partial insolvency.' Beach also made the mistake of defending his policy of not redeeming too much debt by pointing out that Consols stood substantially above par. It was therefore impolitic to redeem them at such a high rate, with such redemption carrying the threat of driving them still higher. Unfortunately Consols then proceeded disloyally to plunge, leaving the argument looking threadbare. Beach's sins in the 1899 budget were not by any standards very heinous. Probably a major part of his trouble was that, unless they are peculiarly commanding and exciting figures, which Beach was not, the public become bored with a Chancellor, or the occupant of any other office, after a maximum of about four years.

In any event, Beach approached the next three years of unprecedently accelerating expenditure with a somewhat diminished authority. The £118 million of 1897–8 went to £144 million in 1898–9, £193 million in 1899–1900 and £205 million in 1900–1 (and never again on its route to the present expenditure total of *c.* £300,000 million did it fall below £150 million, except marginally and briefly in the financial year 1905–6). Beach adjusted to the burden competently rather than heroically. He left approximately three-quarters of the additional expenditure to be covered by loan rather than by taxation. He increased income tax in three instalments from eightpence in the pound to 1s 3d. He stiffened the duties on spirits and beer, as well as those on tobacco and tea. He reverted to two old taxes, one on the imports of sugar, which raised the substantial sum of £6.5 million, and the other on *exports* of coal, which had last previously been tried, and for three years only, as long ago as the 1840s government of Sir Robert Peel and which brought in the more modest sum of £2 million. It did however give more than its money's worth in the amount of theoretical fiscal controversy which it aroused.

In this respect it was almost matched by his revival in 1902 of the shilling 'registration' duty on corn and flour imports which had been got rid of by Chancellor Robert Lowe in the first Gladstone government, and the eventual fallout from this change was ever greater. It produced £2 million in revenue, which was neither massive nor negligible. Beach's claim was that the duty was too small to be protective, and he must at least have convinced himself of this, for as was soon to be demonstrated he was a resolute Free Trader, and certainly had no intention of being the Chancellor who undid Peel's 1846 achievement. However even the registration duty was provocative, and was seen as such by Beach's successor, the still more rigidly Free Trade C. T. Ritchie, who proceeded to repeal it in his first and only budget, and by so doing acted as a catalyst to Joseph Chamberlain's departure from the Balfour Cabinet and the debilitating split which led the Unionist party towards and over the precipice to its 1906 massacre.

The strong impression given was that, in his last three budgets, those of 1900, 1901 and 1902, over which these various tax increases were spread, Beach was desperately scraping the barrel to increase or revive conventional sources of revenue. As a result he followed Goschen away from the steady fiscal policy since Peel and Gladstone of concentrating indirect taxes on as few items as possible. He was much criticized for this, as also (the reverse side of the same coin) for not being willing to increase existing taxes sufficiently drastically to make a major contribution to paying for the war out of current revenue. 'We have a government which dare not tax the poor and will not tax the rich' was one taunt which was made against Beach as a war Chancellor. In the debate on his sixth (1901) budget, it was pointed out that of the then £170 million cost of the war only £27 million had been raised by additional taxes. The rest was left for the future to bear.

It follows that Hicks Beach was a great borrowing Chancellor, and at this he was very successful. His two principal loans, one of £30 million in 1900 and the other of £32 million in 1902, were both about ten times oversubscribed. These successes opened him to some criticism for having offered the loans on too favourable terms, but this criticism could be countered by the argument that the much more dangerous risk was that of a failure. What is striking about the budget debates during Beach's long reign at the Treasury is that while the leading participants from both sides of the House were happy to argue, mostly with wisdom and good temper, rather abstract questions of the balance between direct and indirect taxation, as well as that between the relative taxable capacities of Great Britain and of Ireland, and the desirability of debt repayment as opposed to tax remissions in easy times and borrowing as against tax increases in difficult times, they all did so from a basis of great confidence in Britain's underlying financial strength. National self-congratulation was the dominant note. First it was the buoyancy of the revenue. The Chancellor even spoke on one occasion of the national achievement that 'at the present moment we raise so magnificent a revenue with so little effort to the country'. Then, when in war the magnificence of the revenue did not prove adequate to dealing with the Boers, it was the strength of the country's credit as exemplified by the success of the two loans which became the object of admiration.

This complacent background might be thought to have made the Chancellorship a comfortable bed on which to recline, but it did not exclude critical comparative judgements, which in Beach's case probably settled around a generality of view that he was neither very good nor very bad, but decent and reliable, although after a quiverful of budgets had been there long enough. This last view he had certainly come to hold himself, and when Salisbury resigned in July 1902 he quickly took the opportunity to go with him.

He was nearly sixty-five. He had no reason to feel a sense of frustrated ambition. Of the thirty-seven Chancellors from Gladstone to Gordon Brown he was in the minority of twelve who never had the premiership seriously within their sights. (Of the other twenty-five, eight actually made it.) He stayed in the House of Commons until the 1905 dissolution. He had removed himself in 1885, presumably fearing the effect of agricultural labourer enfranchisement, from his local East Gloucestershire to become the first member for the new division of Bristol West, that urbane Cliftonian constituency which afterwards sustained a succession of moderate Conservative front benchers from Oliver Stanley through Walter Monckton until it failed William Waldegrave in the Labour landslide of 1997.

In 1903–5 Beach was a firm opponent of Joseph Chamberlain's Tariff Reform campaigns, and in 1909–11, translated to the Lords, he was equally firmly moderate in all the stages of the constitutional crisis which followed Lloyd George's 'people's budget'. He was against the rejection by the Lords of the 1909 Finance Bill, and he was most emphatically a 'hedger' and not a 'ditcher' on the Parliament Bill. On both occasions he not only refused to give his vote to the extreme cause (even though on the first occasion it was embraced by his party leaders), but also spoke with force and authority against rejecting the budget and in favour of accepting the Parliament Bill. He was a natural moderate but also a natural Conservative. He spoke his mind freely, even fiercely, and backed it with his vote, or at least his abstention, but it would not have occurred to him to operate within any other party framework. His grandson, who succeeded him direct in 1916 and at the age of four, was appropriately a much respected Conservative Chief Whip in the House of Lords from 1958 to 1978.

This generation-jumping succession was a result of a series of blows which struck St Aldwyn at the very end of his life. Until the beginning of 1916 he had accomplished one of the most difficult feats for a successful politician (or perhaps for anyone else of achievement), which is to manage a semi-retirement so that it gives at least as much satisfaction as, and maybe more happiness than, the battles to which it is a postscript. It is something which in the past sixty years has been notably achieved by Attlee and Macmillan, but which has eluded Baldwin, Churchill and one or two living former Prime Ministers. Hicks Beach for nearly fourteen years after he left office for the last time was firmly in the former category. His reputation, never very low, went gradually up. He found plenty to do. He became a director and later the chairman of several banks and insurance companies. This made him substantially richer than he had ever been before. He never moved back into Williamstrip Park, but he was able to live at ease in the Coln St Aldwyn manor house, to acquire a decent London house and to hand on the Cotswold estate in a reasonably unencumbered shape. He was a surprising and notably successful chairman of the South Wales Coal Conciliation Board, as intractable a task as it is easy to imagine. The fact that he held it from 1903 to 1915, and that whenever he tried to resign both sides were reluctant to let him go, was a high tribute. He presided over a 1904–6 Royal Commission on Ecclesiastical Discipline and achieved a unanimous report. He was an alderman of the Gloucestershire County Council and became President of the County Councils Association. In 1907 the Dean of Christ Church wished to nominate him for the Oxford Chancellorship, but he somewhat wistfully declined on the ground that Curzon had more 'literary and academic qualifications' than he did. He spent a regrettable amount of time on grandiloquent Freemanonsry offices.

At the outbreak of the 1914 war he became the spokesman of the London clearing bankers and made a notable and hard-working contribution to the calming of the financial panic which threatened the stability of the City of London during that August. It was for this, superimposed on his cumulative record of public service, that Asquith recommended him for his 1915 earldom. Throughout all these thirteen years his health, including his eyesight, was almost unbelievably good in view of the crippling troubles of 1887. He was a trim and vigorous walker and at the age of seventy could still jump a hurdle in a field. His family life was close and apparently easy. He was on good terms with his three daughters, the two married ones as well as the later chronicler of his life. As he left the House of Commons after forty years of membership over the turn of the year 1905/6 he had the satisfaction of seeing his son elected at the age of thirty for his home constituency, the only successful Conservative candidate in Gloucestershire.

In 1913 St Aldwyn's life could hardly have been more externally satisfactory for a man of seventy-six and mildly melancholic temperament. He was esteemed and sought after for more jobs than he could do. His estates had been made over to a trusted son, who was a good quiet MP, broadly of his father's views, who had been married in 1909 to the daughter of another Gloucestershire landowner. Even in 1915, with the war not going well and with Lord Quenington, as that son had become with the earldom, in the Dardanelles, there were compensations. Lady Quenington, leaning just enough on her father-in-law's advice, was learning to manage the estate well. Then, in early 1916, fate turned and there were the most appalling blows. Quenington was in Cairo, having been safely evacuated from Gallipoli. The loose travel discipline of the First World War (although perhaps Lady Ranfurly's diaries indicate that it was not always much tighter in the Second World War) made it possible for his wife to join him. She left Coln just before Christmas (1915) never having been abroad before. In late February in Egypt she contracted typhoid. On 4 March she was dead. In early April St Aldwyn, who had been failing for a few months, took to his bed and passed slowly into an aloof detachment. On 23 April Quenington was killed in an isolated skirmish. Lucy St Aldwyn did not dare to tell her husband. On 30 April he, in turn, died. It was a sad end to a life of conspicuous public service.

C. T. RITCHIE

RITCHIE WAS NOT ONLY A SHORT-LIVED Chancellor – one budget and fourteen months – but also a tentative one, who gave the impression of having called in at the Treasury rather than firmly established himself there. And there was something of this in his whole attitude to politics, even though he was an MP over a span of thirty-two years (with a break of three) and a minister for seventeen of them. In offices prior to the Exchequer his quiet legislative achievements were almost without parallel. Ritchie was always more interested in specific causes than in the 'great game'. He was a poor speaker outside Parliament, little known to the public and not very well to his colleagues either. To find a Chancellor of equal anonymity one would have to go back sixty years to Henry Goulburn in Peel's second government or forward fifty-five to Derrick Heathcote Amory.

Charles Thomson Ritchie was born in 1838 at Broughty Ferry on the edge of Dundee, one of the several younger sons of a well-established jute merchant and manufacturer. His upbringing was commercial but largely metropolitan. His main education was four years at the City of London School, which however he left, to go into the family firm's London office, just before the age of fifteen. This office, unlike his school, was not in the City but in the near East End which gave him an acquaintance and sympathy with poor London which was hardly to be matched by a major politician until Attlee, for different reasons, identified himself with Limehouse. Despite this early switch from Dundee to London, Ritchie retained enough Scottish connection to marry a maid of Perth (fair, one hopes) and to do so before he was twenty. Altogether, although his family was prosperous, his early life was about as dissimilar from that of a traditional nineteenth-century politician as it is easy to imagine.

Moreover he remained almost totally immersed in the Ritchie family business until 1874, when he was thirty-six. Then he came forward, very much as an indigenous candidate, for the large undivided borough of Tower Hamlets. His local commitment together with the Tory upsurge of that year meant that he displaced one Liberal in what had hitherto been a safe seat for them and beat the other into second place (in a two-member borough). What is unclear is why he chose to be a Conservative, which did not flow at all naturally from either his Dundee jute provenance or his East End social concern. Presumably he took seriously Disraeli's *sanitas sanitatem omnia sanitas* appeal and the work in this field which was subsequently accomplished by R. A. Cross at the Home Office and Sclater-Booth at the Local Government Board. Throughout the principal Disraeli government Ritchie remained a back bencher. He devoted his parliamentary work to two issues both of which had constituency resonance. In 1875 he successfully promoted a bill which extended the Bank Holiday Act of 1871 to dockyard and customs house employees. Then he waged a campaign against the bounties paid by Continental European governments to sugar-beet producers with the result of subsidized exports and allegedly unfair competition to both the sugar refiners of the East End and the cane-sugar growers of the West Indies.

Ritchie wanted countervailing import duties imposed by Britain. By 1879 he at least got the appointment of a Select Committee on the problem with himself as chairman. The issue spilled over into the next parliament when by what became a supreme irony his demand for countervailing duties was rejected by Joseph Chamberlain, the new Liberal President of the Board of Trade, on the ground of his attachment to the principle of free imports. Twenty-two years later they clashed to the extent of both resigning from the Balfour government from directly opposite positions. Chamberlain, in a 1903 speech, had the memory to recall that 1880 encounter and the command of both French and wit to call what had happened a *chassé-croisé*.

Ritchie's choice of issues at least helped him to survive the strong Gladstonian surge of 1880 (although relegated to second place) and in 1885 to be elected for the single-member division of St George's-in-the-East when Tower Hamlets was split. In 1892, however, despite the Liberal performance in the country as a whole being much weaker than it had been in either 1880 or 1885, he succumbed, and, after missing nearly the whole of that last Gladstonian parliament, came back, appropriately for a minister under Salisbury, the founder of 'villa Conservatism', as member for Croydon.

He was a member of all the Salisbury governments. In the first and short-lived one he was Financial Secretary to the Admiralty under Lord George Hamilton, who seventeen years subsequently resigned with him (it is a good mark when a minister is able to carry with him those who served under him, perhaps an even better one when he is able to carry those who served *over* him), and even in such a brief tenure of such a junior office managed with patient skill to untie one stubborn and important knot. He presided over a committee which speeded up the rate of construction of battleships by about three times.

On the basis of this success Ritchie was given a substantial promotion a year later when Salisbury formed his second government. He became President of the Local Government Board. But this was only when Henry Chaplin, the Lincolnshire 'swell', had refused the post because it was not in the Cabinet. This distinction was also denied Ritchie until nearly a year later when, on the eve of his introducing what was certainly the most intricate and probably the most important item in that government's legislative programme, he was belatedly admitted. It is difficult not to feel that there was always something a little grudging about Ritchie's numerous promotions. Partly because he was a very reclusive social figure, he was treated rather as the highly competent professional who had to roll the pitch as well as make the runs. But he made a lot of runs with that County Councils Act of 1888. It was a measure of 162 clauses and five schedules which completely and semi-permanently changed the basis of local government in the counties of England and Wales and in London. In the latter respect it succeeded where Harcourt under Gladstone had dismally failed in the previous administration. And these two Liberal statesmen paid generous tribute to his four-month conduct of the bill. Gladstone described his introductory speech as 'a very frank, a very lucid and a very able statement ', and Harcourt at the end of the marathon spoke of 'the ability, the conciliatory temper, and the strong commonsense' of the bill's promoter. It is tempting to comment that if Harcourt had displayed half the 'conciliatory temper' of Ritchie he might have pre-empted such local government reform in 1884 as well as becoming Prime Minister ten years later. But they were by no means a bad couple of testimonials for a new, if by no means particularly young (he was fifty), departmental minister to tuck under his belt. While he did not achieve another bill of quite the same impact he continued for the remaining four years of that government with such desirable and sensible, if hardly blood-tingling, measures as the Notification of Infectious Diseases Act of 1883 and the Allotments Act of 1890.

In some ways it suited him well to be out of the parliament of the short Gladstone/Rosebery governments, for he was not a natural man of opposition. This being so, he was lucky to spend twenty-three and a half out of his twenty-nine years in the House on the government side. When Salisbury formed his third government in June 1895, Ritchie was kept firmly in the lower and more workaday half of the Cabinet, but received the small promotion of becoming President of the Board of Trade and moving up one or two places in the pecking order.

At the Board of Trade Ritchie was just as fecund a minister as he had been at the local Government Board, and if anything even more consensual and therefore permanent in his legislative imprint. Several of his measures sprang out of Royal Commissions or committees of cross-party enquiry, some of them set up by his Liberal predecessor, James Bryce. The Conciliation Act of 1896 established boards for the settlement of industrial disputes. By 1900 (when he left the Board of Trade) 113 disputes had been dealt with and 70 resolved under the Act. In 1898 he personally settled an eight-month-old engineering strike. Also, and as a result of the committee's recommendations, he established a new intelligence branch of the Board of Trade, bringing together commercial, labour and statistical information; legislated to improve the position of boy entrants to the merchant navy, where the decline in the number of British seamen was already causing concern, and did so sufficiently effectively to put the number of entrants up seven-fold within five years; promoted a Railway Safety Act in 1900, as well as a Companies Act of medium-grade importance in the same year.

When he was advanced to the Home Office at the turn of the century, it must have been a relief to the legislative branch of the Board of Trade. He remained for only twenty months as Home Secretary, but did a vast (although largely consolidating) Factory and Workshop Act, as well as a Youthful Offenders Act which, being designed to avoid custodial treatment, would not have commended itself to Mr Michael Howard.

In early June 1902, the South African War had come to an end, and a month later Salisbury resigned, suddenly but not unexpectedly. Hicks Beach insisted on going with him. Balfour, the new Prime Minister, would have preferred Beach to stay, not because they had got on particularly well in the Salisbury Cabinets, but because he and the country were at least well used to him at the Treasury, and it was by no means obvious who he should put in his place. What he ought to have done was to press Joseph Chamberlain, who was reluctant to move, but might not in the last resort have held out, to accept the office. Chamberlain *not* becoming Chancellor was a persistent recipe for the failure of governments. If Gladstone had offered the slot to him in January 1886 he might have got the Home Rule Bill through the Commons if not the Lords. If Balfour had insisted on the move in July 1902 the Free Trade/Tariff Reform split would have taken a different form and might not have had such a stultifying and then destructive effect upon this the last Conservative government for seventeen years.

Not only did Balfour not insist, however, but he then proceeded in the only major Cabinet-making decision which faced him at the beginning of his premiership to make it in a way which was as uncongenial to himself as it was to prove disruptive to his government. Balfour and Ritchie were not remotely made for each other. Neither intellectually or socially did their worlds touch. As at least a tolerable working relationship between Prime Minister and Chancellor is highly desirable for the cohesion of a government, it was asking for trouble to appoint Ritchie. Why did Balfour do it? Ritchie's beavering legislative activity had certainly proved that he was a 'hard-working minister of pedestrian methods', as Balfour's influential secretary patronizingly put it.* He may be thought to have earned preferment, but as he had been given the big step to Home Secretary less than two years before, he could hardly have been a clamant claimant. And there is indeed some evidence that he was reluctant to take his head out of his Home Office blue books. But there is also a suggestion inspired by the Balfour entourage that he was 'as usual' pushing his own claims hard.

Whatever the truth between these two versions, Balfour did not know where else to go and thought of Ritchie as an effective if unprepossessing man of business who must therefore understand the dark mysteries of economics and finance, about which his own ignorance was profound. He moved him across and a little up. Ritchie by this time had become a dedicated Free Trader, which given the way majority opinion in the Cabinet was moving, and given too that Hicks Beach's shilling 'registration' duty on corn imports provided the perfect trip-wire for a row, ought to have made Balfour very cautious about

---

* Gladstone's ex-secretary, Edward Hamilton, who had just become joint permanent secretary to the Treasury, was even more explicitly (and snobbishly) dismissive. 'I trust', he presumptuously wrote to Balfour, 'we may be spared from having to serve a man like Hanbury [then President of the Board of Agriculture, former Financial Secretary to the Treasury] or even Ritchie. The two essential qualifications for the post are common sense and to be a gentleman.'

appointing him. But he allowed his caution only to express itself in engineering a Cabinet December fudge. This permitted Chamberlain to depart for his three months in South Africa believing that a majority decision in favour of the retention of the duty had been taken, together with a disposition to use it as the foundation for colonial preference. Ritchie had reserved his position, arguing that no budgetary decision could be taken so far in advance, and that the Chancellor must retain his prerogative of making his own proposals when he could see the whole up-to-date picture.

Nevertheless it was widely assumed that he would not act provoca-tively against the opinion of most of his colleagues. Nothing could have been more mistaken. As the budget approached he made it clear to the Prime Minister that he was determined to get rid of the shilling duty and would resign if frustrated. Balfour thought that Ritchie had behaved badly and was obviously tempted to let him go. But on reflection he did not feel that the government could afford to lose a second Chancellor within a year. Ritchie then compounded his sin by announcing the change in the most unconciliatory way. The South African War was ten months over, but with expenditure still running at £152 million (although this was £40 million less than two years before) and debt standing at £770 million, the remissions of war-imposed taxation which he felt able to propose were very limited. He would take fourpence off the income tax, bringing it back to elevenpence as opposed to the eightpence at which it had started the war, and he would abolish the corn duty, which his predecessor had introduced only the previous year. All the other war levies, tea, spirits, beer, tobacco, sugar, coal export duty, would have to wait longer for relief – if it ever came.

He also injected as much as he could of both principle and implacability into his announcement of the change:

> Corn is a necessity of life to a greater degree than any other article. It is a raw material, it is the food of our people, the food of our horses and cattle ... I do not think it can remain permanently an integral portion of our fiscal system ... It was the last tax imposed by my Right Honourable friend the late Chancellor of the Exchequer and I know it was imposed with reluctance, and only under pressing neces-sity. In my opinion, being as it is a tax on a prime necessity of life, it has the first claim to be associated with the large remission of the income tax of which I have spoken. I therefore propose to remit the corn duty.

The determination to take the issue head on, and the unwillingness to clothe it in obfuscating language, is curiously reminiscent of the budget forty-eight years later in which Ritchie's successor but fifteen, Hugh Gaitskell, was determined to impose charges on teeth and spectacles and was as indifferent to their effect on Aneurin Bevan as Ritchie was to the effect of his words on Joseph Chamberlain. It was curious not least because Ritchie and Gaitskell were utterly different persons. There was also another important difference in that Gaitskell had the support (maybe a little reluctant) of his Prime Minister and the majority of his colleagues, which Ritchie most emphatically did not. Once he had made his flatly courageous budget statement his days as Chancellor were numbered. In the meantime, however, Balfour had to put up some sort of defence of his Chancellor and did so in terms which were more interesting than persuasive:

> As a matter of fact, we know that under the British Constitution party succeeds party and, as a permanency, this tax could not last. I admit that this is no proof why we should take it off, but if I am right in saying that it would be impossible for our opponents to come in and retain the tax, it is quite clear that there was no hope that Chancellors of the Exchequer of both parties would permanently benefit by the tax, and that these hopes were doomed to disappointment. As soon as it was clear that the tax was to be a bone of contention or a tax which was not objected to simply as a tax, but was a matter of contention between great opposed political forces – it also became clear that it could not be a permanent part of our fiscal system, as the income tax or the tea duty is.

There, lurking behind the surprisingly loose syntax of this presumably impromptu passage, lay a most remarkable if slightly weary doctrine of consensual politics, the power of the opposition, and of the supremacy of the continuing interests of the state over the temporary power of one party. There did not, however, lie an enthusiastic endorsement of his Chancellor. That came more from Hicks Beach, the man whose tax was being dumped after a brief year of life, but whose Free Trade spirit was sufficiently strong that, seeing which way the armies were forming up for a new and more vicious phase of that ancient war, resolutely approved of what the Chancellor had done, while complaining that the real trouble was too high a level of continuing public expenditure, for which, he delicately implied, the Prime Minister, by his lack of support in Cabinet for him and his successor, bore a heavy share of the responsibility.

That year's Finance Bill became law on 30 June, by which time Joseph Chamberlain, having formally and publicly raised the Imperial Preference standard in the Birmingham Town Hall on 15 May, was more of an independent commander than part of the government force. Balfour moved into a typically convoluted defensive tactic. To shift the metaphor from the martial to the aeronautical level, he tried to keep the plane in balance and aloft by shedding parts of both wings. Thus in September Chamberlain (whose weight was much the greatest) resigned from the Protectionist side, and, without knowing this, Ritchie, Lord George Hamilton and Lord Balfour of Burleigh all went from the Free Trade side. Eventually the Duke of Devonshire (ex-Hartington) also went from that latter side, which was not in accordance with plan and upset the balance anew.

Of all those resignations Ritchie's was undoubtedly the one over which the Prime Minister shed the fewest tears. He regretted having promoted him to the Treasury, and he was glad to be rid of him. He appointed Austen Chamberlain in his place and as his father's vicar in the Cabinet. Furthermore it was noticeable that when Ritchie, who like Hicks Beach did not stand again at the 1906 general election and was made a peer in Balfour's resignation honours list, it was a humble barony with which he was rewarded, the only ex-Chancellor for the hundred years or so before life peerages disturbed the traditional hierarchy not to be given a higher rank in the peerage.

His resignation effectively brought Ritchie's career to an end. He was sixty-five and there was no question of the Prime Minister, or any other likely one, again offering him office. He stayed in the House of Commons for only another two and a quarter years. He played an active but not a dominant part in the Unionist Free Food League, which embraced fifty-four members of Parliament. As however it contained all of the previous and more famous Chancellors of both the Salisbury and Balfour governments, except for Randolph Churchill who was dead, and several others who were much better speakers, his was a quiet role. But he had displayed more stubborn and self-sacrificial courage for the cause than had any of the others. And he had his solidly impressive legislative record in other departments behind him. He had barely three months in which to enjoy (or perhaps to resent) his barony. He died in Biarritz, an unlikely terminus for him, on 9 January 1906.

AUSTEN CHAMBERLAIN

BEATRICE WEBB WROTE THAT AUSTEN CHAMBERLAIN was 'dull and closed-minded ... intellectually dense'. But Mrs Webb had a considerable capacity, while seeing parts of the truth with meticulous clarity, completely to miss other parts of it, as well as being a prejudiced witness on Austen because she had been a good deal more romantically stirred by his ruthless and dominating father, Joseph Chamberlain, than by the more epicene charms of Sidney Webb. She was therefore inclined to take out her disappointment that neither she nor 'Brummagem Joe' quite had the emotional nerve to risk a marriage of competing champions (Chamberlain *père* had been between wives at the time of their encounters) in a dismissive judgement of his elder son. It was a way of getting back at the father without denying her own taste in forming the infatuation.

Austen Chamberlain was however a more complex (and more interesting) character than she allowed. He was a man of several paradoxes, the most obvious of which was that he was on the surface a carbon copy of his father but underneath a vastly different (and in many ways more attractive) personality and character. He was the nearest approach to a man-made statesman that the twentieth century has seen. His father, the man who made him, erupted out of Birmingham screw-manufacturing and municipal politics on to the national scene in the 1870s. He had what was until then an unequalled authenticity of local base. He was the first nineteenth-century politician of the front rank to sit for the same constituency throughout a long (thirty-eight-year) House of Commons career. He was very glossy in dress and grooming, but this was partly because he was damned if he was going to be inferior to the metropolitan politicians and the landed magnates in this or any other respect. As tends to be the case in these circumstances he somewhat overdid it, and failed to notice that the grandest magnates – Hartington, Derby or Salisbury – were distinctly unglossy. But at least he just followed, a little over sharply, the sartorial conventions of the age.

Austen Chamberlain, who as a young man faithfully copied the eyeglass, the orchid buttonhole, the wing collar, the stiff cuffs, the frock coat and even the hair parting of his father, then felt that he had to stick to it, and became like a beached whale of Edwardian formality in the 1920s and 1930s. He was one of the last three or four members habitually to sit in the House of Commons with his top hat on his head – and the others were not serious politicians. Typically also he assuaged any forbidding barrier which the habit built up by always raising this silken anachronism in acknowledgement of any reference to himself, friendly or hostile, in the speeches of others.

The somewhat waxwork quality which this formality of dress combined with a stiff and shy manner gave him suggested that if one had ordered a statesman from Harrods it would been a copy of Austen Chamberlain which would have arrived. And, although that emporium had a less dominant position at the upper end of the retail market than it enjoys today, there would have been a certain appropriateness about this. He mostly lived within a few hundred yards of that brown palace in the Brompton Road. Joseph Chamberlain not only represented Birmingham in Parliament but always maintained a large, hideously furnished (late Pullman-style, Margot Asquith called it) semi-country house well within the city boundaries. Austen Chamberlain also represented Birmingham (first its southern suburbs in the shape of East Worcestershire and then, following his father's death, the vacated constituency of West Birmingham), but he never had a house of his own there. He even suffered the indignity, for a Chamberlain, of fighting his last few elections from the Midland Hotel, rather than from a family base. He lived at home both in Birmingham and in London, until he married at the age of forty-two, which was a remarkably long attachment to the parental nest, and particularly for one who, by that time, had been a member of Parliament for fourteen years, a Privy Councillor for four and Chancellor of the Exchequer for two. He supplemented South Kensington with a few rented Kent or Sussex houses in the 1914–18 War and then in 1919 bought a house with the unfortunate name of Twitt's Ghyll, near Mayfield. Here he cultivated a splendid alpine garden – Austen Chamberlain was always much stronger on flowers than on country sports – until 1929 when he decided that for money reasons he had to sell it. He was also always stronger on public service than on ensuring his own prosperity.

Yet it was much more than an authenticity of Midland base which Austen Chamberlain lacked in comparison with his father. Despite the copied trappings he was not just an inferior version as would have been the likely fate of any son of such a figure of ruthless flair as Joseph Chamberlain. He was an utterly different sort of human being, but one who was condemned by a combination of paternal force and filial piety to adopt the appearance and to attempt to fulfil the role of his father. It is remarkable that he survived so well the potential psychological crippling.

Joseph Chamberlain was daring and insolent, with a unique capacity to dictate the agenda of politics. 'You can burn your pamphlets; we are going to talk about something different,' he arrogantly but not foolishly told the Liberal Chief Whip when he launched his Tariff Reform campaign in 1903. His talents were exceptional but mostly destructive, as he showed by splitting first the Liberals and then, nearly twenty years later, the Unionists. He was destructive not merely of parties but of individuals, and left a whiff of brimstone in his trail across both the Dilke and the Parnell scandals. He was not strong on loyalty to friends or political allies, although he valued his relations with heavyweight opponents and formed a degree of friendship across the clash of politics with Harcourt, Morley and to a lesser extent Asquith.

Austen Chamberlain, by contrast, was cautious and conventional. He never thought of injecting a new dimension into the political debate. He was too busy trying desperately to reconcile his father's rash ideas to a moderate position on the issues of twenty or more years later. But he was immensely his father's superior on both decency and loyalty. He was the epitome of the stiff gentleman in politics. 'He always played the game and he always lost it' is a remark as apposite and famous as its provenance is uncertain. Robert Blake attributes it to Churchill, and Beaverbrook, slightly more plausibly in my view, to Birkenhead. Birkenhead was appropriate, for Chamberlain's loyalty to him, when he had become profoundly unpopular and distrusted in the Conservative party, made a major contribution to his own game-losing capacity. Birkenhead illustrates by contrast another and surprising aspect of Chamberlain's character. An almost priggishly upright man himself, Chamberlain liked rather louche associates, not only Birkenhead himself, but also Sir Robert Horne and two or three lesser figures as well.

This was only one of the minor paradoxes about Austen Chamberlain. A more major one was that, utterly different, he always had to live under his father's shadow, and did so without overt revolt. When he made his maiden speech in 1893 against the second Home Rule Bill, Gladstone said that it was a speech that 'must have been dear and refreshing to a father's heart'. And it was reported that Joseph Chamberlain had never looked so moved in public as by this tribute from the great adversary whom he had deserted. In this interplay of the titans Austen Chamberlain might have been forgiven if he had quietly complained (perhaps only to himself) that it was *his* speech which they were at once forgetting in substance and elevating into a symbol of political generosity. And twenty-eight years later, when he made what was probably his most successful speech as leader of the House of Commons, he voluntarily re-created the same syndrome when he wrote to one of his sisters: 'Altogether I am very pleased with myself – not least because of Sir H. Warren's comment that it [the speech] resembled the flashing of Father's own rapier.'

The other great paradox, and indeed trauma, of Austen's life was that he, who was bred and trained like a racehorse to be Prime Minister, and who indeed several times had the winning post more closely within his sights, if not within his psychological capacity, than any other twentieth-century politician except for Rab Butler, was deprived only by death and ten weeks of seeing his younger half-brother, who had been trained much more to become a cart horse, or at best a carriage horse, achieve the accolade which he himself had missed. What was also typical of Austen Chamberlain was that for the last five or so years of his life, when he no longer had even the most tenuous basis for ambitious hopes, his aspirations were generously concentrated upon his brother. It was sad that Neville Chamberlain, always one for harsh realism, hardly bothered during this period to see his elder and previously more distinguished brother.

Austen Chamberlain was born in Edgbaston, the leafy end of Birmingham, on 16 October 1863. His mother, Harriet Kenrick, daughter of another well-known Birmingham Unitarian manufacturing family, died at his birth. His father, who never did anything by halves, married another Miss Kenrick five years later, who having successfully produced Neville Chamberlain and three daughters herself died at the birth of a fifth, effectively still-born, child in 1875. Joseph Chamberlain at the time of Austen's birth was at the halfway point between his arrival in Birmingham from London in order to assist his Nettlefold uncle by marriage, the bearer of another famous Midland metal-working name, in what became a successful screw-manufacturing business and his election as Mayor of Birmingham in 1872. Four years later he became an MP for the town, and in 1880 President of the Board of Trade and a member of Gladstone's second Cabinet. It was an unprecedently rapid rise for a 'new man'.

Despite his stiffness of manner Austen Chamberlain was almost the first politician habitually to be referred to by his Christian name. This was to differentiate him from his more famous father; Winston Churchill, eleven years his junior, was for the same reason probably the second. It may be convenient from here forward to adopt the habit of his contemporaries. 'Austen' as a name at least has the advantage of not striking a spurious and inappropriate note of informality.

At the late age of almost fifteen its bearer was sent to school at Rugby, which meant that he was half, but only half, being pushed off from his Birmingham shore. Like Goschen thirty years before him, Austen had a difficult beginning at Rugby but eventually got on to tolerable terms with the school and was captain of his house (as well as deputy chairman of the governors fifty years later). So far his educational pattern was not different from that in which his brother was to follow, except that Neville never deviated from loathing Rugby. But in 1882 Austen was decisively cast off from Birmingham commercial life by being sent to Trinity, the grandest and the most politically nurturing of the Cambridge colleges, which with its six Prime Ministers is second in this respect only to Christ Church, Oxford, although well ahead in size, wealth and numbers of Nobel prizewinners. Neville, by contrast, was drawn back from Rugby to Birmingham, where he went as a 'day boy' to Mason's College, the egg out of which his father was to hatch Birmingham University a decade and a half later. Birmingham University in its early years had a fairly workaday curriculum, but it was broad compared with Mason College's severe vocationalism. Neville Chamberlain studied metallurgy and accountancy.

Meanwhile Austen at Trinity, while achieving few Cambridge distinctions, broadened his mind into history and literature. When he came down in 1885 he went to France for eight months. Oddly as it seems in view of his later persona, his contacts were almost all with the republican left, and his studies at the 'Science-Po' were far removed from the contemporary Faubourg St Germain world of Proust's Swann. Nevertheless the Paris of the *Belle Epoque* made a profound and favourable impression upon him. Despite his insular style and blood (the Chamberlains were unusual in Britain, even for its city most remote from the sea, in not having a drop of foreign or even Celtic blood in their veins) he greatly took to French life at one of its most attractive periods. He was good at languages, learnt excellent French, and derived pleasure from speaking it, either in conversation or on his feet, for the rest of his life. This was a considerable factor, both in his enjoyment of the Foreign Secretaryship in 1924–9 and in the orientation of his policy.

After a few months at home and by his father's side over the 1886 general election, the first which Joseph Chamberlain fought as a Unionist, Austen set out on his travels again and spent an autumn of two months in Turkey and Greece with his father and elder sister. In February 1887 he went on his own to Germany, and lived in Berlin for nearly a year. Prussian life did not attract him as much as *la vie Parisienne*, but he became familiar with the political and physical shape of the Wilhelmine capital, and learnt (and retained) enough German to be able forty years later to talk to Stresemann and others in their own language. He was undergoing a thorough apprenticeship for statesmanship. At the same age his brother Neville, the future Prime Minister, was trying unsuccessfully to grow sisal in one of the least attractive Caribbean islands.

Back in England Austen did not enter the House of Commons quite as quickly as might have been expected. He became candidate for the Border Boroughs (Hawick, Selkirk, Galashiels etc.) and intermittently nursed those attractive but inconvenient (from Birmingham at any rate) banks of the Tweed for four years. He combined this with living mostly at home, both in Birmingham and in London, and falling undemandingly and in no way improperly in love with his father's new, third and American wife. Mary Endicott was the daughter of President Cleveland's Secretary of War, was somewhat younger than Austen, had arrived in November 1888 and lived on as Mrs Carnegie (having married a canon of Westminister after the death of Joseph Chamberlain) until 1957. She brought a great deal of light and life into the heavily furnished Chamberlain mansions both at Highbury (Birmingham) and in Princes Gate.

In the event Austen never fought the Border Boroughs. Early in 1892 a vacancy occurred in the East Worcestershire constituency, much of which was outer Birmingham suburbs, including King's Norton, Hall Green, Acock's Green and Yardley, which were subsequently incorporated into the city. The sitting member had been expelled from the House after a conviction for fraud, but Joseph Chamberlain was determined both to keep the seat in Liberal Unionist hands and to bring his son home (and to greater electoral safety) from Scotland. The East Worcestershire Conservatives were not enchanted with the prospect of another Liberal Unionist member and the matter was not settled until Balfour (as leader in the Commons) was brought in to tell them that if they put up a Tory against Joseph Chamberlain's son they would wreck the national Unionist alliance and would be directly responsible for letting in Home Rule. They gave way and on 30 March Austen was returned unopposed in one of the last by-elections of that parliament. It was a highly nepotic entry and it was not achieved *en beauté*, but once it had been done there was no further trouble, and Austen's inherent qualities and his instinctive Toryism, unless some doctrinaire issue from his father's past radicalism came up, were such that he had a perfectly harmonious relationship with East Worcestershire until 1914, when on his father's death he was called even nearer to home.

At the fag end of a parliament and at the age of twenty-eight and a half Austen thus entered the House of Commons in which he was to serve without interruption for forty-five years. He was introduced to the House between his father and his uncle but he made no speech before the dissolution of late June 1892. He was then opposed (although not again until 1906) by Oscar Browning, the famous Eton master, King's don and historical writer. But Browning's fame did not make much impact in East Worcestershire and Chamberlain beat him by two to one. In that last Gladstone parliament he became the assistant whip of the Liberal Unionist party, but this did not prevent occasional speaking. His advancement was very much up an interior staircase rather than by storming the tower from outside. When, after the victory of 1895, the Liberal Unionists entered the (third) Salisbury government, as opposed to giving support from outside as in 1886–92, Austen became Civil Lord of the Admiralty. With two very short intervals he was then on one front bench or the other for the next thirty-six years.

After five diligent years at the Admiralty (under Goschen) Austen became Financial Secretary to the Treasury (under Hicks Beach) in a reshuffle following the 'khaki election' of 1900. It was a promotion but not a giddy one. He was still in a junior ministerial post, but in the most senior of them, the one nearest to the threshold of the Cabinet. And twenty-one months later, when Balfour replaced Salisbury as Prime Minister, he crossed that threshold, but again his promotion was well short of the spectacular. He became Postmaster-General and occupied the twentieth and last position in the Cabinet hierarchy. It was something to be in the Cabinet at thirty-eight, but he had no exaggerated view of the importance of his post.

It nonetheless had for him the special quality that it brought him to sit at the same Cabinet table with his father. This coincidence is very rare. Successive generations of Pitts, Peels, Gladstones, Churchills, Cecils, Lloyd Georges, Hoggs, Greenwoods, Benns, to take a few examples, have been Cabinet members, but they have not been so at the same time. The only examples beyond the Chamberlains to the contrary are Lord Derby (the fourteenth earl) and his son Lord Stanley (later the fifteenth earl) in the 1860s and Ramsay MacDonald and his son Malcolm in the 1930s. For Austen, with his intense filial as well as wider family feeling, it had a peculiar significance. When, twenty-two years later, he and his brother came together under Baldwin, he semi-mockingly drafted his own epitaph in eighteenth-century tombstone style. He came up with:

> Fortunate in his family life
> Thrice fortunate in his marriage
> He spent many years in the Public Service
> And sat in Cabinet
> First with his father
> And afterwards
> With his brother.

It did not therefore appear to incommode him that his next and in some ways decisive promotion, for it was the one which lifted him into serious political rank, came hardly at all from the merits of his own performance as Postmaster-General and almost entirely as an eddy from one of the two major turbulences in his father's career. In the winter of 1902–3 Joseph Chamberlain, then in his eighth year as Colonial Secretary, spent three months in *post bellum* South Africa. He came as a conqueror, but also as one who wished to knit the defeated Boers and the victorious 'loyalists' into a united British African nation. While there he brooded on the 'illimitable veldt', cast still wider his unifying views and decided that it was the whole British Empire, particularly the white parts of it, that he wished to bring together in an approach to a customs union.

So was born his last great campaign, that for Imperial Preference and Tariff Reform, which he publicly launched in the familiar arena of the Birmingham Town Hall on 15 May, two months after his return. Whatever its effects on the Empire, where it was also fairly divisive, one institution which it was certain not to unite was the Conservative party. Protection versus Free Trade proved (and could have been foreseen to be) the most divisive Conservative issue since the Corn Laws, and remained so until, after a long interval, it was replaced by Europe. During the decades when it remained more or less on the boil there were always plenty of nominally devoted Conservatives who, whenever the party got into trouble for other reasons, were ready to make the trouble worse by stoking up the fire with a few brands of Protectionist controversy.

Joe Chamberlain did not greatly worry about this, for he was in a class by himself as a party splitter. Austen of course supported his father's campaign. He sat upon the platform at its Birmingham launch, and from then until the end of his life any mention of 'Father's cause' always brought him metaphorically to his feet and saluting. Yet it was pietism more than spontaneous conviction which sustained him. Just as Joe relished the provocation of a disruptive cause, so Austen, left to himself, would instinctively have recoiled from one. He was a natural seeker after party unity, and he also liked being on the *bien-pensant* side of an argument, which Tariff Reform never was.

In these circumstances Austen was lucky in the role which was assigned to him. In September (1903) Joe resigned from the government in order to be free to pursue his campaign without inhibition. So from the other side of the argument did four Free Trade ministers, including C. T. Ritchie from the Exchequer. Balfour's middle course increasingly inclined to the Chamberlainite side, because, lacking firm convictions of his own and trying desperately to propitiate a demoralized party, that was where he decided that the weight of activist opinion lay. He therefore wanted to keep his lines open to the resigned Chamberlain and considered that the best way to do this was to put Austen into Ritchie's vacated place as Chancellor. Austen at first hesitated, thinking that he ought to resign with his father, but when his father firmly told him that, on the contrary, he wished him to be his vicar in the Cabinet, Austen dutifully accepted. Rarely can there have been a more frivolous appointment to one of the greatest offices of state. Rarely can a young man at just forty have been blown further by a favourable side-wind.

Austen was two and a quarter years at the Treasury and introduced two budgets. Given the circumstances of his appointment, the vicarious-ness of his position and the general state of disintegration of the governing party as, after seventeen of the previous twenty years in office, it approached the great electoral smash of 1906, he was not a bad Chancellor. Unlike the time when, sixteen years later and a far more senior figure, he became Chancellor for the second time, he was allowed the normal perquisite of 11 Downing Street. It took him four months to move in, but when he did it was his first night away from the parental roof 'in a house at least for the time being my own', and he immediately wrote to his father to acknowledge this and his other debts to him. It is a bizarre thought that under the old pre-1918 franchise arrangements, which in the boroughs essentially dated from Disraeli's 1867 Act, the new Chancellor of the Exchequer, unless some special dodge had been devised, would not previously have qualified for a vote. When in Downing Street he might have got in under the lodgers' enfranchisement clause, which was however tightly circumscribed in two ways. The accommodation had to have a high rateable value, which qualification No. 11 might have met, and the tenant had to show permanence of occupation, which test Austen as the Chancellor of a doomed government might have failed. In any event he was never there for an election.

His budgets, as might have been expected, were cautious and conventional. But they were also taut and competent. The first, on 19 April 1904, had to accommodate itself to distinctly unfavourable circumstances. It came at the tail-end of a minor recession, which meant that nearly all revenue sources were below estimate – to an aggregate amount of £3.1 million. As expenditure was also £3 million more than had been allowed for this produced a deficit of £5.4 million, or just over 3.5 per cent of the total budget. He dealt with this by raising over 80 per cent of the amount in additional taxation. Two of his three measures were simple, one complicated. He raised £2 million by putting income tax up from elevenpence to one shilling in the pound. And he raised approximately the same amount by an increase of twopence in the tea duty. There was a superficial fairness about these measures: income tax was essentially a middle-class levy, the tea tax a working-class one.

His third source (raising £550,000) was a complicated reshuffling of the tobacco duty which involved technical arguments about the difference between imports in strip and imports of the whole leaf. As tends to be the way with complex taxes more parliamentary trouble flowed from this than from either of the bigger increases. It upset the tobacco trade and it also played on the raw nerve of the time, which was whether it was not partly a protective as well as a revenue-raising device. It contributed disproportionately to the Finance Bill proving slow to get through. The other factor which made in this direction was discontent at the acceptance, in the second year of the peace, of a level of total public expenditure (£140.5 million or £150.5 million if local expenditure were added) which was nearly half as high again as the pattern ten years earlier. Campbell-Bannerman, William Harcourt (in his last budget intervention) and Michael Hicks Beach all spoke in this sense, and took a long time to do so.

The Free Traders, to which category all these three belonged, were quite logically more dedicated to economy in public expenditure than were the Tariff Reformers. The latter were happy to have it demonstrated that necessary commitments demanded new sources of revenue. The Finance Bill's second reading alone extended over ten parliamentary nights, and it was a very tight squeeze to get the bill on to the statute book by the last date (1 August) by which taxes could legally be collected under the budget resolutions as opposed to full legislative authority. Altogether the budget was uncomfortably close to Iain Macleod's pejorative category of those which look better in April than in July. Nonetheless Austen had cleared his most crucial hurdle, which was to avoid seeming like a boy trying to do a man's job. Surrogate although he essentially was, there was no suggestion that he had to run to his father for every decision.

By the time of his second budget the circumstances were easier, mainly because of an unconvenanted reduction in naval expenditure. Trade was better, but it had led to no great buoyancy of revenue. Indeed a combination of errors in different directions which produced an unprecedented accuracy of aggregate out-turn, which was within £20,000, or 0.015 per cent, of his estimate. This was in spite of a shortfall of about £1.3 million, or 4.5 per cent, in the revenue from alcohol, which led the Chancellor to postulate a secular change in national habits. The public, he thought, were turning from drink to railway excursions, although at a latter stage some football enthusiasts (and maybe others too) showed that the two outlets were not necessarily incompatible. He used his surplus to take off the twopence on tea which he had imposed in the previous year and to add £1 million to the sinking fund for debt reduction. Much of the relatively brief budget speech – under two hours, the shortest for many years – was indeed concerned with the details of debt management, a tree the leaves from which curl and wither even more quickly than do those from most other budget subjects.

This budget was closely in accordance with Treasury advice and was calmly well received by what would today be called establishment opinion. The Finance Bill got through the House of Commons much more easily and quickly than in the previous year, although in the Lords, Welby, ex-permanent secretary of the Treasury, described it in surprisingly critical terms as a 'budget of drift'. Chamberlain's relations with the mandarinate were mixed. Edward Hamilton, the Treasury diarist who from 1880 onwards had supplied a sustaining contrapuntal accompaniment to Gladstone's succint account of events, had become joint permanent secretary. He liked Austen's budgets but found him stiff and remote. 'The Chancellor of the Exchequer', he wrote in November 1904, 'never shows now. He never comes up to the Treasury. He sits entirely in Downing Street and therefore does not keep in touch with one. One moreover has no inkling of what his intentions are. He ought to be taking in hand the naval and military estimates. I have served many Chancellors but by none have I been so little taken into confidence as by the present.'

This was a fairly damning indictment, although the reason that he gave for Austen's aloofness was ludicrous. He attributed it 'to a *bourgeois* bringing up at Birmingham', Birmingham, one feels, pronounced almost as Lady Bracknell might have done it. Hamilton then added a prediction for the future whch combined insight and ill-judgement in almost equal proportions: 'I am certain of this – that [Austen's] chances of being leader are *Nil*. If anything happened to Arthur Balfour, the man clearly destined to be his successor is George Wyndham . . .'

Nonetheless Chamberlain had done thoroughly respectably as Chancellor. He had not been remotely innovative, and maybe, *pace* Welby, he had 'drifted' a little, but not nearly as much as the Prime Minister had done on the central fiscal question, and even in the Unionist party's state of electoral extremis (they lost twenty by-elections during the short Balfour premiership and were clearly facing a general election smash) he had resisted any attempt at budgetary bribes to pull back votes.

As a result the office, and his conduct of it, had the effect of propelling him from the status of a cadet politician into that of a heavyweight, one of the three or four on either side who were recognized, not necessarily for their talent or their achievement, but for their rank and for the fact that they were regarded as worthy champions for each other; and this process was enhanced by the impact upon Austen's life made by the events of 1906.

The year began, as we have seen, with the crushing defeat of his party in the January general election. But within that defeat there was a considerable Chamberlain triumph. Joseph Chamberlain, in his last active election, achieved the remarkable feat of holding all seven Birmingham seats solid for Unionism, often with increased majorities. In Manchester and Salford the Unionists lost all nine, in Leeds all five, in Glasgow five out of seven, and in both Edinburgh and Bristol three out of four seats. But in Birmingham the tide was held back with all the authority which eluded Canute. This fully extended into Austen's adjacent territory of East Worcestershire. In his first contested election for thirteen years, which bland history combined with his own manner and dress might have been expected to build up a certain pressure of revolt, and on his party's violent ebb-tide, he won by nearly two to one.

In addition the new opposition party in the House of Commons, attenuated though it had become, was at least two-thirds composed of Tariff Reformers. With Balfour himself having suffered the supplementary humiliation of losing his seat in Manchester, although hastily being made room for in the City of London, Joseph Chamberlain appeared to hold far more cards for the new parliament than did his nominal leader. He did not hold them for long. July of that year was set to be a great month of Chamberlain celebrations – 8 July was Joe's seventieth birthday. The Birmingham festivities were vast. Banquets, garden parties, torchlight processions, fireworks depicting his well-known silhouette and a great meeting in Bingley Hall were all part of the not very restrained jamboree. At the meeting Austen was typically called on to say a few words after his father's oration. But it was the last time he was ever required to perform such a subsidiary public function. Two days later Joseph Chamberlain suffered a crippling stroke. His mind remained intact but both his diction and his movement were affected. He never spoke in public again.

Austen Chamberlain was therefore thrust forward, much sooner than he expected, into the public leadership of the Tariff Reform campaign. But he was not set free, nor with most of his being would he have wished to be. The oracle remained alive for another eight years. Indeed he remained a member of the House of Commons, although one who only appeared (with difficulty) to take the oath at the beginning of each new parliament, of which there were two elected in 1910. Furthermore he sometimes communicated advice or even instructions. And Austen accepted the almost daily obligation to keep his father informed of everything which he saw happening in politics. This he did either through frequent calls at Princes Gate, the London house, or through recess visits to Highbury, the Birmingham house or, in the interstices, through long letters to his stepmother, who transmitted them to her husband. The filial devotion was unchallengeable. But whether Austen preferred the oracle to remain silent or not is a more open question. And whether, if it spoke, he obeyed or attempted to

fudge its comments is also subject to a fluctuating answer. The likelihood
is that on one major question between 1906 and 1914 he obeyed (against
his natural judgement), and that on another he did not.

The other Chamberlain celebration set for July 1906 was that of
Austen's middle-aged marriage. It had been arranged for the 21st, at St
Margaret's Westminster, and took place according to plan, but was
inevitably clouded by the immobilization of the patriarch ten days
before. Austen had been medically ordered in March to take a restorative
holiday in a milder and sunnier climate. In measuring his career it has
constantly to be remembered that, in contrast with his father until 1906,
Austen was always both hypochondriacal and of a 'delicate' disposition.
He had a lot of ailments and he made the most of them. He was often
very tense, he probably did not eat enough, his worry was that his weight
and his blood pressure were too low, and after periods of strain he was
frequently near to nervous collapse.

Sciatica was, however, the main trouble which, at the age of forty-
two, forced him to retreat to Algiers in the spring of 1906. There he
engaged in a plunge to matrimony as quick as it was belated. He met for
the first time Ivy Dundas, the twenty-seven-year-old daughter of a
retired army colonel. They were engaged within a few days, his cabled
announcement to his stepmother being received, as she conveyed to her
own mother, with a mixture of amazed pleasure (for Austen and for Joe)
and quizzical detachment. 'Was it not a good cure for sciatica?' was
perhaps her quintessential comment.

An alternative one might have been surprise that he had ever dared
to do it without first bringing Miss Dundas home to Highbury for
approval. However his unendorsed judgement proved good, and the
result was a happy thirty-one-year marriage, three children and a calm
domestic sustenance for Austen. He was naturally uxorious (perhaps
familial is a better word, as his vast 'diary' letters to his sisters showed)
and it was a good thing that the timing of his wife's entry into the family
meant that she always stood somewhat off-shore from Highbury.
Immediately it involved a new London establishment in Egerton Place,
off the Old Brompton Road. He responded to the excitement of
furnishing some rooms of his own for the first time in forty-three years
(a birthday had gone by since the engagement) with an ingenuous
enthusiasm. 'I feel pretty much as I did when a child on the eve of
Christmas Day,' he wrote before moving in.

During the eight-year Indian summer of Liberalism in government
which then intervened before July 1914 brought both the twilight life of

Joseph Chamberlain and the pre-First World War world to an end, Austen Chamberlain had two major political decisions to make. The first (and the one in which it looked as though he were still seeking instructions from his father) related to the Lloyd George budget of 1909 and the constitutional struggle which arose out of its rejection by the House of Lords. Against the budget itself Austen, although leading for the opposition throughout the immensely long-drawn-out Finance Bill proceedings, was not particularly virulent. There was even a hint that he might have had some doubt, more than Balfour did, about the wisdom of a peers' rejection.

Once the issue moved beyond the budgetary to the wider constitutional plane, however, Austen's position became more bewildering. After the unexpected death of King Edward VII in May 1910, a constitutional conference was set up to seek a consensual solution. Austen was one of the four Unionist representatives. The conference deliberated between June and October, came quite close to devising agreed powers and composition for a reformed House of Lords but eventually broke down on Lansdowne's stubborn refusal to agree to any scheme which did not preserve a second chamber with the will and power to block Home Rule for Ireland, even with an Ulster exclusion. Austen, presaging his attitude on the Irish Treaty of 1921, showed little interest in making the world revolve around the rights of Southern Irish absentee landlords, and took no such extreme position. He was also considerably attracted by the 'grand coalition' proposal which Lloyd George, like an Aladdin exhibiting a cave, suddenly threw into the proceedings in August. It was a Bismarckian approach which animated this memorandum from the Welsh hills, a doctrine of national efficiency underpinned with some radical social policy. This made it attractive to Austen, who thought that it would at least deliver a stronger navy and maybe Tariff Reform as well. Balfour was hostile (he was haunted by the danger of being 'another Peel' and splitting his party), Lansdowne had his head down in anti-Home Rule stubbornness, and the proposal died, as soon afterwards did the constitutional conference.

The second general election of 1910 followed immediately. It made practically no difference to the balance between the Liberal-led majority and the Unionist minority, or to the degree of dependence within the majority of the Asquith government on the Irish and Labour parties. What it did make a difference to were Austen Chamberlain's relations with Balfour. Balfour suddenly announced after consultation with hardly anyone other than Lansdowne that, if victorious, he would not introduce

Tariff Reform without a referendum. Austen 'felt the decision like a slap in the face', but stood to attention and did not repudiate his leader. But when the stalemate election was over there was a strong residue of resentment left in Austen's loyal mind. Characteristically he was ill again after the election and thought to be near to a nervous breakdown. He, however, diagnosed it somewhat differently in one of his brotherly letters: 'But my real illness is known only to Ivy [his wife] and myself. It's Referendum Sickness!' While he utterly rejected a displacement of Balfour as leader ('he stands a head and shoulders above the rest of us'), he was like a trusting dog which had received an unjust kick. This may have pushed him to pursuing over the next eight months an uncharacteristic course of action with an unnatural group of allies. Probably, however, the fact that it was his father's instinctive choice was, for the last time, a still stronger factor.

Joseph Chamberlain's position as a wounded chief, not merely revered but with the fiction of puissance still kept up, was unparalleled. At both the 1910 elections, although incapable of a single act of campaigning and without the faintest hope of being able to participate in the proceedings of the new parliament, he had been returned unopposed for West Birmingham. Even the government party paid him the respect of not putting up a candidate. But it was all a courtly charade, a curious apotheosis for the no-nonsense Radical of 1880. On 2 February 1911 he took the oath in the new parliament. He could not manage a signature. He symbolically touched the pen and then Austen signed on his behalf. Also symbolically he sat on the opposition front bench for a few minutes. He never visited the House again, even though he lived for another three and a half years.

The immediate issue for the parliament was whether or not the peers should accept the verdict of the electorate (which while in no way overwhelming was nonetheless manifestly decisive in the sense that no one could seriously advocate yet a third election) and let through the bill for limiting to a two-sessions delay the right of the Lords to block legislation. By so doing they would obviate the threat of their being swamped by a mass creation of peers to which it was thought (although without absolute public clarity) that Asquith had secured the agreement of the new King (George V). Those within the Conservative party advocating this course of discretion rather than of valour became known as 'Hedgers', and included most of the established leaders of the party.

On the other side were the 'Ditchers', as those who proclaimed themselves willing to die in the last of those channels were happy to be called. Their stance was often more self-deceptive than heroic. 'Essentially, theatrical' was Balfour's phrase for it. The 'Ditchers' persistently persuaded themselves either that the nerve of the King or of Asquith or of both would fail and that there would be no creation, or that, if by chance there was, it would be on the smallest possible scale. Their leading figures were: Halsbury (old and extreme but with sixteen years' experience as Lord Chancellor); Selborne (son of another Lord Chancellor); F. E. Smith; Edward Carson (mordantly brilliant advocate whom Smith, ten years later, was to denounced as displaying – on the Irish Treaty – 'an effort at statecraft which would be immature on the lips of an hysterical schoolgirl'); Salisbury (the much lesser son of a Prime Minister father); George Wyndham (a mixture of cavalry captain and romantic poet promoted – briefly – to be a Cabinet minister, whom some people thought to be Anthony Eden's father); Alfred Milner, who inspired his 'kindergarten', but was doubtfully understanding of English politics; and the two Chamberlains, the father in the background, the son only too much in the foreground.

When a dinner of 600, nominally in honour of Halsbury but in fact organized as a gesture of defiance to Balfour and Lansdowne, took place in the old Hotel Cecil on 26 July, Austen both headed the list of sponsors and made the principal speech of the evening. Its keynote was not extremism, which would have been wholly alien to his character, but a sort of bland obtuseness, which, while by no means always his hallmark, nonetheless sat more easily with him than did defiance. He could not believe that either the King or Asquith intended a mass creation of peers. Therefore the threat should be treated as bluff. His father strongly approved of the conclusion, although probably not the reasoning. He thought that a mass creation was more than likely, but preferred it to surrender. He was dedicated to implacability, and always liked a new twist to the political kaleidoscope. The revolt of the 'Ditchers', despite a difference in reasoning and maybe motivation, therefore produced no friction within the Chamberlain family.

Nor of course did it destroy the Parliament Bill. What it did destroy was Balfour's leadership. He had had more than enough and three months after the divisive vote he resigned, abruptly but not without premeditation. That did not at all suit Austen's book. He had had a frayed-nerve row with Balfour as the critical Lords vote loomed, typically caused by his reacting very defensively to a belief that Balfour had accused him (and the 'Ditchers' in general) of disloyalty, which, in Austen's case, was the equivalent of accusing King Edward VII of encouraging anorexia. But in general he greatly esteemed Balfour, and moreover, while he liked being treated as a crown prince, did not at that stage, maybe not at any stage, like being thrust into a struggle for the throne. 'The blow has fallen and I am as sick as a man can be,' he wrote on 4 November 1911:

> Balfour has definitely decided to resign the leadership . . . sad news to me whatever happens for I love the man, and though . . . he has once or twice nearly broken my heart politically, I can now think of nothing but the pleasure of intimate association with him, the constant personal kindness he has shown to me and the great qualities of mind and character he has brought to the discharge of the tremendous duties of his post.

This hardly pointed to a mood of determined militancy appropriate to fighting and winning a leadership contest. And a letter to his stepmother was even more revealing of his lack of ruthless self-promoting ambition, perhaps even of a lack of confidence in his own ability to do the job. 'I wish', he wrote, 'there were another Balfour, clearly superior to us, and obviously marked out for the post. How gladly I would play second fiddle to him.' On the day when Balfour's resignation was made public (Wednesday, 7 November), however, Austen was the front-runner for the succession. He was Balfour's own choice, he was preferred (perhaps not very strongly) by Balcarres the Chief Whip, by Steel-Maitland the party chairman and by the majority of the members of the shadow Cabinet. Had the loose and rough rules under which Macmillan both emerged as Prime Minister in 1957 and manoeuvred towards Home as his successor six and three-quarter years later been applied, Chamberlain would have come through. But it was thought less necessary to secure a fix in opposition in 1911 than in government in 1963. Matters had, however, to be resolved on or before the following Monday (12 November), for which day a Carlton Club meeting of Unionist MPs had been summoned.

Austen's initial rival was Walter Long. Long was a Wiltshire country gentlemen who was nine years his senior and had been a junior member of Unionist Cabinets between 1895 and 1905. His strengths were that he was a quintessential Conservative, Anglican, landed and foxhunting, who had nonetheless resisted the temptations of extremism or exhibitionism over the Parliament Bill and been quietly loyal to the leadership, even though he and Balfour did not much like each other. His weakness was that no one, except possibly himself, thought that he would be much good as leader. But this did not prevent the large group who objected to Austen on one ground or another from thinking that a leader's provenance was more important than his ability to lead.

Austen, although of a naturally conservative temperament, was not a Conservative. He was still a Liberal Unionist. Nor was he an Anglican, although if ever a man was built to be an unfanatical pillar of the Church of England it was he. Nonetheless he was an hereditary Unitarian. Nor was he even a sportsman. He preferred gardening. Moreover the Carlton Club, that temple of Conservative faith, which a Chancellor moving to the left (very rare) like Gladstone stayed in too long and those moving to the right, like Goschen, Chamberlain himself and Winston Churchill, found it difficult to embrace, was still alien to Austen. When he entered it on the following Monday for the party meeting, it was the first time that he had ever done so. And when, eleven years later, he met another great rebuff, it was in the same damned clubhouse. For those who were not born Conservatives the Carlton spelled nothing but trouble. And to crown it all there was the confused image left by Austen, an essentially moderate and loyal man, having indulged himself, partly to please his father, in disloyal extremism during the constitutional crisis.

So he had a raft of considerations going against him. And these considerations translated themselves into individual defections as the final intervening days succeeded each other. During these days Long firmly held Chamberlain and maybe edged a little ahead. It was going to be narrow. MPs' thoughts turned to the possibility of a compromise candidate. And that, in the shape of Andrew Bonar Law, later 'the Unknown Prime Minister' as Robert Blake so aptly entitled his biography of Law, was determinedly emerging.

Bonar Law's deficiencies were obvious. The first was that in a very status-conscious party he had occupied no office senior to that of parliamentary secretary to the Board of Trade. At least that deficiency was capable of repair. The second was not. This was that he had a narrow although quick and logical mind and was lacking in any sort of charisma. It is difficult to avoid the conclusion that his sufficient asset was that he was thrustingly available and was not either Austen Chamberlain or Walter Long.

On the Wednesday/Thursday Law was lucky if he had forty supporters. On the Monday he was elected unanimously. This was due to the decisions of Chamberlain and Long to withdraw in his favour, which were taken on the Friday. This was thought to have shown high magnanimity on the part of Austen in particular, and was the foundation of his reputation as the great gentleman in politics. It certainly showed that he knew how to retreat gracefully. But, on the substance of the matter, he had little sensible alternative, once it became clear that Walter Long was willing so to act. Long, even though he was thought to be full of animus against Chamberlain, subsequently wrote a notably generous letter saying that he thought Austen's sacrifice 'immeasurably greater' than his own. And it was certainly true that Austen got the main credit.

Yet in a sense the success of Bonar Law was a greater insult to him than it was to Long. This was because Law had, some in an exaggerated form, many of the deficiencies of circumstance which were held against Chamberlain. He was equally non-Anglican, non-landed, non-sporting, non-metropolitan. He was even Canadian, and instead of being a second-generation Birmingham screw-manufacturer (whose father was however the dominant politician of his generation) he was a first-generation Glasgow businessman, whose father had been a Presbyterian minister in New Brunswick. It is difficult not to feel that the bulk of the Conservative party in 1911 just did not want Austen as leader. Had he not withdrawn he might well have been beaten on the first ballot by a short head by Long, with Law still subsequently being the beneficiary. That clearly would have been a much worse outcome for him. The 'devil's bargain' which was twice suggested to him and twice rejected, although not surprisingly for it involved both malevolence and being too clever by half, neither of which were in Austen's style, was that he should swing his support to Long, wait to see him fail abysmally over a year or so and then step into his shoes by acclaim.

Austen's main problem when he withdrew was that of explaining himself to his father and other members of the Highbury family. (He had no problem with his own wife, who instinctively followed her husband's judgement, and was probably also aware after five years of marriage that both his physique and his temperament were lacking in robustness for the strains and buffetings of the high game.) Joseph Chamberlain was a different matter. Perhaps fortunately he was in Birmingham at the time, so communication could only be by letter. The news of Austen's withdrawal was a heavy blow to him. His main biographer, J. L. Garvin, wrote, 'I seemed to hear great heart strings snapping at last in Joe.'

At the time he endeavoured to react calmly and even understand-ingly. 'He received your news', Mary Chamberlain wrote to Austen, 'as he always does in his firm strong way.' He was even further reported as saying that 'Austen could have done no differently.' The import of that sentence turns on whether it was said with the stress on *Austen*, in other words whether it was Austen's gentlemanly but weak character which made the result inevitable in a way that it would not have been had his father or his brother been the contestant. Certainly Neville Chamberlain wrote bluntly, 'For the Party's sake I cannot help wishing you had fought it out...', although going on to soften the impact with a number of assuaging phrases. And Joseph Chamberlain moved in the remaining two and a half years of his life to the sombre view that if one of his sons got to the top of Disraeli's greasy pole it would be Neville and not Austen.

Whatever the effect on father/son relations there can be no doubt that these events were the beginning of the legend that Austen Chamberlain was not only a great gentleman but also an unlucky politician. It would be ridiculous to regard his career as broken. He held major offices over another twenty years, including his most successful and durable tenure, which was that of the Foreign Office between 1924 and 1929. He lasted much longer than either Long or Law, certainly had much greater subsequent success than Long, and arguably than Law, in spite of the latter's brief and unhappy seven months in 10 Downing Street. Yet Austen came to be acclaimed more for his fortitude in adversity and his decency than for his flair. This reputation affected his own view of himself and was also considerably strengthened by the next phase of his ministerial career.

In August 1914, Austen, newly returned – unopposed – for West Birmingham, was passionately in favour of Britain's entry into the war on the side of France. And his fervour made him eager to enter the first Coalition, which was formed in May 1915, without making any selfish stipulations about his office. He or Bonar Law, probably the latter, ought to have been Chancellor of the Exchequer, particularly as Lloyd George was moving to the Ministry of Munitions and the claims of the spindly Liberal, Reginald McKenna, who in fact succeeded him, were far from overwhelming. The Conservatives were unwisely kept to the periphery, with only Balfour as First Lord of the Admiralty getting a post which was central to the war. Law became Colonial Secretary. Austen became Secretary of State for India.

India did not prove rewarding for Austen. During the ninety-year lifetime of that secretaryship of state, between the Mutiny and independence, the relationship of its occupant with the Viceroy was always ambiguous. The Viceroy was appointed, not by the Secretary of State, but by the Sovereign on the advice of the Prime Minister. Once appointed the Viceroy assumed for a span the greatest grandeur of any British subject. Yet the Secretary of State was supposed to exercise political control over him. This was never easy to achieve, partly because of the slowness (even though diminishing) of communication and partly because the Viceroy often assumed more prestige than the minister.

In Austen's case these were compounded by his not knowing much about India, although he had presided over a Royal Commission on the narrow field of Indian currency; by his never having been and never going there during his twenty-six months of office (although this deficiency was far from unique); and by the circumstances of war tilting the balance further than usual in favour of the man on the spot. Above all he inherited a theoretical responsibility for a military campaign in Mesopotamia, over which the Indian government found it difficult enough to exercise any control from Calcutta, and about which he in London was almost entirely impotent.

One phase of that Mesopotamian campaign was a near disaster. The British and Indian troops pushed too far up the Tigris without adequate support and were heavily repulsed. The medical and supply arrangements proved grossly inadequate and a sense of public scandal built up. A Commission of Enquiry was set up with a mainly parliamentary membership. Austen was examined at length but not particularly hostilely on 21 December 1916, which was just after the palace revolution which had led to the replacement of Asquith by Lloyd George. This was an event in which Austen had played a somewhat sleep-walking role. He was dissatisfied with Asquith's lack of 'push or drive'. But this was far from meaning that he had by this stage transferred his allegiance to Lloyd George. 'I take no pleasure in a change which gives me a chief whom I profoundly distrust – no doubt a man of great energy but quite untrustworthy . . .' In this mood he, together with the other two members (Curzon and Robert Cecil) of the group of Conservative ministers which temporarily came to be known as the three Cs, stated their position with an ambiguity which made it easy to misinterpret. Nonetheless they had a considerable influence upon Asquith. But as, in Austen's case at any rate, the ambiguity was in his mind and not merely in his words, the confusion did not upset him too much.

It was therefore to a different government under a different Prime Minister that the report of the Mesopotamia Commission was presented. Austen read it during a ten-day holiday in his favourite Sussex Weald countryside in May 1917, and wrote that there were only two things which marred the perfection of the spring birds and flowers. The one was the boom of the guns from France and the other was the report. He did not however see the report as too devastating: '. . . I do not altogether escape blame, nor the Govt. and other authorities at home, but except in the case of orders for the advance on Baghdad where I share responsibility (for what is declared to be a bad blunder) with the War Committee, I am blamed only for saying in "private" telegrams or letters what I ought to have said in public, i.e. formal, official despatches.'

Nonetheless he decided that he ought to resign. By the standards of today, or indeed of the Lloyd George era, it was a quixotic gesture, and there was no question of the Prime Minister who had survived the Marconi scandal pressing him to do so. On the contrary Lloyd George strongly urged him to stay at the India Office or, if he rejected that, to take the Paris embassy. Austen was attracted by the latter, but rejected it partly on his brother Neville's advice that it would queer his pitch for post-war politics, and partly because he felt that he ought to perform some act of expiation more painful than retiring to the splendours of the rue du Faubourg St Honoré. So he went to the back benches at the beginning of July. In one sense it was a sacrifice, but in another it was a relief. Giving up £5,000 a year (which was then, even with wartime inflation and taxation, a good £150,000 of today's money) was a serious matter in his always shaky financial circumstances. On the other hand, as only too frequently, he was on the edge of his reserves of energy and needed a rest. This took him over the summer and well into the autumn, and was once more in Sussex – he never seemed to go to Birmingham once his father had died, although Neville Chamberlain firmly maintained the territorial base and was indeed Lord Mayor in 1915–16.

Over these months Austen's gentle gardening and reading was done to the comforting hum of his steadily rising reputation. Amid the atmosphere of fixing, intrigue and self-advancement which was at least part of the keynote of the Lloyd George Coalition, Austen seemed to offer a disinterestedness and spirit of self-sacrifice which was otherwise manifestly more prevalent at the front than in Whitehall. Although he continued to dress in the stiffest of the coats from which the hostile military sobriquet of 'frocks' was derived, he looked better than the rest of them. He even began to be talked about during that autumn as Prime Minister in reserve if Lloyd George tripped over himself or, in the smart phraseology of the time, 'was hit by a golf ball'. But Lloyd George was not a man who easily tripped or, although much on the links, naturally got in the way of passing golf balls, and the moment, if it ever existed, was soon past.

Austen's natural inclination was not to take on a government but to rejoin it after a decent interval in an honourable way and in a capacity which would give him a tolerable influence. He was a man more at home in than out. Already in the autumn (of 1917) there was talk of his becoming Home Secretary, but that department held no attraction for him and he apprehended that in the peculiar structure of the Lloyd George government it would not carry membership of the War Cabinet with it. Nevertheless he would probably have accepted. But the offer did not materialize. At the end of March (1918) much the same position arose in relation to the War Office. Lord Derby was thought to be resigning. In the event Derby did not resign, so there was once again an anti-climax.

In mid-April, with the allied forces reeling back towards Paris under the force of the Ludendorff offensive, Austen eventually joined. His title, that of Minister without Portfolio, hardly carried the historic authority of either Home Secretary or Secretary of State for War (particularly with a war on), but it did carry the coveted membership of a War Cabinet of six, of whom only one (Bonar Law as Chancellor) was departmental.

When the Armistice came Austen looked to have had a fairly good war for a 'frock'. He was one of the three Conservatives in the War Cabinet, and he had his highly respectable resignation to his credit. But he had in reality played a peripheral and not very effective part in the direction of the war, and his prestige, which in 1914 might have been regarded (unlike his energy) as roughly comparable with that of his parliamentary vis-à-vis Lloyd George, could no longer hold a candle to that of 'the little Welsh attorney' who had won the war. This reflected itself in the post-war dispositions. The rushed December election with its ruthless use of the 'coupon' for Conservatives and acceptable Liberals, and consequent slaughter of Asquithians, was an apparent triumph for Lloyd George, who had an overall majority of almost 250, although the breakdown into 334 Conservatives, 134 Coalition Liberals and ten miscellaneous supporters contained the seeds of trouble for the future.

Austen was returned unopposed in his father's old division. The unchallenged Chamberlain sway over Birmingham and its adjacent areas was an electoral phenomenon without parallel. As member for East Worcestershire Austen sat through twenty-two years, one by-election and six general elections while having to face only three contests, and winning them all handsomely. Then West Birmingham, working-class rather than middle-class and slum rather than sylvan, allowed four opportunities for polls to go by without a contest.

Austen therefore had an apparently secure local base, but he also had to deal with a Lloyd George who was at the peak of his imperious form and with whom he had not then developed any special bridge to span the natural incongruity of their personalities. The terms on which he was offered his position in the post-election government were distinctly graceless. Bonar Law was determined to give up the Exchequer and exercise his function as leader of three-quarters of the government majority, somewhat Martha-like yet crucial, from the sinecure position of Lord Privy Seal. And he was equally determined that Austen should succeed him as Chancellor. Lloyd George would have preferred Edwin Montagu, his own former Financial Secretary. When however he was persuaded (mainly by Law) to offer Austen the Chancellorship he did so on terms which made it the equivalent of throwing a bone to a dog. There was to be no tenancy of 11 Downing Street, because that would remain with Law as the deputy Prime Minister. And there was to be no Cabinet membership, because that might mean the letting in of a whole range of departmental ministers.

If the first deprivation was disagreeable, the second was intolerable. Austen was always status-conscious in spite of his gentlemanly spirit of self-denial. He could do without office altogether but he was damned if he was going to accept it on second-rate terms, which would certainly be the case if he were a Chancellor outside the Cabinet. Furthermore it was less than a year since he had fought a battle to secure the very issue of his Cabinet status, and doubly furthermore he was not remotely enthusiastic about going back after thirteen years to his old stamping ground of the Treasury. 'I enter an office which I dislike with no circumstance omitted that could increase my distaste for it,' he wrote to one of his sisters a week or so later. The last part of his lament was not by then strictly true for he had stipulated his way into the Cabinet. But his needing to raise the issue at all, combined with Lloyd George having at first blandly said that it did not greatly matter because he as Prime Minister was going to be absent in Paris so much that it might be better to do without a Cabinet, both increased his fear that he would not get much Prime Ministerial support and guaranteed that he made no joyous entry into the peacetime Coalition. In a sad *cri de cœur* to a sister a little earlier, he complained that he had 'no real friend and no-one whom I really trust among the present leaders'.

Austen's second term at the Treasury lasted twenty-six months, exactly the same as his time at the India Office, although ending very differently, and involved three budgets, the last introduced several weeks after he had ceased to be Chancellor and become Lord Privy Seal and leader of the House of Commons. The first budget, on 30 April 1919, was more an attempt to re-establish some sort of peacetime bearings, within which the national finances could be prudently conducted in the future, than itself an exercise in such prudent management. Compared with his previous experience the magnitudes were so different and the uncertainties so great that the Chancellor was like a man rubbing his eyes as, after a foggy passage he came into a view of harbour lights, and tried to decide where he was. What was indisputable was that the national debt which in 1905 had been £755 million, had risen by about exactly ten times to £7,435 million.

The revenue and expenditure position was more complicated but the size of this 'dead-weight debt' meant that, after three-quarters of a century of a declining burden, Austen found himself back in the position of post-Napoleonic War Chancellors, with debt interest pre-empting a vast proportion of expenditure. When he estimated that 'normal' national expenditure (that is, once exceptional wartime items and their hangovers had disappeared) might be £766 million, 52 per cent of it was to go to debt servicing.

The 'normal' £766 million was to be compared with nearly twice that amount which were his actual estimates for 1919–20. However a lot of his expected revenue also came from exceptional sources, mainly the sale of war stores, and offered no contribution to his theoretical 'normal' budget of the future. This also applied to the excess profits duty, which he sensibly held could not be kept at its wartime rate of 80 per cent without both discouraging control over costs and discriminating against new enterprises. But for the moment it inflated revenue, which he estimated as coming out at £1,159 million as against an expenditure of £1,435 million. In order somewhat to narrow this gap, he proposed to raise about £110 million in additional taxation, substantial contributions coming from the spirit duty (up by two-thirds), the beer duty (up by two-fifths) and death duties, which were doubled (to 40 per cent) on estates of over £2 million while remaining unchanged on those under £15,000. This last somewhat egalitarian measure for a Conservative Chancellor becomes more comprehensible when it is remembered that proposals for a full-scale capital levy were then at the very centre of the political debate. The death duty increase was seen as a defence against worse, and Austen indeed fortified his budget speech by quoting Montesquieu's dictum that taxation is that part of citizen's wealth which he surrenders in order to underpin the secure possession of the remainder.

Two of the more interesting items in the budget were of little revenue or expenditure significance. They were of symbolic rather than practical importance. The first related to the land value duties, which had been the most controversial item in that most controversial of all budgets in 1909, when Lloyd George had been the Chancellor and Austen Chamberlain had been his principal adversary. The claims at the time of both sides had been grossly exaggerated. The notorious duties produced neither substantial revenue for the Treasury nor dire consequences for landed estates. By 1919, owing partly to judicial decisions, they had become a dead letter, and had to be amended or repealed. Austen tactfully respected the susceptibilities of his Prime Minister by referring their future to a Commons Select Committee which temporizing act paved the way to euthanasia in the following year's budget.

The second issue was what the Chancellor termed 'the most important feature of the budget', but that could be regarded as coming within the category of a 'he would say that wouldn't he' remark. He introduced a mild degree of Imperial Preference, skilfully contrived to raise neither the bogy of food taxes nor the danger of any adverse effect upon home production. The main practical impact (and loss of revenue – of £2.3 million) was on tea, where there was an abatement of twopence a pound, but as 90 per cent of tea came from the Empire in any event there was little room for an effect on patterns of trade. Empire wines and spirits also received some benefit. It was a fine filial operation, but one carried out, so far as the patient in the form of the consumer was concerned, under a strong anaesthetic.

The Finance Bill of that year got through the House of Commons (in which both the Labour and Liberal oppositions were very weak) by the end of July more or less intact and with the Chancellor's authority neither notably mauled nor enhanced. He had however been optimistic. His deficit, which he estimated at £234 million, turned out to be £326 million.

A year later Chamberlain's 1920 budget made a massive effort to restore sound finance. It added nearly £200 million to a revenue which had previously not been much above £1,200 million. It was relatively more draconian than the budget of 1968 which, although holding the record for increasing taxation by £981 million, did so on a base of about

£7,000 million and amounted therefore to not much more than a half of the percentage increase of 1920. As tends to be the case in these circumstances Austen had to scrape around for revenue, and used one or two surprising sources. Pre-eminent in this category was a sudden lurch in favour of the excess profits duty, which in the previous year he had reduced from 80 per cent to 40 as a step towards phasing out. In 1920, by contrast, he put it up again, this time to 60 per cent. His excuse for the switch of direction was that he had not expected the wartime boom to continue so strongly that excess profits were almost as much a feature of the aftermath as they had been of the war itself. Unfortunately, his misjudgement of the future trend of profits was just as great in 1920 as it had been in 1919, although in the opposite direction. The boom was bust almost before the 1920 Finance Bill was passed, and in 1921 the excess profits tax had to be completely abolished, but not before the Treasury had paid out large sums in refunds to companies which had become loss-making.

Even without prior knowledge of these developments the 60 per cent rate had attracted heavy criticism, partly because it was surprisingly accompanied by a new 5 per cent corporation profits tax. The extension of this to Co-operative Societies ensured that the Labour benches were almost as critical as the Tory ones. The heaviest weight of budget criticism, however, both from within the Coalition and from Asquith, who had just returned to the House after his Paisley by-election victory, was directed against the Chancellor not having acted more stringently on the expenditure side of the equation. His overall budget judgement was not greatly queried, even though it involved providing £234 million for debt redemption. Nor was his decision to raise an additional £70 million from substantial further increases in the excise duties on spirits and on beer, as well as in the stamp duties. Wines, especially of the sparkling variety, were subjected to the first duty increase since 1899 and imported cigars were added in for good measure. It was his acceptance of an overall level of expenditure of £1,184 million which aroused the ire of the 'hard-faced men' behind him. Anti-waste became the fashionable nostrum. Lord Rothermere, always one to exploit any demagogic issue, even put up a few by-election candidates under his label. Both in the House and outside much of the anti-public expenditure rhetoric took the simple form of pretending that great savings could be made by an onslaught on bureaucracy. Austen, equally always one to defend those who worked for him or in other public sector jobs, responded magisterially, 'I have served in more than one Department, and I cannot say how strongly I resent and how bitterly I feel these constant attacks upon the Civil Service.'

By the time of the 1921 budget there had been major changes in both the economic and the political situation. The post-war boom broke abruptly over the winter of 1920/1, and in the spring unemployment, exacerbated by industrial dispute, went to the hitherto unprecedented level of over two million, with another million on strike in the coal industry. This meant that some of the taxation yields which Chamberlain had predicted in the 1920 budget proved disappointing, although his large surplus of nearly 25 per cent above the level of total expenditure was effectively achieved. Whether it was desirable in the greatly changed circumstances was another matter, particularly as a collapse of sterling in early 1920 (down from its pegged wartime $4.75 to $3.20) led to the deflationary effects of a high (7 per cent) Bank Rate. However it never seriously occurred to Austen, or to his colleagues and most of his opponents, that this might raise doubts about his strategy of paying off debt, if possible by curbing expenditure, but if necessary by raising taxes. This was in spite of the fact that in December 1919 he had engaged in some very friendly correspondence with Maynard Keynes about his 'brilliant piece of work', *The Economic Consequences of the Peace*, which he had read with 'malicious pleasure'. (It must be said, however, that Keynes himself was hardly into deficit financing in those early post-1918 days.)

The economic deterioration reflected itself in political reaction. The Coalition government found itself in a position familiar to Austen from the days when, almost twenty years before, he had previously been Chancellor, that of losing nearly every by-election in sight. Lloyd George's magic had gone and with it went the appeal of coalition to many Conservatives. Under Balfour in 1905 party feeling had at least given them a Gadarene solidarity as they headed towards the cliff of destruction. Under Lloyd George it made a good half of them feel that if they were headed for defeat they would prefer to do so under the leadership of one of their own, who might even bring salvation and would at least ensure a cosier defeat.

Into this atmosphere of discontent there was injected in March 1921 the news of the collapse of Bonar Law's health. He insisted on resigning immediately. The inevitable successor to Law was Austen. There was no contest, not only in the sense that no votes were counted, which had indeed been the case in 1911, but also in the sense that there were no conflicting tugs in the minds of any of the electing body. Where they would have gone had Chamberlain not been available is not clear, and this could easily have been the case for there had been two friendly attempts in the previous two years to offer him an honourable exit from British politics. In July 1919, he had been offered the embassy to Washington, and had been tempted, but found his wife unenthusiastic and his son's age (twelve) an insuperable barrier; Edward Grey accepted in his place, so the offer was not a low-level one. Then, in October 1920, when he was offered the Indian Viceroyalty, broadly the same considerations applied; Reading was this time the beneficiary.

As it was he was elected by acclaim and even with genuine enthusiasm in March 1921, the meeting being once again in the ever looming Carlton Club. The unanimity may have been partly because it was an inheritance of Dead Sea fruit. Austen Chamberlain was the only leader of the Conservative party of this century, with the as yet untested exception of William Hague, who never became Prime Minister. The other odd thing about Chamberlain's occupancy of the Conservative leadership, which began by being more acceptable to the run of Conservative MPs than it was to his Prime Ministerial chief ('he's an awful Tory' was reported as Lloyd George's comment on hearing of the choice of Austen), was that this contrast quickly and dangerously reversed itself.

Chamberlain, who had never previously had close dealings with Lloyd George, fell under his spell almost as soon as he had become the second man in the government and the Prime Minister's next-door neighbour in Downing Street. He positively liked a number-two position, and felt more comfortable with a guiding star above him, whether it was his father or the Welsh wizard. This was no doubt one reason why he three times showed so little determination to use that position to climb to number one. But he was nonetheless not a good (as opposed to a dedicated) number two, at any rate in the peculiar circumstances of the post-war Coalition. He was insensitive to his own party and therefore less skilled than Bonar Law had been at keeping it loyal to the Prime Minister. He was too aloof and wooden. Second he was in any event on a collison course with the majority of his followers. The more they became disenchanted with Lloyd George the stronger became his own enchantment, and indeed his conviction that the continuance of the Coalition was the only effective barrier against socialism.

On one important issue, however, the 1921 Irish settlement which led to the setting up of the Free State, he performed a notable act of statesmanship and held the Unionist party (as it was still widely called, not least in Birmingham) steady for sense and peace. At a November 1921 conference of the National Union of Conservative and Unionist Associations in Liverpool (not the easiest of cities for that issue) he made one of the best speeches of his life ('Now and again in the affairs of men there comes a moment when courage is safer than prudence . . .') and crushed a revolt by 1,700 votes to 70. But it was a rare victory, and as the troubles increased – honours scandals, the unpopularity of Edwin Montagu and Christopher Addison, two of the few Liberal ministers, and a rash foreign policy risking war with Turkey – so Austen, although stubbornly loyal, found it more difficult to hold the line. The Coalition became increasingly an affair of Lloyd George pirouetting on the discontented base of the Conservative party. Austen, supported by Birkenhead, Balfour, Horne and a few more junior generals without armies, became more and more isolated.

Within the Cabinet, Baldwin, Austen's apparently stolid Financial Secretary of 1919, who had been promoted to be President of the Board of Trade when Horne became Chancellor in Chamberlain's place, became the focus of disapproval of the Prime Minister. Outside the Cabinet, however, there were a lot of key figures whose minds were moving in the same direction. These were the Chief Whip, the Chairman of the party and its Chief Agent. There were also Salisbury and Derby, the principal hereditary magnates. In addition there was Bonar Law, waiting somewhat uncertainly in the wings. By the autumn of 1921 his health had substantially if temporarily improved and his loyalty both to his former Coalition partner and to his successor as Conservative leader had been weakened by absence. He remained a loose cannon until the approach of the crucial meeting when he aligned himself firmly but not necessarily crucially (they would probably have won without him) with the Baldwin forces. As the session was ending the Conservatives junior ministers demanded a meeting at which they might express their discontent to their seniors. The meeting was conceded, but when it took place Chamberlain confined himself to stiffly telling them that it was unprecedented and irregular, while leaving it to the rougher tongue of Birkenhead to denounce them all for impertinence, stupidity and disloyalty. As an exercise in persuasive leadership it was catastrophic. Baldwin observed the scene with incredulous dismay, and then during his usual two-month summer holiday jerked himself towards open revolt.

This led on to the most famous of all the Carlton Club meetings – once again that oppressive location – on 19 October. Once again Austen was wooden. He might just have got away with the continuance of coalition if he had suggested that it should be accompanied by a change to a Prime Minister from the majority party, exactly as was to happen thirteen years later when MacDonald handed over to Baldwin. Lloyd George had indeed offered exactly this solution to Austen in the previous February, when he had declined, saying that it was much better for the country that Lloyd George should retain the first position. By the autumn he had somewhat shifted his position on this, not necessarily in his own favour, although it was difficult to see what other Conservative from within the government, unless it was Balfour (who was seventy-four), could possible take over. Baldwin, although he was to be in 10 Downing Street within seven months, would simply not have crossed anyone's mind at that stage.

Austen may have been caught in a psychological trap. He was not self-confident enough to believe that without bathos he could replace Lloyd George. But he was more than sufficiently status-conscious to dislike the thought of any other Conservative doing so either. As a result he tried to defend an unsustainable status quo, and did so with the lack of skill which contrasted horribly with the carefully crafted but apparently homespun brilliance with which Baldwin cajoled the meeting. Baldwin dealt very gently with Austen who was present but most damagingly, although not crudely, with Lloyd George who was not:

> [The Prime Minister] is a dynamic force, and it is from that very fact that our troubles, in my opinion, arise. A dynamic force is a very terrible thing; it may crush you but it is not necessarily right. It is owing to that dynamic force, and that remarkable personality, that the Liberal party, to which he formerly belonged, has been crushed to pieces; and it is my firm conviction that in time the same thing will happen to our party ... I would like to give you just one illustration to what I mean by the disintegrating influence of a dynamic force. Take Mr Chamberlain and myself. His services to the State are infinitely greater than anything I have been able to render, but we are both men who are giving all we can to the service of the State; we are both men who are, or try to be, activated by principle in our conduct: we are men who, I think, have exactly the same views on the political problems of the day; we are men who I believe – certainly on my side – have esteem and perhaps I may say affection for each other; but the result of this dynamic force is that we stand here today, he prepared to go into the wilderness if he should be compelled to forsake the Prime Minister, and I prepared to go into the wilderness if I should be

compelled to stay with him. If that is the effect of that tremendous personality on two men occupying the position that we do, and related to each other in the way that Mr Chamberlain and I are, the process must go on throughout the party.

It was quietly devastating and it produced devastating result. On the central political issue of the day and on a personal issue of confidence, the leader of the Conservative party, the party whose secret weapon was said (later) to be loyalty, was defeated in his own party meeting by more than two to one. There was no doubt about the message which Chamberlain had to convey to Lloyd George and Lloyd George had in turn to convey to the King. Lloyd George resigned that afternoon, and never held any office again in the remaining twenty-two and a half years of his life. He did however lead several political initiatives, and often persuaded himself that through some fresh twist of the political kaleidoscope they would lead him back to full power.

The effect on Austen Chamberlain was different. After 1922 he was not a contender for the premiership and was probably happier as a result. He nevertheless remained determined to defend his own perquisites and seniority and was profoundly offended when he thought that Baldwin failed to do this in 1923. The key date for this was Saturday, 26 May 1923, which was four days after Baldwin had been preferred over Curzon for the Prime Ministership. Although the long Chequers meeting between Baldwin and Austen (one and a half hours) passed off with mutual expressions of friendship it went in reality about as badly as it could. Austen expressed himself to Birkenhead as 'deeply wounded', and to his brother he wrote: 'But the discourtesy shown to me down to the last detail . . . was not expected and I profoundly resent it.'

On the substance of the interview he deeply resented both Baldwin's offer to him of the Washington embassy (shades of Margaret Thatcher's thoughts of it for Edward Heath in 1979) and the alternative suggestion that he might join the Cabinet 'in a few months'. In regard to the first, he responded that Baldwin must be unaware that it had been proposed to him in 1919, as had at differing times, the Viceroyalty and the Paris embassy, and that he had turned them all down. As to the latter suggestion, he was certainly not going to be like a delinquent boy put on probation.

Essentially he found it horribly difficult to reconcile himself to his inexperienced former Financial Secretary having vaulted into the top job. Being a basically generous man, he eventually and briefly established a tolerable working relationship with Baldwin. But this always stopped well short of affection and was certainly not advanced by that Saturday afternoon in the Buckinghamshire countryside, which was one of the first baptisms of political fire for Chequers, then very new in its Prime Ministerial role.

There were other attempts at Conservative reunion in the remaining months of that parliament but little was achieved before Baldwin plunged into the ill-judged election of October 1923. Austen was returned for West Birmingham, which had become almost a slum constituency, with a surprisingly secure majority. (It was Neville in the neighbouring constituency of Ladywood who had a close shave.) In the confused situation which followed and led to the first Labour government Austen had no very sage advice to offer. But reunion became easier in opposition. There were no jobs which had to be allocated and no hierarchy which had to be continued or changed. In mid-February, Austen, Balfour, Birkenhead and Robert Horne rejoined the shadow Cabinet. The reserved mood in which they did so was well summed up by Austen's description (to a sister) of a luncheon party of the four of them (plus wives) a day or two after their first reunited meeting: 'A.J.B. was at the top of his form. His description of our first shadow-cabinet sent us into convulsions of laughter and was more complimentary to his old colleagues than to his new ones. But that is now treason!' Austen himself was no master of mocking wit (as were at least two of the participants in that lunch), but despite his public pomposity he had a taste for private iconoclasm.

It was as well that his spirits were revived by occasions like this for he had been very low for much of 1923, in the autumn of which year he became sixty. And lowness increased his shyness, which in turn increased his pomposity. It was to this period that there belongs the story, maybe apocryphal because almost too good to be true, but certainly *ben trovato*, of his dinner at Polesden Lacey, Mrs Ronnie Greville's indulgent house in the Surrey hills. Displeased by the performance of her inebriated butler, Mrs Greville scribbled, 'You are very drunk; leave the room immediately' on a piece of paper and handed it to the miscreant servant, who mistily surveyed the room, decided without difficulty where the message would make most impact, and placed it first on a silver salver and then before Austen Chamberlain.

When the Labour government was driven into yet another autumn election in 1924 which gave a Conservative majority of over 200 and a secure prospect of a full-term government, Austen resumed office on much more favourable terms than he could have thought likely. He became Foreign Secretary, which under a Prime Minister at once insular and lazy, and with his own satiation with the Treasury, offered much the best prospect of an independent and rewarding field of action. He was not given very high precedence in the Cabinet list – only seventh, below both the Chancellor and the Home Secretary, but this was somewhat confusingly contradicted by Baldwin making him deputy leader (under himself) of the House of Commons. Furthermore three of those who had signed his 1922 protest against the Carlton Club decision entered the Cabinet with him, a fourth (Balfour) came in when Curzon died a few months later, and Churchill, unexpectedly elevated to the Exchequer, made a fifth and powerful ex-Coalition Cabinet companion.

The truth, however, was that 1921–2 loyalties were becoming tenuous by 1925, and that these dispositions were more important as a discharge of duty to the past than as a provision of allies for the future. To have got Birkenhead into a Baldwin Cabinet ('If Birkenhead stood alone I would not touch him with a barge-pole,' Baldwin had pronounced in 1923) was a remarkable feat of loyalty and determination. Chamberlain, as this outcome showed, was an ally of a staunchness rarely seen in politics, although it may be noted with a little irony that Birkenhead, once reinstated, was the Cabinet colleague of whom Baldwin's opinion rose most rapidly.

Perhaps in return, Austen had his nearest approach to a burst of pro-Baldwin feeling. He reluctantly admired the deft way in which the Prime Minister handled home policy matters in Cabinet. The reverse side of the coin to Baldwin's home policy skill was that he gave Chamberlain a remarkably free foreign policy hand. There has been no subsequent Prime Minister who, whatever the limitations of his knowledge, has not been captivated by the glamour of foreign affairs and international gatherings. Baldwin was genuinely immune to these temptations. Indeed, particularly at first and before Chamberlain had secured his own authority in the new Cabinet, he leant back too much. 'But *you* are Foreign Secretary . . .' was reputed to be his bland reply when Austen asked for his opinion on some international matter.

The 'Locarno' policy was the core of Austen's late life achievement. When he took over at the Foreign Office he inherited the proposed Geneva Protocol, negotiated between MacDonald and Edouard Herriot, the French Foreign Minister, which was intended to tighten up the Covenant of the League of Nations, to make all disputes compulsorily subject to arbitration, and to put upon all member countries, which however in practice meant Britain and France as the two leading powers, responsible for enforcing sanctions against any aggressor anywhere in the world. Internationalist opinion in Britain, from Lord Robert Cecil, who as Chancellor of the Duchy of Lancaster in the Cabinet was Austen's Foreign Office deputy, through Edward Grey to the Labour party, was strongly in favour of the ratification of the Protocol. Insular English nationalist opinion was not. And this was strongly represented in the Cabinet not only by such stage reactionaries as Joynson-Hicks, the Home Secretary, but also potentially by Birkenhead, the man who ought to have been most grateful to Austen. Austen himself was pro-League, pro-French, and wanted to be a Castlereagh, working within Europe for a balance of power satisfactory to British interests, rather than a Palmerston bombarding from off-shore.

Wisely for a minister with wide general experience coming to a new department of which he had no specialist knowledge, he immersed himself in briefing and reflection for two months before making pronouncements. Although his intelligence was in no way spectacular his shrewdness and his experience led him to seize the essential ingredient of a department success. He concentrated on a realistic policy objective on the central issue of the day – reconciling the French desire for security with the German desire for readmission to the comity of nations – and drove down this central axis with skill and determination.

He judged that he could not get through the ratification of the Protocol, which he thought was a 'bridge too far' for Britain's commitment and economic strength, and used a rather good analogy to defend his negativism. There was concern at the time about the safety of the structure of St Paul's Cathedral. Austen told the House of Commons that he had heard several recipes but that no one had suggested that the best method was to build another dome on top of the existing one. That, he argued, was what the Protocol would do. It was much better to secure the existing foundations.

This was quite a good Conservative argument, combining caution with traditional British dislike of theoretical constructions. But it left him with the need, if his foreign policy was not just to be a series of tactical improvisations, to provide some alternative design. This the Treaties of Locarno, which were for a time regarded as the biggest British diplomatic triumph of the inter-war years, were designed to do.

They were concluded in mid-October 1925, at a conference in that eponymous resort at the Swiss end of Lake Maggiore. The central treaty (there were other associated ones) was between France, Germany and

Belgium and provided for the maintenance of their existing frontiers, including a demilitarized Rhineland, and the settlement of any disputes between them to be by arbitration and without resort to force. This treaty was guaranteed by Britain and Italy. It thus gave Western Europe, on a regional basis, the benefit of the Geneva Protocol, which Chamberlain, partly on the advice of the Chiefs of Staff, had been unwilling to see applied more widely, even to Eastern Europe, despite the presence at Locarno of Polish and Czech delegations. This was one of the weaknesses of the Pact. As Lord D'Abernon, the British ambassador in Berlin, presciently protested, it made the Polish Corridor the danger spot of Europe. And Austen, somewhat presaging his brother's remark that Czechoslovakia was a 'far-away country of which we know little' as well as paraphrasing Wellington, wrote that the Corridor was 'not worth the bones of a single British grenadier'. Fourteen years later D'Abernon was shown to have been the wiser. But even three years before that the western part of the pact was blown up by Hitler sending troops into the Rhineland and neither France nor Britain taking any action.

Locarno therefore did not prove wide enough or strong enough to resist the aggressions of the 1930s. It was nonetheless a brave and constructive 1920s attempt to prevent the circumstances of these aggressions from arising. The constructive side of the Treaties was that they gave the moderate German Chancellor Stresemann something tangible to take home to Berlin and also assuaged French fears to the extent of making it possible to bring Germany into the League of Nations with the full agreement of Paris. A large part of the credit for this must go to Austen Chamberlain, and at the time he abundantly received it. He was greeted on his return with almost the triumphant adulation which Disraeli had received when he brought back 'peace with honour' from Berlin in 1878. Austen was not offered 'a dukedom or a marquisate', as Queen Victoria had then suggested, but he was awarded the Nobel Peace Prize for that year, and at home was given the signal honour of a supernumerary Garter (that is without waiting for a vacancy), which had not been bestowed since the Duke of Wellington, although Disraeli (and Salisbury as well) had received 'vacant Garters' at the time of the Congress of Berlin.

Austen hesitated a good deal as to what, if anything, he ought to accept. There was still the old bugbear about not putting himself in a grander rank than his father had occupied, to whom he continued, accurately in most ways, to refer to as a much greater man than himself. This and shortage of money made him clear that he should not become a peer, and he worried about the 'Sir Austen' which would be involved in being a 'Garter-commoner' (there was no other at the time, although Balfour had been one briefly on his way to his earldom). Perhaps he might become an OM instead. But an offer of this was not forthcoming (only Lloyd George, Balfour and Haldane among politicians had it), and so he settled for the KG.

He also enjoyed the shoals of congratulatory letters, getting honorary degrees from both Oxford and Cambridge, and a general sense of being *hors de catégorie* in the Cabinet, separate although equal in relation to the Prime Minister, and above the departmental mill. He shocked his brother by being too stratospherically preoccupied to attend the crucial 'General Strike' Cabinets of the following spring. In the Europe of the 1920s the British Foreign Secretary was still a grand figure, and Austen, following Curzon (but he had a more effective policy than did Curzon), was perhaps the last holder of the office to live up to and fully to enjoy the ceremonial aspects, not least the progress from London to Geneva via Paris, to which Harold Nicolson in *Some People* gave immortal expression.

Austen enjoyed it all, particularly the francophone atmosphere in which British foreign policy was then conducted. His instincts were excessively pro-French and anti-German. He was easily irritated by the struggling politicians of the Weimar Republic (although he could also speak their language fairly well if he chose) and excessively tolerant of the sometimes intolerable French. He nonetheless believed that he had an essential arbitral function to perform between the French and the Germans, and was no by means entirely deceiving himself in this.

Despite all these temptations to self-satisfaction, and despite his natural pleasure in wallowing in the warm bath of post-Locarno praise, Austen kept his head pretty well. At the height of the adulation he wrote to his sister Ida saying that 'the gilt may [soon] be off the gingerbread and my stock at discount again', and that maybe he would do best to retire on the crest of his wave. Maybe he would have, but this was much nearer to an idle thought than to a realistic intention. Within six months or so he had taken a nasty tumble over his mishandling of a French proposal to compensate the Poles for not giving them any worthwhile security guarantees by offering them a permanent seat on the Council of the League. This so upset their approximate population equivalents, Spain and Brazil, that they withdrew from the League. There was a general sense of mishandling and the repercussions marked the end of Austen's late-life honeymoon. As the government moved towards the

1929 general election Austen began to look and seem one of its oldest and tiredest members (even though Balfour could give him fifteen years). If Baldwin had himself had more energy he might have reshuffled or retired him. By 1928 Austen's Foreign Secretaryship was running down. But it had enjoyed its full hour of triumph.

The 1929 election was an even closer-run thing for Austen in West Birmingham than the 1924 one had been for Neville in Ladywood. He was down to a majority of forty-three. On his canvass returns he was fairly sure he was going to lose, and attributed the likelihood, rather attractively, to the appalling housing conditions and to his own detachment as Foreign Secretary (not that he had ever gone there much when in other offices or none) rather than to ingratitude. With the older generation who had known his father the Chamberlain name still invoked a loyalty which was absent among the younger voters. However, by a mixture of luck on his part and discretion on Neville's (who after his previous scraping home by seventy-seven in Ladywood had retreated to the safety of the bourgeois villas of Edgbaston) the rule that a Chamberlain was never defeated in Birmingham was (just) maintained.

Austen then had a miserable two and a quarter years in opposition. His personal circumstances were discouraging. The shortage of money was so acute that he decided he had to sell Twitt's Ghyll, despite its gardening facilities being both his main recreation and his principal pleasure, and wrote of the rupture in poignant terms: 'Twitt's Ghyll [the ludicrous name never seemed to cause him any embarrassment] was looking lovely on Sunday . . . I shall not go there again, for though the purchase is not completed, we have sold the place and I am so sad at parting from it that I think a visit does me more harm than good.' This left him with nothing of his own for weekends or more extended retreats other than the distinctly non-herbaceous surroundings of Morpeth Mansions, alongside Westminster Cathedral, to which he had moved in 1923 (although he acquired a better London house in Rutland Gardens in the spring of 1930), and no superfluity of desirable staying-away invitations either. Those that came were often from the dubious characters against whom the eminently upright and almost over-proper Chamberlain seemed to have no built-in defences of natural discrimination.

In this category, apart from and far worse than his choice of Birkenhead and Horne as his principal political allies, there was the ghastly Warden Chilcott. Chilcott indulged in every form of vulgar flamboyance as well as scandalously trying to get Indian princes to bribe him to exercise improper influence on their behalf with Birkenhead as Secretary of State. But the Chamberlains, Ivy as well as Austen, found him their favourite host, in Hampshire, on his yacht and for their principal yearly holiday in Corsica, until 1935 when some unspecified but apparently horrific behaviour on his part towards the Queen of Spain proved too much for them.*

Then there was Commander Oliver Locker-Lampson, MP for the Handsworth division of Birmingham and Austen's parliamentary private secretary from 1919. The Commander gave his recreation in *Who's Who* as 'refusing honours'. This would be a surprising entry in any event, but becomes the more so because of his role in Austen's row with Baldwin immediately after the 1929 election, which marked the return of their relations to the hostility and near contempt on Austen's part which had prevailed in 1922–4. Chamberlain pressed for a resignation honour (presumably a knighthood) for Locker-Lampson and bitterly resented it when it was refused on the ground of Lampson's general unpopularity and impropriety. And a decade and a half later I have a strong but imprecise young man's memory of Locker-Lampson improbably trying through my father, who was then Attlee's PPS, to get some favour, maybe the same, from the leader of the Labour party and crying in aid of the prejudices against him in the Conservative party.

In any event Austen (at the age of nearly sixty-six) began his post-Foreign Office life offended with his leader, poor and subject to bouts of gloom which amounted almost to clinical depressions. Nor did any political or more general developments pull in the other direction. Despite his seniority and his Locarno achievement he was not at that stage a popular figure in the Conservative party, either at Westminster or in the country. When attacks were made on the 'old gang' he was thought to epitomize it. In the first foreign affairs row of the new parliament, over the sacking of Lord Lloyd as high commissioner in Egypt, he was up to the eyes in collusive guilt, having been anxious, with the strong support of his officials, to do this well before his successor Arthur Henderson actually did it. He was nonetheless not very sympathetic towards Henderson. He greatly wanted J. H. Thomas, 'a much abler man', as his successor rather than Henderson, another example of his bad judgement of individuals.

---

* The Chilcott information comes from the introduction by Robert C. Self to the admirably edited collection of Chamberlain's letters to his sisters published jointly by the Royal Historical Society and the Cambridge University Press. Self attributes the Queen of Spain information to a 1992 interview with Austen's two surviving children.

Austen was also caught on a difficult edge because the salient feature of Conservative politics in 1929–31 was the attempt of the press lords (Rothermere and Beaverbrook) to destroy Baldwin's leadership by running 'Empire Free Trade' (that is, Imperial Preference) candidates against the official Conservatives in by-elections. This threatened to give Austen a fractured pelvis. He had had more than enough of Baldwin, but his dislike of press lords, dating back at least to 1918, was even stronger, particularly of Rothermere, for he could occasionally be half seduced by Beaverbrook. He was also naturally well disposed towards Empire Free Trade, with its echoes of his father, but repulsed by the mischievous and disloyal nature of the campaign. This left him with only two rafts to which to cling, the one unrealistic, the other unselfish and admirable.

The unrealistic one was that a future Conservative Prime Minister, whether it be Baldwin or a replacement, would again make him Foreign Secretary. The unselfish and admirable one was the way in which he transferred his ambitions from himself to his brother Neville, of whom he might so easily have been jealous. His Chamberlain hubris (it was curious that a family which originally owed its national impact to its onslaught on privilege should for two tight generations, but no more, have assumed an hereditary right to rule stronger than any Russell or Cecil or Cavendish) meant that, once he himself had been eliminated, it was essential that Neville should become leader of the Conservative party, and hence Prime Minister, at the earliest possible moment. This was despite the fact that Austen and Neville had few natural affinities, and from then forward quickly drifted apart.

Over eleven months in 1930–1 three of Austen's principal political associates – Balfour, Birkenhead and Worthington-Evans – all died. Balfour was the one figure apart from his father to whom he instinctively looked up and had done so for nearly forty years. This was in spite of Balfour's lukewarmness on Tariff Reform and other matters. It was, however, a lukewarmness which Austen, left to himself, would have instinctively shared. It was sad that Balfour, *au fond*, found Chamberlain 'a bore'. In Birkenhead Austen saw the gold beneath the dross, but they were allies not cronies. Worthington-Evans was a much lesser figure than either, but an old colleague and 'personally a very good fellow tho' a bit of a bounder in manner', which from someone who spent his holidays with Warden Chilcott was a severe criticism. Their going increased his seniority, his isolation and his melancholy.

In the run-up to the mistaken creation of the National government in August 1931, Austen, curiously uninformed until almost the last moment, inevitably supported Neville's enthusiasm rather than Baldwin's reluctance, although his own interests marched more with those of Baldwin and in favour of waiting for a return of a purely Conservative government, which would also have been much better for the balance of British politics in the 1930s.

Austen then had a last almost disastrous three months in office. The Cabinet of the National government was a schematic artifice of ten – four Conservatives, four Labour and two Liberals. From the Labour party it was difficult to find the four. Any Cabinet minister who defected with MacDonald got in automatically. Apart from the Prime Minister, they were Snowden as Chancellor of the Exchequer, Sankey as Lord Chancellor and Thomas as Lord Privy Seal. From the Liberal party, Lloyd George being laid low with a prostate operation, there were the leaders in each House of Parliament, who got departments more powerful than their political strength: Samuel as Home Secretary and Reading as Foreign Secretary. From the Conservatives the difficulty was to make the choice. Baldwin and Neville Chamberlain chose themselves, the former as Lord President, the latter as Minister of Health and Chancellor-in-waiting. Samuel Hoare as Secretary of State for India and Philip Cunliffe-Lister as President of the Board of Trade were also brought in, but not so much on grounds of individual merit or the pre-eminence of their offices as because they had been helpfully present during the August crisis. Austen Chamberlain was invited to be First Lord of the Admiralty *outside* the Cabinet. He much resented Reading, an older but less experienced man than himself, becoming Foreign Secretary.

He might have done better to refuse this resented offer but being Austen, so essentially 'in' rather than 'out', he sulkily accepted. Matters were made worse by Ivy Chamberlain being abroad for her health. Although said by Austen and others to be a highly supportive wife, she did make a habit of absence at crucial times. Their code of communication went wrong so that she wrote enthusiastically to congratulate him on becoming Foreign Secretary. Neville Chamberlain thought that his resultant embarrassment at having to explain to her his demotion had a lot to do with the depth of his resentment. As he wrote to his sister Ida at the end of the government's first week: 'I have allowed myself to be deeply humiliated, and as I see it, with no advantage to the Government or to the country. It is all very bitter to me . . .' And in the same week at a family dinner with Neville and their stepmother, Mrs Carnegie, the object of his old infatuation, he had shown even less restraint. According to Neville, 'Austen's lips trembled and tears came into his eyes and altogether he made us all very unhappy and uncomfortable.'

There was even worse to come. On 6 September he reported that the Admiralty ran itself and that there was 'only half an hour's work to help me pass the day'. On 15 September he received news that there was trouble in the Atlantic fleet at Invergordon over the pay cuts which had been ordered by the Cabinet and clumsily imposed by a weakened Board of Admiralty. The First Sea Lord was in hospital and the permanent secretary was away. It is difficult to avoid feeling that Austen might have been wiser to find more than half an hour's work a day. As it was, he consoled himself with noting that 'the men, tho' refusing duty, stood to attention unordered when the flag was hoisted each morning or when the Admiral's barge passed a ship'. This seemed much in accordance with Austen's own attitude at the time. In the event the Invergordon 'mutiny' blew itself out fairly quickly, aided by the First Lord getting some financial concessions from the Cabinet of which he was so resentfully not a member. He did not suffer much personal fallout, but it was not a splendid end to his thirty-six-year ministerial career.

The October election went better for him. Not only did his own majority soar to over 11,000 but Birmingham as a whole returned to a solid front of twelve Conservative members, something he had thought he would never see again. This did not do much for his own spirits however. He decided that his own ministerial career was over and before even leaving Birmingham after the election he wrote to Baldwin from the Midland Hotel (a lonely address of passage for a Chamberlain) to renounce any claim to office. As his career, indeed his whole life apart from a little gardening and his pleasure in sightseeing travel, had been so very much a matter of office, this was a heavy step for him to take. He said that he did it to make easier Neville's accession to the Chancellorship (where his brother did indeed quickly replace Snowden) and there was no doubt some truth in this. But he may also have had a shrewd suspicion that if he did not jump he would be pushed. Predictably his withdrawal produced a deep plunge into depression, lethargy and hypochondria.

His gloom was only temporarily lightened by Neville in February 1932 introducing the Import Duties Bill, which was regarded by the Chamberlain family as bringing his father's ship into harbour twenty-nine years after it had started on its voyage. But 1932 was a pretty dreadful year for Austen, made worse by the fact that, once he had ceased to count, Neville took scant notice of him. Already by late November 1931, Austen had written to his sister Hilda saying how much out of things he felt and how he would appreciate a weekly letter of Cabinet news from Neville, no doubt remembering the innumerable such bulletins he had provided for his stricken father a quarter of a century earlier. So far from getting one, he was, by the middle of 1932, lucky if he had a six-monthly social chat with his brother. No doubt preoccupation with the busiest department rather than conscious cruelty was the motive, but the effect added to Austen's general sense of rejection and uselessness. His life seemed to have outlasted its point. A few weeks after his sixty-ninth birthday he wrote: 'I'm tired and disgusted. I wish I were merely drunk.'

Then most unexpected and happily there came a pick-up which persisted for the last four years of his life. His financial circumstances began to ease. He acquired a few moderate quality directorships, of Martin's Bank and of a couple of electricity companies. He also became a paid chairman of the League of Nations Loans Committee when this was formed in June 1932. Perhaps more important from a morale point of view was his decision to try to emulate Lloyd George and Churchill by earning money from his pen and his tongue. He hardly approached their success. His planned lecture tour of America at £140 a talk was cancelled because the organizing agency collapsed, and his obituary of Briand for the *Sunday Times* or his gardening articles for the *Countryman* at £15 a thousand words were hardly major journalistic coups. But he proved to have a gentle writing facility, and his two books of reminiscence, *Politics from the Inside*, which was based on his pre-1914 letters to his stepmother (for his father's eyes), and *Down the Years*, memories and portraits, were modest successes. The latter went through seven impressions. These various sources of income stabilized his finances, but not to an extent which made it possible for him to accept the Wardenship of the Cinque Ports when MacDonald offered it to him in October 1933. Walmer Castle, which was its material perquisite, would have cost nearly £2,000 a year (at least £60,000 today) to maintain, and that he could not contemplate. This was a heavy wrench for he would have much enjoyed the amenity and the prestige of an historic residence on the battlements of England looking across the narrow seas towards the scene of his former triumphs and redolent of figures of the fame of Pitt, Wellington and Palmerston.

Still more important than any of these uplifts, however, was a sudden shift of parliamentary and newspaper fashion which set in during the spring of 1933. For nearly seven years since the turn of the tide from his Locarno triumph, he had been regarded as a pompous anachronism, rating himself more highly than did the cruel market in political reputations. When this discrepancy had shaken itself out, the market was more than ready for a turn and Austen found himself transformed from a fossil into an oracle. As recently as November 1932 he had been complaining that no one took any notice of his speeches, neither MPs to provide him with an audience nor *The Times* to report him properly or discuss his views seriously. Six months, and still more a year later, things were quite different. This transition coincided with Hitler coming to power in Germany, and as Austen was from the beginning very robustly critical of him (although a great deal less so of Mussolini) it was a happy coincidence. But it was essentially a coincidence rather than a question of cause and effect. He did not become *à la mode* because of his resolute criticism of Hitler. But his return to fashion meant that his criticism was listened to with more attention.

He regained his pleasure in attending the House, and felt a new sense of parliamentary purpose. He sat in the corner seat of the second bench below the gangway on the government side of the House, where his father had sat after his resignation in 1903, still in his top hat, and was probably the most influential private member on the overflowing government benches. His views, both on India, which was a central subject of Conversative dispute in those years, and on Hitler, were not very different from those of Churchill, but he managed to give an impression of much more constructive moderation. Churchill acted as the scourge of the government, but Austen as its conscience.

All this made it worthwhile for him to stand again at the 1935 general election, which in 1932 would have seemed pointless. Although his majority came down to nearly half of the inflated 1931 figure it was quite satisfactory, as it should have been with the Birmingham twelve all holding their seats. His constituency was melting rather than swinging; it had lost 10 per cent of its population since the previous election.

Immediately after the 1935 election Austen Chamberlain rode out to his last political joust which, with its strong flavour of anti-climax, satisfactorily (in the sense of completing a circle) epitomized both his strengths and his weaknesses. Following Mussolini's invasion of Abyssinia, the National government had fought the election on a policy of upholding the Covenant of the League of Nations and imposing sanctions on Italy. Three weeks after the election Samuel Hoare, the relatively new Foreign Secretary, went to Paris and concocted with Pierre Laval the Pact which bore their joint names and proposed giving half of Abyssinia to the aggressor. There was an outcry, and Baldwin described it as the worst situation in the House of Commons that he had ever known. Austen was the key figure. He was rumbling hard against the Pact, and could, it was thought, have brought the Prime Minister down.

Baldwin took two protective actions. He made Hoare resign and he saw Chamberlain and said, 'Austen, when Sam has gone I shall want to talk to you about the Foreign Office.' It was a brilliantly sprung trap, illustrative of Baldwin being, in spite of his homespun quality, a most formidable politician. If he had offered Austen £100,000 from the secret funds it would have been rejected with contumely, greatly though Austen could have done with the money. But the hint, even at the age of seventy-two, of a return to high public service, and in a department which aroused such nostalgia, made the saliva flow. The next day he called off his revolt. A day or two after that Baldwin saw him again and said that had it not been for his health and age, neither of which had greatly changed in the previous forty-eight hours, he would have offered him the vacancy, but as it was what did he think of Eden? And perhaps he would like to join as Minister without Portfolio. Austen, not for the first time, was deeply affronted by Baldwin.

After another ten days Austen wrote to his sister that Baldwin was 'self-centred, selfish and idle, yet one of the shrewdest politicians ... "Sly, devilishly sly!" would be my chapter heading [on him].' This final example of lack of determined follow-through, typical though it was, happily did not greatly damage Austen's new reputation. He continued to be respected for the remaining fifteen months of his life. In July 1936 he was entertained by the lobby correspondents, with a lot of MPs as guests, at a luncheon to mark the anniversary of his entry into the House of Commons in 1892. The cover on the menu showed how 'dear and refreshing to his father's heart' would have been his innings for forty-four not out. It was a happy tribute, but, probably unconsciously, it exposed his limitations as much as his achievements. He was always his father's vicar, but performing the conventional rituals out of habit and loyalty than with the fervour of proselytizing conviction.

Nor did the 'not out' last for long. He died in his South Kensington house on 16 March 1937, some say in his library taking a book out of a shelf, others a little less romatically that it was in his bathroom. He was seventy-three and a half, not a great age and after not exactly a spectacular career, but he had managed with dignity and decency to span the political world from Gladstone to Attlee more comprehensively than had anyone else.

H. H. ASQUITH

(as Chancellor)

ASQUITH WAS CHANCELLOR FOR two and a quarter years on his way to the Prime Ministership. Others before and since have had briefer terms: Ward Hunt (February–December 1868), Randolph Churchill, Ritchie, McKenna, Baldwin, Macmillan, Thorneycroft, Selwyn Lloyd, Macleod, but no one with the possible exception of Neville Chamberlain (who was by contrast a long-term Chancellor) was so assuredly on his way from No. 11 (which residence Asquith grandly never occupied) to No. 10 Downing Street.

He was not, however, leader of the House of Commons, which most Chancellors were in the thirty-seven years between the death of Palmerston and the retirement of Salisbury when four and a half out of the six Prime Ministers were peers (Disraeli, straddling both categories, provided the fraction). Asquith, in the ill-judged 'Relugas Compact' into which he had a few months before entered with Haldane and Edward Grey, had tried to create exactly this position – the others were more strenuous than he was himself – with Campbell-Bannerman being relegated to the Lords. But that somewhat walrus-like Liberal leader took his wife's advice of 'no surrender', showed himself to be firm as well as amiable, and the Liberal Imperialist plan to control the government (for such it was) fell away.

After this unpropitious beginning, Asquith and Campbell-Bannerman got along surprisingly well during their brief partnership. Short of allowing himself to look a cipher, the Prime Minister was willing to lean heavily upon Asquith. 'Send for the sledgehammer' was his frequent response to the prospect of a difficult debate in the House of Commons. And his use of this term for Asquith indicated that it was reliable force rather than flights of elegant eloquence that he expected from the Chancellor's oratory.

Asquith's reputation was at that stage very high. He was fifty-three years old. He was a 'new man', sprung from lower-middle-class origins, but he was a polished Balliol classical scholar, and had married (secondly) into the beau monde. He had been a very successful Home Secretary in the last previous Liberal government, ten years before. He was a high-earning barrister, although not quite high enough for the level of extravagance expected by his wife, the inimitable and irrepressible Margot Tennant. In the disputes over the South African War he had taken a position firmly on the right of the Liberal party which gave him a good deal of cross-party respect and support. But he had revived his credentials with the Liberal militants by his leading and on the whole winning role in the clash with Joseph Chamberlain in the Free Trade/ Tariff Reform joust, which had been the main spectacle in the previous two years of politics. He was universally regarded as possessing, in the words of the John Morley-drafted resolution for the Reform Club meeting which in 1908 was to endorse his accession to the premiership, 'strong sense in council, power in debate and consummate mastery of all the habit and practice of public business'.

Asquith introduced three budgets, the third a month after he had become Prime Minister. They were all highly competent and fiscally interesting, although achieving their results with the minimum of sound and fury. In this respect they were the reverse of his successor's 1909 performance. Lloyd George's 'people's budget' of that year was one of the political events of the century, but had less permanent impact on the fiscal future than did Asquith's 1907 budget or on social policy than its 1908 successor.

In 1906 Asquith complained excessively that he was circumscribed by the short time he had been in office and by the fact that the out-turn of the year which was closing had been largely determined by his predecessor (Austen Chamberlain). By 30 April, which was the date of his speech, he had been in office for more than four months, which, particularly as he was such a quick worker, was more than time enough to initiate policy. However he chose to play himself solidly in, which was his style, and did so with commanding impressiveness. Sir Edward Hamilton, the joint permanent secretary to the Treasury, whose general querulousness was then reinforced by his rapidly failing health, wrote in one of the last entries to his famous diary: 'Asquith made an excellent budget speech this afternoon. He never fumbled for a word or for a figure during the whole time he was on his legs. He spoke with such lucidity and fluency as if he had been making Budget speeches all his life.'

The inherited out-turn he had no reason to complain of for it was thoroughly favourable. Revenue exceeded estimate by about £1.5 million and expenditure fell below it by around £1 million. As a result (and with Austen Chamberlain's planned £1 million surplus) he had a realized surplus of £3.5 million. The only aspect of the revenue which was disappointing was the yield from alcohol, which showed a further decline of £600,000. This echoed the experience of Austen Chamberlain in the previous year, but Asquith did not join him in attributing the decline to the growth of railway excursions. He was more cautious about assuming a long-term trend even from the experience of six or seven years. But he did produce some remarkable figures of comparison between 1899–1900 and 1905–6. The consumption of wine was down by 30 per cent, that of foreign spirits (then mainly brandy) by nearly the same amount, home-produced spirits by about 15 per cent and beer by about 8 per cent. Asquith as Chancellor and even more as Prime Minister did his personal best to reverse this trend, and his scepticism about its permanence proved well founded, with buoyancy returning only too strongly in the war years after 1914.

In 1906 he used his surplus to take off the coal export tax which Hicks Beach had imposed at the end of the South African War and reduce from sixpence to fivepence the tea duty, that highly symbolic tax of the late nineteenth and early twentieth century. It was symbolic because on the one hand it limited the comfort of cottage homes, and on the other was the only way in which non-smoking teetotallers, just below the income tax limit, mostly Nonconformist and Liberal, were required to contribute to the financial sinews of the state. Both his concessions were popular, as they were intended to be, with Liberal voters. They were not however of any fiscal intellectual interest. They broke no new ground and offered no pointers to the future. Insofar as these qualities existed in Asquith's first budget – and with all his qualities he was never a great ground-breaker – they lay elsewhere. First he did two paradoxical things. He accepted that a level of *c.* £150 million of public expenditure (£147.8 million plus £9.9 million which went direct to local authorities in this budget) was about the right, or any rate the inevitable, level of public expenditure. On that realistic note he at last began to get a tight hold of it in a way which no Chancellor had done since Harcourt. The intervening three, two of whom had to live through the South African War or its immediate aftermath, had theoretically bemoaned the passing of the old £100 million ceiling while accepting constant further increases, some of them uncovenanted.

For the rest Asquith devoted a substantial part of his speech to debt management, including an issue which then aroused some degree of political passion, although that passion has long been all spent, which was that of specific borrowing on departmental votes and by way of terminal annuities, which were counted by some sleight of hand as outside the national debt, for various public projects, ranging from postal to naval and military works. Asquith abolished the separate arrangements, with strong Liberal support, but with protests from Balfour, who thought the change would militate against public investment. The total net reduction in public debt for which this budget provided was £9 million.

Asquith inherited an income tax of one shilling in the pound levied at a uniform rate above the low (£150 a year) exemption limit and with no distinction made between what he called 'precarious' (that is earned) incomes and 'permanent' (unearned) incomes. He regarded the continuance of the shilling (5 per cent) rate, without such differentiation, as unacceptable in peacetime, but he also stated that 'many experts' thought that graduation would be incompatible with the British method of collecting income tax at source. 'Many experts' meant that he had run up against strong Treasury and Inland Revenue opposition to a change. He accordingly sought to circumvent them by setting up a Select Committee under the chairmanship of Sir Charles Dilke, who as a great radical was assumed likely to be reliably in favour of change. That was as far as Asquith felt able to go in 1906.

The Dilke Committee reported quickly – by July indeed – but not unanimously, because Dilke who had become old, arid and rigid with disappointment (he had greatly hoped to be restored from his wilderness years and included in the Campbell-Bannerman government), would only countenance an entirely different scheme of property taxation, as practised in Prussia and Holland. The majority of the Committee however was very helpful for Asquith. They recommended not only the differentiation which he wanted but also a super-tax above £5,000 a year, which Lloyd George was to introduce in 1909. In 1907 Asquith made differentiation and a degree of progression the centrepiece of his budget. For earned income up to £2,000 (approximately £100,000 today) the rate of tax was reduced to ninepence. For all unearned income subject to tax and for earned income above £2,000 the shilling in the pound rate continued to apply. Although the form in which it was expressed changed, the taxation system retained this differentiation for nearly eighty years.

Mild graduation was also introduced into estate duty. Up to

£150,000 (£7.5 million today) no change was made. An estate of £1 million was to pay 10 per cent rather than 7.5 per cent, and an estate of £3 million or over was to pay 10 per cent on the first million and 15 per cent on the remainder. Thus on an estate of £4 million (£200 million today) £550,000 would be levied. It was bold progression when combined with the new income tax provisions, but it was hardly punitive.

The particular characteristic of Asquith budgets was that each one looked forward to the next. Thus in 1906 he was seeking ways of effecting the income tax differentiation of 1907. And in 1907 he was creating reserves for the beginning of old age pensions in 1908. He could therefore justifiably be regarded as a provident financier who set the budgetary agenda rather than allowing himself to be buffeted around by short-term winds. He used the 1907 budget to propound a mixture of party and non-partisan points. First he laid it down that the governing condition of his fiscal arrangements was that the government was a Free Trade government and that the overwhelming majority of the House of Commons had been elected on a clear Free Trade mandate. This was a good ploy for the Liberal back benchers. Second the demand for social reform was inexorable. But 'if we are to have social reform we must be ready to pay for it, and when I say we I mean the whole nation, the working and consuming classes as well as the wealthier class of direct tax-payers'. This, as good anti-'something for nothing' doctrine, enhanced his reputation as a Chancellor who did not go for easy options. Then he established a strong case for the prudence of Liberal finance. He planned for a record repayment of debt in 1907–8 and in the next year he was able to show that in the post-war Unionist triennium of 1903–5 £27.5 million had been redeemed whereas in the Liberal triennium of 1906–8 the aggregate redemption was £46.7 million. He had therefore established a platform of prudence from which to launch old age pensions, and underpinned it by announcing that he would not make the indirect taxation concessions which his surplus would normally have justified, but would keep the surplus in reserve for next year's bold thrust into the outer space of social security. To a greater extent than any Chancellor had done before, he established a budgetary continuum, breaking down the isolation of one year from another.

This gave legitimacy to his decision himself to introduce the budget of 1908. Superficially at least this was a surprising decision. He had become Prime Minister on 8 April and the budget was not until 7 May. Moreover Asquith, certainly at this stage in his career, was not much of a man for backward glances. His career was advancing too fast for that.

Furthermore it was Lloyd George who was thought of as the showman and Asquith who cultivated the throwaway gesture and the indifference to press and publicity. Yet he was clearly resolved that it should be he who would announce the first small instalment of social security. This took the shape of a pension of five shillings a week (8s 9d for a married couple) for those over the age of seventy whose total income did not exceed ten shillings a week, and who had not disqualified themselves by being criminals, lunatics or (within the previous year) paupers. Reserving the budget to himself was a reasonable precaution, although even with it nearly the whole of the credit for the early welfare state subsequently rubbed off on to Lloyd George.

Whether Asquith had any difficulty about superseding the new Chancellor is not clear from the exiguous official records of those days. In his budget speech Asquith recalled that there was a precedent at the time of Peel, although not since (there was to be another example when Robert Horne succeeded Austen Chamberlain in 1921), and added that both he and Lloyd George thought that it would be a matter 'not merely of personal but also of public convenience' that he should make the statement. Maybe they both did, but Lloyd George, not having then fully established his position as an independent statesman, would have found it difficult to resist a Prime Minister who had just given him such a major promotion.

The other surprising feature of the 1908 budget was that Asquith chose to use his surplus of £3.5 million for a major reduction in the sugar duty. This left a contingency reserve of only £240,000, which in fact proved marginally insufficient, so that the out-turn for the year was the first deficit since Ritchie's 1903 stewardship. This accompanying of old age pensions with the sugar reduction was, as some regarded it, a gilding of the working-class lily. The pensions proposals alone sent some people into a state of semi-dementia. Rosebery's description of them as 'so prodigal of expenditure as likely to undermine the whole fabric of the Empire' must surely stand as one of the great bombinations of the decade. It certainly marked the final disappearance of Rosebery's long receding mild radicalism and also the end of any residual political links between him and Asquith.

The addition of the sugar remission made this the only one of Asquith's three budgets which could be criticized for improvidence. And such criticism it duly received, not only from Austen Chamberlain, who was paid (not literally in those days) to do the job, but also from more independent figures such as St Aldwyn and Cromer in the Lords. The latter with only a little less hyperbole than Rosebery, said that the budget 'would be the ruin of the Free Trade cause'. It was not, although it might have been the ruin, or at any rate the substantial denting, of Asquith's reputation as, in his own words many years later, 'a respectable and conservative financier'. This raises the question of why he was so keen to deliver his posthumous budget, rather than letting the divide between orthodoxy and controversy fall more sharply between him and Lloyd George. But Asquith, like Gladstone before him and Attlee after him, was a statesman whose radicalism it was always easy to underestimate because of his liking for traditional habits of thought and life. What is even more certainly the case is that his overall reputation, for good or ill, must turn on his work as a Prime Minister rather than as Chancellor. This is much more true of him than of Gladstone, whose Chancellorships should and do make a major contribution to his place in history.

DAVID LLOYD GEORGE

LLOYD GEORGE, IN SHARP CONTRAST WITH Asquith, was far from being a short-term Chancellor. He stayed at the Treasury for seven years and eight budgets (the changing circumstances of 1914 called for two), which put him in a category of longevity with only Gladstone, Hicks Beach and Neville Chamberlain among Chancellors of the past 150 years. His first budget was also the most controversial, to some extent in fiscal content, incontestably in constitutional consequence, of any since the financial arrangement for the year were brought together in one (normally) spring statement during Peel's premiership. Yet it is Lloyd George as an extraordinary human phenomenon, which quality reached its apogee only during his premiership, rather than his financial management, innovative but sometimes slapdash although that was, which made the dazzling nature of his personality although on a narrower basis of interests and more opportunistic in style, worthy of comparison with Gladstone and Churchill. His opportunism perhaps brings Disraeli into the equation; otherwise there is no one else, at least from the beginning of the nineteeth century, who is on such a plane of personal magnetism.

This poses problems about how to fit Lloyd George into a book about Chancellors, somewhat accentuated by the fact that forty-four years ago I used much his most interesting budget as the foundation for a book about its consequences called *Mr Balfour's Poodle*. My recipe has been to follow a résumé of his budgets with an appraisal of his extraordinary personality, which, in spite of flaws of character and lacunae of intellect, put him well within the premier league of Prime Ministers. The shape of this essay is consequently different from that of most of the others.

What is certain, and paradoxical, is that the first (1909) and most memorable budget of one of the greatest orators ever to be Chancellor of the Exchequer, was singularly ill-delivered. It nonetheless marked a turning point in politics. Its enactment was the key to the financing of Liberal social reform without a retreat from Free Trade. To secure its defeat was equally crucial to the fiscal case for Tariff Reform, which had become central to the Conservative appeal. The stakes were consequently high, and the stuggle for them dominated the subsequent two and a quarter years of constitutional crisis.

One reason why the budget speech was a technical failure was that it was so long – four and a half hours, longer than any except one even of Gladstone's twelve budgetary effusions – and just beyond the limit of Lloyd George's tense vitality. He needed a half-hour adjournment in the middle. This spoilt the crescendo effect, which had been such a feature of Gladstone's major orations. It did nothing however to diminish the delayed-action impact of the budget's proposals.

What were the proposals of the most famous budget of the century which reduced the dukes in particular to a greater collective state of hysteria than even Home Rule for Ireland had previously been able to achieve? Not only were the sums modest, as was the case with all budgets of the early part of the century, but the proposals themselves were in one or two cases ineffective and as a whole hardly revolutionary. The Chancellor sought revenue of £164 million, as against the £151 million of the preceding year and the £148 million which he calculated that existing taxes would yield for 1909–10. And as the need for the £16 million of additional revenue arose from a combination of Dreadnoughts and old age pensions, the cost of which were likely to grow in the future, it was important that he should close the gap with taxes of which the yield would increase as time went by. His first proposal was for a reduction of £3 million in the sinking fund payment. That was routine for all Chancellors under pressure, and put him in the tradition of Harcourt, Goschen and Hicks Beach. Indeed the sinking fund seemed to exist almost in order to be reduced. Such reductions however had a good deal of sense in them, for the figure had been set at such a high level that it was liable to produce an excessively restrictive financial climate and to drive gilt-edged prices (because of a shortage of stock) through the roof.

Next he proposed to make death duties, and the associated legacy, succession and settled estate duties, bring in another £4 million in the current year, rising to £6.5 million in subsequent years. This involved increases of scale which at the upper end subjected estates of over £1 million to a total duty of approximately 25 per cent. The income tax was adjusted to raise another £3 million. On unearned income the rate went to 1s 2d in the pound or 6 per cent. On earned income it remained at the previous one shilling although those with incomes under £500 were positively advantaged with the introduction of a £10 children's allowance.

More important was the introduction of the super-tax, which the Asquith-instigated Dilke Committee had recommended. This was to be charged at sixpence in the pound (or 2.5 per cent) on the amount by which all income of £5,000 or more exceeded £3,000 (a curious provision which might have been expected to produce considerable marginal disincentive to those with £4,800–4,900 of income. Super-tax was estimated to yield £0.5 million in the current year and £2.3 million in the second and subsequent years. Of all Lloyd George's 1909 proposals this was much the most pregnant with social change. But this was not appreciated at the time, and it was well short of being the proposal which aroused the most controversy.

This distinction was reserved for the land taxes, of which there were three. The first provided for a 20 per cent tax on the unearned increment in land values, which was to be paid either when the land was sold or when it passed at death; the second provided for a capital tax of a halfpenny in the pound on the value of undeveloped land and minerals (these first two proposals were somewhat modified by concessions at the committee stage of the Finance Bill); and the third for a 10 per cent reversion duty on any benefit which came to a lessor at the end of a lease. These taxes were to bring in only £0.5 million in the current year, but an optimism which proved largely misplaced was expressed about future yields. Waves of violent opposition were also aroused. When Arthur Balfour denounced the budget as 'vindictive, inequitable, based on no principles, and injurious to the productive capacity of the country', the land taxes, partly because of fear of the unknown, were central to his vehemence. So they were to Sir Edward Carson's claim that the budget meant 'the beginning of the end of all rights of property', to Rosebery's 'farewell to Liberalism' view that it was 'inquisitorial, tyrannical and Socialistic', and to Lansdowne's conviction that it was 'a monument of reckless and improvident finance'. Rarely can a group of taxes have proved such a mouse out of a mountain. The hopes and the fears were alike misplaced. Eventually, as has been described in the essay on Austen Chamberlain, they died (with the exception of the mineral rights duty) of infirmity and irrelevance in the budget of 1920, the crowning irony being that this was under Lloyd George's own premiership.

Next, the taxation of the road-user became for the first time of moderate importance. For motor-car licences a graduated scale, varying from two to forty guineas according to horse-power, was introduced. (The higher rate was equivalent to nearly £2,000 today, a substantial disincentive to cluttering up the roads with limousines, which some people, such was the wealth of Edwardian England, seemed nonetheless to surmount.) Motor-bikes were to pay a flat rate of £1. In addition a tax of threepence a gallon was imposed on petrol, with a rebate for taxicabs and buses. The yield of this group of taxes was put at £0.75 million, which sum was to be paid into a Road Fund and not used for general expenditure. In the same way the proceeds of the mineral rights duty of a shilling in the pound on mining royalties and wayleaves were to be used to finance a Miners' Welfare Fund.

The last important group of 1909 taxes related to alcohol and tobacco. The liquor licence duties were to be rationalized and increased so as to bring in another £2.6 million. Spirits were to pay another 3s 9d per gallon, which would put the price of whisky up by approximately a halfpenny a glass, and the tobacco duty was raised by eightpence a pound. The combined yield of these two taxes was estimated at £3.5 million, which meant that, when the tax on licensed victuallers was included, the taxes on the drinking and smoking classes, who mostly overlapped, went up by £6.1 million, which was very close to the sum which the dying rich were required to contribute.

These, with a few other miscellaneous changes, were the proposals of the 'people's budget'. It was Lloyd George's own title for it, and he could claim with some justice that, despite his many subsequent streaks of opportunism, he was here true to his own cottage, temperance, Nonconformist background. As he put it in an early recording in which he sought to encapsulate his central budget message:

> I am one of the children of the people. I was brought up amongst them, and I know their trials and their troubles. I therefore determined in framing the budget to add nothing to the anxieties of their lives, but to do something to lighten the burdens they already bear with such patience and fortitude. No necessity of life will be dearer or more difficult to get as a result of the budget. On the other hand, out of the money raised by taxing superfluities, funds will be established to secure honourable sustenance for the deserving old, and to assist our great benefit societies in making adequate provisions for sickness and infirmity, and against the poverty which comes to the widows and orphans of those who fall in the battle of industry.

He also provided a new direction and momentum for the Liberal government, which had previously been dangerously becalmed by a combination of a sharp downswing in the trade cycle and inability to get much legislation through the Lords. The government's weakness *vis-à-vis* the Lords lay in its own unwillingness to face a general election on either licensing restriction or the relief of Nonconformist grievances in education, which issues excited the Liberal faithful more than they did the voters who had deserted the Conservatives in 1906. (After the budget, trade recovered strongly with a good upswing between 1910 and 1913: the budget probably had little to do with that, but at least nonsense was made of Balfour's claim that it would be 'injurious to the productive capacity of the country'.)

The budget and its rejection by the Lords opened up a new terrain of political battle which involved two general elections in a single year, and great bitterness both between parties and within the Conservative party, which was hopelessly divided on tactics (and maybe strategy too) and consumed Balfour's leadership in its internecine warfare. These events also effectively consumed what should have been Lloyd George's second budget in 1910. The Finance Bill of 1909 did not become law until 29 April 1910, exactly one year after the introduction of the budget upon which it was based. The next budget could hardly follow immediately, and when it eventually came, on 30 June, it was not a budget in the normal sense of the term, but more a statement of account, designed to bring the national finance for the two years of 1909–11, fundamentally sound with the strong revenue which went with the trade upswing, but inevitably distorted by the collection of some revenues being delayed by the Lords' rejection, into comprehensible balance. There were, unprecedentedly, no changes in taxation, which is what made it a budget which was not a budget.

If the 1910 budget was a phantom budget, the 1911 budget was almost equally shadowy. It was as though 1909 had exhausted the budgetary energy of even such a dynamic and sometimes flamboyant Chancellor as Lloyd George. Bernard Mallet, the chronicler of *British Budgets*, wrote of it as, of all Lloyd George's budgets, 'the one which attracted the least attention'. As all that it did was to adjust chocolate duties at a loss to the revenue of £45,000, to make a rather bigger concession in the licence duties (perhaps £0.5 million) and a small one in the stamp duty on marketable securities, and as also it was competing that spring and summer with the coronation of King George V and with a mounting Parliament Bill crisis, this was hardly surprising. It was as though, having shot the rapids of 1909, Lloyd George for several subsequent years, while devoting himself to a full participation in broader politics, had no desire to do more than keep the budgetary canoe upright with a minimum of deft strokes.

The 1912 budget was again a standstill budget but the fact that it was possible to carry for the forthcoming year the costs of the introduction of health and unemployment insurance, together with a continued increase in naval expenditure, without either a deficit or increased taxation, was presented, with a good deal of justification, as a triumph for the fiscal management of the past three years. An increase in expenditure from £148 million (the budget estimate for 1908–9) to £186 million (that for 1912–13) had been carried without infringing the Chancellor's 1909 rule of not increasing the burden or anxieties of 'the people', provided they did not smoke and drank no spirits. He had of course been greatly helped by the strong trade upswing, which he saw as continuing at least into 1913. That, although he was much more hesitant about claiming direct credit for it than would be a modern Chancellor, was at least no discredit to him. Revenue in almost all fields, except for the land taxes had proved satisfactorily buoyant and had produced for the financial year 1911–12 a surplus of £6.5 million, the largest ever then realized and a fine start for national insurance.

In these circumstances criticism of the budget was largely confined to technical peripheral issues, and the Chancellor of the Exchequer celebrated by agreeing five days later to buy a thousand shares in the American Marconi Company, which were offered to him by his friend Rufus Isaacs, then the Attorney-General, and the future Lord Chief Justice of England, Viceroy of India and Marquess of Reading. Out of this cloud, which truly justified the cliché of being no bigger than a man's hand, there grew the storm which engulfed Lloyd George (and Isaacs and the government Chief Whip the Master of Elibank, and also, most unfairly, lashed Herbert Samuel the Postmaster-General) for much of the session of 1912–13. Its force was greatly increased by the unwisdom of the first three in denying absolutely their involvement with the shares of the English Marconi Company (which had just been awarded a big Post Office contract) without mentioning their investment with the legally separate but cognate American company.

As a result the storm-battered Lloyd George who presented the budget for 1913 was of much lower repute and morale than the Chancellor who had presented that of 1912. Indeed, had he been serving under a Prime Minister less calmly tolerant and supportive than Asquith, his career might well have been wrecked by Marconi. This was one of the ironies of 1916, just as I believe that Sir Edward Heath has sometimes reflected wryly on the missed opportunity of his contemplated dismissal of his Education Secretary when in 1972 she was at the trough of her public esteem and earning the sobriquet of 'Mrs Thatcher, milk-snatcher'.

To add to Lloyd George's obstacles in the spring of 1913 he was presented with the most difficult budgetary situation since 1909. Naval expenditure continued inexorably to grow (apart from ships the bulk of the expenditure for the Rosyth dockyard fell to be met) as did social security costs. On existing revenue he was confronted with a need for an extra £7.5 million, which could have meant some nasty taxation increases and the undermining of his sedulously cultivated reputation for having provided in 1909 a comprehensive framework of taxation which would withstand all likely peacetime demands. So far from being oppressed by this and by his own troubles he handled the challenge with an insolent nerve reminiscent of Disraeli at his best. He produced a budget which might have been a joint product of a conjuror and a gambler. But the tricks worked and the gamble came off. Contained within this reaction is no doubt much of the explanation of why he went within three and a half years from being in the eyes of most Conservatives (and many others too) a soiled 'little Welsh attorney' to the most hopeful saviour of the nation. And it probably meant also that, even had Asquith been less protective, he would somehow have got up off the ground and weaved his way to rehabilitated success. As it was, he produced the equivalent of a spectacular swerving rugby run (despite the fact that they do not play the game in North Wales) and ended up not only with a brilliant try but also with an almost spotless shirt.

He juggled a good number of figures, did a more than usually convoluted raid on the sinking fund, took a highly optimistic view of revenue trends, eschewed any taxation increase and came out with the rabbit from a hat of a bare surplus of £185,000. Had the gamble not worked he would have added public improvidence to private duplicity among his sins, and even for him the combination might well have proved fatal. But those whom the gods wish to preserve they first make lucky. The £6 million automatic increase in revenue on which he rashly counted turned out to be £9.4 million.

This out-turn ought to have made the late spring and summer of the golden age before the deluge an easy fiscal time for the Chancellor.

On the contrary it was at once strenuous and tantalizing. With a sort of 'seven-year itch' (give or take a year or so) he decided that his sixth budget ought to break some new ground. His restless spirit could not live on 1909 innovations for ever. He decided on a major recasting of local government finance, involving both the transference of local taxation from premises to site values and a greater degree of central government support. In addition the rapacious beast of naval expenditure passed the point up to which it could be contained within existing fiscal parameters. The naval estimates (which had been well under £20 million when Lloyd George first entered Parliament) passed £50 million and the total budget for the first time exceeded £200 million.

That led Lloyd George, who had lost a New Year joust with Churchill on naval expenditure, to do a switch of fiscal approach. In 1913, under Marconi siege, he had been eager to display his dexterity by containing the various demands without tax increases. In 1914, this being no longer possible, he wished rather to ram down the throats of his colleagues the consequences of the Prime Minister's adjudication in favour of Churchill. He persuaded them that another £9.8 million of taxation was necessary. He put income tax up from 1s 2d to 1s 4d, he significantly increased both the total and the progression of super-tax as well as bringing its starting point down to £3,000 (perhaps £150,000 today) and increased death duties on estates above £60,000 so that those of £1 million and more paid 20 per cent instead of 15 per cent. It was a classical direct-taxation budget.

It was however far from being a classically well-presented budget. Lloyd George's oratory, although in some respects second only to that of Gladstone's, was not at its best in an expository role. Asquith summed it up well when he wrote: 'The Budget debate collapsed as L1.G landed the House in a well (or luckily) contrived morass of obscurity in which for the moment everyone was bogged.' More serious than the inadequacies of presentation, equally applicable to the budget of 1909, which had by any standards shown itself to be the most reverberating budget since Gladstone's of 1860, was the effective foundering of the local government provisions of the 1914 budget. There was solid opposition from about forty Liberal MPs and when the Speaker added to the trouble by ruling that the local government grants were outside the terms of the resolution on which the Finance Bill had been brought in, and ought to be reintroduced separately, it was decided that enough was enough and the local government clauses were withdrawn on 22 June. As if to draw attention to the hole that had been knocked in the budget the new maximum rates of income tax, which had been put up to 1s 4d in the spring were brought back to 1s 3d. The changes were presented as a postponement to 1915 rather than a final withdrawal, but as the Finance Bill, even with much of its load jettisoned, only got through four days before 4 August 1914, the postponement became *sine die*.

When European war suddenly loomed Lloyd George, still a little soiled by the Marconi affair and his prestige hardly enhanced by the confusions of the 1914 Finance Bill, found himself in an awkward position. Although he nominally remained hesitant until the evening of 2 August, his inner conviction from a few days earlier (in Frances Stevenson's firm appraisal) was that British intervention was inevitable and probably desirable. He made no attempt to organize a peace party within the Cabinet, for which there were a lot of potential recruits, not only Morley and Burns, who both resigned, but also Simon, Harcourt, Beauchamp, Hobhouse at least, who did not. Furthermore most of his natural supporters among Liberal MPs, in the press and in the country were pacifically inclined.

As he began his precipitate shashay, which was to take him within two months from the anti-militarist 'economist' who still bore traces of his Boer War past to the florid recruiting orator of his famous Queen's Hall speech, and within another two years to the proponent of victory at all costs, so he was lucky to have an early-August task which filled his mind and tested his powers without plunging him immediately into the world of generals, munitions and strategy. The approach to war created near panic in the City of London. Because it was then so pre-eminently the centre of world finance it had a peculiar vulnerability, and if it collapsed into chaos a large part of world trade was liable to collapse with it. By 1 August, in the words of a financial historian (E. V. Morgan) quoted by John Grigg,

> the foreign exchange market had practically ceased to operate, the Stock Exchange was closed, it was impossible to get bills accepted or discounted, the accepting houses and bill-brokers were both in grave danger of having to stop payment, the joint-stock banks were faced with perils of unknown magnitude, and the Bank of England itself found the demands upon it increasing alarmingly, and its reserves very near exhaustion.

Lloyd George knew very little about financial markets, but he had energy, nerve, an intuitive understanding, a gift for improvisation and an ability to make disparate people work together. As a result he was at his best in the days of money tension which followed. He handled with consummate skill the stolid but respected Governor of the Bank, Lord Cunliffe. He mobilized the assistance of two former Conservative Chancellors, Austen Chamberlain and St Aldwyn (Hicks Beach), thereby making it a bipartisan operation. And he even brought in his partner in speculation, transformed into Lord Reading and Lord Chief Justice, who, as someone who had once been 'hammered' on the Stock Exchange, contributed the unusual combination of being streetwise in the City as well as at the top of the judiciary. The Chancellor, who had previously done so much to agitate the City, for the first time succeeded in calming it, and did so in a way which brought him all-round kudos and gave him his first practical experience of working in a coalition framework.

Then, on 17 November 1914, Lloyd George brought in his first wartime budget. Although it was not quite such a damp squib as his second wartime budget on 4 May 1915, it was distinctly unheroic. He threw himself at different stages into a variety of warlike tasks, rallying Liberal Nonconformity to militarism, recruiting the armies, lubricating the flow of munitions, settling labour disputes, even attempting to reconcile post-Easter Rebellion Ireland to Britain. But his heart never seemed to be in financing the war, which was after all his central job during the nine and a half months after August 1914 for which he remained Chancellor of the Exchequer. He was confronted with a position in which expenditure under the pre-war heads was estimated to be rising to £207 million and addition expenditure due to the war was estimated at £328 million for the current year. Revenue had fallen back a little to £196 million from his May estimate. He therefore had to raise by taxation or borrowing an additional £340 million.

After a curious historical survey (curious because it underlined the inadequacy of his proposals) in which he pointed out that over the whole course of the Napoleonic Wars £391 million out of a total wartime expenditure of £831 million had been met by taxation, and that in the Crimean War the comparable figure had been £35 million out of £67 million, he announced extra taxation to the extent of £15 million, plus a sinking fund reduction of nearly £3 million, leaving £321 million to be met by borrowing. It was derisory. Even within living memory Hicks Beach had managed by taxation to contribute £27 million to the £170 million cost of the South African War.

The methods by which Lloyd George raised these derisory sums were first to double the rates of income tax and super-tax, but then greatly to mitigate the effect by saying that the increase would apply only for the last four months of the financial year, in other words the increase would be not 100 per cent but 33.3 per cent. With indirect taxes he operated on the traditional sources of revenue, but again somewhat half-heartedly. He put beer up by a halfpenny a pint, which was substantial but made complicated by a series of minor concessions to the brewers. Spirits he left untouched, on the ground of a possible reduction in yield. Wine he also avoided, partly on 'diplomatic grounds' (presumably relations with France), which did not sound like ruthless war finance. That left him with the problem of 'getting at the elusive teetotaller' who did not pay income tax. He put the tea duty up from fivepence to eightpence a pound. And that, plus some customary juggling with the sinking fund, was broadly it. The tax increases did however amount to £63 million in a full year, that is from 1915–16 onwards.

Lloyd George's next and last budgetary effort, on 4 May 1915, gives the impression that his interests were transcending such mundane and over-familiar problems as expenditure and revenue, and that with eight budgets he had done his duty to the Treasury. The political crisis which forced the formation of the first Coalition government (under Asquith) was on the edge of eruption, with the causal issues being the shell shortage and the Fisher/Churchill quarrel at the Admiralty. Political fluidity always excited Lord George, and his mind was already much on munitions production, which was the portfolio with which he emerged only two weeks after that budget day. One aspect of it impacted directly upon his budgetary approach. He had become almost obsessed with the damaging effect which high alcohol consumption, particularly in areas with big ordnance factories, most notably that around Carlisle, was having on war production. He had persuaded his Sovereign to undertake a commitment to total abstinence so long as the war lasted, thus giving it the much publicized title of the 'King's pledge'. Kitchener accepted the same obligation, and Haldane, the Lord Chancellor, had also been inveigled into participation, and was thought by the Prime Minister, who, needless to say, remained totally detached from such a gesture, to have suffered greatly in energy and good humour as a result.* It was part of Lloyd George's opportunistic skill that, having imposed the

* When Haldane was dropped from the government on 19 May, he considered himself no longer 'confined to soda-water', which provided some consolation for the loss of the Woolsack.

sacrifice upon others, he felt no obligation to accept it for himself, although it must be said that he was always a fairly light drinker.

All this made Lloyd George approach the 1915 budget more as a temperance than as a revenue crusader. He announced a scheme for state control (effective nationalization) of liquor outlets in specified areas together with swingeing increases in the taxation of alcohol. Spirit duties were to be doubled, wine duties quadrupled, the supplementary duty on sparkling wines sextupled (was Carlisle sinking in a sea of champagne?) and heavier beers further penalized. He seemed to pay no regard either to the consequences on yield (the specific object was to reduce consumption) or to the need for political support. The Conservatives were unforthcoming and the Irish Nationalists violently hostile. As a result there was no majority and the taxation proposals, although not the scheme for state control, had to be abandoned. It became a budget built around a huge hole, neither a responsible contribution to the needs of war finance nor a worthy coping-stone to his seven years of a most notable Chancellorship. It was time for a change. Reginald McKenna, his much more pedestrian successor, was left to arrange heavy borrowing during the summer and then to come to the first serious attempt at financing the war in September 1915.

Despite this wholly voluntary but somewhat inglorious end to his Chancellorship it took Lloyd George only another eighteen months to get from 11 Downing Street (of which he retained the use during his tenure of first the Ministry of Munitions and then, after Kitchener's death, the War Office) to the neighbouring house at No. 10. I do not attempt to repeat the well-worn story of the way in which, in early December 1916, Lloyd George supplanted Asquith. It has been crawled over, not only by me in my 1964 life of Asquith, but also by many other writers on the period. Rather, having discharged my intention to give an account of Lloyd George's budgets, I jump to his occupancy of the supreme office and attempt to place him in the gallery of fifty-one Prime Ministers.

There had been thirty-five Prime Ministers before Lloyd George and there have so far been fifteen after him. By all conventional standards he came from a less privileged background than any of those who preceded him although of the fifteen who have followed him the split has been even: seven from much more established backgrounds; seven from circumstances which were socially not very different from his own, although with geography nonetheless introducing a very considerable disparity in the circumstances of their early lives; and Mr Blair straddling the split.

It could therefore be argued that Lloyd George was a clear turning point in the social history of the premiership: before him it was a closed corporation; after him it was a career open to the talents. There are, however, a number of reasons why I hesitate about seeing him as quite such a stark hinge. First there is John Grigg's point, developed not so much in his first volume on *The Young Lloyd George* as in subsequent reflection and comparative studies, that Lloyd George's childhood, judged not by wealth or rank, but by attention and esteem, was in fact a comparatively privileged one, much more so, to take an example from among those who came before him, than was that of George Gordon, fourth Earl of Aberdeen, who was bundled about like a parcel after the early loss of both parents, and educated almost by accident. And, in relation to those who came after him, Grigg has specifically commented that Lloyd George in upbringing was 'definitely more privileged' than Churchill, who in contrast with the combination of cosseting and stimulus from mother and maternal uncle at Llanystumdwy was 'a neglected child, whose father was remote and unsympathetic even before a terrible illness warped his mind', and whose mother 'was feckless and self-centred'.

Second, it is easily possible to exaggerate the contrast between Lloyd George and what came before (particularly immediately before). The difference of background between Asquith and Lloyd George was educational much more than social. It was Asquith's cool Balliol classicism (and his later taste for fashionable life) and not his West Riding childhood which set him apart from Lloyd George. Also, in the previous generation, Joseph Chamberlain, never a Prime Minister but a man who for good or ill (and mostly for ill) had a greater influence upon the course of politics than all but a handful of those who were Prime Minister, had made a brasher 'new man's' entry on to the political scene than did Lloyd George. Chamberlain was rich (although largely self-made) to an extent that Lloyd George or Asquith never were, but in his radical phase in the 1870s and early 1880s his style aroused more antipathy than, except perhaps for the peak of the 1909 controversy, Lloyd George ever did. Perhaps the harsh materialistic tones of Birmingham were more clanging than the imaginative lilt of Gwynedd, but Gladstone's involuntary, almost chemical and to himself damaging antipathy to Chamberlain was far greater than any personal unacceptability which ever beset Lloyd George.

Of the seven post-Lloyd George Prime Ministers who have come from an unprivileged background, three of them (Wilson, Heath and

Mrs Thatcher, all of lower-middle-class and not working-class origin) were burnished with an Oxford education, which, as is suitable for that pluralistic university, affected them in widely differing ways. One of the other four (Bonar Law), although passing a fairly rugged childhood in Canada, was in late adolescence fully absorbed into the prosperous Glasgow commercial classes, so that throughout his political career he counted as rich rather than poor but, despite his remarkable knowledge of the works of Carlyle, was narrowly rather than widely educated.

This leaves those whose early advantages in life were markedly less than those of Lloyd George. They were Ramsay MacDonald, James Callaghan and John Major. MacDonald shared Lloyd George's advantage of being brought up in surroundings which made up in rural beauty for anything they lacked in affluence. In MacDonald's case there was also the romantic mystery of his anonymous father, with persistent rumours although no supporting fact beyond MacDonald's distinction of appearance, that it was some high-ranking laird. In terms of local esteem and intellectual stimulus at home, however, his lot was much worse than Lloyd George's.

The most youthfully deprived of all the fifty Prime Ministers, and therefore the one who achieved the greatest self-elevation, was James Callaghan. The back streets of Portsmouth – no natural beauty there – a widowed and poverty-stricken mother, no particular local esteem, no unusual home stimulus, no particular luck with school teachers, no opening to higher education, all these must surely count as handicaps as great as it is easily possible to imagine. The one early factor which worked in his favour was the opportunity for successful wartime service as a naval officer. Nor could it be said that John Major was markedly more fortunate, although there are certain ambiguities about his background and early life which make it more difficult to dogmatize.

So, although Lloyd George was in 1916 the least materially privileged man ever to have got to 10 Downing Street (but not by a wide margin over Asquith) the humbleness of his circumstances have since been exceeded at least three times. His uniqueness, for he was undoubtedly in some ways unmatched, lay in other directions. First, although here too there was an element of paradox as with the point brought out by John Grigg, he was more clearly influenced by the locality from which he sprang than has been any other politician manifestly of the first rank since the beginning of British parliamentary politics. But the paradox is that while he was indelibly identified in the public mind as a Welshman, and indeed as a rural North Welshman, he was very determined not to be bounded by his Welshness or, after his first decade in the House of Commons, by local issues. It was as a Welshman successfully bestriding the stage of United Kingdom politics and not as a Welsh politician, like many of his contemporaries who were MPs from the Principality, that he saw himself. And indeed it was not merely the national British stage, but the international stage as well, that he successfully commanded, particularly during the four peacetime years of his premiership. With the possible but not certain exception of Winston Churchill (partly because Churchill's fall came at what would have been for Lloyd George the equivalent of early 1919) there never has been a Prime Minister whose name and fame has been more familiar at international conferences.

Let us re-examine his claim to be more identified with a particular locality than any other British politician of the first rank. Once again the most obvious rival would be Joseph Chamberlain. It is curious that the Chamberlain comparison crops up so frequently, for their relations were mostly bitter and never close. Lloyd George was not in Parliament early enough to know Chamberlain in his radical phase, and did not therefore share the ambiguity of attitude – half affectionate memory, half current disapproval – which in the 1890s and early 1900s affected John Morley and William Harcourt. Lloyd George probably regarded Joe as an imperialist ogre and their main points of contact were Lloyd George's damaging attack on the defence contracts of Chamberlain family firms in 1900, the year of the first 'khaki election', and the vicious Birmingham Town Hall reception which met Lloyd George in 1901 in a city under Chamberlain's tight control.

Nor was there much subsequent mellowing, for just as Lloyd George did not arrive early enough to appreciate Chamberlain the radical, so Chamberlain's activity did not survive long enough (he had a severe stroke in 1906 and died in 1914) to encounter Lloyd George in his coalition phase, either its tentative expression in 1910 or its reality from 1916 onwards. When Balfour, F. E. Smith and Austen Chamberlain, the unyielding upholders of the Coalition in 1922, boxed the compass in their attitude to the 'little Welsh attorney', Joseph Chamberlain was dead. And his legatees split in an interesting but confusing way. His older son Austen became Lloyd George's most loyal Tory supporter. By sticking to him at the Carlton Club meeting in October 1922 Austen lost his second and last chance of the premiership. His younger son Neville, on the other hand, was a natural anti-Lloyd George man, distrusting his flashes of innovative genius as much as Lloyd George dismissed the pedestrian narrowness of the man who dominated first home policy and then foreign policy in the 1930s. Neville Chamberlain's two *bêtes noires* of the 1930s were Roosevelt and Lloyd George, not a bad couple to be in from the point of view of either.

Joseph Chamberlain had been born in London, but that was little more relevant than Lloyd George being born in Manchester, and that apart he was as completely identified with Birmingham as Lloyd George was with Caernarvonshire. He represented it in Parliament for thirty-eight years, which was an appreciably shorter spell than Lloyd George's fifty-two years as member for Caernarvon boroughs, but during these nearly four decades he exercised a greater surrounding political sway, running an almost independent duchy in this respect. Nonetheless, I would give the edge of particularity of local identification to Lloyd George. Birmigham has a much bigger population and more economic weight than Caenarvonshire. But it is at the same time more ordinary. It is flatter, both in topography and in vowels, and, in spite of the unmistakableness of the latter, it could not be said to have a separate language. Furthermore, although religio-educational issues played a considerable part in Chamberlain's early career, I do not think the intensity of the clash was quite the same as that which turned Lloyd George and Bishop Edwards of St Asaph into rival champions in the 1890s and over the turn of the century. Lloyd George brought more of an exotic excitement into London politics than did Chamberlain, to whom, even had the dates been right, it would have been impossible to imagine Maynard Keynes referring as 'this extraordinary figure of our time, this syren, this goat-footed bard, this half-human visitor to our age from the hag-ridden magic and enchanted woods of Celtic antiquity'.

The Chamberlain example, with a parliamentary career beginning fifteen years before Lloyd George's, does however bring out how rare in the nineteenth- and early-twentieth-century politics was the constituency faithfulness which both of them exhibited. There was no pre-1914 politician before Chamberlain (and after him Lloyd George) who remained in one constituency or even one region of the country throughout his career. Peel had twenty-five years as member of Tamworth, but he had previously sat for the Irish Midlands borough for Cashel, for Oxford University and for Westbury. Disraeli was latterly similarly settled in Buckinghamshire, but only after Maidstone and Shrewsbury; and Palmerston tried Newport (Isle of Wight), Cambridge University, Bletchingley and South Hampshire before remaining for thirty years in Tiverton. Gladstone, the great campaigner, was equally

peripatetic with Newark, Oxford University, South Lancashire, Greenwich and Midlothian.

Nor did the pattern change in the first half of this century. Balfour
took in Hertford, East Manchester and the City of London, Bonar Law
the Blackfriars division of Glasgow, Bootle, Dulwich and finally the
Central division of Glasgow. The early Labour party was at least equally
footloose. Ramsay MacDonald diluted his Lossiemouth childhood with
Leicester, Aberavon, Seaham Harbour and the Scottish Universities,
while Arthur Henderson flitted from Barnard Castle to Widnes to
Newcastle-on-Tyne to Burnley to Clay Cross. Later the fashion became
more monogamous. Cripps, Gaitskell, Eden, Butler, Wilson, Heath,
Callaghan, Mrs Thatcher, Major, Blair have all been one-constituency
men (or women). Lloyd George's more than half a century of constituency uxoriousness (perhaps making up for his more doubtful display of
the attribute in its literal sense) nonetheless remains unequalled, the
more striking because to some extent after 1922 and wholly after 1931
he was without the support of any national party machine.

Next there is Lloyd George's quality as an orator, which was
obviously a most important tool of his political rise and of his ability,
having risen, to achieve persuasive results. His oratorical skill and power
were not unique among Prime Ministers, but they were such as to put
him in a select category of four or five from about 1850 onwards. This
time limit arises out of the difficulty of imagining in any modern context
the quality of early-nineteenth-century let alone eighteenth-century
orators. Canning, of whom the most famous portrait (by Lawrence) with
his right hand raised is the epitome of declamation, although he is rather
curiously doing it to a completely empty House of Commons and from
the middle of the floor in front of the table and the mace, was clearly a
great phrase-maker. But I find it more difficult to have any idea what
Canning sounded like. The same thing applies even more strongly to
Walpole or Chatham or Pitt. Surrounding Canning there were a number
of Prime Ministers whom one does not associate with oratory. Liverpool's long reign is almost totally barren of examples of either eloquence
or aphoristic quality. Goderich, Canning's immediate successor, shone
neither in these nor in any other respects. The second Earl Grey (of the
Reform Bill) was probably less amiable although more memorable and
did have some approach to eloquence. Melbourne had a considerable
command of aphorism, but of so throwaway and downbeat a nature that
it is difficult to imagine him arousing sufficient enthusiasm in himself to
begin to convey it to an audience.

Then we come to Peel, who was pre-eminently a minister's Prime Minister in the sense that Mahler is a musician's composer or Poussin an artist's painter. The two later Prime Ministers who served under Peel, Aberdeen and Gladstone, as well as most of his other ministers, never escaped his influence. John Morley, who first joined a Gladstone government thirty-six years after Peel's death, said that he could still detect in Gladstone's methods of doing public business two unmistakable habits, even to the phrases, which Gladstone had learnt from Peel, and which Morley had first encountered when reading Peel's letters. Disraeli, who would dearly like to have served under Peel but was never given the chance, nonetheless founded his career on the vehemence of his attacks upon his leader.

There was no doubt therefore about the subjective importance of Peel. Objectively he was also central, in the way that was James Knox Polk, his near contemporary as American President. Polk was the President who, by the annexation of Texas, the acquisition of California and the settlement of the line of the Canadian frontier, ensured that the United States achieved its present shape as a massive continent-dominating quadrilateral. Peel was the Prime Minister who laid the foundations on which mid-Victorian prosperity was erected. The third quarter of the nineteenth century was a solid but, a few Palmerstonian flourishes apart, unflamboyant period of British history. In Britain the fourth quarter of the nineteenth century was very different from the third: from 1875 the competitive position *vis-à-vis* both the United States and Germany came to look distinctly shaky, while imperial commitment and, as the Gladstonians thought, tawdry adventurism grew apace.

There can be no doubt that Peel was a great Prime Minister. But was he a great orator, and did his oratory have enough in common with Lloyd George's to make any comparison meaningful? On the whole, although Gladstone once said that he had known only two perfect things in life, and that one was Peel's voice and the other Palmerston's handwriting, I do not think so. At least superficially Peel was a cold man. Daniel O'Connell's unforgettable remark that 'his smile was like the silver plate on a coffin' is curiously like Aneurin Bevan's calling Gaitskell 'a desiccated calculating machine'. First it was a gross exaggeration and second it is doubtful whether either Peel or Gaitskell were the true targets of the aphorisms. Bevan sometimes said he meant Attlee, and O'Connell that he meant someone whom I have forgotten. It is remarkable how many of the echoing catch-phrases of politics were either never said, or if they were said were applied to somebody other than the accredited targets.

A 'compare and contrast' exercise between the oratory of Lloyd George and Gladstone is however relatively feasible whereas one with Peel is about as meaningless as is one with Chatham, or with Cicero, or with Pericles. Gladstone, despite the length of his speeches, was the first modern political speaker. He was this because he was the first to speak outside the House of Commons in physical circumstances which would have been vaguely familiar to a twentieth-century politician. Gladstone was of course a great parliamentary orator. But unlike all his predecessors he was not exclusively a parliamentary orator. Palmerston, for instance, apart from an occasional appearance at a Lord Mayor's banquet and a hustings speech at Tiverton market place in 1859, hardly ever spoke outside the House of Commons. When the fifth Earl Spencer, a member of all the Gladstone Cabinets, was reluctantly persuaded to participate in the general election of 1885, it was the first time that he had made a political speech outside the Palace of Westminster since his own hustings for the 1857 general election.

From about 1860 owards Gladstone began to change all that. Nearly twenty years before the Midlothian campaign he began a series of provincial progresses which earned him the sobriquet of 'the people's William'. Thereafter the importance of the provincial meeting never looked back until it came to be challenged by television. The Grand Old Man imposed a new pattern at least as much on his opponents as on his supporters. Disraeli in 1872 went to the Manchester Free Trade Hall, and although his style, sardonic rather than uplifting, was immensely different, he allowed himself to be outclassed by Gladstone in neither length nor memorability of phrase. He spoke for three and a quarter hours but the main import was confined to three and a quarter minutes or less during which he compared ministers on the Treasury bench to 'a row of exhausted volcanoes, one of these marine landscapes not very uncommon on the coast of South America'. And fifteen years after that Salisbury was telling his son that 'power is more and more leaving Parliament and going to the platform'. In the next generation, he added, platform speaking would be an essential accomplishment for anyone who wished for major political influence. His son had therefore better cultivate that 'peculiarly difficult and unattractive form of public speaking'.

This accomplishment that son, by Cecilian standards the not very gifted fourth marquess, never achieved, but there were others who did, and the most notable of them, who almost exactly fitted the label of 'the next generation', was undoubtedly Lloyd George. He came into the House of Commons four years after Salisbury's letter and remained a member for a period of unbroken service exceeded only by Palmerston and a handful of obscure members, the even greater spans of both Gladstone and Churchill being interrupted by interludes without a seat. During much of the period Lloyd George was the most famous member of the House of Commons. Yet he was not in the fullest sense a great parliamentarian. He was not comparable in that respect with Peel, with Disraeli, with Gladstone, perhaps not even with Russell, or in this century with Asquith, Churchill or even the unesteemed Baldwin, who at his best could fit the mood of the House like a good pair of old shoes.

Lloyd George was a daring challenger in his young days; a Chancellor and then a Prime Minister of skill and resource in his middle period; and a still dazzling veteran performer in his third phase. (One of these performances I heard; I remember it much as I remember watching Rudolf Serkin play the piano at a New England summer festival a couple of years before his death – the movement of his fingers was even more memorable than the sound.) Yet Lloyd George's greatest feats of persuasive oratory were not performed in Parliament. His long and pedestrian delivery of the most famous budget of the century has already been described. As a war Prime Minister he never used Parliament as a national sounding board in the way that Churchill did in 1940–1, and if anything neglected it. Remarkably few of the anecdotes surrounding his gifts of persuasion relate to parliamentary occasions. Often it was great assemblies much bigger than the House of Commons that for one cause or another he was holding in the palm of his hand – from his radical denunciations of the peers to the working men of Limehouse in 1909, through his 1914 patriotic appeal to the Queen's Hall Nonconformists to cast their eyes up to the awesome pinnacle of sacrifice, or his 1915 address to the Welsh National Eisteddfod, when he explained why there was no need for nightingales west of the Severn, to the 1920s relaunch of Liberal radicalism as expressed in the Land Campaign and the Yellow Book.

Occasionally it was in more intimate fora than Parliament as in the famous (but maybe apocryphal) story of the Paris Peace Conference speech which he began under the impression that it was British policy to allocate a particular strip of territory to Roumania rather than to Hungary, and had already started to advocate this course with eloquence when Philip Kerr passed him a note saying that the agreed British line was in fact the reverse of this. His intervention may have taken a little longer as a result but this apart he was able to dismiss his initial arguments as merely a token of his understanding of the other side's case, and sweep to a triumphant conclusion in favour of the Hungarian claim.

Gladstone could never have done this. He would not have had the impudent flexibility. Disraeli might have brought it off, although in general Lloyd George's speaking quality is much more comparable with that of Gladstone. Indeed, among the Prime Ministerial orators, the one who came nearest to Gladstone must be Lloyd George. For the sheer grandeur of the physical force of his oratory, the edge must be given to Gladstone. But his companion in the ability both to inspire and to gain inspiration from an audience is Lloyd George. The third and rather forgotten figure nearly in this league was Ramsay MacDonald, who in his younger and middle phases could achieve a similar mystical melding with an audience. But MacDonald dealt in somewhat baser metal because his speaking was so unstructured that it was very difficult to report, which was not true of Lloyd George or of Gladstone, in spite of the rippling ranges of the latter's subordinate clauses. MacDonald's tendency even in middle life to windbaggery is well illustrated by the great failure of his 1924 election broadcast, the first occasion that the medium was used by party leaders. Baldwin did it quietly cosseted in a Savoy Hill studio. MacDonald chose to have relayed his uplifting rant at a Glasgow mass meeting, which was as much of a success in the hall as it was a disaster on the air.

The trio of Gladstone, Lloyd George and MacDonald nonetheless did have in common both a spontaneity in their relations with their audiences, which Churchill conspicuously lacked, together with a desire to sound the high notes, which were never attempted by Bonar Law or Neville Chamberlain or Attlee, for example. Moreover the three spontaneous orators were not text-bound. Gladstone devoted remarkably little time to the preparation of his vast speeches. Before a major House of Commons oration he would spend a relaxed first half of the day. Lloyd George, as was more natural, suffered from (or maybe one should more appropriately say profited from) a great build-up of nervous tension before one of his major performances, and no doubt experienced a balancing sense of euphoria afterwards.

The comparison must not be carried too far. There were great differences between Gladstone's speaking and Lloyd George's speaking.

Some of the advantages were on one side and some on the other. Gladstone, even leaving aside his classicism, had a far greater range of knowledge than Lloyd George. By the end of his life he had read 20,000 books, all of them listed in his compendious although cryptic diaries. Lloyd George was not a great reader. This gave Gladstone's eloquence a greater depth of language and width of allusion than Lloyd George, although Lloyd George's images, mostly culled from the Bible or Welsh folk tales or from pastoral memories of his boyhood, were sharper than those of Gladstone. The interplay between Lloyd George and his audiences was more intimate. The audience probably understood more perfectly and enjoyed more what he said to them. In Gladstone's case, although they flocked in great numbers, sat or stood riveted and went away feeling they had had a remarkable experience, a lot must have passed over their heads. It was the flash of his eye, the swoop of his cadences and the sense that he gave them of being part of a grand jury of the nation. But Lloyd George wrapped himself more closely around his audiences.

The more difficult question is about Lloyd George as an administrator and as the head of a Cabinet, whether compared with Gladstone or with any other of the front-rank Prime Ministers. Lloyd George in office, whether as President of the Board of Trade, Chancellor, Minister of Munitions, War Secretary or Prime Minister, undoubtedly showed exceptional qualities of energy and ingenuity. He was consistently buoyant and innovative. His role in the formulation of the insurance legislation of 1912 is a fine example of ministerial leadership. He used the brains and knowledge of others a great deal – notably Charles Masterman as a political aide and W. J. Braithwaite as a civil service one – but he gave them a sense of direction and inspiration as well as the feeling that he had the political clout to make sure that their work would not be wasted. And he could also be cool and neat in a defensive role, as with his already cited handling of the threat of financial panic in the first weeks of the 1914 War.

On the other hand, there were severe critics of his ministerial performance who were not just being politically partisan. R. B. Haldane, Secretary of State for War at the time, later Lord Chancellor, wrote that there were large parts of the 1909 budget which Lloyd George never understood. And Asquith, a criticism which is interesting because it is surprising, thought that Lloyd George lacked political courage. 'Ll.G. kept at Walton Heath by one of those psychological chills which always precede his budgets when he does not feel altogether sure of his

A late 1890s Birmingham equivalent of a Goya 1790s Spanish royal family group:
Neville Chamberlain, Austen Chamberlain, Joseph Chamberlain, and in front,
Beatrice Chamberlain, the eldest daughter, and Mary Endicott, the third Mrs Joseph
Chamberlain, who was younger than Austen.

A good but not quite perfect attempt at a copy: father and son at Westminster,
probably 1897, for the setting is exactly the same as the firmly dated picture of
Ritchie. Did a photographer do a round-up of all members of Salisbury's third
government? Joseph Chamberlain was then Colonial Secretary and Austen
Civil Lord of the Admiralty.

Austen Chamberlain, allegedly relaxing at Twitts Ghyll, his unfortunately named Sussex house, *c.* 1919.

Austin Chamberlain as Foreign Secretary in 1926, with Countess Greffuhle, the daughter-in-law of one of Proust's models for Oriane de Guermantes. Messieurs Briand, Doumer, Sarraut and others are a powerful supporting cast.

The MP and the Washerwomen: West Birmingham, October 1931.

Right: Asquith the young
Home Secretary, drawn
shortly after his second
marriage by Violet
Granby, later Duchess
of Rutland and the mother
of Diana Cooper.

Below: The Asquith family
invade Ireland: a Dublin
group from the 1912 visit.
Front row: Lady Verney,
H. H. A., Margot, Augustine
Birrell, Violet Asquith (later
Bonham Carter). Back row:
Sir H. Verney, Arthur
Asquith, Master of Elibank
(Chief Whip), Elizabeth
Asquith (later Bibesco),
Cyril Asquith, Maurice
Bonham Carter.

Lloyd George's last act of subservience: he visits Asquith at The Wharf, Sutton Courtenay, in May 1916.

Clockwise:

A young Lloyd George with many conquests still to make.

The Chancellor on the way to the House of Commons, flanked by the Financial and Parliamentary Secretaries to the Treasury, Edwin Montagu and Percy Illingworth, the latter also Chief Whip.

The Welsh wizard encamped for a charm offensive. Dame Margaret looks more a conscript than an enthusiast. North Wales, 1915.

The Coalition at work: Lloyd George convinces Lord Derby.

McKenna addresses his constituents – and produces varying reactions.

Reginald McKenna as an eagerly beavering MP, *c.* 1905.

McKenna by James Gunn: an appropriate portrait for a bank chairman's parlour.

ground,' he wrote to Venetia Stanley in 1912. This can of course be dismissed as having no more objective reality than Sir Edward Heath on Lady Thatcher or Lady Thatcher on Mr Major. ('Former Prime Ministers are like untethered rafts drifting around harbours – a menace to shipping,' as Gladstone said of Peel after 1846.)

But this explanation is too easy. In the first place Asquith's letter was written a good four years before he was put into the uncharitable frame of mind with which even the most admirable of men and women are wont to regard the phoenixes which arise from their own ashes. And second, until 1915 at any rate, Asquith was by no means ill disposed towards Lloyd George, and gave his notable support at the time both of his 1909 budget and of his Marconi troubles of 1913. There is a more plausible explanation than either crude prejudice on Asquith's part or full justification. It is this. Asquith, in spite of his fine classicism, his social sophistication and his romantic yearnings, had a good deal of unimaginative Yorkshire phlegmatism about him. In spite of his thirty-two years as member for East Fife (which in any event was one of the least Celtic parts of Scotland), he was always bad at understanding Celts, and particularly Welsh Celts. He thus falsely interpreted Lloyd George's highly strung nervousness before a battle or a speech. This is perfectly compatible with the highest form of courage. It comprises the imagination to feel fear but the ability to go on in spite of it. Asquithian though I am, I therefore almost wholly reject his views here.

The more legitimate criticism of Lloyd George is that he lacked an overall philosophical framework, which could have given more cohesive direction to his several brilliant phases. No one should expect total consistency from even the most distinguished men of government. Great swerving runs are permissible and even necessary. But they ought to be in broadly the same direction. Equally true is that statesmen of the highest eminence have moved great distances across the political spectrum. Gladstone again is the outstanding example. Yet it was a fairly steady evolution in one direction. Lloyd George's phases were more zig-zags than curves. His eruption on to the national scene, followed by nine years as a radical, innovating and more than usually partisan minister, can perhaps be regarded as following naturally one from the other. But then 'the man who won the war', after nearly resigning from the Cabinet over not supporting its beginning, marked a distinct switch of direction, as did even more his performance as head of the peacetime Coalition.

Then in the late 1920s he reasserted his innovating, optimistic, 'it can be done' radicalism with the Land Campaign, his collaboration with Maynard Keynes (that was a reversal of alliances if ever there was one in view of Keynes's devastation of Lloyd George in the *Economic Consequences of the Peace*), the Liberal Yellow Book and 'We Can Conquer Unemployment'. And then there was the last, very unpredictable, very uneven phase from about 1935 onwards: rather taken in by Hitler when he visited him at Berchtesgaden in 1936, but anti-Munich, mainly perhaps because of his dislike of Neville Chamberlain, and during the second war a very old man, but in the eyes of some a potential advocate of a negotiated peace, and maybe even a British Pétain. As a result the single-image imprint is less clear than with Peel or Disraeli or Gladstone or Churchill. These are the men with whom he must be compared. And none of them exceeded the brilliance or the turn of speed exhibited in each of his separate phases.

REGINALD McKENNA

McKENNA IS THE MYSTERY CHANCELLOR. HE was competent, successful and sought after, yet curiously insubstantial. This should make him an intriguing puzzle, but I fear that at the centre of the mystery there lies more of a vacuum than an enigma. He has almost the unreality of a man literally made out of straw (although he never lacked courage), as is illustrated by the photograph of him addressing a meeting, of which the most striking and almost frightening feature is his detachment from the wildly varying reactions which his words provoke upon the features of his principal supporters.

His *insaisissable* quality for me is the more surprising because, although I never saw him, my life almost touched his at a number of points. He sat in Parliament for twenty-three years for the constituency in which I (born two years after his defeat there) was brought up, and which my father, after one intervening successor, subsequently represented. He learnt his early politics at the feet of Sir Charles Dilke, to writing a biography of whom I devoted much of my late thirties, and then in the plenitude of his political success he was one of the three or four closest political friends of his Prime Minister, Asquith, to whom I devoted the same attention in my early forties. Furthermore McKenna held the two great offices of state, Home Secretary and Chancellor, which also constituted my main governmental experience. Yet he has no more solidity for me than the powdered wings of a butterfly. But the metaphor is not altogether apt, for McKenna was never crushed. He was always offered some rewarding new job, culminating when the collapse of Asquithian politics appeared to have left him beached, with twenty-four years as chairman of the Midland Bank. Even during this last period he was twice offered a return to the Chancellorship in a Conservative government. He was tempted but made rather stupid conditions and allowed the offers to lapse.

This is room for explanation here, as about why, despite his high offices and his quarter of a century as an eminently lordship-worthy senior banker, he was never offered a peerage, and also about his somewhat ambiguous family background. It is a pity that he has not been better served biographically. He wrote nothing himself and there is only one book about him, a medium-sized life published in 1945 by his nephew. As his entry in the *Dictionary of National Biography* is also from the same source, there is no alternative shaft of knowledge provided there. This nephew, Stephen McKenna, was a prolific and successful novelist, with nearly fifty books to his credit. His biographical method is argumentative, imaginative and unsequential. He constructs interpretations of what he thinks went on in the minds of his subject and of his principal interlocutors. He does it quite well with much more than a novelist's knowledge of the events and issues of the period, but for providing a factual matrix this method leaves a good deal to be desired. Stephen McKenna's book was also weak on his uncle's provenance (surely a nepotic biography should have managed that) and on his wife, as well as lacking both photographs and an index.

McKenna's father was a Southern Irishman (although born in mid-Atlantic) who had a family connection with Daniel O'Connell, and for whom a London post in the Inland Revenue had been procured by 'the Liberator'. He settled in England in the second year of Queen Victoria's reign, and fairly quickly sloughed off both his Irishness and his Catholicism, while acquiring a French-educated wife and by 1863, when Reginald, the youngest, was born, eight children. O'Connell's nomination did not do much more than get him out of Ireland, for it is difficult to imagine an occupation to which William Columban McKenna was less suited than that of a tax-collecting clerk. He was an adventurer and a speculator. He appears to have displayed full Gladstonian spirit by enlisting as a volunteer to assist the Bulgarian resistance to the Turkish atrocities of 1876. That was a decade after he had lost heavily in the Overend and Gurney financial crash of 1866.

Mrs McKenna's French education had meanwhile become of considerable use to her, for during her middle years she lived much in Brittany, first for her health and then for her pocket, and again in France during much of her eighteen years of widowhood after her husband's death in 1887. She died in the Hôtel Terminus at Mâcon in December 1905, within days of her youngest child first becoming a minister. He too had begun with a francophone education, for until the age of eleven the only schools that he knew were in St Malo, which at least had the advantage of being far from the ravages of the Franco-Prussian War and the Commune. Then, for no very clear reason, he was sent for three years to a school at Ebersdorf near Coburg in the middle of Germany. During these periods his father assisted by Reginald's two elder brothers was trying to restore the family fortune in London. To some extent they were successful. One brother had a very sure financial touch until he died young, and from the late 1870s onwards, in no way hindered by the death of the father, there was an aura of thoroughly adequate London commercial money around the family. At the age of fourteen Reginald McKenna was allowed back for four years at King's College School, London, then in the Strand, from where he gained a mathematics scholarship to Trinity Hall. That rather hidden Cambridge college had long been famous for lawyers, and Leslie Stephen had made it so for rowing too. McKenna fitted in to both aspects of the college's traditions, and, despite his somewhat spindly form, determinedly got himself not merely into the Trinity Hall but into the University boat. Moreover Cambridge that year (1887) won the Boat Race.

Charles Dilke had preceded him by twenty years at Trinity Hall and had been an equally keen oar, although not a blue. Out of this community of *alma mater* and of sporting tastes (there is not the slightest evidence that McKenna shared Dilke's more notorious other tastes) there no doubt arose Dilke's patronage of McKenna and McKenna's political apprenticeship to Dilke. But a perhaps equally sustaining factor was the belief of both of them that the best way to illuminate a subject was to bury it in facts and figures and to give it a slab of blue books for a tombstone. This aspect of both their characters was vividly illustrated by a cartoon *c.* 1900 showing McKenna as Crusoe Dilke's Man Friday with his duties being essentially those of bearing statistical publications behind his master. Dilke, disgraced and losing his Chelsea seat in 1886, got back into the House of Commons in 1892 for the Forest of Dean. He was a great hero of the radical miners of that small coalfield, and his influence may well have spread across the twenty-five miles of agricultural land over the Wye and the Usk Valleys to arouse support for McKenna in the easternmost of the South Wales coal valleys which was the core of the North Monmouthshire constituency. Here McKenna was adopted to fight a by-election just prior to the general election of the summer of 1895. If so it was a great bonus for McKenna, for it provided him with a safe Liberal seat until the political map changed in 1918, although he was far from being the most natural spokesman of the miners, tinplate workers and Nonconformist leaders of Pontypool and Blaenavon.

This election effectively stultified McKenna's brief barrister's career which had followed after Trinity Hall. He earned adequately, but he secured no memorable forensic triumphs. Although he did not become a minister until the age of forty-two, he never took silk. Once an MP he largely concentrated upon the House of Commons. He took Dilke's typically 'strength through work' advice that any man who stuck to his parliamentary last day after day and night after night for ten years should find himself on the Treasury bench at the end. He specialized in the procedural tripping up of ministers. When Austen Chamberlain's budget got into trouble on an attempted discrimination between stripped and unstripped tobacco it was he who exploited the technical gap. He became a parliamentary terrier, skilfully and energetically scoring minor triumphs but exhibiting no great powers of perspective.

He was lucky to do as well as he did when the first Liberal government for ten and a half years was formed in December 1905. He became Financial Secretary to the Treasury, the sole junior minister under the Chancellor in those heroic days, and thus found himself not only in the post which was commonly regarded as the threshold of the Cabinet, but also in partnership with Asquith, manifestly the coming man and with whom his relations were to be peculiarly important. Prior to this 1905 association there had been no particular affinity or connection between McKenna and Asquith.

Asquith however quickly developed a respect and regard for McKenna's cool competence. Their partnership did not last long, for after thirteen months McKenna received from Campbell-Bannerman the first Cabinet promotion of the government and became President of the Board of Education, when Augustine Birrell, a great wit but disastrous minister, became Chief Secretary for Ireland in place of James Bryce who went to Washington as ambassador 'to teach the Senators [constitutional] wisdom'. When, another fifteen months later, Asquith formed his own government, McKenna received another quick step and became First Lord of the Admiralty.

In the same spring of 1908 he further fortified his position with Asquith by unexpectedly getting married (he was forty-five and appeared a confirmed bachelor) to a very young and rather pretty woman who fitted perfectly into the Asquith social circle. Pamela Jekyll, born in 1887, was the daughter of Sir Herbert Jekyll who had built himself a famous Lutyens-designed house at Munstead in Surrey. She was the niece on her father's side of the great gardener, Gertrude Jekyll. More relevantly, she was the niece on her mother's side of Lady (Frances) Horner of Mells Park, near Frome, who had been a close confidante of

Asquith's, particularly after the death of his first wife in 1891, and whose daughter Katherine had married the nonpareil Raymond Asquith in 1907.

There is no doubt that Pamela McKenna, whose company Asquith enjoyed and with whom he had an easy mildly flirtatious relationship, greatly enhanced the status of the otherwise tightly buttoned and over-diligent McKenna at the Downing Street court. She made first Admiralty House and then, after 1911, Smith Square, where Lutyens had been employed to build another house,* one of Asquith's two favourite escapes for small informal dinner parties leading into the inevitable games of bridge to which so many otherwise intelligent people of the period were addicted. Asquith certainly was, although he played indifferently. McKenna, on the other hand, was said to be one of the best players in London, as well as being chess champion of the House of Commons. Perhaps he kept his bridge form below its natural level when he was with the Prime Minister.

Was McKenna not only a favoured companion of Asquith, but also, as his nephew/biographer half assumes, although mingling this bland judgement with occasional shafts of sharp criticism, someone sufficiently in Asquith's mould that he might, had the Liberal party not foundered, have naturally succeeded him in its leadership, or alternatively, had he accepted the offer to return to the Treasury in the Bonar Law or the first Baldwin governments, have succeeded to the premiership of a predominantly Conservative government and led the way out of Europe's financial crisis, a sort of cis-Atlantic Franklin Roosevelt?

These are ludicrous propositions. Asquith and McKenna had in common that they were both cool and quick administrators with an unusual ability to cut their way quickly to the heart of a problem, and to express themselves succinctly. Asquith recognized these qualities in McKenna by over-generously placing him (in early 1915) third in a Cabinet order of merit, below Grey and Crewe but above Lloyd George, Churchill and Haldane. 'Merit' in the context inevitably included a strong mark for not being a nuisance to the Prime Minister, although that this was by no means the exclusive criterion was made clear by both the future war heroes being given positions only just behind the neat McKenna and well above the ruck of the Cabinet.

* Munstead and Lutyens seem to have gone to McKenna's head, and not merely temporarily, for he also used him to rebuild Mells Park after it was destroyed by fire during the 1914 War and to design Sussex houses for each of his sons.

Beyond this cool efficiency and dislike of inflated rhetoric, however, there was little in common between McKenna and Asquith. Even when they cut their way to the heart of a problem they did it in different ways, Asquith taking in the surrounding landscape, while McKenna kept his head down and his eyes exclusively on the equation that he was trying to solve. Asquith always tried to argue towards a solution, whereas McKenna was much attracted by an impasse. Asquith was almost too good at keeping a Cabinet together, whereas McKenna was a natural splitter. In sum, Asquith was a statesman, whereas McKenna was a self-righteous accountant. And as a by-product Asquith had much wider interests and much more tolerant judgement of individuals (McKenna, for instance, could see nothing of virtue in Lloyd George, whereas Asquith, although ultimately his victim, could see a great deal). And, to round it off, McKenna was a prig, which Asquith most certainly was not.

Nonetheless his career greatly prospered under Asquith. At the Admiralty he got on too well with the admirals. In his first estimates season he fought a great Cabinet battle, supported only by Sir Edward Grey, for the laying down of six Dreadnoughts, as the new class of capital ships were onomatopoeically called. This put him into violent conflict with both Lloyd George and Churchill, the latter as President of the Board of Trade not having then come to identify the construction of battleships with a state of grace, and to a lesser extent with most of the rest of the Cabinet. He carried his battle to the brink of resignation before he secured, by an Asquithian sleight of hand, a remarkably favourable outcome. It was decided that four should be laid down at once and another four if if they were held to be necessary. They were, and a struggle between four and six thus resulted in a 'compromise' on eight.

This obviously made him a hero with the admirals. It also put him well on the way to the total of eighteen new battleships which his First Lordship contributed to the British fleet, without which it could be (and was) argued that Jellicoe would have lost the Battle of Jutland. He also ushered in the era of the Dreadnought as much as Henry Ford did that of the popular car. There could be doubts about the wisdom of these achievements. First, the bigger the battleship the more it offended what would seem to be several fundamental rules of warfare: it offered as large a surface as possible to the destroying fire of an enemy, it achieved its own fire power at the maximum rate of expense per gun, and, if sunk, it promised a vast loss of life and blow to morale. Second, it began a naval race which ended with Britain's superiority no greater than it had been at the beginning and had more adverse consequences for expenditure than favourable ones for security. However there was little dispute that McKenna had won his first major battle for the navy.

The second one, in 1911, was a different matter. McKenna got himself rigidly involved in a major strategic dispute about whether in a future war Britain should put a big army on the Continent or should confine itself to a peripheral and mainly naval role. Tied up with this was the question of adequate Admiralty co-operation in the Committee of Imperial Defence. McKenna took the non-cooperative, no-mass-army-on-the-Continent line. This put him into conflict not merely with the 'economists' but effectively with all his colleagues who took an interest in these matters, Haldane, the Secretary of State for War, Churchill, even Grey this time, and eventually the Prime Minister, whose solution was to move McKenna and put Churchill in his place. It was the only one of his four moves between departments which McKenna did not welcome, but he was well looked after by Asquith and it was once again promotion of a sort. He lost Admiralty House (it was lucky that Smith Square was just ready) and he lost the Admiralty yacht. But he got what was at least nominally the senior secretaryship of state at the Home Office.

A few months before there had been seriously contemplated (on both sides) a much more extraordinary appointment for him. This was that he should replace the retiring Sir George Murray as *permanent* secretary of the Treasury. A first reaction is that it would be impossible to imagine a less fructuous partnership than that between him as chief civil servant and Lloyd George as ministerial head of department which would have followed. A second is that the mere contemplation of such a move vividly illustrates McKenna's merman-like status as half-official and half-politician. However, he did not take it – his improving health (after a dangerous appendicitis operation) seems to have been a further mystifying factor in his decision to stick to the ministerial side of the table – and Asquith urged the Home Secretaryship on him as 'one of the most difficult and responsible places in the Government'.

Unfortunately the Home Office, where he stayed for three and a half years, did not excite McKenna. His principal piece of legislation was the Welsh Church Disestablishment Bill, which he had to conduct through the House of Commons in the successive sessions of 1912, 1913 and 1914 before it became law, against the opposition of the House of Lords and under the provisions of the Parliament Act. This coincided with Europe's plunge to war. Its operation was then suspended as a gesture of national unity until 1920, by which time McKenna was out of Parliament, esconced in the City and about as interested in the griev-ances of Cymric Nonconformist tithe-payers as F. E. Smith, one of his principal opponents on the bill, was in the temperance movement. Smith's bombinations against the bill produced from G. K. Chesterton one of the great mocking poems of pre-1914 politics with the refrain of 'Chuck it Smith'. Oddly, however, its last stanza was a still more appropriate satire of McKenna's highly statistical, non-emotional method of conducting the bill, which paid more attention to balance sheets and to discounted stipends than to theology or history, than it was of Smith's exaggerated epigrams:

> For your legal cause or civil
>   You fight well and get your fee;
> For your God or dream or devil
>   You will answer not to me.
> Talk about the pews and steeples
>   And the cash that goes therewith!
> But the souls of Christian peoples . . .
>   Chuck it [Reggie].

There could hardly have been a greater contrast between the way in which Gladstone had conducted the Irish Church Disestablishment Bill forty-three years before and the treatment which McKenna gave to the Welsh. The one was like the swelling up of a Beethoven symphony, the other like the ringing of a cash register. Nevertheless the 1912–14 marathon added to McKenna's reputation for cool, omniscient com-petence.

Nor was the other bill most associated with his name during these years exactly of an inspiring nature. This in official jargon was called the Prisoners (Temporary Discharge for Ill-Health) Bill, but once on the statute book it became universally known as the Cat and Mouse Act. This was designed to deal with the cumulative and almost insoluble problem of suffragettes (usually most respectable ladies) who were convicted and fined for what was often some minor defiance of the law, who then refused to pay and were committed to prison, where they refused to eat. The authorities (and ultimately the Home Secretary) were then confronted with the choice between forcible feeding, which apart from its indignity carried real risks of a possibly fatal accident, or of allowing the prisoner, if determined enough, to starve herself to death.

McKenna was therefore liable to have on his hands the prison deaths of ladies who had originally been convicted of nothing more serious than obstruction through tying themselves to railings and sentenced to only a fine. His projected answer to this was to let them out if they would not eat, and to retain the right to put them in again when they would. Hence the 'cat and mouse' sobriquet which, while there may be no exact equivalence between his behaviour to the suffragette prisoners and that of a cat to a mouse, nevertheless did in a general sense encapsulate the spirit of sporadic pouncing. It was perhaps a contrived and over-ingenious solution, although no one who has had to deal with hunger-striking ladies should criticize anyone else for trying to exercise ingenuity in such a situation.

In the approach to war of July–August 1914, McKenna was reliably Asquithian: not bellicose but fully willing to follow Grey's lead and supplying steadiness which usefully helped to bring others along. He swallowed the contradiction of his 1911 strategy views which were involved in immediately putting a large British Expeditionary Force into France, but the essence of his belief here went subterranean rather than was eliminated, and resurfaced strongly although in a somewhat different form in late 1915 and 1916.

Departmentally he ran into heavy criticism for not interning more enemy aliens, but as so many had already been shut up that Kitchener was complaining he could not spare soldiers to guard them, and as the hysteria extended almost to a demand for the rounding up of dachshunds, McKenna's unemotional rationalism and insensitivity to public opinion was on this issue a national asset. On the whole the Home Office enhanced his reputation. It did not give him public popularity and it did not win him much affection in the House of Commons – he was too self-righteous and know-all for that – but it did show him to be an effective parliamentary fighter and more indestructible than the Dreadnoughts which he had so determinedly launched.

In May 1915 McKenna was a reluctant coalitionist. He agreed with Asquith's view that the addition of Conservative ministers would not improve the efficiency of the government as an instrument for the carrying on of the war, and, unlike Asquith, he thought that conclusive, and could assimilate no wider considerations. Reluctant although he may have been, however, he was also a considerable beneficiary of the formation of the first Coalition. He became Chancellor, which not only gives him his place in this book but also put him in the way of his chairmanship of the Midland Bank, which enhanced the prosperity and, to some substantial extent, the satisfaction of his last twenty-four years. It is very doubtful whether he ought to have been given the Exchequer, not because he was a bad Chancellor – given the weak position of the Treasury in wartime he produced good budgets, although his influence on the general shape of the government was baleful – but because if the Asquith Coalition were to have any real cohesion and chance of success it ought to have had a Tory Chancellor. Asquith used two excuses for not appointing either Bonar Law or Austen Chamberlain. The one was that the Liberal majority would not tolerate a Tariff Reformer at the Treasury. The other was that the job had to be kept warm for Lloyd George, who was only, as it were, seconded to the Ministry of Munitions and retained the right of reversion. This made his replacement a tentative appointment, which meant that he could only give it to a subservient Liberal, and not to the Conservative leader or even to the prickly Austen Chamberlain.

The reasons had a certain validity but not enough. McKenna's Chancellorship was marked by two competent budgets, by his near resignation on a general issue and by his consistently urging Asquith into playing ineffectively hostile hands against Lloyd George. For a champion bridge player he did not show much realistic tactical sense. His first budget was on 21 September 1915, as unorthodox a date as were the circumstances with which he had to cope, and was a much more serious attempt at dealing with the finances of the war than had been Lloyd George's eighth and last budget, introduced on the previous 4 May, when he no doubt already had his mind on other jobs and other things.

This first McKenna budget was much praised for its succinct lucidity. His speech lasted only one and a quarter hours, which was one of the shortest budget openings on record. He began with a stark statement of how much the prospect had deteriorated since Lloyd George's May presentation. Revenue on the existing basis was likely to be £5 million better at £272 million. But expenditure looked like being £1,590 million, an increase of £457 million. Of this sum, which then struck everyone as staggeringly vast, the navy would consume only £190 million as against the army's £750 million – so completely had McKenna been defeated in his 1911 battle to make Britain's role in any future war primarily a naval one. In addition 'external advances' directly related to the war amounted to £423 million.

The gap between expenditure and revenue was clearly a frightening one. Barely one-sixth of the cost of the war was being currently financed.

Neither McKenna nor anyone else thought that this whole gap could possibly be eliminated. What he set out to do was sufficiently to narrow it to that, without throttling business or upending the social structure, the civilian population would be shown to be making at least some degree of sacrifice, and fiscal policy could have some claim to be an instrument of war. Income tax rates were increased by 40 per cent, with the exemption limit reduced from £160 to £130. Super-tax, which started at £8,000, was also to be increased and the graduation somewhat steepened. The end result was that a man with no children earning £3 a week (perhaps £120 today), who had hitherto been exempt, would pay nearly £4 a year; a prosperous professional man with £5,000 a year (say £200,000 today) would pay £1,029; and a magnate with £100,000 (£4 million today) would pay £34,029, or a rate of 6s 10d in the pound. This meant of course that the magnate would be left with £65,971, which made it very different from the effect of Second World War surtax. In addition there was to be a new excess profits tax of 50 per cent on the amount, subject to some rather complicated adjustments, by which profits exceeded those upon which income tax was assessed for 1914–15.

There was also heavy increases in indirect taxation, although these avoided the most obvious targets of spirits, wines and beer, on the ground that they had been heavily hit in the first wartime budget of the previous November. As a result the budget was somewhat regressive, with 50 per cent increases on tea, tobacco, cocoa, coffee, chicory and dried fruits. Patent medicines for some reason or other were singled out to go up by 100 per cent and sugar was also heavily taxed, although with many complications and a net effect of increasing the retail price by about 15 per cent.

McKenna also proposed a series of increased Post Office charges, including the suspension of the halfpenny postage. The Speaker however advised that if these were incorporated in the Finance Bill they would endanger its status as a money bill and consequent protection under the Parliament Act against House of Lords interference, not a very present danger in wartime and with a coalition government. They were consequently transferred to a separate Post Office and Telegraph Bill, although without the suppression of the halfpenny postage, which had aroused too much of an outcry.

The most controversial aspect of the budget, however, was not this but what became known as the 'McKenna duties'. It was an almost classical irony that McKenna, having owed his appointment as Chancellor partly to Asquith's determination not to have a Tariff Reformer at the Treasury, then proceeded in his first budget to introduce the nearest approach to Protection that had been seen for well over half a century. In a coalition government Chamberlain or Law would almost certainly not have dared to be so controversial. McKenna claimed that he was not doing it for protective purposes. He had three objectives, he said: to raise revenue, to reduce the import bill and to discourage unnecessary or luxurious consumption. The duties, he claimed, would assist in the general direction of all three objectives, although, as some critics pointed out, they could not logically do all three at the same time.

What they consisted of were *ad valorem* customs duties of 33.3 per cent on motor cars and motor cycles and their parts, cinema films, clocks, watches, musical instruments, plate glass and somewhat bizarrely, hats. The proposals produced more controversy than revenue. The most important item was motor cars, and as a concession was most foolishly made to exempt those for business use. This took away much of the effect. Plate glass also fell by the wayside as did hats on the interesting ground that it proved impossible to define what was and what was not a hat. Even without hats, the McKenna duties provided a peg for argument which rumbled on throughout the fiscal controversies of the 1920s.

Despite these efforts the contribution of the first McKenna budget to closing the gap between expenditure and revenue was very limited. For the current financial year it brought in only an additional £33 million but for a full and future year the contribution was over £100 million. The borrowing requirement both at home and in America remained immense. Nevertheless this budget was on the whole given a favourable reception and its immediate aftermath probably coincided with the nearest approach to fame and even popularity which McKenna's chilly and reclusive personality was ever to achieve.

His second budget in April 1916, as tends to be the pattern, was somewhat anti-climatic, giving the impression of scraping some few marginal bits of additional revenue without much central design. Income tax both became more complicated and rose to a maximum of five shillings in the pound on incomes over £2,500. It was estimated to bring in an extra £44 million a year, which was substantial. Super-tax, however, was allowed to remain the same. Excess profits duty went from 50 per cent to 60. Sugar went up by another halfpenny a pound and there were other increases on cocoa, coffee and chicory. Motor taxation was increased, and a duty on matches, which had not been tried since Robert Lowe burnt his fingers with it in 1871, was introduced. There was also a whole range of innovative duties on entertainment admissions, on railway tickets, on mineral water, on cider and on perry. Some of them, such as entertainments duty, survived for a long time.

Apart from his budgets the three incidents or issues (they were all rather a combination of the two) which most marked McKenna's Chancellorship were first his bad relations with the Governor of the Bank of England; second his mobilization of the American assets of the Prudential Assurance Company in order to satisfy the demand of J. P. Morgan and Co. (British government agents in New York) for a 25 per cent dollar down payment on the next round of British *matériel* purchases in America; and third his deep dispute, carried as in 1909 to the brink of resignation, about the desirable shape of the war effort, hooked to the specific issue of conscription.

McKenna was a prickly Chancellor. Lloyd George, in spite of his outsider's radical opportunism, got on perfectly well with the stately Lord Cunliffe, who was Governor of the Bank (having been on the court since 1895) from 1913 until Bonar Law procured his resignation in 1917. They successfully weathered the financial storm of August 1914 together. But McKenna, much more naturally attuned to City opinion, quickly quarrelled with him. Within two months of McKenna's appointment Cunliffe was complaining to Asquith about his new Chancellor. McKenna won the battle, and indeed scored a notable triumph over Cunliffe, who was taking the view that matters of foreign exchange were for the Bank and not the Treasury, by his bold skill with the Prudential, but these connected incidents left a minor shadow over his relations with Asquith and a major one over those with Cunliffe.

The conscription issue, which was of a different order of seriousness, reached its peak over the turn of the year 1915 and into the early months of 1916. It was a searing dispute, for it played along two fault-lines in the Asquith Coalition, that between the Tories who expressed their frustration at serving in second-rate posts under Asquith by half believing that he and his supporters were not serious about waging the war unless they embraced conscription almost as an article of faith, and that between Lloyd George (pro-conscription and his erstwhile colleague (almost all against with varying intensity and for a variety of reasons). The conscription issue paved the way for a Lloyd George-led Conservative government, which was what governed the country from the end of 1916 to 1922.

Some Liberals, most notably the Home Secretary, Sir John Simon, who resigned, were against conscription on principle. Some, like Asquith himself, Grey and Birrell, did not much like it, but thought there were worse sacrifices to be made in a war. And then there was a hard partnership of Runciman, the President of the Board of Trade, and McKenna, who took what was primarily neither a moral not a libertarian but an economic case against compulsion. It narrowed down to a dispute about whether Britain could afford to provide sixty-five or seventy divisions (the minimum wanted by the military and the Tories) for France. But in fact it was the old and perennial issue of whether Britain was a European or a peripheral power, intertwined with a conflict between an all-out war and a 'business as usual' approach. Twenty-five years later it was to repeat itself in the difference between Churchill's war and Chamberlain's war. The essence of the McKenna/Runciman view was that Britain must maintain its industrial and financial strength, including its capacity to export. Without this it could not be either the arsenal or the banker of the allied powers. The 'depletion of industry' was the real danger. The French must decide whether they wanted more British soldiers or more British munitions and money. They could not have both.

Asquith, as so often in his unhappy transitional Coalition, was caught in the crossfire. He could not hold the Tories (or Lloyd George) without a crab-like advance towards conscription, and he could not remain in office on tolerable terms if his praetorian guard of McKenna, Runciman and Grey were to desert him. This led to considerable Asquithian impatience towards McKenna, made the worse by his at least half agreeing with him. 'The PM told me', Lady Scott (widow of the great explorer and the future Lady Kennet) wrote on 13 February, 'that the man who had disappointed him most for many a long year was McKenna. Said he proved himself unstable mentally and morally – moreover he hadn't the excuse of a stupid man, nor the excuse of artistic temperament or any such thing – it saddened him.'

McKenna was also subject to a great barrage from Margot Asquith, which is interesting not merely as an example of her complete lack of inhibition but also as showing what weight of loyalty McKenna was expected to bear, at any rate in the fevered mind of Margot.

> 'I can't believe,' she had written on 28 December 1915, 'that you, the most fearless, the most loyal of all Henry's colleagues and above all the most intimate and affectionate, are going to desert him because he is in difficulties. Henry always said to me, "If all my colleagues were to turn on me, McKenna never would." Not till I hear it from your own lips will I believe it.'

McKenna did not resign. He reluctantly went along with the almost inevitable shuffle towards full conscription, but took his revenge, no doubt not consciously, translating his mounting enmity towards Lloyd George (and it started from a fairly high plateau) into such intransigent advice to Asquith that it contributed substantially to the end of the government career of his chief, and, as it happened, of himself. Asquith, in McKenna's view, should assert his authority, bring Lloyd George to heel, and if necesssary sack him from the administration. This was all based on the false assumption that Asquith had a demonstrable indispensability and that he only had to raise the stakes of the game in order to win it. This had unfortunately become far from the truth, as the attitude of the Conservative ministers during the crisis of December 1916 was to make abundantly clear. McKenna's position, both official and personal, gave him plenty of opportunities to press his misappraisal upon Asquith, and he used these opportunities to the full. He was, for instance, closeted with him in the Cabinet room (with Grey, Lewis Harcourt and Runciman waiting outside) at the crucial moment of decision on 4 December, Asquith's penultimate day as Prime Minister.

It was also the political end for McKenna. Three months later, at the pressing invitation of Sir Edward Holden, former Liberal MP and Midland Bank chairman, who had formed a deep admiration for McKenna because of his incisive handling of a difficulty relating to the Yorkshire Penny Bank, McKenna joined the Midland Bank board. At first his commitment was no more than that of an ordinary non-executive director, such as many ex-Chancellors have become. But from the beginning of 1918 it assumed a much greater intensity. He became chairman-designate (Holden wanted to go, and indeed died in 1919) and he devoted himself to learning the details of banking to the extent of sitting every day in Holden's room and observing what he did. His approach to the Midland summit also involved a fairly pompous and in some ways mysterious exchange of statements of intention. First McKenna was requested and undertook 'to give the whole of his time and work' to the Bank. It is not clear how this squared, not only with his continuing commitment as an MP, but even more with his desire to be reelected for Pontypool (as North Monmouthshire had been renamed). Perhaps fortunately the matter resolved itself by his defeat there, not at the hands of a Coalitionist as was the fate of most Asquithians, but by the Labour candidate. He also, on his own initiative, drew up an elaborate coda in which he stated his own lack of desire again to hold office, but recognized that it might become his public duty so to do, and provided that, if the issue were raised, it should be decided not by himself, but by the other directors of the Bank.

This might be thought to have been elevating the chairmanship into a little too much of a papacy and the directors into too much of a college of cardinals. However it did have more practical relevance than what he would have done had he won Pontypool, for in both 1922 and 1923 flies of differing allure were cast over him for a possible return to the Exchequer. But there is not the slightest indication that on either occasion the board of the Midland Bank were invited to make the decision for him. Bonar Law in October 1922, having brought down Lloyd George, had to face the problem of presiding over a government of 'second-rate intellects', in Birkenhead's patronizingly memorable phrase. Some riposted that this was better than a government of second-rate characters, but it nonetheless meant that Law, who although in some ways narrow-minded was by no means immune to such criticisms, was open to the thought of bringing in a strengthening figure from outside. It was, however, Stanley Baldwin, after his Carlton Club triumph the natural inheritor of the Exchequer, who first thought of bringing in McKenna. He claimed not to wish to be seen to benefit personally from his part in the revolt. The offer was accordingly made, but rejected fairly quickly. McKenna did not have a seat in Parliament and did not wish to seek a Conservative one at that stage. Nor did he wish to leave his Bank. But he would make a statement of general support for the new government. For him it had the strong advantage of having been born out of hostility to Lloyd George.

Baldwin became Chancellor. Seven months later Law resigned on the verge of death, and Baldwin, following a couple of days of the often-told tragi-comedy, was preferred over Curzon by the King. While it is unlikely that, had he remained at the Board of Trade instead of going to the Treasury, Baldwin would have been even a candidate for consideration, it does not begin to follow that McKenna, had he accepted in November, would have become Prime Minister. This is assumed in the Stephen McKenna biography, where no allowance is made either for the deep desire of the Conservative party to have one of their own in 10 Downing Street, which was a large part of the motive for the Carlton Club revolt, or for the fact that McKenna was seen as essentially a technocrat and not a leader.

He was a very sought-after technocrat however. Baldwin's own elevation made the Exchequer once again vacant. He first offered it to Horne, who had been the last Chancellor of the Coalition government.

But Horne would not accept office without Austen Chamberlain, with whom Baldwin at this stage badly bungled his relations. So the Horne proposition fell. Baldwin then turned once again to McKenna. Why is not remotely clear. His main fear was the emergence of a centre party and his priority was to avert this. This was sensible enough from his point of view. But McKenna was in no way key to this danger. The ex-Coalitionists were, and it was almost lunacy that in these circumstances he should have wasted the one great plum at his disposal (he was committed to keeping nearly all Bonar Law's Cabinet in office) by dangling it in front of a not very distinguished ex-Chancellor of another party who did not even possess a seat in Parliament. And McKenna's answer on this second occasion, even more amazing than the offer, was that he would probably accept in three months' time when he had had a good convalescence after a nasty attack of para-typhoid. To add a third notch to the mystery Baldwin accepted the terms, and made them possible by himself, widely thought to be one of the laziest of Prime Ministers, carrying on as Chancellor in the interim, and thus accepting a double burden which no one since Gladstone had attempted.

Then, in July, McKenna raised another difficulty. He seemed prepared only to come back into the House of Commons as one of the two members for the City of London. It was as though he wished to symbolize his special position in the government as a great envoy from the financial world. However, the chosen facilitator of this process showed a sudden reluctance to progress from Sir Frederick Banbury to Lord Banbury (although he did exactly that a year later), and the plans for McKenna's return to Westminster and Whitehall had either to be abandoned or further postponed. Baldwin at last showed signs of impatience. It may be that he was becoming less keen on the whole project as his mind moved towards the foolish idea of his Tariff Reform dissolution in the autumn, and, in spite of the 'McKenna duties', there was room for doubt as to where the old Asquithian would stand on that issue. In late August Neville Chamberlain was appointed as Chancellor.

That was the end for sixteen years* of McKenna as a political will o' the wisp. He continued to be a respected banker for the next two decades, whose annual reports were looked forward to as pungent commentaries on the economy and the world, but in his old political haunts of Westminster, Whitehall and even Brooks's he became a sort of twentieth-century Scholar Gypsy, sighted only rarely. It is nonetheless

* But see p. 389 of the essay on John Simon.

difficult to think of anyone looking less like Matthew Arnold's smocked yokel than did McKenna, epitomized by James Gunn's official Midland Bank portrait, with his pinstriped trousers, his high-buttoned black coat, his hard collar and cuffs, his trim erect figure, his domed head and his precise rather than sympathetic features. That was appropriate, for McKenna's trouble was that he was always more precise than sympathetic.

He survived until 1943. Most of the Asquithians died before him: Edwin Montagu, his only rival as a provider of intimate little dinners, in 1924; Asquith himself, followed by Haldane, in 1928, Grey and Birrell in 1933. Runciman lived on to help dismember Czechoslovakia in 1938, and Crewe, Margot Asquith and Lloyd George also out-survived him, but only just. McKenna, however, in spite of his closeness to the chief of the clan, was not really an Asquithian. He was more an exile swept on to the shore of Asquithian Liberalism, coming from no clear homeland and leaving little behind him, but while he was there making the most of his opportunities with talent and hard work, but with neither the exuberance of a young Churchill nor the moral authority of an Edward Grey.

BONAR LAW

BONAR LAW WAS A MEDIUM-TERM Chancellor (for the two wartime years of the Lloyd George Coalition) and a very short-term Prime Minister (seven months in 1922–3), but a long-term leader of the Conservative party (ten years from 1911 to 1921, when he resigned through ill-health, and then the brief postscript of his premiership). He had no more than a clerk's education, although he later acquired a depth rather than a width of reading, and he had some exceptional but narrowly focused abilities. He was born and spent his first twelve years in austere circumstances in what is now the Canadian province of New Brunswick. Then he made a reverse emigration into the cousinly bosom of the rich Glasgow commerical classes. As a result of this he was for the whole of his adult life very comfortably off, even affluent. And his wealth was not entirely self-made.

Nevertheless he was the first leader to exhibit some aspect of the 'poor white' mentality which has been a growing and marked feature of the Conservative party in much more recent times. He was a partisan, sometimes a bitter leader, with a stronger sense of 'we was cheated' than of the natural (and sometimes tolerant) authority of an assured right to govern. He was always, for instance, ill at ease with the Balliol benevolence (even though wholly first generation) of Asquith, and addressed him, both in correspondence and in person, as 'Mr Asquith', whereas the Prime Minister (as he was for the first five years of Law's leadership of the opposition) used the form of 'My dear Bonar Law', which was much more natural to the period.

On the long march back to the Commons after listening to the King's Speech which opened his first session as leader, Law was reported as saying: 'I am afraid I shall have to show myself very vicious, Mr Asquith, this session, I hope you will understand.' Whether or not Asquith 'understood', Law certainly succeeded in being 'vicious', particularly on Irish Home Rule, which was the great issue of the next two years. The viciousness which he displayed was that of a leader who had been born out of three successive defeats for his party, and who had a nasty suspicion that his role might be to suffer a fourth, rather than that of a debonair heir striding self-confidently into his inheritance.

It was not however wholly a contrived or bogus viciousness. He attached a great importance, comparable with that of Harold Wilson, John Major and of few others, to keeping his party together, which indeed had been the basis of his otherwise surprising elevation, and put this consideration above his hope that posterity would regard him as a statesman. And he knew that a partisan opposition to the complacency of nearly a decade of Liberal power was the best way to achieve this. As a Scots Presbyterian he probably did not have much genuine feeling against the disestablishment of the Anglican Church in Wales, about which he felt it necessary to beat up a tremendous fuss. But against its bigger brother of those immediate pre-First World War years, a Home Rule Bill which would have put the domestic concerns of the whole of Ireland under a Dublin parliament, he felt genuine passion.

He was an Ulsterman to his fingertips, more than he was Scots or Canadian, even though he never lived in Northern Ireland. His father had however been born, experienced his first ministry and came back to die at Coleraine in County Down. When Bonar Law told Austen Chamberlain many years later that he had cared intensely only about two things – Tariff Reform and Ulster – he was speaking from the heart. And his most notorious pre-1914 statement to the organizers of the Orange Marches of 12 July 1913, that 'whatever steps they might feel compelled to take, whether they were constitutional, or whether in the long run they were unconstitutional, they had the whole of the Unionist party under his leadership behind them', has certainly left a long-lasting legacy.

Like many politicians (and indeed many individuals of all occupations) Law was full of paradoxes. Although he was a man of considerable commercial property and mostly lived in fairly large houses, he maintained an austere way of life. He was a teetotaller and was almost wholly indifferent to what he ate, except for a great fondness for rice puddings. As a result, invitations to his table were not greatly sought after by those of his colleagues who had the more normal indulgent tastes of the period. On the other hand he was a ferocious smoker, with his object at a meal always seeming to be that of getting through it as quickly as possible in order to be able to light up his cigar.

Most people agreed that he was exceptionally honest and straight-forward, although in December 1916 at one of the most significant confrontations of his life, both for himself and for the future course of British politics, he failed to show to Asquith a vital piece of paper which had been agreed with his (Law's) colleagues, and was subsequently much criticized for that omission by strict Asquithians. What there was even less doubt about was that he had a strong melancholic streak, which expressed itself vividly through his memorably sad eyes. This streak was probably there from the beginning, to some extent inherited from his father who spent much of the last year of his Canadian ministry gazing in inspissated gloom at a dismal river which flowed past his study window. But it was accentuated in later life by the death of his wife in her forties and by the loss of two of his sons in the First World War.

His way of life was almost aggressively joyless. Chess he loved, and to some extent golf and bridge. Music he positively disliked and he was equally indifferent to the visual arts and to natural scenery. He read but not eclectically. By far his favourite author was Thomas Carlyle, with Dickens, Walter Scott and Gibbon securing places in the wake of the sage of Ecclefechan. Conversation without a clear purpose bored him, and, even when the qualification was met, he was hardly either expansive or epigrammatic. All of this makes it surprising that by far his closest companion for the last twelve years of his life was Max Aitken, from 1916 Lord Beaverbrook. They had a Canadian origin in common, but very little else. Beaverbrook, although at times (but mostly after Law had gone) almost as much oppressed by the awful eschatological prospects of humanity as had been, *inter alia*, John Henry Newman and Gladstone before him (although with rather more emphasis upon his individual fate), liked self-indulgence, gossip, the fun of irresponsible conversation, and making mischief. Why he chose to attach his allegiance to such a sad knight in somewhat drooping armour as Law is far from obvious. But, having done so, he served him and sought to advance his career and interests with remarkable fidelity.

Bonar Law had some considerable attributes. He had a quick mind and a phenomenal memory. He could apply himself to a subject, whether it was reading a balance sheet or learning French or grasping compli-cated detail, with great efficiency. And while he had no eloquence and little gift of phrase-making, he could express the instinctive reactions of middle Conservative opinion with a succinct accuracy, and mostly without notes. He even delivered a budget speech from the sketchiest of outlines. He was also good at writing pithy letters. But by no stretch of the imagination could he be called either an imaginative statesman or a great political personality.

He was born in September 1858 on the banks of the Richibucto river. Although he was christened Andrew Bonar Law, Bonar was the christian name by which he was called within the family and later by such political colleagues as were sufficiently intimate with him. It was not the equivalent of the Lloyd in David Lloyd George, which gradually became part of the family name. All Law's own children were plain Law, with no Bonar attached.

When he was two his mother died. She had been a Miss Kidston and although born in Nova Scotia was closely connected (although not so closely as to cause property to pass) with the relatively rich family of that name who lived in Helensburgh on the north bank of the Firth of Clyde and made their money in Glasgow. Soon after her death her sister came out from Scotland to keep house for the Reverend David Law and his five young children. (A very similar arrangement prevailed in Bonar Law's own family a half-century later when he was left with six children, except that it was then *his* sister who came from Scotland to London.) Ten years later David Law remarried, and the sister became redundant. She therefore returned to Helensburgh, taking with her, by agreement, Bonar Law, the youngest of the minister's four sons, with responsibility for his education and future being transferred to her prosperous relations. Thus, at the age of twelve, he ceased to be Canadian and became Scottish, as well as moving from poor manse life in New Brunswick to equally dour and sabbatarian but much more affluent circumstances at the core of the west of Scotland commercial classes.

The education and training he was given, however, was more commercial than affluent. He went for a few years to a small boarding preparatory school at Hamilton and then at the age of fourteen to Glasgow High School, an ancient foundation which after vicissitudes and a century after Law's schooldays strongly revived itself. It has the distinction of being the only day school in Britain ever to have produced more than one Prime Minister.* But he was allowed to stay there for only two years before he was put into the counting house. He was not even allowed to matriculate, or to go to the fine new Victorian gothic pile of

---

* Subject to the possible qualification of how far Westminster School in the eighteenth century, when it produced four, was a boarding rather than a day establishment. Campbell-Bannerman was the other alumnus of Glasgow High School.

Glasgow University, which after nearly 400 years in the old city centre had just arisen on a West End hill, let alone to contemplate Oxford or Cambridge. This severe vocationalism may have contributed to a streak of inoffensive and almost Denis Thatcher-like anti-intellectualism which was a persistent part of his make-up. Keynes captured it perfectly when he wrote of Law at Cambridge making 'a charming little speech given to undergraduates after dinner in which he dismissed with sweet-tempered cynicism everything a university stands for'.

The leading Kidstons, cousins of his mother, into whose office he entered, were as barren of descendants as they were rich. Two of them never married, the third was childless. They jointly ran a Glasgow merchant bank which specialized in the financing of the iron and steel trade. They were ageing in 1880 and they looked on Bonar Law more as heir than as dependant, but in 1885 they decided to amalgamate with the Clydesdale Bank, which meant that, although he later became a non-executive director of that *areopagus* of the West of Scotland industrial and commercial scene, there was no executive role for him there. He nonetheless did very well out of William Kidston and Co. When first the sister and then the widow of the sole married brother died they each left him legacies of £30,000, the equivalent between them of £3 million today. Throughout his political career he was therefore a rich *rentier*.

His ten years of commuting from Helensburgh, lunching in some Glasgow city centre coffee house, and finding his main recreation in snatched games of chess on the suburban train or in the chop-houses, therefore served him well, particularly as during some of these train journeys he got to know William Jacks, Liberal MP for Leith, who in spite of the political gap (for Law was always an instinctive and dedicated Tory) offered him a partnership in the successful firm of iron traders which operated on the Glasgow Royal Exchange rather in the way that those in cotton did in Liverpool and those in pork bellies did in Chicago. To this firm, which one of his brothers also joined, he contributed a natural shrewd trading sense combined with a reputation for straight dealing, and he gained from it his practical knowledge of commerce and his sense of political touch with the business community, as well as a very substantial income.

He also suffered some considerable embarrassment when in 1915, fourteen years after he had severed his connection with the partnership except for continuing to use it as a deposit banker holding any cash balances which he fluctuatingly accumulated, William Jacks and Co. was prosecuted for trading with the enemy. They were the agents for providing Canadian iron ore for Krupps and a cargo for that destination had been unloaded at Rotterdam on 11 August 1914. Prosecutions were mounted against three of the partners, including Law's brother, but the charge against the younger Law was eventually dropped. The other two partners were convicted at Edinburgh and sentenced to short terms of imprisonment.

No one suggested any direct responsibility on Bonar Law's part, but the case hung oppressively over him during the period when the first (Asquith) Coalition government was being formed, and is thought to have been a contributory reason why, as the leader of a party with as many seats in the House of Commons as the Liberals, he allowed himself to be fobbed off with the peripheral office of Colonial Secretary instead of demanding a more central position such as the Chancellorship. (It is a strange thought that, during the birth of that on the whole unhappy and unsuccessful government which lasted from May 1915 to December 1916, the Prime Minister and leader of the Liberal party was preoccupied with the break-up of his great epistolatory relationship with Venetia Stanley and the leader of the Conservative party almost equally obsessed with the disgrace of the firm which had made his business career.)

In spite of his full-time education having been both brief and narrow, Law did manage to lift his head out of the counting house. He went to some lectures sponsored by Glasgow University, and was most impressed by the philosopher Edward Caird, who later became Master of Balliol. He heard Gladstone take time off from the Midlothian campaign to deliver his Rectorial Address, and was fired, not with enthusiasm for the Grand Old Man (he was too firm a Tory for that), but with ambition to be elected to such an office and to be able to address such 'a great meeting'; and he was indeed elected to the Glasgow Rectorship forty-eight years later, although he did not then emulate the grandeur of Gladstone's 1879 address.

At about the same time he joined the Glasgow Parliamentary Debating Association which was typical of a number of such societies founded in the provincial cities in that age of earnestness and of respect for the House of Commons. It ran a mock parliament, meeting weekly, with all the paraphernalia of a Speaker, a mace, a government, an opposition, bills, constituencies to which members were allocated, and even a sort of Hansard. Law learnt a lot from his participation in its proceedings, as he also did from his slightly macabre habit of attending all bankruptcy proceedings (quite frequent in the rumbustious Glasgow commercial climate of the 1880s and 1890s) when William Jacks were creditors, and making a point of speaking. He bizarrely claimed, in a way which somewhat foreshadowed his debating style, that this also was very useful parliamentary training.

What, however, was not at all clear was how, with the minimum of strictly political activity, he suddenly emerged as Conservative (or Unionist as it was mostly then known, particularly in Birmingham and Scotland) candidate for the Blackfriars and Hutchesontown division of Glasgow at the 1900 general election. This seat, one of the seven into which the city had been divided in the 1885 redistribution, spanned the Clyde, and took in on the north side much of the old town between the Cathedral and the river. It was thought to be Liberal territory, as it had been since its separate inception, even on the ebb-tide of 1895. They were looking for 'some qualified Conservative who was willing to lose'. The 'khaki election' of 1900 upset this pessimism. Imperialist sentiment in Glasgow during the South African War was strong enough to sweep Law in with a 25 per cent majority over the incumbent but not distinguished Liberal member.

Law took becoming an MP with great seriousness. He gave up his business career, except for a few very part-time directorships, such as that of the Clydesdale Bank. As he had built up a capital position which gave him an income of c. £6,000 a year (approximately £300,000 at present-day values), which was not bad for a barefoot boy from the backwoods of New Brunswick, this was no great financial sacrifice, but it nonetheless marked a different approach from that of many 'business' MPs of that epoch. He continued for another nine years to keep his main base in Helensburgh, but for each parliamentary session he rented an anonymous London house, mostly in South Kensington. When he was in Onslow Gardens in the early 1920s, Curzon referred to him as living in 'those benighted suburbs'.

When Balfour replaced Salisbury as Prime Minister in July 1902 (which involved no dismantling of the dominance within the Conservative party of the 'Hotel Cecil'), Law, after a very brief back-bench experience became parliamentary secretary to the Board of Trade under the Presidency of Gerald Balfour, the new Prime Minister's younger brother, and thus yet another Cecil on his mother's side. Law enjoyed the junior job and made the most of his opportunities in his three and a half years there. His duties were not onerous, but he was highly competent at them and also earned some national repute by being an able auxiliary of Joseph Chamberlain in the Tariff Reform controversy.

This religious war, which convulsed the Conservative party in the first decade of the twentieth century rather as the European issue was to do in the last decade, temporarily unseated Law. His vote in Glasgow fell by over a quarter, and he was not one of 157 MPs to which the Conservative party, having governed for seventeen out of the previous twenty years, had succeeded in reducing itself. However he had done well enough both as a junior minister and as a quietly partisan propagandist to stand high in the queue for an alternative winnable Conservative seat. Balfour, defeated in Manchester, had obviously the highest claim and came back for the City of London in March 1906, but Law was not far behind him, and in May was returned for Dulwich, that leafy and then Conservative redoubt of south-east London. He thus began a Cook's tour of constituencies, starting and ending in Glasgow, but otherwise paying little respect to geographical affiliation, which was a feature of his only medium-length (twenty-three-year) career in the House of Commons.

Robert Blake, who never makes a loose judgement, says with surprising firmness that those next three years 'were perhaps the happiest period in Bonar Law's life'. This should no doubt be seen against the background that happiness was never Law's strong suit. Nevertheless it makes sense only on the basis that Law was naturally an opposition-minded politician who preferred the essentially negative game of wrecking the Liberal government's legislative programme, which with the assistance of the House of Lords the defeated Conservative rump very successfully did, to the more constructive opportunities of office.

However it also marked the fact that he had become an effective parliamentary debater, never attempting any sweep of oratory or ideas, but able to speak effectively and without much preparation on a wide variety of subjects. It also meant that he liked making propaganda speeches in the country, of which he did a great deal, becoming after the incapacitation of his hero Joseph Chamberlain one of the foremost Tariff Reform propagandists. He liked the sense that he was rising in his party, and that, after the disaster of 1906, his party was also rising in the country.

The reason this relatively buoyant period was sharply limited to three years was that his wife became ill during the summer of 1909, and died, almost under the knife of that great surgeon, the first Lord Moynihan, in Leeds in October. This tragic loss (she was only forty-three) occurred very soon after he had affected a permanent move of his household from Helensburgh to London. He had acquired at the surprisingly favourable price (even at 1909 values) of £2,500 a substantial lease on Pembroke Lodge, a large house with an even larger garden, just off Edwardes Square in Kensington. The new metropolitan spaciousness accentuated his sense of being bereft. He never married again, and there is no evidence of his ever contemplating it. Insofar as the gap was filled at all it was filled by the unlikely combination of his sister Mary Law and Lord Beaverbrook. There is a vivid story (admittedly from Beaverbrook's own pen and dating from late 1910 or early 1911) illustrating both Law's loneliness and the balance between its two assuagements. Mary Law said to her brother, 'I don't like the growing influence of Max Aitken here' (Clementine Churchill was to express almost exactly the same sentiment to her husband twenty or thirty years later). Bonar Law, who was reading on a sofa, took off his spectacles and said, with devastating quietness, 'Do let me like him.' She never interfered again, and when she died in 1929 she left Beaverbrook £3,600 and her house, which might be regarded as a classic example of sending coals to Newcastle.

In the 'people's budget' and Parliament Bill disputes Law was a solid, partisan Conservative loyalist. He had little lateral vision, rarely saw trouble coming around a corner, but himself caused no trouble in his party. He was in favour of the Lords' rash rejection of the budget, but when this brought his party up against the searing but predictable choice of whether in the summer of 1911 to fight and see the House of Lords swamped or to surrender, he was, together with Balfour and Lansdowne, in favour of surrender. The only unorthodox action which he took during this period was to agree under party-machine pressure to abandon his safe and convenient Dulwich seat for the second 1910 election in order to lead a Tariff Reform campaign in Lancashire. At first it was proposed that he should fight Ashton-under-Lyne, but with a curious capacity for self-inflicted punishment he left that constituency, which was won, for Max Aitken, and himself accepted North-west Manchester.

This was already a blood-stained battlefield, for it had been won by Winston Churchill from the Tories in 1906, lost by him in a Cabinet-promotion-induced by-election in 1908, and reverted to Liberal in the first 1910 election. There it stayed in the second election of that year. Bonar Law was defeated by 445 votes. He had led but not conquered from the front. Fortunately Lord Derby the Tory 'King of Lancashire' had promised to find him a safe refuge if the Manchester ploy went wrong. If necessary, he said, his own brother would vacate Ormskirk. It was not necessary. Bootle, a surprisingly safe Tory seat, became available and Law was comfortably back in the House of Commons by March. He was member for that Merseyside constituency throughout the long 1910–18 parliament, but he never fought a general election there. For the 1918 (and 1922) contest he returned to Glasgow, where the Central division with its then large business vote made it a much safer haven than had been the Blackfriars division.

Nineteen-eleven was a remarkable year for Law. Immediately after his return for Bootle he was asked to join the shadow Cabinet. In June he became a Privy Councillor (in the Coronation list). And in November, when Balfour, having led his party in three general election defeats and fed up with the ungracious fractiousness of many of his followers, slipped out of the leadership, Law was elected, without a vote but not without contention. The circumstances of his election have been described in the essay on Austen Chamberlain. Balfour resigned on 7 November. During the next twenty-four hours Law would have been lucky if he could have counted forty supporters (out of the 274 MPs to which the Conservatives had recovered from their nadir of 1906). On 12 November he was unopposed. This was essentially because of the combination of his own determined ambition (egged on by Aitken) which kept him firmly in the contest and the Conservative party's terror at the prospect of a close and divisive contest between Chamberlain and Walter Long. So they both withdrew, Chamberlain because he did not have the fire of battle in his belly and because he thought that being just beaten by Long would be more of a humiliation than a joint withdrawal in Law's favour; and Long because he too did not savour the prospect of a narrow victory, and was perhaps even beginning to appreciate what an inadequate leader he would have made.

What was and remains clear, however, is that Law was chosen, even though unanimously, much more as a result of the demerits of Chamberlain and Long than for his own positive qualities. This did not mean that he was necessarily a bad leader. Indeed, in the context of 1911–21, for his tenure in this office was far from short, he was probably the best leader they could have got. He adjusted himself well to the vastly changing circumstances of the decade. It was ironic that he began as one of the most partisan of all opposition leaders and then spent four and a half years, a period which gave him his greatest claim on the gratitude of the state, as an effective and loyal second-in-command to Lloyd George who at the beginning of the period would have been regarded by the majority of Conservatives the most dangerous and objectionable, as of all the Liberal ministers, with the possible exception of Churchill, which again was not without its ironies.

From 1911 to 1914 he was overwhelmingly devoted to satisfying his party rather than to seeking a reputation for statesmanship. He was not in fact an extremist. He had a pragmatic rather than an ideological mind. But he saw his duty as being the servant rather than the master of his party. He sought to give them what they wanted, and above all to avoid the schisms which had plagued the Balfour regime. He attached far more importance to this than to observing old-style political courtesies. This was despite the fact that it was leading exponents of the old style, Asquith until 1916 and Balfour until 1921 or 1922, for whom he felt the greatest instinctive respect. Yet he did not believe he could or should emulate them, and therefore struck out for a different shore.

That shore was mostly an Irish, and particularly an Ulster one. The Home Rule Bill on its three-lap course, made necessary to give it the protection of the Parliament Act, dominated the sessions of 1912, 1913 and 1914. The best that can be said for Law's leadership during that period was that he made no attempt to play both sides of the street, to get plaudits for public intransigence while privately hinting that he was more moderate than he sounded. (In fact he was; much earlier than Lansdowne, for instance, he would have been willing to settle for full Ulster exclusion, while recognizing that a Dublin parliament had become inevitable.) He made no effort to please those outside his own party. It was not only towards Asquith that he showed himself 'very vicious'. His clear intransigence was equal in all directions. In May 1912 he dined at Buckingham Palace, and took a certain pride in saying afterwards: 'I think I have given the King the worst five minutes that he has had for a long time.' He did this by suggesting that a possible exercise of the royal legislative veto should be considered and that, whichever way King George V decided, 'half your subjects will think you have acted against them'. The King's best chance, he added, at once sombrely in manner and frivolously in content, was that the government should be out within two years.

Exactly at the end of the two years, with the government showing no signs of being satisfactorily (from his point of view) out, he was equally unyielding and unpleasing before Mr Speaker Lowther. One of the appalling scenes of parliamentary disorder which characterized those pre-1914 years had broken out. Old Cecils vied with new Smiths in their discourtesy alike to the Prime Minister and to what was at least thought to be the tradition of the House. Lowther, who was both a Conservative and by then an experienced Speaker, publicly asked Law, perhaps a little unwisely, whether the parliamentary hooliganism had his assent and approval. Law rose reluctantly and said: 'I would not presume to criticize what you consider your duty, Sir, but I know mine, and that is not to answer any such question.' It was in its way a good answer, and illustrated his quickness on his feet, but could not be said to have been emollient.

During these three years Law bore awful risks of being the first party leader (and one who trailed no clouds of glory from previous achievement) to threaten the framework of consent which had, almost uniquely, characterized British politics, at least at the governing class level, since the Glorious Revolution. Before the so-called 'mutiny' at the Curragh he had been seriously playing with the idea of getting the Lords to reject the annual Army Act, and thus to deprive the government (and the state) for two years of the use of any military power. It was a desperate remedy, which no party leader with wider than a tunnel vision would have contemplated. Luckily for Bonar Law and the respect for the Conservative party the blundering stage farce of the Curragh intervened. The joint (but not co-ordinated) foolishness of Colonel Seely, Secretary of State for War, and General Paget, Commander-in-Chief in Ireland, hobbled the government's military power against Ulster without any need for Bonar Law's rash contemplation of subversion. Seely resigned and Asquith took over the War Office for five months until European war brought Kitchener into Whitehall. Asquith's cool Prime Ministerial administration restored order in the War Office. Nonetheless the Curragh incident satisfied Law that the army was already a fragile enough instrument for coercing Ulster (if that was ever in the mind of ministers) without his needing further to contemplate tampering with the Army Act.

The mere contemplation of it, however, combined with imprecise but menacing statements that 'there are things stronger than parliamentary majorities', and his trying to put into the King's head the exhumation of a 200-year-dead royal veto, fully justifies Asquith in describing him as having furnished 'for the future a complete grammar of anarchy'. Law's preference at this stage for narrow party interests rather than a wide statesmanship was vividly illustrated by his November 1913 preference (expressed in a letter to Walter Long) for failure rather than success in secret peace talks which he had been holding with Asquith. 'From a party point of view', he wrote, 'I hope the Nationalists will not agree, for, if they do, I am afraid that our best card for the election will have been lost.' And this must be seen in the context of his apprehending the most dreadful consequences from mutual intransigence, including the real danger of civil war.

In all these circumstances Law was at one level (at another he was to suffer terrible personal loss) saved from an impossible political impasse by the outbreak of the 1914 War. From the beginning of the eruption of the international crisis he was determined, quite independently of the invasion-of-Belgium issue, that Britain should fight at the side of France, and throughout the long four and a quarter years he was resolute for victory, subordinating nearly all party considerations to achieving it. As a result he emerged in 1918 with a new persona. The dedicated servant of his party had become the dedicated servant of his country, the loyal and almost indispensable second-in-command of the Welsh wizard whom he had previously regarded with suspicion and disapproval. It was the war which made his leadership into the modest and long-lasting success which it eventually was – modest not least because it was achieved essentially as an auxiliary general and not as a full commander-in-chief. While it would be a ludicrous and cynical piece of *ex post* contrivance to suggest that his motives for so strongly supporting Britain's entry into the war were selfishly careerist, there can be no doubt that his political interests and his policy marched strongly alongside each other in July – August 1914.

The formation of the Lloyd George goverment in December 1916 was also crucial to the build-up of Law's reputation, and here again he was lucky rather than far-sightedly intriguing. At the last moment he played a decisive role in toppling Asquith and making Lloyd George Prime Minister. But this was not part of a settled plot, or even of a long-term disposition. He persisted, almost to the last day, in believing that Asquith was the better, indeed almost the indisputable, head of the government. He would have been willing once the Conservatives had decided to go into coalition in May 1915 to perform an equally supportive role for him as he was later to do for Lloyd George. But he never had a chance of achieving that. He and Asquith were too incompatible. They were like ships which passed in the night, close but without contact. This was more at the volition of Asquith than of Law. The Asquith government, with a still nominally united Liberal party, was of course much less dependent upon Conservative support than was the Lloyd George government, which was essentially made up of the icing of himself and the marzipan of a few Liberal ministers on top of a solid Conservative cake. But beyond that Asquith just could not bring himself either to like or to respect Law. This was partly prejudice and partly the justifiably low opinion which he had formed of Law's handling of the Irish question. 'The gilded tradesman' was one of Asquith's names for Law (although there was not much of the glitter of gold about either his appearance or his style); 'he has the mind of a Glasgow Bailie' was another of his dismissive judgements. In any event there was no chance of Asquith and Law forming a close and constructive partnership.

Nor, superficially, did Law and Lloyd George seem much more likely a pair. With Lloyd George's mercurial and intuitive brilliance and Law's head-down chessboard application to problems, they were even less like each other than Law and Asquith, who at least shared a certain phlegmatism. But with Lloyd George there developed a compatibility of opposites, who knew they each needed the other, which had never been present with Asquith. They settled down remarkably smoothly to Mary and Martha-like roles. Mary of course had the glory, but Martha had the solid domestic position.

Law under Lloyd George was Chancellor of the Exchequer, a full member of the small War Cabinet (the only departmental minister to be so) and the first non-Prime Ministerial (when the Premier was not a peer) leader of the House of Commons, which Lloyd George hardly ever attended. Law also controlled the bulk of the government's majority, which gave him a position much stronger than that of Attlee, itself by no means negligible, in the Second World War. It was very different from that of being a peripheral Colonial Secretary under Asquith.

At least half of Bonar Law's energies were occupied with political management, both of the House and of his party's predominant contribution to the government's majority rather than with Exchequer affairs. As leader of the House he was highly successful, emollient (in contrast with his previous style) and skilful. As a party manager his performance was more mixed. One of his qualities or deficiencies was that he simply could not understand why men wanted honours. This lack of comprehension cut both ways. 'Oh, if he wants it, let him have it,' he was inclined to say. But I doubt if he would have put up with the worst excesses of the post-war Coalition in this respect, which occurred after his resignation through ill-health. And his personal behaviour was wholly consistent with these dismissive views. He was one of the only five Prime Ministers of the last 150 years who accepted no honour or ennoblement before, during or after (admittedly a very brief period in this case) his occupancy of 10 Downing Street. The others were Palmerston, Gladstone, Ramsay MacDonald and Neville Chamberlain.

To balance his semi-absorption in more general political matters was the fact that in wartime a large portion of the Chancellor's peacetime duty was in abeyance. No longer was he expected to exercise a reign of terror over the spending departments, and in particular the service ones. His task was turned into the more limited one of accepting the costs of the war, financing as much as he reasonably could out of increased taxation (which however remained moderate compared with 1940–5 levels) and sustaining the large remaining gap by skilful borrowing, both at home and abroad. As has already been described, Law's immediate predecessor at the Treasury, Reginald McKenna, left the national finances in somewhat better shape than had been the case when he had taken over from Lloyd George eighteen months earlier. (And Law showed strong signs of recognizing this by ignoring his lack of affection of Asquithian Liberals in general and trying to bring back McKenna as Chancellor when he formed his government in 1922.) Nevertheless barely a quarter of the total 1917 budget of approximately £2,200 million was covered by taxation, as opposed to the nearly 50 per cent which had been so covered in the Napoleonic Wars, although even with this relatively better performance the finance of the first half of the nineteenth century had been distorted by a staggering debt service burden.

In these circumstances Law's first budget, on 2 May 1917, cannot be accounted as even approaching an heroic effort. He attempted three very conventional tax increases, but a large part of two of them was whittled away before the Finance Bill became law. Entertainments duty, only a year old, was to be increased by about 30 per cent. Tobacco duty, last increased in McKenna's first budget, was to yield another £6 million. And excess profits duty was to go up from 60 per cent to 80. The estimated overall outcome was a total revenue of £639 million (up £65 million on the previous year) leaving £1,652 million of the total expenditure to be covered by loans. In his winding-up speech at the end of the budget debate the Chancellor suddenly and boldly announced a tax on dogs. This was apparently in response to the report of a Committee of the House published only the day before which commented adversely on the drain of dog food on the national food resources. Mallet and George, the compilers of the third and relevant volume of *British Budgets* published in 1929, commented: 'The proposed dog surtax had a mixed reception and was subsequently dropped.' The experience also suggests that Law's almost off-the-cuff habits of budget delivery had its disadvantages as well as its impressiveness. Robert Blake tells us that he delivered the next year's – the 1918 one – from sketchy notes on 'two small double sheets of writing paper'.

Nor did the original budget proposals for increases in existing taxes, presumably better thought out than the sudden swoop against dogs, fare much better. Before the Finance Bill became law on 17 July the entertainment duty increases were modified and postponed, the addition to the tobacco duty was reduced by a half, and the yield of the excess profits duty was materially diminished by the acceptance of amendments relating mainly to the shipping trade and to Co-operative Societies.

Bonar Law's first budget could not therefore by any standards be regarded as draconian. Indeed he somewhat resiled from the courage of his predecessor, although benefiting greatly from the yield of his predecessor's impositions. There was however one McKenna battle which he pursued with implacability. McKenna, as we have seen, had trouble with Lord Cunliffe, the Governor of the Bank of England, who had come to believe his indispensability entitled him to treat Chancellors as passing inconveniences. McKenna had temporarily brought him to heel. But with Lloyd George Prime Minister, with whom Cunliffe thought he had formed an unshakeable partnership as a result of their successful joint handling of the August 1914 financial panic, and no doubt under-estimating Law, the Governor had another rush of mega-lomaniac blood to his head. He picked a quarrel with the Treasury over the operation of exchange control and wrote to the Prime Minister, 'The London Exchange Committee [over which Cunliffe presided] is therefore a mere cypher entirely superseded by Sir Robert Chalmers [joint permanent secretary of the Treasury] and Mr Keynes, who in commercial circles are not considered to have any knowledge or experience in practical exchange or business problems, and I am convinced that, short of a miracle, disaster must ensue . . .'

Believing that he had thus secured his 10 Downing Street flank, he then orally demanded of Law the dismissal of Chalmers and Keynes. It was a preposterous demand, and he quickly discovered that he had grossly miscalculated the balance of forces. It was the sort of situation in which Bonar Law was at his best. He told Lloyd George that there were three possible solutions: first that he resigned the Chancellorship, second that Cunliffe resigned the Governorship, and third that Cunliffe kept his shell of authority but within it surrendered so completely that he gave a written undertaking that he would resign whenever the Chan-cellor wanted him to do so. Lloyd George, when confronted with this position, had no doubt to which partnership he attached more importance, a sentimental one of three years before or an actual one with the leader of the party which provided more than two-thirds of his majority. Within four months Cunliffe was out and replaced by Sir Brian Cockayne as Governor.

Bonar Law's second and last budget, delivered on 22 April 1918, was more courageous than his first, although not up to the implacable gallantry with which he had routed Lord Cunliffe. It was also intellectually more interesting than its predecessor of 1917, because although victory looked far from imminent that April, with the last German offensive getting near enough to Paris to bombard the city with a great gun, it attempted, on the basis of some highly dubious figures, to peer forward into peacetime finance. And this was not only a theoretical exercise because it provided the basis on which Law justified the size, substantial in themselves but puny in relation to the current scale of expenditure, of his taxation increases. Total expenditure for the financial year 1918–19 he estimated at almost £3 billion, more than the entire national income for 1913–14. Revenue, which had proved buoyant, mainly as a result of price inflation, he put at £842 million. This meant a borrowing requirement at the hitherto unprecedented figure of £2,130 million. It also meant that the burden of debt carried into peacetime was likely to be nearly £8 billion, with a consequent debt service charge of approximately £380 million. It also meant that throughout the war successive Chancellors would have financed 26.9 per cent of expenditure from revenue, while he hoped in the year then beginning to have somewhat improved on the average by producing a modest increase to 28.3 per cent.

Looking to the future, and it was here, perhaps inevitably, that his figures achieved an heroic dubiety, he calculated necessary peacetime expenditure at £270 million as against the £173 million pre-war figure. This was to include a special allowance of £50 million for war pensions but to exclude the likely annual debt service charge of £380 million, appallingly high in relation to the other total of £270 million, which brought the total to be financed post-1919 to £650 million. Then, by some to me inexplicit calculation, he decided that, of his £842 million of current revenue, only £540 million would be available for peacetime finance. On the basis of this highly hypothetical gap he decided that he ought to raise £114 million in additional taxation, £110 million to close the gap and £4 million to show he was a conservative financier. As, obviously, the more he could finance the war effort by additional revenue the better it was for the future, there could be no objection to the principle of additional taxation. But it was an extraordinary and unconvincing method by which to calculate how much he should do.

There were nine methods by which he proposed to raise the £104 million, plus a tenth thrown in as a sort of *bonne bouche* but not counted upon to make a contribution to the magic figure. First postal charges went up. Second the stamp duty on a cheque was to be doubled from a penny to twopence. This petty charge, which increased revenue by only £0.75 million, caused more trouble than all the rest of the increases put together. But at least Law by holding firm did better than Hicks Beach, who had been defeated on such a proposal at the time of the South African War. (It was perhaps with this history in mind that I decided not to reduce but to eliminate the charge, still then at twopence, in the 1970 budget, when the proposal was strongly opposed, but only within the then privacy of the Cabinet, by Barbara Castle; stamp duty on cheques, whether one way or the other, obviously aroused strong feelings.)

His next two direct taxation proposals were more serious. Income tax went up from five shillings (25 per cent) in the pound to six shillings (30 per cent) but with no increase for incomes under £500. This was calculated to produce £41.5 million – a very substantial sum in the budgets of those days. And the maximum rate for super-tax went from 3s 6d to 4s 6d in the pound, with the lower exemption limit reduced from £3,000 to £2,500. As a result the total charge on incomes above £50,000 went to 10s 6d in the pound, still vastly lower than the rates of the Second World War, or the subsequent thirty-five years.

Next he turned to alcohol and doubled both the spirit and the beer duties, which between them were to produce £25.5 million. Wine he left alone. Tobacco, however, despite his half-retreat of the previous year, he subjected to a further increase in duty of about 23 per cent. Pipe tobacco (then a major part of the trade) and cigarettes were made not only more expensive to buy but also more expensive to light. Matches went up from three farthings to a penny a box. The ninth item was an increase in the sugar duty, in itself highly regressive but which he claimed was justifiable in the context of the budget as a whole, with the effect of putting up the retail price from 5¾d to 7d a pound.

He also had a tenth item, which he put forward more tentatively in that he did not set a figure for its likely yield, did not therefore count it as a contribution towards his £114 million, and announced that he proposed to leave the settling of some of the details to a Select Committee of the House. This tenth and supplementary proposal was a special tax on luxuries. He had wanted to do this the previous year but had been persuaded that the practical difficulties were too great. Since then, however, the need for revenue had increased and the French government had shown the way. They had introduced a 10 per cent tax under three heads: first on articles such as jewellery which were inherently luxuries; second on articles such as clothes which became so only when their prices exceeded a certain limit; and third on hotels, restaurants and other service establishments which were judged by some more or less objective standard to be clearly in the luxury class. Law proposed that the British scheme should broadly follow the French lines, but that the rate should be 16.6 per cent rather than 10 per cent because the French also had a turnover tax, which we did not. The exact definitions of category were to be drawn up by the Select Committee.

It was taxation by imprecision, and not unnaturally it foundered. At the committee stage of the Finance Bill, although this year, in sharp contrast with the last, he had no trouble with his other proposals, exception was taken to voting for a tax, the details of which had not been settled. The Chancellor therefore allowed the clause to be negatived, while promising to reintroduce it (in a separate bill) when the Select Committee had reported. When this was achieved, in mid-October, he announced that it was too late in the session to proceed, but expressed the hope that the tax would be resurrected in the following year's budget. It was not. Nor did the whole saga amount to a skilled or elegant piece of fiscal innovation. Indeed his two budgets were probably the least impressive part of Law's performance (on the whole judged to be effective and reputation-enhancing) during the two years when he was Lloyd Georges principal wartime adjutant. The authority within the government which the Chancellorship brought him was greater than the authority and decisiveness which his seniority brought to the Treasury's central task of budget-making.

It was not therefore surprising that, as soon as the war was over and the 'khaki election' won, Law was determined to give up the Treasury and concentrate upon his responsibilities as leader of the House of Commons as well as of the party which as a result of that election had then come to supply nearly three-quarters of the government's massive majority. He transferred to the office, in itself a sinecure, of Lord Privy Seal, but to the considerable dismay of Austen Chamberlain, his successor as Chancellor, retained 11 Downing Street as both a symbol of and a practical contribution to the unique closeness of his partnership with Lloyd George. It was neither an equal nor a subservient partnership, but somewhere between the two. Lloyd George became used to him and developed with him a stable and mutually supportive relationship not totally unlike that of the Prime Minister with his long-standing and perhaps long-suffering wife, Dame Margaret Lloyd George. Law and Dame Margaret both enjoyed certain prerogatives because they were necessary supports, but these did not extend to an approach to equality or to a relationship infused by interest or excitement.

Law in turn admired Lloyd George, but by no means unconditionally. Keynes, who wrote one of his always penetrating and sometimes accurate biographical essays about Law in 1921, thought that it was because Law had a mind and a taste geared to admire success. So long as Lloyd George was successful Law was a faithful lieutenant. When he ceased to be so, which change bore a remarkably close relationship to Law's resignation from the government and temporary withdrawal from active politics in the spring of 1921, so the admiration declined until it turned itself into the fatal (for Lloyd George) Baldwin/ Bonar Law blow delivered at the most famous of all Carlton Club meetings in October 1922.

During the first year after the armistice Lloyd George was almost wholly occupied with the Paris peace talks. He did not once answer questions in the House of Commons until November 1919. Bonar Law was left in almost unsupervised charge in Parliament and in Whitehall. He took the responsibility with courage and resource. He was good at settling inter-departmental disputes, he did not hesitate to speak forthrightly to Lloyd George when he thought it necessary, and he was almost brilliant at holding up the end of the government with narrowly focused debating arguments. Again to quote the Keynes essay,

> Mr Bonar Law was difficult to answer in debate because he nearly always gave the perfectly sensible reply, on the assumption that the pieces visible on the board constituted the whole premise of the argument, that any attempt to look far ahead was too hypothetical and difficult to be worth while, and that one was playing the game in question *in vacua*, with no ulterior purpose except to make the right move in that particular game.

He was much less good at lifting his head from the chessboard and looking to more distant perspectives. Sometimes that served him well. In the early months of 1920 there was a strong move for 'fusion', which was the word of the day, between the two parties which made up the

Coalition. Lloyd George and Balfour were in favour, as were many back-bench MPs. Bonar Law was cautious ('I do not like the idea of complete fusion if it can be avoided') and pleased when there was also opposition from some of the Coalition Liberal ministers. So the project faltered and then died. Had it succeeded Lloyd George would not have fallen, and Law would never have been Prime Minister.

At about the same time the Irish issue again became dominant. The fourth Home Rule Bill was introduced in that spring of 1920. It was satisfactory from an Ulster point of view, provided the basis on which the Stormont Parliament was set up, and was therefore acceptable to Law. But it was miles behind the times in the degree of independent power which it offered to Dublin. Pre-1916 it might have been acceptable, but not afterwards. Asquith, newly returned to the House, was highly critical of the bill. Bonar Law replied to him in what was widely regarded as one of his most impressive debating speeches. Without a note or other sign of preparation he rejected each one of Asquith's just delivered points and was rewarded with a great ovation from the government benches. But it was very much one of his confined chessboard speeches. He had moved some way from his 1912–14 rigidities, but that was largely because he was keeping up with the movement of the political game. He gave no imaginative leadership. The only success in the South which followed from the bill was the 'success' of the Black and Tans. He did not display either the insight or the courage that his successor as leader, stiff old Austen Chamberlain, did a year and a half later when, at the time of the Irish Treaty, he confronted the Conservative party conference in Liverpool.

Law may not have been an imaginative statesman but during the immediate post-war years he was a dedicated and efficient maid-of-all-work to the Prime Minister. Lloyd George, not merely during the six months of the Paris peace talks, when he was hardly ever in England, but subsequently as well, was heavily concentrated on the world scene and frequent international conferences which were a feature of those years. Law managed the House of Commons, often presided over Cabinets, and accepted general responsibility for domestic policy at a time when the exhilaration of victory was turning into post-war disillusionment, when labour unrest was rife, when the boom burst and unemployment soared. All of this took a toll on Law's health. He began to look even sadder and less ebullient than usual and then, in March 1921, when delivering a Glasgow Rectorial Address, often a testing occasion, he lost his famous fluency and, as usual without a text, seemed not to know what to say next. It transpired that he had dangerously high blood pressure and was on the verge of a complete breakdown.

Medical opinion was insistent and unanimous. He could survive only with several months of complete rest. He resigned from the government a few days later on 17 March 1921, and retreated first to Cannes and then to Paris for nearly six months. The hold of France, and of the French Riviera in particular, on in other ways insular British politicians of the 1920s was extraordinary. It was true of Lloyd George, of Balfour, of Austen Chamberlain, of Churchill. And even Baldwin had his Aix. In any event Gallic comforts and relaxation had a beneficial effect on Bonar Law, and by the autumn his health was said to be fully restored. (There was apparently no connection between this and the cancer which killed him two and a half years later.) The consequences of this 1921 attack was probably more permanently damaging to the government than to Law himself. The *Financial News* showed great shrewdness when it wrote of his resignation as 'probably the beginning of the end of Coalition Government'.

So, with a fuse of nineteen months, it proved to be. Austen Chamberlain, whatever his other virtues, was a less skilled minder of the Conservative shop. Lloyd George's luck began to desert him and his government in its fifth and sixth years became accident-prone and scandal-ridden. Bonar Law, with a certain Scots canniness, had held on to his Glasgow parliamentary constituency, in contrast with the behaviour of Stafford Cripps thirty years later, who in not dissimilar circumstances renounced in one swoop both the Chancellorship and his Bristol constituency (thereby creating the vacancy which launched the political career of Tony Benn). His continuing membership of the House gave Law a quietly looming presence. He and Lloyd George became detached from each other in the way that people who are not natural soul mates but whom circumstances have brought closely together often do when those circumstances are removed. Perhaps also, if Keynes was right and he was a success-worshipper, he went off Lloyd George when success began to elude him. Law did not oppose the government in Parliament. He voted, for example, for the Irish Treaty in June 1922. But he managed in a way that was subtle in result, even if not necessarily in intent, to give the impression that it was loyalty rather than spontaneous enthusiasm which made him do so.

Law was not the instigator of the Carlton Club revolt. It was phlegmatic young Stanley Baldwin (young in the limited sense of being ten years Law's junior and in no way until then one of the sixth form of politics) who did that. Law's contribution was rather to skulk in his South Kensington house, consulting his conscience, his doctor, Max Beaverbrook and anyone else who cared to go and see him as to whether he would attend the Carlton Club Meeting, and if so what he would say when he got there. His position was assumed to be crucial because he was the only man among the Conservative anti-Coalitionists who could be thought of in advance as a serious potential Prime Minister. And as the new government when it was formed was dismissed by some as being the 'second eleven' or the 'cabin boys' taking over from the admirals, this was an important consideration. Yet Law's intervention may not have been as crucial as it was commonly thought to be at the time. When it at last became known on the day before the meeting that he would attend and speak against the continuance of the Coalition his decision came as a tremendous boost to the anti-Lloyd George and anti-Austen Chamberlain rebels. But this is different from saying that the outcome would have been different had he stayed away. The result of the vote was a massive 187 for breaking the Coalition with only 87 accepting Chamberlain's contrary recommendation. It is difficult to believe that fifty or more votes would have swung the other way had Law not been present. The state of Conservative discontent with the Coalition – on a whole variety of grounds, too adventurist a foreign policy, honours scandals and above all a feeling that their party was being used as a platform for the flashy but increasingly unsuccessful pyrotechnics of Lloyd George – was too widespread and too deep for that. Furthermore Law did not in fact give a very resonant lead at the Carlton Club. His speech was not nearly as memorable or effective as that of Baldwin. It was received with great enthusiasm, but that was because of who he was, and the party trust which he had acquired over the years, rather than because of what he said. What he said was convoluted rather then inspiring, gave the impression of considerable conflict within his own mind, but at least ended up with a clear indication that he would vote against the Coalition, although 'very reluctantly'.

Why was his mind so full of conflict, leading to his decision being so long postponed? There were I think two separate conflicts, the one a matter of public policy, the other one of private convenience. On the first he greatly disliked being 'disloyal' both to Lloyd George after their long years of partnership, and to Austen Chamberlain, more perhaps as his successor leader of the Conservative party than as an individual, because they had never been exactly made for each other. Against this there was his conviction that Chamberlain, still more bedazzled by

Lloyd George than he himself had been, was leading the Conservative party to a smash. And, except under the exigencies of war, Law had always been primarily a party man. Once the pieces were clearly assembled on the board there was not therefore much doubt as to how he was going to resolve this issue. But he did it without pleasure.

The second conflict arose from his hesitancy over whether he still had the health or the energy fully to re-enter the political arena. He saw accurately that if he was to play any role in the impending crisis he had to envisage becoming Prime Minister. The alternative was to recognize that he had become a permanent semi-invalid and to withdraw entirely from politics. This manichean approach expressed itself by his drafting during the days of indecision not only the outline of the speech which he in fact made but also a letter to his constituency chairman resigning his Glasgow seat. Probably he had an intuitive awareness that the active course would not be compatible with long life. Probably, also, it was inevitable that he was going to choose the path of public duty, and of course ambitious fulfilment. But he did so with a genuinely heavy heart.

At five o'clock on the afternoon of the day of the Carlton Club meeting he was summoned to Buckingham Palace, presumably with a view to his immediate installation as Prime Minister. Law said he could not do this until he had been elected leader of the Conservative party, which event did not take place until four days later. Meanwhile the King had to wait. It was a symbolic little drama. Prime Ministers from Rosebery in 1895 to Attlee in 1945 used the Palace against their party. Law used his party against the Sovereign. Perhaps it was the result of being born a Canadian. He regarded the Conservative and Unionist party as having at least as much mystical significance as His Britannic and Imperial Majesty King George V.

At the party meeting, held either for delicacy or convenience at the now defunct Hotel Cecil rather than the Carlton Club, Law was elected without opposition, proposed by Curzon and seconded by Baldwin. But it was *nemine contradicente* rather than by unanimous acclaim for there was no question of a leading Conservative Coalitionist, Chamberlain, Balfour or Birkenhead, or even Horne or Worthington-Evans, rising with the habitual hypocrisy of party nuptials to propose, second or even support. However, he was anointed by the spiritual authority of the party machine and then went on to Buckingham Palace to kiss hands with the temporal authority.

He was sixty-four years old, a year younger than Churchill in 1940 but other than him and Neville Chamberlain the oldest Prime Minister in the whole series of fifty-one from Walpole to Blair, ever to take office for the first time. And his health was clearly fragile. Perhaps for this combination of reasons he never gave any impression of getting pleasure out of his premiership. Earlier he had undoubtedly been ambitious, and no doubt in 1922 he had some sense of a career fulfilled. But there was more duty than joy about it. He moved into 10 Downing Street but he never used Chequers, the recently bestowed country residence, having a profound indifference to the countryside, English or Scottish, maybe stemming from the hostile face which it had presented to him in New Brunswick.

The government which he formed was not an impressive one, nor much moulded to his own taste. He secured only three of his erstwhile colleagues from Lloyd George's Cabinet. Of a Cabinet of sixteen, seven were peers, much the highest proportion this century, and several of them hereditary magnates rather than working politicians.* And whatever Law's weaknesses, an excessive respect for the territorial aristocracy was not one of them. He had all the traditional preference of the Glasgow-educated West of Scotland commercial classes for their own business values rather than for the different style of Eton and Oxbridge lairds. Perhaps his greatest coup in government-making was to get Neville Chamberlain, somewhat to the chagrin of his half-brother Austen, to join as Postmaster-General, thereby strengthening the sound ministerial competence of the administration and at the same time somewhat tipping the balance back towards business values. (Why on earth, it may be asked, did he not put Chamberlain in the Cabinet, which rank the Postmaster was quite often given, and whose numbers at sixteen were hardly inflated?)

Cabinet weakness put upon Law himself (assisted by Hogg) an exceptionally heavy House of Commons burden. It was a paradox that, while in Whitehall he was resolved to disperse the centralized almost presidential power which Lloyd George had assembled, winding up the 'garden suburb' behind 10 Downing Street which had been created to house additional staff, and encouraging departmental ministers to take

---

* It was of this government that there was invented the story of Derby reassuring Devonshire, or maybe vice versa, that, although the Cabinet was weak in Commons debating power, there was no need to worry because they had procured the services of a clever lawyer called 'Pig' who would deal with most of the difficult issues in that House; there was a foundation of fact in that Sir Douglas Hogg (later the first Viscount Hailsham), although not in the Cabinet at that stage, was a peculiarly active and reliable Attorney-General.

greater independent responsibility, in the House of Commons the reverse was true. Lloyd George had been a super-terrestrial god, only occasionally visiting earth. Bonar Law had to be a workaday parliamentarian, not only constantly on the front bench (Baldwin followed him in this) but taking the burden of answering too many tiresome routine debates.

Partly as a result, but perhaps even more because of Law's doubtful health and his depressive nature, it was not only the debates but most of his short premiership which was tiresome to him. His major, almost his sole, satisfaction was achieved and behind him four weeks after the Carlton Club meeting when he won the 15 November election, thereby vindicating his judgement by showing, for the first time since 1900, that the Conservatives could win independently. In fact they were in a substantial minority of votes cast, but with a three-way split in the opposition they secured 344 seats against 138 for Labour, 60 for the Asquithian Liberals and 57 for the Lloyd George ones. Within three months that triumph had dissolved into one of the greatest humiliations within his own government that a British Prime Minister can ever have experienced.

The settlement of war debts among the allies and the interrelated question of German reparations was one of the most pressing issues of early 1923. During the war Britain had borrowed a great deal from the United States and had lent an almost equivalent amount on to the other allies, mainly France and Italy. Law believed firmly that all-round cancellation between the allies was the only sensible solution. But United States opinion, in an inward-looking and brashly commercial mood, was not at all inclined to let Britain, America's primary debtor, off the hook. 'They hired the money, didn't they?' was the instinctive response of the Harding administration. The French (and maybe the Italians) had no intention of paying the British until they got what they regarded as adequate reparations out of the Germans, about which they remained in British eyes as unrealistic as they were vindictive. Their unilateral occupation of the Ruhr in January 1923, at once expressed their frustration and, on any rational basis, reduced rather than increased the German ability to pay.

This left the Law government with a difficult issue to resolve in Washington. They were partly committed to payment by the so-called Balfour Note of July 1922. Beyond this there was a general Whitehall and City of London desire to preserve British credit in the United States, and also to make the Americans as disposed as possible to assist in European currency stabilization, Germany then being in a frenzy of hyperinflation. In these circumstances the Chancellor of the Exchequer (Baldwin) accompanied by the Governor of the Bank of England (Montagu Norman) set off in the last days of 1922 for a month's negotiating visit to Washington. Law very reluctantly authorized Baldwin to go to a limit of £25 million a year to get a settlement. As soon as he got there Baldwin in consultation with Norman and Auckland Geddes, the 'political' and Lloyd George-appointed ambassador, realized that this offered no hope of a settlement. He therefore tabled an offer going to £34 million. The Americans countered by accepting this for ten years but adding an extra 0.5 per cent interest and thus bringing the annual total up to £40 million for the remaining fifty-two years. Baldwin, who was in fact a much more considerable and wider-visioned statesman than Law, as the next fifteen years were to show, wanted to accept the terms as the best available. This was rejected (unanimously) by a rump Cabinet of the Prime Minister and six other members. Baldwin was therefore forced to return without concluding the matter, but when he landed at Southampton he displayed a mixture of nerve and naivety by outlining the terms to waiting journalists and making clear his own determination that they should be accepted.

This pre-empting might have been expected to create a Cabinet current against Baldwin. But when that body met two days later he argued his case sufficiently persuasively that the Prime Minister, arguing strongly the other way, was left almost isolated. Only Lord Novar, the Scottish Secretary and not exactly a heavyweight figure even in a lightweight Cabinet, was said to be with him. Law then threatened resignation. The Cabinet then adjourned to give the opportunity for reflection; it could not do much else in the circumstances. Such a calm process was hardly aided when on the following morning its members read in *The Times* an anonymous letter denouncing the terms and signed 'Colonial'. It was notable for the use of almost exactly the same phrases and arguments which the Prime Minister had deployed at the previous day's Cabinet, and was indeed written by him.

The reaction of the Cabinet was the equally unprecedented one of holding a meeting in the Lord Chancellor's room at the House of Lords, at which everyone was present save only for the Prime Minister – who was presumably not invited. There they decided, again with only the Scottish Secretary dissenting, that they should put a collective pistol to the Prime Minister's head. A deputation of three (Lord Chancellor Cave, Devonshire and Baldwin) went to urge him to abandon resignation but also to insist that he abandoned his stand against Baldwin's settlement. They found him less adamant than on the previous day for he had discovered in the meantime that City opinion, fickle as so often, and for the interpretation of which he relied upon the ubiquitous McKenna, had swung round and was now in favour of the terms. The Prime Minister's retreat was announced and accepted with relief at a five-minute Cabinet that afternoon. The fact that the Cabinet had formally to be summoned at all, and then the perfunctory briefness of the meeting, made it almost like the symbolic handing over of a sword at a surrender ceremony.

Beaverbrook, who knew Law better than did anyone else outside his family, took the view that from that abject moment there began the final collapse of his health. Whatever may be the medical validity of that dramatic judgement, the incident certainly gravely weakened his internal authority and obliterated any vestiges of enjoyment which he was getting from his premiership. Thereafter he felt more a prisoner of his reluctant retreat from sundering the first Conservative government for seventeen years than a commander-in-chief surrounded by loyal divisional generals. The very odd choice of the word 'Colonial' for his semi-pseudonymous signature pointed to a sense of outsidership as well as a reversion, near the end, to his beginnings.

'Thereafter' did not last very long. The 'surrender' Cabinet was on 30 January. In March the government suffered three heavy by-election defeats and the Prime Minister's health was causing serious concern. It was hoped that the Easter holiday might cause it to improve, but when Parliament reassembled on 10 April his voice was too weak to answer questions, and after a public attempt he handed over the task to Baldwin. On 27 April he told the King that he had been advised to try a month's Mediterranean cruise. Baldwin would lead the House of Commons, Curzon would preside over the Cabinet. He left on 1 May. He got worse and not better on the voyage, and abandoned the ship at Genoa on 8 May. He went first to Aix-les-Bains, where his old friend Rudyard Kipling was deeply shocked at his appearance. The ever-faithful (to Law) Max Beaverbrook came out and arranged a Paris medical rendez-vous in the Hôtel Crillon to which that most eminent of politicians' doctors, Sir Thomas (later Lord) Horder, was summoned from London. That consultation took place on 17 May and resulted in a fatal diagnosis.

Bonar Law returned to London on 19 May and resigned on the 20th. His main concern at this stage was that he should not have to advise the King on his successor. He saw considerable although different disadvantages to the two possibilities of Curzon and Baldwin. He assumed it would be Curzon, although probably his reluctant and marginal preference was for Baldwin. But a stronger emotion was his desire to avoid responsibility for the choice. This avoidance, despite some attempted meddling to distort his views in Baldwin's favour by that most inappropriate of private secretaries, Colonel Ronald Waterhouse (inappropriate because he was both clumsy and sinister), Law achieved. It was Balfour's advice, perhaps aided by some natural instinct on the part of the bluff King to prefer the apparent stolidity of Baldwin to the complex grandeur of Curzon, which determined the outcome.

Bonar Law lived another five months, including a period of some remission in the summer, when he went to Brighton and even to Le Touquet. He was buried in Westminster Abbey, where surprisingly few Prime Ministers lie. The last previous one had been Gladstone, and there has since been only Neville Chamberlain. It was a great political/state funeral. At the dispersal of the ten pall-bearers, who apart from the Prince of Wales and Beaverbrook were the mandarins of British politics, Asquith is alleged to have said that it was fitting to have buried the Unknown Prime Minister by the side of the Unknown Soldier. This aphorism, which does not sound to me quite authentically Asquithian for the occasion, at least gave Robert Blake the title for his first and excellent biography. Nonetheless Bonar Law could perhaps more justly have been called the Sad Prime Minister. Most premierships – and indeed many lives – end sadly. Law's was without much joy at the beginning or in the middle, and sadness imbued almost his whole political career. But he inspired a good deal of affection and respect in those who worked closely with him.

Sir Robert Horne

Sir Robert Horne was a Chancellor whom it is easy to forget. Indeed I remember to my shame that during the Glasgow Hillhead by-election of 1982 on a 'canvas walkabout', on which the object was of course to establish points of conversational contact with the electorate, I was asked by an elderly man if I recalled which previous Chancellor of the Exchequer had been member for the constituency. He was bowling me the equivalent of a long-hop, and I, whose mind is excessively cluttered with the minutiae of political careers, totally fluffed it. I barely remembered the existence of Horne, and had certainly not connected him with the constituency whose franchise I was then so urgently seeking. Such ignorance probably cost me one vote, or at least left a potential supporter disappointed with my lack of response.

Yet I ought to have had fixed in my mind at least one thing about Horne (although not one happily which would have automatically connected him with Hillhead) and that was Baldwin's very memorable description of him as 'that rare thing, a Scots cad'. Baldwin, although in many ways a nice man, was quick to make disapproving moral judgements, whether of the 'hard-faced men who looked as though they had done well out of the war', or of those 'who made a million quick' deserving to be 'in gaol rather than in the House of Lords', or later of King Edward VIII. It is however uncertain what alleged turpitude on the part of Baldwin's immediate predecessor at the Exchequer provoked his pungent but sweeping judgement.

Probably it was to do with Horne's style and character rather than with his Treasury performance. Despite his Scottish manse origin, Horne was something of a minor Birkenhead, fond of high earning, high spending, hard drinking, irreverent conversation and London night clubs. He never married, but he was very social and in particular liked the society of smart women. He could not rival his exemplar Birkenhead as a master of mordant wit, but as an anecdotalist he was unmatched.

His entry in the *Dictionary of National Biography* described him as 'debonair, alert and sprightly', 'in much request socially', but leaving no mark which was 'permanently distinctive'. The author of that surprisingly sparkling 900-word essay which is almost the only permanent record of Horne's life, was Lord Macmillan, the Scottish Law Lord who presided over the Committee on Finance and Industry set up by MacDonald in 1929. He had been a near contemporary of Horne's at Glasgow University and in their early days at the Scottish bar, and wrote about him with a mixture of affection and slightly mocking, amused semi-admiration. It was appropriate that Horne's only recorded address for the last decade or so of his life was 69 Arlington House, Piccadilly, London W1, the apartment block which had recently been constructed on the site of Salisbury's old town house, and where Beaverbrook also had his latter-day London apartment.

It was a long way, psychologically even more than geographically, from Slamannan, the south Stirlingshire mining town/village where his father was minister of the established Presbyterian Church. Slamannan, almost exactly halfway between Glasgow and Edinburgh, was in one of the least attractive parts of Scotland, a little but not much better than Airdrie and Coatbridge to the west of it or Falkirk to the north. Here Robert Stevenson Horne was born in February 1871. Horne moved to the east for his schooling at George Watson's College (where John Anderson was a decade after him, David Maxwell Fyfe another two decades after that and David Steel another three and a half), and to the west for his university. But he was essentially a West rather than an East of Scotland man. Glasgow University was his real *alma mater*. He had all the quick-talking fluency which still characterizes its debating style rather than the taciturn gravitas in which Anderson was to specialize.

From its twenty-year-old gothic halls above the banks of the Clyde he graduated in 1893 with first-class honours in mental philosophy (what other sort was there?), having been president both of the University Conservative Club and of the Students' Representative Council, two offices which it was easier then than today to combine. Next he taught philosophy for a year in the University College of North Wales at Bangor. Then he went back to Scotland, was admitted to the Faculty of Advocates and gradually built up a very sound Glasgow-based commercial and shipping practice. He became a KC in 1910, in which year of two general elections he was on both occasions unsuccessful Conservative candidate for his native county of Stirling.

The contests were not wholly in vain. He was a great networker, using his natural bonhomie to advance his legal, business and political contacts. At the outbreak of the 1914 war, aged forty-three and with a good but not spectacular advocate's career behind him, he was still confined to Scotland, although reaching to get out. From this point of view the war served him well. He advanced as a protégé of Sir Eric Geddes, one of the breed of 'new men' whom Lloyd George advanced rather as, on a much grander scale, Napoleon did his marshals. Geddes, however, was an odd patron for Horne, because he was four years younger and came from no more established a background. However Horne worked with Geddes on railway organization behind the front in France (with the rank of lieutenant-colonel), then in the Department of Materials, and finally (for the war) dealing with labour relations in the dockyards and similar establishments of the Admiralty. The irony was that Lloyd George depended upon Geddes as a problem-solver and that Geddes in turn depended upon his older assistant actually to get the knots untied. In 1921, a few months after he had become Chancellor, Horne repaid the debt, or maybe retaliated against Geddes, by making him chairman of a committee on public expenditure and thus immortalizing him as the wielder of the 'Geddes axe'.

For the election of December 1918 Horne was chosen as the Coalition Conservative candidate for the newly created Glasgow constituency of Hillhead, which showed that his two forlorn fights in Stirlingshire as well as his careful cultivation of contacts had paid off well. Hillhead was, as it remained until its substantial extension eastward for the 1987 election, followed by its sundering and demise for the 1997 one, essentially Glasgow's West End, an expression much more used there than in London and carrying a residential rather than, as in the latter case, an entertainment connotation. It was middle- and upper-middle-class Glasgow, centred around the core of the semi-mansions of Kelvinside, and as such provided Horne with a safe Conservative haven for the seven general elections which he fought there.

Horne was immediately made Minister of Labour, and was thus one of the handful of politicians who delivered his maiden speech from the despatch box on the government side. He was never a commanding parliamentary orator, but he was competent on his feet in the House of Commons, as with everything else which he did. And he handled with a cool and non-provocative skill the explosive industrial atmosphere in the mines and on the railways, which were then the country's two largest sources of employment. He provided an earlier and slightly harder-line version of Walter Monckton's emollience in the same job in the second

Churchill government. His non-ideological fixing capabilities were much appreciated by Lloyd George, and he received two promotions in the two and three-quarter years for which the Coalition lasted. In March 1920 he succeeded his old chief Eric Geddes as President of the Board of Trade, and in April 1921 he succeeded Austen Chamberlain at the Exchequer, and was himself succeeded at the Board of Trade by Baldwin. Although he did not have much individual political clout his usefulness had secured his entry into the top echelons of the Conservative party. Selwyn Lloyd's position thirty-five years later comes to mind.

Horne was responsible for two budgets, but introduced only the second of them. This was a convoluted consequence of the handover at the Treasury having taken place fairly close to budget day. Austen Chamberlain became leader of the Conservative party within the Coalition and abandoned the Chancellorship on 21 March. The budget was due on 25 April. In these circumstances it would have been possible to imagine one of two consequences. Horne might have introduced the budget saying, modestly rather than disloyally, that it was really Chamberlain's budget and that he was merely the mouthpiece. Or Chamberlain might have followed the precedent set by Asquith in 1908 and, while no longer Chancellor himself, made the speech on the ground that he had done the work.

What in fact occurred was less comprehensible. Chamberlain did make the speech, but not on the ground that it was his budget. On the contrary he specifically stated that the budget was Horne's and not his construction. Horne however was so busy as the government's most skilful and experienced industrial negotiater, with the actual coal strike and the threatened sympathetic action by the railway and transport workers ('black Friday' when the putative triple alliance collapsed was on 15 April 1921), that he 'delegated' delivery of the budget speech itself to his leader. This showed both that Horne was not a very ambitious politician, for to miss such an opportunity for self-projection with one's own budget was cavalier, and that Austen Chamberlain was an uncomplaining old trouper: to present someone else's budget was more trouble than fun.

In truth, however, there was not very much to present in the 1921 budget. It was variously described as 'humdrum', 'prosaic' and 'singularly uninteresting'. This was primarily because, apart from the abolition of the excess profits duty, an intention which had been announced in February, there were practically no revenue changes, and it is always such changes that attract the most attention in the strange annual festival of budget day, which achieved such a position in the national life during the classical period of British politics that W. P. Frith should have painted it as a matching canvas to his Derby Day. Apart from the anti-climatic abolition of EPD the only changes were the reversal of the surcharges on champagne and cigars which had been imposed in the previous budget and had proved counter-productive for revenue yield. Austen Chamberlain who had been responsible for the previous year's decisions contradicted the view that politicians never apologize. 'Let others learn by the mistakes which I committed,' he unequivocally said.

The main attention in the debates on the budget and its accompanying Finance Bill, which Horne conducted, was on debt redemption and on trying to reconcile post-war levels of expenditure with pre-war assumptions. Debt had multiplied by more than ten times and expenditure was up to between five and six times the pre-1914 level. There was of course some inflationary element in both these figures, but the rate of inflation had been nothing like that which came to prevail fifty years later. The 1920s value of money was never less than a half that of the late Victorian and Edwardian years. Many felt they were out of sight of land and without a working compass, like early navigators. So the excitement about the increased burden of debt and expenditure was understandable. It was wholly shared by the Labour party, although they at this stage wished to solve the former problem by a swingeing capital levy. Out of this climate of apprehension there arose the Geddes Committee, which Chamberlain announced in the budget speech but for which Horne must bear the principal responsibility, particularly as he had been so closely associated with Eric Geddes.

Horne's second budget was presented on 1 May 1922. It came after a year of collapsing prices and mounting unemployment. The post-war boom was wholly deflated. The budgetary consequences of this were obviously profound. Expenditure was below estimate by £57 million, but revenue was even more reduced. The Inland Revenue receipts as a whole were down by the enormous sum of £111 million, nearly 20 per cent of the total. Of the component Inland Revenue items only death duties were macabrely up: income tax, super-tax, corporation tax, excess profits duty were all significantly down. The nominal surplus of £177 million announced for the year by Chamberlain in 1921, although with a suitable note of caution, turned out to be only £45.5 million.

Variations in the debt position were of a labyrinthine complication. On the one hand the rise in the exchange value of sterling from the $3.20 to which it had fallen in early 1920, when the wartime peg was taken off, to $4.40, the typically perverse reaction of the foreign markets to the deterioration of almost every aspect of the 'real' British economy, had led to a massive automatic benefit on the overseas front. The liability to the United States which would have been £1,302 million at the low rate of exchange had come down to £947 million. It may be doubted that many of his listeners followed the complexity of these explanations, as indeed may be the extent to which Horne himself, despite the lucidity of his lawyer's brain, was in full charge of the detailed navigation.

What however is indisputably the case is that the bold reversal of policy which he proceeded to announce towards the end of his speech was very much his own decision. The financial year 1920–1 under Austen Chamberlain had been a tremendous year for the repayment of debt, and even 1921–2 had made some attempt to continue in this direction: £322 million had been provided in the two years combined towards this end. With budget totals of around £1,000 million in each year this was a prodigious effort, which Horne said had undoubtedly been right in the circumstances. No doubt as a member of the Cabinet throughout he could say no other, and his point had force in relation to the 1920 budget, but it is difficult to see why the 1921 circumstances, with the boom already three months bust, were relevantly different from those of 1922. For 1922–3 in any event he struck out on a course of premature semi-Keynesianism. He did not go as far as deficit financing, but he did announce that the time for budget surpluses and debt repayment was at least temporarily past. With unemployment over two million, with the professional and middle classes enduring heavy taxation burdens, with industry suffering an unprecedented depression, 'no sound canon of finance would be infringed if the government were content to raise sufficient revenue merely to meet expenditure'. Stopping all debt repayment would obviously involve the suppression almost before it had started of the new general sinking fund, and indeed some new borrowing in order to meet the demands of some special sinking funds, but the government should not shrink from that provided the overall burden of debt was not increased.

With no debt repayment obligation he had a surplus of £38 million to dispose of and he used it rather more than to the full, and in a way which looked more even-handed than it in fact was. He reduced the standard rate of income tax from six shillings to five shillings in the pound (from 30 to 25 pence in modern parlance) and he remitted one-third of the tea duty, directed to producing a saving to the consumer of fourpence a pound. The income tax concession cost £32.5 million and the tea one £5 million, which eliminated all but £700,000 of his surplus. As however the combined full-year costs of the two tax reductions were £57.5 million there was an element of imaginative accountancy in pretending that he was in reality budgeting for even the smallest surplus.

This budget was on the whole badly received, certainly on the sparsely populated Liberal and Labour benches of that parliament, but also to some extent among the massed ranks of the Coalitionists. A common thread was a metaphorical gathering up of dowagers' skirts at the brazen irresponsibility, almost the loucheness, of Horne's perform-ance. The implied thought was that it was typical of the decadent decline and fall of the Lloyd George empire. Asquith began the disapproval. The only legitimate ground, he magisterially pronounced, for tax remissions, however desirable in themselves, was an excess of estimated revenue over estimated expenditure and that was far from being the case with Horne's 'fictitious surplus'. Philip Snowden, the arch-priest of balanced budgets and debt reduction at all costs, had still not returned to the House after his 1918 defeat, and Horne was therefore spared the lash of his harsh tongue. J. R. Clynes, leading the Labour party at that stage, was more muted, but he fired an arrow which, although this took a little time to become apparent, was of a deadly accuracy. He cast grave doubt on the validity of the budget estimates on both the expenditure and the revenue sides. He was abundantly justified, for the budget's assumptions turned out to be some of the most inaccurate in the history of British budgets, and sufficiently so as to render irrelevant much of the 1922 argument. Revenue was up by £3.5 million, although with wild variations in the component elements, so that the relative accuracy of the total was almost entirely accidental. At the same time expenditure was down by nearly £100 million, slightly more than 10 per cent of the total.

Some other Labour guns fired in support of Clynes but chose their targets with less than the leader's (maybe accidental) skill. Colonel Josiah Wedgwood thundered most loudly against the class aspects of the budget, which was one for 'railway shareholders, farmers, millionaires, excess profiteers, super-tax dodgers and [mining] royalty owners', but not for the workers. Oswald Mosley, then in transition from the Conservative as which he had been elected to the Labour member he was about to become, delivered a particularly vehement denunciation of the evils of borrowing in order to reduce taxation, which was ironic in view of the fact that, eight years later, he resigned from a Labour government, and set off on his journey to fascism, because that government would not embrace deficit financing in order to attack unemployment (although it must be said that he then advocated using the deficit to finance investment and not to reduce taxation).

The Finance Bill giving legislative shape to the 1922 budget went through without a government defeat (there had been one the previous year), although with the Labour party voting against both its second and third readings, and with many small concessions, for beyond its strategic lines here discussed it had been a restless budget, making many minor changes to the established patterns of taxation, and providing many enjoyable hours for tax specialist lawyers in the House of Commons, and many lucrative ones for those outside. It became law on 20 July, and thereafter the Coalition government approached its iceberg of the repudiating Carlton Club meeting (on 19 October) with erratic speed.

After the fall of the Coalition Horne remained a loyal Coalitionist, which was morally if not opportunistically the most impressive time to remain so. He may have appeared a 'Scots cad' to Baldwin but he certainly did not do so to Austen Chamberlain, who was just as reputable if somewhat less subtle a judge of decency. For the six months of the Bonar Law government Horne had little option but to stand out from it as automatically as did Chamberlain, Balfour and Birkenhead. But when Baldwin replaced Law in May 1923 the flexibility of politics was illustrated by its being the Scots cad (Horne) rather than the philosopher king (Balfour) or the first gentleman of politics (Austen Chamberlain) or the English cad but more swashbuckling wit (Birkenhead) whom he tried hardest to entice into his government. The Chancellorship was wide open, indeed it remained so for four months while McKenna, unlike Horne, dithered. But Horne had first refusal. And refuse he firmly did. At first he tried to pretend that his loyalty to his recently acquired business associates precluded this. But they, generously rather than thankfully I think, offered to release him and he was forced to fall back on his real reason, which was that he would not enter a government without Austen Chamberlain. He was more loyal to Austen than was his half-brother Neville. And as Austen was equally loyal to Birkenhead, who had become anathema to the core of Conservatism, a real impasse to Conservative unity, close-woven in Chamberlain with a mixture of loyalty (to political friends not to the party) and personal prickliness, was created.

As a result of his 1923 refusal Horne never held office again. He paid a greater price, even though he was the first sought after, than any of the other three major Coalitionists. But his business compensations were manifold, even if his associates had put country before boardroom in 1923. He became a director of the Suez Canal Company, of the P & O Steamship Company, of Lloyds Bank and of Commercial Union. He was chairman of Burmah Oil. In 1934 he became chairman of the Great Western Railway, hardly a geographically appropriate niche for someone who was still MP for the Hillhead division of Glasgow.

During the fifteen years after his loss of office he remained a slightly shadowy major businessman/back bencher of a type which was always present in the House of Commons from about 1868 to 1950, but which has since disappeared. Horne was unusual among them because he had held high office, but he did not make great impact in this decade and a half. His viscountcy was one of the last peerages conferred by his old critic Baldwin. Horne was very much a talented Scottish boy on the make. He was better than a cad but not quite a statesman.

STANLEY BALDWIN

(as Chancellor)

STANLEY BALDWIN INCONTESTABLY QUALIFIES FOR THE shortest
of these essays. This is not at all because he was an insignificant figure.
Indeed he was in most ways, despite his indolence, the dominant
politician of the inter-war years. But his Chancellorship was brief – just
over nine months, doubled with the premiership for the last three of
them. It called forth no great display of financial powers or interest, and
it left him with no continuing special concern with financial policy. As
party leader he stood back from his Chancellors just as much as he did
from his Foreign Secretaries. Nor were these nine months necessary to
make him Prime Minister, except insofar as they gave him a little more
seniority. But seniority could not have been the reason he was preferred
over Curzon when Bonar Law's health collapsed. Nor was there any
suggestion that it was because he was thought to have proved himself a
financial wizard. On the contrary, of the two most famous remarks about
him, Churchill's 'he was the most ruthless and astute politician of his
day' and F. E. Smith's (Birkenhead) 'he takes a leap in the dark, looks
round, and takes another', his performance at the Exchequer put one
much more in mind of Smith's than of Churchill's. There was something
of blind man's bluff about it, and it would be as inadequate a basis for
judging his whole career as was to be Churchill's own performance in
the same office less than two years later.

The still more compelling reason for the shortness of this essay is
that in 1987 I published a book about Baldwin. That too was short,
more a biographical essay than a full-scale biography, but it provided a
vehicle for such insights as I thought I had and such judgements as I
felt able to make. These obviously should not be repeated, and I must
therefore confine myself, as with Asquith and for the same reasons,
to describing in a little more detail than in my books the subjects'

actions in the not overwhelmingly important Treasury chapters of their lives.

Baldwin moved back from the Board of Trade to the Treasury, in which for four years until March 1921 he had been Financial Secretary under Austen Chamberlain, in October 1922. He became the vice-captain (at least so far as the Commons was concerned), of a government of the 'second eleven' as, with Balfour, Austen Chamberlain, Robert Horne and himself excluded, Churchill was graciously pleased to put it. Short though the time was before Baldwin moved up to the captaincy, he managed to be involved as Chancellor in three different enterprises, each of which revealed a different side of his effective but idiosyncratic political style.

The first was his negotiation of an American war debt settlement. This was a tangled, delicate and dangerous issue. Baldwin's handling of it has been described in the Bonar Law essay, for it involved him in the most desperate conflict with the Prime Minister, which nearly led to the break-up of the government. This was avoided only by Law reluctantly acquiescing in a most humiliating retreat. He had taken a terrible tumble, and lost a lot of his spirit as well as of his authority. Baldwin, by contrast, had shown a sort of innocent determination, which had worked, and in consequence was seen as moving to fill the power gap which the Prime Minister was leaving empty. It was noticeable that in his next major speech, which was on 16 February 1923, in reply to a Labour amendment in the debate on the King's Speech at the opening of the session, his speech was very much that of a leader and not of a departmental minister. He ranged wide, not only giving a strong defence of the American debt settlement which was so repugnant to his Prime Minister, but also seeking to describe the basis of the government's foreign policy. He envisaged not just the possibility but the certainty of a future Labour government – 'when the Labour party sits on these benches' was one of his phrases, and one which very much expressed the cross-party emolli-ence which was becoming part of his oratorical stock-in-trade. And he ended with a homily, trite or profound according to taste:

> Four words, of one syllable each, are words which contain salvation for the country and for the whole world, and they are, faith, hope, love and work. No government in this country today which has not faith in the future, love for its fellow-men, and which will not work and work and work will ever bring this country through into better days and better times, and will ever bring Europe through, and the world through.

The eloquence was by no means perfectly wrought, with something of a dying fall at the end, but it was nonetheless a notable speech. It was the first of a whole series of his ruminative House of Commons disquisitions, at once homespun and high-flown, which, whatever else could be said about them, rarely failed to capture the ears of his listeners. They were the epitome of the Baldwin style, which helped to make him Prime Minister three months later and then to keep him, even if with quite a lot of downs as well as ups, in the leadership of his party for the next fourteen years.

His one and only budget came on 16 April. As a speech it had the two virtues of being relatively short (only just over an hour and a half) and occasionally self-deprecatingly funny. Yet in substance it now gives the impression of sleep-walking. The out-turn for the year 1922–3 had been much more favourable than had been expected. Horne had budgeted for a bare surplus of £706,000 but had achieved one of £101.5 million. Revenue was up by £3.5 million, but the fact that it bore any close relation to the estimate seemed to have been purely accidental. Excess profits duty, for example, which had been estimated to produce £27.8 million in fact produced only £2 million. On the other hand there was an unexpected clearing-up of arrears of income tax and surtax, which meant that the Inland Revenue as a whole was £36 million above estimate.

The major contribution to the unexpected surplus came from the expenditure side, which was £98 million below estimate. Interest on Treasury Bills was nearly £30 million below estimate and the service departments were down by £27 million. Baldwin, who could not of course be held responsible for Horne's loose estimating, took the view that while this out-turn was unplanned it was nonetheless all for the best. Reductions in public expenditure had been widely urged. When they occurred it must be a good thing. It was unnecessary to look gift horses too closely in their mouths. He had reached a fine vantage point, and the fact that he did not know quite how he had got there did not matter too much until, like Tamino and Papageno in the *Magic Flute*, it became a question of finding his way back.

For the moment, however, he was able to use the vantage point to distribute some bonuses. Income tax came down from five shillings in the pound to 4s 6d. There were Post Office concessions with a reduction in the cost of a letter which, while it did not quite restore Rowland Hill's penny post, brought it down to a penny halfpenny, where it remained until some way into the Second World War. The cider tax was abolished and the beer duty was reduced so that, with some contribution from the brewers, the price to the public fell by a penny a pint. This reduction of what Philip Snowden, the Labour financial spokesman, described as 'the greatest agency of temperance reform ever seen in the country' put that total abstainer into a great state, and even Asquith, who did not exactly fall into the same category as Snowden, thought that a reduction in the sugar duty would have been more appropriate.

Snowden however, unusually for him, exposed a weak intellectual flank by reacting equally violently against Baldwin's *ballon d'essai* in favour of a betting tax. The Chancellor thought the Exchequer needed for the medium term some new source of revenue, and betting seemed to him the most promising avenue up which to look. But Baldwin pleaded lack of time in office, with the interruptions first of an election and then of the American negotiation, as reasons why he had not been able to give the matter sufficient study to reach a definite conclusion: he proposed therefore to refer it to a House of Commons Select Committee. But even this tentativeness allowed Snowden to denounce the idea of making respectable by taxation 'the second greatest curse of the country'. As in his calendar the even greater curse was drink, it was not obvious, as Baldwin was able gently to point out, to reconcile with this view his passion for a high duty in beer.

A large part of the budget speech was devoted to debt management, inevitably a highly technical and therefore, except for *aficionados*, a fairly boring subject. There was ample justification for giving the subject this degree of attention. The 1914–18 war had had the effect of putting the structure of budgets back to a shape not very different from that which had prevailed between the end of the Napoleonic Wars and the Peel/Gladstone reforms. Debt charges in Baldwin's budget amounted to £350 million or 43 per cent of the total expenditure estimates of £816 million. In addition the level of floating or unfunded debt (at over £1,000 million in 1922 but down by £220 million in the year under review) had been causing concern, and as there were some formidable maturities, necessitating reborrowing, the state of the gilt-edged market was of crucial importance.

It was also the case that nearly everyone, across the spectrum of politics, believed that the route to national salvation lay through the reduction of the national debt. Snowden and the Labour party certainly did. They had used it as one of the principal justifications for a capital levy. But when they came to office in the following year Snowden jettisoned the capital levy but continued to believe in debt redemption by, for most, more painful means. Asquith was equally for paying off debt, although not for the capital levy. Almost the sole contrary voice was that of the ex-Coalition Liberals, of whom Sir Alfred Mond had become economic spokesman and who expressed a policy of benign self-indulgence. The objective should be to water the roots of investment and enterprise. It was therefore more important to reduce taxation than to produce budget surpluses and to redeem debt.

Baldwin in 1923 also produced a new sinking fund arrangement to replace that which Stafford Northcote had introduced in 1875 and which had survived, although often in very battered form, for forty-eight years. Sometimes Chancellors had been borrowing in order, *inter alia*, to keep up the sinking fund commitment, which was *Alice Through the Looking-Glass* finance. But the virtue, such as it was, of the 1875 arrangement was that it had a built-in accelerator. As debt was reduced so this sinking fund reduced it still further. It was a sort of compound interest in reverse. Baldwin's new sinking fund – of £40 million a year – was on the contrary a straight-line payment, analagous with simple interest, which would not gain momentum as the debt was reduced, and which would not achieve its elimination in under 150 years. Asquith and Lees-Smith, a Labour member referred to with respect in *British Budgets* as 'a professional economist', were both critical on these grounds.

Baldwin therefore had good reason for devoting so much of his speech to debt management. This nonetheless resulted in it giving the impression, its asides apart, to a greater extent than almost any other budget speech, of being written by officials and read, almost parrot-like, by the Chancellor. He nevertheless read it in a sufficiently characteristic Baldwinesque style that it did him no harm at all. Within five weeks of its delivery he was Prime Minister. As he then followed Bonar Law in wanting that elusive ex-Liberal Reginald McKenna to be his Chancellor, and as McKenna, whatever his other virtues by this stage may or may not have been, liked having the Chancellorship on offer rather than actually accepting it and would not make up his mind for several months, Baldwin, commonly thought one of the most indolent of Prime Ministers, had for the first time since Gladstone to double the two jobs until August. However he semi-demoted and semi-promoted William Joynson-Hicks (the 'Jix' to whom he later gave the opportunity to be the least liberal Home Secretary until Mr Michael Howard) from Postmaster-General to Financial Secretary of the Treasury (but with a seat in the Cabinet, which he had not had before) and left him to carry through the Finance Bill.

Just before his departure for his long annual holiday at Aix-les-

Bains, always the most sacred moment of the year, Baldwin got tired of waiting for McKenna and appointed Neville Chamberlain Chancellor. The latter's first stint at the Exchequer was very brief and he was, as we have seen, one of the only three in this series (Iain Macleod was a fourth) who had a Chancellorship without a budget. But later, still under Baldwin's leadership, he became almost as powerful a Chancellor as Lloyd George had been under Asquith. Baldwin meanwhile moved towards his bizarre decision to throw away his large majority within six months of becoming Prime Minister in the unsuccessful Protectionist election of November–December 1923. His reputation, which deserves to be considerable, rests neither upon his Chancellorship nor upon the first and briefest of his premierships.

Philip Snowden

THE MOST INTERESTING BUT NOW NEARLY the most hidden of the inter-war Chancellors was Philip Snowden. In both the MacDonald Labour administrations and for the first month or two of the National government he was a powerful, famous, cantankerous and rigidly orthodox head of the Treasury. He had a bitter and unforgiving streak in his nature, which, while it could perhaps be explained by the permanently crippling illness which struck him down at the age of twenty-seven, could not thereby be wished away. As he was also self-righteous and narrow-minded, he could not be called an attractive man. But he had a powerful persona, and he is well worth disinterring from the rubble of neglect and obscurity which has fallen upon his career and his character, at once defiant and defensive.

He was essentially a Pennine evangelizing socialist, his early life, and indeed his later constituencies, alternating between the Yorkshire and the Lancashire sides of that low mountain chain, where a sense not merely of insularity but of remoteness from Leeds or Manchester achieves an intensity disproportionate to the height or the distance. Later in life he settled in semi-manorial, semi-suburban circumstances, somewhat mirroring Lloyd George's movement from Criccieth to Churt, among the pine trees and sandy soil of upland Surrey, with a good part of his socialist fervour and generous hopes draining away into that peculiarly porous ground.

Philip Snowden was born in July 1864 in the hamlet of Ickornshaw which was part of the parish of Cowling, seven miles west of Keighley and only two or three miles short of the watershed and the Lancashire border. It was a location which made the Haworth of the Brontës, also about seven miles distance to the south-east, seem almost lush and close to the bright lights of West Riding urbanism. The cottage of his birth, although solid with well-matured dark Yorkshire stone, stood insecurely on a precipitate ledge. It epitomized the ability of Pennine villages, less than a thousand feet up, to give an almost Tibetan impression of being on the roof of the world. Snowden, like them, developed a habit of looking down on softer locations and weaker mortals.

Snowden's father was a weaver with intellectual tastes and a good small library. He was in a sense an aristocratic artisan with high skill and a tradition of independence, but it is difficult to believe that in such a remote location and with wool, even if less so than cotton, becoming a large-scale factory industry, he was not becoming a marginal producer. This indeed proved to be the case for in 1879 the Cowling mill collapsed and the family were forced to move across the county boundary to Nelson. Philip Snowden went with them, even though he, unlike his sisters, had not been employed in the bankrupt Cowling mill, and even though it involved the end of his brief career as a very young pupil teacher. From Nelson he got a job in an insurance office in Burnley. And from there he obtained by competitive examination in 1886 entry into the lower ranks of the civil service. He became a second-class assistant revenue officer dealing with excise questions, at a salary of only £50 a year plus about £30 of expenses. It was a post which brought him security, entry by the modest end into the middle classes, and the prospect of a quiet life interspersed with some promotions, but with these likely to stop well short of the administrative top.

He appeared to enjoy his five years as an excise official, despite his life-long aversion to the beers and spirits, measuring the strength and quantity of which was his primary duty. He was sent to widely scattered bases; Liverpool (for training), then Aberdeen with its sub-station in Orkney, Carlisle and Plymouth with its Redruth sub-station. It was a good broadening for a future national politician who had hitherto been very geographically confined. In August 1892, while at Redruth, he was stricken with a severe ailment of the spine which led to a paralysis of the legs, a long bed-bound period, and the end, after twenty-six months of sick leave, of his civil service career. During the summer leading up to his illness his duties had involved a lot of bicycling round the Cornish lanes, and a theory was developed, mainly by Snowden, but sympathetically considered by his professional superiors and even the Treasury itself, that his condition might have been induced by a bicycle bump. But this theory owed more to a desire for a generous disability settlement than to objective medical diagnosis. It seems more probable that he was infected by a tuberculosis of the spine similar to, but less well treated, than that which afflicted Alec Douglas-Home during the Second World War. The bicycle-accident theory faded and he was invalided out of the

Inland Revenue Department in 1893 with a gratuity of only £31. He did not return to the public payroll until just over thirty years later when he became Chancellor of the Exchequer.

There is no suggestion that he held his parsimonious termination against the Treasury. It would have been illogical had he done so, for he was instinctively a parsimonious Chancellor, indeed the most consistently so since Gladstone. It would have been most unlikely that anyone in his position would have done better had he himself already been in charge. In general indeed he took fate's cruelty with more fatalism than bitterness. The course of his illness was that, having gone home to his mother in Cowling when it struck (she had returned there from Nelson following the death of his father in 1889), he had been forced to spend a year or even eighteen months effectively bed-ridden. At times it was difficult for him to achieve even the elevation necessary to read, let alone to write, although as a result of great effort, assisted by a contraption of an ingenious local joiner, he began during this period what was subsequently a long-continuing journalistic habit. Towards the end of this period of purgatory he regained the ability first to get out of bed and to stand, then to hobble, and finally to walk, slowly and with manifest difficulty, but if necessary for quite long distances. He stabilized at this level of activity for the next forty years until in his early seventies he again began to lose the use of his legs. During these relatively good decades he was habitually dependent on two sticks.

I do not think that these vicissitudes, bravely accepted and to a considerable extent brilliantly overcome, were the cause of Snowden's mordancy and the contemptuous invective which he became so easily inclined to display against either a political opponent or a critic within his own party. Rather it was that they gave to these outbursts a frightening, almost a supernatural force. With his powerful shoulders, twisted body, thin face and occasional rather sweet smile he became a man whom it was not only dangerous to cross but whose approval, because it was so abstemiously given, was also greatly valued.

He also became a high ethical socialist, the epitome of the proselytizing spirit which, 'owing more to Methodism than to Marx', characterized the early Independent Labour Party. This was a vital if sometimes turbulent tributary to the surge to government of the 1920s Labour party. The ILP, although national in intent and substantially so in achievement before declining at the end of its life into being a Clydeside rump, was, almost as much as Snowden himself, a Pennine product. It was born in Bradford in January 1893 and many of its early triumphs (and setbacks) were experienced in the textile towns and villages of West Yorkshire and East Lancashire.

It also came at almost exactly the right time for Philip Snowden. As a young man he had not been particularly interested in politics. When he lived in Liverpool in 1886, his first experience of a big city, he wrote with excitement and even hyperbole ('it is a city which possesses every attraction') of the libraries, the art gallery, the concerts, the opera and the literary lectures, but not of how much Liverpool support there would be for the conversion of Gladstone, its most eminent son, to Irish Home Rule. Snowden was a Liberal – with his Noncomformist Cowling background he would have found it very difficult to be anything else – but he was up to this stage a fairly cool one.

Nevertheless at the key point, a few months after the Bradford birth and at exactly the time when, his civil service career formally ended, his recovery had proceeded far enough for him to begin to look for another mainspring to his life, an invitation from a Liberal organization precipitated his conversion to socialism. He was invited, at the instigation of a relation, to lecture to a body no more prestigious than the Cowling Liberal Club. The subject was to be socialism, it no doubt being assumed that he would refute its doctrines. As he had plenty of time he prepared most carefully. He first read a rather neutral work, Kirkup's *Enquiry into Socialism*. This set his mind moving favourably as a result of the analysis rather than the argument. Then he plunged much deeper into the subject, reading American and German as well as English authors, but never Marx.

Eventually, such was Snowden's implacable all-or-nothing approach, he sold the little library of about 200 works of literature which he had built up during his civil service years in order to replace them with the classics of early socialist propaganda. The lecture came out as a paean of praise for ethical idealistic socialism, fuelled by a vision of the unity of humanity rather than by class warfare. It was the first of many hundreds, if not thousands, of such talks of uplift which he was to give. It may have surprised the audience, although it apparently temporarily converted the chairman.

From the acorn of this lecture there quickly grew the vast oak of Snowden's proselytizing activity. From about 1895 to 1905 he was a full-time peripatetic propagandist. The only respite from his endless soap-boxing (his summer meetings were mostly in market squares, although his winter ones frequently in dimly lit Noncomformist or Co-operative halls) was his political journalism. He first edited a Keighley

Labour journal (and indeed moved into the town from Cowling in order to do this) at a 'salary' of eight shillings a week. Then he became responsible for the national weekly *Labour Leader*, typically putting it together on ill-lit railway journeys from meeting to meeting across the North of England.

Much of his life was lived on the station platforms and buffets portrayed half a century later (but they had not changed much in the meantime) by the Carnforth Junction of *Brief Encounter*. But his rendezvous were with local socialist militants rather than with doctors' wistful wives. A typical Snowden evening around the turn of the century would be arrival around dusk at a gaslit and smoky station, a difficult (for him) walk of perhaps a mile (cabs too expensive) to the meeting place clutching his sticks and Gladstone bag, an inspirational address of at least an hour, followed by questions and discussion, and then a retreat to the kitchen hearth of a keen local supporter who had a bed (or occasionally half a one) to spare, and who would assemble two or three other local enthusiasts. Snowden, although fortified by no liquid stronger than tea, would then regale his small audience with reminiscence, anecdotes and ILP gossip for two or three hours before retiring to his humble berth. On these occasions his private charm took over from his platform mordancy, which he had nonetheless made uplifting and memorable. The Tennyson couplet of 'Ring out the darkness of the past, Ring in the Christ that is to be!' was the core of one of his favourite perorations.

In his earliest speaking days he had specialized in bitter personal attacks, which even if they eschewed Marxist methodology did not do much to promote class harmony. Thus at Keighley in 1895 he excoriated the composition of the Liberal party in Parliament. It was composed of 'horse-racing aristocrats like Rosebery; of sinecure-hunting lawyers like Gully [who had just become Speaker]; of 40,000 acre landlords like Acland; of £12,000 a year mining-royalty-owners like Sir Wilfred Lawson; of speculative company promoters like [A. J.] Mundella; of brewers like Sir James Stansfield; and of millionaire labour exploiters like Sir Isaac Holden [the local member]'. After this election, however, he announced that the time for the platform denunciation of opponents was past, although it had been necessary in the previous phase. Although the logic of this was far from clear, the new rule did to some considerable extent determine Snowden's own pattern, and he concentrated much more on the 'sunny uplands' of contented and co-operative living to which socialism would lead.

These ten years or so, essentially his thirties, were for Snowden physically exhausting and financially straitened, but emotionally satisfying. The schedules were killing and the normal fee was five shillings a lecture. With the many column inches of his ill-paid journalism this brought him up to not much more than £2 a week of income. Apart from his few years in Keighley, his home base remained his mother's house (or rather one of many of them, for she was constantly moving) at Cowling, not the most convenient railway hub for a roving propagandist.

However there were considerable longer-term benefits, as well as short-term privations, which flowed from this decade. He became a most accomplished speaker, almost always able to hold and grip an audience, whatever its level of sophistication. He applied himself most carefully to the technique of speech-making, claiming in particular that open-air speaking (which he liked) need not be a strain on a properly cast and modulated voice. He was also highly sensitive to the different disciplines of speech which were called for from different sizes of audience, about five gradations being necessary. He was equally interested in the content of his speeches. He was an elevating, and often an abstract, but never a ranting orator. Although he almost always spoke without notes he worked out the structure of his speeches very carefully and his accumulation of fact and argument from these years of propaganda proved an effective reservoir for his subsequent speeches in the House of Commons, where he soon came to be regarded as a formidable participant.

His unflagging and widespread journeying also gave him a bedrock of respect and affection throughout the ILP, which was later of much value to him as his always intransigent views developed in a more right-wing direction. The militant supporters were prepared to take a lot on trust from the Philip they had known and almost worshipped. His combination of being a great man on the platform and then a warm conversationalist at the fireside was a powerful recipe for leaving a trail of loyalty behind him.

His gifts and dedication also made him increasingly in demand for ILP tasks and offices. He was a member of its national committee from 1898 and its chairman for a three-year spell from 1903. He was adopted as parliamentary candidate for his native Keighley division for the 1895 general election, but did not eventually go to the poll owing to lack of funds. A nominated candidate had then to meet his share of the official expenses of the election, returning officer's fee etc., which meant that he would have had to find £160 (approximately £8,000 in today's money) before spending a penny on his own campaign. His first real contest was across the Pennines at Blackburn in the 1900 'khaki election'. In this two-member constituency he polled well but did not win. His vote of 7,095, as against 11,247 and 9,415 for the two successful Conservatives, was the largest vote which until then had been polled by any socialist candidate throughout Britain. There was no Liberal candidate. Black-burn, although industrial, had been a Tory stronghold since Disraeli's day.

Snowden's campaign was even more impressive than his vote. It made an almost revivalist impact on A. G. Gardiner, later editor of the Liberal *Daily News* and official biographer of Sir William Harcourt, who was then a local journalist. 'Philip Snowden wrought a miracle,' Gardiner wrote in a work of reminiscence many years later. 'That election will never be forgotten by those who witnessed it. It was like a sudden wind stripping the leaves of the forest.... Philip Snowden's name was on every lip, his sayings ran like rumour through the weaving sheds and the streets.' A good sample of his oratory at this stage, a little sententious with distinct Gladstonian undertones, but carefully crafted with clean sharp phrases, is provided by the following passage. He was refuting an attack on his patriotism in relation to the South African War, and announced that he declined to have his possession of that quality judged by the standards of Joseph Chamberlain:

I am a patriot. It is because I love my country and am jealous of her honour; because I want to see her the home of freedom and the friend of small nationalities, because I want to see her honoured and respected for righteousness that I decline to approve a course of action which has indelibly stained our national honour and lowered our prestige among the nations of the world.... I am no 'little Englander'. I am all for a great England. I want to see an England great in the health and happiness of its people, great in the strength of righteousness of its manhood, great in the vistas and beauty of its womanhood, great in the innocence and protection of its children, great in the splendour of its public works, great in its arts and literature. I wish to see a great England whose courageous sons shall leave her shores, not to the beating of the martial drum, but like David Livingstone who never shed one drop of human blood. I wish to see those adventurous sons of a great England go forth to win, by love and example, all those victories of Peace which are more renowned than [those of] War.

In 1902 Snowden was persuaded to be the candidate at a Wakefield by-election and polled, respectably rather than spectacularly, 1,979 votes against 2,960 in a straight fight with a Tory. In 1903 he was strongly promoted for the candidature in a Clitheroe by-election. It was a tempting seat for him, both because it included his late boyhood home town of Nelson and because there was a prospect of winning. But such a victory depended on relations with the local Liberals, and eventually Snowden withdrew in favour of the weavers' leader, David Shackleton, who as a non-doctrinaire trades unionist was more acceptable to them, and who in the eight years for which he held the seat proved himself a most able artisan representative in Parliament, as well as going on, most surprisingly, to become the first permanent secretary of the Ministry of Labour. The value of the prize which Snowden forwent is illustrated by the fact that Shackleton, once the Liberal deal had been struck, was given an unopposed return at the by-election.

Snowden then reconcentrated his electoral attention upon Blackburn. Even in this traditional Tory town however, and despite the much vaunted independence of his socialism, a not too explicit alliance with the Liberals was crucial to his electoral success. The national deal which was struck between Ramsay MacDonald as secretary of the Labour party, to which the ILP had become a tributary, and Herbert Gladstone the Liberal Chief Whip was as crucial to Snowden's success in Blackburn as it was to MacDonald's own election in Leicester. The essence of this deal was to allow a limited but substantial number of Labour candidates to run in double harness with a Liberal in two-member boroughs which were naturally disposed (certainly in 1906) to elect non-Conservatives. Such an arrangement secured the return not only of MacDonald in Leicester but also of Keir Hardie in Merthyr Tydfil, and was to bring in J. H. Thomas for Derby in 1910.

It undoubtedly increased the scale of the Conservative defeat in 1906 but it also, according to some, allowed the trojan horse of the Labour party into the Liberal keep and thereby contributed to the end of Liberalism's short century as a party of government. The Labour candidates could get in simply by holding on to Liberal coat-tails, typically finishing second with the Tories in third and fourth places. In Blackburn Snowden had to use the coat-tails to get to the starting line, but then to use a special appeal of his own, essentially directed to non-Liberal working men, to get from the starting line to the winning post. The psephological geography is vividly illustrated by the details of the 1906 Blackburn result:

Hornby (a popular and sitting local Tory): 10,291
Snowden: 10,282 (only nine votes behind)
Drage (an imported Tory): 8,932
Hamer (an unobjectionable but unexciting Liberal): 8,892

It was a remarkable result for 1906, with a Conservative at the top
and a Liberal at the bottom of the poll. But no less interesting was the
provenance of Snowden's successful and almost triumphant support.
He shared 7,871 votes – his essential bedrock support – with Hamer. He
had 1,504 'plumps' – those who voted for him and for no one else.
He shared 822 votes with Hornby, the popular Tory. And he even
shared 86 votes, thereby showing that there is rarely a limit to the
eccentricity of human choice, with the unpopular and virulently anti-
socialist Drage. But none of this would have availed had the Liberals put
up a second candidate in Blackburn. They would no doubt both have
lost, but so, just as certainly in these circumstances, would Snowden.

When therefore he first arrived in the House of Commons in the
great Liberal dawn of February 1906 his position was paradoxical in a
way that was curiously analogous with that of the British 'independent'
nuclear deterrent. He was one of twenty-nine Labour members, a new
phenomenon on the political scene, to some extent buttressed, to some
extent rivalled, by the miners' group of fourteen MPs who remained
outside the Labour party, as the Labour Representation Committee had
just rechristened itself, together with eleven other Lib/Labs. The
twenty-nine by contrast were at least nominally wholly independent of
the Liberal party, and if there was one man who was most symbolic of
that independent purity it was Philip Snowden. Yet, and this is where
the nuclear analogy applies, he was as dependent upon lack of Liberal
opposition for his Commons seat as the British were upon US means of
delivery for their 'independent' deterrent.

This did not prevent the eight and a half years of his pre-First
World War parliamentary career being markedly successful (perhaps
Polaris was too: it served its purpose without ever coming near the firing
of a missile). Before he began this phase of his career, however, an event
of considerable significance in his life had occurred. In March 1905,
Ethel Annakin had married him. This is the apposite way in which to
describe both the event and the union, the latter lasting for thirty-two
years. He was forty and she was twenty-four. Miss Annakin was the
daughter of a Harrogate building contractor, who partly to escape from
her parents had become a schoolteacher in Leeds. From there she

erupted into West Riding progressive politics in 1903, giving lectures in Keighley and elsewhere, fastening her interest upon Snowden, who offered the twin attraction and challenge of being national chairman of the ILP as well as an apparently confirmed bachelor. In 1904 she moved from Leeds to a school and lodging at Nelson, nine miles from Cowling, in order to be able to visit more frequently and easily the Snowden household, an attention which was cordially disliked by the maternal Mrs Snowden.

Although so much the *demandeuse* she was a young woman of striking good looks, tall, golden-haired, with elegant features and enveloping eyes. She had very strong views – anti-alcohol, pro-women's rights, and was at that stage militantly socialistic, although much later, she was at least an abetter if not the instigator of Snowden's move to the right. She also brought a whiff and a swish of Harrogate sophistication into the cottage life of Cowling, but it was not exactly that of the secure upper-middle-class. Although she was not close to her father, his status as a speculative house-builder told a lot about her style. When a quarter of a century later she was able fully to avail herself of the Court opportunities of a Cabinet minister's wife and then of a viscountess she always wore one or two ostrich feathers too many. And when she unwisely attempted to compete with Mrs Sidney Webb as an arbiter of the proper behaviour for the wives of 1920s Labour ministers she was simply playing outside her league.

Nevertheless she was a woman of ideas, force and some originality, who became sufficiently in demand as a lecturer, primarily in the United States, that she was able by the 1920s to buy and set up their Surrey country house out of her earnings. And one of her strongest 1903–5 ideas was the desire to marry Philip Snowden. She got him, if not exactly to the altar, at least to the Otley register office on St Patrick's day, 1905. With his crippled state and her almost excessive 'health and beauty' appearance there was inevitably a sense of the princess and the frog, even though Snowden's features had a far from crapulous strength and dignity. As there were no children of the marriage it was also suggested that the relationship must have been ethereal (or political) rather than physical. But Snowden was much less incapacitated than Franklin Roosevelt, in which distinguished case the ethereal did not entirely take over.

Snowden's success in the 1906 and subsequent parliaments was based on his being at once the most feared and the most respected Labour member. He was harsh, not least in his denunciations of others, and he was long in his speeches, which sometimes extended to the quasi-Gladstonian length of one and a half hours. Aided perhaps by the fact that the shadow Chancellor, Austen Chamberlain, never had his heart in opposition, Snowden's third-party budget critiques came to be an accepted and eagerly awaited feature of such debates.

He began in curious House of Commons circumstances, making his maiden speech on 12 March (a very respectable month's interval after his election). He spoke on a general Free Trade motion, which had the effect that, Labour independent though he was, he was welded by his own convictions (which on his subject persisted longer than almost anyone else's) into a relatively pro-Liberal position, although he was careful to stress that while Free Trade was a necessary condition for a successful economy and a satisfactory society it was certainly not a sufficient condition, as was shown by the gross inequality and poverty which had distinguished its heyday. Free Trade was right but not a substitute for socialism.

The speech was a moderate success. It was favourably commented upon by the majority of newspapers. But it left at least two people dissatisfied. The one was Snowden himself, who stated in his *Autobiography* that he had never been able to bring himself to read the Hansard report of it. And the other was the parliamentary sketchwriter (John Foster Fraser) for whom Snowden had the highest respect. Fraser wrote that it 'was the poorest contribution which Parliament [he meant the new parliament] has had from any of the Labour representatives'.

In the circumstances of that parliamentary day it was amazing that Snowden got any press notice, favourable or unfavourable. It was the day of Balfour's re-entry into the House after his defeat in Manchester at the general election and his retreat to an artificially induced vacancy in the City of London. He celebrated his return with a logic-chopping speech of somewhat faded elegance which called forth Campbell-Bannerman's famous put-down ('Have done with the foolery . . . Move your amendments, and let us get to business') and first stamped the new Prime Minister's authority upon the new House. Then, immediately after Snowden sat down, F. E. Smith rose to make the most famous and sardonic maiden speech of the century. (Neither of them seemed remotely concerned with the allegedly so traditional convention that first speeches should not be controversial.)

While the honours for that day undoubtedly rested with Smith, a balance can be struck by saying that he never again made quite such a good speech. Snowden, on the other hand, improved greatly. He recorded that, despite his vast outside speaking experience, it took him two years to feel at home on his feet in the House of Commons, and he did not press hard during that period of acclimatization. He spoke only once again in 1906 after his maiden effort, and he never remotely suffered from verbal diarrhoea. But he gradually made for himself a considerable parliamentary position. Members, including the most eminent – Balfour was very faithful – came in to hear him, and he became one of the fixed points of the chamber, often referred to in the speeches of others.

His weakness as a parliamentarian, perhaps as a human being, was his inability to return the respect which he aroused in others. This was particularly so in relation to his Labour colleagues. As is so often the case in politics he found it easier to get on with his opponents, while reserving his contempt and even enmity for his honourable friends. Among the twenty-eight other Labour members with whom Snowden sat in that 1906 parliament there were two men who were by any standards major politicians. They were Ramsay MacDonald and Arthur Henderson. They were utterly different from each other, MacDonald's faults being vanity and cloudiness, while Henderson's were complacency and stolidity. Yet Snowden despised them both with an even light. To him MacDonald was an untrustworthy windbag and Henderson an unimaginative party agent jumped up into being an intriguing whip. Somehow the two judgements cancelled each other out and left Snowden at least as much damaged by them as either of his objects of obloquy. For all his other virtues he was not a good colleague, either in those pre-1914 years nor in the Labour governments of the 1920s.

There was among the Labour MPs a fourth figure of equal note, and perhaps even greater charisma, in the shape of Keir Hardie. He was a propagandist at least as powerful as Snowden himself, but no good as a parliamentarian, and would have been a disaster as a minister, which however he would almost certainly not have allowed himself to become. To Hardie, the most impractical of the four, Snowden was prepared to defer, even though in general and increasingly as time went on it was for those who would not face realities that he felt most contempt. It is difficult to avoid the conclusion that through Hardie he was able to revere his own past while seeing in him no rival in the present nor threat for the future.

The mechanics of life developed relatively smoothly for Snowden between 1906 and 1914. Miss Annakin was good at them. After their marriage they lived for a time in Leeds, and remained there during his first couple of sessions as an MP. Then in the autumn of 1907, when she did the first of her profitable lecture tours of America and he spoke, without material profit, in more than forty English, Scottish and Welsh towns, they abandoned Leeds and moved first to a West Kensington flat and then, after another couple of years, to a Golders Green suburban house. There they remained for fourteen years until Tilford in Surrey was acquired in 1923. Golders Green was thought to be convenient for Westminster (and indeed Arthur Henderson lived in the same Woodstock Road for a time), but it is difficult to see how, with a necessary change of Underground line and then a significant and (for Snowden) difficult walk from Golders Green station it was remotely so. Lambeth or Kennington would have been much more so and cheaper too. Woodstock Road was the equivalent of Attlee's Stanmore. Labour members, diligently although they remained in the House of Commons until late at night, seemed to like tube journeys. What it did mark was Snowden accepting both middle-class and metropolitan status.

In these circumstances it was fortunate that he fairly comfortably surmounted in Blackburn both the two elections of 1910. The results exhibited an odd pattern. In the first, with the Liberal tide ebbing nationally a long way from the high point of 1906, a new Liberal candidate went to the head of the poll, with Snowden only 200 votes behind. It was a Liberal/Tory reversal of the 1906 result. But the important thing for Snowden is that he showed he could survive in either circumstance. So he did in the second 1910 election, when all the other candidates were new, even the previously triumphant Liberal having decided after only ten months that he preferred the practice of international law (in which he operated with distinction) and residence in Paris to the House of Commons and a Lancashire borough. With him out of the way, Snowden, for the only time in his five-elections life in Blackburn, seized (by eight votes) the place at the top of the poll, although his margin over the Conservative candidates weakened. For this second election he had arrived late and without his wife, for they had jointly embarked on a three-month lecture tour of the United States, and she was left behind to complete the schedule. Neither his lateness nor her absence prevented it being his most successful Blackburn election.

These tours, led by her, were becoming a significant part of Snowden life, and indeed of Snowden family income, even before the results burgeoned into the Surrey house. Ethel Snowden had started alone in 1907, but they jointly did this 1910 one and a still more extensive one four years later. These pointed to a growing international reputation, which was in some ways surprising, for the fields of Snowden's House of Commons activities were severely domestic. He believed in peace, but it could also be said that he was very close to believing that the best way to preserve it was to have as little as possible to do with diplomacy and with foreign and defence policy. On the other hand he was deeply involved, again to some extent at the instigation of his wife, with temperance and with women's suffrage, two subjects which ranged beyond the strict confines of socialist politics, and which also had a considerable resonance in America.

Nineteen-ten brought a few losses of Labour seats from the gains of 1906, but also the adhesion of the substantial group of miners' MPs, who had previously remained detached, so that there was a settling down into a substantial group of around forty. They were however increasingly bound, not by formal affiliation but by circumstance, to the Liberal party. Paradoxically the strength of the Liberal pull arose out of the new weakness of that party. It had lost its dependent majority. It could only continue to govern by grace of the Irish Nationalist and Labour parties, and, while the former party was bigger, the latter had a more intimate and across-the-board interest in the continuance of non-Tory government. The constitutional struggle had to be seen through to the curbing of the powers of the Lords; this was a necessary preliminary to the implementation of almost any part of the Labour programme. And there was also a more direct and selfish Labour dependence upon Liberal bounty. The Osborne judgement of 1908–9, declaring it illegal for trades unions to use their funds for political purposes, had wrecked the basis of Labour party finance. The party had been seriously hobbled in the 1910 elections. Until this was rectified (as it substantially was by an Act of 1913) the Labour party was more a beggar at the Liberal table than it was an arbiter of the fate of Asquith. It could not withdraw its support without cutting its own throat.

This dependence greatly irked Snowden. Although in many ways he was a natural Gladstonian and ended up in the late 1920s as more the political heir of the Grand Old Man than almost anyone else after the death of Morley in 1923, his pre-1914 attitude was that of prickly independence, which set him apart from either MacDonald or Henderson. It was perhaps the major contradiction of Snowden's career that he was at once a man of government and a lone wolf. He was always in favour of 'sound finance' and he came not merely to disagree with but to despise those of his colleagues and supporters who would not face up to its consequences and to what he saw as other realities of power. Yet he was never a good team player. He was too egocentric and dogmatic. But his dogmatism, even in those early days, did not necessarily make him an extremist. He was idiosyncratic as well as egocentric, and it was never wholly predictable which way he would jump on an issue. He was, for instance, basically cool in his attitude to trades unionism. One reason that he remained for so long so attached to the ILP (until he flounced out of it against its impracticalities in 1927) was that, unlike the Labour party itself, it was not a trades union party. His hostility was based partly on an almost snobbish view that trades union leaders were unimaginative clod-hopping fellows (like Henderson) and partly on a sophisticated and well-argued theory that strikes did more harm than good, even to the strikers and even when they were nominally successful. He was therefore deeply opposed to the wave of industrial unrest, with a strong syndicalist undertow, which marked 1911–12. They were certainly no route to the socialist commonwealth. He anticipated Tony Blair by at least eighty years in his desire to see an arm's-length relationship between the Labour party and the unions.

At the same time he was singularly unsuited to be the bo'sun of a small boat keeping diligently alongside the liner of Liberalism. He expressed his impatience by leading a group of four Labour members in an attack on Lloyd George's Insurance Act of 1912, commonly regarded as the most important piece of pre-1945 social legislation. Snowden and his three cohorts were vehemently against the contributory principle. Social advance should be paid for out of general progressive direct taxation. His breaking of ranks on this issue, for the bulk of the Labour party was solidly in favour, caused at least as much resentment in his own party as it did among the Liberals.

On several issues, however, and those the most central to his parliamentary interest, notably financial management, Snowden was moving somewhat but in no way extravagantly to the right in those immediate pre-1914 years. He was also perhaps getting a little bored with third-party politics and with the absence of any real prospect for either himself or for his ideal of a gradual, peaceful, parliamentary advance to a socialist commonwealth. His detachment was expressed by he and his wife planning a massive almost year-long round-the-world lecturing and sightseeing tour, of which the centrepiece was to be a three-month participation in the New Zealand National Prohibition (of alcohol) Campaign. While it might have been thought better to leave the New Zealanders to decide these grave matters for themselves, the participation of the Snowdens was apparently regarded as sufficiently desirable for the financial underpinning of the whole trip to be forthcoming.

They left Liverpool for Canada on 10 July 1914. It was six days before Snowden's fiftieth birthday, which climacteric may have had something to do with his desire for a complete and long change of scene. It was also nearly halfway between the Sarajevo assassination and the outbreak of the war to which it tortuously led, and which might have been expected to disrupt their plans more than they allowed it to do. They heard of Britain's declaration of war in Glacier National Park in the US state of Montana. Although Snowden had been rhetorically prophesying for years that war was the inevitable consequence of great armaments and balance-of-power diplomacy, he received the news that it had actually arrived with surprise and even incredulity. Fortified by a cable from Henderson (as Chief Whip) telling him that he need not return – the pro-war Henderson had every reason for not wanting the predictably anti-war Snowden back – the Snowdens continued calmly on their elaborate tour. The calm was temporarily interrupted in Portland, Oregon where Snowden suffered both from food poisoning and from a newspaper headline which credited him with having advised British soldiers to shoot their officers. This he certainly had not done, for he had been too ill to say anything, but Mrs Snowden may have made some less that discreet remarks.

After obtaining a more or less satisfactory retraction, they proceeded across the Pacific to New Zealand, completed their three months of temperance campaigning, spent a fortnight in Australia, reluctantly abandoned India and South Africa, but made a leisurely return across the United States, and arrived in Liverpool only in early February, having been absent for a full six months of war. It was an extraordinary act of detachment for a leading member of Parliament who had very strong views on and against Britain's participation in the conflict.

Opposition to the war had the effect of rekindling his interest in politics in general and in particular in the Independent Labour party, from which he had previously been rather drifting away. In the federal Labour party itself he was always in a minority, crushed when it came to a vote by the often truculently pro-war strength of the unlovely trades unions. But the ILP was dependably anti-war. He rejoined its national committee in 1915 and became chairman for the second time in 1917–20. These circumstances also had the effect of jerking him back several notches towards the left. They did not prevent his strong rightward move in the 1920s, but they did mean that it started later and from a much further leftward point than would have been the case had there been no war in 1914–18.

Yet his opposition to the war, while determined and courageous, was circumspect, even fastidious. He was not an absolute pacifist and he recognized the need for a country to defend itself and to have adequate but not excessive means with which to do so. He thought there was never a need for Britain to have got involved in 1914, but, this having mistakenly been allowed to happen, all possible opportunities for negotiation should be seized with a view to bringing the war to an end on honourable but not abject terms. While there had been plenty of difference in their positions in 1915 (publicly at least Snowden did not have one in 1914, except on enforced total abstinence in New Zealand), by late 1917 he and Lord Lansdowne (in his famous *Daily Telegraph* letter) were saying much the same thing from opposite ends of the political spectrum.

Even in 1915, however, Snowden stated his position with some delicacy and moderation. He went direct from the Liverpool landing-stage to Blackburn (after seven months' absence that was perhaps the least that he could do) and addressed 2,000 of his constituents in a theatre. He explained that he would not participate in the Mayor of Blackburn's recruiting campaign because:

> I am not going to ask any man to do something for me which I am not able to do for myself. The consequences are so serious that I believe the decision should be left entirely to the individual conscience. If a man thinks it wrong to go, he ought not to go and he ought not to be persecuted. If a man thinks he should go, then he ought to go, and I honour the man.

These two sentences neatly laid down the lines of Snowden's conduct for the remaining three and three-quarter years of the war. He did not stir up trouble and he never came near to being prosecuted for incitement to disaffection. But he was firmly for peace and when conscription came, in the parliamentary opposition to which he took a leading part, he was indefatigable in defending the rights of conscientious objectors. Through a relentless use of parliamentary questions he exposed the frequent expressions of blind prejudice on the part of those appointed to judge their cases. He was particularly good against the judicial shooting of soldiers whose nerve had gone or occasionally of conscientious objectors which was such a disfiguring aspect of military discipline on the Western front in the First World War. But his main parliamentary activity was devoted to criticizing the laxity of war finance and the vast burden of debt which was being built up as a result of the refusal to match the conscription of men with the conscription of wealth.

Yet a curious paradox was that, accompanying those highly oppositional activities, he spent a significant portion of his time in the war years on a government-appointed job which could be regarded as helpful to the war effort. He had long been regarded as a desirable catch for committees of enquiry. Between 1906 and 1913 he was appointed to one departmental committee (on the jury system), no less than three Royal Commissions, the first on canals and waterways, the second on the civil service and the third, which might perhaps be regarded as no great favour, on venereal diseases. Then in 1915, almost as he got back from New Zealand, Lloyd George got him to be part of a small committee which, under the chairmanship of Herbert Samuel, drew up in about ten days of intensive work a plan for the complete nationalization of the drink trade. At a cost of £250 million it sounded a good bargain, although as the aim was to reduce the trade rather than to increase it the investment might have found itself stultified. When this scheme foundered Lloyd George set up a Liquor Control Board with very wide powers, which, *inter alia*, produced the Carlisle and Gretna state control scheme, which persisted into and over my first period as Home Secretary in the 1960s, as well as regulations for the drastic restriction of the hours both for public houses and for off-licences.

Snowden became a member of this board, of which the chairman was Lord D'Abernon, an all-purpose public servant who was later to be ambassador in Berlin. The other members included such disparate notabilities as Lord Astor, Neville Chamberlain and Lord Leverhulme. Snowden, whose heart was in the work, accepted a good deal of executive responsibility and undertook sometimes on his own or with one other member visits of inspection and effective decision to various problem areas. It was faintly reminiscent of Andrei Sakharov, who in the Russia of Brezhnev when he had become the best known of all the 'refuseniks', was able to travel round the country on his pass as a Hero of the Soviet Union and thus get privileged travel to the trials of other dissidents.

None of this availed Snowden when it came to the second 'khaki election', that of December 1918. Although he had retained good relations of mutual respect with his (mostly differing) constituents during the war, much more so for instance than MacDonald had done in Leicester, and although (or perhaps because) the electorate had been fortified by the women for whose voting rights he had striven so hard, he was slaughtered in Blackburn. It was back to a position much worse than in the first 'khaki election' of 1900. He polled 15,000 votes against the 32,000 of the Liberal Coalitionist, Sir Henry Norman, whom he had led to a joint victory in 1910, and the 30,000 of a Conservative naval commander and VC who had somewhat crudely been brought in to emphasize Snowden's anti-combatant status.

The curious effect of the 1918 election upon the Labour party was that, although it increased its numbers to sixty-eight and, with the destruction of the Asquithians and the abstention from attendance of Sinn Fein, made it the largest opposition party, it also cut off the heads of all its tall poppies. Not only Snowden but also MacDonald and Henderson went down. William Adamson, a respected but anonymous Fifeshire miner, became leader until 1921, when he was replaced by J. R. Clynes, who although more considerable was not exactly of a quality to set the blood racing. Snowden therefore had no serious loss of competitive position to fear from his rejection by Blackburn. It was merely boredom and the loss of his £400 a year parliamentary salary with which he had to contend.

He was fairly well fortified against both. He had his continuing chairmanship of the ILP for the first year and a half, after which he became treasurer of that organization, although by then moving out of sympathy with the more left-wing Clydeside-activated post-war spirit of the ILP. What he mainly did, however, was to sit at home in Golders Green and to pour out a stream of political writing. He produced three books, innumerable pamphlets and a lot of journalism, some of it a labour of love (as with his supervising editorship of the *Labour Leader*, which however ended abruptly when he quarrelled irreparably with the executive editor wife of his old pioneer friend, Bruce Glasier), some of it well paid as with a notable series of articles, later syndicated, which he wrote for the *Morning Post*. He was thus well able to support himself, and, if there was any doubt about this, his wife's earnings could be more than underpinning.

All these writings were designed to reassure rather than to shock, and were particularly directed towards conciliating the middle class. He was almost a premature harbinger of today's New Labour. As much consideration would be given to a man in 'a black coat' with £500 a year (then a good middle-class income) as to someone in a 'fustian jacket' with £2 a week. The majority of electors, he asserted, would never vote for a Labour government unless they were assured that it would be controlled by common sense and moderation. And that, he was confident, would be the case. 'I should expect a Labour government', he wrote with true prescience, 'to err rather on the side of conservatism than of "extremism".' Almost certainly only one measure of nationalization would be possible in the first parliament of such a government, and priority would no doubt be given to mines or railways.

Despite this growing and genuine moderation he retained a certain implacability, although in defence of new positions. There was still more than a touch of the old Robespierre of 1906. This was shown in the way he absolutely severed his connection with the *Labour Leader* as soon as the quarrel with Katherine Glasier arose. It was shown at the formal level by the fact that he never once entered the precincts of the Palace of Westminster during the four years when he was not a member. And it was shown above all in his violent hostility to the development of the Bolshevik revolution in Russia, which was the central cause of his growing estrangement from the ILP.

Ethel Snowden was an important agent in this process. The period 1919–22 was the peak of her independent political career. Under the Arthur Henderson/Sidney Webb 1918 constitution of the Labour party she had been elected one of the first women members of the party's National Executive Committee. She used this position primarily to play an international role and became very well known in Europe, as she already was in America, because of her lecturing. She travelled a great deal during those first post-war years, while her husband mostly (but contentedly, it appears) sat scribbling in Golders Green. By far her most important journey was as a member of a 1920 TUC/Labour party committee of enquiry in the Russian regime. She was deeply disillusioned, and forcibly expressed her opinion both there and on her return. She was the only woman on quite a large delegation, but she easily outstripped all the others including Bertrand Russell, who was surprisingly part of the party, by the attention which her views received. This in itself aroused jealousy and animosity, which was increased by her shrillness.

She published a successful book called *Through Bolshevik Russia*, the tone of which can be gauged from a preliminary interview which she gave to the *Evening Standard*. She said that conditions in Russia were 'closely approximate to some phases of slavery', and she announced her opposition to Bolshevism because 'it is not Socialism, it is not democracy, and it is not Christianity'. There was undoubtedly much sense and truth in what she said, but it was strong meat at that stage for the optimistic idealism of many comrades.

The ILP retaliated by refusal to continue to nominate her for the Labour party executive, an act for which Philip Snowden never forgave them, and which marked a decisive step in his rupture with the organization which he had partly created and which had nurtured his early career. Although he had begun by expressing sympathy for the Russian revolution, in its October as well as its Kerensky phases, and had been strongly opposed to British military intervention on behalf of Poland and against Russia as late as August 1920, Snowden had nonetheless become increasigly critical of the Russian regime even before his wife's journey. He was wedded not only to Miss Annakin but also to parliamentary democracy and to gradualism, and he did not see much sign of either of them in Leninism. These views however were greatly strengthened both by her revulsion and by the criticism which it provoked in left-wing circles at home. It is difficult to believe that Snowden did not sometimes find his wife an embarrassment, but he was ideologically (and in other ways) an immensely loyal husband, and from 1920 onwards anti-Bolshevism was an important part of his political motivation. He was set on a course which made his most famous and most resented 1931 election remark ('This is not Socialism,' he said of the Labour programme. 'It is Bolshevism run mad') a not wholly illogical destination.

For the moment, however, his chief desire was to return to the House of Commons as a Labour member. This he achieved at the 1922 election which followed the break-up of the Lloyd George Coalition. He had committed himself to win back Blackburn, but the prospects for that were not encouraging, and when in early 1922 he was offered the nomination for Colne Valley, one of those half-urban, half-rural Pennine-straddling constituencies in which he felt most at home, he was delighted to respond to a draft from the national committee. Colne Valley when last it had been fought on a three-cornered basis in 1909 had returned Victor Grayson, a maverick socialist populist who had infuriated his colleagues before losing the seat at the 1910 general election and then disappearing from human records as completely as Lord Lucan was to do sixty-four years later.

This left a stain of loucheness on the socialist cause in the Colne Valley, but Snowden was the best possible candidate to expunge it, and he won by a majority of 1,200 votes in 1922, and then built it up to

1,900 in 1923, 3,200 in 1924 and 9,100 in 1929, his last election. It was an impressive and satisfactory progression. In 1922 the Labour party returned 142 members to the House of Commons, which meant that the prospect of government, obviously not in that parliament but in a proximate one, became real and enticing. As this developed so the assumption that Snowden would be the only possible choice as Chancellor of the Exchequer became almost universal. The Labour party needed to build up confidence, above all in its financial management, and there was no one who could hold a candle to him in this respect.

There is no doubt moreover that from here forward this became his legitimate ambition. He was never obsessed by self-advancement. But he did have a strong feeling, a contempt indeed, for those in the Labour movement who shied away from the responsibilities of power. And in this case this clearly meant being prepared for the Treasury. Yet he was capable of being swayed by even stronger and less admirable emotions. The first major decision he had to influence was the choice of a new leader. All the defeated stars of 1918 had been returned. Clynes was *in situ*, but was challenged by MacDonald. There was no doubt, even at the time let alone in retrospect, that MacDonald's ability for levering the Labour party into government was vastly greater than that of Clynes. Yet Snowden tried to get the ILP to support Clynes, and when he failed still did so himself. MacDonald was nonetheless elected, but only by a majority of two votes.

Snowden's persistent distrust and dislike of MacDonald was an extraordinary phenomenon. They were of course very different personalities, although MacDonald was at least superficially the more attractive one. But the evolution of their political positions marched remarkably in step. It was their styles not the substance which produced the conflict. Having started as itinerant propagandists they both took naturally to the parliamentary arena after 1906, and were both moving to the right in the pre-1914 years. They both courageously opposed the war, which naturally pushed them both back leftwards. But it did not pull them together. Snowden in his *Autobiography* (published in 1934) quoted at considerable length and with mocking malice the admittedly remarkably vague and flatulent letter which MacDonald had written to the Mayor of Leicester (the analogue to Snowden's more forthright response to the Mayor of Blackburn) in 1914. It was curious and obsessive to drag up 300 words of someone else's prose after twenty years.

Then in 1918 they both suffered electoral defeat and four years out of Parliament for their semi-pacifism, and then both came back in 1922 for different seats and dedicated to broadening the class appeal of the Labour party and preparing it for government. But none of this, nor even, looking nine years to the future, their being two of the small and reviled band of Labour Cabinet ministers who entered the National government, brought the slightest breath of warmth or respect, at any rate on Snowden's side, to their relationship. It is difficult to believe that his mind was not perverted by jealousy and the bitterness which flowed from it. The only thing to be said for this unadmirable constancy was that at least it showed that Snowden could put his implacability above his ambition, for MacDonald's thrust to fame was essential to making the Labour party a 1920s party of government.

During his two short parliaments as an opposition member for Colne Valley, Snowden made a number of notable speeches, on reparations from Germany, on which he was good and clear-headed, and on unemployment, on which, except for drawing attention to the sufferings of the unemployed, he was not at all good, for his main recipes were nationalization, likely to be neutral in its effects, and sound finance including the most rapid possible reduction of the national debt, likely to have positively adverse results. Then in March 1923, he staged a great set-piece theoretical debate, of a sort it is now very difficult to imagine taking place in the House of Commons. He put down a straight socialist/capitalist motion, couched in calm and moderate terms ('this House declares that legislative effort should be directed to the general super-session of the capitalist system by an industrial and social order based on the public ownership and democratic control of the instruments of production and distribution') but nonetheless going to the heart of the ideological dispute. He spoke for over an hour, apparently holding a full House in easy command, and was then replied to by Sir Alfred Mond, later the architect of Imperial Chemical Industries, in what Snowden described as 'an extremely clever and amusing speech'. The courtesies of knightly combat were obviously observed. Later in the debate many of the most prominent members of the House spoke. The whole occasion attracted widespread outside attention, including a several-column report on the front page of the *New York Times*, an indication not only of the inherent interest of the debate, but also of the greater attention then paid in America to British affairs.

The general election of the following autumn was both in its provenance and in its outcome one of the most curious in British political history. Baldwin, after only six months as Prime Minister and with a thoroughly satisfactory majority behind him, suddenly decided that he needed Tariff Protection in order to combat unemployment and that this need imposed upon him the obligation to dissolve a parliament which was barely a year old. The election of December 1923 was, in Snowden's own words, 'fought solely on the question of Protection'. The result was that Protection was defeated by 8.7 million votes to 5.5 million. The 5.5 million translated themselves into 255 Conservative MPs, and the 8.7 million produced 191 Labour members plus 158 representatives of a nominally reunited Liberal party.

The Labour party was less than a third of the House of Commons, but it was nonetheless the logical party of government. The Conservatives had been defeated on what its leader claimed was the dominant issue of the day and it could not just carry on as though nothing had happened. Moreover Asquith, who, although the leader of the smallest party, nonetheless controlled (insofar as he could control Lloyd George) the situation, made it clear in a speech before Christmas that he was not prepared to bridge the Free Trade Protection gap by any arrangement with the Conservatives, but that he was prepared to facilitate a Labour government coming to office and to give it conditional support. The correct constitutional doctrine, he pronounced, was that the two opposition parties should unite in defeating the government and that the larger of them should then take office. As Lloyd George agreed with him on both points there was thus far no difficulty. What would of course have offered a much better prospect of a stable administration would have been a Labour/Liberal coalition, but as the new party was anxious to be free of the leading strings of the old, and as Asquith could hardly be expected to be excited by the prospect of serving under MacDonald, this was not seriously considered.

There remained open – but not for long – the question of whether the Labour party would, in these very restricting circumstances, be prepared to take office. In his *Morning Post* series of articles Snowden had argued that such a minority government would be disastrous for the future of the Labour party, and that the best course would be for it to stand out and force a Conservative/Liberal coalition. But a combination of the dominance which the Free Trade issue had assumed and the enticement offered by the actual imminence of office changed his mind. In the key pre-Christmas discussions he offered no resistance – rather the contrary – to Labour taking office. (It should be remembered that this new parliament was not due to meet until mid-January, and that Baldwin, perfectly properly in view of the uncertainties, had decided not to resign immediately but to wait to see whether he was turned out on an amendment to the King's Speech.)

The key meeting was a dinner at the Pimlico house of the Webbs on 12 December. Beatrice, perhaps surprisingly, allowed herself to be banished for the occasion, and the others present besides Sidney were only MacDonald, Snowden, Henderson, Clynes and J. H. Thomas. There was quick and unanimous agreement that Labour should take office, although the mood was probably well caught in Beatrice Webb's *Diary*, where she recorded, following Sidney's account to her, 'that they have all, except Henderson, "cold feet" at the thought of office, although all of them believe that JRM ought not to refuse'. There was then a loose policy discussion, of which the main outcome was that controversial measures from the capital levy to nationalization should be dropped. Snowden, whom it was assumed would be Chancellor, although nothing specific was said to him (or to anyone else), indicated that some reduction of food taxes might be possible provided that the most rigid economy was enforced, in other words that there was no question of an expansionist programme to reduce unemployment.

Over the following couple of days MacDonald, supported by these powerful barons of the Labour movement, got the endorsement of the TUC General Council and of the National Executive of the Labour party for his acceptance of office, while also preserving, a little more shakily, the traditional prerogative of a 'capitalist' Prime Minister to choose his own Cabinet. Partly, perhaps, in order to avoid erosion of this right, he then disappeared to Lossiemouth, his birthplace on the Moray Firth, and remained there for over two weeks. In one sense this was a sensible rest between the election and the pressures of 10 Downing Street. In another, however, it was alienating him from the barons who had been his essential defenders, for they found themselves as much in the dark as anyone else, and in particular did not know what offices they were likely to occupy.

His treatment of some of them was distinctly cavalier. This applied particularly to Henderson, who was unique in having serious experience of Cabinet office. Nevertheless MacDonald's first proposition was that he should stay outside the government and devote himself to the organization of the party in the country. Admittedly Henderson had just lost his parliamentary seat (he had a remarkable propensity to do this; he did so in 1918, in 1922, in 1923 and in 1931, when of course nearly everyone did, but his record nonetheless suggested a carelessness with constituencies. However MacDonald's next proposal for Henderson was hardly tailor-made for someone outside the House of Commons. It was that he should become chairman of the Committee of Ways and Means, in other words deputy Speaker. Eventually, after a good deal of ill-feeling, he became Home Secretary.

Snowden, although escaping such insults, was not treated particularly graciously either. He received no direct intimation that he was to be Chancellor until 20 January, two days before the change of government and six and a half weeks after the election. Nor was he given the normal but not invariable Chancellor's perquisite of 11 Downing Street. That was reserved for Clynes, who as Lord Privy Seal became effectively leader of the House of Commons, leaving MacDonald, who remained nominally so, freer for the Foreign Office, which he had rashly decided to combine with the premiership. MacDonald had originally wanted J. H. Thomas, the shrewd vulgarian who was general secretary of the National Union of Railwaymen and had appointed himself a sort of court jester to King George V, to have this job, but the protests, particularly as they could be couched in such flattering terms to himself, drove him off it. Thomas became Colonial Secretary, and Webb, who was no parliamentarian, completed the deployment of the sextet by becoming President of the Board of Trade. Haldane, MacDonald's best catch from outside the Labour party, returned to the Woolsack from which he had been ejected nearly nine years before.

Snowden was both sworn of the Privy Council and received his seals of office on 23 January 1924. To perform both the ceremonies on one day was unusual but not unique for a Chancellor. Disraeli had been in the same position in 1852, and indeed that first Derby government, which was immortalized as the 'Who? Who? ministry' following the Duke of Wellington's expressions of incredulity as the list of names was read out to him, contained fewer existing Privy Councillors than were mustered in the Labour invasion of 'new men'. (In 1852 there were only three: Derby himself, Lonsdale and Herries; in 1924 there were six: Clynes, Henderson, Thomas, Haldane, Parmoor and Chelmsford, but not MacDonald.) For this auspicious occasion, when the protocol instructions were silk hat and frock coat (there was always a great deal of agitation through this government about exactly what ministers were to wear), Snowden managed to produce out of his own resources both the hat and a cutaway coat, but his frock coat, he regretted to say, he had sent to a jumble sale a few years earlier.

Snowden installed himself in the Treasury, then on the corner of

Downing Street and Whitehall, where the Cabinet Office now is, and with his own office the very grand Queen Anne's Throne Room, now principally used for non-Prime Ministerial Cabinet committees. Between Snowden and the 1920s Treasury officials there was a true marriage of like minds. Thirteen years later his immediate successor, Winston Churchill, wrote in his *Great Contemporaries* essay on Snowden: 'We must imagine with what joy Mr Snowden was welcomed to the Treasury by the permanent officials . . . he was the High Priest entering the sanctuary. The Treasury mind and the Snowden mind embraced each other with the fervour of two long-separated kindred lizards, and the reign of joy began.'

By 1937 Churchill perhaps felt a need to get his own back on Treasury officials to whose advice he had succumbed too easily, but there was nonetheless much truth in his satire. In 1924 Sir Warren Fisher was an authoritative permanent secretary, Sir Otto Niemeyer was the most penetrating brain in the next rank of officials, and P. J. Grigg, whose subsequent career took him to be first the official and then the political head of the War Office in the Second World War, which was a time when running the War Office really mattered, was the Chancellor's principal private secretary. Grigg wrote in his 1948 memoirs the absolute tribute that 'Of all the Ministers I have ever known [and he had been private secretary to five Chancellors] he [Snowden] was easily the most popular with the civil servants who worked for him.' And he proceeded to give a very succinct and convincing account of why this was so: 'In the first place, he was the ideal of what a Minister should be in that he gave a very clear lead on all questions of policy, interfered rarely, if at all, in matters of administration, gave decisions quickly and unequivocally, and then defended his decisions against all-comers with confidence and vigour – and nearly always with success.'

There was one other functionary with whom relations for a Chancellor are almost as important as with his permanent or his private secretary, and that is the Governor of the Bank of England, although until 1946 the Governor was not strictly a public servant. The Governor in Snowden's day, and indeed from 1920 to 1944, was Montagu Norman, with whom it is hardly an exaggeration to say that Snowden fell in love. Norman called on Snowden during his first evening in office. Snowden affected to believe that he had no previous idea what he looked like. Would he be like 'the hard-faced, close-fisted, high-nosed' figure whom he had often seen portrayed in caricatures of international financiers? 'There came into my room a man so different! He might have stepped out of the frame of a portrait of a handsome courtier of the Middle Ages. It took but a short acquaintance with Mr Norman to know that his external appearance was the bodily expression of one of the kindliest natures and most sympathetic hearts it has been my privilege to know.'

This ease, indeed happiness, of department working relationships assisted Snowden in the presentation, three months after he had taken office, of a budget which was, within the limitations of its assumptions, accomplished and popular. He regarded his primary duties as the reduction of the national debt and the defence of the purest principles of Free Trade. As a third priority, but subordinate to the other two, he wished to reduce the burden of indirect tax, particularly where it fell upon food. There was simply no place in his scheme of thought for giving the budget more than a purely fiscal role and using it for wider social or economic purposes, such as trying to reduce the level of unemployment, which currently stood at 11 per cent. A little later that session he gave a public definition of a Chancellor's function, which was as honest as it was starkly negative. 'It is no part of my job as Chancellor of the Exchequer', he said, 'to put before the House of Commons proposals for the expenditure of public money. The function of the Chancellor of the Exchequer, as I understand it, is to resist all demands for expenditure made by his colleagues and, when he can no longer resist, to limit the concession to the barest point of acceptance.'

T. P. O'Connor, accomplished journalist and the only Irish Nationalist MP to sit for an English constituency – for forty-four years for the Scotland division of Liverpool – in appraising Snowden's budget speech 'as a Parliamentary performance' said, 'unhesitatingly, that it was the best since Gladstone'. O'Connor had the advantage of being almost the only member left who had actually heard Gladstone budgets, but with his emphasis on form rather than content perhaps did not appreciate that the milk of Gladstonian doctrine ran more purely through Snowden's veins than through those of any intervening Chancellor. The only difference was that the Grand Old Man himself, confronted with the circumstances of 1924, might have been a little less rigid than was Snowden.

Snowden's budget was to an exceptional extent an untrammelled internal Treasury production. He was determined to defend an extreme version of the isolated prerogative of the Chancellor. Most ministers were afraid of the mordancy of his tongue, as well as being intimidated by precedents they did not fully understand. And with the Prime Minister, who ideally both supports and acts as a litmus paper for a

Chancellor, he was hardly on speaking terms. MacDonald was in any event preoccupied with Foreign Office as well as head-of-government business.

Snowden inherited an unusually favourable budgetary situation. As against the bare £2 million surplus for which Baldwin had budgeted in 1923, the outcome was a surplus of £48 million, the difference accounted for by £28 million of reduced expenditure and £18 million of excess revenue. The savings were mainly due to falling prices and, in the case of the service estimates, poor recruitment and slow start of works. Falling prices did not point to good trade. In the case of the revenue excesses, which were curiously widely spread, inaccurate estimating seems to have been the main cause, although as a touching tribute to the cosy cottage atmosphere of national finance in those days other explanations were dredged up, such as that the spirit-duty surplus of £6 million was due to the long cold winter and the increasing popularity of whisky as a remedy for influenza. In any event the result, coupled with the budgeted sinking fund provision, meant that he was able to announce a total debt reduction for the year of £127 million, which was formidable, although of course not much due to Snowden.

The outlook was a little less certain, as is the way with the future. Snowden claimed that he had secured a reduction of £31 million in the estimates for 1924–5. But this was from first bids, which were themselves somewhat higher than the 1923–4 result, which was not perhaps surprising in view of the underspendings of that year. Snowden's budget speech implied that he had been an iron Chancellor. Others, most notably Sir Godfrey Collins, MP, the Glasgow publisher of bibles and dictionaries, said that he was being far too lavish with the (sometimes) fighting services.

Whatever the exact merits of the argument, Snowden estimated that existing tax rates would give him a surplus of £38 million, after fulfilling the substantial sinking fund commitment. He proceeded to announce remissions of taxation which amounted to £34 million for the current year (leaving him with a surplus of £4 million) but the cost of which would rise to £40 million in subsequent years. This, he thought, the secular buoyancy of the revenue would be more than enough to sustain. This small and eminently bridgeable gap was the only risk that he took.

His main reductions were concentrated on indirect food and (non-alcoholic) drink taxes. He reduced the sugar duty from 2¾d a pound to a penny halfpenny. This was his most expensive concession and cost him nearly £18 million. He also halved the tea duty at a cost of £5 million.

Cocoa, coffee and chicory were treated similarly. Dried fruits (primarily prunes in those days) were also given a reduction, which enabled him to claim that his proposals were 'the greatest step ever made towards the realization of the cherished Radical ideal of a free breakfast-table'. Sweetened table waters (mainly children's ginger-pop and similar forms of bottled gas) had their duty abolished, but unsweetened ones, such as soda-water and Apollinaris, which were thought to appeal to more sophisticated or at any rate more affluent tastes, continued to bear duty. The changes made, apart from the abolition of the friendless corporation profits tax (at a cost of £2 million but rising), were very deliberately slung against regression. Thus his cutting of the return from entertainments duty by a half was almost all concentrated on the cheaper seats, abolition up to sixpence, heavy reduction up to 1s 3d, no concession over that.

This of course made the detail of the budget, the proposals he actually announced, highly palatable to Labour and radical listeners. But the psychological relief to the prosperous and even more the wealthy was in fact much greater. They were not disposed to argue about whether the budget was too kind to sweet-tea addicts or whether champagne might have been treated as generously as ginger-pop. These questions were far outweighed by their relief that he had left direct taxation broadly alone: nothing extra on income tax or on surtax or on death duties, merely a more generous tax allowance for widowers with housekeepers (somehow a very Snowden-like concession) and a glancing opinion that at 4s 6d (22.5p) in the pound income tax was too high, but that nothing could be done about it in the current year. And the capital levy, a hot political issue for the previous four years, had disappeared far down wind.

This was the artistry of this highly conventional but not pedestrian budget. What it did benefited the 'have-nots'. What it did not do relieved the 'haves'. Many of them had worked themselves up into a state of expecting the first socialist budget to mean the end of civilized life, or at any rate of aristocratic and high bourgeois life, and when it did nothing of the sort they could scarce forbear to cheer. Snowden's claim that 'the budget is vindicative against no class and against no interest' was well founded. He followed this with a high statement of fiscal principle which, although perhaps contractually void for vagueness, had a ring much more of Gladstone than of Dalton or Cripps about it: 'Though I have always held and declared that the State has the right to call upon the whole of the available resources of its citizens in case of national need, I have equally held and declared that the State has no right to tax anyone, unless it can show that the taxation is likely to be used more beneficially and more economically.'

When Snowden sat down there was a great fluttering of order papers (a rare but intoxicating occurrence which the Chancellor, perhaps fortunately, cannot easily see from his position of exhausted collapse) not only from the Labour but from much of the Liberal benches as well. Asquith endorsed the budget as 'proceeding upon a thoroughly sound financial basis'. Other compliments, both in the House and in the press, were freely forthcoming. The sighs of relief from Eaton Square to Lombard Street were clearly audible at Westminster, and the Chancellor when he wound up the budget debate was able to say jocularly but without arousing derision (although he might have done better to have left it to others to make the comment) that he had heard there was a move to erect a statue to him in the City. Even Beatrice Webb, who was not naturally a fan of Snowden's (it was difficult to know who was a fan of whom in that first government of comrades), confessed to error. 'Philip has had a great triumph,' she wrote in her diary, '. . . we were wrong about [him] . . . he has turned out to be the best available Chancellor.' Some Labour members, but those probably the more foolish, were apparently urging a dissolution in the wake of the budget's popularity.

There were, however, two aspects of the budget which, behind the first wave of euphoria, aroused more criticism. The first alleged that he had been over-optimistic, and that, in place of the small covenanted surplus, the year would end up with a big deficit. This proved wholly ill-judged. The year turned out, probably as much by luck as by judgement, almost uncannily close to what he had predicted. The second provided the main item of Finance Bill controversy. He repealed *en bloc* the so-called 'McKenna duties'. These, it will be recalled, had been introduced in 1915 by a Free Trade Chancellor, not it was stressed to protect British industry but to discourage the purchase in wartime of manufactured articles, motor cars, motor cycles, musical instruments, clocks, watches and cinematograph films.

The duties had since been continued by a series of four more or less Protectionist Conservative Chancellors. They yielded only £3 million a year, but behind them the nascent motor industry, concentrated in the Midlands, was moving to successful mass production. Snowden acted dogmatically and with very little consultation, but on the whole got away with it. Some of his colleagues were horrified when they first heard of the proposal on the morning of budget day. The motor industry, needless to say, was up in arms, and not greatly assuaged by the counterbalancing concession of a £0.5 million reduction in motor licence duties. But in the outcome the growth of the industry registered no visible check. It was part of Snowden's strength and of his weakness that he would not greatly have cared if this had been the result. Free Trade was right, the 'McKenna duties' were wrong, and that was it.

The Conservatives naturally chose to make their abolition the main point of their attack. It brought together the needs of opportunism and of ideology. It produced some fraying at the edges of both Liberal and Labour loyalty. But Baldwin's amendment was nonetheless defeated by sixty-five votes. He did not move it at all viciously. One of Baldwin's troubles was that he was always too good-tempered in opposition – the fact that it meant even longer holidays more than outweighed any sins of the government. Thereafter the Finance Bill proceeded relatively easily and was law by 1 August.

By this time Snowden was greatly enjoying being Chancellor. By the test of whether Labour was fit to govern he had been a brilliant success. Only John Wheatley, the militant Clydesider who brought remarkable administrative flair to the Ministry of Health, and MacDonald himself as Foreign Secretary, in which office up to this point he was much better than as a leader and co-ordinator of the government, could begin to hold a candle to him. Presenting his budget to a House of Commons which contained five former Chancellors (three of them former Prime Ministers as well) he had shown that he could do it as well as any and better than most. In the circumstances a degree both of hubris and of desire to retain office on his part was neither surprising nor objectionable. He was consequently furious when what he regarded as gross political bungling by MacDonald resulted in him (and his colleagues) being out of office, and with a decisive majority against them, within thirteen weeks of his bringing his budget proposals triumphantly into harbour.

The Chancellor and the Prime Minister had a semi-public dispute during August over the handling of the 'Dawes Plan' to deal with reparations and to get some stability back into the collapsed German economy. MacDonald had worked skilfully to promote an approach to Franco-German harmony, and as a lubricant for the process proposed some small sacrifice of British claims (which were not in any event being paid) in favour of France. Snowden, foreshadowing the still more virulently chauvinistic attitude which he was to display at The Hague

Anti-clockwise from above

A seditious afternoon in the country, Blenheim, 23rd July 1912: two mountebanks, an old trout, an actress manqué and our sad knight (from left to right: the Duke of Marlborough, Lord Londonderry, Mrs F. E. Smith, Bonar Law and Smith (later Birkenhead).

Bonar Law leaves the most famous of all Carlton Club meetings with J. C. C. Davidson, October 1922.

Bonar Law with his self-appointed Sancho Panzo, Lord Beaverbrook, 1923.

Right: Robert Horne: a bland Chancellor on the eve of his 1922 Budget.

Below: Three Chancellors together: Austen Chamberlain, Robert Horne and Winston Churchill, *c.* 1922.

Top left and above: Stanley Baldwin in town; and country (both 1923).

Left: Reluctantly in London, August 1931; Baldwin in search of a resumed holiday, Neville Chamberlain of a National government.

Above: Snowden's birthplace: the high Pennine village of Ickornshaw.

Right: Ethel Snowden before she acquired the ostrich feathers.

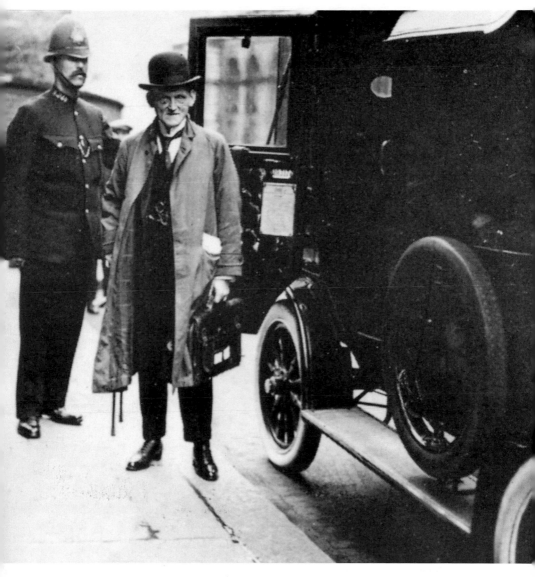

Snowden in Downing Street at the time of the first Labour government.

Above: Fishing on the Don, August 1935.

Right: The Man of Munich, with his *vis-à-vis*, September 1938.

conference five years later, when the Dawes Plan had become the Young Plan, was bitterly resistant. His position was highly perverse. He kept within hailing distance of his ILP past by claiming to be against reparations altogether. But if they existed he was not going to allow Britain to sacrifice a fraction of an ounce of its pound of flesh in favour of the grasping French. He in effect repudiated the Prime Minister's policy in a *Manchester Guardian* interview published on 21 August.

This dispute, with Snowden both in form and in substance much more in the wrong than MacDonald, merely produced an even worse than usual underlying feeling. It was not the cause of the *dégringolade*. That was the role of the Campbell case, in which the forensically brilliant but politically inept Attorney-General, Sir Patrick Hastings, first allowed the launching of a prosecution for sedition against J. R. Campbell, the acting editor of the Communist *Workers' Weekly*, and then withdrew it after some sort of intervention or at least discussion of the case with the Prime Minister. Political convenience, it was alleged, was being allowed to suborn the proper independence of the Attorney when acting in his judicial capacity. The Prime Minister's handling of the issue at a couple of his question times was singularly unconvincing. Snowden subsequently described MacDonald's performances as 'intolerant, evasive and prevaricating'. This led on to a debate for which there were two motions down. The first was a straight Conservative vote of censure. The second was a Liberal amendment asking for an enquiry by a Select Committee. The amendment was intended, by some of its supporters at least, to throw a lifeline to the government. Snowden wanted to accept it and keep the government alive. MacDonald, whom Snowden thought feared enquiry more than defeat, insisted on opposing both. As a result he went down by a huge majority, and on the next day a general election was announced for 29 October.

The campaign began with the Labour party on the wrong foot and continued to go consistently badly. Latterly the dominant issue was the probably forged Zinoviev letter, which conveyed instructions from the head of the Comintern for the stirring up of insurrection in Britain. The Foreign Office had published it without taking instruction from or even warning MacDonald, their political head. (I do not think this would have happened in Snowden's Treasury.) And once again MacDonald handled the matter with a mixture of ineptitude and shiftiness. It probably made more difference to the morale of the campaign than to the result, which was largely produced by a shift of votes from Liberal to Tory. The Labour vote actually went up by nearly 25 per cent, but in

a period when there were great fluctuations in the number of constituencies uncontested this in itself did not mean much. What was more
significant was that the number of Labour seats went down to 152 and
the number of Tory seats went up to 411, which meant a full parliament
of opposition for Snowden and his colleagues.

Snowden's sense of self-righteous bitterness (never difficult to tap)
was increased by the fact that his own majority in Colne Valley nearly
doubled, whereas MacDonald's in Aberavon was more than halved. His
private comment (to F. W. Jowett,, an old Bradford ILP colleague and
the defeated First Commissioner of Works) was of 'the great opportunities we have wantonly and recklessly thrown away by the most
incompetent leadership which ever brought a Government to ruin'.
Ethel Snowdon, wholly typically to be found on a Canadian lecture tour,
put her husband's thoughts fully into the public domain by proclaiming
that 'the British Labour party has been the victim of the worst leadership
of modern times'. Snowden thus terminated his first and nine-month-
long period of office with his own reputation more enhanced than his
respect for his principal colleagues.

In opposition Snowden found himself shadowing Winston Churchill
who had just 're-ratted' to the Conservative party, and whom Baldwin,
with unexpected and somewhat ill-directed generosity, made Chancellor
of the Exchequer. This suited Snowden very well. The change brought
about by his experience of high office combined with his move, under
his wife's aegis, to the sylvan delights of the Surrey hills at Tilford, was
that he became an enthusiastic member of what might today be called
the premier league of politicians. The scribbling puritanical hunchback
of Golders Green became if not exactly the squire at least one of the
sages of the country beyond the Hog's Back. Lloyd George was his
neighbour to the south-west (as were the Webbs but he chose to see less
of them) as Beaverbrook was to the north-east. He enjoyed visiting both
of them, and it is an open question whether or not Beaverbrook
persuaded him that a gentle sipping of champagne was essentially
compatible with the temperance which he had preached since his youth.

But that was not significant. No one was going to seduce Snowden
by a direct undermining of his standards. Nor had he taken to a
luxurious way of living. Eden Lodge was a proper small house in the
country, with about ten rooms giving plenty of space to have people to
stay. But neither the furniture nor the catering was lavish. Mrs Snowden
displayed signed photographs of the King and the Queen, but Snowden

himself stuck in his study to Siegfried Sassoon (not the most obvious choice for him) and Keir Hardie, buttressed by a few other old ILP associates, but conspicuously not MacDonald. Snowden himself was estimated to have a journalistic income of about £2,000 (say £80,000 today) during these years. He had switched from eleemosynary articles for Labour periodicals to writing occasionally for several of the main national newspapers and quite often getting his work syndicated abroad. In addition Ethel Snowden became a governor of the BBC at the end of 1926 (a Baldwin appointment) and was paid the surprisingly large sum of £750 a year for this very part-time commitment. So there was perfectly adequate money for his spending needs, of which the most indulgent was his liking for travelling by chauffer-driven motor car, which in view of his lameness was very natural.

Although all this was a far cry from his hobbling between railway stations and Co-operative halls of thirty years before there was no danger of Snowden becoming a slave of the fleshpots. His temptations were more subtle ones: first his finding the Treasury and Bank of England establishments more intelligent and interesting than his party colleagues and caring more for their good opinion; and second his increasing conceit of himself (by no means entirely misplaced) as an independent statesman who exchanged insults or compliments with other members of this chosen race, but took no comparable notice of his colleagues or followers. This tendency was both accentuated and epitomized by his resigning in 1927 from the ILP, which he claimed had become redundant in the modern Labour party, but of which in fact the main sin in his eyes was its takeover by Clydeside proletarianism.

Being opposite Winston Churchill suited him well from every point of view. Churchill was undoubtedly a member of the chosen race of statesmen, so that there was no question of Snowden sullying himself by wrestling with a chimney sweep. Churchill also had the advantage, in this context, of knowing much less about finance than did Snowden. Their duels became eagerly awaited parliamentary set-pieces, battles of grandiloquence with mordancy. The clash of their styles was not made less enjoyable by the absence of much divergence on policy. Churchill's most vital (and damaging) decision was to put the pound back on the Gold Standard at the pre-1914 parity. Snowden managed to wrap himself round an opposition notion criticizing the timing but was in fact whole-heartedly in favour of the substance of the decision, wished he had been able to do it himself and thereafter (until the ark sank six years later) treated it as part of the ark of the covenant. Churchill in return extended his respect to Snowden. When in 1929 he became Chancellor of Bristol University, Snowden was on his inaugural list of honorands.

Just as the return to Gold was the dominating decision of the mid-1920s, so the General Strike was the dominating event. Snowden was totally opposed to it. He had long been sceptical of the value of strikes, even in a strictly industrial context. In a political context and as a political weapon, which a general strike inevitably was, he thought their use not merely unwise but nearly insane. Even he, with his taste for provocative courage, however, did not think he could say that, or anything near to it, during the battle. It would have been the equivalent of desertion in the face of the enemy, for which the death penalty to his deep disapproval had been so freely used during the First World War. So he kept absolutely quiet. There was some suggestion that he was ill, but if so, his illness was more diplomatic than clinical. It was not perhaps his most heroic hour, but was a remarkable feat on the part of the Labour party's principal economic spokesman, and (in the appreciation of most of the public; Clynes was nominally so) second man, to maintain total public silence during the nine days of the Strike.

Of course his absence of support was noticed, and a few more notches were marked on the scale of Snowden alienation from the left and even the centre of the Labour party. A year later, however, he came back into partisan politics like a thunderclap. He had something of the quality which Aberdeen attributed to Gladstone of being 'terrible in the rebound'. The Conservative government's revenge for the General Strike was the Trades Disputes Bill of 1927. Snowden was even more against the revenge than he was against the provocation. Against this bill he delivered what Lloyd George considered the greatest speech of his parliamentary career. It was certainly one of the longest, lasting ninety minutes, and holding a large House throughout. It became the *locus classicus* of the case against the bill. It had a force and an authority which no other Labour spokesman could match. For sheer quality 'our Philip' was indispensable.

When the 1929 election gave Labour its second opportunity for government Snowden was thus, despite having moved to the right of almost any party member except for MacDonald, who cordially and reciprocally disliked him, an automatic choice for the Chancellorship. It was simply impossible to imagine anyone else usurping his claim. That election nominally put Labour in a much stronger position than it had occupied in 1924. It had won the election and not merely seen the

Tories lose it as on the previous occasion. Although Labour did not have an independent majority it was the largest party and the only possible government, except for the variant that Labour could have led a coalition with Lloyd George and the fifty-nine Liberal MPs, which might have been better both for itself and for the country. But Labour exclusivity, and perhaps Liberal prickliness too, ruled this out. There was no range of possibilities as in 1923–4 and Baldwin recognized this by resigning immediately in 1929 rather than waiting to meet Parliament.

Nonetheless the second Labour government was in reality more precariously placed than the first. As its leading figures celebrated their victory and argued with comradely viciousness about the dispositions of offices, they were like a lavish picnic party laying out the rugs and the victuals on a cliff-top promontory which was about to fall into the sea. Ministers were sworn in on 8 July (1929), which was just sixteen weeks before the great crash on the New York Stock Exchange and six months before British (and other) unemployment figures took off into an upward spiral of unprecedented intensity. Unlike 1924 Snowden had no immediate budget-making pressure upon him, although he had taken a dismal view of the national finances in a discussion with MacDonald over the formation of the government, and he opined that after the extravagant ebullience of Churchill at least three budgets would be necessary to get them right.

This sombre view did not prevent his celebrating his return to office with a profligate display of chauvinist populism. The Young Plan, designed to achieve a final settlement of the reparations issue which had so damaged Europe both economically and politically during the previous ten years, was due to be endorsed at an August international conference in The Hague. Months, even years, of careful preparation had gone into the enterprise. The previous Conservative government was firmly committed. The essential points of the tentatively agreed scheme were some reduction in German liabilities in return for their promise of prompt payment; France to evacuate the Rhineland; and Britain, as a price for those objectives which it had long sought, to accept a limited adjustment (about £2 million a year) in its receipts in favour of France and Italy.

Snowden, accompanied by Henderson the new Foreign Secretary and William Graham the President of the Board of Trade and at that time his closest friend in politics, set out for the Dutch capital on 4 August, a date which might have reminded the participants of Europe's capacity for self-destruction. It was the first time that Snowden had been on the continent of Europe since 1907, and the first time ever that he had taken part in an international conference. This inexperience in no way inhibited him from dominating the proceedings. He pushed aside Henderson who was not normally negligible ('I might as well go home,' the Foreign Secretary said after one particularly rough encounter with the granite Chancellor, and received the unyielding reply of 'That's about it, Arthur'). He insulted the chief French delegate. He demanded 'his money back' in a way that foreshadowed Margaret Thatcher's negotiating technique at Dublin and in other capitals fifty years later. Then having delivered these opening pleasantries, he retired to his room from which the Japanese delegate, who had surprisingly taken on the role of intermediary between Britain and Europe, tried, vainly for several weeks, to extricate him. He long resisted all compromise. He ruined (which would hardly have upset him) the Prime Minister's holiday at Lossiemouth, where MacDonald was harried by Foreign Office reports that his Chancellor was wrecking his (and Henderson's) central foreign policy aim of Franco-German reconciliation.

He did not however need special Foreign Office intelligence, for the English newspapers, thin on news in a holiday month, focused on The Hague and treated Snowden like a national boxing hero. Eventually by sheer intransigence he achieved 75 per cent of what he had been demanding and saved Britain a notional £1.5 million a year for thirty-seven years. Long before 1966, however, the victory had been subsumed in a number of other international events, such as the Second World War, to which misfortune the failure of The Hague in 1929 to improve goodwill in Europe made a minor contribution. It was an expensive £1.5 million. This was not however appreciated by the superficial currents of British public opinion. They welcomed Snowden back as a victorious fighting cock. There was a big crowd at Liverpool Street station on a Sunday morning. The City of London made him a freeman, and the King and Queen invited him and Ethel to Sandringham for twenty-four hours and presented them with a book-stand and tea-table made by the estate gardeners; a fretwork present seemed appropriate.

During the next eight months Snowden, having gone a good way to snuffing out the internationalist desires of both the Prime Minister and the Foreign Secretary, turned his snuffing-out attention to the home front. Between January and April 1930, while unemployment rose from 1,500,000 to 1,700,000, he killed any hope of the Labour government pursuing other than the most orthodox of financial policies. On the formation of the government, J. H. Thomas, who in spite of his buoyant careerism seemed consistently to draw the short straw in Cabinet appointments, was made Lord Privy Seal and put in charge of a team of middle-rank ministers to combat unemployment. Sir Oswald Mosley was an impatient member of this team, and in January 1930 he put forward a Cabinet paper which advocated vigorous premature Keynesianism. Snowden was horrified. The correct rule must be that in hard times the government, like a prudent private citizen, drew in its belt. Any concept of counter-cyclical deficits was profoundly antipathetic. 'I am a man of a saving temperament,' he said at about this time. And his seniority and prestige were such that Mosley did not stand a chance against him. The Mosley memorandum was crushed within the Labour party, and when Mosley tried outside tools, first the New Party and then the British Union of Fascists, he did not achieve much with them either.

Then, in his 14 April budget, Snowden scuppered the hope not only of the Labour government producing a counter-cyclical expansionist policy but also of its using direct taxation for a sustained egalitarian drive. In itself the 1930 budget was by no means a bad one. He whipped up a great passion about the precarious state in which Winston Churchill had left the nation's finances. But he did this more to create a climate of apprehension in which he could get through some tax increases than to score partisan points. The year for which Churchill had last budgeted ended up with a deficit of £14.5 million as against the £4 million surplus of his estimate. But as this was after a debt repayment of £50 million it was not a remotely serious matter, even without raising the issue of whether, with soaring unemployment and weak revenue returns owing to poor trade, debt repayment was in any way desirable. But Snowden's every instinct was the other way. He made a moral crusade out of deflationary finance: 'As long as I hold this position,' he proclaimed, 'I am determined, however burdensome it may be, that this country shall pay its way by honest measures . . . I will not leave my successors to pay my bills. . . .'

So, by an inverted cooking of the books based on giving an absolute priority to debt repayment, he managed to manufacture a prospective deficit of £42 million, and to propose taxation increases to cover it. With one small exception they were all on the direct side and had a distinctly progressive tinge to them. The standard rate of income tax went up from four shillings to 4s 6d, but with assuaging adjustments which meant that a married man with three children would not pay until his income reached £882 (perhaps £28,000–£30,000 today). Surtax was increased from ninepence to a shilling at the beginning of the scale, with the top rate (charged on the slice of over £50,000 a year) rising from six shillings to 7s 6d, that is to a maximum total tax rate of twelve shillings in the pound, significantly higher than anything today. Death duties on estates of over £2 million went from 40 per cent to 50. The small indirect exception was an increase of a penny a gallon in the beer duty, which he claimed should have no effect on the retail price. By these means his somewhat artificial deficit was turned into an estimated surplus of £2 million. (It was not achieved, for the gathering momentum of the slump produced shortfalls in most of the main items of revenue.)

Snowden accompanied his 'hard' budget proposals with three statements *obiter*. First, he committed himself to get rid of all food taxes in the course of the parliament, which he optimistically saw lasting another four years. Second, he announced legislation for land valuation, which would make it possible to bring in land taxes to which he had been attached since he had heard Henry George speak at Aberdeen forty years earlier. Third, he announced that his income tax and surtax increases were the last in this field that he would propose in that parliament except 'in unforeseen circumstances'. The 'unforeseen circumstances' loophole was a fairly wide one, but it was nonetheless extraordinary that he should have twice shown such a predilection for committing himself for several budgets ahead, and for doing so, in the latter case, in a way that alienated a lot of left-wing support. It was taken as giving notice that the modest 1930 increases in income tax and surtax sealed off any further attempt on the part of that Labour govenment to produce socialism by redistributive taxation. It was a direct contributory cause of the decision of the rump of the ILP effectively to detach itself from the Labour party.

The deterioration in both the budgetary and the general economic situation during the next year was probably the worst with which any Chancellor, certainly any peacetime Chancellor, has ever had to contend. And the political weakness of a minority government combined with a collapse of Snowden's own health, which set in about Christmas 1930, made the landscape even bleaker. By then unemployment was above two million and would be almost two and a half by the time of the 1931 budget. And Snowden's strenuous efforts for budgetary propriety of the previous April had been undermined by revenue shortfalls and by the devastating impact of the numbers out of work on the Unemployment Insurance Fund, which was forced into borrowing at the rate of nearly £1 million a week.

After several weeks of unspecified illness at the beginning of the year Snowden came back in late January to try to square a very difficult circle. His 1931 budget strategy could have accepted living with a deficit and justifying it on the ground of the extraordinarily depressed state of the revenue. But this was directly alien to his thought. Furthermore he believed that there was a particular obligation on Britain, as the home of the world's primary financial and trading centre, to maintain budgetary probity. Otherwise, aided by the City of London's vulnerable habit of borrowing short and lending long, there might well be collapse of confidence. This was bankers' wisdom, which Snowden found easy to accept.

Another route out of his morass would have been increased taxation. But he was inhibited here both in the direct and the indirect directions by his foolish pledges. He might in any event have found increases difficult to get through the House of Commons. The Tories would have voted for a revenue tariff, but for nothing else, and quite a lot of Labour members, as well as a few Liberals, would have agreed with them that this was the best route. But certainly not Snowden, whose dogmatic attachment to Free Trade was unshakeable.

So he was left trying to solve his problems by economies. This was a possible but stony road, particularly after he had indicated to a meeting of the parliamentary Labour party that he had no intention of cutting unemployment benefit, despite the fact that the slump had caused the cost of living to fall by 10 per cent. This opened up a dilemma. If he was going to get serious economies through the Labour party he had to create an atmosphere of deep apprehension. However, scaring his back benchers was also liable to scare the bankers who held mobile funds in London, and thus precipitate the trouble which the whole enterprise was designed to prevent. But Snowden, who rather liked gothic horror stories, and was indeed something of a character in one, decided to take the risk.

At the end of January he instigated the publication of a Treasury report on the Unemployment Insurance Fund which contained the following knell of doom: 'Continual State borrowing on the present vast scale without adequate repayment by the Fund would quickly call in question the stability of the British financial system . . .'. It was a curious procedure for a Chancellor to encourage an announcement that financial policy was set on a disaster course.

Two weeks later he followed this up in an even more bizarre way. The occasion was a Conservative motion of censure against the laxness of Labour public expenditure policies. The Liberals, whose attitude was crucial for the survival of the government, played it in a way reminiscent of the Campbell debate six and a half years earlier. They put down an amendment calling for the appointment of an independent committee of enquiry. This was however less sensible in 1931 than in 1924, for there were dark patches in relation to the Campbell case which an independent enquiry could well have elucidated. Such was not the case in relation to public expenditure and prospective deficits. The facts were known. What was at issue were policy decisions going to the centre of political dispute and government responsibility. Was budget balance desirable in a slump? Was unemployment benefit to be cut? If not, what other major economies were to be made? However a Labour government, having fallen on its rejection of the more sensible motion in 1924, decided to accept the less sensible one in 1931.

What was even less understandable was the way in which Snowden chose to play the debate. In reply to Sir Laming Worthington-Evans, neither the most provocative of Tory debaters nor the best remembered of inter-war statesmen, he launched a violent attack on Tory financial laxity over most of the previous decade. Never perhaps the most difficult thing to do, he reduced the House to a bear-garden. Then, having established his partisan credentials, he completely changed his tone and gave the most sombre warnings to his own followers. The outlook was awful, and the problems could be solved not by party bickering, 'which would be resumed later', but only by a united effort.

It was a bewildering speech, and despite the opening rodomontade was better received by Liberal and Conservative than by Labour members. That he had been able to produce such an abrupt change of tone and atmosphere between the two parts of his speech demonstrated both his exceptional power as a House of Commons personality and a developing imbalance in his behaviour. Already by this time he had effectively cut himself off from Cabinet consultation or discipline. He acted entirely on his own both in launching the Treasury insurance fund bombshell and in delivering the 'double-whammy' speech. After the latter he became even more detached because he developed a bladder infection which required surgical intervention (severe in those days) followed by an extended convalescence at Tilford. It was probably the longest withdrawal of a minister in office until 1953, when Churchill's stroke and Eden's surgical visit to Boston left a still more truncated government.

In March 1931 questions began to be asked in Parliament about who was in charge of the Treasury, to which the answer was that Snowden was. It was not so much that Chancellor's control over the Exchequer (on strategic issues at any rate) was lost as that all Cabinet control over the Chancellor was sundered. Eventually he appeared in London on the Friday before a Monday budget and made a presentation to the Cabinet, rested for the weekend in 11 Downing Street (restored to its normal cancellarian tenant in the government of 1929 as opposed to that of 1924), and then hobbled into the House of Commons on the Monday afternoon, creating a considerable drama as to whether he would be able to get through the speech. As a good theatrical prop William Graham, the President of the Board of Trade and still for another few months the Chancellor's faithful acolyte, was provided with a speaking copy, so that, if Snowden collapsed, he would be able to carry on.

Snowden did not collapse, and indeed in his *Autobiography* dismissed the view that this was ever likely. The speech was relatively short and the budget both a stop-gap and an anti-climax. By his acceptance of the Liberal amendment in February he had very largely put financial policy into commission for the spring and summer season. But the composition of the 'independent enquiry' more or less guaranteed that when it came back into the open it would do so on terms deeply inimical to radical, let alone socialist, solutions. The Prime Minister and the Chancellor were jointly responsible for the appointment of Sir George May, the just-retired secretary of the Prudential Assurance Company, as chairman, and for filling the other places with equal representation of the three parties, which meant the government party being in a less than 30 per cent minority on a committee set to pronounce on the most sensitive current issue of politics.

May was a very odd choice. He represented the most conventional upper-middle-rank City opinion. The government might have done better with Snowden's old love Montagu Norman, had he been available, or with a great private financier of flair. As it was they created a time-bomb ticking away under them and due to explode at the end of July, well known to be financially the most dangerous time of the year. But it was not ready to explode by the time of the late April budget, and Snowden confined himself to putting up petrol by twopence a gallon, making one or two internal adjustments and coming up with a nominal surplus of £134,000, which was not only negligible but, as he added gloomily, unlikely to be realized. For the rest they must wait for May (Sir George) and July (end of). A worse count against the budget than this *attentisme* was that, with unemployment climbing steadily towards three million, it launched into an elaborate and irrelevant scheme of land taxation. This at least kept the House of Commons occupied for most of the summer.

The May report was published on 31 July just as Parliament was adjourning. It had been a summer of reports. They were mostly chickens coming home to roost. In June there reported the so-called Gregory Commission, specifically dealing with the Unemployment Fund, which recommended a cut of 30 per cent in the rate and the rigid confinement of the benefit to forty-six weeks, after which the Poor Law must take over. In mid-July came the report of the Macmillan Committee which made serious long-term recommendations and the deliberations of which led Keynes and Bevin to meet and appreciate each other, no insignificant achievement. Its constructive nature procluded it being taken much notice of in that summer of febrility. Purely accidentally it was the day of the Macmillan publication that the serious withdrawal of funds from London began. To anyone who was Chancellor in the 1960s, let alone later, the sums sound puny. In the first bad week the Bank of England lost £22 million in gold. Twenty-five years later that could have gone in the blink of an eyelid between 3.00 and 3.05 on a moderately bad Friday afternoon. In 1931, however, it was enough to create an excited official and political climate for the reception of May.

May said that there would on present policies be a deficit of £120 million (and nobody much noticed that this would be after providing £50 million for debt reduction) and that the position could be contained only with economies of £96 million, which amounted to no less than 20 per cent off supply (broadly non-debt servicing) expenditure, of which two-thirds (£66 million) should come off unemployment benefit. The crisis curiously hung fire for the first couple of weeks of August, perhaps a tribute to the importance attached to holidays. MacDonald went to Lossiemouth, and others, except for Snowden who remained at his Treasury desk, in various other directions. A very high-level Cabinet committee (MacDonald, Snowden, Henderson, Thomas, Graham) was set up to consider May, but arranged its first meeting only for 25 August.

An accelerating loss of gold upset this leisurely time-table. Mac-Donald was brought back to London on the morning of Tuesday, 11 August. From then until Monday, 24 August when the National government was formed, the crisis raged, at any rate in the breasts of ministers and the few opposition leaders (mainly Neville Chamberlain; Baldwin, after appearing briefly in London on 13 August was on holiday at Aix-les-Bains) who were available. The Bank of England, led by Harvey, the deputy governor, was also in a high state of excitement. (The famous and Snowden-beloved Montagu Norman had got so agitated earlier in the summer that he had retired hurt with a nervous breakdown. It was not a very impressive performance at the most challenging point of his twenty-year governorship.) The role of the Bank was to arrange with their New York agents, J. P. Morgan and Son, a sufficiently large loan to avoid 'the deluge' (in Snowden's phrase) which would submerge sterling. Acting nominally as messengers, but ones with monopoly rights on transatlantic communications, these two financial institutions achieved the position of joint arbiters of what was and what was not acceptable in British government policy.

Within the government discussions were first conducted in the framework of the five-man Cabinet economy committee. Snowden was still pursuing a tactic of uttering dire warnings rather than proposing attainable solutions. He advised that the prospective deficit (for 1932–3 and therefore not immediately compelling, eight months before even the beginning of the financial year) was not May's £120 million but £170 million, and that this must be eliminated by a mixture of economies and taxation. But £50 million of it was contributed by the sinking fund, which he resolutely refused to see eliminated or even reduced. This was the first of the two rigidities which he contributed to testing the government to destruction. The second was that when it came to a stark choice between a cut in unemployment benefit and a revenue tariff he refused to contemplate the latter, the significance of which was that it was at one stage preferred by sixteen out of twenty-one members of the Cabinet, including his closest Cabinet friend and hitherto devoted ally, William Graham. There was a bitter personal split as a result, which, such was the burning force of Snowden's personality to the few exposed to its direct rays, many people thought contributed to Graham's death at the age of forty-four five months later.

'At one stage' is an appropriate phrase for the complications, confusions and shifting positions of those thirteen days which brought to a juddering end the first phase of Labour as a governing party. Downing Street was as shrouded by fog as any battlefield during that period when there was more agony than comprehension. It is a criticism of Snowden that he did not set out the facts more clearly and consistently.

The main confusions were that the May Committee recommended £96 million of economies, that Snowden recommended £78 million, while often giving the impression that this was not really enough, and that the Cabinet had only firmly accepted £56 million, although in talks with both the opposition leaders and the Bank of England it was sometimes suggested that they had gone to £78 million. The £56 million essentially came from a stop on the road-building programme, a good hardy annual for public expenditure exercises but socially unobjectionable, and cutting the salaries of public employees, schoolteachers providing the bulk of the savings, by 20 per cent. The essential difference between this package and the £78 million was a 10 per cent cut in unemployment benefit. (A 20 per cent cut would have got near to the £96 million.)

It is easy to see why an unemployment benefit cut was such a traumatic issue for a Labour Cabinet. It was bad enough that the main impact they had made on the unemployment problem, which had been a main point of anti-Conservative attack in the 1929 election, was to increase the numbers out of work from 1.3 million to 2.5 million. If on top of that they were to reduce by 10 per cent (or even worse by 20 per cent) the money benefit of what was, on the whole rightly, presumed to be the poorest group in the community, it was going to be a staggering record. Against this Arthur Henderson for instance, very much a man of government but also a man of stolid force, took an absolute stand.

How could Snowden, who could justly say, 'I have been in active political life for forty years, and my only object has been to improve the lot of the toiling millions,' take the opposite view? For forensic ballast he could rely on the argument that the cost of living had fallen by a little more than the 10 per cent since 1929, so that there was no real cut. But at a more profound level of motivation his essential approach was that bad times necessarily meant hardship and that Labour could prove its political maturity only by being prepared to press the hair shirt on itself and on its natural constituency with as much courage as Tories or Liberals. In any event he rather liked hair shirts.

There is no evidence that Snowden was eager for a coalition government which would ensure his own continuance at the Treasury. He always took a quietest view about his own career, based partly, it must be said, on a self-confident belief in his own near indispensability. On the key night (23 August), when the ultimatum came from New York via the Bank of England, when the Cabinet refused to meet the terms, when MacDonald went to Buckingham Palace to resign, and then conferred in 10 Downing Street with the opposition leaders, Snowden just went to bed in No. 11. When at the end of the following morning he was asked by MacDonald if he would serve in the new National government he made three stipulations: first that it would be strictly temporary for the purpose of dealing with the financial crisis, and would then dissolve itself; second that there would be no controversial party legislation during this brief lifetime; and third that there would be no 'coupon election'. MacDonald gave all three assurances, whereupon Snowden, without any request for further reflection, agreed to serve, alongside among the Labour Cabinet only Sankey the Lord Chancellor and J. H. Thomas, the patriotic vulgarian and 'Lord Boiled-shirt' of Low's cartoons. In view of his immediately preceding role and attitude it would have been very difficult for Snowden to have done anything else.

Two days beforehand he had written to his chairman in Colne Valley telling him (for publication) that he did not intend to stand again for that or any other constituency. That decision, together with his health (which was again deteriorating) and his age (he was sixty-seven) obviously precluded his continuing into a long Chancellorship, but as he had just stipulated that there should be no snap election it did not avoid his having to deal with the immediate crisis. This he believed that he handled almost exactly as he would have done in the previous government had he been able to secure adequate Labour support. In his emergency budget of 8 September he proposed £81 million of additional taxation. Income tax went up from 4s 6d to five shillings, with reductions in the marriage and children's allowance. Surtax was increased by 10 per cent. Beer went up by a penny a pint, petrol by twopence a gallon and cigarettes by a penny a packet. But there was an important difference on the savings side. He accepted, partly on the advice of Neville Chamberlain, whose financial responsibility he trusted more than that of his 'spendthrift' former colleagues, a reduction of £19 million in the sinking fund, a course which he had previously treated as the road to perdition. This meant that he had to find only £70 million for economy cuts, broadly the agreed £56 million plus the 10 per cent cut in unemployment benefit. On this basis he claimed that he had eliminated the deficit, balanced his budget and repulsed the threat to the pound and to British credit.

Unfortunately the international financial community did not take an equally sanguine view. The £80 million loan from New York (and Paris), the need for which had caused so much trouble in the previous month, was nearly exhausted, and tentative enquiries showed that more would not be forthcoming. Then, on the day that he wound up the budget debate there occurred the Invergordon mutiny – against pay reductions – in the Home Fleet. This was a further blow to hesitantly recovering confidence. Those responsible for the movement of international funds loved public expenditure reductions but not their consequences. There was a second wave of heavy withdrawals from London, and within four days Britain was forced off the Gold Standard and into an effective 20 per cent devaluation. Snowden explained this in a curiously ambivalent broadcast, his rehearsal of Harold Wilson's 'pound in your pocket' attempted reassurance of thirty-six years later: 'The consequences are bound to be disagreeable. In some ways they may be serious. But they will not be disastrous or catastrophic. The pound will not go the same way as the mark or the franc.'

He was not ambivalent about where the fault lay. It lay with the Labour party, for his former colleagues in which Snowden was at this time developing a shrill and bitter contempt that shocked even Mac-Donald. It changed Snowden's mind about a 'coupon election'. He now wanted one in order to smash them. This paranoiac dislike he first expressed publicly at the end of the budget debate on 15 September:

> I have noticed during the last two or three days that I have been sitting here, being able for the first time to see the faces of my old associates. I have admired the way in which they have cheered to keep their spirits up [this expressed with sneering sarcasm], and I have admired those who have done that knowing – knowing – that only a few weeks possibly remain before this place that knows them now will know them no more.

Then, two weeks later, in the final speech of his quarter-century in the House of Commons, he rose (or sank) to an even greater outpouring of bile. He was particularly contemptuous of the speech of Attlee, who had immediately preceded him in the debate. It was a curious conjuncture between the Labour party of the future and the Labour party of the past. This led up to the dramatic part played by Snowden in the election campaign which began on 5 October and ended on 27 October. During these twenty-two days Snowden addressed no public meeting and hardly left 11 Downing Street, but he nonetheless made an impact on the campaign, and probably upon the result, at least as great as that of any party leader.

He sat in his lair, for such it certainly came to seem to his victims, issuing press statements and messages of support to selected candidates (he even sent one to William Graham's opponent in Edinburgh), but above all preparing and delivering his 17 October broadcast. This ranks with Churchill's 1945 'Gestapo' performance as one of the two most notorious political broadcasts of the century. But whereas Churchill's was counter-productive, Snowden's was devastatingly successful. He began in graphic and dire terms: 'In front of me as part of the wireless arrangement is a red light, and a red light is a warning of danger to be avoided: I am going to give you this warning tonight.' Towards the end he described the Labour programme as 'the most fantastic and impracticable document ever put before the electors', and added, to repeat his most famous phrase: 'This is not socialism. It is Bolshevism run mad.' And then, in what was surely a work of supererogation, as well as being deeply discreditable, especially for someone who had lived through and complained about the Zinoviev letter scare, he rounded off his campaign by issuing a statement of innuendo, which was at once menacing and meaningless, about a possible Labour threat to Post Office Savings Bank deposits.

The result was superficially all he could have hoped for. The Labour vote held up surprisingly well against the appalling battering to which it had been subjected and was down by only 7 per cent compared with 1929. But the British electoral system (to which it must be said that Snowden, as a determined advocate of proportional representation, had always been opposed) performed a spectacular exaggerating role and produced a House of Commons with 554 National government supporters of whom 473 were Conservatives, against a Labour rump of 52. He more than fulfilled his prophecy that his erstwhile supporters, whose faces he had so disliked gazing upon, would soon be strangers to the House of Commons.

Yet at a more profound level he had very much cut off his nose to spite his face. Free Trade was the last historically radical cause for which he cared, but he had helped to produce the most overwhelmingly Protectionist majority for at least ninety years. The political group with whom he was beginning to feel most affinity were the Samuelite Liberals (the Simonite Liberals had become both Protectionist and crypto-Tory), but he had helped to reduce his new friends to a rump even smaller than the Labour party, and one which moreover had no springs of recovery within it. And he had left himself no alternative if he wished to continue in politics (and he had nothing else to do) but to go to the House of Lords. This he duly did in November 1931, becoming Viscount Snowden of Ickornshaw. There are obviously worse old people's refuges than 'that upper home of bliss'. But it was a sad apotheosis for such a sea-green incorruptible, particularly at a time when he was highly vulnerable to charges of self-seeking. The despised (in Snowden's eyes) MacDonald permanently avoided the seductions of a peerage. Snowden had the grace never to like the Upper House. But Ethel Snowden, it was said, much enjoyed being a viscountess.

For a year the new viscount continued unhappily in the government as Lord Privy Seal. Then, in September 1932, he and Samuel and Archibald Sinclair resigned against the ratification of the Ottawa Imperial Preference agreements. Thereafter his main pronouncements were through the columns of the *Sunday Express* by courtesy of his friend and semi-neighbour Lord Beaverbrook. In 1934 he produced two volumes of autobiography which were more readable than charitable. He spoke only once in the House of Lords, which was in July 1934 when he delivered an embarrassingly bitter denunciation of MacDonald. At the 1935 general election he moved into alliance with his nearer neighbour Lloyd George and made an election broadcast, much more constructive and less vicious than in 1931, but alas also much less effective, on behalf of the Liberal party.

It was curious that these two old intransigents from the radical redoubts of Britain, one from the crags of the Pennines, the other from a remote valley of the Lleyn peninsula, should have been brought together for their last election in an alliance formed in the very different surroundings of the 'soft-muffled' Surrey hills. Lloyd George's achievements were incomparably greater than Snowden's, but as a personality Snowden was not much inferior, equally idiosyncratic and far more difficult. He died in May 1937.

WINSTON CHURCHILL

(as Chancellor)

WHEN CHURCHILL BECAME CHANCELLOR, ON 5 November 1924, he was three weeks short of his fiftieth birthday. Although two years previously he had been severely ill, losing, as he put it, both his appendix and his seat in Dundee almost simultaneously, and although another two years after the end of his Treasury spell he was to receive a heavy battering when knocked down by a car in New York, his four and a half years at the Exchequer, the first half of his fifties, were a period of maximum vigour. Perhaps for the first time since his dismissal from the Admiralty in 1915 he felt securely anchored in a great office and in a government with a good prospect of tenure. He was not again to have such a test or such an opportunity until 1940. Then the scale was clearly greater, but he was already sixty-five years old and the vigour was not so unforced.

Baldwin's offer to Churchill of the second position in the government was a great surprise (and mostly an unpleasant one) to the Conservative party, and a considerable (but wholly pleasurable) one to Churchill himself. He had not been a nominal Tory since 1904. He had made his early career as a swashbuckling young Liberal minister, the virulence of whose anti-Conservative oratory had been rivalled only by that of Lloyd George. He had been forced out of the Admiralty by a Bonar Law *démarche*. And when in 1917–22 he gradually got back to high status, although not to his pre-Dardanelles prestige, it was as a Liberal Coalitionist. He had unsuccessfully fought the 1923 election, which ended Baldwin's first government, as a determinedly anti-Protectionist Liberal. However he strongly opposed Asquith's decision to put in the first MacDonald government, and from the beginning of 1924 he began to move firmly towards the Conservatives. He introduced a hiccup into the process, with typical rashness, by fighting in March 1924 a by-election in the Abbey division of Westminster against an official Conservative candidate, although with considerable Conservative support, including a useful if slightly ambiguous letter from Balfour. There, in the most floodlit of political jousting grounds, he had achieved vast publicity and defeat by only forty-three votes.

The experience did not however stop his move to the right. He made his expedition to Canossa on 7 May when he went to Liverpool and addressed a big Conservative meeting, his first for twenty years, and then delivered at least a partial recantation of his Free Trade beliefs. He thus made himself available to be a Conservative-sponsored candidate, and there was a good deal of eagerness to have him, both because of the drawing power of his oratory and because of the effective virulence of his anti-socialist invective. His eye flickered around various constituencies, but when he eventually settled, like a bumblebee on a flower, it was on Epping, and it was indeed a substantial settling, for it or that part of it renamed Woodford remained his constituency for the last thirty-five years of his parliamentary life. Nevertheless he insisted on fighting it not as a Conservative but as a 'Constitutionalist', although his independence did not prevent his being adopted by the local Conservative Association or his playing a full part in the Conservative campaign outside Epping.

The election over, and with 419 seats triumphantly won for the Conservatives, Churchill undoubtedly hoped for office, and for substantial office. The Treasury nevertheless exceeded his expectations. There was an element of luck in the disposition. The grand job was offered to Neville Chamberlain who, preferring the Ministry of Health with its workaday but wide and constructive reform-inviting responsibilities, declined, and with Churchill his next caller Baldwin illustrated his 'leap in the dark' propensity (see p. 245) by offering it to him. The story that, when Baldwin mentioned the Chancellorship, Churchill thought it was the Chancellorship of the Duchy of Lancaster (only the third in the hierarchy of sinecure offices) is apocryphal, but like most apocrypha not entirely without foundation. It was Sir Stanley Jackson, cricketer and currently chairman of the Conservative party, to whom Churchil spoke on his way out (the interview being at Conservative Central Office) who, when told the news of his Chancellorship, thought that Churchill must, be talking of the Duchy.

It was therefore for Churchill a surprising, lucky and only marginally secured appointment in his new party. All this might have been expected to have two consequences. One of them was a sense of gratitude towards Baldwin, and this at a naturally somewhat declining level was lively for several years. The other in most people would have been a respect for the household gods of his new party and a caution in asserting himself in a new field of departmental authority of which he knew little.

A signal example of Churchill's impudent genius was that he showed no such respect or caution. He assumed the authority within the government of the Treasury as though he had the combined experience of Gladstone, Disraeli, his father and Harcourt, and he behaved towards his colleagues as though he had the most unassailable of Conservative credentials. Occasionally he overdid the self-confidence, as when, set to preside over a Cabinet committee during the General Strike, he began by assuring the other two principal members, Joynson-Hicks, the Home Secretary, and Worthington-Evans, the War Secretary: 'I have done your job for four years, Jix, and yours for two, Worthy, so I had better unfold my plan.' His experience was of course vast, and rivalled in that government only by Balfour, who was failing, and by Austen Chamberlain, who made himself remote as Foreign Secretary; but that experience had been acquired within the bosom of the Conservative government's opponents.

This did not give him a moment's pause. The overwhelming impression which emerges from the records of his first few months at the Treasury is of the explosive release of a vast store of energy and of an outpouring of a flood of memoranda and letters, which, whether internal to the department or to the Prime Minister or other colleagues, bore his unmistakable personal stamp. Most such communications within a government are written in a flat prose style which is sometimes given the label of civil service-ese. This is unfair, for civil servants, asked to draft hurriedly, mostly have no knowledge of what style their ministers would adopt in the unlikely event that they attempted to draft such documents themselves. They therefore naturally cleave close to a safe coast without headlands or cliffs. Churchill, on the other hand, obviously did both his own drafting and showed a remarkable capacity to dictate (for such was his habit) resonant aphorisms, which not even the most literary and confident civil servant would have dared to compose on his behalf.

On 28 November 1924 when he set out his views on direct taxation in a nine-page letter advocating remissions in the middle and at the lower end to Sir Richard Hopkins, then the chairman of the Board of Inland Revenue, later permanent secretary to the Treasury, he concluded, 'As the tide of taxation recedes it leaves the millionaires stranded on the peaks of taxation to which they have been carried by the flood. The smaller class of Super Tax payers get a progressive relief. . .'. On

1 December he wrote to the Foreign Secretary saying that he proposed to demand payment of overdue French and Italian war debt objectives, which 'will mean worry for you – sulky instead of smiling Ambassadors'. In contesting the naval estimates (of which more later) he minuted the secretary of the Cabinet (Hankey) asking whether it was not provocative to increase the number of submarines based at Hong Kong from six to twenty-one. 'Suppose the Japanese owned the Isle of Man, and started putting 21 submarines there!' A week later he wrote to Baldwin saying that to accept such Admiralty demands would be 'to sterilise and paralyse the whole policy of the Government. There will be nothing for the taxpayer and nothing for social reform. We shall be a Naval Parliament busily preparing our Navy for some great imminent shock. Voilà tout!' Then two months later, when he was vigorously contesting the determination of the Bank of England and the official Treasury to return to the Gold Standard at the pre-war parity, he wrote to Sir Otto Niemeyer (Treasury controller of finance): 'I would rather see Finance less proud and Industry more content.'

This spate of highly personal outpouring and his general vibrating certainty struck people in differing ways. His wife's Christmas comment to Professor Lindeman was a good central judgement: 'Winston is immersed in thrilling new work with the Treasury officials whom he says are a wonderful lot of men.' These Treasury officials and those of the Bank were stimulated by Churchill, although finding him less amenable and more time-wasting than his immediate predecessor Snowden had been. Among his senior colleagues Austen Chamberlain was determined to be friendly, and Birkenhead had been for many years, despite their previous difference of party, his most compatible companion, many of their habits being similar.*

Earl Beatty (Admiral of the Fleet and current First Sea Lord) supplied, as the naval-estimates argument unfolded, a view of Churchill from a different angle. 'That extraordinary fellow Winston has gone mad,' he wrote on 26 January 1925. But ten days later he added: 'It takes a good deal out of one when dealing with a man of his calibre with a very quick brain. . . . A false step, remark, or even gesture is immediately fastened upon, so I have to keep my wits about me.' However it was

---

* Churchill's self-indulgence was however more controlled, so that he was able to outlive Birkenhead by thirty-five years. During the 1920s the latter could not exactly be described as a 'crony' because that implies a degree of client relationship, and Birkenhead was by contrast probably the last close associate who could stand up to Churchill as an equal.

from Neville Chamberlain, who might have been Chancellor in Churchill's place had he not preferred the Ministry of Health, that there came the most striking 'insider' portrait of Churchill's Cabinet performance in his early Conservative days. Chamberlian wrote to Baldwin at the end of August, 1925:

> Looking back over our first session I think our Chancellor has done very well, all the better because he hasn't been what he was expected to be. He hasn't dominated the Cabinet, though undoubtedly he has influenced it. . . . He hasn't intrigued for the leadership, but he has been a tower of debating strength in the House of Commons. . . . What a brilliant creature he is! But there is somehow a great gulf between him and me which I don't think I shall ever cross. I like him. I like his humour and vitality. I like his courage. . . . But not for all the joys of Paradise would I be a member of his staff! Mercurial! A much abused word, but it is the literal description of his temperament.

On Baldwin himself Churchill's influence was at this stage great. Churchill was warmed to gratitude towards the Prime Minister, and the Prime Minister, even though good at not being dazzled by Lloyd George, allowed himself to be temporarily dazzled by the man who was to be Britain's other great war leader of the century, second in time but first in historical repute and in the sweep of his accomplishments. This came out in the tone of Baldwin's letters to Churchill. Their style was different from his usual ones. It was almost as though he were determined to amuse his Chancellor and to try to elevate himself to his level of sophistication and verbal felicity.

Thus, when Herbert Samuel had been summoned from the Tyrol to see the Prime Minister at Aix-les-Bains in the summer of 1925 in the hope that he would accept the Chairmanship of the Coal Royal Commission, Baldwin reported to Churchill at Chartwell: 'The infant Samuel [which curiously was the joke name for this somewhat prematurely portentous statesman with which Asquith had tried to amuse Venetia Stanley ten years before] duly arrived as the clock was striking six on Monday evening. Cool, competent and precise as when he was first lent to the temporary world by an inscrutable providence, it was the work of a moment for him to grasp our position in all its manifold implications. Aix is very full: so are most of the people here,' he amiably concluded his letter. 'The hotel buses discharge 'em at the baths and they look, many of them, as if you stuck a fork in them, a rich gravy would burst forth.'

In spite of this epistolatory familiarity the social lives of Baldwin and Churchill did not much overlap. They nonetheless saw each other frequently, for Churchill developed the habit of walking through the two connecting doors of 10 Downing Street on his morning progress from No. 11 to his room in the old Treasury building, and mostly calling in for a few minutes' chat with the Prime Minister on the way. This greatly contributed to their never seriously quarrelling for the four and a half years of the government, although that peace did not long survive its defeat. The habit certainly helped to get Churchill through his first few months as a Conservative minister, when he was engaged in at least four major disputes within the government, as well as in the preparations of his first budget and in the conduct of delicate war-debt negotiations with the French.

The most dangerous of the disputes for Churchill was the naval-estimates one. This was because here he not only performed an extraordinary *volte face* from his position twelve years before when he had almost broken the Asquith Cabinet with his demand for a *bigger* navy but also because in his 1925 demand for a *smaller* navy he took on Baldwin's closest friends within the government. Bridgeman was First Lord of the Admiralty and Davidson was its Financial and Parliamentary Secretary. A major Cabinet row rumbled on for nearly a year, with threats of resignation from these two ministers as well as from the admirals, but not from Churchill, which was perhaps part of his strength. Eventually Baldwin steered skilfully towards a solution which was somewhat more on the Admiralty's than on Churchill's side, but at least the Chancellor escaped without either humiliation or great ill-will.

The second dispute was with Steel-Maitland at the Ministry of Labour, and to a lesser extent with Neville Chamberlain at Health, about the provisions of the widows' and orphans' pension insurance scheme which Churchill was determined to introduce in his first budget. Steel-Maitland argued strongly that it was too generous and too early in the parliament, and on the latter point at least Chamberlain agreed. Churchill however got his way on both issues. The third dispute was with the other Chamberlain (Austen), who was a much older friend than Neville, and who complained bitterly that when, formulating his 'Locarno' policies, he had suffered (without adequate support from Baldwin) two unsatisfactory Cabinets in early March 1925, Churchill had contributed considerably to this unsatisfactoriness. At that stage Churchill was against any entangling commitment to France, who 'could stew in her own juice without it having any bad effect on anybody or anything at all'. France must make a real peace with Germany before we need do anything for her. In Weimar Republic days there was a certain sense in this but it was certainly not an attitude calculated to make a Cabinet ally of Austen Chamberlain who was however remarkably forgiving and gave Churchill a lot of budget support.

The fourth dispute was much the most interesting, even though it did not spill from the Treasury and the Bank into the Cabinet arena. Nearly all the *bien-pensant* sources of advice were unanimous that it was Britain's interest and duty to return to the Gold Standard and to do so at the pre-1914 parity. In the written exchanges which ensued Churchill's minutes were masterpieces of pungent questioning whereas the replies took refuge in a misty higher wisdom. On 29 January 1925 Churchill wrote a minute and circulated it to Montagu Norman, Otto Niemeyer (already described) Lord Bradbury (permanent secretary of the Treasury throughout the First World War, who had a few months earlier succeeded Austen Chamberlain as the chairman of the joint Select Committee of both Houses on Currency and Banking which had been specifically charged with pronouncing on the wisdom or otherwise of a return to Gold) and R. G. Hawtrey (who in forty-one years in the Treasury made himself almost more of a legend even than Niemeyer as a pundit of international finance. The spirit in which this minute was received is well expressed by its becoming known in the Treasury as 'Mr Churchill's exercise', which combined a hint of admiration for its strenuousness with more than a hint of impatience at its naivety, and by Bradbury's comment: 'The writer . . . appears to have his spiritual home in the Keynes–McKenna sanctuary [the Cambridge economist and the ex-Chancellor who had become Midland Bank chairman were the most prominent sceptics] but some of the trimmings of his mantle have been furnished by the *Daily Express* [that is, Beaverbrook].'

The direct replies, as opposed to the oblique comments, were splendid examples of substituting superior wisdom for rational argument. Niemeyer said that to refuse the fence would be to show that Britain had never really 'meant business' about the Gold Standard and that 'our nerve had failed when the stage was set'. Norman, the great Governor, was even more sublimely bland. In the opinion 'of educated and reasonable men', he wrote, there was no alternative to a return to Gold. The Chancellor would no doubt be attacked whatever he did but: 'In former case [Gold] he will be abused by the ignorant, the gamblers and the antiquated industrialists; in the latter case [not Gold] he will be abused by the instructed and posterity.'

Churchill's doubts took a lot of subduing. And his combination of energy and self-confidence made him a formidable fighter of a rearguard action. Niemeyer's reply to Churchill's first memorandum was written on a Saturday (21 February). Churchill in turn replied to this with the purest milk of expansionary doctrine:

> The Treasury has never, it seems to me, faced the profound signifi- cance of what Mr Keynes calls 'the paradox of unemployment amidst dearth'. The Governor shows himself perfectly happy [with] the spectacle of Britain possessing the finest credit in the world simul- taneously with a million and a quarter unemployed. Obviously if these million and a quarter were usefully and economically employed, they would produce at least £100 a year a head, instead of costing up to at least £50 a head in doles.

And he composed his reply at length and with great speed. 'Forgive me adding to your labours', he concluded, 'by these Sunday morning reflexions.'

Whatever else Churchill was he was not a lazy minister. Of the near-contemporary Chancellors, Snowden would have accepted the advice without argument, Baldwin might have mulled it over during a quiet Sunday-morning walk with Tom Jones, and Austen Chamberlain, tending his rock garden at Twitt's Ghyll, might have complained in a letter to a sister that he was being pushed, but would never have provided a polemical riposte without an official draft.

Churchill encouraged the argument by more than epistolatory means. On 17 March he set up a dinner-table jousting ground. He always liked argument over the knives and forks. Despite his cavalry subaltern's background the concept of not talking ship in the mess was totally alien to him. He always sought to combine his enthusiams of the moment with his perennial indulgences. Champagne should be inter-mingled with controversy and brandy with a recipe for action, if it could be attained. To this dinner he summoned Keynes and McKenna, the two sceptics on Gold, whose 'sanctuary' he was thought to inhabit, together with Bradbury (the author of the phrase) and Niemeyer.

The sixth participant was P. J. Grigg (principal private secretary to five Chancellors before eventually becoming permanent under-secretary and then Secretary of State at the War Office), who recorded that the encounter lasted until after midnight (foreshadowing Churchill's later habits) and that at the end 'the ayes [that is the pro-Gold forces] had it'. Keynes took a rather abstruse point about the discrepancy between

American and British prices and also between American and British phases of economic development being too great for an open currency system. McKenna showed that *le trahison des clercs* could embrace not only clerks of banks but their chairmen as well. On the merits he strongly supported Keynes but at the end he sold the pass by saying that as a matter of practical politics Churchill had no alternative but to go back to Gold.*

As the Gold battle unfolded so there was a sense of even such a rumbustious character as Churchill being swept downstream by the force of a compelling current, protesting but nonetheless essentially impotent. The Treasury was against him, the Bank was against him, the Committee presided over first by Austen Chamberlain and then by Bradbury was against him. Snowden, his Labour 'shadow' was against him. Baldwin, much respecting Montagu Norman, in fact played no part in the decision, but would have been against Churchill had he attempted to decide otherwise. The two tufts of ground – Keynes and McKenna – on which he attempted to stand proved, for varying reasons unsatisfactory footholds. The momentum of conventional wisdom swept them away. Churchill's 17 March dinner was the last attempt at a stand. The decision was not so much taken as finally assumed a day or two later, although not formally announced until the budget on 28 April.

The whole story was a remarkable example of a strong not a weak minister (for there was nothing of Mr Hacker being manipulated by Sir Humphrey Trafford in his civil service relationships) nonetheless reluctantly succumbing, ineluctably adjusting himself to the near unanimous, near irresistible flow of establishment opinion. Two further points are worth mention: first the secrecy with which the dispute was carried on – during two months it hardly spread outside the Treasury, let alone outside the government; and second, the ability of such a near unanimous concentration of advice to be wrong, or at least sufficiently myopic as to produce highly undesirable lateral consequences. This Churchill vaguely perceived: his corner-of-the-eye perspective was far superior to that of Norman or Niemeyer, Bradbury, Austen Chamberlain or Philip Snowden. But in dealing with economic affairs his confidence at that stage, while fully up to writing iconoclastic letters and minutes, did not extend to a persistent overruling of all the pundits.

* Reading Grigg's account I was much reminded of the disastrous dinner which in 1962 I arranged between Jean Monnet and Hugh Gaitskell. Prandial encounters are not a universal solvent.

As a result there was committed what is commonly regarded as the greatest mistake of that main Baldwin government, and the responsibility for it came firmly to rest upon Churchill. Keynes, for instance, wrote a pamphlet of which the obvious and resonant title for him to choose was *The Economic Consequences of Mr Churchill*. In a sense this allocation of blame was unfair, but only in a sense. Churchill was deliberately a very attention-attracting Chancellor. He wanted his first budget to make a great splash, which it did, and a considerable contribution to the spray was made by the announcement of the return to Gold. Reluctant convert although he had been, he therefore deserved the responsibility and, if it be so judged, a considerable part of the blame. An irony was that by up-valuing the pound Churchill threw a destructive spanner into the works of Baldwin's industrial policy, although had he not done so Baldwin would almost certainly have interfered for the only time in financial policy and pushed him towards accepting Montagu Norman's advice.

This advice however ran directly counter to the emollient policy towards the trades unions which the Prime Minister proclaimed on 6 March 1925 in one of the two outstandingly successful speeches which he delivered in a quietly oratorical career.* This was his 'Give peace in our time, O Lord' speech, which led to the withdrawal of a Conservative anti-trades union private member's bill and sent his leadership to its apogee of repute. Churchill wrote to Clementine: 'I had no idea he could show such power.' However the worst possible contribution to industrial peace in our time was to make things more difficult for already suffering traditional export trades, cotton, shipbuilding, steel and above all coal, which was precisely what was done by the return to Gold at the pre-war parity. Churchill's reluctant decision within a few weeks of the Baldwin speech which had so impressed him, and entirely in accordance with Baldwin's own desires, made it almost inevitable that 'peace in our time' became the General Strike in fourteen months.

With Churchill, budget days were given even more a sense of occasion than was usual, with the surrounding ritual more than fully matched by the *élan* with which the speeches themselves were delivered. On these occasions he not merely did a routine display of the 'Gladstone box' at the door of 11 Downing Street, but then proceeded down Whitehall to the House of Commons, accompanied by Robert Boothby

---

* The other was his abdication *pièce justificative*, gently devastating of the former King Edward VIII, which he delivered nearly twelve years later.

his parliamentary private secretary,* and by a rotating group of family members, a posse of policemen and a tail of respectful members of the public. On these occasions, despite all his budgets being well into April, he displayed a fine variety of overcoats. His great astrakhan-collared one he appeared to put away after the equinox (although it reappeared surprisingly early in the autumn), but he had at least two others and rarely ventured out without one of them.†

When the procession had safely arrived at the House, Churchill entered with a flourish an expectant chamber without the overcoat but with Boothby, the box and the speech, and proceeded to deliver it for *c.* two hours. In form at least the first one was very well received, Horne and Snowden, for example, paying it extravagant compliments. Its oratorical style was high-flown and so characteristic that it could hardly have come from any other lips, but was relieved by mordant pin-pricks, both of himself and of others. One of his new sources of income for the Exchequer was the restoration of the 'McKenna duties' of 1916, which Snowden had removed in the previous year, and which he proposed to fortify with a new tax on silk, natural and artificial, both foreign and domestic, but with a distinct preference for the home producer. 'These duties', he proclaimed, 'do not fall on the masses of the people. They do not touch the necessaries or interfere with the modest comfort of daily life.' Then, in order to get round the embarrassment that as a Free Trade Chancellor in a Protectionist Cabinet he might be seen as a pushed-around pawn (not perhaps very likely), he added: 'To some these duties are a relish, to others a target, and to me a revenue.'

He was determined to present the budget, despite its substantial remissions for high earners (and to a lesser extent for large owners) as a 'condition of the people' enterprise, well in the tradition of his pre-1914 partnership with Lloyd George. (Indeed there was some Whitehall criticism of his poaching announcements which would have more appropriately come from the Ministry of Health.) Yet the terms in which he spoke, undoubtedly with genuine compassion, of the risks and sufferings of 'the little people' now strike a note of patrician condescension. Of course the social assumptions of the 1920s were very different

---

* Boothby was not there for the first one, being appointed only in late 1925.
† Such caution was indeed a habit of inter-war politicians. When the whole Cabinet went out to meet Neville Chamberlain on the return of his aeroplane from Munich in 1938, few of them risked the tarmac without such protection, despite the date being no later than 30 September. And the argument that suits were much thicker because houses were much colder is hardly valid in relation to overcoats in the open air.

from those of the post-Second World War world, but even allowing for this, there are visible in the 1925 budget some of the archaisms which contributed to the defeat of 1945. 'The average British workman in good health, full employment and standard wages', he said,

> does not regard himself and his family as an object of compassion. But when exceptional misfortune descends upon the cottage home with the slender margin upon which it is floated, or there is a year of misfortune, distress or unemployment, or above all the loss of the breadwinner, it leaves the once happy family in the grip of the greatest calamity. Although the threat of adversity has been active all these years, no effective provision has been made by the great mass of the labouring classes for their widows and families in the event of death. I am not reproaching them, but it is the greatest need of the present time. If I may change to a military metaphor, it is not the sturdy marching troops that need extra reward and indulgence, it is the stragglers, the exhausted, the weak, the wounded, the veterans, the widows and orphans to whom the ambulances of state aid must be directed.

The 'ambulances of state aid' amounted to the removal of an earnings restriction to the ten shillings a week old age pension available at sixty-five (as against the five shillings a week at seventy which Asquith had introduced in 1908); to a new ten shillings a week for widows for life; to five shillings a week for such a widow's eldest child and three shillings a week for her other children; and seven and sixpence a week for full orphans, all of these children's pensions to cease at the age of fourteen and a half. The long-term costs were extremely complicated, and Churchill managed to make them even more so by bringing in as an offset the future decline in war pensions, which he confidently announced, a supreme irony for the great warrior of the Second World War, should be down from the current £67 million to £32 million by 1945. He liked gazing eloquently into the future, but was not always actuarially convincing. Mallet and George in *British Budgets* commented magisterially: 'It is perhaps improbable that these somewhat unsubstantial calculations of the burden which future generations might have to bear were taken much more seriously by the House than they were by their author.' For the moment however the costs were small – perhaps £5 or 6 million a year for the remainder of the parliament and were handsomely covered by the surplus of nearly £37 million which had been given him by a combination of Snowden's caution and his own new revenue duties.

This surplus he used for some fairly dramatic reductions in direct taxation. Surtax (or super-tax as it was still called until 1928) he proposed to reduce by £10 million in a full year, which was substantial in relation to a tax the total yield of which was little more than £60 million. He balanced the rich-favouring aspects of this concession by recouping an almost equivalent amount from an increase in death duties beginning with estates of £12,500 (about £400,000 today) and falling with increasing severity up to estates of £1 million (£30 million today). He could therefore claim that he was transferring the rich man's burden from income to capital, from the living to the dead, and thus encouraging enterprise at the expense of the frozen hand of established property rights. Such a balancing transaction eased the presentation of his major concession of the budget, which was a reduction of the standard rate of income tax from 4s 6d to 4s in the pound (from 22.5p to 20p), which of course was of substantial benefit to the rich, not only as individuals but also in the capacity of many of them as shareholders, for income tax was then the principal form of company taxation. So far as individuals were concerned Churchill juggled with allowances so as to give proportionately the biggest relief at around £500 a year, which was then a good lower-middle-class income, but the absolute relief, particularly when added to the super-tax change, was of course incomparably greater for the rich. Philip Snowden, in uncharacteristically harsh (towards the right) terms for that stage in his life, described it as 'the worst rich man's budget ever presented', but Arthur Ponsonby, the Labour son of Queen Victoria's long-term private secretary, was probably nearer the mark and certainly neater when he wrote that while Churchill's 'sympathy for the poor was eloquent, his sympathy for the rich was practical'.

Nevertheless the budget, which was rounded off by a somewhat bathetic removal of the duty on Empire dried fruits together with the introduction of a wine, sugar and tobacco preference in that direction, which cost £1.75 million, broadly secured a good reception. Even apart from the massive but extraneous additions of the pensions and Gold announcements, it was a 'big budget' and one which, raising many hares, led to considerable Finance bill difficulties, particularly with the silk duties. These difficulties were, needless to say, rumbustiously confronted by Churchill, and the whole enterprise substantially enhanced his prestige both inside and outside the government.

This meant that he was prominently concerned with the coal crisis, which in one form or another dominated the life of the government for eighteen months from the summer of 1925. He was largely the cause of the trouble, for the return to the 1914 parity was devastating to the coal industry (which then employed a million men). But he was also looked to as a provider of a possible solution. In July he was made chairman of a special Cabinet committee to consider the nationalization of mining royalties, which it was thought offered one approach to the reorganization of the industry. But this was not going to deal with the immediate problem, which was that the employers (or 'the owners' as they were appropriately and collectively known) who were in Birkenhead's judgement of a year later the most stupid body of men he had ever encountered,* reacted to the new parity as predictably as did Marshal Göring when he heard the word 'culture' and reached for their guns in the shape of announcing a national lock-out from 31 July unless the miners accepted a substantial reduction in wages.

The miners themselves, living for the most part in close-knit and isolated communities, were the most battle-scarred fighting troops of organized labour. They may not have been led with brilliant tactical skill but they had their own solidarity and great emotional command over the Labour movement and were therefore dangerous adversaries. Baldwin, who had more foresight as well as greater social conscience than the coalowners, did not want a conflict. Nor did Churchill. He proposed to Baldwin a Royal Commission on the future of the coal industry, which under the chairmanship of Herbert Samuel deliberated for the next seven months, and readily agreed, despite being engaged in a desperate search for economies in government expenditure, that a subsidy, estimated at £10 million but which in fact turned out to be £19 million, should be paid to the industry to tide over this period. By these means were both the miners' lock-out and the General Strike postponed from July 1925 to May 1926. It was in some ways a pre-run of the 'low case' for the Munich settlement thirteen years later. In 1925–6 however with the Miners' Federation, a much less dangerous and more sympathetic adversary than Hitler, Churchill was on the side of appeasement. 'We were not ready' (in 1925) Baldwin subsequently told his chosen biographer.

When Churchill came to present his second budget on 26 April 1926, he was therefore suspended between the publication of the Samuel Report on 11 March and the outbreak of the General Strike on 4 May. (The Report proposed the nationalization of mining royalties, amalgamations and some closures, government aid for research and marketing,

---

* He had until this encounter reserved the honour for the leaders of the Miners' Federation.

considerable welfare provisions and a sharp rejection of the owners' typically Bourbon-like proposals for both longer hours and less pay. However Samuel also considered that with the retention of the seven-hour day and with a falling price index – seven points down in the year – a reduction in wages was reasonable.)

Churchill additionally had all the difficulties inherent in a second budget after a considerable triumph with the first, which are at least as great as those of writing a successful second novel. On top of that he himself was beginning to suffer from some of 'the economic consequences of Mr Churchill'. Even before the revenue havoc of the General Strike itself and the long months of coal strike which persisted even when the general challenge had been called off, the budgetary situation was extremely tight. The £19 million of coal subsidy turned a small surplus into an awkward deficit. He had seen this tightness coming in his 1925 speech, but it was nonetheless the case that the intervening year, the coal subsidy entirely apart, marked a climacteric in thinking about public finance. Hitherto it was thought that an £800 million budget was a post-war aberration, and that with a determined Chancellor and a full return to normality it could be got back if not to the £197 million of 1913–14 at least to somewhere approaching equidistance between the two figures.

This was always a pipe-dream. Apart from anything else the post-war debt charges of over £300 million (compared with £24 million in 1913–14) rendered it totally impracticable. But impracticability does not always dull aspiration. It was one of Churchill's perhaps involuntary services that he bust this illusion. After great strivings at economy the net effort, as Sir Robert Horne cruelly pointed out, was that, beneath convoluted attempts at paring the figures, actual expenditure, with the coal subsidies excluded, had risen between 1924–5 and 1925–6 from £795 million to £805 million. Thereafter the £800 million was a fact of life – until it passed £2,000 million in the second 1939 budget and £100,000 million in 1981–2.

Churchill's room for manoeuvre before this second budget was small. He nonetheless prepared for it with great energy but no extensive concentration upon Treasury work. From November onwards he was fighting a vigorous even if not notably successful (as Horne's comment makes clear) battle to get down the departmental estimates of his colleagues. This did not preclude him from advocating a sweeping measure of House of Lords reform (which made short shrift of the rights of hereditary peers) before a November committee on the subject, with the resulting scheme to be submitted to a referendum. He took a long Christmas holiday at the recently acquired and largely rebuilt Chartwell, with a number of his favourite people, Edward Marsh, his pre-war private secretary, and Professor Lindemann, his new guru, to stay, and with his recreational hours punctuated by a vigorous exchange of memoranda with the Treasury. Then on 20 January, having negotiated an Italian war debt settlement in the preceding week, he went to Leeds and addressed the annual Chamber of Commerce banquet. For some reason this Leeds banquet seemed to be a favourite place and occasion for Chancellors to make their last major speech before the period of pre-budget purdah. I used it in 1970 to dampen expectations following the turn-round of the balance of payments and in the run-up to an election. Churchill used it in 1926 for a more high-flown appraisal of the future:

> Prosperity, that errant daughter of our house who went astray in the Great War, is on our threshold. She has raised her hand to the knocker on the door. What shall we do? Shall we let her in, or shall we drive her away? Shall we welcome her once again to our own fireside settle, or banish her once more to roam about among the nations of the world? That is the choice that will be before the British people in these next few anxious months.

These sentences sufficiently impressed King George V that he sought Churchill's permission to use them in a speech of his own.

On 31 January Clementine Churchill went to the South of France for a long winter holiday (as was her habit at the time) but this had no diminishing effect on the scale of her husband's political hospitality. For the weekend of 6/7 February he had to stay two Cabinet colleagues plus his Financial Secretary. For the next weekend he invited no fewer than six *prominenti* including Sam Hoare, then Secretary of State for Air, who wrote a memorable account of the visit:

> I had never seen Winston before in the role of landed proprietor. Most of Sunday morning we inspected the property, and the engineering works on which he is engaged. These engineering works consist of making a series of ponds in a valley, and Winston appeared to be a good deal more interested in them than in anything else in the world.

He is convinced, Hoare added,

> that he is to be the prophet to lead us into the Promised Land in which there will be no income tax and everyone will live happily ever

afterwards. The trouble is that he has got so many schemes tumbling over each other in his mind, that I am beginning to wonder whether he will be able to pull any one of them out of the heap.

The budget, ten weeks later, gave him very little opportunity for pulling anything out of the heap. It was all juggling with small amounts and adjustments to the sinking fund in order to preserve a reasonably provident posture without going back on his major concessions of the previous year. Nor were the opportunities for eloquence great, although he did his best with poor material. No one except Churchill, I think, could have moved from reviewing both the performance of the exchange rate following the return to the Gold Standard and the working of the new silk duties by saying: 'Now, having lingered for a few moments in the regions of silk and gold, we proceed to the more severe stages of our journey.'

The main severities were a betting tax of 5 per cent and a 'raid' upon the Road Fund, to which revenue had risen to the substantial sum of £21.5 million, and in relation to which the motoring lobby had succeeded in building up an assumption that, contrary to the doctrine against the hypothecation of revenue, it should all be reserved for roads. Churchill was rightfully scornful of this. 'Such contortions', he had written in a Treasury memorandum, 'are absurd, and constitute at once an outrage upon the sovereignty of Parliament and upon commonsense.' He brushed aside the special pleading of the Home Secretary (Joynson-Hicks) who was President of the Automobile Association, took £7 million that year and arranged for what he regarded as a fair future allocation between the Exchequer and the Road Fund.

Most of this became of minor relevance only a week later when the General Strike began. Churchill, as we have seen, had been a 'moderate' in the summer of 1925 when the question was that of curbing the intransigence of the coalowners by the appointment of the Samuel Commission and the payment of a temporary subsidy. And he was to be a 'moderate' again in the summer of 1926 when Baldwin, after a virtuoso performance during the eight days of the General Strike, fell into a state of exhausted lassitude and retired hurt to Aix-les-Bains. During this sojourn he left Churchill, in no way exhausted, in charge of the negotiations to end the coal strike, which continued for six months after the General Strike, of which it had been the cause, had been called off. But during the General Strike itself Churchill's mood was of the utmost bellicosity and, some of his colleagues thought, utmost irresponsibility as well. 'He thinks he is Napoleon ...' Davidson wrote to Baldwin. It was perhaps more a throwback to a longing to be at the enemy, reminiscent of Brigadier Ritchie-Hook in Waugh's *Sword of Honour*, which had made him on a visit to Walcheren in 1914 seek to resign from the Cabinet and take personal command of the Marine division there, for which he had no relevant training. However it was also a foretaste of the spirit which gave him his lion's roar of defiance in the terrible summer of 1940.

In 1926, against a less formidable enemy, this spirit aroused more apprehension and exasperation than admiration. When the first convoy brought food into central London from the docks Churchill wanted it to be escorted by tanks with machine guns strategically placed along the route. He wanted to commandeer the BBC and use it as a government propaganda agency. It was therefore a relief to his colleagues when his energies were to some extent corralled within his chosen task of running the *British Gazette*. This was an official publication produced from the offices and with the plant of the *Morning Post*, while it and the other newspapers were more or less on strike, and which by the last day he got up to a circulation of 2,200,000, a formidable achievement.

He did this at the expense of tense relations with all the main newspaper proprietors (Burnham *Telegraph*, Astor *Times*, Berry *Sunday Times* and Cadbury *Daily News*), who apart from anything else did not like having their stocks of newsprint commandeered. H. A. Gwynne, the editor of the *Morning Post*, suffered more directly and accused Churchill of charging about the *Post* offices and upsetting both the editorial staff by 'changing commas and full stops' and the printing staff by pretending that he knew better how to work the machines. So far as the content was concerned he provoked even such an almost excessively moderate man as Walter (later Lord) Citrine, the general secretary of the TUC, who ten or twelve years later was happy to appear on anti-appeasement platforms with Churchill, to describe it as 'a poisonous attempt to bias the pubic mind'.

Yet, when all these criticisms are made, there was probably no one else who could have mounted such a vigorous enterprise to fill a dangerous information gap. Two months later, in a retrospective House of Commons debate on the Strike he again performed as no one else could have done and delivered a wonderfully emollient piece of self-mockery. A Labour member had threatened a renewed trial of industrial strength against parliamentary legitimacy. In the closing minute or so of the debate Churchill began to reply to this in the most portentous terms: 'I have no wish to make threats which would disturb the House and cause bad blood.' Everyone nonetheless waited for the most horrendous announcement that the thunderbolts of Zeus were at the ready. 'But this I must say. Make your minds perfectly clear that if ever you let loose upon us again a General Strike, we will let loose upon you – another *British Gazette*.' It was a brilliant *coup de théâtre*. He sat down in a burst of laughter which was equally strong from both sides of the House and the corner of what might have been a dangerously bitter recriminatory debate was at once confidently and self-mockingly turned.

There were three phases to the 'summer' coal negotiations, which in fact extended well into the autumn until at last, both sides having stubbornly resisted a settlement, the owners with consistent intransigence, the Miners' Federation more variably, the strike eventually petered out, broadly on the owners' terms, on 20 November. During the first phase Baldwin was still in England and nominally in charge, although with his attitude best summed up by his mid-July remark; 'Leave it alone – we are all so tired,' and with Churchill as usual being more than willing to fill with his energy any adjacent vacuum. Then on 22 August Baldwin was medically ordered away in a state of nervous prostration and stayed at Aix for the next twenty-four days.

This was Churchill's great window of opportunity. He had two adjutants, Arthur Steel-Maitland, the not very effective Minister of Labour, and George Lane-Fox, the Yorkshire country gentleman who was much too close to the owners to be a good Secretary of Mines. Neither of them really agreed with Churchill's approach, which they thought was too interventionist for the government, too favourable to the miners and too bullying towards the owners. But such was the force of his personality that he largely swept them along with him. Gusto took over. The Harold Wilson beer and sandwiches in 10 Downing Street approach to industrial disputes was foreshadowed forty years earlier in the early autumn of 1926 by champagne and oysters at Chartwell and the Savoy Grill. A. J. Cook and Herbert Smith, the miners' leaders, were too dour to be so entertained, but everybody else, the reluctantly following ministerial colleagues, the leader of the opposition Ramsay MacDonald, coalowners from Lord Londonderry to D. R. Llewellyn, and relevant officials, above all the *éminence grise* and ever-recording Tom Jones, were all swept into that regime of energetic optimism and indulgent hospitality. And the more champagne that he consumed with every party to the dispute except for their unclubbable leaders, the more favourable Churchill became to the miners and the less well disposed to the owners.

There were tangled cross-currents. The owners believed in profits and Churchill believed in the authority of the state. When therefore Churchill wanted a tripartite conference with the government as the balancing force and the owners refused, he thought it was almost *lèse-majesté*. There was a strong surface dispute on the issue of a national as opposed to 'district' agreements. The terms have now faded, but they had great emotive impact at the time. The owners wanted to be free to pay lower wages in the less profitable districts with the seams which were harder to work. The Miners' Federation was passionately attached to equality of treatment, both because they thought that natural justice demanded at least as great a reward for working a difficult seam as for working an easy one, and because they saw it as the key to the unity and strength of the Federation.

Then there was a still more powerful undertow, which was based on the view (correct so far as it went) of the owners and of the majority of the government that the miners were on the brink of being starved into a crushing defeat. It was therefore better to wait a few months for this to happen than to seek a possibly face-saving solution. Churchill's contrary view was that the country was suffering debilitating economic bleeding and that it was the duty of government to staunch the flow at the earliest possible moment. It was during this phase that he was first recorded as having coined the aphorism 'defiance in defeat, magnanimity in victory'. And there was the final cross-current that several devoted Baldwinites (Davidson, who was with his hero in Aix, Hankey the secretary of the Cabinet, and even Tom Jones, who combined his love of Baldwin with a reluctant admiration of Churchill's brilliance and a somewhat sentimental commitment to the left and hence the cause of the miners) were worried that Churchill might achieve a too early settlement which would leave the Prime Minister upstaged by his too successful lieutenant. They were making plans to get Baldwin back to share in any glory which might be going. The same apprehension informed a comment by Jones during a winding up by Churchill of a coal debate on 27 September, which Baldwin had opened rather pedestrianly: 'During [Churchill's] brilliant performance the P.M.'s face was turned towards the official Gallery, and covered with one of his hands. He looked utterly wretched, much as Ramsay does when L. G. is on his legs.'

In fact the protective apprehension of the Baldwinites was misplaced. Early September offered Churchill's best hope of achieving a settlement, and by his end of September oration it was effectively extinct. When his hopes were high he had put heavy pressure on the coalowners. At an afternoon and early-evening meeting on 6 September he had harangued and argued with them over fifty-six pages of official transcript. But he had failed to move them. The President of the Mining Association, Evan Williams, was a hard-line and limited South Wales owners' man, but he was good at standing up to fast bowling. Moreover, when several of Churchill's colleagues (including his friend Birkenhead) came to read the transcript, they thought he had tried to exert illegitimate pressure. As they gradually came back from holiday they constituted a phalanx against him on the Coal and other Cabinet committees. Churchill was able to keep some part of the reins in his hands for a little time after Baldwin's return on 15 September. But by the end of that month he was less in the driving seat, except for his ability to make by far the best speeches in the House of Commons. And in the third phase, which extended throughout October and for most of November, he became a prisoner of the view of most of his colleagues (curiously only the shadowy figure of Sir Laming Worthington-Evans, the War Secretary, was consistently with him) who by this stage much preferred victory for the coalowners to a negotiated settlement.

Nevertheless his sustained pacific effort while others were on holiday stands in sharp contrast both to his bellicosity during the General Strike itself and to the reputation which long followed him in Labour and trades union circles. In South Wales in particular, he was seen as the man who 'sent the troops to Tonypandy' against the miners in 1911. His mainspring was such that, if a problem was set before him, he could not fail to try to solve it. He might do so wisely or unwisely. But to say, as Baldwin had, 'Leave it alone – we are all so tired,' was simply outside his range of choice. At this stage in his life, and indeed in most others, except perhaps in 1951–5, he was irremediably pro-active.

As soon as the miners' strike was over, even if not in the way he would have wished, he switched his attention to two months of strenuous writing to finish the third volume of *The World Crisis*, which complete work Balfour memorably described as 'Winston's brilliant autobiography disguised as a history of the universe'. Then, when he returned to England from a long Mediterranean holiday on 29 January, Churchill applied himself to the preparation of his 1927 budget.

This third budget was a thing of threads and patches presented with even more brio than its two predecessors. Baldwin showed both generosity and a perceptive edge of description when he wrote that evening to the King: 'The [crowded] scene was quite sufficient to show that Mr Churchill as a star turn has a power of attraction which nobody in the House of Commons can excel ... [The Chancellor] came into the House beaming with smiles, having apparently filled the role of Pied Piper of Hamelin from Downing Street. . . .' And his opening words had a pungent impact which at least postponed the falling asleep of his large and distinguished audience. 'We are met this afternoon under the shadow of the disasters of last year. The coal strike has cost the taxpayer £30 million. It is not the time to bewail the past. It is the time to pay the bill. It is not for me to apportion the blame. My task is to apportion the burden. I do not assume the role of the impartial judge. I am only the executioner.'

As an executioner however he cut off very few heads, not at any rate those on necks famous or stiff enough to cause much commotion. Translucent pottery was to contribute £200,000, motor-car tyres £750,000, matches £700,000, wines (mainly by adjusting the borderline at which they came to count as fortified down from 27 to 25 degrees) £1.25 million, and tobacco £3.5 million. The Road Fund was again to be raided, but in a peculiarly complicated way, and various windfalls were to be procured by, in his own phrase of the previous year, 'a judicious shaking of the tree'. These, in the form of a speeding up of the dates of payment, yielded the amazingly large sum of nearly £20 million. But they were unrepeatable of course, and thus a source of slightly bogus finance. By these and other ingenious twists he managed to turn a prospective deficit of £21.5 million into a prospective surplus £16.5 million, nearly all of which he devoted to raising the sinking fund to the very high level of £65 million, while still leaving himself with the little scalp of a surplus of £1.5 million.

Baldwin summed it up as neatly as anyone could by writing (to the King): 'His enemies will say that this year's budget is a mischievous piece of manipulation and juggling with the country's finance, but his friends will say that it is a masterpiece of ingenuity.' No one contested the view expressed in *British Budgets* (an unusual form of comment for this staidly factual work) that it was 'two and a half hours of extraordinarily brilliant entertainment'. For some of his colleagues, maybe smarting under his attempts at boisterous leadership during the strikes, there was too much tinsel. Lane-Fox called it 'a cheap jingle' in a letter to the Viceroy, and L. S. Amery, who was frequently disposed to be critical of Churchill (perhaps because of an 1887 ducking in the Harrow School swimming bath) wrote a catalogue of complaint to Baldwin ending in a request for Churchill's removal from the Treasury. In Parliament, however, as was perhaps suitable to a ragbag budget, the arguments and criticism from both sides were all over the place rather than converging on a single vulnerable point, and the Finance Bill moved through more or less unmolested to become law on 29 July.

Well before this date Churchill had begun to cast his mind forward to the 1928 and indeed the 1929 budgets, which it was assumed would fall within the parliament and within his Chancellorship, although they would obviously be the last two within the former and probably the latter as well. He was eager to make as big a splash as possible. In 1925 he had sought to mark a return to normality by a delayed removal of some of the burdens of direct taxation, the weight of which would never have been contemplated had not 1914 transformed the world of 1913. In 1926 and 1927 he had been heavily constrained by industrial strife. Nineteen-twenty-eight was his first chance to make a cavalry advance across open country (he was always much given to thinking in such military metaphors), and he intended it to be a dashing and a massive one.

Following the return to Gold and in the aftermath of the strike the British economy was performing flaccidly. He wanted to give some dramatic and wide-impacting stimulus to economic activity. The best route he could see was via a lifting of the burden of local rates – total in the case of agriculture, which was already 75 per cent favoured, and with a new relief of the same figure of 75 per cent for all industry, heavy or light, prosperous or failing, as well as for freight-carrying railways, canals, docks and harbours. This would require a *masse de manoeuvre* of approximately £30 million, a very big sum in relation to the budgetary aggregates of those days, and this he proposed to provide partly by enforcing economies upon the departments, particularly the Admiralty, and partly by a substantial new tax on petrol.

He saw this financial scheme as opening the way to a major reform of local government – certainly the most important since 1886, 'perhaps since 1834'. This was of course much more Neville Chamberlain's business than his own, but he was never a great respecter of departmental frontiers, and in any event hoped to make Chamberlain into an enthusiastic ally, which to some extent he did. The local government reorganization would gradually require finance beyond the £30 million, and it was therefore important to develop buoyant sources of revenue. Petrol taxation showed every sign of being this.

The scheme was obviously bold. It was also ingenious and to some substantial extent a product of his own fertile mind. The person with the best claim to be a co-parent was – surprisingly for the time – Harold Macmillan, who had made seminal suggestions along these lines to him about two years before. Churchill launched the internal consideration of his plans by firing off three major memoranda, one down, one up and one lateral. The downwards one went to A. W. Hurst, a then powerful Treasury official whose subsequent career did not greatly prosper. From him he demanded flesh for his bones. Two days later he addressed eleven pages to the Prime Minister. They were couched in terms of high political strategy. The government was becalmed, but with menace ahead. Only by seizing the initiative with his great scheme could the clouds be dispersed and the storms weathered: 'we have to dominate events lest we be submerged by them'. The third memorandum, on the day after that, went to Neville Chamberlain, his most important Cabinet ally and/or adversary. It was skilfully directed to the great strengthening of responsible and economical local government to which it could lead.

Having launched these three salvoes, and with the scheme in the centre of his mind, he then proceeded to take a summer and autumn holiday the length of which exceeded even one of Baldwin's Aix-les-Bains six week sojourns. But both the pattern and the purpose were quite different from Baldwin's. Baldwin went to Aix in order to cut himself off from his colleagues and so far as he could shut political thoughts out of his mind. He made a point of never reading a newspaper there. Churchill went to Chartwell or elsewhere in order to lengthen the stride of his political work, but not greatly to reduce its quantity, and, so far from shutting himself off, he persuaded as many as possible of his colleagues and henchmen to visit him, to receive his ever generous hospitality, to listen to his views and to watch his manifold other activities, from painting to bricklaying.

He was effectively away from the first week of August to the third week of October, mostly at Chartwell, but interspersing his Kent weeks with a short cruise in Beaverbrook's yacht to Amsterdam, a few duty days with the King at Balmoral, ten days in Venice with his wife (who was there for most of the holiday) and a short week of salmon fishing in the North of Scotland with the Duke of Westminster. Throughout he was summoning and working on Treasury memoranda, as well as pursuing his other interests. In late September he had Sickert down to Chartwell to advise him on his painting technique, and on top of everything else he was dictating large chunks of *My Early Life*, an autobiographical volume which he started that summer and published in 1930.

None of this deflected him from pushing with exceptional determination his derating initiative. A substantial minority of ministers are essentially supine. They take advice too slavishly, although advice in the majority of cases is better accepted than rejected. Then there is a middle group who sceptically query official advice but who end up in the sensible but not inspiring position of the eighth Duke of Devonshire, whose main contribution to his latter-day Cabinets was to say 'Far better not'. Those capable of both overcoming official opinion and of pushing ahead against the caution of colleagues are very rare, but Churchill was emphatically in this category, as was spectacularly illustrated by his derating proposals.

The Treasury, apart from Hurst, was to say the least cool. They would have preferred him to devote any surplus which he could muster to debt reduction. He had some, although not many, Cabinet allies and the general goodwill but not firm commitment of the Prime Minister, who was still somewhat in thrall to the force of Churchill's personality and also thought that the adventurousness of the Chancellor's scheme might give a puff of revival to his flagging government. But the exuberance of Churchill's undiscriminating attacks on the departmental estimates of his colleagues were not calculated to make friends. 'No more airships, half the cavalry and only one-third of the cruisers,' he wrote to his wife on 30 October. (As with the Gladstones, posterity is lucky that the Churchills spent so much time apart but on close epistolatory terms.) He continued: 'Neville is costing £2½ million more and Lord Useless Percy [Lord *Eustace* was President of the Board of Education] the same figure, and we are opening a heavy battery against them this week. It is really intolerable the way these civil departments browse onwards like a horde of injurious locusts.'

The most dangerous adversary was Neville Chamberlain, both because of his stubborn but impressive application to detail, in direct contrast with the grand sweep of Churchill's style, and because of his crucial departmental position. Chamberlain himself provided a penetrating retrospective account of the struggle, as well as of his view of Churchill, in a letter which he wrote to Irwin (later Halifax) in India on 12 August 1928. (There is some irony in the fact that Chamberlain and

Halifax, who were to be his only two Conservative colleagues in the small War Cabinet which confronted Hitler in the desperate days of 1940, should thus have corresponded about him less than twelve years before.)

> When these [derating] proposals came to me I declared my approval of the principle that industry should be relieved of a part of its rates, but I strongly objected on Local Government grounds to any plan which completely severed all connection between industry and industrial interests and Local Government. It appeared to me to be most dangerous if a large part of the Community were given to understand that they were unaffected by any inefficiency, extravagance or corruption in Local Government . . .
>
> Over this point we had numerous battles. I accused Winston of reckless advocacy of schemes the effects of which he did not himself understand. He accused me of pedantry and of personal jealousy of himself. At times feelings became rather acute. But I had one advantage over Winston of which he became painfully conscious. He could not do without me. Therefore in the end I was the sole judge of how far to go because whenever I put my foot down he was helpless. As a matter of fact I only put it down once and he gave way directly. But it was a very harrowing time for me and to tell you the truth, Edward, Winston is a very interesting but d----d uncomfortable bed fellow. You never get a moment's rest and you never know at what point he'll break out. . . . In the consideration of affairs his decisions are never founded on exact knowledge, nor on careful prolonged considerations of the pros and cons. He seeks instinctively for the large and preferably the novel idea such as is capable of representation by the broadest brush. Whether the idea is practicable or impracticable, good or bad, provided he can see himself recommending it plausibly and successfully to an enthusiastic audience, it commends itself to him. . . .

It was not an unperceptive description, even though obviously written with some bias, and it conveyed a good sense both of the strains of 1927–8 and of the reasons which later made Chamberlain so loath to take Churchill into his government until war had actually broken out. All winter long and into the early days of the spring the noise of battle rolled, and the outcome was not wholly satisfactory to either side. Chamberlain got his way on preserving some financial link between industry and local government, and Churchill got his way, almost at the last moment, on extending derating to railways, to which Chamberlain and several others had been strongly opposed. The finally agreed scheme was enough Churchill's own for him to be able to present it to

Parliament with a great flourish and in a three-and-a-half-hour speech on 24 April. This fourth budget was on the whole well received, although it and the preceding arguments had clearly taxed his great but sometimes dramatically exhaustible reserves of energy to the limit, as was shown both by half an hour's suspension of the sitting (for the first time in a budget speech since Lloyd George's 1909 marathon), and by his being struck down by a violent influenza four days later. This attack prevented his replying to the budget debate and not only kept him in bed for more than a week but required nearly a month of convalescence.

He was however back for the Finance Bill and the associated rating legislation, which proved complicated to get through, with the former not becoming law until 3 August. By this time Churchill's mind was already well into his holiday tasks, interspersed with a few thoughts for his next budget. He had started on yet another volume of *The World Crisis*, this one dealing with the Treaty of Versailles and the aftermath, and his civil engineering interest had turned from dams and ponds to bricklaying, for which he acquired a surprising facility. As a result he reported to Baldwin in early September: 'I have had a delightful month, building a cottage and dictating a book: 200 bricks and 2000 words a day' – an output which should have satisfied anyone.

While his own political thoughts may have been turning towards the budget of 1929, however, those of an uncomfortably large number of his colleagues were engaged with how they could get him out of the Treasury before the election of that year, which could not be postponed into 1930, and which in fact took place at the end of May. The view of Churchill's old school-fellow Amery that his replacement at the Treasury by Neville Chamberlain 'would be worth twenty or thirty seats at least' may have been exaggerated, and stemmed in Amery's case from his obsessive interest in getting a Baldwin commitment to general Protection, to which he saw Churchill (cf. Kenneth Clarke's brake on Tory anti-Europeanism in the 1997 election) as a major obstacle. But it was much more widespread than Amery, and embraced Neville Chamberlain, Baldwin's close friends Davidson and Bridgeman, and to some extent the Prime Minister himself.

The glamour of Churchill's coruscating phrases, both in memoranda and in oratory, was beginning to wear off, there was a feeling that he had in any event been at the Treasury long enough (only four Chancellors had previously produced as many as five consecutive budgets), there was a fear that he might be building up an unwelcome claim to succeed Baldwin as leader, and, above all, he had ruffled the feathers of too many colleagues. That July, for instance, he had played a major role, against the views of such a venerable figure as Arthur Balfour, in getting reconfirmed the 'ten-year rule', under which defence planning proceeded on the basis that no major war threatened within ten years. Germany was of course still the Germany of the Weimar Republic and even on a narrow time chart ten years did not expire until July 1938, two months before Munich. It was nonetheless an ironical position for the alarm-bell of the 1930s to have taken up.

There was no serious suggestion that Churchill should be dropped from the government. He was too good a trumpet and too dangerous an adversary for that to be mooted. It was a shift to an equal or almost equal position which was under consideration. Probably the most canvassed idea was that he should become Secretary of State for India, but the Viceroy poured very tepid water upon this (it was remarkable how much of Irwin's time seems to have been spent in receiving or sending letters about Churchill), which was probably as well in view of the deeply obscurantist position on India to which Churchill devoted most of the five years after the fall of the government. The Foreign Office was also a possibility. Clementine Churchill in a remarkable but undated letter of this period wrote to him of the need for a replacement for Austen Chamberlain who 'is just an animated cardboard marionette'. But, in what the future made another great irony, she continued, 'I am afraid your known hostility to America might stand in the way.'

In the event Baldwin's indolence avoided all these awkward choices. He lacked the energy to do a major reshuffle before the 1929 election, and after it he lacked the power. So Churchill approached (and just passed) the unusual milestone of his fifth budget. He did so with unabated enthusiasm. He did not have a great deal new to announce beyond the abolition of his own unsuccessful betting tax and a couple of modest election 'bribes': the bringing forward of agricultural (but not industrial) derating by six months, so as to encourage grateful farmers to rush to the polls, and the abolition (for the time being only as it turned out) of that old King Charles's head of the tea duty, at the moderately serious cost of £6.25 million. But he allowed this paucity of substance to inhibit neither the length nor the brio of his speech. Once again it was in the three-hour range, this time without a break, and filled with a sweeping if tendentious survey of his whole record since 1924 accompanied by denunciations of both the Labour and the Liberal (Yellow Book) proposals. It was perhaps the greatest *tour de force* of his five budget speeches. It was bricks without much straw. But it inspired the chroniclers of *British Budgets* to refer to its 'scintillating rhetoric' and the *Sunday Times* to call it 'the most brilliantly entertaining of modern Budget speeches'.

It did nothing to avoid or even, it seems likely, to mitigate the Conservative defeat which came six weeks later. This could not, on the evidence of his previous written comments, have been a great surprise for Churchill, and may even have been a relief, for it averted the danger of his demotion from the Treasury. He nonetheless greeted the results, which he curiously chose to observe in 10 Downing Street in company with Baldwin, with a typically pugnacious partisanship. Tom Jones wrote a famous description:

> At [one] desk sat Winston doing . . . lists in red ink, sipping whisky and soda, getting redder and redder, rising and going out to glare at the [tape] machine himself, hunching his shoulders, bowing his head like a bull about to charge. As Labour gain after Labour gain was announced, Winston became more and more flushed with anger, left his seat and confronted the machine in the passage; with his shoulders hunched he glared at the figures, tore the sheets and behaved as though if any more Labour gains came along he would smash the whole apparatus. His ejaculations to the surrounding staff were quite unprintable.

His impact upon the internal scene of defeat was therefore just as powerful and just as idiosyncratic as had been the external impact of his long Chancellorship and his first Conservative office. His great virtues had been the generosity of his sympathies together with the force of his oratory and personality. His great defect had been the lack of any persistent sense of direction. And the dominant impression left by this important yet branchline phase of his life was of his pulsating energy, breadth of interest and rash self-confidence, towards the public and his colleagues at least, if not always towards himself or his pillow.

NEVILLE CHAMBERLAIN

NEVILLE CHAMBERLAIN IS THE ONLY MAN since Gladstone who was twice Chancellor of the Exchequer and then Prime Minister. He therefore occupies an important place in the gallery of Chancellors. Indeed his career is of sufficient significance that I was tempted to put him in the category in which for reasons varying from case to case I have placed Asquith, Lloyd George, Baldwin and Churchill, and concentrated upon his performance at the Treasury, without attempting to see his life as a whole. However I swung away from this, mainly on the grounds that I had never previously written anything of the remotest significance about Neville as opposed to the other Chamberlains, and that it is the contrast between the impressions given by his performance in different offices which are of the most interest in interpreting his elusive personality.

Where, however, space can be saved is that his family background, education and experience as a young man are sufficiently dealt with in the essay on his very different half-brother that I need start with him only on the threshold of his late-beginning political career. In the autumn of 1911, at the age of forty-two, he achieved his first elected office as a Birmingham City councillor. By that time his father, after thirty years at the fulcrum of British politics, was a crippled giant; and his brother, only five and a half years Neville's senior, had been Chancellor of the Exchequer, and was just about to be the front-running (although not the successful) candidate for the Conservative leadership.

Until then Neville Chamberlain appeared to have been content as his central activity to run two middle-grade and typical Birmingham companies of the period. The first was Elliott's, subsequently absorbed into ICI, which employed 700 men in making brass, much of which was exported to Benares to be turned into fantastic and holy shapes. The second was Hoskins', with only seventy employees, but more highly skilled, which sent men to the Clyde or the Tyne or even Genoa to fit cabins made in Birmingham into naval or mercantile vessels. Somewhat later he became an active director of the Birmingham Small Arms Company and imposed a very forward workers' welfare policy upon this substantial company. He gave it a very different spirit from that which sustained the activities of Sir Bernard and Lady Docker in the 1940s and 1950s. Its name was a curiously appropriate one for absorbing some of his energies. The Birmingham part of it goes without saying. Second, he was always unsentimental about arms and the arms trade. And if BSA was 'small' by virtue of the sort of munitions it had been formed to produce rather than in relation to the scale of its operations, it was at least locally concentrated. He liked his enterprises to be sufficiently so that he could keep control over them. He refused the high-prestige offer of a directorship of the Great Western Railway, which, although it kept its own station in Birmingham through and well beyond Chamberlain's lifetime, was basically a West Country and South Wales operation.

He was also concerned to keep adequate time for his wide range of local voluntary activities, embracing the University, the hospitals, the Territorial Army and even Sunday school teaching, although religious faith as opposed to social improvement was never a very lively factor in his life. He was also the resident representative of his father and his brother in Birmingham. At least when Parliament was in session, he was the sole (and very solitary) occupant of Highbury, the *rus in urbe* villa which his father had constructed in the southern suburbs. This almost ambassadorial role is important to understanding the mixture of patricianism and modesty in Neville Chamberlain. It would be too much to say that he was a Medici remaining in Florence when his family had gone to Rome to become Popes, but it is nonetheless the case that when he went on to the Birmingham Council in 1911 it was very different from his father doing so in 1865. The father was a new man thrusting his way up. The son did it out of a sense of duty and almost conferring a favour, although condescension was not at all his style. As he expressed it to a business partner: 'I rather expect to go on to the City Council next autumn . . .'

When he joined the Council ten of his kinsmen had already been Mayor. The area over which the writ of the Council ran had just been greatly extended so that the Birmingham population rose as a result of boundary changes from 525,000 to 840,000. It became the largest local authority outside London in England (Glasgow was a little bigger in those days) and the Chamberlain tradition and ethos demanded that it should be not only the biggest but the best and most positively governed city of provincial England. Furthermore with its 40,000 back-to-back houses and generally foetid conditions in the inner wards, where the annual death rate was twenty-four per thousand compared with nine per thousand in the suburbs, the city was ripe for another wave of municipal reform such as his father had led in the 1870s. He quickly became chairman of the Town Planning Committee and changed the pattern of housing estates as well as greatly increasing their extent. Within three years he was an alderman and within five was elected Lord Mayor.

By then it was wartime and this, combined with his name and executive temperament, gave him more the stature and function of a Continental or American mayor than the 'Buggins's turn' figurehead role which has been normal in English local government. He was re-elected for a second term in November 1916. Lloyd George's jibe, made many years later, that the ceiling of Chamberlain's talents was to be 'Lord Mayor of Birmingham in a lean year' was singularly away from the bull's-eye. Whatever his limitations of horizon, Neville Chamberlain was a very good Lord Mayor for any year, and indeed might have done better for himself, his city and maybe his country by staying there several years longer.

Just before the beginning of this municipal phase of his life, Chamberlain had married. He was almost forty-two, the same late age to within a few months to which his brother Austen had also waited. The marriages of both the brothers were felicitous, long-lasting and moderately fecund, which makes it the more remarkable that they should both have delayed so long. The obvious explanation would be the strength of the paternal link – of the four daughters of Joseph Chamberlain, it may be noted in passing, only one ever married – but Neville might have been expected to be more immune to this than Austen, for he lived a substantially different life, and made no attempt to be a carbon copy of their father.

The other surprising aspect of Neville's marriage was how he ever met his bride. (It was in fact through a Canadian aunt by marriage who had, through her second marriage, formed an equally remote connection with the family of the future Anne Chamberlain.) Although more than secure among the Unitarian elite of Edgbaston he was still living a very provincial and urban life. He liked fishing and trees and birds, but not the more aggressive country pursuits, and he had no residence outside Birmingham. His wife's provenance could hardly have been more different. Her father was Major William Cole of the 3rd Dragoons, who lived at West Woodhay on the borders of Hampshire and Wiltshire.

Her mother had been Mary de Vere of Curragh Chase, Co. Limerick, and her brother, Horace de Vere Cole, was one of the most famous practical jokers – and winners of wagers when bringing them off – of Edwardian England. He once impersonated the Emperor of Abyssinia and, accompanied by a suite equally appropriately disguised (which amazingly included Virginia Woolf), got himself and his companions given almost a full naval review off Weymouth. However, Anne Cole seemed wholly content to settle down to a much more serious-minded life in Westbourne Road, Edgbaston.

This almost exclusively Birmingham life lasted just under six years. In December 1916, a couple of weeks after Lloyd George's accession to the premiership, Neville Chamberlain was wrenched out of Birmingham, partly through the bumbling goodwill of his brother and partly through the new Prime Minister's frenetic energy and desire for dramatic appointments. A Director-General for National Service was required to administer a manpower policy which it was hoped would be defensible and would get more men into the army without too much weakening of industry. At the prompting of Austen and of Alfred Milner, Lloyd George was persuaded that Neville Chamberlain would be, or at least sound, a good man for the job. His relations with labour were at that stage excellent. He had a burgeoning reputation for crisp efficiency. And his description as Lord Mayor of Birmingham carried a sense of sustaining down-to-earth provincial strength.

The method of his appointment provided a good illustration of the way in which at least some senior ministers, with the adrenalin flowing, like to operate. After a day in London dealing with a municipal loan flotation, Chamberlain was pulled out of a Euston-to-Birmingham train and rushed to see the Prime Minister, who wanted a decision in ten minutes. The somewhat theatrical drama would not have mattered had it been accompanied by precision in the terms of his appointment. But Neville claimed that, even after a further two talks with Lloyd George, he did not know whether his writ ran in Ireland and/or Scotland, whether he had authority over those who had volunteered for munitions work, and if he was to be paid a salary or be treated himself as a volunteer.

There was no suggestion that he should become an MP, which might have strengthened his position, although as a crowning anomaly he was to have a parliamentary secretary to answer for him in the House of Commons. He was half the head of a quango and half a low-ranking minister. It was a recipe for failure, and a failure the whole arrangement rapidly turned out to be. It led quickly to the second of the three bleakly unhappy periods of Neville Chamberlain's life. The first was when the sisal would not grow on the West Indian island to which he had been sent in 1894–6 to supervise the making of some money for the family, and the third, obviously, came with the collapse of his policy, his parliamentary support and his health in 1939–40.

What exactly went wrong in 1917? A clear account is difficult to find. Professor Keith Feiling, for instance, Chamberlain's first serious posthumous biographer, who in an impressionistic way generally conveys a clear enough picture is simply incomprehensible on what were the exact subjects of policy and administrative clash. All that is indisputable is that Chamberlain operated in deepening gloom from an office in the St Ermin's Hotel, Westminster, a building conducive to gloom in the best of circumstances. Dimly through the fog there also emerges the impression that Chamberlain had been given a highly political job without any political power, that the War Cabinet failed to support him in arguments with other departments, and that he showed little adroitness in rallying support. He believed that Lloyd George had let him down and he retained a life-long distrust and dislike of the 'Welsh wizard' as a result. But it is difficult to reject some of the adverse comments which Lloyd George made in his (1934) *War Memoirs*. Chamberlain, he wrote, was 'a man of rigid competency' with 'a vein of self-sufficient obstinacy' and 'no great breadth and boldness of conception'.

Whatever the exact merits Chamberlain quickly recognized that he had made a mistake, and after seven months retired hurt to Birmingham, rejecting both the offer of a knighthood and local suggestions that his Lord Mayoralty might be revived. He was deeply depressed. 'My career is broken,' he wrote towards the end of l917, and at about the same time in one of his long unfailing weekly letters to a sister he came very near to a hopeless self-pity:

> Every now and then a feeling of almost irresistible nausea and revulsion comes over me at the thought of all the drudgery, the humiliation, the meanness and pettiness of that [political] life, and of the hopeless impossibility of getting things done. And then I grind my teeth and think if it hadn't been for my d----d well-meaning brother I might still have been Lord Mayor of Birmingham, practically in control of the town and about to enter upon my third year of office.

Of the two points of interest in this extract the first is the note of controlled exasperation with Austen. The second point was why on earth, in view of his expression of dislike and almost contempt for the political process, was his main rebound response to his retreat from Whitehall a decision to enter the House of Commons. The likely explanations seem to be a desire to get his own back and to prove that he could succeed even in the foul and filthy air of metropolitan politics.

It was still the case that for a Chamberlain to feel a desire for Parliament was for him to command its fulfilment. With seven seats (to be made twelve in 1918) at the disposal of the Birmingham Unionist Association it was almost like a sultan entering his harem, inappropriate although such a self-indulgent simile sounds in relation to Neville Chamberlain. First it was arranged that, at the general election, he should replace the member for the Central division, the old John Bright seat after the splitting of the city in 1886. But when the seven seats became twelve he shifted his preference to Ladywood, which was a neighbour to the West division, to which Austen had moved from South Worcestershire on the death of their father in 1914.

When Neville Chamberlain took his seat in February 1919 he was only a month short of his fiftieth birthday, the most advanced age by quite a wide margin at which any future Prime Minister has ever entered Parliament. Somewhat surprisingly in view of his 1917 stricture on metropolitan political life, as well as his somewhat reclusive personality and critical, even mordant, cast of mind, he took to the House of Commons remarkably enthusiastically. Of course he came in with both the advantages and the disadvantages of a well-known name. His father was still vividly remembered as the dominant parliamentary personality between the retirement of Gladstone in 1894 and his stroke in 1906. His brother was currently Chancellor and soon to be leader of the House. And Neville Chamberlain himself had been almost a minister for six months. He did not start as a tyro. Nor did he start as one of the hard-faced men of business who (in Baldwin's phrase) looked 'as though they had done well out of the war' and who dropped into the House only when they could spare the time from trying to do well out of the peace.

Chamberlain was assiduous, both in Birmingham and in Westminster. He became almost a full-time back-bench MP. He went on a lot of committees and he made a lot of speeches, mostly in minor debates on detailed questions about which he was well informed. He also made friends in the House, and the trio with whom he was particularly close – Edward Wood (Irwin and then Halifax), Sam Hoare and Philip Lloyd-Graeme (later Cunliffe-Lister, then Swinton) – suggests that he had good taste, or at least a good eye for those who were capable of becoming his future senior colleagues.

He paid meticulous attention to Ladywood, and was critical of Austen for neglecting West Birmingham. Indeed Neville was at this period, and perhaps always after Austen's failure to seize the leadership in 1911 and then compounding the sin by pushing him into the bosh National Service job at the end of 1916, critical of Austen on a number of points. He was full of family feeling (although not quite as full as Austen himself), but also of impatience at Austen's unoriginal pomposity. Neville's chief fear at getting fully embroiled in national politics was that it would inevitably bring him into conflict with his brother. In a *familial* and nostalgic way Neville was fond of Austen, but after about 1914 he never much respected him.

In January 1919 he wrote to a sister after an unsatisfactory brotherly conversation, 'The fact is I always said that if I went into the House we should differ and we are bound to do so because our minds are differently trained. He thinks me wild and I think him unprogressive and prejudiced.' This was written with a spurt of anger, but even a year later, when he was half making a joke and half showing a surprisingly demanding gourmet side, there was not much sign of rapport, let alone respect:

> I went to see Austen, who gave me a very bad and meagre dinner: smelts, snipe, cheese! No wonder he looks hollow-cheeked if that's how he feeds himself. I thought I might attract some information of interest about the political situation but he had absolutely nothing to give and as he didn't ask why I was in town, I didn't tell him.

There were several paradoxes about these early years of Neville Chamberlain in the House of Commons. Objectively, if he was to make up for his late entry and realize his full potential (and there was no false modesty which led him to do other than set that very high) he had to be a middle-aged man in a hurry. Yet a combination of his own prejudices and pride led him to stand back from the government of which Lloyd George was Prime Minister, his brother a leading member and himself at least a nominal supporter. He refused a GBE in the 1918 New Year's honours list. He refused junior office in early 1920, proffered by Bonar Law on Lloyd George's behalf. He seemed to be in an impasse. He did not want to be in a Lloyd George government, yet he could not work publicly against it, particularly when in 1921 his brother became its principal Conservative supporter.

He then had extraordinarily good luck. For this he ought to have been deeply grateful to Stanley Baldwin, with whom however his subsequent relations were as typically edgy as are those between most politicians who occupy the numbers one and two positions within the same party: Rosebery and Harcourt, MacDonald and Snowden, Attlee and Morrison, Macmillan and Butler, Wilson and George Brown. Baldwin's Carlton Club revolt in October 1922 ruined Austen Chamberlain's leadership of the Conservative party but made Neville Chamberlain's career, and made it so dramatically that he advanced within a single year (and within only five and a half years of his first election to the Commons) from stymied back bencher to Chancellor of the Exchequer. To add to his luck this result was achieved without his having to take any action of his own. He did not even have to cast a vote at the crucial Carlton Club meeting, for he was away in Canada. Had he been there he would probably have felt it necessary to have added one vote to the minority of 87, although all his instincts and his interests would have been with the majority of 187. They did the job for him. With one bound he was free, free from Lloyd George, free (up to a point) from his brother, free from Coalition politics, which he instinctively disliked, partly for good reasons (honours scandals among others) and partly for bad ones (a priggish inability to appreciate Lloyd George's quality behind the screen of his opportunism).

It was ten days after the Carlton Club meeting before Neville Chamberlain reached Southampton from Canada. Already an election had been arranged for 15 November and he went straight to Birmingham to prepare for the contest. Bonar Law was by then far advanced with the formation of the first purely Conservative government for seventeen years. He offered Chamberlain the Postmaster-Generalship, outside the Cabinet. Neville was anxious to accept. The obstacle was Austen, already in Birmingham for his own campaign, but heavily bruised by his Carlton Club humiliation, and certainly not well disposed towards either Bonar Law or Baldwin, the new Chancellor. The post offered was, curiously, the first senior one which Austen himself had occupied, although *in* the Cabinet, at the beginning of the Balfour government. But this made him no better disposed to his younger brother mingling with the agents of his defeat. A most awkward Birmingham family dinner ensued. There was a touch of moral blackmail from both sides. But Neville, the stronger character, played the higher and more risky card. Very well, he said, he would refuse the offer, but it would follow logically that, having refused office from Lloyd George, to do so again from Bonar Law would mean that his political career was at an end. He would withdraw from Parliament. Austen collapsed, as Neville must have had a pretty shrewd hope that he would.

Neville Chamberlain threw himself into the Post Office – it was the sort of detailed and limited administrative task which he liked – but he did not stay there long enough to make much impact. Just over four months later he was promoted to be Minister of Health in place of Arthur Griffiths-Boscawen, whose ministerial career, in a way half paralleled only by C. F. G. Masterman and Patrick Gordon Walker, foundered on his losing his seat at a general election and failing to win the bye-election which was subsequently found for him. But even at Health the suddenly upwardly mobile Chamberlain stayed only five months before he reluctantly became Chancellor of the Exchequer.

In May 1923 Bonar Law, stricken with a cancer of the throat, terminated his half-year of unhappy and undistinguished premiership. Chamberlain's surprising preference would probably have been for Curzon rather than Baldwin as his successor, but as he was not consulted it did not much matter. Baldwin at first combined the Chancellorship with the premiership, mainly because he had been infected with the current fever (perhaps more a sleeping sickness) of waiting for McKenna. When McKenna was very slow to arrive, and when Baldwin in any event was beginning to recover from the virus, he approached Neville Chamberlain in August.

As Baldwin then plunged in October towards both Protection (which was welcome to his Chancellor) and the second (and lost) general election within a year (which was not welcome) it was not a fructuous Chancellorship. There was no budget and not much else either. But it meant that Neville had had a remarkable year's surge to the front rank of politics. Even though Austen's fame was to be temporarily warmed by the sun of Locarno it was the cross-over point for his influence compared with that of his half-brother. It also meant that he had brief experiences of both the departments which he was to dominate, Health for four and a half years, the Treasury for five and a half years, during the next, and best, fourteen years of his life. On the whole, with his admirably workaday approach – he was still happy to leave the trappings to Austen – he preferred the Ministry of Health to the Treasury.

Chamberlain's full 1924–9 parliament as Minister of Health is widely considered the most productive period of his life, although his second Chancellorship from 1931 to 1937, with Britain, as in the mid-1990s, doing relatively well in a period of weak world performance, was also ministerially impressive. It did not however have the constructive social-reform drive of the earlier period. In the autumn of 1924 he returned to that vast sprawling Department of Health (more so even than the Department of the Environment is today) with a clear legislative programme in his mind. On 7 November, he circulated to the Cabinet a list of twenty-five bills which he wished to carry over a four-year period. His colleagues were half impressed and half dismayed. But the former emotion gained over the latter as he proceeded relentlessly to get his way. Twenty-one of the twenty-five were law (plus a few other uncovenanted measures) by the time of the 1929 dissolution.

They were in no way demagogic bills, as with some recent spurts of legislation. They were designed, within a framework of financial discipline, to improve the condition of the people, not to win plaudits at party conferences. One of the more important, the Rating and Valuation Act, which reduced the number of rating authorities from 12,000 to 600, confining the power in Chamberlain's own words to 'the real living bodies of today', the county, borough and district councils (many of which were Labour controlled), was distinctly unpopular with the local Tory activists who thereby lost their function. So too were several aspects of his late 1928 Local Government Bill (perilously close to a general election) which got rid of the Boards of Guardians for Poor Law relief and transferred their powers to the local authorities.

Neville Chamberlain was a true heir of his father's 'gas and water' socialism period on the Birmingham Town Council. (He wrote ironically of Samuel Hoare and himself as being 'the only socialists' in the 1922 Conservative government.) This was despite his lack of Joseph Chamberlain's charisma, world vision and destructive ruthlessness. Neville was a Conservative insofar as he disliked the sentimental liberalism which he saw as permeating both the Liberal and Labour parties, but he was also a very bossy reformer. He believed in big government, 'the supervisory State' as he once put it with approbation, subject to one important limitation. He believed passionately in local government. It was as much part of his visceral creed as the higher statecraft was to a Salisbury or business values to Sir Alfred Mond. Local government, he said in one memorable phrase, belonged to the people 'standing between them and ill health and injustice'. A good efficiently run county, town or city council, even if Labour controlled, earned his instinctive respect, and a bad one, whether George Lansbury's 'open hand at the till' Poplar or a dozy hierarchical county council, his equally instinctive contempt.

Why, with this outlook and when he was carrying through such progressive measures as widows' pensions and a successful public and private housing programme, did he not begin to rival his Prime Minister, Stanley Baldwin, in acquiring a centrist constituency in politics, and a sympathetic relationship with the Labour party? The answer I think lies in his developing, even during this 'progressive' period, the narrowly intolerant habit of mind which, even had his central policy not ended in abysmal failure, made him such a divisive Prime Minister ten years later. It was splendidly summed up in his own straightforward but possibly puzzled recording of a massive but gently administered rebuke given to him by Baldwin. 'Stanley begged me to remember', he wrote on 19 June 1927, 'that I was addressing a meeting of gentlemen. I always gave him the impression, he said, when I spoke in the House of Commons, that I looked on the Labour party as dirt.'

His neutral recording of this remark might be regarded as evidence that he took the rebuke serenely. Yet nine months later, in another letter to a sister (his devotion to such correspondence was a striking but by no means solitary example of his admirable private character) he showed himself incorrigible on the point: 'their [the Labour members'] gross exaggerations, their dishonesty in slurring over facts that tell against them, and their utter inability to appreciate a reasonable argument, do embitter my soul sometimes, and if I seem hard and unsympathetic to them, it is the reaction brought about by their own attitude'.

Chamberlain was a very efficient departmental minister, and a genuine and effective reformer, but a very self-righteous one with a narrow imagination, and markedly short on ability to appreciate minds which did not work like his own. However there can be no doubt that his long stretch as Minister of Health substantially and deservedly enhanced his reputation. Towards the end of the government he arranged two changes for his future, both of them mildly surprising. First he settled with Baldwin that in the reshuffle, which was expected before the election but which, thanks partly to Baldwin's indolence, never took place he should become Colonial Secretary. Apart from a nostalgic attachment to his father's last office it is difficult to see the sense of this arrangement. Neville Chamberlain was very domestically orientated and his strongest feeling towards the colonies must have been distasteful memories of the West Indies in the mid-1890s.

Second he changed his Birmingham constituency to Edgbaston. Ladywood, like West Birmingham, Austen's neighbouring seat, was part of the old core of the city, where Joseph Chamberlain's influence had been strongest and where his memory most lingered. However, they had both also become almost exclusively working class and marginal even for Chamberlains. Edgbaston was safe, and it was a highly rational move, unlike the projected one to the Colonial Office. It was nonetheless odd that Austen, whom Neville was increasingly inclined to criticize for neglecting Birmingham, should have stayed in the exposed segment and held it intact to the end of his life in 1937, while it was Neville who retreated to bourgeois security.

The move probably saved the continuity of his parliamentary career, for the Labour party won Ladywood in 1929. As Neville Chamberlain always claimed that he hated opposition, taking no pleasure in the game of politics, and was solely interested in administration and legislation, this was presumably in the short run a mixed blessing for him. But his presence and influence in 1931 (combined with that of King George V) profoundly altered the course of politics (in a way that was even more of a mixed blessing) as well as the shape of his future career. During the two and a quarter years of that ill-fated second Labour government Chamberlain was half the principal lieutenant to Baldwin, who was himself having a miserable time with his own party, and half his most dangerous critic. They neither of them liked opposition, but for quite different reasons. Baldwin disliked it because haranguing a government did not suit his ruminative emollient style. Chamberlain, naturally critical and often harshly partisan, would have been quite enthusiastic about this aspect of being leader of the opposition, a position which, rarely but not uniquely for a Prime Minister (Lloyd George, Macmillan and Eden are the other twentieth-century exceptions), he never occupied. He simply regarded speech-making as unrewarding (whereas Baldwin governed much more by mood-creating orations than by hard decisions) and found winning debates afforded no compensation for the frustration of losing power.

Chamberlain wanted to be loyal to Baldwin, to whom he referred as his friend as well as his leader. But he was ambitious, although like his father more for power than for place, he was over sixty years old and he was convinced he could do the job better. When Baldwin's leadership ran into its third and most acute crisis in October 1930, this combination of circumstance and belief proved too much for him. With suitable but not excessive reluctance he came to the view that Baldwin should go. In his capacity as Chairman of the Conservative party, which post he had occupied for the previous six months, he received a wounding (to Baldwin) memorandum from the Chief Agent saying that 'from practically all quarters' he heard the view that the leader ought to go, and hinting strongly that the Chairman should be the replacement. Chamberlain disseminated the criticism widely by consulting half the shadow Cabinet as to whether or not he ought to worry Baldwin with the document.

Eventually Chamberlain sent it to him at the same time as the news was coming through that the St George's division of Westminster – peculiarly favourable territory for the Rothermere/Beaverbrook-financed rebels – had become vacant and that the official Conservative candidate had withdrawn, preferring to run rather than fight. It was thus a highly vulnerable moment for Baldwin and at his first meeting with Chamberlain after the receipt of the memorandum he agreed to step down. Then he dined with two of his closest political friends (Bridgeman and Davidson) and changed his mind. Instead he was going to fight on every possible front and with all guns blazing. He would resign his safe Worcestershire seat and himself be the candidate for St George's. Early the next morning he resummoned Chamberlain and told him of his new plans. The party Chairman and putative successor was aghast at the prospect. 'Think of the effect upon your successor,' he tactlessly remonstrated. 'I don't give a damn about my successor, Neville,' was Baldwin's conversation-ending response.

That was a definitive moment, not only for Baldwin's routing of his opponents within his own party (although he did not have to fight St George's – Duff Cooper did so on his behalf) but also for his relations with Chamberlain. The use of Chamberlain's Christian name at the end was important. It gave a different balance to the sentence, and expressed controlled exasperation, an assertion of seniority and an indication of who was going to be boss in the future. Thereafter for the remaining six and a half years of his leadership it was obvious that Baldwin would go in his own time and not before. Chamberlain's energy, efficiency and bossiness would be given plenty of scope, not least because it contrasted so sharply with Baldwin's laziness, but he would be unwise to push his authority too far or in future to think of Baldwin as his friend as well as his leader.

Chamberlain had probably become convinced of the desirability of a coalition government by the end of July 1931. In opening an economic debate on the 30th of that month he noticeably pulled his punches against Snowden, whose harsh puncturing of the illusions of his Labour followers had earned Chamberlain's respect, even though he differed sharply from Snowden's stubborn attachment to Free Trade. Indeed one of the attractions for Chamberlain of a coalition was the thought that, in spite of the predilections of Snowden and indeed of Herbert Samuel the Liberal leader, the logic of Britain's weak trading position would drive it inevitably towards Protection, maybe with a tinge of Imperial Preference, and thus enable him to vindicate his father's last campaign. He was also attracted by the prospect of forcing an 'irrevocable split' in the Labour party, without which he was by no means sure of Conservative prospects for the next election.

Baldwin's attitude was quite different. As late as 22 August it was described as follows by his faithful henchman J. C. C. Davidson: 'S.B. was deeply reluctant to envisage a new coalition. He had destroyed one and did not wish to form another. Neville Chamberlain became very impatient with S.B.'s attitude.' Baldwin had further reasons, both public and private for being unenamoured of a national government. It cut against his central political strategy of the 1920s. He had worked for a stable balance in politics, with a large, moderate and 'responsible' Labour party sharing power, although preferably not on an equal basis, with his own brand of paternalistic Conservatism. To cut off from the Labour party its most moderate leaders, and to leave the bulk of it as a wounded and resentful animal, but one with an almost inevitable power of recovery, was to fly in the face of that strategy.

In addition Baldwin did personally very badly out of the National government. At the end of the 1930–1 parliamentary session he had every reason to expect that within a matter of months, at most a year or so, he would again be Prime Minister with at his disposal, to put it at its lowest, 10 Downing Street, Chequers and a full salary (which he needed, for the slump had reduced to rock bottom the value of the shares of Baldwin Ltd). But he ended up as only the third man in the government hierarchy, without Chequers or No. 10, and, as Lord President, with a salary of only £2,000 instead of the £5,000 of most of the others.

All this being so, why did Chamberlain, whose tactical sense was sharper but whose strategic sense was less wise than Baldwin's, get his way over his leader, particularly as the latter had so recently enjoyed his triumph of the spring accompanied by resentment at Chamberlain trying to push him around so bossily? In part the explanation lies in Baldwin's addiction to holidays and Chamberlain's devotion to duty, and in part too it lies in pure ill-chance. When the session was over Chamberlain went fishing on the Tummel in Perthshire. Baldwin, a little later, went to France. They both came back to London when the crisis broke on 11/12 August. The difference was that Baldwin was

determined to be off again, and that Chamberlain was equally determined to stay. His house was closed, the Carlton Club was closed and
he was forced to operate from a small bedroom in its annexe. He might
have been said, had it not been the coldest and wettest August that
anyone could remember, to have 'sweated it out' (assisted by Samuel
Hoare, his co-opted adjutant) in London for the remainder of the
month. Baldwin, by contrast, was back across the Channel on that same
evening. His attitude, admittedly as described by Chamberlain in a letter
to a sister, was disengagement at almost all costs: 'Anyway the decisions
are left to me as S.B. is not coming back. I think he would agree that
crises of this kind are not his forte.'

In fact Baldwin did come back, reaching London late on 22 August.
By then he found the cards heavily stacked against him. When he saw
the King on the following afternoon he was asked whether, as Samuel
the Liberal leader had already done, he would agree to serve in a
subordinate capacity under MacDonald and thus save the country. His
whole character and political stance gave him little alternative but to say
yes, much though it was against his instinctive and probably better
judgement. Had he got there earlier he might have been asked a less
direct question and been able to divert the pressure. Had he not been so
keen on holidays he might have prevented Chamberlain seizing total
control of the Conservative influence, which was a crucial ingredient in
the outcome. As it was, those last two weeks in August 1931 set the
pattern of British politics for nearly a decade, and did so in a way which
was almost as deleterious to Baldwin as it was to the national interest.

The new government came in with an emergency three-party
Cabinet of ten members, pledged to maintain the parity of the pound
and then to dissolve itself, and on no account to have a 'coupon election'.
In fact it abandoned the parity on 19 September, held an election on 27
October, which was still more of a pre-emptive strike against its
opponents than was Lloyd George's 'khaki' poll of December 1918, and
lasted with only mild processes of mutation until May 1940.

On the formation of the emergency Cabinet of only ten, Chamberlain became Minister of Health for the third time. After the election, in
a Cabinet reverting to normal size, he succeeded Snowden as Chancellor. This second Neville Chamberlain Chancellorship, in contrast with
his first, was both long-lasting and exceptionally powerful. There was a
curious devolution of power within the National government. Mac-
Donald, although he began to deteriorate heavily in early 1934, a full
year before he handed over the premiership to Baldwin, was during

1932 and 1933 Prime Minister in substance as well as in name, and performed reasonably well internationally and as chairman of the Cabinet. Nevertheless Baldwin, commanding the parliamentary troops, was inevitably an unusually powerful second-in-command. He concerned himself with the House of Commons, with India, with defence (somewhat fitfully), and with the crisis management of issues which suddenly blow up and as quickly subside. Baldwin in turn delegated unusually to his own deputy. Economic, industrial and social policy he left almost entirely to the Chancellor of the Exchequer. Chamberlain therefore exercised even in the early 1930s a wide suzerainty. From the early part of 1935 onwards it became still wider. His influence upon defence and foreign policy then became paramount.

From the beginning, however, his control over budgetary and economic policy was complete. Baldwin was schooled by nature and MacDonald by Snowden into non-interference in such matters. Chamberlain's first exercise of cancellarian power however related to tariff policy rather than to budgetary policy. Although the 1931 election had been fought on an open policy so far as the Protection/Free Trade issue was concerned, with the Conservatives in the government for, the Liberals against, and MacDonald asking for a 'doctor's mandate', the general assumption was that a combination of a substantial trade deficit, mounting unemployment and the collapse of world trade (which had fallen to one-third of its 1929 value) would enable the Protectionists to achieve the triumph which had eluded them in 1904 and 1923 and bring to an end Britain's nearly ninety-year tradition of Free Trade.

The Samuelite Liberals, who had been reinforced in the enlarged Cabinet by the inclusion of Donald Maclean and Archibald Sinclair, although with Reading dropping out, were vehemently opposed, and so was Snowden, who had acquired special prestige by the virulence of his attacks on his former colleagues during the election, and was also respected by Chamberlain as an 'iron Chancellor'. But the other ex-Labour Cabinet members were amenable, as were the Simonite Liberals, with Runciman, who had become President of the Board of Trade, in a key position. And the Tories Ministers were unanimously in favour. Their only major figure who might for historical reasons have been doubtful was Churchill, and he was outside the government.

Chamberlain's task, to which his clear but narrow-sighted decisiveness was very well suited, was to make sure that the Cabinet majority prevailed over the minority. He was quite prepared to lose the Samuelite Liberals on the way, although he would have preferred to keep Snowden.

First, in November 1931, he got through an Abnormal Importations Act, which allowed almost any rate of duty to be temporarily imposed if there was evidence of forestalling while the government was pondering what its permanent policy should be. Then he got himself made the chairman of a strong Cabinet committee to formulate recommendations for correcting the adverse balance of trade. This committee came out, although not unanimously, in favour of a permanent general revenue tariff of 10 per cent. There were to be exceptions downwards both by category of goods and for reasons of Dominion and Colonial preference, and also upwards to a limit of 100 per cent for industries which needed safeguarding (steel was the outstanding example) on the special recommendation of a Tariff Board. Sir George May, our old friend from the days of the Labour government's agony, became the chairman of this Board.

The Free Traders in the Cabinet came very near to resignation, but were persuaded instead to accept the constitutionally unprecedented 'agreement to differ'. They stayed in the government, but did not support its policy. There was no repetition of such Cabinet laxity for another forty-three years, until the minority in Harold Wilson's second Cabinet was allowed the same rights of dissent in the European referendum campaign of 1975. And then in the John Major Cabinet, on the same European issue, there was not so much an agreement to differ as running *de facto* disagreement without the Prime Minister either conferring consent or enforcing discipline.

Chamberlain announced the new policy to the House of Commons on 4 February 1932, which he described in a private letter as 'the great day of my life'. Its greatness had of course much to do with his strong family feeling. After twenty-nine years he was vindicating his father's policy. Gruff and unemotional though he mostly was in public, he did not hesitate on that day to stress the paternal aspect of the matter. He brought Joseph Chamberlain's widow and surviving daughters to the gallery. He used his father's Colonial Office red despatch box for his notes. And he ended with a deliberately sentimental, although somewhat stiffly constructed peroration:

> There can have been few occasions in all our long political history when the son of a man who counted for something in his day and generation has been vouchsafed the privilege of setting the seal on the work which his father began but was forced to leave unfinished. . . . I believe he would have found consolation for his disappointment if he could have foreseen that these proposals, which are the direct and

legitimate descendants of his own conception, would be laid before the House of Commons, which he loved, in the presence of one and by the lips of the other of the two immediate successors to his name and blood.

Neville Chamberlain was sufficiently proud of this passage that, four years later, he copied it out on request and in the most beautiful script, as clear as it was flowingly neat (he had well the best Prime Ministerial handwriting since Asquith) for the autograph collection of the future King George VI. He had certainly implemented one part of his father's programme, and Austen Chamberlain's gesture of coming down from his back-bench perch of discontent and publicly shaking Neville's hand at the conclusion of his speech, while a little sententious, was not out of proportion to the occasion. The second and equally important part of Joseph Chamberlain's grand design, an interlocking and mutual system of Imperial Preference, had to await the outcome of the Ottawa Conference which was due to begin in late July. In the meantime Dominion goods were excepted from the British tariff. Imperial solidarity however proved a goal about which it was much easier to orate than to negotiate.

A delegation of unprecedented strength sailed for Canada on 13 July. It included seven members of the Cabinet, headed by Baldwin with Chamberlain and Hailsham (the latter with energies surplus to his departmental responsibilities at the War Office) harnessed as the work horses of the team. And Chamberlain at least was clearly determined that it should not be a beano for the others. Throughout the voyage he insisted 'on continual conferences, re-drafting Baldwin's opening speech and drawing up a series of general propositions for the approval of the Conference'.* All this hard work did not do much good. The Dominion Prime Ministers disappointed Neville Chamberlain in 1932 even more than their predecessors had disappointed Joseph Chamberlain when they came to London in 1906. The Canadian R. B. Bennett, who on his home ground acted as chairman, was the central disappointment but Bruce of Australia and Coates of New Zealand were not much better. The flavour of the disappointment is perhaps best captured by Chamberlain reserving his accolades for the delegations of India, South Africa and the Irish Free State.

However, after a great deal of brinkmanship, some sort of success was achieved by 20 August, thanks largely to the assiduity of Chamberlain

* Iain Macleod, *Neville Chamberlain* (1961), p. 159.

and the ingenuity of Hailsham. But it was hardly a triumph for imperial unity. A cynical summing-up could be that enough discrimination was achieved to give the Americans a running grievance, but not enough to produce any great stimulation of Empire trade. It was also enough finally to drive the Samuelite Liberals and Snowden out of the government, but Chamberlain did not regard the three who went from the Cabinet as any great loss, even Snowden's 1931 services having begun to fade into the background.

Besides his two Tariff Reform ventures Chamberlain's first year as Chancellor had contained a couple of other heavy strains on both his energy and his nerve. His first budget was on 19 April and was on the whole badly received. He was of course still dealing with the consequences of an immensely severe trade depression which meant, for instance, that Inland Revenue receipts for 1932–3 were likely to be nearly another 10 per cent below even the 7 per cent downward-adjusted level which had been made to them in Snowden's September budget. Nevertheless a bare surplus had been achieved, even after the provision of £32 million for the reduction of debt, which seems in retrospect an extraordinarily perverse pressing on of the hair shirt. This was made the more so by the fact that the budget speech was interspersed by several dirges about the deleterious effect in a depression of high indirect taxation. The beer duty for instance, which Snowden had increased by thirty-one shillings a barrel in September, was manifestly counter-productive, with the revenue yield significantly lower than it had been with a lower duty in the late 1920s.

More arguably Chamberlain also thought that the burden of direct taxation had been pushed up against the 'practical limits' for maintaining the revenue. But, like a rabbit transfixed by the headlights of an oncoming car, he did not feel that he could move away from danger. This was the crux of the criticism of the budget. Chamberlain had persuaded himself that it was his duty to be a St Sebastian showing his public spirit by the number of arrows he could absorb in his back. But he had no ideas for getting out of the way of the arrows. His self-righteousness also became a little cloying. Britain was setting an example to the world by the stringency of its economy measures. The budget had been balanced, admittedly with unemployment at nearly three million and rising, and the trade deficit had been eliminated, admittedly at the lowest level of imports and exports for a generation, and he was going to do nothing to impair these achievements.

Almost the only upbeat note which he introduced into the budget speech came when he congratulated the British income taxpayers on the patriotism with which they had promptly paid their crippling tax bills. And almost the only time when he warmed to his subject was when he announced that the next quarter of an hour of his speech would not be agreeable listening. In fact the taxation changes that he announced were minor; the main – and regressive – one was the reimposition of the duty on tea which Churchill had repealed in 1929. More significant was that all the 'emergency' imposts and cuts in public sector salaries which Snowden had imposed in September 1931 were kept rigidly in place.

It was these which made *The Times* describe the budget as one of 'puritanical severity'. And it was from that budget that there came Chamberlain's image as an efficient but deadening funeral director, which reached its apogee five years later in a brilliant aphorism of Aneurin Bevan's when Neville took over from Baldwin as Prime Minister: 'In the funeral service of capitalism, the honeyed and soothing platitudes of the clergyman are finished, and the cortège is now under the sombre and impressive guidance of the undertaker.'

The debate on the 1932 budget was largely carried on within the Conservative party, for the flat-on-its back Labour party was exiguous both in numbers and in financial expertise. Sir Robert Horne, whose authority had come to rest more upon his position as a spokesman of big business than as a former short-term Chancellor, delivered the most noticed and ground-breaking speech, the impact of which on modern ears is increased by the idiosyncrasy of the doctrine propounded. The great objective of the government, he said, both domestically and internationally, should be to raise prices. To this end the exchange value of the pound, which had fallen from $4.89 before September to about $3.20, should be prevented from rising. The fall in prices, which in their two plunges, one after 1921, the other after 1929, had brought them below their 1913 level, but with much higher costs of production, had, among other deleterious effects, the result of nearly doubling the real burden of the national debt, and this at a time when its servicing was consuming 41 per cent of total government expenditure was hardly a negligible matter. Horne broke out of the head-down assumptions of the Chamberlain budget, although like most critics without responsibility he could be accused of being much stronger on analysis than on recipe for cure.

The strains of the budget produced one of Chamberlain's worst ever attacks of gout, his perennial and indulgent-sounding malady, although undeserved by his lifestyle. He was absent throughout much of the

Finance Bill, which was ably conducted by Major Walter Elliot, as his Financial Secretary was then described by Hansard. He even contemplated resignation on the ground of long-term ill-health. But he was almost as much of a false resigner as Gladstone had been under Palmerston, and this was not taken too seriously. He was back for the final stages of the Finance Bill, which became law (very early) on 16 June, and in Lausanne for the opening of the war debts conference on the following day.

At both appearances his status as a weary but indomitable Titan, carrying the honour of his country and the problems of the world upon his shoulders, was enhanced by his appearing, not exactly as a 'goat-footed bard' in Keynes's famous phrase about Lloyd George, than which few descriptions would have been less appropriate to Chamberlain, but at least as a semi-lame Savonarola, with one foot in a gout-boot. At Lausanne he was accompanied by MacDonald, although his growing sense of indispensability made him see it rather the other way round. 'The P.M. is I think getting to rely on my help very much,' he wrote to his sister Ida on 4 July. 'He has a good deal of difficulty in following the more technical side and he doesn't understand French, so he likes to have me about and in fact won't conduct any conversations with the other delegations without having me there too.' (This picture of himself as the sophisticated cicerone leading MacDonald by the hand through the labyrinth of Europe might have been more convincing had he not subsequently confessed that he himself could not speak French at all easily, but 'could understand it', a frequently expressed cliché which runs counter to the hard fact that it is much more difficult to understand the nuances of a language well enough to be able sensibly to negotiate in it than it is rudimentarily to speak it.) Then, in much the same self-praising genre, he wrote to another sister in October of the same year, 'it amuses me to find a new policy for each of my colleagues in turn'. (Perhaps, just as it was said to be difficult for a man to be hero to his valet, so was it too easy for him to be one to his sisters.)

At Lausanne he opened firmly for all-round cancellation of war debts. This being unacceptable in principle to the French, he was then forced to look for more serpentine methods of dispersing the enervating weight of reparations, which he effectively did by about 6 July. This result was greatly assisted by the surprisingly good and close relations which he had succeeded in establishing with Edouard Herriot, the Radical Socialist from Lyon who was part of the République des Camarades, but one of the very best parts of it.

In the middle of the Lausanne Conference he returned to London for a few days to announce the major debt-conversion scheme on which he had been working for some time: £2,000 million of 5 per cent War Loan was converted into a 3½ per cent stock. There was a 92 per cent acceptance at the new rate, which exceeded expectations, saved the Exchequer £40 million in interest charges (over 5 per cent of the total budget), and perhaps even more importantly moved the great mass of high-interest-bearing debt which, in his for once vivid phrase, had been 'hanging like a cloud over the capital market' and preventing any general move to lower rates. The success of this operation, which was a deserved personal success for Chamberlain, was also an important step towards the cheap money which was one of the best features of the British economy in the 1930s, and a major factor in the private-house construction boom which gained momentum a year or so later.

After 1932 Chamberlain was not again subject to such a demanding series of events (the achievement of the general tariff, the sombre budget, gout, the Lausanne debt conference, the debts-conversion operation, the Ottawa Imperial Conference, the resignation of the Liberal minsters) until well into his premiership. His clear if sometimes narrow-sighted powers of decision, contrasted with the differing mistinesses of his Prime Minister MacDonald and his party leader Baldwin, made 1932, when he was sixty-three, the year when he firmly established himself as the man of power, if not particularly of popularity, within the somewhat amorphous mass of the National government.

The budgets of 1933, 1934 and 1935 followed in an orderly and unexciting way. In April 1933, with the unemployment peak of just over three million (in relation to the size of the insured population a far worse proportion than would be represented by the same figure today) only a month or so past, he was much criticized for his continued rigidity. There were no concessions of any significance, just a prim scepticism. Any adventurism, whether played with by young Tory ministers and MPs, to whom he contemptuously referred as 'the Boys' Brigade', or advocated by Keynes, *The Times*, the *Daily Mail* and the *Daily Express*, was firmly dismissed, and its burial accompanied by a fanfare of national complacency: 'Of all countries passing through these difficult times the one that has stood the test with the greatest measure of success is the United Kingdom.'

There were indeed several foreshadowings of John Major's defensive propaganda up to and around the 1997 election in Chamberlain's presentation of those days. He was aware of and resented the fact that many looked upon him as dull. 'There are some who think that I am over-cautious, – timid, Amery calls it – humdrum, commonplace and unenterprising. But I know that charge is groundless, or I should not have been the one to produce . . .' (there followed a catalogue of four or five claimed innovative measures; the recipient of this letter was again a sister). Then in a speech at Cambridge he was plaintive about 'the false suggestion that this is a safety-first government destitute of new ideas [when it is] in fact continually introducing changes of a really revolutionary character'. And in 1935, when a measure of recovery was certainly under way, he illustrated his 'Britain's booming' theme with a simple consumer-society test which was more statistically impressive than medically reassuring. The British people, he said, 'had sweetened their lives' with 80,000 tons more sugar than in the previous year, and had also smoked 2,600 million more cigarettes, spent £2.75 million more on entertainments attracting duty and 'washed away their troubles' with an extra 270 million pints of beer.

In fact, however, his economic policy, although founded on a financial caution which produced a moderate (but doubtfully appropriate) budget surplus for each of the difficult years of 1932–3, 1933–4 and 1934–5, would have appeared excessively corporatist and *dirigiste* by the standards of Mr Major, and maybe by those of Mr Blair too. He was certainly not a Free Trader and he was not really a market economist – it is indeed difficult to be one without the other. On the contrary he instinctively used his powers and influence in favour of amalgamations and managed markets. The measures of which he was most proud were, first, the protection and cartelization of the iron and steel industry, with a considerable increase in its output; second, the provision of £35 million of public money for the publicly owned monopoly of the London Passenger Transport Board, an investment which gave Britain for a time the most efficient and the most design-conscious underground system in the world; third, a big revival in protected agriculture, with an increase of 44 per cent in the acreage under wheat, which brought it to its highest level since the 1890s opening up of the prairies, and with sugar-beet cultivation becoming, with a public refining board, as highly protected as it was tightly organized; and fourth, the provision of crucial state finance so that the giant Cunard hull which became the *Queen Mary* should be completed (very much a personal Chamberlain initiative) with the subsidy also used as a lever to promote a merger of the Cunard and the White Star lines. Most businessmen, particularly those in politics, preached competition for others while seeking monopoly for themselves. Chamberlain, an ex-businessman, was unusual in promoting near monopoly for others, at any rate in the depressed trading conditions of the mid-1930s, while welcoming with his usual hubris highly competitive politics for himself.

In his budget of 1934, which in a Dickensian literary flight he described as the end of *Bleak House*, with a prospect of *Great Expectations* to come, he removed the additional sixpence on the standard rate of income tax which had been imposed in 1931, restored the traumatic cut in unemployment benefit of that crisis year, and also halved the cuts in the pay of state and local government employees which had accompanied it. In the 1935 budget he restored the other half, while making only a fairly modest claim for the achievement of the past three and a half years. 'Broadly speaking,' he said, 'we may say that we have recovered in this country 80 per cent of our prosperity.'

Although Chamberlain was to remain at the Exchequer for another two years, this 1935 budget marked an important break-point in the history of the 1930s. First it was soon followed by the end of MacDonald's premiership and thus of the early phase of the National government. Under Baldwin for the next two years the government did not become better or worse (although it would have been very difficult to imagine 'Ramshackle Mac', in his friend Lady Londonderry's cruel phrase, trying to nudge King Edward VIII into abdication) but it became increasingly difficult to see it as anything other than a Conservative government with a thin slice of Simonite Liberals, natural eliders to the right in any event, added like a poor ration of *foie gras* on a *tournedos rossini*.

The 1935 budget and the subsequent major Cabinet reshuffle were also the gateway to the 1935 general election, which the government won only slightly less handsomely than it had done in 1931. Labour representation increased, but only to 157 MPs. Even more important were the compelling demands from 1935 onwards of the need for rearmament expenditure on the mind of Neville Chamberlain. He could rigidly resist the demands (from Lloyd George *inter alia*) for public works à la New Deal as a cure for unemployment. Roosevelt and Lloyd George were his twin *bêtes noires*, and when he could get them both in the same sights he was particularly scornful of the chimerical nature of their quack remedies. But the straight-ahead clear-sightedness of his mind made him give an altogether different order of priority to the need to strengthen Britain's defences.

Hitler had been in power since January 1933, but it was only after about two years that he began to seem a serious external menace.

Chamberlain's mind was naturally attuned to a strong defence policy. It was in line with his father's latter-day imperialism and with his own Midlands arms-manufacturing background. Furthermore the Labour party's ambiguity on the issue (resist aggression but do not spend money on defence) aroused his particular contempt on grounds equally of simplistic logic and natural partisanship.

Chamberlain was strong on both. A splendid example of his partisanship was provided on 29 April 1933 when he wrote (as usual to a sister) after reading Volume II of Garvin's life of his father: 'I particularly admire the way Gladstone is treated. The wickedness of the old man, his cunning and treachery, and his determination to get his own way while he has time, are plain to see. I feel my old resentments burn up again as I read.'

At the end of 1934 there had been a strong attempt to make Neville Chamberlain Foreign Secretary in place of Simon, whose poor performance in that role was thought to be dragging the Conservative cause down with him. Chamberlain had resisted this, showing a considerable shrewdness about the location both of his own talents and of power within the government. He added the odd argument that he could not afford the expenses of the Foreign Office, never previously (or subsequently) deployed and which does not seem compatible with the tenancies of, say, his brother Austen or Arthur Henderson, neither of whom had as secure a financial base as Neville.

Remaining firmly fixed at the Treasury did not prevent some flexing of Chamberlain's foreign policy muscles. The Disarmament Conference finally collapsed in January 1934. Although it had never attracted Chamberlain's enthusiasm, offering too hazy a hope for his precise intelligence, its end, together with the new and menacing noises coming from Berlin, made him realize that the low and declining British military expenditure of the 1920s was a thing of the past. By March 1934 he was writing of 'the staggering prospect of spending 85 million £ on rearmament', which was hardly in itself enticing to a precise and conservative Chancellor. Indeed before embracing the need he made a surprisingly strong ploy in a collective direction, strongly advocating for six months or so what he called a 'limited liability force', but which would in effect (and he did not dodge the term) be an international police force. It would not be universal but be associated with mutual frontier guarantees by 'say Germany, France, Italy, U.K., Poland and Czechoslovakia'.

Equally he was at first in favour of strong sanctions against Italy when Mussolini embarked on the Abyssinian adventure in 1935. With his black and white mind he was willing to bite on the bullet of oil sanctions, the only ones likely to be effective, and from which many of his colleagues shied away as being therefore too dangerous. But he also put in a safety net, rather like the award to Shylock of being able to have his pound of flesh but not a drop of blood. He would only participate in sanctions to the extent that the French did too, and the chances of their whole-hearted support with Laval, followed by Flandin as Foreign Minister, were minimal. And then, in June 1936, when sanctions had failed and Mussolini had been allowed to destroy the not very secure mechanism of the Abyssinian state, he was the first to speak out brutally and resolutely. The continuance of ineffective sanctions, he said, was 'the very midsummer of madness'. He liked pointing out the absence of emperors' clothes. Thereafter he placed no reliance on the League or on any collective arrangements. It was on a combination of strengthening Britain's defences, above all its air force, and seeking bilateral accommodation with both Hitler and Mussolini that he set his faith. The alliance with France he accepted (although never feeling the romantic infection of 'French flu' which long affected both his brother Austen and Churchill), but not wishing for wider entanglements. And the shuffling of responsibility between London and Paris at the time of Hitler's reoccupation of the Rhineland in the spring of 1936 did not suggest that even that limited partnership was in very good working order.

Meanwhile Baldwin's third premiership was running its brief course. The new Prime Minister's first task was to win the election and this was satisfactorily achieved in November. Baldwin's spirits and vitality, never very high throughout this final phase of his career, were then further depressed by the fiasco of the Hoare/Laval pact and what was thought to be his weak, almost contemptible handling of it. Throughout the first nine months of 1936 he was very low, and from June to October was effectively suffering or convalescing from nervous prostration. His most popular decision of this period was to fix and announce the date of his retirement, which was to be May 1937.

There was no substantial doubt that Chamberlain would be his successor. There was however a curious combination of conflicting Tory emotions. There was quite widespread regret that he had not succeeded MacDonald direct in 1935. He would hardly have provided a change of generation (MacDonald was born in 1866, Baldwin in 1867 and Chamberlain in 1869), but at least a change to greater vigour. But when MacDonald went, the King just sent for Baldwin, which was still the constitutional and Conservative party practice of those days. Second, and despite this, there was in 1937 a sense of inevitability rather than enthusiasm about Chamberlain's succession. There were said to be many MPs who would have preferred Sir Thomas Inskip (the Minister for the Co-ordination of Defence), whose appointment to that office had been described as the most unconvincing since Caligula made his horse a consul, which suggested that their preference was the rough equivalent of saying they wanted anyone other than Neville.

Nonetheless Chamberlain's succession was one of the only four almost effortless ones this century. The other three were Balfour in 1902, which led to the electoral disaster of 1906, although with some considerable half-hidden achievements on the way; Asquith in 1908, which led to one of the longest and most productive peacetime premierships; and Eden in 1955, which led to Suez. The record of inevitable successions, with the exception of Asquith, was not a good one. Probably, however, Chamberlain's three-year appendage to the long leadership of Baldwin was more akin to Callaghan's succession to Wilson, which was not effortless. It began, like Chamberlain's premiership, with the virtue of a greater tautness of government. Nevertheless they both ended, in the context of history, as postscripts to the much longer if not necessarily more distinguished reigns of their predecessors, Baldwin and Wilson. And both their premierships ended badly, unlike the unforced retirements of their respective predecessors. The country's prospects in May 1940, which was Chamberlain's legacy, were however a great deal worse than the privations of Callaghan's 'winter of discontent', of which so much has been made.

In that summer of 1937 Chamberlain was sixty-six and a half, and among a small handful of Prime Ministers who had first taken over 10 Downing Street as late in life as that. Despite this late start at the summit Chamberlain came to his final short and disastrous phase with an exceptionally active and productive fifteen years of political service behind him. Had he retired with Baldwin and let the leadership pass to a younger generation, he would still have been a considerable figure, and indeed a more creditable one, in inter-war history. Campbell-Bannerman, Baldwin, Attlee, Home, Heath, Thatcher and Major would have left little mark if, after other offices, they had not attained the topmost rank. Chamberlain was emphatically not in this category. He was more like Eden in this respect: *omnia consensu capax imperii nisi imperasset*. (Everyone believed him capable of being an emperor until he actually became one.)

In one sense he began well. There were numerous tributes to the improved tone which he gave the Cabinet. There was a similar reaction when Callaghan took over from Wilson thirty-nine years later. At the same time, and surprisingly for one so experienced and so generally competent, he left a nasty departmental mess for his successor as Chancellor (John Simon) to clear up. Chamberlain had announced in his 1937 budget a new National Defence Contribution along the lines of the First World War excess profits tax, in other words not on profits as such but on their growth. His intention was the worthy one of preventing the owners of industry doing too well out of rearmament. But the method chosen was tailor-made to produce manifest inequity and to freeze the pattern of British business. The proposal provoked strong opposition, in Parliament (from the government's own back benchers), in the press and from representative business institutions. Indeed the last group volunteered to produce the same amount of revenue from a straight additional tax on *all* profits. Simon (obviously with the concurrence of the new Prime Minister) had to organize the retreat. Three weeks into his Chancellorship he announced a major recasting of the Finance Bill along the lines proposed by the industrial interests.

The whole chapter was far from being a nice house-warming present for Chamberlain as he moved into 10 Downing Street, but he was too intent on putting his own pattern upon the government for it to be much more than a passing irritation. In particular he was concerned to reassert Prime Ministerial control over foreign policy – in a way that it had not existed, except for the nine months when Ramsay MacDonald actually was his own Foreign Secretary, since the fall of Lloyd George – although this was not a precedent which Chamberlain would have wished to cite. Baldwin, particularly in the two years of his third and final premiership, was a very easy-going head of government. And even in the plenitude of his power and energy in 1924–9 he had rigidly refrained from interfering in Austen Chamberlain's Foreign Office principality.

Neville Chamberlain had no intention of continuing the non-intervention from which his half-brother had so signally benefited. The Foreign Secretary whom he inherited was Anthony Eden, who had served for eighteen months under Baldwin and was to last another nine under Chamberlain. Eden was young (nearly thirty years Chamberlain's junior), vain, prickly in private although urbane in public, and very conscious of his own almost iconic popularity. Although enjoying his high office, he was combustible material in any dispute about prerogatives with the Prime Minister.

Nevertheless Eden did not display overt resentment at the tightening of Downing Street control. 'I do hope that you will never for an instant feel that any interest you take in foreign affairs, however close, could ever be resented by me,' he wrote to Chamberlain as late as 9 January 1938. It must of course be allowed first that, while letters are likely to be a truer indication of settled states of mind than transcripts of telephone calls, ministers in jobs they like, unless engaged in a critical dispute, tend to err on the side of amenability in writing to the Prime Minister; and, second, that to deny a resentment is almost to confirm its near existence. However the letter showed that Eden had ingested Chamberlain's two 'sinews of command' changes without approaching boiling point. The first was the switch of Sir Horace Wilson into a foreign affairs role. Wilson's nominal position was that of chief industrial adviser to the government, after a spell as permanent secretary of the Ministry of Labour. Baldwin had however brought him into 10 Downing Street in a general advisory role. But he neither sought much advice on foreign affairs nor looked to Wilson to give it. Under Chamberlain Wilson quickly acquired much of the influence which a combination of Charles Powell and Percy Cradock had under Mrs Thatcher, and his actitivies were heavily concentrated on external issues. By the time of Chamberlain's three excursions to Germany in September 1938, which led up to the Munich Agreement, his role had become central. He, and no Foreign Office minister or official, was present at the crucial talks between Chamberlain and Hitler.

For a possible effect on ministerial relationships, however, the comparison which most springs to mind is not with Powell or Cradock but with Professor Walters, Mrs Thatcher's economic guru, whose influence had such an explosive effect upon her relations with Chancellor Nigel Lawson. Wilson did not however appear to have a comparable impact upon Eden. Nor did the change in the Foreign Office itself which was engineered at the New Year of 1938. Sir Robert Vansittart, who had been permanent under-secretary since 1930 but was two years short of retirement and who was strongly against the appeasement of Germany, partly for good and partly for bad reasons, was shunted upstairs. He became chief diplomatic adviser to the government, and Sir Alexander Cadogan, thought to be more amenable (but obviously no one at that time knew of the extreme acerbity of his comments on all politicians in his wartime diaries) became PUS. This new disposition appears to have suited both Chamberlain and Eden, although the latter should have been more wary, for it had the perverse effect of making the chief industrial adviser in 10 Downing Street a far more powerful influence upon the government's diplomacy than was the chief diplomatic adviser in the Foreign Office.

Six weeks or so later the row which led to Eden's resignation broke out. No doubt there had been a gradual accumulation of grievance, as is almost invariably the case with resignations. The immediate causes were however fairly precise. Chamberlain wanted to press ahead with bilateral talks with Mussolini, which would necessarily involve the *de jure* recognition of the Italian conquest of Abyssinia. Eden was very doubtful of the wisdom of this and the issue was complicated by some 'stage farce' manoeuvring, which Eden thought was deliberately behind his back, in which Grandi the Italian ambassador in London, Ivy Chamberlain, Austen's widow who was wintering in Rome, and Sir Joseph Ball, a Conservative Central Office/M15 figure, all played a part. Interlinked with this was Chamberlain's rejection of a somewhat hazy Roosevelt proposal to summon an international peace and security conference in Washington. Chamberlain, privately but decisively, poured cold water upon it on the grounds that it was not clearly thought out, which it was not, and that it would 'excite the derision of Germany and Italy', which in view of what happened to both their regimes within seven years under essentially Roosevelt-deployed power was not a consideration notable for either relevance or prescience. More immediately he thought it would get in the way of his eagerly sought talks with Italy.

Eden, with wider vision, thought that anything which embroiled the United States with Europe, however tentatively, was worth more than a minuet with Counts Grandi and Ciano. And Churchill retrospectively gave greater force to the same thought when he wrote in his *War Memoirs* of Chamberlain's rejection of Roosevelt's flicker of an initiative as 'the loss of this last frail chance to save the world from tyranny otherwise than by war'. Chamberlain's attitude to the possibility of Eden's resignation, which came over the horizon about 17 February, is well summed up by three sentences which he wrote in a continuous long diary entry which he dated '19 to 27:2:1938'. First he recorded that Ivy Chamberlain 'had written to me of the strong dislike and distrust with which Eden was regarded [in Rome] and the general belief that he did not want better relations'. Second, 'I told Horace Wilson on Friday morning [18 February] that I was determined to stand firm [a curious phrase to use for a resolution to appease] even though it meant losing my Foreign Secretary'. Third, and for the same day: 'I told A.E. that he had missed one opportunity after another of advancing towards peace; he had one more chance, probably the last, and he was wanting to throw it away.'

Eden resigned on 20 February. The Cabinet overwhelmingly supported Chamberlain. The country was more split. But with the vast parliamentary majority, with an election at least two years away, and with Eden's very hesitant handling of his position off-shore of the government (Michael Heseltine did a good deal better after 1986, even though Eden ended up, disastrously, with the premiership and Heseltine did not), Chamberlain's authority was not seriously shaken, and the consequent changes further increased his grip on foreign policy.

Halifax became Foreign Secretary. R. A. Butler became the sole representative of the Foreign Office in the Commons, and Chamberlain, in order to meet strong opposition criticism of this arrangement, undertook to answer major Foreign Office questions himself. This was a burden for a Prime Minister (and one which Baldwin or Attlee would have been very reluctant to accept), but Chamberlain never minded burdens, and it gave him, as it were, a statutory right of full interference. The relationship of Halifax (the 'Holy Fox' in the title of Andrew Roberts's admirable biography of him, written with all the perceptive discrimination of youth, before success and ideology began to take over) to the person of Chamberlain and the policy of appeasement is a complex and fascinating subject. Not merely in the first flush of his appointment but for some time thereafter he was undoubtedly an easier Foreign Secretary for the Prime Minister than Eden had been. He accepted a wholly subordinate role and when Chamberlain began his shuttle diplomacy to Germany seemed content with seeing the Prime Minister off on the (London) tarmac with a wave of his bowler hat and helping to welcome him back with cheers when he returned. He was however in advance of Chamberlain in deciding that, so far as Hitler's behaviour was concerned, enough was enough. He was harder against the Godesberg terms, more brutal in form although the others were equally so in substance, which Hitler intermediately put forward between Berchtesgaden and Munich. And when Hitler tore up any idea of a binding agreement and occupied Prague in the spring of 1939, he was growling hard. Partly as a result of this, a large section of the Labour leadership would most mistakenly have preferred him to Churchill as the new head of the government in May 1940.

Yet there was a paradox. Chamberlain's self-righteous and self-centred conviction that appeasement deserved success, that Hitler indeed owed it to him, made him more reluctant to acknowledge the collapse of the policy in the spring of 1939. But Halifax's deep streak of Christian pessimism made him even more of an appeaser for all seasons than was the Prime Minister. When the war was six months old, when Hitler had resolutely refused 'to miss the bus' (in Chamberlain's spectacularly ill-chosen phrase of early April 1940), when the Norwegian campaign had been lost as well as the debate which followed it, Chamberlain knew that the game with Hitler was up. Indeed very soon after accepting the Lord Presidency in Churchill's War Cabinet of five, he delivered a broadcast of almost hysterical loyalty to his successor and hatred of Hitler, 'that wild beast who has sprung out of his lair'.

Halifax, perhaps because he had never shared Chamberlain's facile optimism about a permanent peace between Britain and Germany, was a more determined defeatist and persistent appeaser. His analogue to Chamberlain's denunciation was a homily saying that the best thing he could recommend to the British people was the habit and power of prayer. And in the desperate days at the end of June 1940, he initiated a day and a half of Cabinet discussion, only very reluctantly and for a short distance supported by Chamberlain, about the possibility of a negotiated peace, which might preserve England, not as an empire or as a world power, but as a little island of gentle landscape and civilized and hierarchical manners off-shore from a Nazi-dominated Europe. The other three, Churchill, Attlee and Greenwood, were resolutely opposed, and with Chamberlain eventually swinging to them there was a firm four-to-one majority against any such approach. But it was not surprising that at the end of the year Churchill seized an opportunity to pack Halifax safely off to Washington, where, to complete the paradoxes, he gradually and loyally achieved an outstanding success as the ambassador of Britain's resistance.

Broadly speaking, therefore, Chamberlain was able to pursue almost unimpeded his own foreign policy between the resignation of Eden in February 1938 and the collapse of such limited faith as he had reposed in Hitler in the spring of 1939. It was not a policy imposed on a reluctant Cabinet. Most of its members supported it enthusiastically. This was particularly true of Simon and Hoare, who with Halifax and Chamberlain himself constituted a solid inner core. Nevertheless it was very much Chamberlain's policy. He was the instigator and often the executant of it. He was a strong and pro-active Prime Minister. It would, for instance, have been impossible to imagine Baldwin behaving as

Chamberlain did at the height of the Czech crisis in the second half of September 1938. Apart from anything else he would never have got into an aeroplane and flown three times to Germany.

Without Chamberlain the approach to the Munich settlement would not therefore have evolved in the way that it did. And as that was the epitome of his attempt at peace by appeasement it is fair that it should be central to any judgement of his foreign policy. It should be said straightaway that, even with the knowledge that it led not to an era of peace but to Hitler's subsequent aggressions and exterminations and to a six-year war in the early part of which Britain teetered on the edge of the greatest defeat in its history, there is a substantial 'low case' for Munich. The trouble is that it was not the case which Chamberlain was seduced by a mixture of hubris and applause into making.

By the 'low case' I mean that it was a depressing but necessary (and therefore wise) temporary arrangement. We were in no state to fight, so the argument runs. We had few aeroplanes and no adequate framework of air-raid precautions. The country was still not reconciled to the inevitability of war as was shown by the vast out-pouring of relief which greeted Chamberlain's throwing of the Czechs to the wolves. The French were blowing hot and cold, the Russians were unpredictable, Roosevelt was not likely to be of much help, even for *matériel*, before the 1940 election, at which, in 1938, there was no reason to think that he would even be a candidate. And, worst of all for British traditionalists, discouraging messages were coming in from the Dominion governments; New Zealand might be all right, but Canada, Australia and South Africa were very wobbly.

Not all these factors moved favourably in the course of the next year. France remained shaky and Russia moved from being unpredictable to being a partner in the Nazi/Soviet pact. Exactly how the balance of armaments between Britain and Germany moved is a matter for dispute, but we at least had the Anderson shelters and enough planes not to lose the Battle of Britain in 1940. Where the movement was most favourable was in the growth of a unity of inevitability in Britain and in a dramatic stiffening of Dominion opinion. All of this goes some way to justify the Halifax view that Munich was 'a horrible and wretched business – but the lesser of two evils'.

It certainly does not justify the view into which Chamberlain allowed himself to be pushed without too much difficulty that he was a prince of peace and that Munich was not a tactical withdrawal but a great and imaginative long-term settlement which almost guaranteed the future.

What else was he doing when he waved his piece of paper at Heston aerodrome? Or later when he told the crowd outside his house, 'This is the second time in our history that there has come back from Germany peace with honour. I believe it is peace for our time'? After the emotional and physical strain of the past few days, and responding to almost hysterical acclaim, it was natural that he should succumb to temptations of rhetoric, although Disraeli was almost the most incongruous of all the Prime Ministers for Chamberlain to summon up for comparison. Much more important however, was the complete incompatibility of what he there said, and went on saying in less dramatic and euphoric shape for many months to come, with the 'low' and sustainable case for Munich. If he was merely making a tactical withdrawal in order to prepare on more favourable ground for a necessary conflict in the following year, it was the reverse of what he ought to have been telling the British people.

Chamberlain remained Prime Minister for nineteen months after Munich, eleven of them in peace and eight of them in war. In neither phase was he near his best. He had no public inspirational quality, although he attracted the loyalty and affection of those who knew him well, from Jock Colville to King George VI, both of whom (and some others too) took several months to adjust in May 1940 to the mountebank style, as they were inclined to regard it, of Churchill. Chamberlain continued to be an efficient administrator, and imposed an orderly queue on competing service demands at the turnstile of rearmament. But he lacked any breadth of tolerance. Halifax at the time of the Czech crisis wanted him to broaden his government, certainly to the extent of bringing back Churchill and Eden into Conservative communion and maybe to that of including the Labour and Liberal leaders. This however had elements of Groucho Marx's club joke about it. He did not want them, and they would not have joined, under him, if he had invited them. His appointments of 1938–9 were Lord Stanhope in place of Duff Cooper (resigned over Munich) as First Lord of the Admiralty in October, John Anderson, wisely authoritative but with nil public impact, as Minister of Home Security in November, and Leslie Burgin, so little known even at the time that he could hardly be described as forgotten, as Minister of Supply in January. Yet, when immediately after the outbreak of war he was at last persuaded to bring in Churchill as First Lord, he and Chamberlain got on remarkably well, so much so that Simon, until then the Prime Minister's principal Cabinet confidant, felt his nose put out of joint.

Chamberlain sustained the outbreak of war with what can best be described as a sombre self-regarding dignity. His broadcast on Sunday, 3 September 1939 was a remarkable example of all these attributes: 'You can imagine what a bitter blow it is to me that all my long struggle to win peace has failed. Yet I cannot believe that there is anything more or anything different which I could have done which would have been more successful.' He sustained the same note when the shadows began to close upon his premiership after the Norway débâcle. Superficially he was unfairly a victim of that defeat. Churchill was as much to blame as he was. But time was running out for one and beginning for the other. In the crucial debate he appealed to his friends to support him. It was an ill-judged but not a ludicrous appeal. He had a lot of friends, but matters had become too grave for friendship to be determinant. And, as in September 1939, the note struck was too personal.

He took a good deal of persuading that he ought to go, but once he was so convinced (the highly Chamberlainite Kingsley Wood playing a brave and maybe crucial role in this process) he accepted the final defeat without rancour, as he did the last terrible six months of his life. He fell in May, he was stricken by desperate illness in July, he resigned as Lord President in September, he died in November. The only thing in which he was lucky at the end was that he was removed from the scene, so that when, a little later in the war, scapegoats were sought for the failure of appeasement and preparedness the accusatory beam fell upon the living Baldwin and not upon his dead successor.

Neville was at once the most successful, the most reviled and the most miserably ending of the Chamberlains. He was probably also the most clear- but narrow-sighted of them. Nineteen-forty brought the dynasty to an end, seventy years after it had erupted on to first the Birmingham and then the national scene, which was rather longer than the Kennedy span in Massachusetts and Washington, although both the virtues and vices of the two families could hardly have been more different.

SIR JOHN SIMON

SIR JOHN SIMON (the 'Sir', as with several ex-law officer knights, Sir William Harcourt – despite his already described initial reluctance to take the title – Sir Stafford Cripps, even Sir Geoffrey Howe, assumed the status almost of an additional Christian name, so that he sounded half-naked without it) became Chancellor of the Exchequer when Neville Chamberlain became Prime Minister in June 1937. This was part of a long Indian summer, although one of fluctuating weather, in which, after fifteen and a half years out of office, Simon reappeared in Whitehall at the age of fifty-eight and spent the years between then and seventy-two in an unprecedented tour around all the major offices of state – except for that of Prime Minister. James Callaghan, forty years his junior, was his only rival on the historic-offices sightseeing bus, although Callaghan, not being a lawyer, which Simon most conspicuously was, had to miss a visit to the Lord Chancellorship. Callaghan became Prime Minister instead, an office for which the otherwise omnicompetent Simon was never seriously considered. This was because Simon throughout a long ministerial career, which spanned thirty-five years, was to an unusual and possibly unjust degree neither liked nor trusted.

In the circumstances his considerable, superficially even dazzling, success was a remarkable achievement, although one which seemed to give him little pleasure. He was always looking for the few things that he could not attain: in politics a route to the supreme office and the ability to inspire followers; and in more private life making chilling and ineffective attempts at an easy camaraderie which constantly eluded him, which indeed, it would almost be true to say, he unconsciously repelled with every step he took in the direction of achieving it.

Examples of his fellowship-repellent quality (except at All Souls College, Oxford, where, using the word in a different sense, he obtained one in 1897, and actively retained it for the remaining fifty-six years of his life) are enshrined in a series of anecdotes or remarks made up in varying proportions of the amusing and the blood-chilling. Asquith, who was his first head of government, gave him the private sobriquet of 'the Impeccable' and, after a series of chance social encounters, complained that 'the Impeccable' was becoming 'the Inevitable'. Neville Chamberlain, who was his penultimate head of government and the one to whom he felt himself closest, wrote many years after Asquith: 'I am always trying to like him, and believing I shall succeed when something crops up to put me off.' Hugh Dalton, admittedly a strong political opponent and a man with a liking for harsh and clanging phrases, who himself shared some, but by no means all, of Simon's characteristics, including the look of a worldly prelate and a propensity to call people by the wrong Christian names, referred to him as 'the snakiest of the lot'. A profile of Simon written for the *New Statesman*, also politically hostile of course, spoke of 'many of those who have shivered as he took their arm'. Harold Nicolson, more (politically) neutral, made the word flesh by recording in his diary for 19 October 1944: 'As I walked out [from St Paul's Cathedral] I felt my arm gripped from behind. It was the Lord Chancellor . . . God, what a toad and a worm Simon is!'

Lloyd George, with whom until 1931 Simon shared at least nominal membership of the same party and a mutual antipathy which in politics can only be achieved in such proximity, coined two of his most famous pieces of invective for Simon. In the summer of 1931, before the formation of the National government, when Simon resigned the Liberal whip and became a Tory ally, Lloyd George spoke of Simon's effective crossing of the floor in terms which began with a display of tolerance. He did not object to Simon changing his opinions: 'Greater men have done it in the past, but . . . they, at any rate, did not leave behind them the slime of hypocrisy in passing from one side to another.' Then on an occasion less precisely documented, he observed that Simon had 'sat on the fence so long that the iron has entered into his soul'.

Simon's failures in friendship were rarely for want of trying. He embarrassed a mid-1930s Cabinet by inviting his colleagues to call him 'Jack'. J. H. Thomas, the irrepressible ex-railway union leader who was soon to be disgraced by the passing on for gain of budget secrets, was the only one who could bring himself to do so, although Neville Chamberlain got rather awkwardly as far as 'John'. Then, in the early post-1945 years, Simon endeavoured to strike up an improbable friendship with G. D. H. Cole, the too-prolific but socially fastidious Left Book Club author of the 1930s who had become a professorial fellow of

All Souls. Returning from a weekend at that college on a Monday morning, Simon encountered Cole on the platform of Oxford station and greeted him with his well-known false bonhomie. As the London train came in, Cole, disapproving of Simon and eager to make a display of semi-proletarianism as well as to escape, said, 'I must get along to my third-class [for such was then the description of the modern standard class] compartment,' and disappeared down the platform. Simon, determined not to be frustrated in his search for ecumenical companionship, announced that he always travelled 'third' himself and loped after him. In those days railway tickets were neat little cardboard rectangles about two inches by one, first-class ones virginally white, third-class ones more earthily green. When the ticket-collector came round they both, with varying degrees of embarrassment, produced white tickets.

Simon's barren and bloodless memoirs, published under the title of *Retrospect* in 1952, were of interest primarily because they exposed his fatal capacity to turn even his substantial if partial triumphs into anti-climatic ashes. He had full respect for worldly success and 'glittering prizes' in the phrase coined by Birkenhead, his Wadham College contemporary, but in many ways his temperamental opposite. An unusual proportion of the prizes he did achieve. Yet, as Nicolson, varying the metaphor, put it in his review of *Retrospect*: 'The nectarines and peaches of office dropped one by one into Lord Simon's hands; he describes them as if they were a bag of prunes ... [He] manifests no pleasure [in himself].' A still more mordant summing up of the unsym-pathetic poignancy of Simon was supplied by George Edinger, a notable journalist of the 1930s: 'Often he would touch with his finger-tips the ivory gates and the golden – and he never got inside. Perhaps he annoyed the gate-keeper by slapping him on the shoulder and calling him by the wrong name.'

It all sounds a little too bad to be true. Simon was very clever, with one of the best analytical brains of his generation, although lacking both originality and power of decision. Once he had analysed a problem and outlined the various courses of action he had done about as much as he could contribute towards its solution. As he was also very hard-working, this lucidity of analysis made him a brilliant advocate, particularly in complicated commercial cases before high-ranking judges; he was less good before juries. But as these cases were precisely those which attracted the highest fees he was widely thought during the somewhat intermittent periods when he devoted himself principally to the law to be the highest earning of all the famous advocates of the

1920s. As Lord Chancellor in the 1940s he discharged the judicial aspects of that office with as great a distinction as any of this century's occupants of the Woolsack. His indecisiveness did not seem here to inhibit him.

Both the bar and the bench, however, were for Simon very second-rate occupations compared with politics and government. And here his lack of decisiveness and self-conviction more than outweighed his forensic skills. Particularly when he was Foreign Secretary between 1931 and 1935 he emerged as clearly deficient in the central qualities necessary in a powerful and successful senior minister. He was the antithesis of, say, Ernest Bevin, who meshed with his officials so that *they* strove hard to put *his* far-sighted and original but often inchoate ideas into a persuasive and coherent form which *he* then proceeded to drive through the Cabinet and to defend with massive truculence before Parliament, party and public. Simon was often the despair of his officials, went before the Cabinet without knowing his own mind, had a solution imposed upon him by others, and, perhaps not unnaturally in the circumstances, defended it only weakly in public.

Yet, breaking the normal rule that people most like doing those things at which they are best, he set public service well above his legal triumphs. He was not grasping for money. He had enough, although in 1933 he sold the rather grand manor house near Banbury which he had acquired twenty-two years before as a young (thirty-seven) KC MP, and transferred to a more modest establishment alongside a suburban golf-course. And he never appeared to hesitate about accepting a public assignment at vast 'opportunity cost' whenever one of sufficient import-ance was suggested. He was also reported to be unobtrusively generous, to All Souls College, to young barristers and to the children of his less fortunate contemporaries. And he was, without question, an exception-ally devoted son to his mother, who lived until 1936, when Simon was sixty-three.

Perhaps Simon's real trouble was that there was something in his personality which made people, by no means necessarily his enemies, suspect his motives even when he was acting disinterestedly. Neville Chamberlain had explained his devastating remark about trying to like him but not succeeding by writing: 'He has a certain air of – what is it – *slyness* which is rather disconcerting in a man of the first rank.' Thus when in his early political career he nearly resigned as Attorney-General rather than accept British entry into the 1914 War, and when seventeen months later he actually did resign against conscription from the high office of Home Secretary, to which he had been promoted at the unusually young age of forty-two and which he had occupied for only seven months, he was by any normal standards putting principle before careerism. Yet on the first occasion he was widely accused of sophistry for agonizing without eventually going, whereas Lloyd George, the evolution of whose position during those late July and early August days of 1914 was not very different from that of Simon, was allowed far more licence as he bounced within a few weeks from potential leader of the 'keep Britain out' faction to unrestrained recruiting orator, and then became the agent of victory at all costs.

At the end of 1915, on the other hand, it was Simon who actually resigned and by so doing condemned himself to an occluded middle-age. From the age of forty-two to fifty-eight, he, a natural man of government, was without any Whitehall perch. By contrast it was his allies in the conscription argument, Edward Grey, McKenna and Runciman, who reluctantly stayed in the government until they were all swept out with Asquith a year later. Yet, once again, it was Simon who got the most criticism. The almost inescapable conclusion is that Simon was something of a Dr Fell figure. It was not so much what he did as the way in which he did it. He was a man whom people loved to hate, and whose unctuousness and somewhat charmless impeccability made him more enemies than his clear intelligence and high sense of public duty made him friends. As a result, difficult though it is not to enjoy the denigration, he was probably often unfairly judged.

John Allsebrook Simon was born in 1873, a year after F. E. Smith, a year before Winston Churchill, ten years after Lloyd George, six years after Stanley Baldwin, four years after Neville Chamberlain, into a lower-middle-class household in Manchester. His father was a Congregational minister. He was an only child. His parents removed to Bath when he was ten. After another four years he went on a scholarship to Fettes College in Edinburgh, a boarding school nearly as far removed from Bath as any in the United Kingdom, except for the fortunately still-unfounded Gordonstoun and Gladstone's Episcopalian enclave Glenalmond. The tradition of Congregationalism was peripatetic, with ministers rarely being allowed to settle at a single church or even in a single locality for long periods. Even so the choice of school was carrying respect for movement to extremes, particularly as there was no Scottish connection in the Simon family. The tradition of Fettes was austere and athletic but it was also academic and, in its Edinburgh way, non-provinical. Simon gave it a start as a political breeding ground. In the three following generations it has produced two other Chancellors of the Exchequer (Selwyn Lloyd and Iain Macleod) and one Prime Minister (Tony Blair).

Although hitherto a 'mother's boy', taught a good deal at home and rather unused to other children, Simon seems to have absorbed the harshnesses of Fettes without undue early repining and to have ridden them with dominance as his five years there progressed. He became head of the school, was esteemed by both his housemaster and the headmaster, won most available prizes, and left with an open scholarship to Wadham College, Oxford. Even his sporting performance was good, although not brilliant. He retained a visiting affection for Fettes throughout his life, which was natural for his uneasiness in individual human relations directed him towards corporate loyalties, as with All Souls.

His choice of Wadham perhaps owed more to his having failed to get an equivalent scholarship at Balliol than to more positive reasons, but it was nonetheless fortunate, for he participated in and helped to make a memorable period in the history of that then small college. He and F. E. Smith arrived on the same day in October 1891, just as sixteen years later they were simultanously to become very young King's Counsel. While the strata of their social backgrounds were not very different, Smith's only a little higher in the middle class, their background ethos could hardly have been more different. Although neither manifested much religious faith they epitomized the difference between 'chapel' (Simon) and (Erastian) 'church' (Smith), as between temperance and the drinking classes, between sanctimoniousness and irreverence, between Simon's studied suavity and Smith's fondness for the brutality of the bludgeon as well as the precision of the rapier, between Simon's liking for the arguments of persuasion and Smith's for those of epigram and coruscation. They were united in their determined pursuit of the great prizes of political life and by their belief that the best route to that end, for young men of higher talent than birth, was via the law. The canard that they tossed up to decide who would join which party is not only untrue but wholly implausible. Although Simon, partly by dint of a much longer life, ended up at least as far to the right as Smith had been, their youthful (and persisting) styles left no room for doubt as to which would be attracted to the tradition of Gladstone and which to that of Disraeli.

They both became President of the Oxford Union and they both secured firsts in their final honours schools, although Simon achieved the edge by getting his in Greats, whereas Smith's was in the more vocational Jurisprudence. Simon was always somewhat the more polished scholar, which was symbolized by his securing in 1897 an All Souls prize fellowship, while Smith had to settle for becoming briefly a law don at Merton. They also, more surprisingly, played in the same Wadham rugby fifteen, in which the brightest star was C. B. Fry, the third member of that Wadham constellation, who, as clever as either of them but more athletically dexterous, chose to devote much of his life to sporting rather than party games.

After a brief few months as a *Manchester Guardian* trainee leader writer under C. P. Scott, Simon went to London at the end of 1898 and devoted himself to building up his general common law barrister's practice. He began as hesitantly as do most young barristers (£27 of earnings in his first year) which made it the more surprising that he married in 1899. His wife had been an early Oxford woman don, a niece of the historian J. R. Green and herself Vice-Principal of St Hugh's College. They had three children in little more than three years. The growth of his practice easily sustained this rapid increase in his family. But his wife's health did not. The third birth, that of a son who survived as the second Viscount Simon until 1994, killed her. Simon was naturally devastated, and there is some curious hint that as she had not been given normal medicines, maybe owing to an homeopathic fad on his part, guilt was added to grief. His experience of being left a widower with young children was not an uncommon one at the time, peculiarly and inexplicably so for politicians – Harcourt, Dilke, Joseph Chamberlain (twice), Asquith – but there is some suggestion that it may have affected Simon more permanently than it did the others and accounted for at least part of his coldness and false bonhomie. Certainly it meant that for several years, apart from trying to do his best as a single-parent father, he wholly immersed himself in eighteen hours a day of courts and briefs.

He did not marry again for over fifteen years. It was alleged that towards the end of this period he tried hard to get Mrs Ronnie Greville, the great hostess of Polesden Lacey, to marry him. Robert Boothby indeed claimed in his 1978 memoirs that Mrs Greville had shown him the spot in the park there at which Simon had fallen on his knees and implored her (in vain) to accept him. It must be said that this story comes to us with the benefit of a double filtering through minds well endowed with dramatic imaginations. L. S. Amery, however, always friendlily disposed across politics to Simon since they had been jointly elected at All Souls, provides some corroboration. He claimed that

Simon wrote Mrs Greville a letter saying that he would in consequence of his rejection 'marry the next woman whom he came across'.

This was not exactly an appropriate description for Kathleen Manning, whom he married in Paris in December 1917. She was the widow of a Dublin doctor and had for several years been the governess of Simon's then nearly grown-up children. He might however have done better to have made the purely random choice which he threatened. Kathleen Simon's most interesting feature was that she was a determined anti-slavery campaigner, who had also been a midwife in the East End of London. For the rest she appears to have been a lady of unfortunate appearance with a gift for tactless remarks, who from the late 1930s onwards became a near-alcoholic. Her health was not good during the latter period, but she nonetheless outlived her husband by a year, as he survived her various idiosyncrasies with tolerance and kindness. She may, however, have contributed to the attraction for him of the single-sex All Souls of those days.

Early in his widowerhood Simon became adopted as Liberal candidate for Walthamstow, then nominally a county division of Essex but in fact an urban sprawl with an unusually large electorate tacked on to the north-eastern side of the poor London boroughs of Hackney and Stoke Newington. There was a sitting Unionist member, but in the great swing of 1906 Simon was comfortably elected. In 1910, with the Liberal tide on the ebb, he had to face three more elections there within a year, two as a result of the rapid-fire constitutional-crisis dissolutions, and the third, an intervening by-election, because of his appointment as Solicitor-General and the pre-1918 rule which made those accepting government office reseek the mandate of their co-consituents. He survived all these contests.

Mr Solicitor, by a double paradox, had to be not only a barrister but a 'Sir'. Simon, who at that time counted as an advanced radical, made an attempt at resisting the knighthood, but his scruples were brushed aside by Asquith, as those of Harcourt had been by Gladstone. Simon, the youngest law officer for seventy-five years and not enthusiastic about being given a legal rather than a more political appointment, nonetheless made a considerable success of his new job. He coped easily with the legal aspects – court appearances for the government and on one occasion for the King in his libel action against Edward Mylius, who had accused him of bigamy, the handling of public enquiries, as after the *Titanic* disaster, and internal advice – while taking a more active political role in general debates than was normal for the junior law officer. He was nothing if not a highly effective lawyer. In October 1913, when Asquith defiantly continued the tradition of allowing the Attorney-General (Rufus Isaacs) to succeed to the pillow of the Lord Chief Justiceship (in spite of his embroilment in the Marconi scandal) Simon was his almost automatic successor.

Following the precedent of Isaacs, he was given membership of the Cabinet with the Attorneyship, a flattering but not altogether desirable arrangement, for it confused the formulation of policy with the giving of advice upon its legality and with the other quasi-judicial functions of the Attorney. It also put upon Simon a much greater if collective responsibility for general policy than would have been the case had he, as with many Attorneys, been outside the Cabinet. Filling a semi-technocratic role and hoping for a vacancy in either the Lord Chancellorship or the Lord Chief Justiceship, they had frequently done no more than subscribe to the general tenets of their party in a way that did a back-bench MP.

Simon on the other hand, and perhaps surprisingly in view of the highly careerist reputation which he subsequently acquired, took a more active part in Cabinet disputes and showed his head above more parapets than did several of his lay colleagues. Thus, within three months of his promotion, he was deep in the dispute with Churchill about the 1914 naval estimates, caballing with Lloyd George (an uncertain ally), McKenna, Samuel, Hobhouse and Beauchamp, and sending Cabinet notes to Asquith as tendentious (and presumptuous) as the 'loss of W[inston] C[hurchill], though regrettable, is *not* by any means the splitting of the party'. Simon carried his opposition nearer to resignation – his own (not Churchill's, greatly though he desired that) than did any of his allies. Lloyd George, indeed, when he began to move towards compromise, referred to Simon as 'a kind of Robespierre', and Asquith to him as organizing 'a conclave of malcontents'. It was curiously rash (or maladroit) for an ambitious law officer with over thirty years of office-seeking ahead of him to succeed before he was forty-one in irritating Asquith, Lloyd George and Churchill, the three most notable Prime Ministers of the half-century over which his own political career extended. It suggests flat-footedness rather than 'snakiness' (in Dalton's much later phrase).

This naval dispute was a dummy-run for Simon's semi-public agonies at the 1914 outbreak of war. Once again he started with Lloyd George as a half-ally, but quickly lost him. Morley and Burns, who had not been leading in the naval dispute, resigned quietly without causing resentment. Beauchamp wobbled as much as Simon, but in spite of being the owner of Madresfield, the bricks and mortar model for Evelyn Waugh's Brideshead, did not much matter. Asquith undoubtedly wanted Simon to stay, and for reasons somewhat more flattering than a simple desire to keep down the number of resignations. In his famous order of Cabinet merit which he drew up to amuse Venetia Stanley in early 1915 he put Simon equal seventh (with Lewis Harcourt) and added that 'his curve is moving steadily upward, now that he is convalescent from the malaise of last autumn'. From the adverse consequences of that malaise Asquith had been skilful as well as urgent in trying to save Simon. As he wrote to him on 3 August 1914, a day when the Prime Minister could hardly have been disposed to carry on unnecessary masculine correspondence: 'I have thought much over what you said this afternoon. I fully realise your point of view. And I am most anxious that, whatever I ask you to do, should not in any way compromise your future. In that respect, I think I can fully safeguard you.' Thus was a hint of promotion held out. But Asquith was not crude enough to let that obtrude. He also stressed that Simon had 'something that nearly approaches to a public duty . . . to remain'.

Simon stayed, and suffered in the eyes of some (C. P. Scott of the *Manchester Guardian*, Charles Masterman, the High Church radical, and Henry Hobhouse, the Postmaster-General, for instance) for having havered and even played a career-advancing game at a moment of national peril. This was unduly harsh. To hesitate in this way and very nearly to retreat into the wilderness of the back benches (which was not just play-acting as was shown by his actual resignation in December 1915) was far from being the most obvious careerist step. What seems much more likely is that Simon genuinely agonized in August 1914 but that his holier-than-thou earnestness of manner made the way in which he did so profoundly irritating to at any rate some of his colleages. As Dr David Dutton, in his excellent 1992 biography of Simon, perceptively puts it: 'It was perhaps the first illustration of the difficulties Simon had throughout his career in convincing people that his actions at important times were dictated by creditable motives.'

In spite of the echo of complaint against his self-righteousness contained in the private label of 'the Impeccable' which Asquith pinned upon Simon, there is no evidence that the Prime Minister reacted intolerantly to the 'malaise'. At any rate he more than lived up to his hint of future promotion. Indeed he emptied a cornucopia on to Simon's smooth and unctuous head. When the first Coalition was being formed in May 1915 (and coalition-forming is by its nature likely to be more a time of sacrifice than of promotion for members of the previous exclusively governing party) Asquith began by offering Simon the Lord Chancellorship, a staggering legal advancement for a lawyer aged forty-two, who had been a 'silk' for only seven years. Then, when he discovered that Simon did not want another legal as opposed to a political appointment, and in particular did not want to weaken his Prime Ministerial chances by shutting himself up in the House of Lords, he made him Home Secretary, the senior secretaryship of state.

In this first period at the Home Office (he returned twenty years later) Simon served for only seven months. He scored no triumphs (they would not have been easy to achieve in that department in wartime) and he was responsible for no major disasters. He was buffeted by trying to maintain a balance between freedom of expression and the authority of the state in wartime. He tried weakly to defend the Union of Democratic Control against the depredations of the Director of Public Prosecutions under Sir Edward Carson, who was his own replacement as Attorney-General, and satisfied neither the libertarians nor the authoritarians. He demonstrated that his liberalism fell short of Voltaire by proposing to ban *The Times* and the *Daily Mail*, both Northcliffe-owned, but, unsurprisingly, failed to get Cabinet support.

A great part of his energies was however directed to non-departmental business: the fighting of the battle against conscription. In this struggle he was united with most of the Liberal ministers who remained in prominent positions in the Coalition. There were however at least three exceptions: Lloyd George, whose swing to 'victory at all costs' was making him the leader of the compulsionists, a role which was an essential foundation for his emergence as an acceptable Prime Minister of the second and largely Tory Coalition; Churchill, temporarily in semi-eclipse, but whose combative ebullience led him in the same direction; and Asquith, who had the wider responsibility of holding the government together, but was also reluctantly coming to the view that a comprehensive war effort was incompatible with voluntarism.

Ranged on the Simon side were KcKenna, Runciman and Grey. But McKenna and Runciman at least, although feeling very strongly on the issue, were impelled by arguments different from those of Simon. Simon believed that conscription was incompatible with his view of the liberal state, an indefensible invasion of the rights of the individual. McKenna and Runciman believed that any further diversion of men from industry to the army would weaken the economy and pervert our true strategic role, which should be primarily that of a naval power sustaining our land allies with munitions and money. Grey believed something between the two, but was in any event hesitant about opposing anything claimed to be necessary to win the war for Britain's participation in which he, more than anyone else, was responsible.

Simon's objection was therefore more one of principle than that of Runciman and McKenna, and there was a certain logic in his being the only one to push it to actual resignation. Inevitably he was once again accused of a self-indulgent self-righteousness, but it was difficult (although not impossible, as several sharp comments proved) to sustain the view that it was a chessboard career move of subtlety. He no doubt did not foresee the long-lasting nature of the wound he was inflicting upon himself, but he can hardly have believed that to leave the Home Office before he had made any mark there was other than casting his bread on the most hazardous of waters. In his memoirs he admitted that his resignation had been a mistake.

At the time he may have been disappointed that others did not resign with him, but within a year all his potential co-resigners – and Asquith as well – were involuntarily ejected, so that for the last two years of the war he had the somewhat sterile fellowship of the large Asquithian rump in the House of Commons. It was somewhat sterile because they were anxious to wound but afraid to strike, and when they did, as in the 'Maurice debate' of May 1918, it was at once not very effective and near to signing their own parliamentary death warrants. Asquith, Simon and the majority of the group were slaughtered in the 'coupon election' of December 1918. Simon lost Walthamstow by a majority of over 4,000. In the meantime he had enlisted in the Royal Flying Corps for about a year from the summer of 1917. He served as a staff officer close to Trenchard, and was involved in frequent missions to Paris, during one of which, as we have seen, he married Mrs Manning. His object in enlisting was at least partly to show that it was compulsion and not service that he was against.

After his defeat, Simon's practice at the bar burst into a second flowering even more luxuriant than that which had made him a law officer at thirty-eight. He was varyingly estimated to earn between £30,000 and £70,000 (about £900,000 to £2.1 million at present values) whenever he chose to apply himself. He was also politically active, made a lot of speeches in the country, and fought a by-election in Spen Valley at the end of 1919, just before Asquith was returned for Paisley. Simon was unsuccessful on this occasion, to the great satisfaction of

Lloyd George who, behind the scenes, had devoted what were for a preoccupied Prime Minister surprisingly strenuous efforts to keep him out. Lloyd George's candidate split the 'bourgeois' vote and let Labour in. Simon nevertheless stuck to the constituency, reversed this result in the 1922 general election and remained member for the division, several times with very narrow majorities, despite having no Conservative opponent from 1924 onwards, over six general elections and until the end of his House of Commons career in 1940. The geographically uninformative nature of the constituency's name concealed the fact that it was between Huddersfield and Bradford in the west and Leeds and Dewsbury in the east, was made up mainly of scattered Yorkshire industrial communities centred on Cleckheaton, that it contained neither a packed-in proletariat nor rich suburbia but a lot of rather socially indeterminate people, Nonconformist ministers, schoolteachers, small tradesmen, local government officials and others of the sort among whom Simon had been brought up. It should have been well suited both to himself and to the individualistic Liberal message which he still preached, and up to a point it was. His earnestness went down well in Cleckheaton, although his style was a little too suave and metropolitan.

However it was one thing to find a constituency and another to find in the shifting sands of 1920s politics a role which was worthwhile in relation not only to his own inherent abilities, but also to others' view of him. The House of Commons then contained many members with a much stronger position in the national life, independently of whether they were or were not in office, than is the case today. This applied to an industrialist like Sir Alfred Mond, Liberal MP but currently engaged in bringing together Imperial Chemical Industries, to an academic like H. A. L. Fisher, to a trade union leader like J. H. Thomas, to advocates of the quality of Simon or Patrick Hastings and to redundant but notable ex-ministers like Lloyd George or Robert Horne. No one expected them to behave like aspiring junior ministers, to attend regularly or to try to make their names at committee stages. Perhaps the only recent example of someone in a similar position is Sir Edward Heath. Their presence strengthened the House of Commons in public esteem, but it also presented them – the stars with strong outside commitments, with a problem of not appearing like beached whales whose self-esteem exceeded their quality – and the House collectively with the problem of treating them with adequate respect and giving them the ability to shine without totally departing from the fiction of a Parliament of equals.

Simon, who re-entered the House as a member of a group of less than sixty Asquithians, was successful in re-establishing his position as an effective debater and a parliamentary big gun. He had no difficulty in seizing the attention of the House, and he made several speeches on general issues, socialism, unemployment, Ireland, the League of Nations, which attracted favourable attention. He became in effect deputy leader under Asquith and temporarily returned his briefs in order to concentrate on this. As Asquith was already seventy, the deputy's post obviously carried the strong hope of a fairly early accession to full leadership. But of what value was this to a man of Simon's abilities and ambitions? The answer was clearly not much without a major Liberal revival. And even the hope of achieving that without Liberal reunification was clearly utopian. Apart from anything else the Asquithian rump, without the financial resources of the Lloyd George fund, could not afford to fight, let alone win, enough seats to make them a serious challenger for office. But Simon had no enthusiasm for Liberal unity, first because of his antipathy to Lloyd George, and second because, with Lloyd George back in communion, his own ticket to succeed Asquith became valueless; Lloyd George was barely sixty and full of vigour.

The result was that the confused politics of 1922–4, with three general elections in two years, produced little more than one satisfaction for Simon, which was that, as the Liberals swung from sixty seats (plus fifty-seven Lloyd Georgeites) in 1922 to 157 (after reunion) in 1923 and then down to an abysmal forty in 1924, he held on to his seat in Spen Valley, while all about him his colleagues were losing theirs. Even Asquith went down in Paisley in 1924. But this was of little use when there were only forty to lead, and when in any event Lloyd George in Carnarvon Boroughs was more impregnable. After the 1924 election Asquith, maintaining the nominal party leadership, went to the House of Lords, Lloyd George was elected leader in the Commons by twenty-six votes to nine, and Simon, having sat sullenly on the sidelines during this vote, decided he ought to spend more time with his briefs.

Simon's liberalism up to this stage had not been so much right-wing as backward-looking. More than almost anyone else he looked back to Gladstonian issues, although his political style with its sinuous high legalism had little enough of the GOM in it. It was also a sterile approach. Thus he was happy to vote to put the first Labour government in at the beginning of 1924. But no sooner had he put them in than he wanted to put them out. It was he, appropriately, who moved the amendment on which that government fell in the following October. By

John Simon launching the 1935 election campaign with MacDonald and Baldwin.

Simon as Chancellor with his rarely seen second wife, 1938.

Kingsley Wood as a rather heavy Parliamentary Secretary to the
Ministry of Health, 1928.

More cherubic as Chancellor with his wife on Budget Day, 1941.

Dalton as Labour candidate for Cambridge, 1922, *aet* 35.

Dalton exercising his well-known button-holing technique (on James Walker, a trade union member of the Labour party National Executive), Bournemouth, May 1940.

'The old conjurer almost at the end of his repertoire': Dalton on Budget Day, November, 1947.

Late joys on a Vosges mountain weekend escape from Strasbourg with his well-chosen young protégés, Anthony Crosland, Denis Healey and James Callaghan (plus a Belgian lady who just happened to be in the hotel), 1950.

so doing he hardly performed a great service for the Liberal Party, and he certainly brought to an end the period in which he could hope to use that party, to which he had been firmly attached for the past thirty years, as a vehicle for re-creating the successful political career which he had rashly thrown away in the last days of 1915.

If a date from which Simon began to become a Tory is sought, the answer must be the early months of 1925, following the disastrous Liberal result at the end of 1924 and Lloyd George's subsequent election as Commons leader in Asquith's place. And if a date when he began to make himself an attractive asset to his new partners be also sought, it must equally surely be 6 May 1926, the fourth day of the General Strike. Simon spoke late at night in the House of Commons. It was not a full House, but the impact of his words, particularly on the Labour and trades union leaders, was nonetheless profound. He argued that the General Strike, being an action not against an employer but against the state, was not a strike but an insurrection, and as such was clearly illegal and unentitled to the privileges conferred by the Trades Disputes Act of 1906. Every trades union leader involved in incitement to participation in the so-called General Strike was therefore in breach of contract and in consequence liable to damages 'to the utmost farthing of his personal possessions', as, *con amore*, Simon put it.

The powerful impact of this speech provokes at least three reflections. First, the decline of the House of Commons is such that it is difficult to imagine any speech, certainly no back-bench speech, having today a comparable effect. Second, the impact was a tribute to Simon's legal authority and an underpinning of his position, even when his strictly political career seemed at a dead end, as one of a limited number of oracles of the nation. Third, it illuminated the ambiguity of the position of most trades union leaders. So far from being dedicated revolutionaries they were much nearer to seeing themselves as pillars of the state, loyal subjects of King George V, with modest bourgeois aspirations for themselves and their families. Illegality was as morally unwelcome to them as was materially the thought of being sued 'to the utmost farthing' of their possessions. Lenin, and maybe Robespierre, would not have cared. Sir Arthur Pugh (about to be chairman of the TUC) and the Right Honourable J. H. Thomas did.

The consequences of Simon's speech were also great. It helped to break the Strike and therefore produced some Conservative gratitude, although that emotion has never been an outstanding Conservative characteristic. Almost equally quickly it broke the Liberal party. Reunion had lasted a bare three years. Lloyd George, to some extent a prisoner of his lucrative American journalistic contracts (half-a-crown a word – that is, £125 a thousand, perhaps £4,000 today – it was awesomely and enviously whispered that he was being paid) and was there writing more critically of the government than of the strikers. The Liberal shadow Cabinet then attempted portentously to discipline Lloyd George. (For a shrinking party of forty members to continue with the fiction of a shadow Cabinet was in itself a fairly portentous thing to do.) Their motives were partly loyalty to Asquith, who was firm that the Strike had to be defeated, and partly inherent distrust of Lloyd George. But they had become unrepresentative of many of the back-bench Liberal MPs and of party activists in the country. Both these categories had some sympathy with Lloyd George on the merits of the dispute.

They also saw the party's need of him, a need which was made greater by Asquith suffering a stroke in the immediate aftermath of the General Strike and almost on the eve of the annual meeting of the National Liberal Federation, which was intended to act as a grand jury for the condemnation of Lloyd George. But by a remarkable feat of jiu-jitsu, Lloyd George ended up not as the condemned man but as the presiding judge. When Asquith insisted on resigning the overall leadership in October, Lloyd George picked it up without a struggle. This suited Simon extremely ill. It was in effect a final check to his attempt to be a leading post-war Liberal politician. It was largely the result of his own limitations. The fading of Asquith (who died in February 1928) was wholly predictable. Had Simon's popularity begun to match his ability, Lloyd George would not have been inevitable. As it was, Simon had no basis on which even to offer a choice.

Simon responded to this end of his Liberal road in a variety of ways, at once symbolic and somewhat contradictory. First he gave what was perhaps his most distinguished display of his style as a high-quality advocate. He appeared before the Privy Council for the government of Newfoundland (then an independent Dominion) in a Labrador boundary dispute with Canada. The lucidity of his presentation was said to be breathtaking. It was as though he was underlining that, whatever else was at fault, it was not his intellectual command. Then, having demonstrated his mastery of the advocate's art, he proceeded to relegate it below the public service by announcing his permanent retirement from the bar. This was on his appointment as Chairman of the Indian Statutory Commission, a parliamentary body promised by the India Act of 1919 to consider what further reforms (if any) had become necessary and desirable. In fact the Commission proved a sterile and ineffective body, but Simon's ready acceptance of the chairmanship, which occupied much of his time during 1928 and 1929, showed that he was eager for public appointment. The Commission was sterile and ineffective partly because it had no Indian members, which vitiated in advance its authority with Indian opinion, and partly because it was outflanked by the Viceroy (Irwin, later Halifax) who came out for the goal of Dominion status before its report was ready. That left the Simon Commission standing on an isolated tuft of ground with the stream of history swirling past it. This was despite the fact that one of its quieter members was Major C. R. Attlee, who two decades later was to give India independence almost with the stroke of a pen.

Although Simon despaired of the Liberal party and was willing to accept the heavy commitment of time which was involved in the Indian chairmanship, this did not mean that he wished permanently to give up British politics. On the contrary he was anxious to secure his future in the House of Commons. And the way in which he sought to do this gave a clear guide to his developing orientation. As a *quid pro quo* for undertaking the Indian job he successfully pressed for a guarantee from the government that he would not be opposed in Spen Valley by a Conservative in the forthcoming 1929 general election. His excuse for making the request was that he would as a result of long absences in India have little time for his constituency. But there was more to it than that. In fact he was never again to be opposed by a Conservative. There was no basis on which they could have done so. Although never nominally bearing the label, he became a far stauncher Tory than many of those who did.

It took him a few years to make an overt move. From the beginning of the 1929 parliament and the second MacDonald government he was steadily opposed to any Lib/Lab co-operation, and whenever the Liberal MPs went into different voting lobbies (which was fairly frequently) he was always to be found in the more right-wing one. Then in June 1931 he formally resigned the Liberal whip, taking with him Ernest Brown, a future Minister of Labour, and one or two others. This was only a couple of months before the collapse of the Labour government and MacDonald's surprise emergence as head of a 'National' government. Simon was an enthusiastic supporter and by this time was able to bring with him about half the parliamentary Liberal party, including Runciman and Hore-Belisha. He did not however get into the first National Cabinet. Samuel and Reading secured the two Liberal places (out of ten). Simon responded by redoubling his support for MacDonald in his new guise. He swallowed the need for a tariff, he set up the National Liberal party, designed to work almost unconditionally, unlike the Samuelite Liberal party, with the Conservatives, and he offered both to move a vote of confidence in the new government from the back benches and, perhaps a little rhetorically, to give up Spen Valley in favour of the Prime Minister if he had difficulty at Seaham Harbour.

After the landslide election Simon got his reward. In early November he replaced Reading at the Foreign Office, where the former Viceroy's tenure had been so short that in those days when British passports were issued not only in the name of but also under the facsimile signature of the Foreign Secretary, 'Readings' were so rare as to become collectors' items. Simon had taken nearly sixteen years to regain the Secretary of State status which he had thrown away in 1915. But once back he was like Charles II, although he did not have much else in common with the 'merry monarch', determined not to depart again on his travels.

His next fourteen years of continuous office began with three and a half of them at the Foreign Office. Although there was general agreement, both at the time and subsequently, that he was a bad Foreign Secretary, he took a great deal of shifting. His strengths were his own limpet-like quality and that, as long as Ramsay MacDonald was Prime Minister (which covered the whole of Simon's Foreign Office span), he had a valuable protector. MacDonald had an obvious interest in keeping senior ministers of non-Conservative provenance. They made him feel less isolated in the vast sea of 473 Conservative MPs who dominated his majority. A switch of Neville Chamberlain from the Exchequer to the Foreign Office, which was the most canvassed solution, was particularly unattractive to the Prime Minister. Chamberlain was efficient but intolerant of those whose minds were less sharply and narrowly focused than his own, in which category he certainly placed MacDonald. It was bad enough to have Chamberlain running from the Treasury an increasingly wide area of industrial and social as well as economic policy. But at least there were areas of government in which MacDonald did not claim great expertise. To have Chamberlain taking an equally tight grip on foreign policy, which was very much MacDonald's field of interest, would have been unacceptable.

This gave Simon a certain negative strength, which he badly needed, for the belief that he was the weakest link in a weak government, so far from being confined to his left-wing critics, was remarkably widespread. In 1933, and again towards the end of 1934 after a brief period of remission, his performance was highly criticized by such a diverse company as the two Chamberlain brothers, Anthony Eden, Lloyd George, Nancy Astor, Walter Runciman, David Margesson (government Chief Whip), Winston Churchill, Vincent Massey (Canadian High Commissioner) and General Smuts.

What made him so widely perceived as a bad Foreign Secretary? It is sometimes suggested that his fatal flaw was his forensic training and experience. Simon, the theory went, put the coping stone on the evidence that great advocates make hopeless Foreign Secretaries. The trouble with this theory is that there are no examples, one way or the other. Apart from Reading's ten weeks, Simon was the first lawyer Foreign Secretary since Canning over a hundred years before, and Canning, although a great politician, was never much of an advocate. Since Simon there have been only another three, Selwyn Lloyd, Geoffrey Howe and Malcolm Rifkind. Lloyd was rather bad, Howe rather good, and in Rifkin's short tenure the signs of greatness were sparse. But what is clear is that up to and well beyond Simon there has been no evidence on which to construct a general theory. There have been far more lawyer Chancellors of the Exchequer than lawyer Foreign Secretaries: Harcourt, Asquith, Lloyd George, McKenna, Simon himself, Cripps, Selwyn Lloyd, Howe, Clarke in the last hundred years alone, with about an average incidence of success and failure.

Nevertheless there were some attributes which Simon had acquired from his legal work which were thought to contribute to his unimpressive performance as Foreign Secretary. First, he was much better at analysing a problem than solving it. He laid out the facts, lucidly, even persuasively, but not with the passion of conviction. It was then for the court to decide. And the court in that context meant the Cabinet. Thus (as Neville Chamberlain complained) he was constantly seeking instructions from the Cabinet rather than imposing his own consistent policy upon it. He once informed his permanent under-secretary (Vansittart) that 'while I have no great admiration for my own judgement, I do believe in my powers of deductive reasoning'. He also, again according to Chamberlain, gave the impression that he was always speaking from a brief, although doing it with great technical skill, which skill might however equally easily have been applied on the other side.

He could also occasionally let his advocacy run away with him and argue a case, not necessarily his own, far more strongly than he should have done. Probably the most self-damaging speech of his life was in this category. It was delivered in Geneva to the Assembly of the League of Nations in December 1932 at the height of the crisis provoked by the first serious post-1918 aggression, that of Japan against China which led to the turning of Manchuria into the Japanese puppet state of Manchukoa. It was understandable that Simon and the rest of the National government had no intention of fighting for Manchuria. As 'a far away people of which we know nothing', its inhabitants were in a much more remote class than the Czechs to whom Neville Chamberlain applied these unforgettable words six years later. But Simon could at least have expressed firm if ineffective disapproval of the Japanese aggression. Instead of this he was so anxious to show that there was some fault on both sides that he stated the case for the Japanese government about as persuasively as he had stated that for the government of Newfoundland five years before. This caused profound misunderstanding and offended almost everyone – except the Japanese. The speech led to the label of 'Man of Manchukoa' being tied around his neck.

Nor did he have any counterbalancing triumphs. The Disarmament Conference foundered, Hitler came to power and took Germany out of the League, Britain's prestige at Geneva plunged heavily from what it had been in the days of either Austen Chamberlain or Arthur Henderson, Simon's two immediate predecessors, and this deterioration was wholly uncompensated by any improvement in Anglo-America relations, either with the Hoover or with the Roosevelt administrations. Insofar as there were any laurels won by British foreign policy during these years they were placed on heads other than Simon's. MacDonald took the lead at the Stresa Conference in April 1935 (a very short-term success) and Eden, Simon's junior minister at the Foreign Office, was a much more popular and adroit Geneva figure. In that multilateral meeting point the sanctimoniousness of Simon's personality outweighed the suppleness of his brain; as a result he always disliked going to the city of Calvin and Rousseau, which briefly became such a crossroads of the world.

Altogether he was lucky (for his pride not for his reputation) to survive as Foreign Secretary as long as he did, and he was lucky also in his fate when at last the major reshuffle came. In June 1935, with an election looming, Baldwin replaced MacDonald as Prime Minister, Samuel Hoare, who as Secretary of State for India had skilfully parried Churchill's assaults on his policy, replaced Simon as Foreign Secretary, and Simon replaced Sir John Gilmour, a now forgotten Scottish Tory, as Home Secretary. Admittedly he was only back at the age of sixty-two where he had been at the age of forty-two. But there had been a lot of previous talk about his being dropped altogether, and it was a major department. Once again he benefited from his status as a non-Conservative. With Baldwin becoming Prime Minister and MacDonald retreating into the shadows, Simon as the leading National Liberal could hardly be simultaneously demoted without the fig-leaf being snatched away from the government's claim to be National. Slightly bewilderingly indeed, Simon was given the bonus of being made deputy leader of the House of Commons, although it was revealingly stipulated that the title should go to Neville Chamberlain after the election was safely won (but it did not).

Even more bewildering was the fact that Simon's reputation, which seemed about to go through the floor when he left the Foreign Office, picked up considerably at the Home Office. It is difficult to say exactly what he achieved there, but he avoided major disasters and gave the impression of being in charge. Legislatively his main measures were a Factory Act, which was desirable, but something of a ragbag, and the Public Order Act of 1936, which was thought to have dealt coolly with the threat posed by Oswald Mosley's uniformed marches. As a penal reformer Simon did not compare with his successor, Hoare, who in spite of his 'black' reputation, first as the co-author with Laval of the notorious pact and then as the most suitable man to send as ambassador to Franco during the war, was probably the most liberal Home Secretary between Asquith and Butler.

Simon spent much of his time on the royal aspects of the Home Secretary's wide range of responsibilities. He was mostly good with sovereigns and their consorts. When the present Duke of Kent was born in 1935 he was one of the last Home Secretaries to attend a royal accouchement. At the time of the abdication he was an admirable Sancho Panzo to Baldwin's Don Quixote. He was dependably censorious of King Edward VIII and rich in constitutional lore to sustain his and the Prime Minister's positions. When Baldwin made his apparently informal yet brilliantly contrived post-abdication speech to the House of Commons, it was to Simon that he turned round, as though to underline the spontaneity with which he was searching his memory, and said, 'It was that day, was it not?' And in 1937, after the Coronation of King George VI, the KCVO which he had earned in 1911 from King George V, for dealing with the Mylius libel, was advanced to GCVO for his part in the smooth arrangements for the ceremony.

By the time of the next change of premiership, that from Baldwin to Neville Chamberlain in May 1937, and the reshuffle which followed,

Simon, so far from again being in danger of relegation, was promoted to be Chancellor of the Exchequer. He was even being discussed as a possible successor to Chamberlain, not merely at the Treasury but, for the future, in 10 Downing Street. As he was only three and a half years Chamberlain's junior this might have seemed a tight succession. But as Chamberlain himself was only two years behind Baldwin, and Baldwin only one behind MacDonald, the obstacle looked far from fatal in that government of old men.

Simon's Chancellorship embraced both the apogee and the collapse of appeasement. It continued for eight months of 'phoney war' and thus became associated with a half-hearted war effort. But it began well. Surprisingly for a Chancellor under Neville Chamberlain who was an authoritarian Prime Minister and who had himself been a long-term and successful head of the Treasury, Simon began as a powerful Chancellor. This was contrary to the habitual experience of those who served under a Prime Minister who had himself long presided over the department to which they succeeded. It was not much fun being Chancellor under Gladstone, Lloyd George or even Macmillan, nor Foreign Secretary under Salisbury or Eden. But Simon blossomed under Chamberlain, partly because their minds for a period became closely attuned. They both set more store by peace than by international honour, and they both believed that sound finance and business competence, which Simon with Runciman and McKenna had sought to uphold in 1915 and the restoration of which had been Chamberlain's achievement since 1931, were almost as important to national defence as front-line aircraft and troops for an expeditionary force.

In addition Simon was a first-rate flatterer and, to those not put off by what even the unastringent Sir Thomas Inskip called his 'soapiness', was an adjutant who combined intelligence and knowledge with almost unfailing sycophancy. He became the cheerleader for Chamberlain and appeasement. It was he, just as he had been Baldwin's fall man in his abdication speech, who was inevitably on hand to pass Chamberlain the note from which he dramatically announced the summoning of the Munich Conference to the House of Commons. It was he who led the Cabinet out to Heston airfield to wave him Godspeed. And it was he who on Chamberlain's return poured such Cabinet unction on his head as to play a major part in turning the highly arguable 'low case' for Munich into the unsustainable and discreditable 'high' one: a necessary tactical retreat was one thing, the elevation of the Prime Minister to a prince of peace was another.

Chamberlain, who was almost as lonely a man as Simon, although a stronger one, was too susceptible to this adulation. Having been highly and shrewdly critical of Simon's weaknesses in 1933–5, he temporarily approached friendship with him in 1937–9. This gave Simon a powerful position in the Cabinet. Of the inner group of four (the two 'friends' plus Halifax and Hoare), who ran the government's foreign policy and much of the rest as well, he undoubtedly occupied the second position, both in fact and in the eyes of the press and the public. This had its disadvantages as well as its advantages. When the appeasement ship was torpedoed by Hitler's invasion of Prague and takeover of the rump of Czechoslovakia in March 1939, Simon's reputation went down with it, almost as much as did that of Chamberlain, who at least had the ballast of continuing to be Prime Minister and leader of the Conservative party. When Labour and Liberal politicians proclaimed ukases against those with, or at least under, whom they would not serve, Simon figured almost as prominently as Chamberlain. Halifax, and to a lesser extent Hoare, escaped such full obloquy. Indeed a number of Labour front benchers showed an ill-judged desire to make Halifax Prime Minister.

On the other hand this number-two position, together with his special relationship with the Prime Minister, gave Simon great Treasury power, which he exercised with some independence. If he said 'no' to a departmental minister, it meant 'no', unless Chamberlain contradicted him, and that happened rarely. The key question is whether he used this power to slow down rearmament (not because he wished to sabotage but because he was loath to disrupt the economy for a war which he hoped would never come, and which, if it came, he saw as more likely to be sustained by an economically strong Britain than by an arms-bristling one) or did he merely reject or retard many demands of Duff Cooper at the Admiralty, Hore-Belisha at the War Office and Kingsley Wood at the Air Ministry in order to marshal a more orderly but at least equally effective programme? It is a question to which there is obviously no definitive answer.

In Simon's favour several arguments can be deployed. Once rearmament became the order of the day (just about when he became Chancellor) there was obviously a danger of Duff Cooper's cruisers, Hore-Belisha's Territorial Army divisions and the need to keep within hailing distance of the Germans in front-line aircraft (the item which commanded most Cabinet support and which proved itself the most vital in 1940) rushing at the same bottleneck and creating more chaos than results. To this extent the heavy Treasury scaling down of the demands of the service departments was a sensible rationalization rather than complacent defeatism. Furthermore, until about the middle of 1939, Simon was able to carry the Prime Minister with him. And Chamberlain, who believed in rearmament as well as in appeasement, was a man who, within his confines, had a clear and hard sense of efficiency in the machinery of government.

Alongside his efforts to preserve financial discipline Simon presided over and financed, with a mixture of taxation and borrowing, a level of peacetime expenditure which had previously been unimaginable. Expenditure passed the £1,000 million mark in the 1938 budget, as compared with £894 million in Neville Chamberlain's 1936 budget and the £864 million of Snowden's 1931 budget, when the Labour government was said to have allowed the unemployment fund to debauch the public finances. Nevertheless the £1,000 million was only a brief staging post on the way to £2,000 million, reached in the emergency budget which Simon presented at the end of September 1939, three weeks after the outbreak of war; and this had risen to £2.7 billion by his last budget in April 1940. At that stage Simon was covering £1,250 million or 46 per cent by taxation, while leaving just over a half to be financed by borrowing. This was a somewhat more provident performance than those achieved by his predecessors in the First World War or even in the Boer War.

His methods of raising revenue were orthodox but by the standards of the day drastic. In his (1938) first budget (in 1937 it had been his Finance Bill but Chamberlain's budget) he put income tax up from five shillings to 5s 6d in the pound, and increased the indirect taxes on tea and petrol, including other forms of oil. In 1939 income tax remained unchanged, although surtax was modestly increased, as were the indirect taxes on motor cars, sugar and tobacco. This budget was just over a month after Hitler's occupation of Prague brought to an end any realistic chance of appeasement offering a long-term hope as opposed to a pause in the descent to war. Yet it was in no way a war budget. The first of those came five months later when Simon put the standard rate of income tax up another two shillings (to 7s 6d in the pound) and accompanied it with considerable increases in the duties on alcohol, tobacco and sugar and the introduction of an excess profits tax at the rate of 60 per cent. By the somewhat soporific standards of the 'phoney war' months it was not a bad preliminary bite at wartime finance. Shortly beforehand he had slipped through, under the camouflage of so much else happening, one of the quietest fixed-rate devaluations in British history. Sterling was brought down from $4.89 to $4.03. It was a sensible move, and it was adept of him to do it with so little fuss.

Nevertheless his position after the spring of 1939 became vastly weaker than it had been in his high days of 1937 and 1938. He became the symbol of the foot-dragging approach to the war. His pronounced unpopularity was erected into an excuse almost as big as that of the Prime Minister for the opposition parties not joining the government. Archibald Sinclair, the leader of his old party, launched a direct and damaging attack upon him as having been for more than seven years 'the evil genius of British foreign policy'. Dalton, Attlee and many government back benchers as well were frequently inveighing against him. And, worst of the lot, there was some fraying of his relations with Chamberlain, who told the Cabinet secretary that he found the Chancellor 'very much deteriorated'.

This fraying was accelerated at the outbreak of war when Churchill joined the Cabinet. He and Chamberlain got along surprisingly well, and this reduced Chamberlain's dependence on Simon. According to J. R. Colville, who devotedly served Chamberlain before reluctantly (at first) transferring his loyalty to Churchill in the summer of 1940, the Prime Minister was actively playing in the first months of the war with the idea of replacing Simon as Chancellor. There was even a revival of the hardy 1920s annual of sending for Reginald McKenna, aged seventy-six. Then Lord Stamp, the economist chairman of the LMS railway, despite being a peer, was clandestinely summoned to 10 Downing Street, with a view to his taking over the Treasury; he was killed in a 1941 air raid. And Captain Margesson, the formidable but hardly statesmanlike Chief Whip, was sufficiently worried by the damage done to the government by the weakness of Simon's performance that he contemplated the sacrifice of taking over the job himself.

Simon's fourth budget, presented in late April 1940, was therefore a test in which he needed to succeed more than averagely well. He did not. He proceeded without much imagination along the conventional road. Income tax he kept at 7s 6d, and the main *Punch* cartoon of the week, often in those days a good indication of middle patriotic opinion, was predicated on the view that it ought to have been ten shillings. Income tax allowances were reduced, postal charges were put up and so were the duties on tobacco, alcohol and matches. He also invented purchase tax, which had a long and useful fiscal life ahead. But he rejected Keynes's idea for a forced loan and earned a coruscating *Times* letter of rebuke from the master as a result. There was also criticism from, *inter alia*, L. S. Amery and Aneurin Bevan.

This budget left him, which he probably would have been in any event, a sitting target for the major reconstruction of the government which came within three weeks. Many, including probably himself, thought that he would be out altogether under a Churchill premiership. And Simon did indeed, while urging Chamberlain to stand firm for his own office, offer to exclude himself and take Hoare with him. But, with his extraordinary cat-like capacity for sinuous survival, he not merely hung on but was deposited in the fourth of his great offices of state, the Lord Chancellorship.

The way in which he acquired this historic position was at once an act of generosity and an insult. Churchill was determined that Simon should be as far removed as possible from the conduct of the war, and, it must be added, from himself as well. Thus, not only did he keep Simon permanently out of the War Cabinet, in spite of his being the second most experienced member of the government, but then, at the end of the war and with the break-up of the Coalition, he still kept him out of the more normal-sized Cabinet of sixteen members in the 'caretaker' government. It was an exclusion which had never been experienced by any previous Lord Chancellor since the beginning of Cabinet government. Provided these conditions were met, however, Churchill was prepared to recognize Simon's legal quality and even to be reasonably magnanimous as well. The leader of the Labour party concurred. On the Woolsack, Attlee said, Simon 'will be quite innocuous'.

The Lord Chancellorship is an office which is a standing contradiction to the doctrine of the spearation of powers. Its occupant is head of the judiciary, normally a full and powerful member of the executive, and presides over one branch of the legislature. His Court precedence is so high that he comes above the Prime Minister at Buckingham Palace occasions, and there is a balancing amount of panoply associated with his installation and subsequent activities. The hollowness of the shell was more than usually apparent at a time when Germany was crushing France and hurling British troops back to Dunkirk, when Simon himself had to accept the final collapse of his highest political hopes, and when the House of Lords, to preside over which he was made a viscount and dressed up in full-bottomed wig, knee breeches and buckle shoes, was assuming such a minor role that, during the war years, it rarely met for more than an hour at a time. Moreover it was so thinly attended that, when a bomb destroyed the Commons chamber a year later, the removal of the Lords into the dolls'-house surroundings of the King's Robing Room, in order that the Commons might have their chamber, aroused hardly a ripple of interest or protest.

Simon accepted with patience his demotion (for such it was), took the flummery without excitement, and wisely decided to concentrate on the judicial aspect of the Lord Chancellor's work, which aspect most maintained its value in wartime. In addition, when he was called upon to do so, he defended with dexterity the government's decisions, in the making of which he had been allowed to play virtually no part. The almost court-like atmosphere of the vestigial Lords was well suited to his ability to speak elegantly and persuasively to a brief. Occasionally also he undertook a special task for the government, such as the interrogation of Rudolf Hess or the chairmanship of the Royal Commission on the Birth Rate. But it was in presiding over the two supreme courts, the House of Lords, in practice reduced to five Law Lords, and the Judicial Committee of the Privy Council of which the Lord Chancellor is *ex officio* president, that he made by far his greatest mark. Few Lord Chancellors ever, and certainly none since him, have sat judicially so frequently or so impressively as Simon. In 1943 alone he delivered forty-three major and complicated judgements. He presided with an easy authority over a distinguished collection of Lords of Appeal in Ordinary, most of whom had twenty years of judicial experience, whereas Simon had been away from the law since his final retirement as an advocate in 1928. The tribute of R. F. V. Heuston, who carried on from Atlay the chronicling of the lives of the Lord Chancellors, is absolute: 'As a judge in the highest tribunal Simon was superb.'

At the end of July 1945 there came not only the deposition of Churchill but also the end of this phase of Simon's career. The latter was of course a miniscule event compared with the former. It was also at once less absolute but more final. Simon never held office again. In 1951, when Churchill returned to Downing Street, he preferred first Asquith's youngest son who declined and then a fairly obscure Law Lord, Gavin Symonds, as Lord Chancellor. On the other hand Simon was able to go on sitting judicially for several years. What he was not allowed to do was to become a British nominee to the inter-allied tribunal sitting at Nuremberg. Attlee blocked him and explained his objection in a very direct letter to Simon. After acknowledging Simon's legal strength, he wrote: 'There is, however, one objection. The fact that you were a member of the British Government before the war might give an opportunity to war criminals ... to raise all kinds of extraneous matters relating to past history.'

Simon retaliated with, or was diverted into, vigorous anti-socialist campaigning. At each of the three general elections of his remaining years he distributed his many speaking engagements widely across the country. He also tried hard to arrange a full merger between his Liberal National remnants and the Conservative party. Churchill was unenthusiastic. He seemed more interested in prospecting for the support of the independent Liberals by speaking for Lady Violet Bonham Carter in Colne Valley, the Pennine twin to Simon's old constituency of Spen Valley. Simon, as often before, was the partner with whom no one wanted to dance. He did however manage to get a place for Liberal Nationals on Lord Woolton's ball-card; they retained Conservative support in their existing seats.

All Souls College became more and more imporant to Simon. His wife was still alive, but with her heavy drinking, frail health and (superficially at least) unattractive personality she was more of a burden than a comfort or a companion. Simon was an uncomplaining and devoted attendant, but he preferred his weekends at All Souls. In 1948, when Sankey died, he was appointed High Steward of the University, a post which traditionally goes to the most distinguished living Oxford jurist, and which he fully deserved. He was never suggested for the Chancellorship of the University, although this may have been because the timing did not fall out well for him. When Edward Grey died in 1933 and Halifax was elected, Simon was in the trough of his Foreign Office unpopularity, and when Halifax in turn died in 1959 and was succeeded by Macmillan, Simon was himself already four years dead. But it is doubtful if he would in any event have been at all widely supported. His paper qualifications, as for the premiership, were immense, but there was the old fatal flaw that nobody much wanted him.

In 1952, after much difficulty, he produced his volume of memoirs. He died in 1954.

SIR KINGSLEY WOOD

KINGSLEY WOOD WAS CHANCELLOR FOR THE forty core months of the Second World War. He was a Chamberlainite appointed by Churchill at the beginning of his premiership. At the Treasury he was a highly competent and innovating but not a politically towering head, and this was exactly as he had been in several other departments. Yet he is not so much a forgotten as a never well-known Chancellor. On the day of his wholly unexpected death in September 1943 (he was the only one in this gallery to die in office and, such is the preservative quality of power, the only Chancellor to do so apart from Charles Townshend in 1767), I was transferred to a new unit in the army, and in the mess that evening thought his achievements, his death and its likely consequences would be promising subjects of conversation with my hitherto unknown fellow officers; but none of them seemed to have heard of him.

This was less than Wood deserved, for starting from modest beginnings he was a remarkably effective minister at a time when it was not easy to break into the Conservative hierarchy from outside. Such a handicap never prevented his being given and making a success of difficult and even crucial jobs, not only the Exchequer at the peak of the wartime financial challenge but the Air Ministry in 1938–40, when a rapid increase in the fighting strength of the RAF was at the centre of the rearmament need. He never failed in a challenging job. Yet he never became a heavyweight politician. He was highly effective but he remained essentially a small man. It was not just a question of height, for no one would ever have said that of Napoleon, or even of Lloyd George. He was liked, he was even respected, but he was never either revered or feared. He was cherubic.

Howard Kingsley Wood was born at Hull in August 1881. His father was a Wesleyan minister, who was fairly quickly moved to Wesley's Chapel off the City Road, Finsbury, one of the cathedrals of Methodism, where he was allowed to remain for the unusually long

Wesleyan tenure of nine years. Thereafter Kingsley Wood was almost as much of a Londoner, politically and geographically, as his near contemporary, Herbert Morrison. His formal education was confined to the Central Federation Boys' School (another Wesleyan establishment) in Cowper Street, EC1, from where he went straight into solicitors' articles, was admitted in 1903 with the accompaniment of honours and a high prize in his finals. He quickly set up his own City firm, which became Kingsley Wood, Williams, Murphy and Ross, specializing in industrial insurance law. This firm's premises contained until recently almost the only remaining relic, pictorial, lapidary, biographical or autobiographical, of the childless man (although with one adopted and surviving daughter), who only a half-century ago occupied what is traditionally (even if not actually at the time) the second most important position in a British government. It was a 1928 oil painting by A. T. Nowell, and even that now seems to have disappeared.

By 1911, when he was elected for Woolwich to the London County Council, Wood had established a satisfactory practice and was well on the way to making himself the legal panjandrum of industrial insurance. He represented the companies in the negotiations occasioned by the Lloyd George Insurance Act of that year, and was substantially responsible for bringing them into the scheme. As the war years went by he became president or chairman of almost every representative industrial insurance body in London, and when he was knighted in 1918 at the unusually early age of thirty-six it was essentially for his work in this field. Even on the LCC his committees were insurance and old age pensions, supplemented by housing.

At the Lloyd George 'khaki election' of December 1918, Wood became Conservative MP for West Woolwich, which in the post-1945 years was a swinging constituency but which sustained him throughout the seven inter-war general elections and therefore to the end of his life. He quickly began a classical career of gradual advancement up the ladder of political promotion, except that the early rungs were not orthodoxly Conservative. He became parliamentary private secretary to Christopher Addison, a Coalition Liberal (later a Labour leader of the House of Lords) who was the first Minister of Health, and as such the chosen agent for the building of 'homes fit for heroes'. When Addison was first shunted as a failure and then resigned from the government in dudgeon, both events in the spring of 1921, Wood stayed on under Sir Alfred Mond, another Coalition Liberal. When the Coalition broke up in October 1922, and was replaced by the first Conservative government for seventeen years, Wood was offered no position. In 1924 however he became parliamentary secretary (that is a paid member of the government and not just a voluntary aide as is a PPS) under Neville Chamberlain, again at the Ministry of Health, and stayed with him in that post for four and a half productive years. In 1928, an unusual honour for a parliamentary secretary, he became a Privy Councillor.

In opposition he was an effective critic of the second Labour government. His style was that of a keen but not a bitter party man, more akin to a Whitelaw than to a Tebbit. That his party credentials were good, however, was shown by his election in 1930 as chairman of the National Union of Conservative and Unionist Associations. After these marks of favour and popularity he was perhaps disappointed on the formation of the National government in August 1931 to find himself only a parliamentary secretary once again, this time to the Board of Education, with Sir Donald Maclean, the Liberal deputy leader, as his ministerial chief. This and his experiences with Addison and Mond suggest that he was thought to be good at working across party boundaries.

After the landslide victory of the National government, however, there came what was perhaps his biggest breakthrough. He was made Postmaster-General almost immediately after the election, and began the task of putting commercial vitality into the tired bones of St Martin's-le-Grand. There was already some call for the hiving off of the Post Office. Its privatization was however regarded as a bridge too far. There were few, even among the most right-wing Tories who made up the massed cohorts at the command of Captain Margesson, the famed and feared Conservative Chief Whip of the whole of the 1930s, who would have contemplated such a relaxation of the sinews of the state as to push Post Offices out of the town centres into the back-street corner shops in which they now find themselves. On the contrary the decade was one in which handsome if unoriginal neo-Georgian Crown offices became a central feature of innumerable market and industrial towns. There was, however, some call for the Post Office to be devolved from a government department to a quango. Wood set up an independent committee to advise on this. It reported against, but in favour of a more commercial approach. This Wood sought to achieve by creating a new post of director-general, and by negotiating with the Treasury a new financial arrangement in which the Post Office contributed a fixed sum to the national finances and kept any profits above that for reinvestment.

Beyond this Wood devoted his main attention to the telephone service, which had hitherto been the weakest arm of the Post Office. By the skilful use of publicity, at which he was always adept, he secured a proportionately greater increase in telephone subscribers than was taking place at the time in any other country. He also secured some more specialized and maybe fortuitous triumphs. The GPO film unit, which he constituted in 1933, achieved a high aesthetic reputation for the making of documentaries, of which John Grierson's *Night Mail* was the most famous.

Wood's success was recognized by his being asked in 1933 to join the Cabinet, while retaining his Postmaster-Generalship, and by his being promoted to be Minister of Health in place of Hilton Young, later Lord Kennet, in the June 1935 reshuffle, when Baldwin took over the premiership from MacDonald. Minister of Health in those days was at least as much a Minister of Housing as a Minister of Health, and as the housing boom of the 1930s was one of the two most powerful locomotives (rearmament was the other) of such recovery as took place this was an appointment of which the importance, as with Harold Macmillan in the analogous job from 1951 to 1954, exceeded its hierarchical position. In addition Wood's party standing continued to advance. In addition to his 1930 appointment as Chairman of the National Union of Conservative and Unionist Associations, he was put in charge of the government's campaign publicity for the 1935 general election. Here he exercised his almost unique gift of being a committed partisan politician who did not arouse much animosity among his opponents. At the beginning of 1938 his party standing was further underlined by his being elected to succeed Baldwin as Grand Master of the Primrose League.

A month or two later, in the reshuffle which followed Anthony Eden's resignation from the Foreign Office, he was given a more onerous task than looking after primroses and became Secretary of State for Air. On the face of it this was a surprising appointment. Wood had hitherto been one of the most domestic and civilian of ministers, far removed from any defence or foreign policy involvement. But his old department chief Neville Chamberlain, who had been Prime Minister since May 1937, presumably thought that if he could enrol telephone subscribers and get houses built so he could also produce aeroplanes. And on the figures, maybe fortified by catching a tide which was already rising, he notched up another very successful two years, and in what was much the most crucial department that he had so far occupied. When he went to the Air Ministry in March 1938 Britain's monthly production of front-line military aircraft was running at eighty. When he left it in

April 1940 the monthly figure had advanced to 546. It is of course easier to double or quadruple a small rather than a large number, but his achievement nonetheless looked impressive.

His immediate subsequent career was however bewildering. In that spring when the 'phoney war' came to an end, first in April with the German invasion of Denmark and Norway, and then in early May with the still more formidable sweep through the Low Countries and northern France, he announced that he was exhausted, and his faithful master Chamberlain arranged for him to swap jobs with Sir Samuel Hoare, who was currently occupying the sinecure office of Lord Privy Seal. Only three weeks later the British defeat in Norway led to the famously damaging House of Commons debate of 8–9 May, at the end of which the government majority fell heavily. In the aftermath of this Wood showed that he in turn was not only a faithful but a courageous friend to Chamberlain and told him affectionately but firmly that it was right and becoming inevitable that he should resign.

The advice was taken and Churchill became Prime Minister on 10 May. Whether or not out of gratitude for Wood's influence, which if not absolutely decisive was an important contributory factor, Churchill then proceeded to make Wood Chancellor of the Exchequer in his new government. The appointment had a certain neatness. It enabled him to get rid of Sir John Simon, hitherto at the Treasury and exile him from any real contact with the war effort to the Woolsack. Hoare left the government prior to becoming ambassador in Madrid, where it was thought that he had the best chance of getting on with Franco. This freed the Privy Seal for Attlee, who coming in as the leader of the minority partner in the Coalition required both membership of the small War Cabinet (at first of only five) and a non-departmental office. Furthermore Hoare's removal from the Air Ministry without there being any question of Kingsley Wood going back there enabled Churchill to distribute the service ministries among the Labour, Liberal and anti-appeasement Conservatives. A. V. Alexander went to the Admiralty in place of Churchill himself, Archibald Sinclair, the Liberal leader, went to the Air Ministry, and Anthony Eden went to the War Office.

Churchill was not of course remotely making Wood the number-two man in his government, as is often the case when a Prime Minister appoints a Chancellor of the Exchequer or has one thrust upon him. Wood was not at first offered membership of the War Cabinet, but he came in in October 1940 and was then dropped from it for no apparent reason – the big reshuffle of February 1942. In May 1940, however, Wood was being given a big departmental promotion and responsibility, with Churchill reposing in him more confidence than he bestowed on any other Chamberlainite, except paradoxically for Chamberlain himself. And Wood on the whole well repaid the trust. He did not inspire the country. He did not bestride discussions within the government. But he was mostly a highly competent and responsible wartime Chancellor.

He introduced four budgets. The first was in July 1940, that month of deathly calm at the centre of the storm, when Britain stood most alone, after the temporary exhilaration of Dunkirk and before the inevitable onslaught – certainly by air and probably by invasion as well. It was an emergency budget in the sense that it was designed to supersede Simon's last regular spring one. But it was widely judged to make an inadequate contribution to dealing with the extreme emergency with which Britain found itself confronted. He did little beyond bringing into operation the beginnings of purchase tax which his predecessor had announced in April, accompanied by the first powers for the compulsory deduction of income tax at source. (This was not PAYE, which was to be Wood's last achievement at the Treasury, for it related in practice to tax on incomes which had accrued many months or even a year or so before.) This hardly made the budget the equivalent of 'fighting them on the beaches', and it passed with little notice. There is no mention of it, for instance, in either Churchill's voluminous *Second World War* or in J. R. Colville's *Fringes of Power*.

Colville was by no means an admirer of Wood's, as almost his next subsequent (29 August 1940) reference to him shows:

> Kingsley Wood came about [air-raid damage] compensation, and proved himself the perfect yes-man. Afterwards I enjoyed listening to his pandering to Beaverbrook and Brendan [Bracken] both of whom flattered him and treated him as an inferior being.

During this fateful summer of 1940, however, Wood may have done more for the future of British economic policy, both internal and external, than a more adventurous budget would have accomplished. In mid-June he set up a council of economic advisers, not in itself a very original or formative step, but one which led, quite quickly, to Maynard Keynes as one of its members moving into the Treasury. Keynes stayed there until his death five and three-quarter years later. He was thus near to the centre of British economic policy-making over the key period for the financing of the war, for the Bretton Woods conference in 1944, and for the negotiation of the American loan, following the abrupt termination of Lend–Lease in the autumn of 1945. He occupied a room next to the future Governor of the Bank of England, Lord Catto, and in consequence, particularly when he was occasionally reluctant to give an opinion, became internally known as Lord Doggo.

Wood's Chancellorship is strongly reminiscent of that of Selwyn Lloyd, his successor but eight. An uncommanding personality, as Colville condescendingly brings out and in this respect like Lloyd, Wood was also a considerable innovator, again like Lloyd. Lloyd, a dull Chancellor in contemporary judgement, created the consensual National Economic Development Council, which lasted more than twenty-five years until it was destroyed by Norman Lamont. He also created the 'regulator', a useful instrument by which indirect taxation could be varied up or down by 10 per cent without legislation, an economic weapon of utility and flexibility.

Wood's next budget, in the spring of 1941, showed some considerable signs of Keynes's influence. This budget broke new ground in two respects. It endeavoured for the first time to match the country's real resources with the claims upon them and not merely to raise money for Exchequer outgoings, and it also introduced the concept of the state pulling in resources when demand was heavy and pumping them out again when it was slack. The standard rate of tax went to ten shillings in the pound, accompanied by a reduction in allowances which meant that two million more became liable, and made income tax, which it had never been in its previous 150 years of fluctuating existence, a majority and not a minority tax. This was balanced by the introduction of post-war credits, so that part of the tax became a form of forced saving rather than a simple levy. In theory this was highly intelligent, although as there was no post-1945 slump in contrast with the post-1918 experience, but on the contrary full and sometimes overfull employment for nearly the next thirty years, the repayment of the credits proved an inconvenient commitment for successive Chancellors. The same principle was applied to the excess profits tax. Twenty per cent of this was also to be refunded after the war.

This truly innovating budget of 1941 was rounded off by the introduction for the first time of an attempt at serious national income statistics. The 1942 and 1943 budgets followed broadly the same precepts. By the time of the latter Wood was financing nearly £6 billion of public expenditure compared with totals of less than £1 billion which had prevailed until 1938, and was covering just about half of it by taxation. This compared well with previous wartime performances, and was also made more tolerable for the future by the average cost of borrowing being kept to around 2 per cent. There were of course inflationary tendencies in the economy, but these were combated by a series of surprisingly effective measures of control, including an expensive food-subsidy programme, which held the cost of living steady at no more than 30 per cent above the pre-war level.

It was a record of effective quiet competence, which was made the more remarkable by the fact that Wood's pre-war reputation had been largely based on flamboyance of presentation. At the Treasury he gave the strong impression of being more interested in the substance than in the form. He became the reverse of that derisory old Texas label of 'all hat and no cattle'. He had plenty of cattle to show, and he was about to add substantially to the herd, in the shape of a carefully and clearly worked-out scheme for PAYE (Pay as you earn) which was a highly desirable concomitant of income tax affecting nearly every adult employee and not just a fringe of professional men and *rentiers*. Others, notably Paul Chambers, later chairman of ICI, contributed much technical ingenuity, but it was Wood who gave the essential ministerial leadership. It was hard and ironic that he should have died on the morning of the day on which he was to announce this important change to the House of Commons.

Yet despite his steady confidence and occasional adventurousness Wood remained essentially a departmental and limited politician. It is impossible to imagine him being even considered for the leadership of the country at war, for which his Treasury successor John Anderson became the recommended candidate, had Churchill and Eden perished together. He was a small man, in manner as well as in size, who did big jobs and did them surprisingly well. He deserves a larger niche in history than that left by one now disappeared oil portrait.

SIR JOHN ANDERSON

FOR MOST CHANCELLORS IN THIS SERIES the Treasury was either the clear peak of their career, as with Harcourt, Hicks Beach, McKenna, Snowden or Kingsley Wood, or else an essential stepping-stone to their getting further, as with Asquith, Lloyd George or Neville Chamberlain. John Anderson is unusual in being in neither category. It would be quite possible to remember him while forgetting that he had ever been Chancellor. This is partly because his Treasury work lay in the shadow of the war, but even more because he did such a range of public service jobs – and nearly all with conspicuous success – that any one thread gets lost in the skein. He was the epitome of the ambitious and diligent young man from Scotland, entirely Edinburgh-educated apart from one year in Leipzig, who inevitably rose to the top of any tree that he touched.

Yet it would be a mistake to call him many-faceted. Indeed until his second wife, whom he married when he was almost sixty, made his portentousness a little more glossy and launched him into society, his non-working life was very narrow. Throughout the peak of his civil service career he regularly caught the same train home to Sutton, Surrey. Official blue books monopolized his reading, and his own publications were confined to his collected speeches as Governor of Bengal. He was the opposite in these respects of Winston Churchill, the other figure whose Chancellorship might be forgotten without any danger of memory missing the man.

Anderson was a public servant of unique gravitas, skill and reliability, and as such was greatly admired (Harold Macmillan, admittedly subject to hyperbole of the occasion when unveiling Anderson's bust by Epstein, suggested that he was admired 'perhaps more than any man who has come into our lives'), and became increasingly the first choice for any difficult job which was going. He richly deserved his Order of Merit, one of the only five to be given to non-Prime Ministerial politicians since the war, although typically and slightly irritatingly he always denied being a politician. He was also mostly liked by those who worked closely with him, but less so by those more remote. In the War Cabinet, for instance, both Attlee and Bevin felt friendliness as well as respect for him, but Churchill, although heavily dependent upon him for the efficient running of the home front, had little desire to see him when he did not have to.

The question which remains undecided was how deep-rooted was Anderson's humourless pomposity. Was it the core of his being, or was it just a superficial trait which made him an engaging caricature of himself like Ted Heath's curmudgeonliness or Attlee's taciturnity or Rab Butler's feline asides? The evidence is conflicting. There is the story of his habitually opening War Cabinet committee meetings, the presiding over of which was his forte and marked the peak of his service and influence, with such redundant homilies that the Home Secretary (Herbert Morrison) closed his eyes and murmured to the Minister of Production (Oliver Lyttelton), 'Wake me when prayers are over,' and that Lyttelton recorded the remark with heartfelt appreciation. There is the earlier and equally authenticated account of his rebuking P. J. Grigg, his nearest approach to a civil service co-equal, who addressed him on an official occasion in India by his Whitehall sobriquet of 'Jonathan'. 'You forget yourself, Sir James,' he pontificated. (His other, less friendly, Whitehall names were 'Jehovah' and 'pompous John'.)

Then there are my own exiguous personal memories of him. We overlapped in the House of Commons for two years, and sometimes spoke, with immensely different weights of authority, in the same economic debates. Anderson was not light of touch in the House. I remember Attlee giving great pleasure (on the Labour benches at any rate, but probably not exclusively there) by saying that Anderson's somewhat flat-footed intervention in the post-devaluation debate of 1949 reminded him of 'the Carthaginians [employing] a heavy, sagacious and most amiable animal called the elephant but unfortunately the elephant ran the wrong way and disordered the ranks'. Rather less amiably Anderson liked to deliver highly disputable opinions with the self-righteous condescension of someone who had special access to incontrovertible truth.

A more engaging (and last) memory comes from nearly a decade later. For the sixteen years of his second marriage Anderson lived in London in his wife's Lord North Street house. These Westminster houses were (and are) more notable for their elegance and convenience of locality than for their solidity of construction. They were more suited to the bird-like Lady Waverley, as his viscountcy had then made her, or to his near neighbour and successor as chairman of Covent Garden, Garrett Drogheda, than to his own frame. Ava Waverley had asked me to lunch in order to discuss the mystery of Sir Charles Dilke. Lord Waverley was not joining us for lunch, but as I arrived he came down the stairs with a purposeful tread and in his habitual wing-collar, black coat and striped trousers before putting on his hat and setting off to what one felt was some more serious occasion. Both the house and I shook a little as he reached the ground floor, and it was easy to believe that whatever wisdom he was setting off to impart would be accepted with submission and maybe with gratitude as well.

Anderson was born in July 1882 in the heart of middle-bourgeois Edinburgh, just south of the Meadows, within hailing and speech-pattern distance of Morningside. It was as separate from the eighteenth-century elegance of the grand lawyers' houses in the New Town as it was from the slums of Craigmillar. His father, David Anderson, who lived to within nine years of John's own death, ran stationery, photography and leather-goods shops in the Princes Street Arcade, which he later sold to Valentines, the postcard-makers of Dundee, in which firm he then became a director and partner for nearly fifty years. John Anderson's mother was of German ancestry, five years older and slightly higher up the social scale. The Andersons moved in two stages a little further out, but John Anderson was able to walk to George Watson's College, then alongside the Meadows, throughout the eleven years that he spent in first the junior and then the senior part of the school.

He achieved almost all available honours, as he did in the four years which he subsequently spent at Edinburgh University. His bent in this first bite at Edinburgh University was strongly scientific and led on to his year of chemistry at Leipzig, then the academic Mecca for the subject. When he came back to Edinburgh for a year in 1904 he did economics and political science in order to prepare himself for the highly competitive civil service entrance examination. He appears to have been pushed in this direction and away from becoming an academic scientist, partly because it would quickly give him a salary on which he could marry Miss Chrissie Mackenzie, 'the girl next door', on whom his heart was very firmly set, and partly because Edinburgh regarded it as the natural goal for its brightest students.

He duly went to London and took the examination in the summer of 1905. He is reported as not merely having come top but as having secured the highest mark ever with one anonymous exception. His subsequent career certainly leaves no reason to doubt these achievements, although there often seem to have been a remarkable number of angels who have managed to dance on the topmost point of this needle. (And as Keynes in the adjacent year managed to come only fourteenth there may also be room for doubt as to how precise a test of originality of intellect the examination presented.) What however is surprising is that with the field presumably wide open to his preference, he then went to the Colonial Office rather than, say, to one of the two core departments with which he was subsequently to be so prominently associated. The Colonial Office, just free of the dominant reign of Joseph Chamberlain, then had a higher prestige (although Chamberlain's style of braggadocio never was Anderson's) and he might, with his Edinburgh background, have felt a sense of mission for the Africa of Livingstone and Cameron.

In fact, however, Anderson was a strictly London-based colonialist, and never once went to a colony during the six and a half years he spent in that department. He was secretary to two committees of enquiry, one into Northern Nigerian Lands and the other into West African currency, but he serviced (and probably dominated) them both from Whitehall. Already his gravitas was becoming legendary. The assistant under-secretary of state, Sir Vandeleur Fiddes, whose own personality was said to be nearly as impressive as his name, was credited with the view that when holding an official conversation with Anderson he felt like a peccant schoolboy being admonished by the headmaster.

In 1912 at the age of twenty-nine Anderson was seconded to Lloyd George's new National Insurance Commission. This marked the start of his remarkable capacity, without any evidence of undue striving on his part, always to find himself at a focal point of administrative challenge. Although the beginnings of social security had met with a vague general political welcome, there were many interest groups who would have been happy to see the scheme sink into a morass of bureaucratic chaos, and there were plenty of opportunities for this in the launch of the new venture. Sir Robert Morant, veteran of Balfour's Education Bill and a civil servant of Anderson's energy and power, but much more erratic and difficult to work with, was in charge, and Anderson had both to conciliate and to control him, twin tasks which W. J. Braithwaite, intended to be the other star of the new venture, signally failed to perform. Morant's only recorded complaint against

Anderson was that 'he was always so damned right'. A year later he got a big promotion to be secretary of the National Insurance Commission.

In the first two years of the 1914 war Anderson collected a few special assignments (plus, one day in the street, a white feather, which deeply hurt him; how could it be thought that he was not fulfilling his highest national duty by remaining in Whitehall?), but it was not until the beginning of the Lloyd George government that he was given his central wartime role. He became secretary to the new Ministry of Shipping, which began from scratch under the 'political' control of a Glasgow shipowner, Sir Joseph Maclay, who knew about ships but little about government or indeed politics. Anderson, who was in the reverse position, had to form an alliance of the traditions of Glasgow and Edinburgh in order to help Maclay through the jungle and needless to say did so with skill and success. The tasks of the new ministry were vital, for shipping losses in 1917 were a victory-threatening menace.

After a few months of winding up his shipping responsibilities, mainly by advising on the disposal of the German mercantile marine at the Paris Peace Conference, Anderson was given his equivalent of demobilization and made available for peacetime service. For the next three years he was shunted with bewildering rapidity, but ever upwards, or at least to a temporarily more crucial post. At first he was made second permanent secretary (under Morant) following the birth by amalgamation of the Ministry of Health, which was oddly named for it was more a ministry of housing and local government and of the poor law, but which nonetheless persisted within its wide boundaries until after Aneurin Bevan's period in the Attlee government. Anderson saw the Ministry through its launch but little more. On 1 October, all in the same year of 1919, he was made chairman of the Board of Inland Revenue. This was a high-prestige post, partly because of its salary and partly because it operated unusually free of ministerial control, and it was presumably thought that Anderson's services had been so outstanding as to deserve the bonus. It cannot have been thought that time was rushing past him and must be caught by the forelock. He was thirty-seven.

He remained in charge of the Inland Revenue for seven months. During this period he at least twice demonstrated his quality and style. After four months in office he gave evidence to a Commons Select Committee, nominally on the then active subject of capital taxation but in fact on the whole functioning and tradition of the Board. He had with him Richard Hopkins, a more experienced Revenue man and later permanent secretary of the Treasury under Anderson's own Chancellorship. But it was only after he had answered more than 500 questions that he turned to Hopkins for any fact or opinion. Then he had a dispute with the tax inspectors who objected to his policy of promoting on merit rather than seniority. He received a deputation and treated it courteously but negatively. The aggrieved inspectors then tried to whip up a campaign of protest in Parliament and press. Anderson regarded this as improper civil service behaviour and came down heavily on the offenders. Omniscience at the head and discipline in the ranks, the latter even fortified by fear, were his hallmarks.

Perhaps the reputation for sternness so established contributed to his next appointment, which came about in circumstances at once tragic and dramatic, and with another bewilderingly quick turn of the wheel. On 9 May 1920 his wife died during a cancer operation. She had not been ill for long, and the circumstances of her death suggest that it came as a sudden blow rather than as the execution of a lingering sentence. There is also every indication that the thirteen years of their marriage had been a period of full domestic felicity. The blow to Anderson was therefore a heavy one, to which he reacted with a more than Roman fortitude. In effect, he never spoke of his first wife again until twenty-one years later, when he poured out a moving account of this first courtship and marriage, clearing his mind as it were, to his second wife before proposing to her. More immediately it made him anxious for a change of life from the Strand and Sutton, and by 16 May he was in Dublin, having accepted an offer of the joint permanent under-secretaryship of the Irish Office. The other half of the joint arrangement was an urbane 'Castle Catholic' James MacMahon, but there was no doubt that Anderson was intended to be the sharp end of the partnership, to tighten up the lax administration of Dublin Castle, and to be both the principal adviser and the principal agent of the 'no-nonsense' Canadian, Harmar Greenwood, a typical product of the Lloyd George era, who had just become Chief Secretary.

Anderson remained in Ireland for twenty months. As this was the peak of the 'troubles', with Arthur Griffiths and Michael Collins organizing a campaign of classical and cold-blooded terror against the occupying power, and with the Black and Tans providing more provocation to the enemy than protection for the British garrison, Anderson as both a symbol and the director of that garrison was obviously in a position of extreme and exposed danger. He was of course heavily protected, but as protection can never be proof against a determined assassin willing to lose his own life, of whom there were many in Ireland at the time, this was of limited value. And the experience of his predecessor of thirty-eight years before, Thomas Burke, who was the real target of the attack which killed Lord Frederick Cavendish, underlined the nature of his exposure. There can be no doubt that Anderson reacted to this sustained risk with exceptional courage and steadiness.

Steadiness was an even more valuable quality in the circumstances than would have been bursts of manic courage. But Anderson contributed much more than even the higher forms of fearlessness. First he kept his team together well, showing more capacity for leadership than in any of his previous posts. But beyond this he demonstrated a sophisticated capacity to accommodate himself to the fact that the British government's policy alternated between suppression and negotiation. This was partly because such opportunism was endemic to the Lloyd George regime. But it was also because it was endemic in any colonial or semi-colonial situation. Anderson and those who worked closely with him were occasionally cynical about their political masters, but they never got into the position of regarding negotiation as parleying with treachery. They knew that a negotiation had to come, and when it did they were impatient against the preliminary view of the Cabinet in London that it must begin with Sinn Fein surrendering their arms.

When he returned to England in early 1922 it was for the moment to the Inland Revenue chairmanship from which he had been seconded. But it was for an even shorter period than had been the result of his previous mostly unsought translations. In March of that year he became permanent under-secretary of the Home Office, and settled into that high post for a span of ten years with a clutch of no less than seven Home Secretaries whom he was to serve, or, as some might think it could be more aptly put, who were to serve under him. He was still not quite forty, and apart from his remarkable experience had accumulated honours without precedent for one so young and so modestly born. He had been made CB at the age of thirty-five, KCB at the age of thirty-six, an Irish Privy Councillor at the age of thirty-eight, and was about to be made GCB at the age of forty.

He took all these baubles, as he did their more serious side, which were his great promotions, with an olympian calm. But there is an engaging story from his early Home Office years which shows him as a little more vulnerably proud. His private secretary (later as Sir Frank Newsam himself the permanent under-secretary of the Home Office for nine years) recorded Anderson arriving one morning with a suitcase and explaining that it contained his full regalia, including Irish Privy Councillor's uniform and Bath collar and mantle, into which he proposed to change before receiving his father and mother who were both exceptionally in London and were coming to call on him. 'They have never seen me in it,' he added simply.

Another anecdote, not documented or wholly precise but freely circulating in the Home Office during my first Home Secretaryship and surely at least *ben trovato*, relates to his same early years as permanent under-secretary and to his firmness with ministers as well as to his sparing style on paper (he never wrote much in the way of memoranda or minutes). A junior Home Office official had begun the consideration of a policy issue by writing an analytical paper which outlined two possible courses and ended by recommending Course A rather than Course B. He initialled the paper, let us say, C.W.D. His immediate superior disagreed violently, not only preferring Course B but excoriating Course A. The file then made its way upwards, all the senior officials up to and including Anderson endorsing B. Then the Home Secretary of the day (probably W. C. Bridgeman) hesitantly wrote, 'I rather agree with C.W.D.' The next and concluding note on the file was 'I have spoken with the Home Secretary. He no longer agrees with C.W.D. [signed] J.A.'

Contrary to what might have been expected Anderson neither worked long hours nor took files home during his years at the Home Office. He habitually arrived at 10.15 a.m., worked steadily until 1.15, when he walked across the park to lunch at the Reform Club, returned at 2.45 and departed at 6.15. This was despite the fact that his life in Sutton, where he had a series of houses on a rising suburban scale, must have become fairly barren. It had never been very externally exciting, being confined to golf and bridge and suppers before or after these pastimes with a handful of three or four Scots in exile like himself. It had no doubt been redeemed by his intense connubial affection. But that was gone. When the blow had struck, and he had been left with a son of nine and a daughter of four (whom he in turn had quickly if temporarily left by departing for Ireland, where of course they could not follow), the situation had been saved by one of his wife's younger sisters, Nellie, abandoning her training as a nurse at St Thomas's and moving in to take charge of the Sutton household.

For twenty-one years she devoted herself to looking after her brother-in-law and her nephew and niece. She was apparently painfully shy, and this together with Sir John's demeanour and despite all the hysteria of the period about deceased wives' sisters, may have provided complete protection against prurience. Nevertheless, when Anderson married his second wife it left Nellie in bereft circumstances, not financially for Anderson saw to that, but so far as the purpose of her life was concerned. It is difficult to believe, however, that she could have made Sutton life very gay for Anderson in the 1920s. It is therefore the more remarkable that he stuck to it so diligently.

When, however, the offer of a dramatic change came in 1931 he was more than ready for it. He was proposed for the Governorship of Bengal, the largest and most difficult of the three Indian Presidencies. The difference between them and the other provincial governorships in British India was that the Presidencies – Bengal, Bombay and Madras – were traditionally reserved for politicians and grandees, whereas the others were the fruits of service in an Indian Civil Service career. Anderson was of course a civil servant (although not of the ICS) and neither a politician nor a grandee, and it was a more considerable change of life for him than for nearly all his predecessors when he entered into a new domain of four official residences at Calcutta, Dacca, Darjeeling and Barrackpore, two special trains and two river yachts to move him between the four, a vast retinue and a salary of £20,000 a year.

Bengal was at once the most populous, metropolitan (the Viceregal court still spent quite a lot of its time in Calcutta) and difficult of the provinces. It had been partitioned by Curzon in 1905 and stuck together again under Minto in 1912. The Muslims were a majority but the Hindus were over 40 per cent and dominated the Calcutta metropolis. The Presidency's finances were in a great mess, not through extravagance (public services were much less advanced than in the other two Presidencies) but because of an unsatisfactory financial relationship with the government of India, under which, broadly speaking, the central government got the proceeds of the buoyant taxes and the Presidency only of the inelastic ones. Furthermore, and to complete the unhappy picture, terrorism was rife. There was a serious assassination attempt on the retiring Governor between Anderson's acceptance and his arrival in India, and there was to be one on Anderson himself two years later. Judges were being murdered in their courtrooms and officials and police chiefs in their offices. When Anderson went to Buckingham Palace for a departure luncheon and to receive yet another high decoration (the GCIE), King George V asked him with more perspicacity than encouragement, 'What is wrong with Bengal?', and suggested that he might, when he had appraised the situation, write a personal memorandum for the King.

This gave him the incentive to produce one of his few significant 'own hand' state papers. In June (that is a couple of months after his arrival) he despatched seventeen pages to the King. Its main practical benefit stemmed not from what the King did with it but from the fact that such high-level interest made Anderson apply more schematic thought to what he wanted to achieve during his Governorship than he might otherwise have done. And the conclusions with which he emerged were the fairly obvious ones that suppressing terrorism was essential but not enough in itself and that the financial position of the province must be improved. Insofar as he was welcome in Bengal it was largely because of his anti-terrorist reputation from Ireland. But he had the sense to see that the situations were very different. 'Anyone who says the conditions here are like Ireland is talking through his hat,' he wrote to his father. 'Repressive measures alone will never destroy terrorism,' he wrote to the King. Nevertheless he did, as in Ireland, help to get a grip on the situation by improving the morale of the administration, and by his own displays of imperturbable personal courage. He even became known, perhaps more in London than in Calcutta, and improbably in view both of his shape and of the ponderous nature of his movements, as 'the tiger of Bengal'.

He also achieved considerable practical progress in negotiating by stages a substantially more favourable financial position for Bengal in relation to the government of India. He did not exactly arrive in India with a ready-made reputation. The Viceroy (Lord Willingdon) for instance had never heard of him when his appointment was proposed. But he knew how to present a case persuasively within the parameters of a government machine and, even when he was putting him down, he was good at impressing P. J. Grigg, the Finance Member. When they had both departed from India, Sir Jeremy Raisman, Grigg's successor, said, 'Now that John Anderson has gone, the days when Bengal can bamboozle the government of India are over.'

His governorship was widely accounted a success. When the five years were over he was pressed, even though he did not get on with the new Viceroy (Linlithgow), to stay on for six months in order to see into place the new constitutional arrangements under the 1935 India Act. He eventually arrived back in England on 11 December 1937. Whatever their effect on Bengal the five and a half years had considerably changed John Anderson. He had become for the first time a figure known to the informed public. There would have been no danger in 1937 of Willingdon's rough equivalent in some other part of the world, say the British ambassador in Washington, not knowing who he was. Furthermore his tastes had altered and his horizons had widened. There was no eagerness to get back to Sutton and the 6.15 p.m. train.

His life in Bengal had continued to be fundamentally a lonely one but it had become less narrow. His family, such as it was, could not mostly be with him, partly on security grounds, although paradoxically his daughter (aged eighteen and his chaperoning sister-in-law were on a visit and closely present at the racecourse assassination attempt in May 1934. But he lived in almost continuous proximity with his 'official family' of military and civilian secretaries, ADCs and so on, and this forced him into a greater intimacy and more relaxed atmosphere with them than anything he had fostered with his Whitehall subordinates. There is some indication that he even allowed and enjoyed a respectful degree of teasing. I doubt if there was quite the upper-class boisterousness of small dinners at the Viceregal court of a few years before, when Lord Irwin (Halifax) liked to blow his hunting horn and watch young Lord Stavordale jump over the chairs, but there was probably some desire for imitation of that style among the ADCs. With the majority of those with whom he came into official and even social contact, however, he maintained what was sometimes called his 'howdah manner'.*

Another new element in his life was provided by the stream of fashionable visitors who on a winter trip through India were delighted to spend some time as a guest in one or other of the Bengal government houses. One such example was Mrs Ronnie Greville, the redoubtable chatelaine of Polesden Lacey, who was still going strong twenty years after her refusal of Sir John Simon's offer of marriage, and was happy to add another Sir John to her collection of lions. She lent him Polesden Lacey for the honeymoon following his second marriage. Most of the foci of the new social life which greeted him on his return were however staider than Mrs Greville. He seemed to be regarded as a suitable *vis-à-vis* for Queen Mary at dinner parties and even for weekends. The Abercorns, the Athlones, the Willingdons were typical hosts, although there was also a leavening of Lady Cunard and Lady Colefax.

---

* The comment, delivered in the almost Welsh lilt which is characteristic of modern India, 'very fine man, but always talks to you from top of elephant', might have been invented for Sir John, but in fact comes from forty years later when the Raj was well dead and the high commissioner (to one of whom the phrase in fact related) was the highest British official in the sub-continent.

Still more striking than the widened social life to which he returned was the range and quality of the job offers which he received. Already before leaving India he had turned down a request from the Prime Minister that he should become high commissioner in Palestine. If he was to go on in the public service he would prefer to have stayed in Bengal, as he had been pressed to do. But he felt he must look to his own private affairs. He joined the board of the Midland Bank with the accompanying inducement that he might soon succeed the perennial McKenna as chairman. (He never did, for he was soon otherwise occupied and McKenna obligingly stayed on until past his eightieth birthday.) He also became a director of Imperial Chemical Industries, of Vickers, and of the Employers Liability Assurance Corporation, as fine a clutch of 'blue chip' directorships as it is possible to imagine. He was thus financially secure, and at a much higher level than anything he had previously known in England. He rented a house in Chepstow Villas, Notting Hill, and a little later acquired an Edwardian semi-mansion with ten acres of ground near Merstham, a few miles beyond Sutton.

His main re-entry exercise, however, was much more surprising than any of these. He became an MP. Ramsay MacDonald's death had created a vacancy in one of the three seats with which the graduates of the Scottish Universities were then represented in Parliament. The approach first came to him when he was at sea on the way from India from Sir John Graham Kerr, who was one of the other sitting members for the constituency and a Unionist or Conservative. Anderson sent a temporizing reply saying that an immediate answer would have to be 'no', but that if he could take soundings when he got home he might become favourably disposed. What he meant was that he wanted first to be convinced that he would win – he obviously had no interest in a losing contest – and secondly to explore the extent to which he could keep himself free of a party label. This was partly because he thought it improper for a former civil servant to become too partisan and partly because he thought himself as more a Gladstonian Liberal than a Conservative.

What he really wanted, it might fairly accurately be postulated, was to get Conservative votes, and then to be available for service in a predominantly Conservative government, without having to bear the Conservative label. The smokescreen with which he satisfied himself was a fairly thin one. He ran at the invitation of the Scottish Unionists, but he did so as a National candidate. He was thus able to start his election address with the statement 'I am not a Party man.' Two sentences later he qualified this with 'But I present myself as a convinced supporter of the National government,' thereby defining his position on the pro- or anti-Neville Chamberlain divide, which was the central issue of political controversy at the time. Anderson therefore put himself firmly on the other side from the Labour and Liberal parties, as well as nearly all genuine independents plus such Conservatives as Churchill, Macmillan and (perhaps more doubtfully) Eden, who resigned as Foreign Secretary literally as the Scottish Universities votes were being counted.

Anderson's was therefore far from being a non-partisan candidature. It was however a successful one, and he was well ahead of the field, which was composed of one Scottish Nationalist (Gibb) and two independents, all of them Scottish academics. The result after a transferable vote count was:

Anderson: 14,042
Dr Frances Melville: 5,618
Professor Dewar Gibb: 5,246
Sir Peter Chalmers Mitchell: 3,804

He took his seat – as a back bencher – on 1 March 1938. The slight falseness in the colours under which he had been elected, as an independent who was not very independent, as a non-Conservative whose Conservatism was more dependable than many of those who took the party label, almost exactly foreshadowed his conduct during his twelve career-advancing years in the House of Commons, and indeed his subsequent five in the House of Lords.

His first couple of months as an MP, however, created more friction than friendliness with the Prime Minister. Anderson was offered the chairmanship of Imperial Airways, on a more or less full-time basis. It was an odd proposition to make to a man who had just won a by-election, particularly as, although it formally came from the Imperial Airways board, Chamberlain was behind it, and indeed much of Anderson's correspondence about the matter was with him. Anderson accepted in principle on the basis that he would not resign his so recently acquired seat, but would announce that he would not stand again and would heavily restrict his parliamentary activities in the meantime. However there was dispute both about his other directorships and about his demand that the government should take public responsibility for having pressed him into the job. Eventually Chamberlain (perhaps cumulatively influenced by the Palestine refusal as well, decided that Anderson was becoming more trouble than he was worth, and turned to Sir John Reith instead. Churchill's 'wuthering height' from Glasgow and the BBC was for the moment preferred to 'Jehovah' from Edinburgh to Bengal. Churchill at this stage was not particularly in favour of either panjandrum. When Anderson made his maiden speech in June his private comment was 'elephantine platitudes'.

The speech was about air-raid precautions (an old subject of Anderson's in the 1920s when the need was less pressing) and was garnished by a somewhat sententious quotation from Browning. It was listened to by a large and on the whole respectful House, although Megan Lloyd George's immediately following compliment that it made her wish he had never left the Home Office might be regarded as back-handed. *The Times* printed the speech in full, Anderson noted with satisfaction.

Perhaps its main significance of his speech was that it set the course of his ministerial activities for the next two and a half years. Already he had been asked by the Home Secretary (Hoare) to preside over a small parliamentary committee (there were only three other members) to prepare a scheme for the evacuation of the non-essential population from the big cities in the event of war. It was a task which almost exactly suited his qualities of forceful energetic chairmanship and tidy administration. The committee met twenty-five times during June and July, examined a total of eighty-three witnesses and presented its finished report to the Home Secretary by 26 July. This led on directly to his designation as Civil Regional Commissioner for London and the Home Counties, obviously the most important region, when the Czech crisis made September 1938 a month of impending war. The Munich settlement temporarily removed that threat, and Anderson after two executive weeks installed in New Scotland Yard returned for a few more weeks to his status as back bencher extraordinaire.

Typically, he voted for Munich – the boat must not be rocked – and, equally typically, he did so without enthusiasm. This made him just eligible for inclusion in a Chamberlain Cabinet, and on 1 November he became Lord Privy Seal with a special supplementary designation as Minister for Civilian Defence. This responsibility he took sufficiently seriously – there were few tasks to which he did not accord this honour – that within ten days he had taken the first steps towards creating the monument which has most kept his name alive in history. The Anderson shelter, which with its curved corrugated roof became a feature of so many British back gardens during the next six years, was not personally designed by Sir John, but it was created by his old Edinburgh engineering friend (Sir) William Paterson under his very close inspiration and direction. Paterson was in America when the Department of Civilian Defence (later Home Security) came into being on 10 November. Anderson went to Waterloo station to meet the boat train which brought Paterson back, and to make sure that he got his nose straight to the grindstone, or at least to the design board. Three months later the first operational shelter was installed, and by the outbreak of the war, just over six months after that, one and a half million had been manufactured and made available.

This was a prodigious and valuable feat of organization, but Anderson's general ministerial performance was more mixed. He was heavy-footed in Cabinet and in the House of Commons. 'Don't talk to us like niggers,' was once shouted across the floor at him, thereby indicating both that political correctness was not at a high premium among Labour MPs in 1939 and that Anderson's parliamentary manner left something to be desired. Nevertheless he got a major Civil Defence Bill through in the summer of 1939, and at the outbreak of war changed places with Hoare, who reverted to the sinecure office of Lord Privy Seal, while Anderson became both Home Secretary and Minister of Home Security. Despite these responsibilities he (unlike Hoare) was not made a member of Chamberlain's War Cabinet of nine. This was compensated for by his satisfaction at being the political head of the major department of state on which he had for such a substantial period been the official head, a unique double in the history of the Home Office, and one only paralleled in another department of state by his once rebuked colleague P. J. Grigg at the War Office.

Eventually however the Home Office proved the site of his one career setback. He survived in that post over the formation of the Coalition government in May 1940, perhaps luckily, for Churchill had no reason to be enthusiastic about him. He had been too middle-of-the-road in India and too content with Chamberlain at home. His reaction to the revolt against the Prime Minister which followed from the Norway débâcle was typical of a powerful but cautious administrator without political imagination. He thought it was 'irresponsible' to provoke a political upheaval which could only confuse the country and comfort the enemy. He was by no means alone of course in initially preferring Chamberlain to Churchill and then gradually changing his mind over the summer of 1940, but there was no basis other than his performance as a minister on which Churchill owed him anything. Such performance rests not only on the formulation and implementation of policy, but also on its presentation, both to Parliament and to public. The last requirement marks an essential difference between a permanent secretary and a Secretary of State and it is not perhaps surprising that this was Anderson's vulnerable flank. It exhibited itself on two issues during the five months for which he was Churchill's Home Secretary.

The first was the internment of enemy aliens, mostly refugees. During the period of the 'phoney war' Anderson had pursued a sane and cautious policy on this. He had set up a system of tribunals which up to 1 March had led to 62,244 exemptions from all special restrictions, 6,782 exemptions from internment but not from movement restrictions, and 569 internments. As soon as the war became more intense, however, he was subject to a mounting wave of pressure for more drastic action. The popular press were in the lead but were not alone. They were joined in mid-May by the *Manchester Guardian* and in June Churchill sent Anderson a peremptory minute urging less dawdling. Britain was of course facing the imminent threat of invasion, and imaginations were excited by tales of Vidkun Quisling in Norway and of numerous enemy agents, some of them allegedly disguised as nuns, in the Netherlands.

Anderson then somewhat overreacted. On 1 June he revoked most exemptions, and by the late summer internment camps, for which the Isle of Man was a favourite location, became full of those with impeccable anti-Nazi credentials. Italy had also entered the war and this produced a fine crop of *maîtres d'hôtel* and *maîtres d'orchestre*, as well as more humble practitioners in gastronomy and music. A good number of them perished when the *Arandora Star* was torpedoed on her way with a refugee cargo to Canada. Public opinion then began to turn the other way, and by the time of a House of Commons debate on 22 August, 1940 (which I heard from the public gallery) Colonel Josiah Wedgwood, the intrepidly independent Labour potter, was able to strike a chord with his mordant parody of a War Office communiqué saying that after some gallant but fatal action by resistance fighters on the Continent 'the next of kin have been interned'.

Anderson was probably not guilty of more than a lack of quickness on his feet which meant that he was always moving a little clumsily behind the current wave of opinion, but it was not a good preparation for the next and more severe test of his presentational and persuasive qualities. The 'deep shelter' issue which had been quietly simmering away at least since the spring of 1939, when a powerful committee under Lord Hailey came out against them, erupted into a boil when the

London blitz began on 7 September 1940. Its first political casualty was John Anderson's Home Secretaryship. He was removed from the Home Office on 8 October. He was resolutely opposed to deep shelters, in which hard doctrine he was almost certainly right. To construct them on a scale commensurate with the size of the population which needed to be protected would have been hopelessly expensive and diversionary in men and materials – money did not much matter at that stage. It might have encouraged the development of a 'shelter mentality', with people taking to the catacombs as soon as they heard the sound of a siren, and production being devastated. And the risks of a direct hit on a crowded cavern with concentrated carnage beyond even the clearing-up capacity of the emergency services were considered to be unacceptable.

These were all powerful, rational arguments which were not invalidated by the unorganized (indeed disorganized) rush to the tubes which took place and resulted in conditions of considerable squalor during that September. There was also a substantial press and local agitators' campaign in favour of deep shelters. The Communist party, opposed to the war until Hitler's invasion of Russia nine months later and at the time by no means negligible in the East End, made it their campaign of the autumn. Churchill was seriously concerned about the breakdown of civil society in East London, and his concern was not assuaged by the Home Secretary's methods of dealing with the issue. Anderson organized a conference of editors and metaphorically read the riot act to them: Their patriotic duty was to drop the campaign. They were not impressed.

Herbert Morrison had been Minister of Supply since the formation of the Coalition and had shown a great flair for publicity. More substantially he had been a powerful and successful leader of the London County Council from 1934, and was a Londoner of Londoners, the son of a Lambeth policeman and himself an MP at that time for South Hackney. He was also a politician to his fingertips, a worthy grandfather of Mr Peter Mandelson. Churchill's decision to replace Anderson with Morrison at the crisis of the blitz and of East London morale was therefore one of his best Cabinet dispositions.

He did not demote Anderson. He made him a member of the War Cabinet (of eight) which he had never been as Home Secretary (although Morrison was to be so later) and by relieving him of departmental responsibility freed him for the most successful and influential role that he was ever to play, that of the great chairman of Cabinet committees.

Nevertheless it was the one and only time in his life when he was superseded in a job, and he was quite sensitive enough, in spite of his portentous carapace, fully to appreciate this.

It was also appreciated in wider circles, as I can personally testify. In that autumn there opened in George Street, Oxford, a restaurant which was lush by the standards of the time and which called itself Anderson's. The head waiter had some of the gloomy bloodhound-like appearance of Sir John, as well as wearing clothes at least equally formal, if a shade more shop- or soup-soiled, than those of our hero. It gave us exquisite if immature pleasure to pretend that this lugubrious figure was Anderson himself, forced to recover from his supersession by a little moonlighting from his light duties as Lord President. The supreme fantasy was to address him, fairly *sotto voce*, as 'Sir John'. This little piece of undergrad-uate nonsense indicated both that Anderson had by then become something of a known public figure, which he had hitherto never been, in spite of his quiet triumphs from Dublin to Calcutta, and that he was regarded as having suffered a setback.

Needless to say he was far too solid on his feet and robustly self-confident in his mind to be unduly cast down by that. He noted it sadly. That was all. 'I should like to have seen the [Home Office] job through,' he said to his parliamentary under-secretary as he left that department. He remained Lord President for almost three years, gaining during this period an astonishing ascendancy over the whole machinery of home front government. He became, in the not exaggerated claim of his biographer, 'one of the three [ministers] most important in the conduct of the war, the others being the Prime Minister and Ernest Bevin'. This might have made for jealousy with Attlee, who for much of the time (from February 1942 to September 1943) was in a semi-peripheral position as Dominions Secretary, although also leader of the minority party in the Coalition and with varying formality entitled to the label of deputy Prime Minister.

Anderson succeeded, however, in gaining the lasting and amicable respect of Attlee, who enjoyed a little gentle teasing of him (as with the joke about the elephant or when earlier he referred to a Cabinet committee waiting for its chairman as 'Jehovah's witnesses'), but who for the rest of Anderson's life disliked going strongly against him. This was a considerable feat on Anderson's part, but it and his other achievements were all gained well within the Whitehall labyrinth and made little impact on the outside world. In a wider forum he was often clumsy, as most notably in his opening of the debate on the Beveridge

Report in February 1943. He then gave such an impression of unimaginative foot-dragging as to produce the biggest Labour revolt in the history of the Churchill Coalition. Ninety-seven Labour members voted against the government and only two Labour non-office holders voted in its favour.

Even within his favoured field of presiding over committees and of the untying of administrative knots, he suffered from a lack of originality and creativity. Every ball was played straight down the middle with deadly aplomb. Again to quote his distinguished and solitary biographer, Sir John Wheeler-Bennett, who deserves great credit for having produced in 1962 almost a soufflé of a book about Anderson:

> in [his] calm lay both his strength and also a certain weakness. His imperturbability seemed sometimes to be carried to the point of unwillingness to think ahead; his analytical and administrative cogency to be matched by a lack of creative power; his fairness and balance to arise to some extent from a lack of excitement or any feeling of involvement.

There was however one issue during this period in which he certainly became involved and which indeed even aroused his excitement. This was his second marriage, which took place in the Chapel Royal, St James's Palace on 30 October 1941. Three weeks before he had informed his father of the impending event with the measured calm of a Whitehall minute. He waited until the third page of his regular letter to convey the essential item:

> I don't usually have much news. I have this week, however, one item that will surprise you and may perhaps startle you. I have decided – not in any undue haste – to marry again. The lady is a widow – aged 45 – whose husband died five years ago. He was in the diplomatic service. Her name is Mrs Ralph Wigram. I expect we shall be married very quietly within the next two months.

His next letter showed signs of irritation with Edinburgh provincialism which meant that his father, not unnaturally, had never heard of Mrs Wigram. 'There was a good deal about her in the London papers, and I thought, wrongly as it seems, that you would have seen similar reports.' There were some things to know about Ava Bodley, as she had been born. Her father, J. E. C. Bodley, moved from being private secretary to Sir Charles Dilke (to a belief in whose innocence from the sexual charges levelled against him he remained dedicated) to writing a notable history of modern France, and his daughter was brought up in a very francophone and francophile atmosphere. In 1924 she had married Wigram, who was both rich and talented, but misfortune had dogged their marriage. He was stricken by polio in 1926 and died in 1936, while their only child was a severely handicapped son, born in 1929, who lived until 1951. In her Sussex house she cared for him devotedly but was nonetheless able to live a life of wit, fashion and high political contacts from her house in Lord North Street. Anderson had met her soon after his return from India full of prestige as the 'tiger of Bengal'. She was a considerable lion-hunter (and no doubt willing to take in tigers as well), who it was widely believed would like to have married Harold Macmillan as her third husband in their mutual old age. He would have fulfilled at least one of the qualifications which Ava's close but insolent friend Gladwyn Jebb felt that Anderson lacked when, on rumours of her second engagement, he sent her a telegram saying, 'Do not do it. I assure you he will neither be Prime Minister nor Viceroy.'

For a year or so after Anderson and Ava met such an engagement seemed infinitely remote. In 1940 he began to find reasons for going with surprising frequency to Lord North Street or some other encounter ground, but he remained on terms of gruff formality, never calling her anything other than 'Mrs Wigram', never expecting to be addressed as anything other than 'Sir John', and indeed, so she subsequently complained, hardly ever addressing a remark directly to her. Then in July 1941, he suddenly and insistently announced his arrival for a late-night call, poured out an account of his early life and first marriage, said that the complication of a second marriage would be too great, but asked her to join with him in a chaste but faithful spiritual union for the rest of their lives. This proposition was unattractive to her, but when by September he moved to a more conventional proposal she accepted him. The marriage gave every sign of being successful, lasted sixteen years and transformed Anderson's life, materially, socially and maybe even emotionally.

In late September 1943, when Kingsley Wood died suddenly, Churchill at first intended to make Oliver Lyttelton Chancellor, but overnight he decided he could not spare him from the Ministry of Production and Anderson was transferred to the Exchequer for the last year and a half of the war, although retaining some of his more general responsibility, such as that for the Economic Section of the Cabinet Office and, most notably, for the Tube Alloys/Manhattan atomic project, for the consequences of which indeed he kept an important advisory role for three years into the Attlee government.

Anderson was sixty-one when he went to the Treasury. Only two Chancellors this century, Ritchie and Simon, had been older than him when they began, although Neville Chamberlain was a year and a half senior when he began his second and much more significant term at the Exchequer in 1931. After Anderson, among the twenty subsequent Chancellors, only Macmillan has been older, and he only by a margin of a few months. But when it is considered how much lay before Macmillan at this stage it can hardly be held that Anderson's age began to mean failing powers. On the other hand he was unlikely to be an adventurous or light-hearted Chancellor. His style was not liable to bear much relationship, to take examples from both the past and in relation to him in the future, to that of Lord Randolph Churchill or Mr Kenneth Clarke. But that would have been so almost as much at the age of thirty-one as at that of sixty-one.

His two budgets could not be regarded as exciting. Indeed the follow-on work from Wood's 'Pay as you earn' innovation which he did in the autumn and winter of 1943–4 made much more impact than either of them. Somewhat reluctantly and under pressure Anderson agreed to extend PAYE, which had been intended only for weekly wage earners, first to monthly salary earners up to a limit of £600 a year and then to all salary earners without limit. His 1944 budget was on 25 April. It was unusual in that he answered Treasury parliamentary questions in the morning (the House of Commons as a wartime gesture was endeavouring to squeeze its sittings into the hours of daylight) then went home to lunch, rather as Charles Dilke had reported the troops of the Paris Commune doing in 1871, and came back at 2.45 to deliver his budget. It lasted two hours, and there is some difficulty in retrospect in seeing exactly how he filled the time.

There were no changes in taxation. When he announced that his prescription was 'the mixture as before', timing this to coincide with his taking a sip of his specially prepared budget potion, this was regarded as an exceptional foray into light-hearted witticism. He no doubt thought that with income tax at ten shillings in the pound and surtax rising to an additional five shillings in the pound he (or rather Kingsley Wood) had done what he could with direct taxation, and that further increases in indirect taxation would bear heavily on the cost of living, which was a sensitive issue at the time. Indeed the point of most substance in

Anderson's speech was his announcement that the government could no longer guarantee to use subsidies, mainly on food, to hold the basic cost of living to between 25 and 30 per cent above the pre-war figure. The margin of tolerance would have to go to between 30 or 35 per cent. Either target zone was a considerable *dirigiste* achievement with wages rising quite fast and other inflationary pressures. Even with this additional burden on government expenditure, however, the internal national finances were not in a bad state for the fifth year of a total war. Revenue was estimated at £3,102 million as against £5,967 million of expenditure, which meant that a much higher proportion of war costs were being currently financed than in either 1914–18 or the South African War.

The main change announced by Anderson was the introduction in relation to the depreciation of industrial assets of initial allowances at the rate of 20 per cent. This could be regarded as lifting his eyes to the post-war world, and also enabled him to fill a substantial part of the speech with a wise lecture about the difference between research and development and the desirability of seeing that one followed from the other. The speech received a remarkably good reception. The appropriate note for congratulating Anderson was almost perfectly caught in a message which Queen Mary sent through a lady-in-waiting about his follow-up broadcast: 'It made the financial position of the country vividly clear to the lay mind, and Her Majesty particularly appreciated the judicious mixture of warning and encouragement!'

By the time of Anderson's second and last budget, exactly a year later, the war in Europe was almost won, and he with his special atomic knowledge should have been more optimistic about the subsequent length of the Japanese conflict than almost anyone else. However he used a phrase at once curious and ultra-cautious about the future. The nation, he opined, had not yet reached the stage at which he as Chancellor should begin to consider his task in relation to post-war taxation. He therefore merely noted that revenue was up by £163 million over the previous year, expenditure up by rather less, and the deficit down by £25 million. Again he made no taxation changes, which should await 'a comprehensive review of the probable course of post-war expenditure and of the system of taxation in relation to it', which might however come in much less than a year.

Anderson could never be accused of rushing things, but he handled them with such effective and deliberate speed that his internal reputation was at its peak during these early months of 1945. On the eve of departure for Yalta Churchill wrote formally and in a rather convoluted way to the King to advise that if he and Eden were by chance both killed on the journey Sir John Anderson should be sent for. Nor did he suggest that this should be merely a stop-gap appointment. He continued, without great prescience: 'It is very likely there will be a substantial Conservative majority in the new Parliament; but it by no means follows that the majority would not accept Sir John Anderson as Prime Minister with or without his acceptance of the Leadership of the Conservative party.'

At the end of May the coalition broke up and its component parts returned to their battle lines for the election which took place on 5 July. Anderson had no difficulty about continuing as Chancellor in the Conservative 'caretaker' government which followed, and indeed made one of the election broadcasts on behalf of the Conservative party. Nevertheless he once again presented himself to the Scottish Universities as a non-party candidate. The result for him was a comfortable return. Under the transferable-vote system of proportional representation which prevailed in the university seats it looks from the published result as though he was equal second in the contest for three seats. In fact however he was well ahead on first preferences with Sir John Boyd Orr, the nutritionist, who counted as a somewhat left-of-centre progressive as a good second. Sir John Graham Kerr, who had originally persuaded Anderson to stand but had not done much in the meantime except for a little quiet zoology, and was at the age of seventy-six standing as a straight Unionist, was a poor third to begin with and needed a lot of transferred second, third and even fourth preferences to get above the quota.

This election brought to an abrupt and final close Anderson's six-and-two-third-year ministerial career, but it left him with another four and a half years to go in the House of Commons. He accepted without wincing membership of the otherwise purely Conservative shadow Cabinet, while continuing to cling on to the 'independent' label which deceived nobody but himself. Whatever he called himself, however, he was ill suited to opposition, and assumed something of the air of a beached whale on that front bench. Why did he continue? In his case probably no doubt because of a sense of public service. Partly also because he was able to combine that public service with a good ration of private reward. He was anxious to make some money and he gradually, while still an MP and indeed a member of the shadow Cabinet, rejoined his old boards of ICI, Vickers and Employers' Liability Assurance (although not the Midland Bank, which, in spite of McKenna and other later refugees from Westminster to the City, he thought inappropriate for a former Chancellor), and added to them the Southern Railway (for a brief pre-nationalization sojourn), Hudson's Bay Company, the Canadian Pacific Railway and a few other less resonant names.

Much his most important outside activity, however, was the chairmanship of the Port of London Authority, which he accepted as early as January 1946. The Port was still a major and visible, although heavily war-damaged, component of the life of the capital city, and Anderson approached it almost with the circumstance (and more than the pomp) of a Chirac turning from the premiership of France to the mayoralty of Paris. He was a dominant and effective head of the Authority, particularly in its external relations, but it was for the high style which he imposed, a long call from the modest austerities of Sutton, that he is best remembered in the present epoch of built-over wharves and warehouses and largely deserted river. He insisted on a salary much larger than that of a Cabinet minister even though with his other commitments he was manifestly devoting only half time to the PLA and his predecessors had been unpaid. He inherited an office and boardroom of an opulent dignity comparable with that of the Bank of England and imposed an entirely new culinary regime which made the Authority's board dining room stand out as a Lucullan oasis in the drab post-war world. By a supreme irony the Inland Revenue (can there have been any aggrieved juniors left from Anderson's period as chairman over a quarter of a century before?) tried to challenge the lavish free luncheons for board members as a benefit which ought to be taxable. They were routed by Sir John.

The greatest perquisite however was the Authority's small river yacht, which nonetheless sat sixty for lunch or dinner, and, under the combination of Anderson's gravely benignant hospitality and Lady Anderson's wide social trawl, frequently did so. The boat was originally intended as a survey vessel but came increasingly to ply relentlessly up and down the tidewater reaches of the Thames with a fine company of political, diplomatic, literary and otherwise fashionable lions, between whom Ava fluttered with avian agility. It was indeed when the craft was in attendance at the University Boat Race in 1951 and she was deep in conversation with the Prime Minister (Attlee, who with his loyalty to all institutions with which he had been associated was an eager Boat Race attender) that the question of Anderson's transference from the House of Commons to the House of Lords seriously arose.

Until then he had persisted in believing that the university seats although abolished by Labour would be put back by the Conservatives. Attlee brusquely told Lady Anderson that this would not happen. Churchill, whatever he had said, would never take the trouble or endure the odium of putting back a 'fancy franchise'. And he proved quite right. Anderson had been offered safe Conservative seats in Surrey or in Ulster, but he rather quaintly still did not want that label or an ordinary constituency. So it was the House of Lords or nothing for him, and there he ended up in the New Year's honours list of 1952. It was the first list of the new Conservative government, and his ennoblement came after something of a contretemps as to whether he was to be in that government or not. He could equally well have got the peerage had Labour remained in office.

The contretemps arose out of Anderson's probably still hoping to be Chancellor again. He was sixty-nine, but Churchill himself was almost seventy-seven. Oliver Lyttelton (once again) also hoped to be Chancellor, but eventually R. A. Butler got the job. Churchill tried to sugar the pill for Anderson by offering him an 'overlordship', a sort of vague supervisory role over the Treasury, and the Board of Trade and the Ministry of Supply as well. This was repugnant to Butler and unattractive to Anderson. He was not much excited by being Chancellor of the Duchy of Lancaster, which was to be his title and was only the third of the sinecure offices, but more substantially the whole arrangement struck him as being contrived, artificial and doubtfully constitutional. So he declined.

His peerage as an ex-Chancellor and Lord President was automatically a viscountcy. Indeed, in view of his great wartime services and unique previous career, he might well have been regarded by traditional standards as pushing an earldom, which his 1943 successor as Lord President, Lord Woolton, was to receive four years later. When there was some College of Heralds objection to his continuing to be called Anderson he decided that if he had to find a territorial title he wanted an Edinburgh one, and apparently regarded Waverley as a satisfactorily indigenous 'auld Reekie' name and not merely a post-Walter Scott commemorative one. So he became the only peer of the railway age to be called after a station; Queen Victoria and W. E. Forster (of Bradford) had termini named after them, but that was the other way round, and they were not peers.

Anderson spoke with moderate frequency in the Lords for the next five years, and on a wide variety of subjects from whether or not Britain should continue to manufacture heroin (he was in favour) through the setting up of independent television (he was against) to the death penalty (he urged its retention). But his forte was more the chairmanship of deliberative committees of enquiry than the exchange of debating speeches in the second chamber. He investigated the problems of the export of works of art, and to this day the 'Waverley Rules' are accepted as the criteria for deciding whether a work of art is of such national importance that its sale abroad should at least deferred while a domestic home is sought. It was typical of him that, with the minimum of visual taste, he should nonetheless be capable of guiding a committee towards a lasting and on the whole sensible bureaucratic framework within which others could take aesthetic decisions. He applied himself as much to the causes and lessons of the East Coast floods of February 1953 as to the continuing problems of atomic energy. But there was one enquiry over which, to his deep resentment, he was not allowed to preside. In early 1952 he was nominated to fill a vacancy in the chairmanship of the Royal Commission on the Taxation of Profits and Income. The Labour party protested vigorously. In his years on the front opposition bench in the House of Commons he had taken very strong and partisan views on the points most directly at issue. He could not believe that any view of his was other than objective truth, and certainly not partisan; after all, he was not a nominal Conservative. Furthermore he thought that the Labour motion of regret ignored the debts of gratitude to him which Attlee, Morrison, Dalton and his other wartime colleagues should have accumulated. Nevertheless he felt obliged to withdraw.

The other great interest of his last decade was the chairmanship of the Royal Opera House, Covent Garden. He had taken this on in succession to Maynard Keynes in 1946. It was in many ways a strange appointment, for he was almost tone-deaf and had very little aesthetic appreciation of either opera or ballet. But it was also a successful appointment. During performances he was often asleep in the Royal Box, where he and Ava entertained almost as lavishly as they did on the PLA boat. But he was never asleep during meetings of the board or its committees, and his weight and reputation made him a most powerful and skilful defender of the needs of the Opera House.

He was such a general panjandrum in the early 1950s that a story developed (or was invented) of a delegation from an East European country who visited London and, arriving by water, were received by the chairman of the Port of London Authority. In the afternoon they visited the Advisory Committee on Atomic Energy and were received by the chairman. In the evening they were entertained at Covent Garden and were received by the chairman of the Royal Opera House. They went home convinced that Britain was run neither by Attlee nor by Churchill, but by a man of whom they had never previously heard called Lord Waverley.

Anderson's health held well until he was seventy-five, and he had a satisfying approach to old age. At about the time of his peerage he and his wife moved Sussex houses, going to Westdean, an 1830s house set in the South Downs near Alfriston, which they had coveted over ten years before. Here he took to breeding bloodhounds, which in view of his own appearance indicated a greater sense of humour than that with which he is mostly credited. Honours continued to descend upon him. But by the Oxford Encaenia (honorary degree ceremony) in June 1957 he had begun to feel disagreeably unwell. By August he was seriously ill. He then went downhill quickly and died at the beginning of January 1958. A few weeks before, when it was thought he might not even last a few days, the Order of Merit had been conferred upon him in hospital. 'The civil service will be pleased about this' was his curious throwback of a comment. He had indeed been a remarkable civil servant, but not for the last thirty-six years of his life.

HUGH DALTON

ANDERSON APART, HUGH DALTON WAS THE only figure in this series whom I knew, and I knew him well. I liked him, contrary both to the fashion of the time and to most of the judgement of history, but I did not admire him in the way that, of his immediate successors, I did Stafford Cripps, who with his frosty eminence I knew less well, or Hugh Gaitskell, to whose memory I remain devoted, and whom I knew still better than Dalton.

Why include Dalton, particularly as bringing him in pushes me beyond the natural break-point of 1945, makes my numbers uneven and introduces the inevitably unbalancing factor of personal recollection? These disadvantages are outweighed by his being more a politician of the 1930s and of the war and its immediate aftermath than of the full post-war world; by his having become (in spite of Professor Ben Pimlott's excellent biography and subsequent diary editing) a somewhat neglected figure; and by my never having previously written anything of more substance than a book review about him.

Although now neglected, Dalton was certainly not anonymous during the nearly twenty years of his high prominence, which began about 1935. No collective political cartoon was then complete without his long but not wholly elegant body, shining pate and faintly sinister smile, which gave him the air of a very worldly prelate, figuring prominently in it, and needing no label of identification. Pimlott captured the spirit of Dalton's latter-day appearance peculiarly well when he wrote:

> There was a clown-like element, later tragi-comic, which made those who admired him despise him at the same time ... Physically he was becoming odder: his body more top-heavy and head gleamingly polished, his voice more thunderous, his [rolling] eyes more disconcerting.*

* Maynard Keynes, who was his senior by four years at both Eton and King's reacted

Although he was born fifteen years too late to have been a possible contributory model, there was more than a touch of Anthony Powell's Widmerpool about Dalton. He had indeed received his adolescent education in that Thames-side academy which had nurtured, not only Powell himself and most of his early characters, but at the time of Dalton's schooldays nearly half the Prime Ministers of Britain. Superficially he was just the noisiest and the most self-confident of the little band of upper-class recruits which the Labour party received in the 1920s. Yet there were always ambiguities about both Dalton's self-confidence and his class bearings.

Dalton was in fact very class-conscious in a rather uneasy way. He once rather shocked me by dismissing Herbert Morrison as 'a board schooligan'. Dalton's own background was ecclesiastical semi-courtier. His paternal grandfather, like his father, had been a clergyman. His mother was the daughter of a minor country gentleman in Neath, Glamorgan, which was where Dalton himself was born in 1887. However his father cast off from parochial duties in 1871 when he became first tutor and then, as it was at once grandly and severely called, 'governor' to the two sons of the Prince of Wales (later King Edward VII), the elder Prince Albert Victor who became Duke of Clarence before dying in 1892, and the younger Prince George of Wales, who became King George V. He gave them a strict and largely naval education, as was indicated by the two books which he published around these years: *Sermons to Naval Cadets* and *The Cruise of HMS Bacchante*. After this signal service he was made a canon (and steward) of St George's, Windsor, where he lived from 1884 to 1931, conceiving the future Labour Chancellor in 1886 and booming his way around the Windsor cloisters for nearly the next half-century.

He and his son were not close. They were separated by a wide generation gap of forty-eight years, and by sharp differences of apparent orientation. Yet they were very like each other: vigorous, eager to do good provided this did not mean curbing their indiscreet and slightly malicious tongues, generous but not very sensitive, and above all booming. Hugh Dalton made the library corridor of the House of Commons almost the exact equivalent for him of his father's Windsor cloisters. He loved pacing up and down that corridor, pouring out to

---

to this aspect of his physique and personality by christening him 'Daddy Dalton', not intended as a term of filial respect. Partly as a result of this and other brush-offs from that great economist Dalton never became a full Keynesian.

one of an interchangeable group of young companions (to whom it was highly flattering) a series of wild indiscretions.

I recall in particular such a pacing exchange *c* 1954, when after a meeting of the National Executive Committee (then a crucial organ – or at least battleground – of the Labour party) he began by saying that he wanted to tell me exactly what had happened that morning. He had proposed and Jim Callaghan had seconded a motion that anyone who betrayed the secrets of the NEC should be severely censured, maybe asked to resign or to suffer some still more formidable but equally unenforceable penalty. 'It was carried', he continued, 'by thirteen votes to five [or some such majority], and I must tell you, if I can remember it exactly, who was in the [admirable] majority and who was in the [contemptible] minority.' It was of course one of the many ploys made by the right of the Labour party in those days of anti- (or pro-) Bevanite *furia* and illustrated Dalton's acute sense of 'our side' and 'their side', as well as his somewhat less developed sense of irony about his own actions.

His determination to cast himself off from the somewhat soggy shore of such a 'Church and King' background did not easily give him firm alternative ground. He was suspicious of the upper class, contemptuous of the middle class and nervously patronizing of the working class. I also recall an occasion, again *c.* 1954 and in that inevitable library corridor, when he seized upon a passing Labour MP for a northern constituency (as he was himself). 'How are you, Bert?' he boomed, and held him for some time. I stood a little impatiently alongside. The encounter over he turned to me and said, 'You will never get anywhere in politics until you learn to call that man Bert.' I said, 'I don't think you are quite right, Hugh. Apart from anything else his name is Horace.' He was only semi-abashed, as he took me off to the slightly delayed dinner to which I had been summoned. That was part of the teasable and (away from his father) easy generation-crossing side of his personality (he was thirty-three years older than me) which made him capable of laughing at himself and highly enjoyable to be with.

Yet beneath his ebullience there was a deep melancholia. His family life was jejune in the extreme. His relations with his father have already been described. His mother engaged neither his interest nor his affections. He had one sister, four years younger than himself, who disliked him as a child and allowed political differences in later life to produce implacable personal hostility. Her children, his only surviving relations, were never allowed to meet their uncle. His own marriage provided little compensation for this chill. When he was twenty-six, he married an intelligent, brisk Fabian of high bourgeois origin and means, who was nonetheless as free of family affiliations as he was. They had one daughter, who died, searingly, at the age of four, which tragedy separated rather than united them. At times in the 1920s and 1930s they achieved a successful political partnership. But in the Second World War and over the period of his high political success they separated completely. Ruth Dalton went to work first in Manchester and then in France. She returned and looked after him in his decline with an aseptic care. The great emotional involvements of his life were with Rupert Brooke in his twenties and with Anthony Crosland in his sixties. Neither fully reciprocated his feelings.

This emotional black hole meant that while he was gregarious he was also a lonely man. He mostly sought the company of other people more than they sought his, although he was always a forthcoming and often an engaging companion. 'Got Attlee to dinner' was a recurrent note of his wartime diaries, never 'Attlee got me to dine.' He also compensated for a certain sterility in his life with a clamant Housmanism, with metaphors of the battlefield, of youthful strength and of early death all a little too easily to hand. Just as Housman's poetical style could be parodied into 'What, still alive at twenty-two, a fine upstanding lad like you,' so Dalton's oratorical style, although sadly less neat, had similarly parodiable elements. His capacity to tear a passion to tatters was well-illustrated by the over-blown peroration of his speech to the Labour party conference at the beginning of the 1945 general election campaign, which however scores marks for the accuracy of its final confident prophecy:

> I believe we stand on the threshold of a new age of hope. I believe that the spirit which today has been running through this conference, the spirit of hope and determination, a flame burning in every heart among the delegates to this conference, a flame burning in each heart ready to go forth to the bloodless battles after the bloody battles for which – how glad we are to know it – very many of our Service candidates have come back, living and unscathed, though leaving behind on those battlefields many beloved dead, will carry us to victory. The flame is burning in the hearts of all of us survivors of the battle, of the blitz and of those peacetime hard years, and we will carry forward into the battle that is very soon to come the same determination which we of the Labour movement have shown in this war. We will go forward from this conference passionately determined that when the roll is called our

men shall be there, our vote will be cast, and on the day of the count of those votes there shall be, for the first time in our history, a Labour and Socialist majority in our Parliament.

I was present and had the impression that by the end the audience was at least as exhausted as Dalton himself. However he had sustained what he saw as one facet of the political role which he had set for himself, that of being a shouting cheerleader for the Labour party, showing that he could make as much patronizing noise as any Tory. He had also satisfactorily secured his return to the National Executive Committee. And this, together with the two wartime ministries over which he had on the whole successfully presided, and his general abilities, gave him a strong claim to very high office in the event of his somewhat bombinating prophecy of Labour victory being fulfilled. Yet Dalton's ambition was always qualified. He never saw himself as leader of the Labour party. It was other people rather than himself that he was almost obsessively intriguing to make party leader. This was not because of excessive modesty (although he did not suffer from excessive vanity either), but because by some process of inverted snobbery he instinctively wanted to replace 'rabbit Attlee' (whom he consistently underestimated) in 'his little Victorian villa at Stanmore' with someone lower down rather than higher up the social scale, in 1935 Morrison, in 1947 Bevin. It was the old cricket hierarchy turned upside down. Dalton thought that he was at least as good a performer as most if not all of the others, but was precluded from captaining England because he was a gentleman, which, as a final irony, he rather doubtfully was.

Yet Dalton had many virtues. He was not bitter about his setbacks and not jealous about his successors. He thrust forward Hugh Gaitskell, who had been his private secretary during the war, to a higher position than he ever himself achieved with a selflessness which was nearly unique in politics. He was dedicated to trying to promote the political careers of his young associates (and by no means only those by whom he was romantically excited, although perhaps a little more extravagantly in their case). The brutal side of his indiscreet and resonant tongue he reserved for his contemporaries – Morrison, Shinwell, John Strachey, a very mixed bag, were especial and dependable recipients of his disapproval – and perhaps as a result he had remarkably few friends in his own generation, although this was balanced by the reciprocated loyalty (always a good test) of those who had worked for him, most notably Gaitskell and Gladwyn Jebb. He played a major role in containing and reversing the Labour party's march to the wilder shores of lunacy in the early 1930s (a fifty-year recurrent fever, it may be thought, which at least offers the happy prospect of no recurrence until 2030). And he was by no means as bad a Chancellor as, somewhat provoked by his own provocative and clanging phrases, is his unfair reputation.

Edward Hugh John Neale Dalton was born in August 1887, and had a highly conventional education, very similar to that of his seven-year junior fellow politician as well as fellow inhabitant of the no-man's land between the upper and the upper-middle class, Harold Macmillan. He went to Summer Fields, which compared with the Dragon School was the less dons' children-orientated of the two Oxford preparatory schools. From there he failed by a fairly narrow margin to get an Eton scholarship and entered an Oppidan house in 1901. He had an adequate rather than distinguished Eton career, winning a prize or two, showing little interest in or capacity for games, not getting into Pop and, as a rather happy result, not looking back on his schooldays as the best of his life. He had no strong anti-Eton reaction, and in later life defended it on the splendidly negative ground that it performed the great service of getting boys away from their parents.

He much preferred King's College, Cambridge, where he went with a closed Eton exhibition in mathematics in 1906, and therefore on the high tide of Edwardian Liberalism, although at school he had been more politically attracted by Joseph Chamberlain's imperialism. King's had then half emerged from its earlier status as no more than an outpost of Eton in Cambridge, although the two foundations of Henry VI retained close links for another half-century, but not much beyond that. King's despite its 'nave-only' cathedral of a chapel which dominates the Cambridge skyline, was much smaller than Trinity. But it was the only college which could hold a candle to this larger neighbour in drawing power on those, both dons and undergraduates, who either came from established positions of family and fashion or were to attain resonant eminence. It liked to think that while Trinity might be allowed the greater diligence and achievement in the disciplined pursuit of the Cambridge speciality of empirical enquiry on the frontiers of knowledge, King's was developing into a more sensitive repository of human values (which a harsh critic might have described as aesthetic experience plus personal relations – often homosexual, for there were few women involved – equals the good life). The epitome of this outlook was E. M. Forster who had gone to King's eight years before Dalton, but its guru was the philosopher G. E. Moore, who confused the picture by having become a Trinity undergraduate in 1891 before, as a fellow there, publishing *Principia Ethica* in 1903. This treatise, written with simple clarity and innocent force, became the lead text for all the far from simple convolutions of Bloomsbury. The other key figures in this matrix were Goldsworthy Lowes Dickinson, liberal humanist who invented the phrase 'League of Nations' and King's don since the 1880s, and Maynard Keynes, who despite much common background was never Dalton's real friend and always disposed to make his economics look pedestrian and his sexuality clumsy.

Dalton, who was not on the whole lucky either in love or in politics, had the one piece of good fortune that on his first day at King's he met Rupert Brooke. Brooke was as much from the womb of Rugby School as Matthew Arnold had been when he went to Balliol just over sixty years before. (Both their fathers had been schoolmasters there, although Thomas Arnold of course far the more eminent.) Rupert Brooke however was much more of a natural cult figure than Matthew Arnold, if by no means a better poet. Dalton struck up a radical alliance with him. For a time it worked splendidly, and may even have provided the happiest period of Dalton's life (although he subsequently put his whole King's four years in this category). They both became Fabians in early 1907, and organized a dramatically successful meeting for Keir Hardie in the Cambridge Guildhall. But after a bit their partnership began to fray. The sad fact was that Brooke was more sought after than Dalton, and was somewhat torn away by the flattery, and maybe by other factors too.

Dalton's Cambridge career, like his Eton experience, was essentially *proxime accessit*. In King's he was by no means negligible. In the University he was a figure of interest, attracting for example a *Granta* profile, and a frequent and powerful Union debater. But no more than at Eton did great contemporary honours come his way. He got only a third in Part I of the mathematical tripos (and a second when he switched to economics), he was defeated several times in Union elections, and although he was instrumental in setting up the Carbonari, a King's dining club, he never got near to following Harcourt and becoming an Apostle. That somewhat self-regarding Cambridge society, although it became a little later as great a spawning ground of spies as of geniuses, naturally absorbed such diverse approaches to the latter category as Bertrand Russell, Lytton Strachey and Keynes, as well as, most provokingly for Dalton, Rupert Brooke, whose intellect was not of that level.

Dalton left Cambridge in 1910, and from then until early 1915, when he joined the army, his life meandered through a flat landscape. This was against his natural desires, for his tastes were always for rough walking over hills and crags, and gothic rather than classical. He was a natural Lake District man, although the nearest he ever got to establishing himself there was his Durham constituency of Bishop Auckland. The flatness of his pre-1914 life arose mainly out of his lack of clear sense of what he wanted to do. He began by reading for the bar, and was eventually 'called', although with an unimpressive entry mark. He had no legal vocation. The strongest pull upon him was that of the London School of Economics. This was very much a fledgling school at the time, founded only sixteen years before, mainly on the intiative of Sidney Webb and still having little more than a thousand students. It nonetheless gave Dalton more of a solid intellectual base than Cambridge had done. At King's he had an emotional flowering but did not find any very firm intellectual feet, hovering between the influence of the patronizing Keynes and that of A. C. Pigou, 'tall and handsome like a viking', who was at once more orthodox and more interested in equality than Keynes ever was, which was almost exactly Dalton's own position. At LSE he learnt far more economics than he ever had at King's, and did it under the aegis of Professor Edwin Cannan, a notably unadventurous thinker. In the hot summer of 1911 he won the Hutchinson Research Studentship at LSE, which was the first real academic distinction which he had achieved, and LSE remained an important base of his life for the next quarter of a century. It never made him a professor, although he was largely instrumental in promoting Lionel Robbins as Cannan's successor but one (the one being very brief) and thus setting the School off in a Free Market economics direction, which made it a natural home for Friedrich-August von Hayek when he came to England in 1936. On the political-science side the mixture of Marxism, radical utilitarianism and starry-eyed regard for the famous from Baldwin to Roosevelt which activated Harold Laski was equally unattractive to Dalton. It was a remarkable mix, and a good example of academic tolerance.

There were, however, two limitations which need to be set to the love match between Dalton and LSE. First, he was never on the staff before the First World War. He nearly was, but when a lectureship became vacant in 1913 a social worker in the East End called C. R. Attlee, four years his senior but, as Dalton continued to think for many decades, intellectually his inferior, was preferred over him. Second, although LSE provided him with a wife (Ruth Fox had been a student there), his romanticism was still essentially centred on his King's life. It was spectacularly illustrated by a note which Rupert Brooke wrote to him immediately after his honeymoon: 'I am as free as the wind on Thursday night. Are you? You can shelve your wife.' Dalton did, and he and Brooke dined together alone. But it was not the beginning of a 'shelving' of his wife for the renewal of old passions. It was in fact the last time that he ever saw Brooke, who died of fever on a Greek island a year later, but who nonetheless had been in 'England the one land I know, where men with splendid hearts may go; and Cambridgeshire of all England, the shire for men who understand' for a full six months after that dinner without ever renewing his contact with Dalton. It was an epitome of Dalton's tragedy: flickering from his wife like a moth to the flame, but the flame going out before he could be seriously singed.

Dalton had no doubt about his support for the 1914 War. His instinctive militarism and his incipient anti-Germanism coalesced to make that certain. But his early army career was bathos. Unlike R. H. Tawney and some others of the patriotic left, he felt no compulsion to serve in the ranks, but having secured a commission he somehow got himself deployed in the least martially spirited and most unfashionable echelons of the army. He was not only in the Army Service Corps – the grocers of the army – but in that section of it which was attached to the 'bantam' division, made up of those who were below normal physical requirements for the army. It was not as though like his fellow Etonian George Orwell, twenty years later, he positively welcomed this lowering of social status. On the contrary, he was acutely and snobbishly aware of the social deficiencies of his fellow officers. One was 'ill-at-ease with gentlemen', another would 'suck his teeth' and 'bring other vets to meals'. In this company he spent 1916 in France, listening to the guns of the Somme, almost the bloodiest of all battles, while never actually engaging with the enemy or being in a position of real danger.

Perhaps inspired by the sound of these guns, Dalton began an intrigue to get transferred to the artillery (from then through to the end of his parliamentary life, forty-five years later, every initiative, selfish or unselfish on Dalton's part – and many of them were the latter – always assumed the characteristics of an intrigue). When this eventually succeeded it was to a heavy artillery unit which was sent off to try to prop up the Italian front against the Austrians in the eastern Dolomites. This experience was both an inspiration and a revelation to Dalton. Freed of tooth-sucking RASC majors in the base areas of Picardy and Flanders, he took to Italy, to his romantic vision of the descendants of the soldiers of the Risorgimento and to the mountains of Venezia Giulia, not so much like a duck to water as like an eagle to gothic scenery.

Although his main battle experience was to be part of the chaotic retreat from Caporetto, this was compensated for by the successful subsequent restabilization of the line. His sixteen months in Italy left him a strong italophile, a sentiment which even survived a 1932 meeting with Mussolini, although it perished three years later, at least so far as the Italian government was concerned, with the Duce's Abyssinian adventure. This pro-Italian prejudice (for there was always a good deal of prejudice in all Dalton's judgements) fitted in with an equally favourable bias towards Slavs, particularly Poles, and a balancing anti-teutonism, which persisted throughout his life and at times, and those times not confined to the Hitler period, became almost obsessive. His Italian service also produced his first published book (although pre-war he had done a lot on what subsequently became *Some Aspects of the Inequality of Incomes*) entitled *With British Guns in Italy*, a title which, while accurate, was also faintly bombastic. It was written in an optimistic 'Georgian' style owing much to Rupert Brooke, and was well received in a quiet way when it came out in May 1919, which was just in time before a more disillusioned mood set in.

By then Dalton had switched to a pursuit both of a parliamentary seat and of a job, academic or administrative, which would provide him with a moderate salary, engage his interest and enhance his reputation. His pursuit was more relentless than rewarding. The first results were the Labour candidature for Cambridge and the Cassell Readership in Commerce at the London School, the latter continuing to be his base until 1935. The Cambridge candidature was more short-lived. He fought a by-election there in early 1922 and lost by 4,000 votes. For the general election in the autumn of that year he transferred to Maidstone, not an obviously better Labour prospect, and he exchanged his second place in Cambridge for a third, but with all the candidates within a thousand votes of each other.

For the 1923 general election, which led to the first Labour government, he was offered the choice of two Cardiff seats and chose the wrong one, losing by 700. He travelled back in the same railway compartment as the MP for Aberavon who was to be Prime Minister within six weeks, but as he cordially disliked Ramsay MacDonald that was hardly adequate compensation. Then in July 1924, two-thirds of the way through the short Labour government, Dalton fought another by-election in the Labour-held seat of Holland-with-Boston in south Lincolnshire. No doubt on an ebb-tide he lost it by 800 votes and it was no longer Labour-held. Finally at the general election of November 1924, he alighted, like an airliner running out of fuel, on the highly proletarian seat of Peckham in south-east London. Proletarian or not it had returned a Tory by a miniscule majority in 1923, which Dalton, against a stronger tide than in Holland-with-Boston in the summer, was able to turn into a favourable majority of 900. His five elections in three years had been more frenzied than commanding and it was with relief to himself, and probably also to the Labour party national agent who had been harried to get him in, that he at last arrived in the House of Commons. He was thirty-seven. Despite this electioneering frenzy, however, he succeeded in this phase of his life in completing and publishing his *Principles of Public Finance*, which was his main academic achievement, which continued to sell as a text book for many years and in many countries, and which in combination with his other activities was a great tribute to his energy.

Peckham by no means settled his constituency problems. In the House of Commons he settled quickly into the boisterous patronizing style which continued to be his hallmark, and was particularly successful at irritating the Tories, but not at making them like or even respect him. From his own side he received early recognition, being elected to both the Parliamentary Executive (Parliamentary Committee or 'shadow Cabinet' as it later came to be called) and the National Executive of the Labour party within his first two years. These successes, however, soon came to be overshadowed by a long-running and debilitating faction fight within his Peckham constituency, in which he got far too closely involved, which indeed built up to an obsession in his mind, and which by 1928 led to his deciding to give up the seat and seek another one. The dispute was nominally about whether the agent should be sacked, which Dalton tried but failed to do, and indeed produced an outcome in which the agent in effect sacked him. Dalton's fault was far from being constituency neglect. It was rather a display of tactless hyper-energy, getting himself far too deeply involved in the local disputes of a constituency which had the advantage and disadvantage of being only a penny tram-ride away from Westminster.

At first Dalton had very good luck in his search for another constituency. He fixed his eyes firmly on the North-east (he had had enough of constituents within that penny tram-ride) and for a time hovered between Gateshead and Bishop Auckland but settled on the latter, where the sitting Labour MP, Ben Spoor, was conveniently and considerately planning to retire at the next general election. Dalton was adopted for that fairly safe Labour seat, which also had the advantage, for Dalton's romanticism, of having Durham miners on or under the ground and Pennine uplands on the western horizon. Unfortunately Spoor's helpfulness was not wholly dependable, for he died in the Regent Palace Hotel and in circumstances requiring an inquest on 22 December of that year. Dalton, spending almost a last Christmas with his father in the Windsor cloisters, was distraught, not with grief but with anguish, that fate, having so generously given, should so capriciously take away. As a sitting member he could not be a candidate at the by-election. But his wife could. And this was the somewhat ruthless decision which was arrived at. Mrs Dalton, although not very well at the time, fought a spirited campaign and was returned on 8 February with a majority of 7,000. She was an MP for thirteen weeks, during which period she exhibited some parliamentary activity, but when the dissolution came on 10 May loyally surrendered the seat to her husband, who, fortunately, managed to put the majority up by another thousand. Although she was an enthusiastic member of the London County Council there is no suggestion that Ruth Dalton wanted to continue as an MP. There may nonetheless be some room for doubt about how much she enjoyed being treated as an expendable piece of linen, quickly consigned to the laundry basket.

However Dalton had survived the two hiccups and was safely back in Parliament for what he (mistakenly) thought was a seat for life and eager for office in the second Labour minority government, which was the outcome of that 1929 election. As in 1923, he was once again on the train which bore the Prime Minister-elect back to London. MacDonald, at least as peripatetic as Dalton, had moved his constituency to Seaham Harbour, and when the 5.15 p.m. from Darlington pulled out on 31 May it contained not only MacDonald, who had to make speeches to the crowds at York, Doncaster and Grantham, but also one of the most eager candidates for office in his government, as well as Harold Macmillan, defeated at Stockton-on-Tees, who according to Dalton, ineffectively attempted at these stops to call for three cheers for Stanley Baldwin.

'I have a few words with J.R.M., but only a few, on the train,' he typically and just a little sadly recorded. But his main lobbying effort on his own behalf was to be conducted not direct but via Arthur Henderson, who inspired Dalton's genuine and consistent fealty but who had first to win his own battle over J. H. Thomas to become Foreign Secretary. When he had won this Henderson was happy to have Dalton as his parliamentary under-secretary (only one junior minister for the Foreign Office was thought necessary in those days), and indeed there is some suggestion that he appointed him unilaterally, telling the unesteemed MacDonald (by him and Dalton at least, even if not by the crowds at LNER stations) that it was laid down by statute that the parliamentary under-secretary was appointed by the Secretary of State and not by the Prime Minister.

Dalton's two and a quarter years at the Foreign Office consolidated his alliance with Henderson, to whom he was very loyal, increased his confidence although not his powers of conciliation at the despatch box in the House of Commons, and gave him the habit of bullying officials, which became one of his most notable characteristics as a minister. Broadly he made only two Foreign Office allies. The one was Gladwyn Jebb, his peculiarly self-confident twenty-nine-year-old private secretary, who knew how to stand up to him, and the other was Sir Robert Vansittart, who became permanent under-secretary after a few months. Vansittart and Dalton both had a touch of the 'outsider' about them, although Vansittart was a more sophisticated one despite the embarrassing titles which he gave to most of his twenty-four books, and were drawn together partly by this and even more by the fact that they were both deeply anti-German.

In the 1930s, when Vansittart was the source of a good deal of leaked information to Dalton, this put them on the anti-appeasement side, but made them less good counsellors for the post-war settlement. Dalton's Foreign Office immersion also kept him relatively free of the internal quarrels of that unfortunate 1929–31 government, although when the break-up came in August 1931 he had no hesitation (and not merely on grounds of departmental loyalty) in staying with Henderson and not going with MacDonald, and indeed expressed himself most violently against those whom he regarded as traitors. When the election came in October 1931, Dalton to his considerable surprise was rejected, although only by a margin of 750, in his 'seat for life' of Bishop Auckland.

As a result he was not one of the rump of fifty-two (Lansbury, Attlee and Cripps being the only ex-ministers of any significance among them) who had to hold the opposition fort in Parliament. He nonetheless played a central role, and a steadier one than any of these three, in rebuilding the party outside Parliament, and in pulling it back from that plunge to extremism which is such a frequent accompaniment for parties of either the right or left, of crushing electoral defeat.

The unexpected loss of Bishop Auckland was naturally a considerable blow to Dalton, but his position after the calamitous election was not nearly as devastating as that of many of his defeated colleagues. He still had his LSE readership with its modestly substantial salary to which to return. He had his wife's significant private income, its value enhanced, as was the case with most *rentiers*, by the sharp increase in the value of money which was one result of the slump. There was no question of his being without a job or having to reduce his easy but not grand lifestyle. The sub-Bauhaus-style walking lodge with which he had in 1930 scarred a particularly fine brow of downland five miles east of Marlborough, together with a rather bleak flat in the purlieus of Westminster Cathedral, were still perfectly well within the Dalton means. And he retained his position on the National Executive, indeed moving to a relatively stronger position within a weakened party.

From these bases he strenuously resisted the embrace of a cataclysmic approach to socialism, the probable remoteness of which was to be compensated for by its completeness. This embrace led Stafford Cripps to announce that 'the one thing that is not inevitable now is gradualness' and it even led Attlee to write and say some things which would have sounded very odd in 1945, let alone 1995. Dalton stood very firm against any half-baked Leninism, expressing himself most clearly in his 1934 book with its significantly chosen title *Practical Socialism for Britain*. 'I discount heavily,' he there wrote, 'in this common-sense and politically mature country, all panic talk, whether from right or left, of an "inevitable crisis", and all theatrical nightmares of violent head-on collisions, wrecking the train of democracy.' And later in the same work he set out his own utilitarian and anti-manichean political philosophy: 'Socialism is a quantitative thing. It is a question not of all or nothing, but of less or more.' This approach achieved general Labour party endorsement three years later, when Dalton, by then back in Parliament, and enjoying a successful year giving an exceptional influence to the office of party chairman, got his ideas and his practical proposals, which formed much of the basis of what the 1945 government did, endorsed in *Labour's Immediate Programme*.

On these domestic issues he worked in fairly close alliance with Herbert Morrison, leader of the London County Council since its capture by Labour in 1934, who had also returned to the House of

Commons at the 1935 general election. After that election, indeed, Dalton manoeuvred, vigorously but ineffectively, to get Morrison elected as leader over Attlee's head. (This was ironical in view of how equally hard Dalton used his influence against Morrison both in the late 1940s and at the time of Morrison's last and humiliating throw for the leadership in 1955.) On foreign and defence policy, however, Dalton in the 1930s was harder-line than Morrison (or Attlee) and he looked outside the parliamentary Labour party for his principal ally and found him in Ernest Bevin, already the dominating trades union leader, who was buttressed (although they did not get on) by Walter Citrine, the general secretary of the TUC. This was a line-up which appealed to the 'brutal realist' side of Dalton's character. He liked the thought of being in alliance with the real men of the Labour movement against the waverers and quaverers among the MPs. It should have led to giving Dalton a store of credit with Bevin when they became colleagues first in the wartime Coalition and then in the post-war Labour government. But on the contrary, owing to that old persistent flaw in Dalton's personality and/or character, it had the unfair result more of subordinating him to Bevin than of increasing Bevin's respect for him.

The first of the foreign policy points at issue was resistance to the wave of quasi-revolutionary pacifism which swept the Labour party in the aftermath of the 1931 defeat and reached its apogee at the October 1933 party conference. This was two years after the outbreak of the Sino-Japanese war and eight months after Hitler's accession to power. Nevertheless a resolution announcing that the Labour movement would take no part in any war and would resist its outbreak by the proclamation of a general strike was moved by Sir Charles Trevelyan and carried unanimously. Immediately afterwards, however, an orthodox collective security speech from Arthur Henderson was warmly applauded.

This attempt to wallow in the warm luxury of having it both ways was anathema to the clear and sometimes harsh mind of Dalton, and he was able to promote substantial progress away from it at the conference two years later. In October 1935 the Italian invasion of Abyssinia faced the Labour party with the question of whether it was prepared to support the League of Nations in meeting this aggression with sanctions which might lead to war. The leader of the party (Lansbury) tried to resist this on pacifist grounds, but was swept aside and into resignation. Stafford Cripps, still in his extremist period, deployed an alternative, not strictly pacifist argument which was at once more convoluted and more defeatist. He proclaimed that nothing worthwhile could be accomplished in international affairs until all capitalist governments had been replaced, and that in the meantime it was dangerous for a workers' party even to try.

Both the Lansbury and the Cripps positions were defeated by majorities of approximately twenty to one. So far, so very much so good for the Dalton view. But this was a long way from settling the question of the Labour attitude to British national armaments. Germany was rearming furiously and the British government announced the beginning of a balancing-up programme in February 1936. Dalton thought this was at least a start in the right direction, but failed to carry the parliamentary party with him, despite being shadow Foreign Secretary. At the end of that July the party repeated what had become its reflex action of voting against the service estimates. 'We *are* unfit to govern,' Dalton wrote privately. He decided to invoke the 'conscience clause' in the parliamentary party's constitution which was normally thought to apply only to drink, gambling and religion, and to abstain. The survival of the country, he mordantly suggested, was at least as strong a candidate for conscience as pubs and betting shops. Two other front benchers abstained with him.

This semi-heroic action (abstention not being the most glorious of positions) did however reap a considerable benefit the next July (1937). Dalton then succeeded by the most strenuous canvassing in producing a majority for abstention in a thinly attended parliamentary party meeting. By forty-five to thirty-nine (which meant that over seventy did not vote) the party moved away from its traditional opposition posture to an official abstention on the service estimates. Nevertheless the view of a large segment of the Labour party, including some who were to be valiant members of Churchill's War Cabinet, remained of the comfortably soggy view (in the circumstances of the late 1930s) that an effective policy of collective security would diminish rather than increase the need for British national armaments.

As the threat of Hitler mounted, with the *Anschluss* with Austria in the spring of 1938, the Munich surrender in the autumn and the obliteration of the rump Czech state in the spring of 1939, Dalton as foreign affairs spokesman held the Labour party on a resolutely anti-appeasement course. This was the phase during which Vansittart, though shunted by Chamberlain to the spurious position of 'chief diplomatic adviser', gave Dalton a great deal of secret briefing. Dalton was also a self-appointed liaison officer with the Tory anti-appeasers. While the subtlety of his manoeuvres in this direction may be doubted, they at least showed an ecumenical approach (rather at variance with his normal party exclusivity) to the urgent task of bringing down Chamberlain. However his credentials in the Churchill and Eden camps were considerably weakened by his accepting the Labour decision to vote against the limited measure of conscription which the government introduced in April 1939. (The reason why he did not even abstain on the occasion may have been that he was currently engaged in getting Cripps – and Aneurin Bevan – expelled from the Labour party for ignoring party decisions and therefore did not wish to expose a flank of his own; if so, the difficulty of combining the roles of party boss and international statesman were thereby vividly illustrated.) Despite a few blemishes, however, Dalton's 1930s record, domestically and internationally, was more consistently sensible and courageous than that of almost any other leading Labour figure, and the period was one of the most creditable and most satisfying of his life.

Once war had come Dalton was in favour of the Labour party entering the government, provided it was under almost any Prime Minister other than Chamberlain. However when the first real opportunity for such a concatenation occurred, in the Norway debate at the beginning of May 1940, he was cautious about seizing the opportunity for what proved to be one of the decisive House of Commons votes of the century. He did not believe there would be enough Tory dissidents to endanger the government and he feared that Chamberlain might respond to the ineffective attack with a snap election in which the Labour party would be slaughtered. However he freely accepted the majority Labour decision to vote, and when the result turned out so much better than he expected (forty-one Conservatives voted with the opposition and sixty-five abstained or were missing unpaired), he was restlessly energetic in his inter-party anti-Chamberlain canvassing, but wobbling, like most of the rest of his Labour colleagues, between the merits of Halifax or Churchill as a replacement. He was eager to be in a coalition government in a senior position (he did not wish 'to wash bottles for anyone', he told Attlee in a taxi), but had to wait four days before his appointment came through. During this period he was at Bournemouth for the Labour party conference and was brilliantly described (by Vera Brittain) as 'pacing like a caged panther [through] the lounges of the Highcliffe Hotel'.

At 6.00 p.m. on the evening of Tuesday, 14 May, on the fifth day of Hitler's *Blitzkrieg* against Holland, Belgium and France, the panther was released from his agony by a telephone call from Churchill offering him the job of Minister of Economic Warfare, outside the War Cabinet, which at that stage only had five members, but fully in charge of an independent even if recently created department, and one which was directly engaged with the war effort. Dalton accepted with gratitude and left by the next train to London.

Dalton remained Minister of Economic Warfare for the twenty-one most crucial months of the war. The organization that he took over was mainly that of a ministry of blockade, with many of the officials brought over from the Foreign Office, which provenance neither made Dalton pro-them nor most of them pro-Dalton. In July 1940, as a result of a sustained Whitehall battle, he succeeded in extending his domain to include the organization of subversion and political warfare in the enemy-occupied territories. In bureaucratic terms this meant that he was put in charge of SOE, the Special Operations Executive. More dramatically it meant that he was in charge of undermining the Axis powers from within, both by propaganda and by terrorist-style sabotage. 'And now set Europe ablaze,' Churchill is reported to have said when he reluctantly accepted this extension of the boundaries of Dalton's power.

For these tasks Dalton had considerable advantages. He had energy, a liking for command and responsibility, a reasonable knowledge of Europe and a natural bellicosity: he wanted to engage the enemy and not just to sit and wait for something to happen. But he also had some disadvantages. He could be more bullying than strong. He made enemies more easily than he secured allies. And, above all, he could not command the liking of Churchill. This was in many ways unfair, because he remained deeply loyal to Churchill throughout the five up-and-down years of the Coalition government. Churchill was the only one of his three Prime Ministers against whom Dalton did not intrigue. Yet he could not handle Churchill. He was at once nervous and bombastic in speaking to him. As a result he did not often get the opportunity to do so. One mishandled Sunday lunch at Chequers throughout the twenty-one months was his ration of hospitality.

As a first result he had to rely in any disputes which got to War Cabinet level on mobilizing Attlee to give him Labour support. Attlee was remarkably loyal at doing this. But Dalton ought not to have been so tribally dependent. With his anti-appeasement and pro-rearmament pre-war record, with his social background, with his buoyant bellicosity and natural ability, he ought to have made his own cross-party allies. Instead he got involved in bitter Whitehall 'turf' disputes with Duff Cooper and Brendan Bracken (the Prime Minister's closest crony) as successive Ministers of Information, and ultimately with Eden. Against this line-up Dalton, even with Attlee's support could not win, and he was lucky when it was resolved, in February 1942, by his being transferred to the perfectly acceptable post of President of the Board of Trade.

In that sprawling department he spent the last three and a quarter years of the war, and was probably more content there in spite of its mainly home front problems than in MEW, which had originally so attracted him with the romanticism of its cloak-and-dagger activities. The Board of Trade waters were less shark-infested for him. This was despite his beginning with a major row with Tory back benchers over his aborted scheme for coal rationing and then his plans for the effective requisitioning of the mines, a good halfway house to nationalization, which he substantially achieved. He was better backed on these issues by the other senior Labour ministers, Bevin, Morrison and Cripps – the last not nominally 'Labour' at the time. Churchill was not much interested, and Dalton there encountered no direct and dangerous adversary comparable with Bracken.

In June 1942 he thankfully got rid of coal to a new Ministry of Fuel and Power, and as peace began to loom was able to devote much of his energy to a location-of-industry policy, using a mixture of carrot and stick to take industrial development to the areas of heavy peacetime unemployment, instead of, as before the war, watching some of the unemployed be drained away from Scotland, South Wales and the North-east of England to Slough and Dagenham. He just got through a Distribution of Industry Bill in the last days of the parliament. This policy was popular with Labour MPs both because of its objective merits and because a high proportion of them came from areas which stood to benefit. One such area was Bishop Auckland, indeed the whole of County Durham. Rarely has a minister brought by entirely legitimate means such large and tangible benefits to his own constituency. Throughout the quarter-century after the war the fullest of full employment was maintained in what had until 1940 been an area of massive unemployment. In 1932 the unemployment rate in the North-east region was 38 per cent. In 1951 it was 1.5 per cent.

Dalton therefore ended the war with high Labour party prestige and an established position as a controversial but effective departmental minister. He was not sanguine about the 1945 election result. He expected a Churchill victory and several years in opposition. But when the Labour landslide occurred he was obviously well poised to fill one of the great offices of state, and he had the unique quality of being, on paper at least, equally well qualified by his previous experience for either the Foreign Office or the Exchequer. This ambidexterity was illustrated by Attlee making him Foreign Secretary on the morning of 27 July, and indeed telling him to pack a thin suit for the Potsdam Conference, to which they were to proceed on the following day, and then making him Chancellor in the afternoon.

The reasons for the switch have long been the subject of intense speculation. None of the reasons given, including Attlee's own retrospective reflections a decade and a half later, completely hold water. The explanation is probably that the reasons were cumulative, with no single one being decisive. This seems certainly the case with Attlee's immediate justification to Dalton that Bevin and Morrison got on so badly that they had to be kept from getting in each other's way on the home front. If this had validity it was just as great in the morning as in the afternoon.

Something the same applies to the antipathy of King George VI to having Dalton as Foreign Secretary. The King, no doubt influenced by some family sense of betrayal that Canon Dalton's son should have turned out as he did, and maybe as well by some personal frisson of dislike, such as Hugh Dalton was only too liable to arouse, particularly in those (for example Churchill) with whom he was not at ease, indisputably wanted the switch. And from a personal point of view there was sense in his preference, for the Foreign Secretary sees far more of the monarch than does the Chancellor, who leads a workaday life, more cut off from the court than any other of the top five ministers. Furthermore the King had expressed himself to the new Prime Minister on the issue in unusually strong terms. According to the minute of Sir Alan Lascelles, the royal private secretary: 'Mr Attlee mentioned to the King that he was thinking of appointing Mr Dalton to be his Foreign Secretary. His Majesty begged him to think carefully about this, and suggested that Mr Bevin would be a better choice.' But that audience took place on the previous evening (July 26) and could not therefore in itself have been the decisive element in the switch. If it had been, Attlee would not have made his morning offer to Dalton.

What were the other factors? 'With whom did C.R.A. lunch?' Dalton suspiciously wrote in the margin of his diary. Churchill, it was imaginatively suggested. But the answer appears to have been the more prosaic one that he did so with his wife, and Violet Attlee was a very non-political spouse, who probably thought of both the contestants as in their different ways equally loud-mouthed and unhouse-trained for the quiet family life, interspersed with occasional chintzy hospitality, which she liked. So it was non-prandial exchanges which counted, and these took place with Sir Edward Bridges, Cabinet secretary (but also permanent secretary of the Treasury, and therefore, if he was anti-Dalton, liable to at least mixed views as to whether he wanted him at home), possibly Sir Alexander Cadogan, the PUS at the Foreign Office, William Whiteley, the Chief Whip, and Herbert Morrison. Morrison subsequently claimed to have warned Attlee that Dalton's 'uncontrollable temper' – which, as opposed to his ill-calculated bluster with civil servants, I never noticed – made him unsuitable for the Foreign Office. But Morrison at that time, because of his own machinations to put himself in Attlee's place, was unlikely to have been treated as a trusted adviser.

So it was a tangled story, added to by Attlee's own explanation that he came to the conclusion (which his visit to the first part of the Potsdam Conference may well have instilled in him) that the Russians were going to be awkward and that Bevin would be better at standing up to them. Again, one may comment, why over lunch-time? However decisions need have no single cause and good as well as bad ones are often arrived at as a result of an uncovenanted moment when issues suddenly clarify themselves and emotional certainty imposes itself on the conflicting intellectual arguments which had already been there. And, as Ernest Bevin was indisputably outstanding among the British Foreign Secretaries of the century, the decision must be counted a good one.

So Dalton had to unpack his thin suit and repair to what can often be the chill of the Treasury rather than to the summer heat of the Brandenburg plain. On the whole he took very well the juddering change of track, although with a natural and unsatisfied curiosity as to exactly why it had happened. Fifteen years later he recorded that he was 'not unhappy, or disappointed, for more than half an hour. I swallowed my fate in one gulp.' This may have been putting a retrospective brave face upon it, but for a year and a half Dalton had a better time at the Treasury than he would have been likely to experience at the Foreign Office, particularly with unwelcoming officials who, *per contra*, adored Bevin. At the end of 1945 he had a hard time when, following the abrupt end of Lend-Lease and the disappointment that Keynes's negotiating skills had not proved more productive, he had to defend the unsatisfactory terms of the American loan, with the unrealistic and (for Dalton in particular) highly damaging commitment to restoring the full convertibility of sterling by the summer of 1947. Dalton, together with Attlee and Bevin, did not waver in his view that the loan was essential.

With this issue temporarily out of the way, Dalton then entered on the high tide of his Chancellorship. He later referred to it as his 'Annus Mirabilis'. During this period he wrote, 'I was gay, confident, tireless, influential and on the whole successful.' Nineteen-forty-seven by contrast was his 'Annus Horrendus', or alternatively a 'pig of a year'. The high tide really began with the October budget of 1945, the first of his four, of which two were irregular or autumn ones, outside the then normal spring pattern. But there was a vast difference between the 1945 budget, freely introduced to mark the financial beginning of a new peacetime era, and the November 1947 one, introduced under relentless pressures by an exhausted Chancellor and marking by a petty quirk of fortune Dalton's end at the Treasury, which consummation, although not the reason for it, was by then by no means wholly unwelcome either to Dalton or to his principal colleagues.

The direct taxation changes in Dalton's first two budgets are best considered together. What he did not do was more significant than what he did. He maintained, as a matter of policy more than of necessity, and as no other Chancellor would have been likely to do, the full rigour of wartime redistributive taxation. He took two and a half million at the lower end of the scale out of income tax, but he increased both surtax and death duties. As a result Britain faced the post-war world with a top rate of tax of 97.5 per cent, a rate unmatched elsewhere, with fewer than a thousand people with post-tax incomes of over £4,000 (perhaps £100,000 today), although some of course maintained a much higher standard of living through the manipulation or depletion of capital. The proportion of disposable national income remaining in surtax payers' hands was reduced from 7.2 per cent before the war to 3.3 per cent.

The October 1945 budget was also notable for the beginning of the Daltonian phase of cheap money. This was not a new policy. It had been Treasury orthodoxy since 1932, and had contributed substantially to the house-building boom of the mid-1930s, and to the fact that the Second World War left nothing like the debt service incubus on budgets which was the legacy of the First World War. When therefore Dalton tightened the noose on short-term rates by reducing the interest on Treasury Bills from 1 per cent to 0.5 and on Treasury Deposit Receipts from 1.125 per cent to 0.675 there was little reaction from either the Tories in the House of Commons or the financial press. It was nonetheless an important step, cutting at a stroke the interest charge on the floating debt by nearly a half.

In 1946 he pushed the cheap money policy further. He moved against medium- and long-term rates. In October he announced that he proposed to convert 3 per cent Local Loan Stock into 2.5 per cent Treasury Stock, redeemable in 1975 or later at par. It was no more than Goschen had done, but Dalton was a more flamboyant, although not a vainer character than Goschen, and made the mistake of provocatively boasting about it. 'Never before, in a cash issue,' he announced, 'have H. M. government borrowed so much for so little for so long.' It chimed in with his remark in the 1946 budget speech that he would find whatever money was necessary for 'useful and practical' development area schemes 'with a song in my heart'. He repeated the phrase at Neath, his birthplace, three months later, so that it cannot be regarded as just an exuberant *lapus linguae*. And indeed it stemmed, although this proves nothing, from his *With British Guns in Italy*, when he had used it to describe his emotional reaction to advancing across the River Piave in 1918. The policy on which he based the vaunt was perfectly sensible, but he was nonetheless giving an obvious and terrible hostage to fortune if things generally went wrong.

Nemesis was invited but took some time to come. The new stock was floated on 4 January 1947 and went to a mild premiums at 100.25. By 4 February, at the beginning of the fuel crisis, it was only down to 95.75, but by Dalton's last weeks at the Treasury in November 1947, battered first by that crisis and then by the disaster of sterling convertibility, 'Daltons', as they were unfortunately called, were down to 84. The long rate had gone back to 3 per cent, from where he had started. The very cheap money policy blew itself out at almost exactly the same time as did Dalton's Chancellorship. Throughout he had acted in accordance with official Treasury and Bank advice, and if there was blame to be attached, they deserved it as much as he did. They did not however write his speeches, certainly not the most clamant passages in them, and these passages were part of the trouble. If they did not cause the retreat from ultra-cheap money, they at least made it more humiliating.

The Bank of England had been nationalized as one of the early legislative acts of the Labour government. Dalton moved the bill in October 1945, and it became law in the following January with a vesting date of 1 March 1946. It was the first swallow of the post-1945 public ownership flock, but it was nonetheless more symbolic than practical in its effects. It was Labour's revenge on the City of London and on Montagu Norman as its inter-war high priest for the restrictions which the Labour minority governments had suffered at their hands. But it was a very light penalty which was exacted. The Bank retained a great deal of practical independence, much more, for instance, than the Banque de France, and continued to be more the embassy of the City to the government than vice versa. Dalton on the whole had good relations with the first nationalized Governor, Lord Catto, who, almost needless to say, had also been the last non-nationalized Governor. Once again, however, the Chancellor could not avoid involving him in a clanging sentence of propaganda which might have been more appropriate to a Labour party regional conference than to the annual Mansion House dinner for City Bankers and Merchants, which was where he delivered it. 'Lord Catto and I flew back most comfortably across the Atlantic under the efficient auspices of BOAC,' he said, 'one newly nationalized service thus lending wings to another.' Nevertheless it was Cripps, commonly regarded as his more orthodox and responsible successor, and not Dalton who once referred to the Governor of the Bank as 'my creature'. Creatures or not, Governors remained effectively unsackable, unlike those in France, who were moved in and out by a combination (in the Fifth Republic) of the President and the Minister of Finance like professional footballers being moved to and from the substitutes' bench by a self-confident manager.

In spite of this jibe, Cobbold, Catto's 1949 replacement, got on well with Cripps, Gaitskell and the Conservative successors until he in turn was succeeded by Lord Cromer in 1960. That earl's relationship with the incoming Labour government of 1964 was, apart from Bonar Law/ Cunliffe, the worst in the history of the Chancellor/Governor balance (although the tension then was even more with the Prime Minister), and it was probably a relief to all parties when his term ran out in 1966. He was replaced by Sir Leslie O'Brien, who came from the warp and woof of the Bank administration and not from the grand City establishment. But Cromer was not sacked, and it would not have occurred to me that, had O'Brien been difficult, which he most emphatically was not, dismissing him before the end of his term (which was in fact extended) was a possible option. The adverse effect upon the ever-ailing sterling of the forty post-war years would have been simply unacceptable.

So Dalton's bill cheered the Labour troops more than it hobbled the Bank. The cheering was a large part of his objective. As he wrote in his third (1962) volume of autobiography: '[It was] one of my constant aims to radiate confidence all through the Labour Party, to rid it of inferiority complexes, and to keep the parliamentary troops behind me in good heart.' And for a time and to a remarkable extent he succeeded. Throughout 1946 he was undoubtedly the most popular senior minister with the government back benches. This was partly because he was near to being the most unpopular one on the Tory benches, a status which he gave every sign of welcoming, although it of course weakened his authority and left him without any reserve of opposition goodwill when things came to go badly.

That, in 1947, they most certainly did. The seven-week freeze-up which started in the last ten days of January had already by the end of the first week in February resulted in the cutting off of electricity from industry, offices and domestic consumers for the five daily hours of heaviest consumption, and was driving temporary unemployment up to two and a quarter million, which it reached before the wind changed and the thaw came in mid-March. Dalton blamed Shinwell, the combative but administratively slapdash Minister of Fuel and Power, who had indeed been grossly improvident. Many others in the press and on the Tory benches were more inclined to blame Dalton, who was a bigger target and the most visible economic minister. This was somewhat unfair, and had the effect of turning Dalton's wholly justified criticism of Shinwell's inefficiency, which criticism was shared by many other ministers, into an obsessive personal hatred, which never left him for the rest of his life. The birth of this obsession may have been assisted by Dalton passing this first period of major setback suffering acute physical discomfort from an outbreak of inconveniently placed boils – with which he had been afflicted, but less badly, at previous periods of strain and discouragement. Dalton's rallying of ministerial opinion against Shinwell was sufficiently successful that, in October 1947, he got him demoted to a job outside the Cabinet and Hugh Gaitskell, his own wartime private secretary and latterly Shinwell's junior minister, appointed in the senior's place. This ensured that Shinwell fully reciprocated Dalton's long-term hatred.

The domestic energy and unemployment crisis had an adverse effect on exports, which made the balance of payments outlook, and in particular the all-important dollar prospect, look still less satisfactory as the days ticked away towards 15 July, when the pledge of full sterling convertibility, judged essential to get the American loan in 1945, had to be implemented. In any event, even without that commitment, the loan was draining away only too fast. Half of it had been drawn in the first eleven months. As the dread date for payment approached, Dalton became like a Faust who had sold his soul to the Devil, and was haunted with the awfulness of the prospect. That was no doubt a large part of the reason for his psychosomatic neuroses of the time.

It was at once his weakness and his strength as a Chancellor that he had a very compartmentalized mind. This had been true of him academically. He saw particular issues very clearly, but he would not have been remotely capable of bringing together the 'two sides of the moon' in the way that was done by Keynes's *General Theory*. Burke Trend, his private secretary at the time and later the secretary of the Cabinet, said that 'he wilfully shut his eyes to the relation between internal and external finance'. The weakness of this myopia was obvious, and he paid for it the price of being ill regarded by conventional wisdom in the gallery of Chancellors. Its strength was less obvious but equally real. He could or would not see the connection between balance of payments and sterling weakness with the domestic programme of the Labour government. The National Insurance Act or the National Health Service or food subsidies did not directly cost dollars. Nor did the nationalization of coal or electricity or gas or railways. He therefore saw no reason why, however menacing the external economic situation, the government should not press on with its promised programme. He was determined not to be another Philip Snowden, whose orthodoxy had made Gladstone look spendthrift.

The result was that Dalton's stewardship of the national finances ended in personal humiliation. His successor was endowed with a slightly exaggerated halo, which Cripps nonetheless wore with aplomb, while Dalton was awarded an equally exaggerated forked tail, which he in turn carried without pleasure but with surprising dignity. The parallel result, however, was that the Attlee government left a decisive imprint on Britain as one of the two great radical reforming governments of this century (or one of the three if Mrs Thatcher's opening to the right is also included), whereas with a more cautious Chancellor in its first years its mandate-fulfilling impulses might easily have run into the sand. And as major legislation changes, particularly if they flow with the current of the time, are much longer lasting, for good or ill, than success or failure in the short-term management of the economy, Dalton's myopia cannot be counted an unmitigated misfortune.

He was prepared to act decisively and courageously when he could see a clear connection between home consumption and the dollar problem. Thus the April 1947 budget was dominated by his swingeing increase in the price of cigarettes, made as they were mostly of Virginia tobacco, which went up by nearly 50 per cent, with no health-risk support at this time. He was also severe on the import of American films. As the main leisure occupation of the British population of the period was smoking cigarettes while waiting in cinema queues, these were not the actions of a feeble or populist Chancellor. It was simply that he could or would not see the connection between high but non-dollar-consuming levels of demand at home, whether public or private, and a weak balance of payments.

With overseas expenditure, however, particularly military overseas expenditure, he had no difficulty in seeing the connection, and where he did exhibit weakness as a Chancellor was in launching frequent *démarches* against over-extended commitments, and then allowing his waves of protest to disintegrate on the rock of Ernest Bevin, against whom Attlee was always loath to sum up a discussion. Dalton made some progress, and the February (1947) decisions to put the responsibility for propping up expenditure in Greece and Turkey firmly into the lap of the Americans had important consequences for the acceptance by the United States, after a brief post-war respite, of a world role. But its geo-political repercussions exceeded its direct impact upon the British budgetary position. Commitments still remained world-wide, the numbers in the services qualitatively different from pre-war, with a great concentration of both military and relief expenditure in Germany. This brought together a number of Dalton's prejudices when he complained (privately) about having to squander 'his dollars' on 'Strachey's food and Shinwell's fuel' for 'Bevin's Huns'. But he never put his foot down quite hard enough.

This was partly because he retained a mixture of admiration for and fear of Bevin, combined with an envy of his job. Perhaps after all he could get back to where he had hoped to be in 1945 and escape into the comparatively green fields of the Foreign Office from what had become for him the prison-house of the Treasury. But he was also realistic enough to see that he could not supersede Bevin against Bevin's will. His best hope was to make him Prime Minister and step into his Foreign Office shoes. He always under-estimated Attlee, who lacked both the upper-class noisiness and the working-class roughness to which Dalton's tastes ran. And he had been genuinely dismayed by what he saw as the lack of assertive grip displayed by Attlee during the economic/military arguments of that spring and summer.

So, fairly disastrously, Dalton took the opportunity of a long drive back with Bevin from the Durham Miners' Gala, then a great occasion in the Labour calendar, to try to hatch a plot. Some politicians try to intrigue in success, which is natural if not admirable. Others, and Dalton was not alone in this, try to do so in failure, which is perverse. Dalton found it difficult not to do so in all circumstances, and on this occasion, when he was flat on his back both politically and psychologically, he tried almost as a reflex action to revive his spirits by pouring sedition into Bevin's capacious ear. It is easy to imagine these two ailing and exhausted statesmen, the one great the other not negligible, keeping each other going, almost as though drugs were being injected by the stimulus of political manoeuvre, leaning together in the back of the large black ministerial Humber as they pounded on that July Saturday night down the long stretches of an unmodernized A1.

What they had in common was the prospect of intractable problems on return. They were entitled to a little malicious relaxation on the way. The difference was that Dalton took it seriously and Bevin did not. Bevin liked complaining about all his colleagues, as he did on this occasion about Morrison, Cripps and Attlee. But he was fundamentally loyal to Attlee, partly but not entirely because he was a satisfied power and thought that he had the Prime Minister under control.

Dalton was not a satisfied power. As much feared dates have a habit of doing, 15 July had come and gone without producing a sudden haemorrhage, but the drain from Britain's exiguous reserves in the dog days of that hot summer of 1947 was nonetheless unsustainable. The underlying position, even without the enforced convertibility, was unsound, and sterling holders realized that the window of opportunity for conversion into dollars might be only briefly open. As a result they made inevitable its early closure, which was announced on 20 August, just as Dalton was hoping to begin his holiday. The only event which revived his spirits during that month, which embraced his sixtieth birthday, was that he met Tony Crosland for the first time.

Against this sombre background there was performed a *danse macabre* which was one of the least edifying chapters in the history of that notable Labour government. Dalton had started it with his ill-judged motoring conversation with Bevin at the end of July, which was so ill judged that he had effectively hobbled himself, and the main subsequent participants were Cripps, who had the strength that he was prepared to confront Attlee direct, and Morrison, who had the weakness that he was prepared to support any plot which ended up with himself as Prime Minister, which no one else wanted at that stage, but not one with a different result. Bevin, the biggest fish, lurked in the shadows. Attlee looked the most vulnerable, but by remaining relatively still allowed the contortions of the others to cancel themselves out around his area of calm in the centre of the storm. The result was that Attlee emerged unscathed, that Morrison lost his weakly exercised economic responsibilities to Cripps, who exercised them strongly, and that Dalton as a result ceased to occupy the clearly leading economic position which he had previously enjoyed. The only remaining qualification is that Dalton had ceased, for several months previously, to enjoy it. He was ready to see someone else take part of the burden. Nevertheless a situation of unstable equilibrium, comparable with that between Callaghan and George Brown nearly two decades later, had been created, the resolution of which might have been bloody had it not been for the events of November 1947.

By early October Dalton, with his spirits still low and the American money still draining away, had come to the reluctant conclusion that he ought to have a deflationary autumn budget. Otherwise the measures to stimulate exports and reduce imports which were already planned and were announced (significantly not by Dalton but by Cripps) on 23 October, were bound to lead to an inflationary situation at home. Cripps's speech set the clear objective of halving the dollar gap by the end of 1948, and left no doubt that, while there was a substantial gleam of hope on the horizon in the shape of the Marshall Plan, which had been tentatively launched in the previous June but was still not a reality, there would be need for some intermediate reduction in the standard of living. Dalton's task had become the almost subordinate one of devising the measures to implement this reduction.

In the circumstances he set about this with determination and diligence. The date was fixed for 12 November, and the measures then announced, in a short speech which lacked all Dalton's normal bounce, made a greater contribution to the new period of austerity than anything which Cripps himself, who had become the very symbol of that austerity, ever did. Dalton's budget was criticized at the time for being inadequate (which was partly because by then he could not dissociate himself from his reputation for jaunty improvidence). In fact he was neither jaunty nor improvident on 12 November. He and the Treasury substantially under-estimated the revenue-raising and inflation-reducing efforts of his measures. As a result, when Cripps came to introduce his April 1948 budget, he inherited a surplus of £319 million, entirely due to Dalton's taxation measures, and himself added only £11 million to it.

By what measures did Dalton achieve this result? They were most succinctly summarized in the single, fatal sentence that he addressed to a friendly journalist on his way into the chamber: 'No more on tobacco; a penny on beer [there was also an increase on whisky]; something on dogs and [football] pools but not on horses; increase in purchase tax, but only on articles now taxable; profits tax doubled.' This indiscretion, at once wild yet venial, led to that now defunct London evening newspaper the *Star*, for whom the lobby correspondent worked, publishing an informed and accurate budget forecast in an edition which was on a few streets and sold to a handful of customers approximately twenty minutes before the changes were publicly announced by Dalton in the House of Commons; there was no evidence that any of these few casual purchasers used the report for speculative trading. But the indiscretion led to Dalton's resignation of his office (and his replacement by Cripps) within twenty-seven hours of his ill-fated conversation. This was despite the fact that when the issue was raised in the House on the day after the budget and Dalton had delivered a blame-taking but insouciant confession of guilt it had been well received and Churchill had offered him 'sympathy' and approved of 'his very frank manner'.

The whole series of events amount to one of the most bizarre episodes in modern British politics. The initial error was only made possible by a most unfortuitous combination of circumstances, but that is of course nearly always the case with fatal motor accidents, for example. Had the House of Commons not then been still sitting in the Lords' chamber, Dalton would not have entered by a way which exposed him to temptation or harassment; had Douglas Jay, who was supposed to be 'looking after' Dalton, not been sent off to see that there was a glass of water beside the despatch box he would presumably have headed off the fatal conversation; had John Carvel – the incontinent journalist – not been asked by a colleague to put to Dalton the boring and totally innocent question of whether he proposed to drink rum and milk, as on previous more boisterous occasions, he would never have approached him at all.

Beyond that, however, there was the trivial nature of the fault, only beginning to be significant by being so characteristic of Dalton. In the context of the last decade or so, when budgets are mostly published (or at least fairly accurately forecast, and done so on leaks) not twenty minutes but sixty hours beforehand, such a tumble of a Chancellor seems almost unimaginable. Nor is it a question just of a recent degradation of standards. Lloyd George in the Marconi scandal was far more blameworthy and more technically vulnerable than Dalton was in 1947. If Asquith had applied the rigid standards of Attlee, he might not have had the challenge of Lloyd George to face in 1916, he might not have fallen, not at any rate in a way which spilt the Liberal party.

Why, then, did Dalton so urgently tender his resignation – having offered it at 2.15 before his reply to the question in the House he went back to see the Prime Minister in the early evening to press its acceptance – and why did Attlee accept it with so little remonstrance? The answer I think must lie, as Professor Ben Pimlott argued with a wealth of detail in his 1985 biography, in Dalton's realization that he was no longer emotionally or physically up to doing the job, and that Attlee, with a parallel awareness of this harsh fact and with no great liking or debt to Dalton to balance it, was also anxious to use the opportunity to get rid of him and to install Cripps in his place, who looked the coming man, although he was to last barely three years in office and to die over a decade before Dalton.

To go beyond this, however, and argue that Dalton deliberately used Carvel as an agent to secure his release would be unconvincing. Although he had in both September and October dropped resignation hints in his diary they were probably more rhetorical than determined. Apart from anything else it never occurred to him that Carvel would publish, and certainly not that he would do so with such expedition as to gain the twenty-minute lead over his own public statement. What was more the case was that Dalton's low morale was making him careless and accident prone. In any event the contrast between his 'song in the heart' on the 'high tide of success' in 1946 and his humiliation (inner humiliation at least, for his prompt and over-fastidious resignation earned him a lot of immediate public sympathy) in 1947 could hardly have been more dramatic.

Immediately he suffered something very near to a total collapse. But six weeks at his Wiltshire house restored equilibrium and some energy. He lived another fourteen years, but although he occupied two middle-rank Cabinet offices between 1949 and 1951, he never remotely regained the position either in the Labour party or in national politics which he had previously occupied. He saw it all with realistic clarity and sad acceptance at the time. 'All the rest, I thought, would now be anti-climax: cross-currents in the shallows. With some interest, no doubt, some influence, occasional excitement, some opportunity to put some of my ideas into practice, and the happy continuance of friendships. But anti-climax all the same.'

'And I was not far wrong,' he added in the last volume of his autobiography, published in February 1962, the month of his death.

Select Bibliography

Lord Randolph Churchill

Winston Spencer Churchill: *Lord Randolph Churchill*, 2 vols, Macmillan, 1906

R. F. Foster: *Lord Randolph Churchill: A Political Life*, Oxford University Press, 1981

Robert Rhodes James: *Lord Randolph Churchill*, Weidenfeld & Nicolson, 1951

William Harcourt

Arthur Armstrong, article in *Dictionary of National Biography*, 1901–1911 volume

A. G. Gardiner: *The Life of Sir William Harcourt*, 2 vols, Constable, 1923

George Joachim Goschen

Arthur D. Elliot: *The Life of George Joachim Goschen, 1st Viscount Goschen*, 2 vols, Longman, Green, 1911

Sir Michael Hicks Beach

Lady Victoria Hicks Beach: *The Life of Sir Michael Hicks Beach*, 2 vols, Macmillan, 1930

C. T. Ritchie

Richard Jennings, article in *Dictionary of National Biography*, 1901–1911 volume

Austen Chamberlain

David Dutton: *Austen Chamberlain: Gentleman in Politics*, Ross Anderson Publications, 1986

Charles Petrie: *The Chamberlain Tradition*, The Right Book Club, 1938

Charles Petrie: *Life and Letters of Sir Austen Chamberlain*, 2 vols, Cassell, 1940

Robert Self (ed.): *The Austen Chamberlain Diary Letters*, Oxford University Press, 1996

D. R. Thorpe: *The Uncrowned Prime Ministers*, Dark Horse Publishers, 1980

H. H. Asquith

Margot Asquith: *The Autobiography of Margot Asquith*, 2 vols, Eyre & Spottiswoode, 1920 and 1922

Mark Bonham Carter and Mark Pottle (eds): *Lantern Slides: The Diaries and Letters of Violet Bonham Carter, 1904–1914*, Weidenfeld & Nicolson, 1996

Michael and Eleanor Brock (eds): *H. H. Asquith: Letters to Venetia Stanley*, Oxford University Press, 1962

Earl of Oxford and Asquith: *Fifty Years of Parliament*, 2 vols, Cassell, 1926

Earl of Oxford and Asquith: *Memories and Reflections*, 2 vols, Cassell, 1928

Roy Jenkins: *Asquith*, Collins, 1964

Stephen Koss: *Asquith*, Allen Lane, 1976

Mark Pottle (ed.): *Champion Redoubtable: The Diaries and Letters of Violet Bonham Carter, 1914–1915*, Weidenfeld & Nicolson, 1998

J. A. Spender and Cyril Asquith: *Life of Herbert Henry Asquith, Lord Oxford & Asquith*, 2 vols, Hutchinson, 1932

David Lloyd George

Lord Beaverbrook: *The Decline and Fall of Lloyd George*, Collins, 1963

John Campbell: *The Goat in the Wilderness*, Jonathan Cape, 1977

William George: *My Brother and I*, Eyre & Spottiswoode, 1958

John Grigg: *The Young Lloyd George*, Eyre Methuen, 1975

John Grigg: *Lloyd George: The People's Champion*, Eyre Methuen, 1978

John Grigg: *Lloyd George: From Peace to War*, Methuen, 1985

Frances (Countess) Lloyd George: *The Years That Are Past*, Hutchinson, 1967

Richard (2nd Earl) Lloyd George: *Lloyd George*, Frederick Muller, 1960

Donald McCormick: *The Mark of Meslin: A Critical Study of David Lloyd George*, Macdonald, 1963

Frank Owen: *Tempestuous Journey: Lloyd George and his Times*, Hutchinson, 1954

A. J. P. Taylor (ed.): *Lloyd George: A Diary by Frances Stevenson*, Hutchinson, 1967

A. J. P. Taylor (ed.): *Lloyd George: Twelve Essays*, Hamish Hamilton, 1971

A. J. P. Taylor (ed.): *My Darling Pussy: The Letters of Lloyd George and Frances Stevenson, 1913–41*, Weidenfeld & Nicolson, 1975

Reginald McKenna

Stephen McKenna: *Reginald McKenna, 1863–1943*, Eyre & Spottiswoode, 1948

Bonar Law

Robert Blake: *The Unknown Prime Minister*, Eyre & Spottiswoode, 1955

Dr Tom Jones, article in *Dictionary of National Biography*, 1922–1930 volume

Sir Robert Horne

Lord Macmillan, article in *Dictionary of National Biography*, 1931–1940 volume

Stanley Baldwin

A. W. Baldwin: *My Father: The True Story*, George Allen & Unwin, 1936

Stuart Ball: *Baldwin and the Conservative Party: The Crisis of 1929–36*, Yale University Press, 1988

Keith Barnes and John Middlemas: *Baldwin*, Weidenfeld & Nicolson, 1969

H. Montgomery Hyde: *Baldwin: The Unexpected Prime Minister*, Hart-Davis MacGibbon, 1973
Roy Jenkins: *Baldwin*, Collins, 1987
John Raymond (ed.): *The Baldwin Age*, Eyre & Spottiswoode, 1960
Robert Rhodes James (ed.): *Memoirs of a Conservative: JCC Davidson's Memoirs and Papers, 1910–37*, Weidenfeld & Nicolson, 1969
G. M. Young: *Stanley Baldwin*: Rupert Hart-Davis, 1952
Kenneth Young: *Stanley Baldwin*, Weidenfeld & Nicolson, 1976

Philip Snowden

Colin Cross: *Philip Snowden*, Barrie & Rockcliff, 1966
R. C. K. Ensor, article in *Dictionary of National Biography*, 1931–1940 volume
Philip Snowden: *Autobiography*, 2 vols, Ivor Nicholson & Watson, 1932 and 1934

Winston Churchill

Martin Gilbert: *Winston S. Churchill*, vol. V: *1922–39*, William Heineman, 1976
Martin Gilbert: *Churchill: A Life* (single volume summary), William Heineman, 1991
P. J. Grigg: *Prejudice and Judgement* (memoirs), Jonathan Cape, 1948
J. M. Keynes: *The Economic Consequences of Mr Churchill*, Hogarth Press, 1925

Neville Chamberlain

David Dilks: *Neville Chamberlain*, vol. I: 1869–1929, Cambridge University Press, 1984
D. H. Ellerton: *The Chamberlains*, John Murray, 1966
Keith Feiling: *Life of Neville Chamberlain*, Macmillan, 1946
Iain Macleod: *Neville Chamberlain*, Frederick Muller, 1961
R. A. C. Parker: *Chamberlain and Appeasement*, Macmillan, 1993

Sir John Simon

David Dutton: *Simon*, Aurum, 1992
R. F. V. Heuston, article in *Dictionary of National Biography*, 1951–1960 volume

Sir Kingsley Wood

Helen Palmer, article in *Dictionary of National Biography*, 1941–1950 volume

Sir John Anderson

Arthur Salter, article in *Dictionary of National Biography*, 1951–1960 volume
John W. Wheeler-Bennett: *John Anderson, Viscount Waverley*, Macmillan, 1962

Hugh Dalton

Hugh Dalton: *Call Back Yesterday: Memoirs, 1887–1931*, Frederick Muller, 1953
Hugh Dalton: *The Fateful Years: Memoirs, 1931–1945*, Frederick Muller, 1957
Hugh Dalton: *High Tide and After: Memoirs, 1945–1960*, Frederick Muller, 1962
Ben Pimlott: *Hugh Dalton*, Jonathan Cape, 1985
Ben Pimlott (ed.): *The Political Diary of Hugh Dalton, 1918–40 and 1945–60*, Jonathan Cape, 1986
Ben Pimlott (ed.): *The Second World War Diary of Hugh Dalton, 1940–45*, Jonathan Cape, 1986

General

Edmund Dell: *The Chancellors: A History of the Chancellors of the Exchequer, 1945–90*, HarperCollins, 1996
Bernard Mallet: *British Budgets, 1887–1913*, Macmillan, 1913
Bernard Mallet and C. O. George: *British Budgets, 1913–1921*, Macmillan, 1929
Bernard Mallet and C. O. George: *British Budgets, 1921–1933*, Macmillan, 1933

Index